SHARON K. TUGGLE *Vassar College*

Assembler Language Programming: Systems/360 and 370

 SCIENCE RESEARCH ASSOCIATES, INC.
Chicago, Palo Alto, Toronto, Henley-on-Thames, Sydney, Paris, Stuttgart

A Subsidiary of IBM

Library of Congress Cataloging in Publication Data

Tuggle, Sharon K
  Assembler language programming, systems/360 and 370.

  Includes index.
  1. Assembler language (Computer program language)
2. IBM 360 (Computer)—Programming. 3. IBM 370
(Computer)—Programming. I. Title.
QA76.73.A8T83   001.6′424   74-84276
ISBN 0-574-19160-7

Appendixes 3, 5, and 6 and form X28-6509 are reprinted by permission of International Business Machines Corporation.

TABLE OF CONTENTS

PREFACE

This text covers Systems/360 and 370 Assembler Language, as used on both OS- and DOS-based operating systems. Where important, the differences in the two families of operating systems are discussed; for example, job control language and input and output instructions. Where possible, the tone of the language used in the text is conversational, allowing the student to interact with the author as if attending a lecture. Questions that are likely to arise in the reader's mind are carefully anticipated, and answers or explanations discussed at that point.

At the end of each chapter is a series of questions that can be used as a self-testing device. Following the questions, most chapters have a series of exercises that can be assigned as formal problems or done as inclass exercises to solidify the information presented. In addition, at the end of most chapters is a quick-reference list for easy location of specific items, terms, or instructions.

The book is divided into three parts: Introduction to Computers and Computer Programming, Introduction to Assembler Language, and Program Management and the Assembly Process. Part I contains an explanation of punched cards, flowcharts, and loops. It provides a good introduction for students taking their first course in programming. (For those who have had some previous computer experience, such as a course in one of the higher-level languages, this part may be reviewed, or skipped all together.)

Part II contains all that a student needs to know to code problems of simple to average complexity. Chapter 3 contains an explanation of the basic components of Systems/360 and 370, chapter 4 explains the representations of data within the machine, and chapter 5 describes how to define storage and constants. Chapter 6 presents the student with his first machine instructions, the move instructions. This is followed by chapters 7 through 10, which cover the three different types of arithmetic instructions—fixed-point binary, packed decimal, and floating point—along with the conversion instructions necessary to make input data ready for calculations and prepare output data for printing. In part II, transfer of control—branches and jumps—is also explained.

If further detail is desired and more time is available, part III contains many topics of interest to the individual who wants to understand more about assembler language and its more advanced capabilities. Topics covered are: the assembler's scanning process and the two passes of the assembler, the handling of absolute and relocatable values, and the fundamentals of addressing. Chapter 14 goes into collecting data into tables and how they are referenced (index registers) and some of the more complicated branch instructions (BAL, BALR, BXH, and BXLE). Chapter 15 covers program sectioning and linking—the whole area of handling subroutines.

Chapter 16 treats the areas of debugging and dump reading. Chapters 17 and 18 cover the remainder of the machine language instructions—those involved in the manipulation of bytes and bits within bytes, and the powerful special-purpose instructions (ED, EDMK, EX, TR, TRT) and the instructions found only on System/370.

The last four chapters, 19 through 23, each contain topics that can enrich any course. Each can be covered in depth or just introduced. The topics are: DSECTS, Job Control Language, Input and Output, macros and the macro language, and virtual storage. There is very little interdependence in part III. These chapters can be discussed in any order or interleaved with the chapters in part II.

The contents of this book comply with Course B2, Computers and Programming; and the majority of Course B1, Introduction to Computing, as set forth in the 1968 Course Curriculum, recommended for Academic Programs in computer science by the ACM Curriculum Committee on Computer Science. It can be used in either a one-semester course or a two-semester course, through expanded use of the topics in part III.

I want to express my sincere thanks and appreciation to all who have been so helpful in the completion of this text: Shirley Mayewski and Pat Caswell, for their patience in typing the manuscript; to my reviewers, whose comments were so helpful in making this a better book: G. G. Casper, Weber State College; Carl Eckberg, California State University; Marilyn Bohl and William Lewis, of IBM; as well as Sallyann Hanson and Eric Weiss; also to Jim Budd, whose attention to detail has made this a better book.

To the computer-center staff at Vassar College, and to my many students, who suffered through the preliminary drafts, I give my appreciation. Most of all, I wish to thank my parents, Eleanor and Cully Krenek, who forged in me the habits and attitudes to accomplish this task, and my husband, Mike, who provided moral support and editorial comment.

S. K. T.

PART I

Introduction to Computers and Computer Programming

CHAPTER 1

Introduction to Computers

Since the beginning of time, man has been forced to adapt to an ever-changing environment. Today's environment is changing rapidly, in part because of the development and expanded uses of the electronic digital computer. And today, as often in the past, some people fear that advances in technology will encroach on their friendly, familiar environment. Man's first reaction to a new and powerful invention is frequently fear and apprehension. He fears for his job, his safety, and his security. It is understandable, then, why many people fear the computer.

And yet the computer, when reduced to its simplest components, is easy to understand. It is made up of relatively uncomplicated parts. Men build into the computer a language—that it understands and follows; to communicate with the computer, we need only to learn that language. Anyone knowing the computer's language can tell it exactly what to do, step by step. Built into the computer is the ability to perform any number of operations when given a sequence of orders. Change the sequence of orders, and the computer performs a different sequence of operations.

Give the computer no orders and it just sits there—an inanimate box of wires, circuitry, and switches. It needs you, the programmer, to tell it what to do.

Note: The remainder of this chapter, as well as all of chapter 2, may be review if you can already program in a higher-level language such as FORTRAN or PL/1. If so, you may wish to skim them.

DATA PROCESSING SYSTEMS

A *data processing system* is a network of machine components capable of accepting information, processing this information according to plan (a program), and producing the desired results. Regardless of what type of equipment is used, all systems perform the same five basic functions:

Input	makes data available to the system
Storage	provides devices into which data can be entered and held and from which it can be retrieved at a later time
Control	the order for performing basic functions
Processing	arithmetic operations or other manipulations on data
Output	the results

One example often used to illustrate the use of these terms is the preparation of an electric bill. Each customer of an electric company has a meter that registers the amount of electricity he uses. At periodic intervals a company representative reads the meter. This reading and the one taken for the previous billing period, make up the input. These two readings are stored, and the results of any calculations produce the customer's bill. The processing of data involves:

1. subtracting last month's meter reading from this month's reading to determine the amount of electricity used
2. multiplying the amount of electricity used by the rate charged for it
3. calculating any taxes or discounts that may be applicable

The output is the entry into the company's accounting records and the customer's bill. The control function is performed throughout the entire operation. It determines the sequence of the other functions. It ensures that subtraction is performed before multiplication by the rate, and it sees to it that taxes and discounts are applied before producing the bill.

The data processing system described above might involve only human processors, human and mechanical processors (such as adding machines), or human, mechanical, and electronic processors (computers). If only human processors are used in the system, the brain of a human being controls the entire operation. As long as the human can read the handwriting of the meter reader and has access to the accounting records, he can take the input, perform the proper calculations in his head or on a piece of paper, and write out a bill.

If the electric company expands, so that it is no longer feasible to perform all the basic functions by hand, the company could purchase adding machines. If, as time passes, the area the company services becomes a booming metropolis, hiring more people and buying more adding machines becomes impractical. The decision is then made to introduce a computer and let it perform the repetitive task of processing mountains of bills.

When a human being is processing data by hand, there is a great deal of latitude in the inputs and outputs that can be interpreted and produced. However, while input numbers scribbled on scraps of paper are fine for human processors, they have no meaning to a computer. A computer requires *standardization* of its input.

STANDARDIZATION

The data used in conjunction with nonhuman processors, computers in particular, needs to be standardized in two ways:

1. standardization of the medium on which the data is recorded
2. standardization of the method by which data is recorded on the medium

The medium must be standard in size, quality, and composition. The basic and most frequently used medium in the data processing industry is the *Hollerith* punched card, which is shown in figure 1-1. It is rectangular in shape and measures $7\frac{3}{8}$ inches by $3\frac{1}{4}$ inches (18.6 by 8.3 cm). The corners of the card may be squared, rounded (to prevent wear), or cut off (to make sure that no cards in a deck are upside down or backwards).

Rectangular holes may be punched into a card. There are 12 horizontal rows and 80 vertical columns on the card, thus 960 positions where a hole may be punched. The rows are numbered 12, 11, 0, 1, 2, 3, 4, 5, 6, 7, 8, and 9 from top to bottom on the card. On an IBM punch card, the 80 columns may be identified by column numbers in two locations: at the bottom of the card and just below the zero row. The numbers 0–9 fill each of the 80 positions in each respective row. Punches in any of these 10 rows are referred to as *numeric*

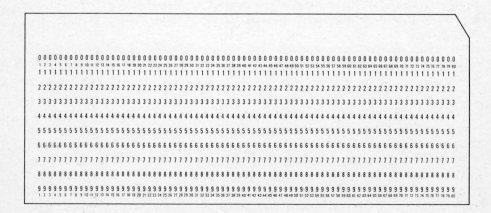

Fig. 1-1 The 80-column punch card

punches. Punches in the 11 and 12 rows as well as the 0 row are referred to as *zone punches.* This gives punches in the 0 row two different meanings, depending on the character punched in that column.

The numbers 11 and 12 are not shown in the 80 positions of their respective rows, but these are above the row of zeros—the 11 row directly above the 0 row, the 12 row above the 11 row (near the top of the card). Thus the top of the card is frequently referred to as the *12-edge* and the bottom as the *9-edge.* The character that is punched into a particular column can be printed at the top edge of the card.

The standardization of the method by which data is recorded on the medium has two separate components:

1. the *character set*—a set of graphic representations (characters) whose total number is fixed
2. an established correlation between a unique combination of punched holes and a character that it represents

The punched-card character set used in the IBM Systems/360 and 370 consists of 10 digits, the 26 characters of the alphabet, and 27 special characters. These 63 characters and the combination of punched holes that represents each are shown in figure 1-2.

These are the combinations of punched holes that represent the Hollerith system of coding data. In this code each of the 10 digits is represented by a single numeric punch in the row. Each letter of the alphabet is represented by two punches—one zone punch and one numeric. Notice that the alphabet is

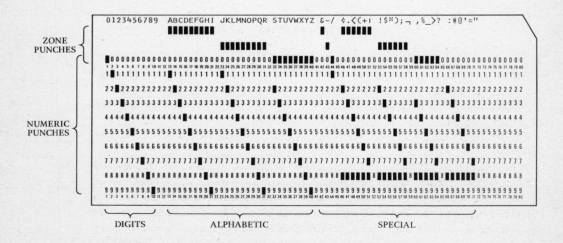

Fig. 1-2 Systems/360 and 370 character set

divided into three groupings. The letters A-I all have a 12-zone punch with a numeric punch, the letters J-R have an 11-zone punch, and the letters S-Z a 0-zone punch.

The 27 special characters are represented in the Hollerith coding system by a single punch, two punches, or (in most cases) three punches. Except for 3 special characters (&, -, and /), they all have two numeric punches with one of the two being the 8-punch. (Data represented in this code will be converted into another code before it is placed in the storage of the computer. This code will be discussed in chapter 4.)

THE USE OF PUNCHED CARDS

Putting data in machine-readable form on punched cards is usually done on a keypunch machine: depressing a key on the keyboard punches the corresponding combination of holes into the card. To be used as input to a computer program, data items must be punched in areas of the card reserved for the particular categories of data called *fields*. For example, the payroll department of a firm keeps certain data on all employees: name, department number, and rate of pay. To process its payroll by computer, the company must set up a standard card format providing for three separate fields on each card, one for each of the data items above. Specific columns of the cards will be set aside for each of the three fields. Each of the cards is referred to as a *record*; it is a collection of related data items, treated as a unit. Thus, the three fields could be set up in a record as follows:

Columns	Field
1–15	employee's name
25–30	employee's department number
40–44	rate of pay xx.xx

Each card or record contains the three related items for a particular employee. The payroll records for all the company's employees are called a *file*, a collection of related records treated as a unit. Figure 1-3 shows the relationship between field, record, and file.

A second example illustrating these terms can be related to the electric company discussed earlier.

The data items on the card in figure 1-4 are the name John C. Doe and the numbers 1845.6 and 1722.4. The fields are: customer name in columns 10–35, the new meter reading in columns 40–45, and the old meter reading in columns 50–55. Each card is a record containing information about one customer. Information for each customer is punched into a separate card, but the same columns or fields are used for each kind of data item on each card. The collection of all the customer records is the company's payroll file.

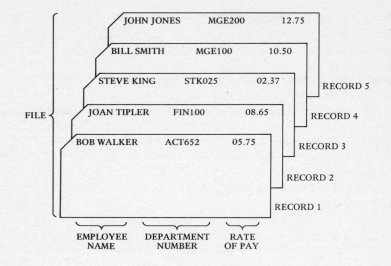

Fig. 1-3 Relationships between *field, record,* and *file*

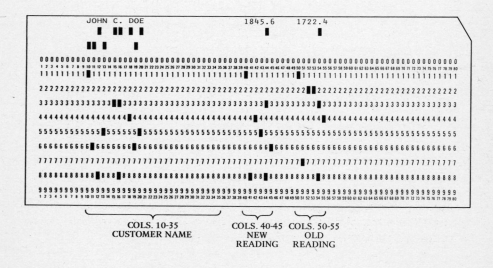

Fig. 1-4 Example of electric-company record

Punched Cards as Input to a Data Processing System

When used as input to a computer, the cards within the electric company's file are placed in a *card reader,* which is an input device attached to the computer. The card reader mechanically reads the card and detects the holes punched in it. In this way the data items are placed in the storage of the computer. Then the calculations are performed and the results are placed in storage. The results are then taken from storage, converted into human-readable form, and printed on a paper document by a *printer*, which is an output device attached to the computer. All this is done under the watchful eye of the control function of the computer. Each record is read from the card reader in the same manner, and the same calculations are performed for each one until all of the records have been processed—the *end of the file* is reached.

Figure 1-5 shows the interrelations of the five basic functions of data processing systems. The input function is supplied by the card reader, the output function by the printer. The storage, process, and control functions are supplied by the computer.

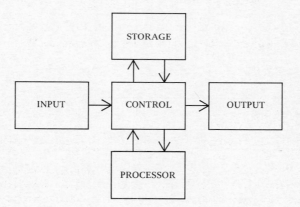

Fig. 1-5 Five basic functions of data processing systems

Notice the importance of the control function: it is the system's nerve center. It ensures that the plan—the program—is followed and that the other basic functions are performed as required.

STORED PROGRAM CONCEPT

The set of orders, or instructions, necessary to perform the reading of the electric company's records, the calculations, and the printing of the results is called a *program*. The job of preparing these instructions and of deciding the order in which they are to be performed is called *programming*.

Once a program has been written, it is punched into cards in a standardized format. Then it is read and stored in the computer's storage. This means that not only is the data stored in the computer's storage before being used in calculations, but the program that indicates which calculations are to be performed is also stored in the computer. Computers that have this capability are known as *stored program computers*. The IBM Systems/360 and 370 discussed in this text are stored program computers.

The control function of a stored program computer includes reading the instructions one at a time from punched cards and placing each instruction sequentially in storage. When all instructions have been read, the program is stored in a block of the computer's storage. Then the control function fetches the first instruction, interprets it to determine the desired action, and sees to it that this action is performed. Having done so, the control function then fetches, interprets, and executes the second instruction.

Instructions are fetched one after another from the computer's storage and executed sequentially until the last instruction in the program has been executed. At this point, the program has performed the function it was designed to perform, and the control function can proceed to the next program.

QUESTIONS

1. What five basic functions are performed by all data processing systems?

2. Why is the control function so important?

3. Why is it that the incorporation of a computer into a data processing system usually requires some alterations to the data serving as input to that system?

4. What are the two ways in which the data used by nonhuman processors must be standardized?

5. The Hollerith punch card has space for _____ rows and _____ columns.

6. How many punches are required to represent a number in a column of a card?

7. How many punches are required to represent any one of the 26 letters of the alphabet in a column of a card?

8. Describe the relations among the following terms: (1) field   (2) record   (3) file

9. What is indicated by the end-of-file condition?

10. Explain what is meant by the stored program concept.

11. What is meant by sequential fetching and execution of instructions?

12. Is it true that the instructions (as well as the data those instructions manipulate) must be in the computer's storage before being executed?

EXERCISES

1. What characters are punched into the following columns of the card shown in figure 1–6?

   column 1:
   column 5:
   column 20:
   column 25:

2. Which holes in the column of a card will be punched to represent each of the following characters?

   digit 8
   digit 0
   letter P
   letter G
   special character /
   special character +
   special character =

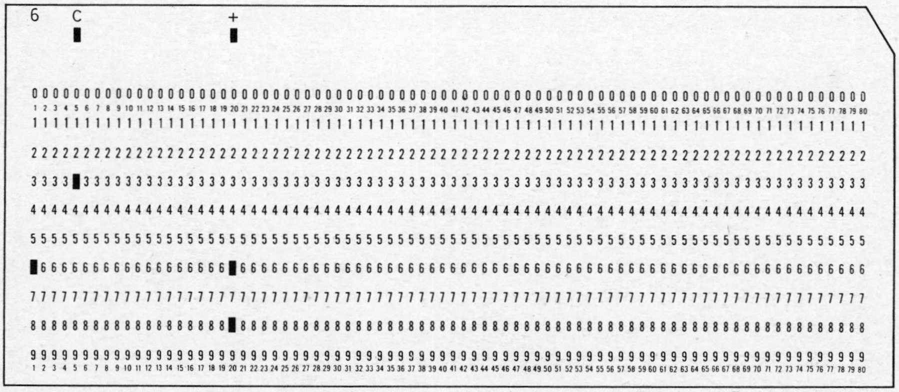

Fig. 1-6 Punched card for exercise 1

CHAPTER 2

Basic Computer Programming Techniques

PROBLEM SOLVING

Programming is a skill requiring that problem solutions be broken down into steps and expressed in a language understood by a computer. The programmer follows the same steps in programming that he uses in solving every problem that confronts him in everyday life. Take the example of giving a small child directions on how to get from his house to the local grocery store. This is a very young child. He is unable to read, and he has never been to this grocery store. Figure 2-1 is a diagram of the area in which both the house and the grocery store are located.

First, analyze the problem. You must consciously or unconsciously break down the problem into a series of instructions you will give the child. Since the child cannot read, you must phrase the instructions in terms of items he can recognize along the way, in a language he understands.

1. Turn left at the sidewalk.
2. Stop at the traffic light and turn right.
3. When the light is green, cross the street.
4. The grocery store is just past the ice cream shop and across the street from the post office; the grocery store is a green building with boxes filled with fruit in the window.

These directions seem simple enough. Yet, implicit in them are many pieces of general knowledge this child has already learned which it is assumed he will

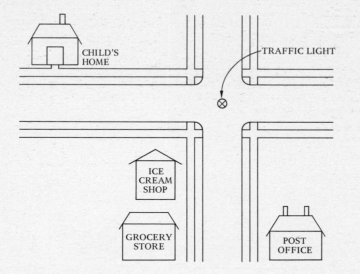

Fig. 2-1 Diagram of grocery-store problem

use in applying them. A left turn or a right turn means a turn of 90°. "Stop at the traffic light" means stop at the curb. When a traffic light turns green, one should always look left and look right before crossing the street. Past experience has taught the child many things that he applies to his current situation.

When setting up a series of instructions to use a computer to solve a problem, no assumption of any general knowledge can be made. The best way to think of a computer is that it is extremely simpleminded; in fact, as you learn to program you will discover that a computer follows every instruction exactly as you give it. Told to turn left (if it could), a computer would continue turning left in a circle until told to stop. It must be told to turn left 90°.

Instructions to the computer must be given in the language that it understands. The set of instructions given to the young child is not exact enough for the computer. Every instruction for the computer must direct it to perform one finite operation. For example:

Starting at the edge of the walk in front of the door:

1. Take one step forward.
2. Check to see whether the sidewalk has been reached.
3. If the sidewalk has not been reached, go back to instruction 1.
4. If the sidewalk has been reached, turn left 90°.
5. Take one step forward.

6. Check to see whether the curb has been reached.
7. If the curb has not been reached, go back to instruction 5.
8. If the curb has been reached, turn right 90°.
9. Check to see if the traffic light is green.
10. If the light is not green, go back to instruction 9.
11. Check to see if traffic is coming from the left.
12. If traffic is coming, go to instruction 11.
13. Check to see if traffic is coming from the right.
14. If traffic is coming, go to instruction 13.
15. Step down from the curb.
16. Take one step forward.
17. Check to see if the curb on the other side of the street has been reached.
18. If the curb has not been reached, go to instruction 16.
19. Step up on the curb.
20. Take one step forward.
21. Check to see if you are passing the ice cream shop.
22. If you are not passing the ice cream shop, go to instruction 20.
23. Take one step forward.
24. Check to see if the post office is directly across the street.
25. If there is no post office, go to instruction 23.
26. Turn right 90°.
27. Check to see if the building ahead is green with boxes of fruit in the window.
28. If the building is not green with fruit in the window (in which case, he never reaches the store), go to instruction 40.
29. Take one step forward into the grocery store.
30. When the groceries are purchased, take one step forward out of the grocery store.
31. Turn left 90°.
32. Take one step forward.
33. Check to see if the curb has been reached.
34. If the curb has not been reached, go to instruction 32.
35. etc., the rest of the instructions to get the child back home.
   .
   .
   .
40. Turn right 90°.
41. Go to instruction 32.
42. End.

BRANCHES (OR JUMPS)

The simplest program is a straightforward sequential series of instructions, executed one after the other until the last instruction is reached. This is the way a computer works. The instructions are placed in the computer's storage, and the computer will always perform the next sequentially stored instruction unless an instruction that transfers control to a different instruction sequence is executed.

Instructions that change the sequence of execution are called *branch* or *jump* instructions. Several branch instructions are contained in the set of instructions for the child in the grocery-store problem. Branch instructions direct the computer to perform, as its next operation, an instruction that is not the next one in storage.

There are two types of branch instructions—conditional and unconditional. There are examples of each in the grocery-store problem. In the *conditional branch*, a test is made for a particular condition. If the condition is met, the branch is taken; if the condition is not met, the next sequential instruction is executed. Instructions 2, 6, 9, 11, 13, 17, 21, 24, 27, and 33 each check to see if a particular condition has been encountered. In instruction 2 the condition being checked is "has the sidewalk been reached?" If the sidewalk has been reached, the next sequential instruction is executed, in this case instruction 4.

Instruction 41 is an example of an *unconditional branch*. No test is made for a particular condition; the branch is taken every time this instruction is executed, regardless of conditions. In this example, instruction 28 checked to see whether the building ahead was green, with boxes of fruit in the window. If this condition was not met, something is wrong. The only assumption that can be made is that the child has not found the grocery store. In this case the child must be instructed how to return home. To do so requires a right turn of 90° (instruction 40) to head him back down the sidewalk toward the traffic light. Once this is done, the instructions that return the child home after purchasing the groceries could be used. Therefore, instruction 41 is an unconditional branch to instruction 32 (the first of the instructions to return the child home). No condition is checked; the branch is to be taken in all cases. This branch to the existing instructions is taken because there is no reason to duplicate instructions when instructions already exist to perform a required series of operations.

In programming it is important to take into consideration any error conditions that may occur. In the problem of the child and the grocery store, the error condition occurs if the child is unable to find the grocery store after following the instructions he was given.

PROGRAM FLOWCHARTS

Flowcharting is a method of displaying the steps involved in the logic of a solution to a problem. The individual operations to be performed, conditions to be checked, and branches to be taken are shown graphically by enclosing required steps in blocks and connecting these blocks with lines.

The flowcharting symbols and their use are given in figure 2-2. These con-

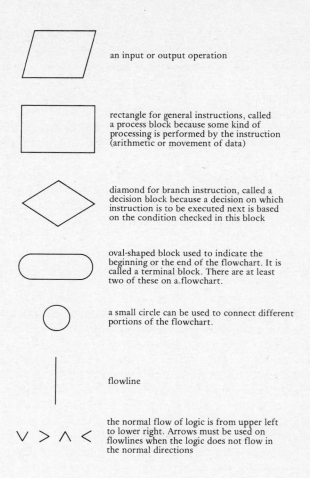

an input or output operation

rectangle for general instructions, called a process block because some kind of processing is performed by the instruction (arithmetic or movement of data)

diamond for branch instruction, called a decision block because a decision on which instruction is to be executed next is based on the condition checked in this block

oval-shaped block used to indicate the beginning or the end of the flowchart. It is called a terminal block. There are at least two of these on a flowchart.

a small circle can be used to connect different portions of the flowchart.

flowline

the normal flow of logic is from upper left to lower right. Arrows must be used on flowlines when the logic does not flow in the normal directions

Fig. 2-2 Standard flowcharting symbols

form to flowcharting standards that have been approved by the American National Standards Institute (ANSI) and will be used throughout this book.

It should be fairly easy to trace the flow of the logic for the grocery-store problem by following the flowline from the start block to the end block (see figure 2-3). Notice that only one flowline enters and leaves each process block. In the case of the decision block, one flowline enters, but as many flowlines may exit from the block as there are answers to the question asked in that block. In most cases, two flowlines exit from a decision block, as is the case in all of the decision blocks in the grocery problem. Each of the flowlines exiting a decision block must be labeled, either to indicate whether or not the condition is met, or to denote what the answer is to the question asked in the block.

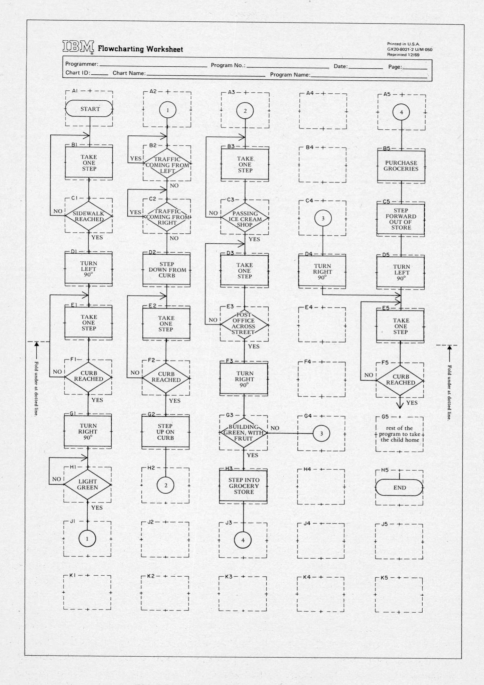

Fig. 2-3 Flowchart for grocery-store problem

Should there be three flowlines exiting from one decision block, one can come out of each of the three corners of the block:

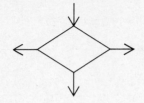

An example of this type of decision would be:

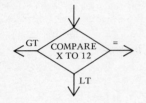

The result of comparing X to 12 could be equal ($=$) or not equal ($\neq$), but in this case the logic of the program needed to know whether X was equal to, greater than, or less than 12. Another way of illustrating a 3-way or more than 3-way decision is:

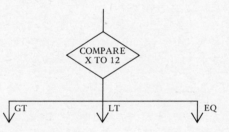

It is important to remember that flowcharts should contain no ambiguity. There should be no doubts as to where the logic is flowing at any point, especially at the points where decisions are made and branches are or are not taken as a result.

PROGRAMMING TECHNIQUES

Programming languages that are used in the preparation of computer programs were developed to simplify the task of writing them. However, the use of a programming language does not in itself guarantee efficient programs. The programmer must adhere to certain basic techniques and practices if he is to achieve a high degree of programming efficiency. One of the common programming techniques is the loop. The reader should gain a firm conceptual grasp of this technique so that he can apply it when programming.

PROGRAM LOOPS

When coding a program that involves a series of operations to be repeated on similar pieces of data, such as records in a file, a programmer has two choices. He may include a separate series of instructions for each record in the file. For example, if he needed to perform addition on two fields and then multiply by a third field in the record, he would need one add and one multiply instruction for each record in the file. If he knew his file contained twenty records, he would code twenty groups of add and multiply instructions, *inline*, meaning one right after the other in his program. This would be a total of forty instructions. There are a few jobs where this inline programming may be the quickest way of solving a problem, but in most applications it presents problems. This type of coding is tedious and prone to errors, and the resultant program occupies a large amount of storage.

The alternative to inline programming is to reuse a portion of the program for each record, that is, a *program loop*. This is an efficient programming practice. A loop may require a few additional instructions for control, but in the majority of cases it occupies much less space than would otherwise be required for the corresponding inline code.

The portion of the program that is reused as the result of a loop is known as the *body of the loop*. Each loop must contain some way of determining when the computer should stop execution of the instructions in that loop and continue execution of another portion of the program. This part of the loop is called the *loop control*; it prevents the instructions in the loop from executing interminably. The loop control consists of a check to see if a particular condition or event has occurred. An example of this is the calculation and printing of the powers of 2 (e.g.; $2^1 = 2 \times 1 = 2$, $2^2 = 2 \times 2 = 4$, $2^3 = 2 \times 2 \times 2 = 4 \times 2 = 8$, $2^4 = 2 \times 2 \times 2 \times 2 = 8 \times 2 = 16$, etc.). Refer to figure 2-4.

Condition-Controlled Loops The body of the loop in figure 2-4 consists of the multiplication block and the print block. The loop control is the decision block. The condition or event which controls the exit from this program loop is the occurrence of a value of X greater than 100. This type of loop is called a *condition-controlled loop*.

Notice that X is assigned a value of one in the first process block of the flowchart. This is the initial value that X must contain before the first execution of the body of the loop. This initialization takes place outside the body of the loop. All counters, conditions, and variables necessary to the proper function of the loop are established during this *initialization* phase.

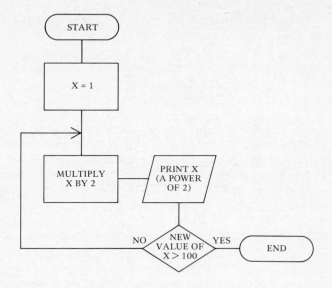

Fig. 2-4 Flowchart of a program loop

Count-Controlled Loops A special type of condition-controlled loop has its exit dependent on the execution of the loop a particular number of times. Such a loop is called a *count-controlled loop*. The exit is dependent on checking a counter—an area of storage set aside and initialized to a particular value prior to the beginning of the loop. Each time through the loop the counter is modified, and the control portion of the loop checks the counter for a particular value.

The counter for a count-controlled loop can be initialized to the number of times the loop is to be executed. In this case, the counter is decremented by one each time through the loop, and the control portion of the loop checks for a value of zero in the counter (figure 2-5). A second method is to initialize the counter to zero and increment it by one each time through the loop, checking for a value in the counter equal to the number of times the loop is to be executed. At times there is a need for a third method, using an initial value of one and a test for a value greater than the largest value desired.

In the above example, the body of the loop consists of the read block and the one process block which processes the record. The loop control consists of the process block which modifies the counter, and the decision block that tests the value of the counter. Again, initialization (setting the initial value of the counter) is done before the beginning of the loop.

Leading and Trailing Decision Loops The test of the counter may precede or follow the body of the loop. The former is called a *leading decision* loop and

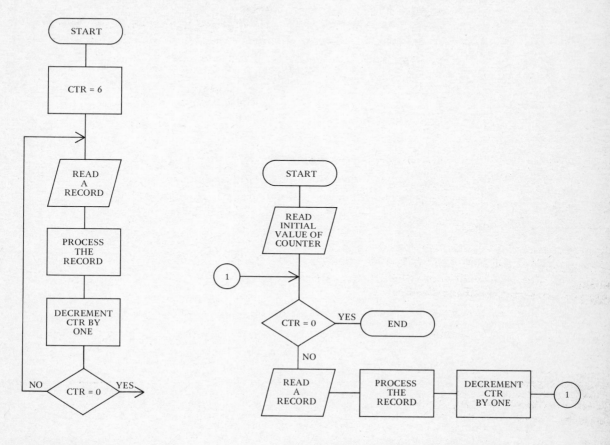

Fig. 2-5 Example of a
count-controlled loop

Fig. 2-6 Example of a leading-decision loop

the latter a *trailing decision* loop. The basic difference between the two is the value for which the counter is checked. Any errors in loop control are generally related to checking for the wrong value in the counter, causing either one extra execution of the loop to be made, or one execution of the loop to be missed.

The big advantage of a loop controlled by a leading decision (see figure 2-6) is that the test prevents records from being read erroneously when zero is the original value of the counter. If the original value of the counter was zero and a trailing decision was used on the loop, the logic would cause a record to be read and the counter decremented by one. The counter would not be tested until it had been decremented and contained a negative one. This is not equal to zero, and an exit would not be made from the loop unless a test was made for counter less than or equal to zero; but, even then, one record would have been read and processed erroneously.

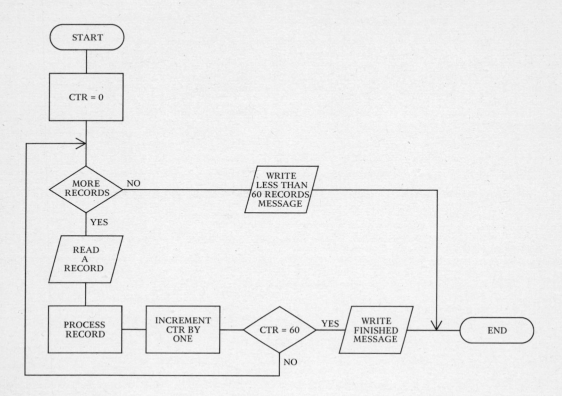

Fig. 2-7 Example of a loop with two possible exits

It is possible for a loop to have more than one exit. A usual case is a count-controlled loop that can also be exited if a certain condition occurs before the expected count is reached. Figure 2-7 shows an example where a file of sixty records is being processed. The programmer expects the file to contain sixty records, but the possibility exists that it contains less, and end-of-file would be reached before the counter reaches a value of sixty.

The program could not process records that do not exist. While the programmer is flowcharting for the sixty records he expects, he still must take into account the possibility that sixty records do not exist. (If more than sixty records exist, only the first sixty are read and processed.)

QUESTIONS

1. Explain in your own words what each of the following terms means to you:
    a. Branch instruction
    b. Flowchart
    c. Inline
    d. Program loop
    e. Condition-controlled loop
    f. Count-controlled loop

2. What is the difference between a conditional branch and an unconditional branch? Give an example of each.

3. Explain generally what each of the following symbols indicates in a flow-chart.

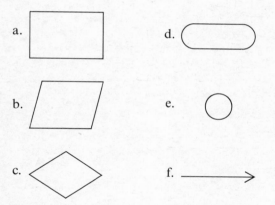

   a.   d.

   b.   e.

   c.   f.

4. How many flowlines may enter a process block? a decision block?

5. How many flowlines may exit from a process block? a decision block?

6. Why is it necessary that a flowchart contain no ambiguity?

7. What are the different parts of a loop called, and what is the function of each?

8. Explain the difference between a leading decision loop and a trailing decision loop, and why a leading decision structure is preferred in some cases.

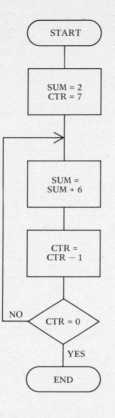

Fig. 2-8 Flowchart for question 9

9. Does the flowchart in figure 2-8 contain an example of a leading or trailing decision loop?

10. In the flowchart shown in question 9, how many times will the body of the loop be executed? What will the value of SUM be when the exit is taken from this loop?

EXERCISES

1. Draw a flowchart that will use a leading decision and count-controlled loop to initialize TOT to a value of 3, increment it by 4 in the body of the loop, until TOT contains a value of 35.

2. Flowchart the process you go through in making a phone call to a friend on a dial phone. (Assume that you already know the number.)

3. Create a flowchart, containing several simple loops, which will give the mouse in the following illustration the logic to locate the cheese.

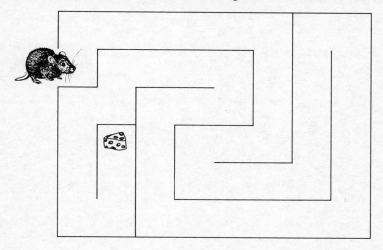

4. Placing yourself at the left front door of your car with your hand on the handle, flowchart the process of getting into and starting the car.

5. Given three numbers represented by the symbols A, B, and C, represent the three numbers in terms of the symbols SML, MED, and LRG. Show in a flowchart the logic involved in sorting the three numbers.

6. Given a cash box containing a finite number of pennies, nickels, dimes, and quarters, flowchart the process used in giving out change for a sale less than one dollar when a dollar bill is given in payment.

PART II

Introduction to Assembler Language

CHAPTER 3

Fundamentals of Assembler Language

INTRODUCTION TO PROGRAMMING LANGUAGES

When a computer is used as the processor for a data processing system, there is a wider need for standardization than simply supplying data in a form acceptable to that system (as discussed in chapter 1). Once a problem is analyzed, its proposed solution must be broken down into a series of steps. These steps are determined keeping in mind how they can be performed within the basic operations built into a computer. Being a piece of machinery, a computer has built into it the ability to perform only a finite set of operations.

To request the performance of one of these basic operations, there must be some way to direct the computer in a language that it understands. Any language conveys information by following rules and conventions to combine symbols into meaningful representations. In the English language we combine alphabetic characters, following the rules of grammar and punctuation, to convey information. In the case of the computer, the only symbolic representations that are acceptable are ones and zeros. Normally, this would give us the ability to convey only two pieces of information, one represented by a one and the other represented by a zero. The way we get around this is to combine ones and zeros into groups.

In Systems/360 and 370, these groups are combined into sets of eight units, giving us the possibility of defining 256 different pieces of information since there are 256 different ways we can combine ones and zeros in groups of eight (from eight zeros through eight ones). Using some of these combinations, we are now able to convey in the computer's language which one of its basic operations we want it to perform. Next we are faced with the problem of how to convey to the computer what data it is to use when performing the operation.

We could have one and only one location where data is stored. Data could be read from an input device into this one special location in the computer's memory. Operations could then be performed on that piece of data, and the result placed back in that special location. Finally, the data could be picked up from this location and written out on an output device. A very simple computer could be designed around this concept.

The limitation of having only one location in memory to store data becomes apparent as soon as a problem of any complexity is to be solved. Therefore, we shall design the computer so that data may be stored in many locations. When you inform the computer which operation to perform, you can also tell it where the data is located. As you might assume from previous discussion, the main storage of Systems/360 and 370 is logically broken into groups of eight units, and each of these groups has an address. Each group is called a *byte* (see figure 3-1). Note that the address of the first byte is zero, and the other bytes are addressed consecutively.

As we give the computer a request to perform an operation, that request can be broken down into two parts. The first part is the combination of ones and zeros that represents the operation to be performed. The second part of the request is the address of the data. These two parts of the request, or instruction, are called the operation code (*opcode*), and the *operand*.

opcode	operand

Although we now have a flexible way to refer to pieces of data, it seems that we are forced to give the computer one instruction at a time. Why not use part of the computer's memory to store the instructions and the other part to store the data? As long as a sequence of instructions, or program, remains in the computer's storage, the sequence can be used repeatedly; and the same plan can be followed to a given end using entirely different data each time.

0	1	2	3
4	5	6	7

Fig. 3-1 Bytes in the computer's storage

MACHINE LANGUAGE PROGRAMMING

A programmer analyzes his problem and hypothesizes a solution. He breaks this solution down into a series of discrete steps to be performed according to his plan. He then sets up a series of instructions for the computer, each requesting that one of the computer's basic operations be performed. This is common to much programming, but the programmer who programs in machine language has a difficult job. He must actually allocate particular storage addresses to pieces of data, making sure he does not assign the same storage address to more than one piece of data, and he must remember the storage addresses he assigns to any data referred to in his instructions. He is required to punch the long series of ones and zeros (which now represent the program, the sequence of instructions, plus the data) into cards—a task prone to error. The program is then read into the computer's storage. The computer is informed that it should begin operations with the first instruction.

The following shows what this type of program might look like:

11001010	00001100	10110111	00001101
0	1	2	3
11101001	00001110	10101101	00001111
4	5	6	7
01101110	00001100	11111111	00000000
8	9	10	11
00000110	00000111	00000010	00000011
12	13	14	15

In this example, each instruction consists of two bytes; a one-byte opcode, and a one-byte operand. There are six instructions in this program and they occupy the bytes with addresses 0–11. Bytes 12–15 each contain a data constant. The byte at address 12 contains a constant of 6, the byte at address 13 contains a constant of 7, and the bytes at addresses 14 and 15 contain constants of 2 and 3, respectively.

The opcodes involved in this program are:

Opcode	Operation Performed
11001010	load the data at the operand address into the accumulator[†]
10110111	multiply the data at the operand address by the contents of the accumulator, placing the result in the accumulator

---

[†]Note: The accumulator is a place in the computer that is used for intermediate storage.

11101001	divide value in accumulator by data at the operand address, placing quotient in accumulator
10101101	add data at the operand address to the contents of the accumulator
01101110	subtract data at the operand address from the contents of the accumulator
11111111	stop executing instructions

Using the above list of opcodes, see if you can verify that this program performs the following sequence of operations:

$$ANS = 6 * 7 \div 2 + 3 - 6$$

Should the programmer encounter an error in his program, he must find the particular combination of ones and zeros that caused the error and change the incorrect instructions. Should he make a mistake in remembering a storage address he assigned to a particular piece of data (or should he insert new pieces of data), he must change all affected instructions.

An error is present in the above example of what a program could look like. The sequence of operations should be:

$$ANS = 6 * 7 \div 2 + 3 - 6 + 7$$

The instruction to add 7 at the end was forgotten, meaning that an extra instruction must be added after the subtract instruction at address 8. This seems an easy enough task, except that such an insertion means that all the data must be moved. This results in all the addresses in the existing instructions that refer to the data in need of change. The altered program becomes:

11001010	00001110	10110111	00001111
0	1	2	3
11101001	00010000	10101101	00010001
4	5	6	7
01101110	00001110	10101101	00001111
8	9	10	11
11111111	00000000	00000110	00000111
12	13	14	15
00000010	00000011		
16	17		

This programming is in the computer's—the machine's—language: nothing but ones and zeros.

SYMBOLIC LANGUAGE PROGRAMMING

Symbolic language programming allows a programmer to use a symbolic name, or *mnemonic*, when referring to a particular combination of eight ones and zeros that represents the opcode of an instruction, and to use symbolic names to reference data locations in the computer's memory. Remembering the symbolic name, or mnemonic, for a particular operation is much easier than trying to remember a particular combination of ones and zeros. Also, by using a symbolic name to refer to a piece of data, the programmer doesn't need to remember the address of the location of the data in storage.

The following illustration will give you an idea of what symbolic language programming involves. This illustration involves the same hypothetical sequence of operations on the identical values as used in the machine language example on page 31.

```
              LOAD   SIX
              MULT   SEVEN
              DIV    TWO
              ADD    THREE
              SUBT   SIX
              STOP
      SIX     DATA   6
      SEVEN   DATA   7
      TWO     DATA   2
      THREE   DATA   3
```

For each symbolic language there is a *translator*, a program that takes the symbolic language program and translates it into machine language. This gives the symbolic language programmer more freedom. He is less tied down by having to remember every little thing about his machine language program. His job is easier, and he can produce more in a given period of time.

To make the same alteration in the above program that was made in the machine language program, the symbolic language programmer need only insert the instruction: ADD SEVEN following the SUBT instruction. All necessary operand address changes would be made by the translator.

ASSEMBLER LANGUAGE PROGRAMMING

In assembler language, which is a type of symbolic language, each instruction is equivalent to one machine language instruction. The advantages are that symbolic names are used to indicate the opcode and the operand, and the translator program keeps track of the location of every piece of data.

As the translator changes the assembler instructions into machine instructions, it looks up the mnemonic in a table that contains mnemonics and machine opcode equivalents. It looks up the symbolic name of the data in another table that contains symbols and data addresses.

The tables used by the translator in its translation of the symbolic language program on page 33 were as follows:

Opcode Table

Mnemonic	Machine Opcode
ADD	01011010
SUBT	01011011
MULT	01011100
DIV	01011101
STOP	11111111
LOAD	01011000

Data Table

Symbol	Address
SIX	12
SEVEN	13
TWO	14
THREE	15

The translator substitutes the machine opcode for the mnemonic opcode and the actual storage address for the symbolic reference to the data. One by one, the translator goes through the program, translating each assembler language instruction into a machine language instruction. When this translation is complete, the machine language program, along with its data, can be placed into the computer's storage; and the running or execution of the program is started. The program so stored is identical to the same algorithm programmed and placed in the computer's storage by a machine language programmer. The difference lies in the time and effort it takes to create the two programs.

BASIC COMPONENTS OF SYSTEMS/360 AND 370

THE BYTE AS THE BASIC BUILDING BLOCK

The storage of Systems/360 and 370 machines is binary in orientation. This means that each basic component of storage is capable of being in either one of two different states: on or off. We represent these states by a one and a zero respectively, the two digits in the binary number system. Stated another way, each component of storage is capable of representing or storing one binary digit worth of data. The term *bit* is short for *bi*nary digi*t* and is used when referring to one of these basic components of storage.

The *byte* (eight contiguous bits) is the smallest piece of storage that can be addressed. Thus, the byte is known by the term *BAU*, which stands for Basic Addressable Unit. Each byte has a unique address assigned to it that reflects its physical position within the computer's storage. The first byte has the address of zero, the second byte one, and so on. When an assembler language instruction makes a reference to storage by using a symbol, the assembler program translates that symbol into an actual storage address.

FIXED- AND VARIABLE-LENGTH DATA

Remember that an assembler language instruction has two parts:

opcode	operand (length)

The first part, the opcode, states which of the computer's basic operations is to be performed. The second part, the operand, states where the data on which the operation is to be performed is located.

The assembler language of the Systems/360 and 370 has two groups of instructions. The difference between the two groups is that one uses fixed-length data and the other uses variable-length data. The opcode that appears in the first part of the instruction reveals whether that instruction uses fixed-length or variable-length data, as well as the operation to be performed.

Variable-length data instructions are probably easier to understand, so we shall examine them first. Among the operations these instructions can perform is the movement of data from one location in storage to another. Since the smallest piece of storage we can address in these systems is the byte, the smallest amount of data that can be moved is one byte; but many more bytes of data can be moved if necessary.

How do we tell the computer how many bytes to move? We do this in the same way we tell it what operation to perform and where the data is located—in the instruction. Therefore we add a third part to the basic instruction format:

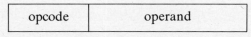

opcode	operand

What lets the assembler program know we are using a variable-length data instruction? The opcode. Where is the data located? It begins with the byte whose address is in the operand portion of the instruction (whether it be a symbol for the storage address or the actual storage address). The length in the instruction states exactly how many bytes of data are to participate in the operation. The operation can begin with any byte and include up to the maximum allowed for that particular opcode.

Fixed-length instructions operate on data that is of specific lengths. Some of these instructions use data that is two bytes in length, some use four bytes of data, and others use eight. These instructions work faster than variable-length instructions because the data is placed at particular addresses in storage called *integral boundaries*—mandatory only on System/360. (As in all addressing, each of the fixed-length data areas is referenced by the address of its first byte).

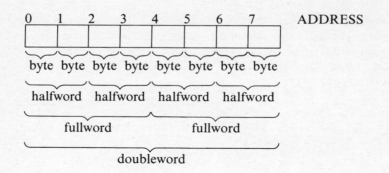

Fig. 3-2 The organization of storage

Integral boundaries mean that the address of a fixed-length area is evenly divisible by the number of bytes in that area. A four-byte area where the address of the first byte of the word is evenly divisible by four is called a *word*. A two-byte area where the address of the first byte of that halfword is evenly divisible by two, i.e., an even number, is called a *halfword*. An eight-byte area where the address of its first byte is evenly divisible by eight is called a *doubleword*. This organization of storage can be seen in figure 3-2.

Zero is the address of a doubleword; zero and four are the addresses of words; and 0, 2, 4, and 6 are the addresses of halfwords. Just as the opcode of the instruction enables the assembler program to distinguish between variable and fixed-length data instructions, the opcode also specifies which length of fixed-length data is to be used: a halfword, word, or doubleword.

The assembler will ensure compliance to the integral boundary requirement for fixed-length areas. The programmer informs the assembler when he requests a storage area for data that that area is fixed in length and treated as words, halfwords, or doublewords. As a result, the assembler will make sure that the address of the first byte of that area is on the correct integral boundary.

REGISTERS

Registers are special areas of storage set aside in the processing unit of the computer. There are 16 general purpose registers in the Systems/360 and 370. These registers are identified by the numbers 0–15. **It is best not to use registers 0, 1, and 11–15. These registers have special uses; to avoid conflicting with these uses, do not refer to those registers in your coding.**[†]

Each register can hold one word (4 bytes, or 32 bits of data). Registers are needed for certain arithmetic operations and have a multitude of other uses in programming. If the data for an instruction is currently held in one of the 16

[†]Note: The special uses for these registers are discussed in chapters 13 and 15.

registers, rather than in a word of storage, that register is named in the assembler language instruction, and the address of the register is the operand of the machine language instruction formed by the assembler. How does the computer know whether the address in the operand is the address of a register or a location in storage? By the opcode.

```
        FIRST                   SET UP FOR AND START EXECUTION
        L       7,SIX           MOVE FIRST VALUE TO REGISTER
        M       6,SEVEN         6*7
        D       6,TWO           6*7/2
        A       7,THREE         6*7/2 + 3
        S       7,SIX           6*7/2 + 3 − 6
        LAST                    END EXECUTION
SIX     DC      F'6'
SEVEN   DC      F'7'
TWO     DC      F'2'
THREE   DC      F'3'
```

The above is a working assembler language program that solves the same sequence of operations performed in the examples on page 31 and page 33. FIRST and LAST are special instructions (used in this text) to start and stop the execution of the program, respectively.

The symbolic names used for the data are identical to those used on page 33. The letters DC following each of these symbols stand for Define Constant. The letter F, following the DC, is the means by which the programmer has informed the assembler translator that each of the constant values are to occupy words (be 4 bytes in length and the first of those 4 bytes located on a fullword integral boundary). The number enclosed within the apostrophes is the value to be placed in the fullword.

The differences in the instructions in this example and the one on page 33 involve shorter mnemonic opcodes and two operands instead of one. Two operands are necessary here because the programmer has 16 general purpose registers to use instead of just one accumulator. He must indicate which of the 16 registers he wishes used in the operation.

You will notice that it appears as if two different registers (6 and 7) are used in this program. This is necessary because the multiply and divide instructions use two consecutive registers to hold the product and the dividend.

ASSEMBLER LANGUAGE INSTRUCTION FORMAT

The assembler language translator is (as we have said before) a program. In order for that program to be able to translate assembler language instructions into machine language instructions, the programmer must follow certain rules and conventions. These rules ensure that the assembler program can determine exactly what action the programmer is requesting of the computer.

THE FOUR FIELDS OF INFORMATION

Since the unit of control in a program is the instruction, the first things an assembler language programmer should learn are the rules for writing or coding an assembler language instruction, which contains four fields of information. These are: (1) name, (2) opcode, (3) operand (the length mentioned earlier as being used with instructions dealing with variable-length data is actually a part of the operand field), and (4) comments. Every field does not have to be present in every instruction. Fields that are present are separated by blanks; no blank may be embedded within a field.

[name]   opcode   [operands]   [comments]

(Brackets [ ] mean that what they enclose is optional.)

The Name Field   The first field, the name, is optional. If you give a symbolic name to an instruction or an area of storage that the assembler is to allocate, this name must begin in column 1 of the coding line or card. The symbolic name consists of from one to eight characters. The first character must be alphabetic; the remaining characters (referred to as *alphameric*) may be alphabetic (A–Z), numeric (0–9), or national (@, #, or $). National characters are specially set aside because there are differences in the symbols used by different countries. For example, Great Britain uses £ (pound) sign instead of a $ (dollar) sign. Symbolic names *cannot* contain special characters (+, /, −, or ?, and so on) or blanks.

According to the rules for symbols, which of the following are valid symbols, which are not, and why are the invalid ones not correct?

a. BETA
b. T
c. FLD A
d. LOC
e. SERIALNUM

f. AREA2
g. MAN#
h. 3LINES
i. C/D
j. PLACE

You should determine that *a, b, d, f, g,* and *j* are valid; *c, e, h,* and *i* are invalid symbols—*c,* because there is an embedded blank; *e,* because it contains more than eight characters; *h,* because it does not begin with an alphabetic character; and *i,* because it contains a special character.

The Opcode Field   The opcode is the only mandatory field of an instruction. It must be preceded by at least one blank. Several kinds of opcodes can be specified:

1. machine language instructions
2. constant or storage definitions

3. instructions to the assembler
4. macro instructions

Generally, machine language instructions predominate in a program. These instructions request that one of the computer's basic operations, such as addition or subtraction, be performed. The other types of opcodes aid the assembler in its job of generating machine language instructions.

The opcode is the most important part of any instruction. It tells the assembler program what to look for in the operand field of the instruction, whether the data is variable or fixed in length, and whether the data is located in a register or in a storage location. The mnemonic used to represent the opcode must be one of the valid System/360 or System/370 mnemonic opcodes. A complete list of valid opcodes is shown in appendix 3 and on the green IBM System/360 Reference Data Card (GX20-1703) or the yellow IBM System/370 Reference Summary Card (GX20-1850).

The Operand Field The operand field of an instruction must be separated from the opcode field by at least one blank. Operands for machine instructions usually represent data. Data may reside in three different places:

1. in main storage
2. in registers
3. as part of the instruction itself (called immediate data)

Systems/360 and 370 instructions have two operands in most cases. A few instructions have three operands. Embedded blanks are not permitted in the operand field; operands are separated from one another by commas. An operand may be specified either symbolically or numerically (i.e., a symbolic name such as LOC, or the numeric identification of a register such as 6). The assembler knows what to expect in each operand and how to interpret a particular symbol or number by the opcode that's used with the instruction.

The Comments Field The comments field may be used for descriptive information that supports and clarifies the instructions. The comments are separated from the operand field by at least one blank.

FULL-LINE COMMENTS

Entire blocks of instructions can be documented by an entire coding line for comments. By placing an asterisk (*) in column 1, you can indicate that the entire line contains only comments. The first thing the assembler checks for in its scan of a line of code in the source program is an asterisk in column 1. If the asterisk is found, the comment is printed on the listing, and that line of input is examined no further by the assembler.

TYPES OR CLASSES OF INSTRUCTIONS

The opcode of a machine-language instruction places that instruction in one of five classes of instructions. The class informs the assembler of the number of operands to expect in the operand field, and whether each of those operands represents data in a register, data in a storage location, or data immediately available in the instruction itself. The five classes of instructions are:

1. RR-type
2. SS-type
3. SI-type
4. RX-type
5. RS-type

The clue to the location of the data is available from the names of the five classes. Each of the letters in the name of the class indicates the location of one of the operands. An *R* indicates data residing in one of the 16 registers. The first class of instructions is the RR-type. Every instruction that belongs to this class of instructions has two operands, and each operand represents data in a register (R).

An *S* indicates data in the computer's storage. The second class of instructions, the SS-type, have two operands—both operands are the addresses of data in storage locations. Each operand can be either an actual storage address or a symbolic name to which the assembler attaches an actual storage address.

An *I* in the name of the class of instructions indicates that that operand consists of *immediate* data. Immediate data is that which is actually a part of the instruction itself. The instruction operand does not contain the address of the storage location or a register where the data is located; the data is in the operand of the instruction. All instructions which have data as one of the operands belong to the SI-type or class of instructions. All SI instructions have two operands. The first is a storage location and the second is immediate data.

The two remaining classes don't follow the generalization (letters in type name corresponding to data locations) as completely as the RR, SS, and SI classes. Instructions belonging to either the RX or RS class of instructions deal with operations between registers and storage locations. Instructions belonging to the RX class of instructions have two operands. The first operand is a register, and the second is a storage location. An *X* is used instead of an *S* to indicate a storage address because the instructions which belong to this class can reference storage locations in a special manner. This special manner involves the specification of actual storage addresses in three separate pieces. Since our references to storage will be made symbolically throughout the first chapters of this book, the assembler will be supplying the actual storage addresses. (For the time being, treat the *X* as if it were an *S*.)

Instructions belonging to the RS class of instructions can have two or three operands, depending on the opcode. If the opcode indicates two operands, the first must be a register, and the second a storage location. If the opcode indicates three operands, the first and second must be registers, and the third a storage location. Examples of instructions belonging to some of these instruction classes:

Instruction Class	Instruction Example	Explanation
RR	LR 6,8	moves data from one register (8) to another register (6)
RX	L 7,LOC	moves data from a word in storage (LOC) to a register (7)
SS	MVC LOC2(6),LOC1	moves variable amount of data from one location in storage (LOC1) to another storage location (LOC2); in this case it moves the contents of 6 bytes of storage

THE CODING FORM

There exists a printed form that can aid the assembler language programmer when coding his instructions: the standard IBM Assembler Coding Form (GX28-6509). This coding form has room to indicate the programmer's name, name of program, data, and other pertinent information at the top. It is printed with eighty columns that correspond to the card columns. Using this form makes it easier to keypunch the coded assembler language statements.

The names of the four fields of an assembler language statement are printed over the columns suggested for use as a particular field (name, columns 1–8; operation, columns 10–14; and operand field starting in column 16). It is best to align similar fields of statements on identical columns. It makes the coded program more readable. See figure 3-3 for an example. The reasoning behind the suggestion that these particular columns be used is based on the maximum sizes of the first two fields. A symbolic name, if used, must begin in column 1 and can be from one to eight characters in length. Column 9 is left blank because the opcode field of an instruction must be preceded by at least one blank. Remember that the blank is used as a delimiter to end each of the four fields

IBM System/360 Assembler Coding Form

PROGRAM: EXAMPLE
PROGRAMMER: TUGGLE

Name	Operation	Operand	Comments	Identification-Sequence
		* START EXECUTION		SKT0010
FIRST	L	7,SIX	MOVE FIRST VALUE TO REG.	SKT0020
	M	6,SEVEN		SKT0030
	D	6,TWO	6 X 7 / 2	SKT0040
	A	7,THREE	6 X 7 / 2 + 3	SKT0050
	S	7,SIX	6 X 7 / 2 + 3 - 6	SKT0060
LAST		* END EXECUTION		SKT0070
SIX	DC			SKT0080
SEVEN	DC			SKT0090
TWO	DC			SKT0100
THREE	DC			SKT0110

Fig. 3-3 The assembler coding form

of an assembler statement. The opcode field therefore can begin in column 10. The maximum number of characters contained in a mnemonic opcode is five. So, columns 10 through 14 allow for this maximum; column 15 is left blank to delimit the opcode field.

Column 16 is generally used as the beginning of the operand field. This field can vary in length depending on the lengths of the symbolic names the programmer chooses to represent the operand locations. Since this field is also delimited by at least one blank, it is best to choose a column such as 35 or 40, or even 45, as the first column in the comments field. The comments field may extend to column 71.

If, for some reason, an instruction will not fit on one line, it may be continued on the next line. The instruction is written up to a convenient breaking point prior to column 72, and a nonblank character is placed in column 72. It doesn't matter which character is placed in this column; it's not part of the instruction. Its only function is to indicate that the following line contains a continuation of the instruction on this line. The following line (the continuation line) must have blanks in columns 1–15, with the continued instruction beginning in column 16. A maximum of two continuation lines may be used under OS based systems and one for DOS based systems.[†]

Look at the coding form (figure 3-3) once more; you can see "Identification Sequence" printed above columns 73–80. The assembler program does not consider columns 73–80 as part of the instruction. Therefore, these columns are available to the programmer for whatever purpose he deems necessary. There are two good reasons for using these columns, particularly when the lines of coding are punched into cards: to identify the program or programmer and to add a sequence number to the cards. Should decks of cards get dropped or disorganized, it is extremely helpful to be able to identify cards and to be able to put them back into order quickly.

A convenient way to use columns 73–80 for both identification and sequencing is to use your initials followed by a three to five-digit sequence number (e.g., SKT0010). An additional good piece of advice is to choose sequence numbers at set intervals; for example, SKT0010, SKT0020, SKT0030, and so on. This allows for easy insertion of additional instructions into the program. For example, an instruction inserted between SKT0020 and SKT0030 may be given the sequence number SKT0025. As you can see, the example above allows for the insertion of up to nine cards between each pair of initially consecutive statements, in case the program needs modification.

[†]OS and DOS are two abbreviations used to refer to the IBM Systems/360 or 370 Operating Systems and Disk Operating Systems, respectively. Operating systems are collections of programs such as control programs and language processors which help you in getting your programs to work on the computer.

OVERVIEW OF THE PROGRAMMING JOB

Becoming somewhat familiar with the process your program goes through from source program to execution will give you an overview of your programming job. As illustrated in figure 3-4, the program you code goes through three steps on its way to producing the results you want.

First, the assembler takes your assembler language program (also called source program or *source module*) and translates it into machine language (also called object code or *object module*). Second, another program called the *linkage editor* takes the object module produced by the assembler, performs a few operations on addresses within the object module, and creates a load module, placing it on a disk Input/Output (I/O) device. Third, the load module is placed in the computer's storage, and the instructions in your program are executed one by one.

In summary, the three steps your program goes through are: 1) assembly, 2) linkage editing, and 3) execution. Each of these steps works with a different form of your program. These forms are source module, object module, and load module, respectively.

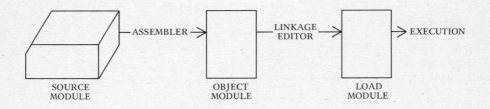

Fig. 3-4 The three steps to program execution

QUESTIONS

1. How many different combinations of ones and zeros can be represented in one byte of storage space?

   256

2. Does the first byte of storage have an address of zero or one?

   ZERO

3. What are the differences between machine language programming and symbolic language programming?

4. Discuss two tables used by the assembler in its translation of the assembler language program into a machine language program.

5. Discuss definitions of the following terms:

    a. Bit — *SHORT FOR BINARY DIGIT*
    b. Byte — *EIGHT CONTIGUOUS BITS, SMALLEST PIECE OF STORAGE ADDRESSABLE*
    c. BAU — *BASIC ADDRESSABLE UNIT*
    d. Integral boundaries — *THAT THE ADDRESS OF A FIXED-LENGTH AREA IS EVENLY*
    e. Word, halfword, doubleword *DIVISIBLE BY THE NUMBER OF BYTES IN THAT AREA*
    4 BYTES, 2 BYTES, 8 BYTES

6. What are the differences between fixed-length and variable-length data?
FIXED LENGTH OPERATES ON DATA THAT IS OF SPECIFIC LENGTH WHILE VARIABLE-LENGTH OPERATES ON DATA FROM 1 BYTE TO MAXIMUM ALLOWED

7. Why is the opcode such an important part of a machine language instruction? *IT TELLS THE ASSEMBLER PROGRAM WHAT TO LOOK FOR IN THE OPERAND FIELD OF THE INSTRUCTION, WHETHER DATA IS VARIABLE OR FIXED IN LENGTH & WHETHER DATA IS LOCATED IN STORAGE OR REGISTER*

8. How many general purpose registers are available on Systems/360 and 370? Which of these should you avoid using?
0-16; D+1, 11-15

9. What are the four fields of information that can appear in an assembler language instruction?
NAME (1-8) OPCODE (10-14) OPERANDS (16-35) COMMENTS (35-71)

10. What are the five classes of machine language instructions, and what does the name of a class tell you about the data used by instructions in a particular class? *RR — 2 OPERANDS & EACH REPRESENT DATA IN REGISTER*
RS, RR, SS, RX, RS *SS — 2 OPERANDS & EACH REPRESENT DATA IN STORAGE. OR SYMBOLIC NAME SI — STORE IMMEDIATE 1st OP STORAGE LOCATION, 2 OP IMMEDIATE DATA*

11. What use can be made of columns 73–80 of a coding line or punch card?
IDENTIFICATION SEQUENCE

12. What are the three steps a program goes through on its way to producing results?
1) ASSEMBLY 2) LINKAGE EDITING 3) EXECUTION

EXERCISES

1. According to the rules for symbols, which of the following are valid symbols, which are not, and why are the invalid ones not correct?

  V a. S
  IN b. TEN%
  IN c. A+B
  V d. W45
  IN e. FORTYFIVE
  IV f. CAN'T
  IV g. 6CENTS
  IV h. LIKE IT
  V i. LOC

CHAPTER 4

Representation of Data

A data processing system manipulates data. Much of this data is in the form of numbers. In using Systems/360 and 370, a programmer deals with three number systems: decimal, binary, and hexadecimal. An easy way to familiarize yourself with these different number systems is through the concept of positional notation.

POSITIONAL NOTATION

DECIMAL NUMBER SYSTEM

The decimal number system will be discussed first, since it is familiar to us because of its frequent use in our everyday lives. The decimal number system, taking its name from the Greek *dekas*—group of ten—has ten digits, ten unique symbols or characters that can be used when representing a number. These are the digits 0, 1, 2, 3, 4, 5, 6, 7, 8, and 9. Every number in the decimal system is comprised of one or more of these digits. The value that each digit contributes to the number depends on its position in that number. For example, the two 5s in the decimal number 55 have two different values based on their positions in the number. The first (leftmost) 5 has a value of 50, and the other 5 a value of only 5. The first 5 contributes 10 times as much value as the second 5 to the total value of the number 55.

$$
\begin{array}{l}
5\ 5 \\
\ \ \ \rule{0pt}{1em} \\
\end{array}
$$

5 5
value = 5
value = 50

We know that the first 5 contributes a value of 50 because it is in the tens position, and the second 5 contributes 5 because it is in the units position. But we must break this down into a more detailed explanation if we are going to understand the other number systems.

In positional notation, the value of the digit in a digit position is determined by multiplying the digit by a certain value. In the case of a decimal number, that value is a power of 10. Ten is thus referred to as the base (or radix) of this number system. The first digit position has a value equal to the digit value itself. The second digit position has a value equal to 10 times the digit value. The third digit position has a value of 100 times the digit value.

$$5 = 5 \times 1$$
$$50 = 5 \times 10$$
$$500 = 5 \times 100$$
$$5000 = 5 \times 1000$$

Stated another way, each digit has the value of itself multiplied by a power of 10 equal to its relative position in the number. We begin with the zero power of ten, and increase by one power of 10 for each digit position.

$$
\begin{aligned}
5555 \\
5 \times 10^0 &= 5 \times 1 = 5 \\
5 \times 10^1 &= 5 \times 10 = 50 \\
5 \times 10^2 &= 5 \times 100 = 500 \\
5 \times 10^3 &= 5 \times 1000 = 5000
\end{aligned}
$$

The powers of 10 are the result of multiplying the number 10 by itself that (the power) number of times.

$$10^2 = 10 \times 10 = 100$$
$$10^4 = 10 \times 10 \times 10 \times 10 = 10000$$

The 2 and the 4 in the previous example are called exponents. An exponent of 1 always results in the number itself. An exponent of zero is a very special case and always results in a value of 1 regardless of what number the exponent is used on ($10^0 = 1$ just as $6^0 = 1$ or $2^0 = 1$).

Numbers with a value less than 1 can be represented in the same manner. Simply remember that the significance of the digit decreases the further it is away from the decimal point. Each digit still has the value of itself multiplied by a power of 10 equal to its relative position in the number. We begin with a power of -1 for the first decimal place and decrease by one power of 10 for each digit position.

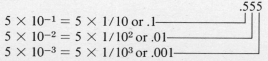

$$
\begin{aligned}
.555 \\
5 \times 10^{-1} &= 5 \times 1/10 \text{ or } .1 \\
5 \times 10^{-2} &= 5 \times 1/10^2 \text{ or } .01 \\
5 \times 10^{-3} &= 5 \times 1/10^3 \text{ or } .001
\end{aligned}
$$

Expanded Form   A decimal number can be represented in what is called its expanded form. This form expands the number to show its value as the sum of the value of *each* digit multiplied by the base of the number system raised to the exponent that reflects the position of that digit within the number. For example, the decimal number 672.36 in its expanded form is:

$$672.36 = 6 \times 10^2 + 7 \times 10^1 + 2 \times 10^0 + 3 \times 10^{-1} + 6 \times 10^{-2}$$
$$= 600 + 70 + 2 + .3 + .06$$

So, in its expanded form, a number is shown as the sum of the values contributed by each of its digits.

Counting   Before advancing to a second number system, one other process we usually do without much thought should be examined: counting. We advance through the range of symbols or digits in the system until the range of symbols is exhausted. We then carry one to the next, more significant, position and start through the range again. In the decimal system, we count from 0–9; once 9 is reached, we carry one to the tens position and begin over with 0 in the units position. This process is the same regardless of the number system in which we are counting:

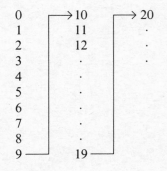

BINARY NUMBER SYSTEM

Due to its importance in modern computer systems, including Systems/360 and 370, it is important that a programmer acquire a working knowledge and understanding of the binary number system. As in the decimal system, the value of a particular digit in a binary number is a reflection of the digit multiplied by the base of the system, raised to a power that reflects the position of that digit in the number. The base of the binary system is 2.

The binary number 101101 in expanded form is:

$$101101 = 1 \times 2^5 + 0 + 2^4 + 1 \times 2^3 + 1 \times 2^2 + 0 \times 2^1 + 1 \times 2^0$$
$$= 32 + 0 + 8 + 4 + 0 + 1$$

Thus the number 101101 in the binary number system is equivalent to (represents the same value as) the decimal number 45. What we have done above is to use the expanded form of the binary to convert it to decimal. Try converting the following to their decimal representation. Subscripts ($_{2~10}$) following the numbers are used to indicate the base of that number.

   a. 110101101_2 b. 10111001_2 c. 111011_2

Respectively, your answers should be:

   a. 429_{10} b. 185_{10} c. 59_{10}

CONVERSION OF DECIMAL TO BINARY

There are two ways to convert a number in base 10 to a number in base 2. The first way is the multiple-division method. The number to be converted is divided repeatedly by the value of the base of the number system to which the conversion is being made. The division operation is repeated on the quotient until the quotient finally reaches zero. The remainder from the first division operation is used as the digit in the rightmost position in the resultant binary number; the remainder from the second division operation becomes the next digit, and so on, until the evaluation is complete. For example, converting the decimal number 45 to binary takes the following division operations:

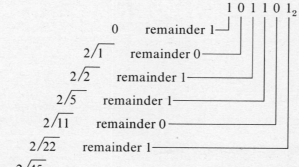

Thus 45_{10} and 101101_2 are equivalent. Convert the following decimal values to binary:

   a. 216   b. 1849   c. 87

See if you get:

   a. 11011000_2 b. 11100111001_2 c. 1010111_2

A second method for converting decimal numbers to binary utilizes a table of the powers of 2 and the expanded form of the binary number:

Powers of 2	Value
2^0	1
2^1	2
2^2	4
2^3	8
2^4	16
2^5	32
2^6	64
2^7	128
2^8	256
2^9	512
2^{10}	1024

We find the value for the largest power of 2 contained in the decimal number, and this yields the most significant one digit in the binary number. This value is subtracted from the decimal number. The value for the largest power of 2 contained in the remainder yields the position of the next most significant one bit in the binary number. For instance, the decimal number 74:

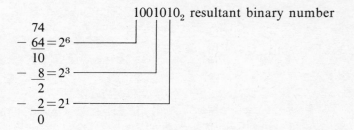

Now with this second method, try converting the following to their binary equivalents:

   a. 1426_{10} b. 936_{10} c. 15_{10}

These binary equivalents are:

   a. 10110010010_2 b. 1110101000_2 c. 1111_2

Hexadecimal Number System

Systems/360 and 370 are binary-oriented. Storage in these systems is based on the use of ones and zeros. It becomes cumbersome, however, to work with so many ones and zeros. Try to memorize the decimal number 362,678. That's not too difficult, but now see how hard it is to memorize its binary equivalent, 1011000100010110110.

We could break up the binary number into smaller groups of bits and represent each group with one symbol, therefore having less symbols to remember. We would be using the new symbols as a shorthand to remember the long binary numbers. The designers of System/360, predecessor of System/370, decided that they would use groups of four binary bits—each as a logical entity. Sixteen different combinations of ones and zeros can be represented by one group of four bits. Therefore, the hexadecimal number system with its 16 different digits came into prominence.

In addition to the ten digits (0 through 9), the six letters A through F are used in the hexadecimal number system. The same rules apply to hexadecimal that apply to the decimal and binary number systems. However, in the hexadecimal number system you count 0, 1, 2, 3, 4, 5, 6, 7, 8, 9, A, B, C, D, E, F. The symbol A is equivalent to a decimal 10, B to a decimal 11, and on up to the symbol F, being equivalent to a decimal 15:

Hexadecimal		Decimal	
0	→10	0	→16
1	11	1	17
2	12	2	18
3	13	3	19
4	14	4	20
5	15	5	21
6	16	6	22
7	17	7	23
8	18	8	24
9	19	9	25
A	1A	10	26
B	1B	11	27
C	1C	12	28
D	1D	13	29
E	1E	14	30
F	1F	15	31

The value that a particular digit contributes in a hexadecimal number is that digit times the base 16, raised to a power that reflects the digit's position. In its expanded form the hexadecimal number 24B5 is:

$$24B5_{16} = 2 \times 16^3 + 4 \times 16^2 + 11 \times 16^1 + 5 \times 16^0$$

Following through with the calculations involved in the expanded form results in deriving the decimal equivalent of the hexadecimal number.

$$
\begin{aligned}
24B5_{16} &= 2 \times 16^3 + 4 \times 16^2 + 11 \times 16^1 + 5 \times 16^0 \\
&= 2 \times 4096 + 4 \times 256 + 11 \times 16 + 5 \times 1 \\
&= 8192 + 1024 + 176 + 5 \\
&= 9397
\end{aligned}
$$

Also try calculating the decimal equivalents for the following:

<blockquote>a. $82C_{16}$ b. $1BC6_{16}$ c. 429_{16}</blockquote>

You should get:

<blockquote>a. 2092_{10} b. 7110_{10} c. 1065_{10}</blockquote>

CONVERSION OF DECIMAL TO HEXADECIMAL

The multiple-division method can be used here as it was to convert decimal numbers to binary numbers. Remember, in this method the number to be converted is divided repeatedly by the base of the number system to which the conversion is being made. The remainders are used as the digits of the new base numbers—beginning at the least significant digit position. In this case the decimal remainders 0–15 are converted to the equivalent hexadecimal digits 0–F. Each quotient becomes the successive dividend until a quotient of zero is encountered, which stops the conversion. For example, 6452_{10}:

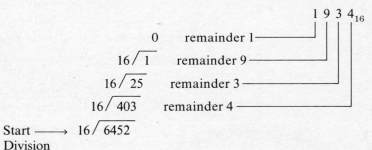

Try a few more for practice:

<blockquote>a. 3179_{10} b. 9680_{10} c. 759_{10}</blockquote>

See if the hexadecimal numbers you calculate are:

<blockquote>a. $C6B_{16}$ b. $25D0_{16}$ c. $2F7_{16}$</blockquote>

THE USE OF CONVERSION TABLES

If a hexadecimal-decimal conversion table is available (see table 4-1), it can aid greatly in the calculations that need to be performed. To use the conversion table, locate the column in it that corresponds to the position of the particular digit in the number you are converting. Note that the lower digits begin at the right and that the X at the top of each column is in the corresponding position in relation to the zeros. Look down the column until you are opposite the hex (short for hexadecimal) digit you are converting. For instance, examine $8CB_{16}$. The 8 is in the third position, therefore look down the third column from the right until you are opposite the 8 in the hex-digit column. An 8 in this position in a hexadecimal number is equivalent to a value of 2,048 in the decimal number system. Look down the second column from the right until opposite the C, and you see that a C in this position is equivalent to 192_{10}. The B in the least significant digit position is valued at 11_{10}. Summing the equivalent values of the three digits, the converted value is $2048 + 192 + 11$, or 2251_{10}.

$$8CB$$
$$800_{16} = 2048_{10}$$
$$C0_{16} = 192_{10}$$
$$B_{16} = 11_{10}$$
$$2251_{10}$$

The same table can be used to convert from decimal to hexadecimal. Search the numbers that make up the columns for the one that is closest to, but not larger than, the number you are trying to convert. Look to the left in the table to see which hex digit will represent this value when placed in the converted number (in the position indicated at the top of that column in the table). Then

TABLE 4-1 Hexadecimal-Decimal Conversion Table

Hex. Digit	Decimal					
	X00000	0X0000	00X000	000X00	00X0	0X
0	0	0	0	0	0	0
1	1,048,576	65,536	4,096	256	16	1
2	2,097,152	131,072	8,192	512	32	2
3	3,145,728	196,608	12,288	768	48	3
4	4,194,304	262,144	16,384	1024	64	4
5	5,242,880	327,680	20,480	1280	80	5
6	6,291,456	393,216	24,576	1536	96	6
7	7,340,032	458,752	28,672	1792	112	7
8	8,388,608	524,288	32,768	2048	128	8
9	9,437,184	589,824	36,864	2304	144	9
A	10,485,760	655,360	40,960	2560	160	10
B	11,534,336	720,896	45,056	2816	176	11
C	12,582,912	786,432	49,152	3072	192	12
D	13,631,488	851,968	53,248	3328	208	13
E	14,680,064	917,504	57,344	3584	224	14
F	15,728,640	983,040	61,440	3840	240	15

subtract this closest value and look for the number closest to the remaining number.

For example, convert $35,682_{10}$ to base 16. The closest number from the table is 32,768; it can be represented by an 8 in the fourth digit position of the hexadecimal number. Subtract the 32,768, and you are left with 2914. The closest number to this is 2816, represented by a B in the third position. Subtract the 2816 and you have 98 left. Since 96 is closest, a 6 in the second digit position suffices. Subtract the 96, which leaves you with a 2 in the least significant digit position. The hexadecimal number made up of these 4 digits you have found is $8B62_{16}$. Check the work by converting in the other direction. Using the conversion table, try the following:

$$1,796,081_{10} \qquad \text{to} \qquad \text{base 16}$$
$$55,219_{10} \qquad \text{to} \qquad \text{base 16}$$
$$3D672_{16} \qquad \text{to} \qquad \text{base 10}$$
$$F63D_{16} \qquad \text{to} \qquad \text{base 10}$$

You should arrive at the following:

$$1B67F1_{16}$$
$$D7B3_{16}$$
$$251,506_{10}$$
$$63,037_{10}$$

ARITHMETIC IN DIFFERENT NUMBER SYSTEMS

Addition and subtraction in the decimal number system are understood by all of us and used frequently in our everyday lives. Now that we are going to be using a computer, we should become familiar with addition and subtraction in the computer's number system—binary—and addition and subtraction in hexadecimal—the shorthand used to represent binary numbers.

BINARY ADDITION AND SUBTRACTION

We need to learn only four different combinations to do binary addition: two zeros can be added, yielding a zero result, a one and zero—or a zero and one—can be added, yielding a result of one, or two ones can be added, yielding a result of zero with a carry of one to the next significant digit position.

$$
\begin{array}{cccc}
0 & 0 & 1 & 1 \\
+0 & +1 & +0 & +1 \\
\hline
0 & 1 & 1 & 0 \text{ plus a carry of 1}
\end{array}
$$

The last possibility merely states that one and one make two ($1_2 + 1_2 = 10_2$).

Examples:

$$
\begin{array}{r}
01010_2 \\
+\ 00100_2 \\
\hline
01110_2
\end{array}
\qquad \text{equivalent to} \qquad
\begin{array}{r}
10_{10} \\
+\ \ 4_{10} \\
\hline
14_{10}
\end{array}
$$

$$
\begin{array}{r}
00010_2 \\
+\ 00011_2 \\
\hline
0101_2
\end{array}
\qquad \text{equivalent to} \qquad
\begin{array}{r}
2_{10} \\
+\ \ 3_{10} \\
\hline
5_{10}
\end{array}
$$

$$
\begin{array}{r}
000111_2 \\
+\ 001011_2 \\
\hline
010010_2
\end{array}
\qquad \text{equivalent to} \qquad
\begin{array}{r}
7_{10} \\
+\ 11_{10} \\
\hline
18_{10}
\end{array}
$$

In this last example we added two ones in the first position. This yielded a zero in that position of the result and a carry of one to the next position. In adding the second-digit positions, we have a one plus a one plus a carry of one; this yields a result of one and a carry of one.

In the binary subtraction, we also have only four different combinations to learn: subtracting zero from zero yields a zero, subtracting zero from one yields a one, subtracting a one from a one yields a zero, and subtracting a one from a zero requires a borrow of one from the next significant digit position and yields a value of one in the resultant number.

$$
\begin{array}{cccc}
\begin{array}{r} 0 \\ -0 \\ \hline 0 \end{array} &
\begin{array}{r} 1 \\ -0 \\ \hline 1 \end{array} &
\begin{array}{r} 1 \\ -1 \\ \hline 0 \end{array} &
\begin{array}{r} {}^1 0 \\ -1 \\ \hline 1 \end{array}
\end{array}
\quad \text{requires a borrow of 1}
$$

Examples:

$$
\begin{array}{r}
011100_2 \\
-\ 001000_2 \\
\hline
010100_2
\end{array}
\qquad \text{equivalent to} \qquad
\begin{array}{r}
28_{10} \\
-\ \ 8_{10} \\
\hline
20_{10}
\end{array}
$$

$$
\begin{array}{r}
{}^0{}_1 \\
01\!\!\!/1001_2 \\
-\ 010100_2 \\
\hline
000101_2
\end{array}
\qquad \text{equivalent to} \qquad
\begin{array}{r}
25_{10} \\
-\ 20_{10} \\
\hline
5_{10}
\end{array}
$$

The second example shows borrowing. In the third digit position we are unable to subtract a one from a zero. In borrowing one from the fourth digit position (8_{10}), that 1 has a place value one power of two higher than a 1 in the third digit position (4_{10}). So when you borrow one from the next digit position, it is really equal to the value two, in the digit position you are currently subtracting. You add the borrowed two to the number you are subtracting from and continue the operation. Try a couple of binary subtraction examples of this type.

$$0101011_2 \qquad 0100101_2$$
$$-\ 0010101_2 \qquad -\ 0011001_2$$

Your answers should be 0010110_2 and 0001100_2, respectively.

HEXADECIMAL ADDITION AND SUBTRACTION

Although the computer itself does not perform its arithmetic operations in base 16, there are times when a programmer finds it an asset to be able to perform such addition and subtraction operations. Hexadecimal numbers are used in *dumps*, which display the contents of storage, and for addresses of storage locations. When trouble arises in the execution of a program, facility with hexadecimal arithmetic can be more than just handy—it can be a necessity.

In performance of the addition operation, the following examples are conceptually the same for the purpose of discussion—they are also equivalent.

$$\begin{array}{c} 434_{10} \\ +\ 385_{10} \\ \hline 819_{10} \end{array} \qquad \text{same as} \qquad \begin{array}{c} 1B2_{16} \\ +\ 181_{16} \\ \hline 333_{16} \end{array}$$

When you add the digits in the first position, you get $4_{10} + 5_{10} = 9_{10}$ and $2_{16} + 1_{16} = 3_{16}$. (Remember how to count in hexadecimal: 0, 1, 2, 3, 4, 5, 6, 7, 8, 9, A, B, C, D, E, F.)

When you add the 3_{10} and 8_{10} in the second digit position of the decimal addends you get 11, but there is no such *digit* as 11 in the decimal number system. Subtract out the base (10), place the remainder in the second digit position in the result, and carry 1×10 to the next higher digit position.

Adding B_{16} to 8_{16} in the second digit position of the hexadecimal addends yields 19_{10}. Subtracting the base (16) places a remainder of 3 in the second digit position of the result, and a carry of 1×16 is made to the third digit position. Try these examples:

$$\begin{array}{c} 4B_{16} \\ +\ 33_{16} \\ \hline \end{array} \qquad \begin{array}{c} 81_{16} \\ +\ 2F_{16} \\ \hline \end{array} \qquad \begin{array}{c} 6C_{16} \\ +\ 26_{16} \\ \hline \end{array} \qquad \begin{array}{c} 54C_{16} \\ +\ 16A_{16} \\ \hline \end{array} \qquad \begin{array}{c} D35A_{16} \\ +\ 41B2_{16} \\ \hline \end{array}$$

Your results should be: $7E_{16}$, $B0_{16}$, 92_{16}, $6B6_{16}$, and $1150C_{16}$, respectively.

In the case of hexadecimal subtraction, when you borrow one from the next digit position, you add 16 to the digit in the position you are working and then perform the subtraction. For example:

$$\begin{array}{c} 875_{10} \\ -\ 318_{10} \\ \hline 557_{10} \end{array} \qquad \begin{array}{l} \text{equivalent and same} \\ \text{conceptually as} \end{array} \qquad \begin{array}{c} 36B_{16} \\ -\ 13E_{16} \\ \hline 22D_{16} \end{array}$$

In subtracting the first digit position, you borrow one from the 7, add 10 to the 5, and subtract the 8 from the 15, leaving a remainder of 7. Applying the same procedure to the hexadecimal number—borrow one from the 6 making it a 5, add 16 to the B, and subtract E (or 14_{10} from 27_{10}), leaving a remainder of 13, or D.

INTERNAL DATA REPRESENTATION

As stated earlier, the basic building block of Systems/360 and 370 is the byte. Bytes are combined to represent numeric, character, or logical data in the computer's storage. The IBM Systems/360 and 370 use four different codes or means to represent data in the computer:

1. character information
2. fixed-point binary numbers
3. decimal numbers
4. floating-point numbers

CHARACTER INFORMATION

Character information can be handled as either fixed- or variable-length data. When the data is used as fixed-length fields, it can consist of one, two, four, or eight bytes. (This format for data will be discussed more fully in chapter 17.)

When variable-length data fields are used, each byte of the area contains the 8-bit code for one character. In chapter 1 we discussed the standardized way data is recorded on the medium of the punched card. This standardization involved a character set and an established correlation between a unique combination of punched holes in the card and the character represented. Now we are discussing standardization in the form of an established correlation between a unique combination of punched holes in a column of a data card and the 8-bit code that represents the character in internal storage. The 8-bit code accepted by Systems/360 and 370 is the Extended Binary Coded Decimal Interchange Code, EBCDIC for short. Each graphic symbol in the Systems/360 and 370 character set (the 10 digits, 26 alphabetic characters, and 27 special characters, including the 3 national characters) has its own unique 8-bit EBCDIC code. Some examples are:

Character	EBCDIC Code
A	11000001
S	11100010
5	11110101
$	01011011
+	01001110

For a complete list of character representations see appendix 3, the IBM System/360 Reference Data Card (GX20-1703), or the IBM System/370 Reference Summary Card (GX20-1850).

Fixed-Point Binary Numbers

A separate, distinct set of arithmetic instructions is provided for each of the three numeric data representations (fixed-point binary, decimal, and floating-point). Fixed-point arithmetic instructions use data in fixed-point binary format. Fixed-point numbers occupy *fullwords* or *halfwords*. Each consists of a sign bit (bit position 0) followed by the integer number. The fullword has 31 integer bits, bits 1–31, and the halfword has 15 integer bits, bits 1–15.

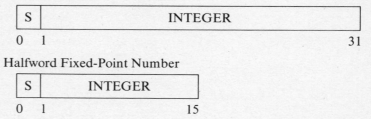

Fullword Fixed-Point Number

Halfword Fixed-Point Number

All fixed-point operands of instructions are treated as signed integers. Positive numbers are represented in their true binary form with the sign bit set to zero.

0000001010010010
hwb (halfword boundary)

Shown above is a halfword containing the fixed-point binary equivalent of 658_{10}.

Two's Complement Notation

Negative numbers are represented in two's complement notation with a sign bit of one. In addition to representing negative binary numbers, the use of two's complement notation simplifies the computer's handling of arithmetic operations. For example, subtraction is performed in Systems/360 and 370 by complementing the subtrahend and the operation simply becomes an addition operation.

The complement of a number is obtained by subtracting each digit of that number from the digit having the highest value in that number system (for a decimal number, this would be 9; for a binary number, 1), and then adding one to the least significant digit of the result. This is sometimes referred to as the radix complement and the name given to the complement refers to the base of the number system involved.

For example, the ten's complement of the decimal number 626 would be calculated as follows:

999	subtract each digit from the
− 626	highest value digit in that system
373	
+ 1	add one to the least significant digit
374	is the ten's complement

The same process is followed for a binary number. For example, the two's complement of 00110101_2 is 11001011_2.

11111111	subtract each digit from the
− 00110101	highest value digit in that system
11001010	
+ 1	add one to the least significant digit
11001011	is the two's complement

If you examine the original binary number (00110101) and the result of the subtraction operation (11001010), you will notice that each digit in the result is just the opposite of the digit in that position of the original number.

00110101	original number
11001010	result of the subtraction

This direct relation between the digits in the original binary number and the result of the subtraction holds true because the binary number system has only two digits. The subtraction of each digit position in the number can result in only one of two possibilities. Either you subtract a 1 from a 1 and the result is 0, or you subtract a 0 from a 1 and the result is 1. The result is always the opposite of the original digit.

Since each binary digit in a binary number is equivalent to a bit, the two's complement of a binary number may be calculated by "flipping" the setting of each bit to its opposite position and then adding one to the result. Thus calculating the two's complement of any binary number involves two simple steps:

1. Flip all bits in the original number.
2. Add a 1 bit to the least significant bit position of the result.

Calculate the two's complement for each of the following binary numbers:

1. 00101111   2. 01110100   3. 00100001

Your calculations should result in (1) 11010001, (2) 10001100, and (3) 11011111.

To extend the concept of two's complements to the representation of negative numbers in the computer's storage, extend the number of digits in the binary number so it corresponds to the number of bits in the fixed-length area of storage. For example, use (1), above, where the original binary number is 00101111. If the area in storage that is to contain this binary number is a half-word, then we would add eight 0 bits on the original binary number making it 0000000000101111. The value of the binary number is still the same, but the number occupies more space.

Remember, the first bit of each fixed-point binary number, whether a full-word or a halfword of storage, is the *sign* bit. The remaining 31 or 15 bits, respectively, represent the binary number. By allowing the sign bit to participate in the calculation of the two's complement of a binary number, the result is that the two's complement has a sign bit of 1, which indicates a negative fixed-point number to the computer. If a halfword in storage contains the binary number 0000000000101111, it contains the binary equivalent of a decimal $+47$. If that same halfword in storage contains 1111111111010001, it contains the binary equivalent of a decimal -47. 1111111111010001 is the two's complement of 0000000000101111.

If you see a halfword of storage such as 1111111111011011, you immediately know that this halfword contains a negative number, because the sign bit is a 1. To find out the true value of that negative number, recomplement it. In other words, flip all the bits and add 1 to the least significant digit position. This creates the same result as subtracting 1 and then flipping all the bits. Use whichever method seems easiest to you.

$$
\begin{array}{ll}
1111111111011011 & \\
0000000000100100 & \text{flip the bits} \\
\underline{+\ 1} & \text{add one} \\
0000000000100101 &
\end{array}
$$

The true value is 0000000000100101_2 (equivalent to 37_{10}). Thus the original halfword in storage is equivalent to a -37_{10}.

What is the decimal equivalent of the contents of each of the following storage areas?

1. 0000000000110100
   hwb

2. 0000011000100111
   hwb

3. 1111111111001001
   hwb

4. 1111111111111011
   hwb

The decimal equivalents you should calculate are: (1) $+52$, (2) $+1575$, (3) -55, and (4) -5.

The formats for decimal numbers and floating-point numbers will be discussed in the chapters which explain the arithmetic instructions provided for these data representations, chapters 9 and 10, respectively.

QUESTIONS

1. What are the three number systems used in Systems/360 and 370?
   1) DECIMAL 2) BINARY 3) HEXADECIMAL

2. Explain briefly what is meant by positional notation. Use the decimal number system to supply examples. *THE VALUE OF THE DIGIT IN A DIGIT POSITION IS DETERMINED BY MULTIPLYING THE DIGIT BY A CERTAIN VALUE* $5=5\times1$ $50=5\times10$ $500=5\times100$ $5000=5\times1000$

3. Tell what value the ones contribute to the total value of each of the following numbers:

   a. 6172_{10} *$=100$*
   b. 816_{16} *$=16$*
   c. 01000_2 *$=8$*
   d. $1A8_{16}$ *$=256$*
   e. 0100000_2 *$=32$*
   f. 176843_{10} *$=100,000$*

4. What are the four means of representing data in the Systems/360 and 370 computers? *1) CHARACTER INFORMATION 2) FIXED-POINT BINARY NUMBERS 3) DECIMAL NUMBERS 4) FLOATING-POINT NUMBERS*

5. What are the 8-bit EBCDIC representations for the following characters?

   a. A *11000001*
   b. 6 *11000110*
   c. —
   d. blank *40*
   e. J *11010001*
   f. & *01011011*
   g. *
   h. S *11100010*

EXERCISES

1. Convert the following numbers to their binary equivalents:

   a. 16_{10}
   b. 8_{16}
   c. $2C_{16}$
   d. 234_{10}
   e. $3AFC_{16}$
   f. 216_{16}
   g. 79_{10}
   h. 111_{10}

2. Convert the following numbers to their hexadecimal equivalents:

   a. 01110101_2
   b. 5826_{10}
   c. 87643_{10}
   d. 11110110_2
   e. 30651_{10}
   f. 111000001001_2

3. Convert the following numbers to their decimal equivalents.

   a. $AC7B_{16}$ e. $87F_{16}$
   b. 1111_2 f. 010111000011_2
   c. 0110101100_2 g. $F26C_{16}$
   d. $3607B3_{16}$ h. $380C_{16}$

4. What are the two's complements of the following?

   a. 01011011_2
   b. 01100110_2
   c. 00000000_2

5. Perform the following arithmetic operations:

   a. 10010110_2 d. $A682B_{16}$
        $+\ 01001001_2$ $-\ 92C6_{16}$

   b. $6AC2_{16}$ e. 10110111_2
        $+\ 4237_{16}$ $-\ 00101011_2$

   c. 01100101_2 f. $56B3_{16}$
        $+\ 00110011_2$ $+\ 15C7_{16}$

6. Since practice is the only means you have to master the performance of arithmetic operations in various number systems, try the following.

   a. 01101001_2 d. $2C76_{16}$
        00111000_2 $3A42_{16}$
        $+\ 10001110_2$ $+\ 13F8_{16}$

   b. $38C72_{16}$ e. 10111001101_2
        $-\ 1A26B_{16}$ $-\ 01001101010_2$

   c. $39B8_{16}$ f. $A67F26_{16}$
        $-\ 38C0_{16}$ $-\ 87C29A_{16}$

CHAPTER 5

Definition of Storage and Constant Description

INTRODUCTION TO DEFINING CONSTANTS

Before using instructions that manipulate data, a programmer must learn how to define *constants*, one form of data to be manipulated:

```
MSG        DC   C'ERROR MESSAGE'
REPEAT     DC   4C'12345'
FIVE       DC   F'5'
TENH       DC   H'10'
DUPL       DC   3F'0'
```

In Systems/360 and 370 assembler language, an instruction with the opcode DC is used to define constants in storage. Constants are fixed values. The general format for this instruction follows:

> symbol or   DC   operand
> blank

The operand field consists of four subfields, which are written in this order:

1	2	3	4
duplication factor	type	modifier	value or constant

While the first and third subfields (the duplication factor and the modifier) are optional, the type and value subfields are mandatory and must be included in order for the instruction to be syntactically valid to the assembler program.

(*Syntactically valid* means that the instruction follows all the rules that govern the structure of the assembler language.)

Examination of the Subfields

Type Subfield   The type subfield is by far the most important, because it specifies to the assembler the type of constant that is being defined. Once the assembler is told the type of constant, it knows how to interpret the value subfield; what to expect, what characters are valid for this type of constant, and what type of conversions it should perform on the value before placing the constant in storage. This is why the type subfield is mandatory, and why it must contain an acceptable type code, such as:

Code	Type of Constant	Internal-Storage Format
C	character	one 8-bit binary code per character
F	fixed point	signed binary number, a fullword
H	fixed point	signed binary number, a halfword

(This list includes only the type codes explained in this chapter.) These codes (C, H, and F) identify the types of constants the reader will need to use in the next few chapters. For a complete list of codes, see appendix 3.

Value or Constant Subfield   The value or constant subfield provides the constant that the other subfields describe. The value subfield is enclosed in apostrophes. Remember that the code that appears in the type subfield determines what characters will be accepted as valid.

The Modifier Subfield   The modifier describes the length, in bytes, of a constant (overriding the implied length, which is explained in the detailed discussion of the character constant). This length modifier is written Ln, with the letter L immediately following the type code, where n is a decimal number representing the number of bytes of storage to be reserved by the assembler for this constant. Appendix 3 lists the implied lengths and automatic boundary alignments, if any, for the various types of constants.

Duplication Factor Subfield   The duplication factor subfield specifies the number of times the particular constant is to be duplicated in consecutive storage locations. It is specified as a decimal number immediately preceding the type code. If the duplication factor is omitted, a value of one is assumed.

Character Constant (C)

This type of constant is used for defining character strings in storage. Headings for reports and error messages are two of its most common uses. Any of the graphic symbols represented by an 8-bit pattern in the Systems/360 and 370 (see appendix 3 for the complete list) can be used. As the assembler examines the character string in the value subfield, character by character, it translates each character into its equivalent 8-bit EBCDIC code and places those eight bits in the next available byte of storage. No special boundary alignment is made; the assembler begins translation with the first character in the string and fills the first byte of available storage with the equivalent 8-bit code. In other words, it left-justifies the constant in the storage space.

If no length modifier is used, the length of the constant (implied length) is just sufficient to hold the specified number of characters. If a symbolic name is given to this constant, the length associated with that symbolic name is equal to the number of characters in the character string in the value subfield. Examples:

1. CHARS   DC   C'AB'

> Two bytes of storage are allocated for this constant. The first contains the 8-bit code for an A and the second the 8-bit code for a B. The name of the constant is CHARS. The length associated with the symbol CHARS is two bytes, because there are two characters between the apostrophes.

> > CHARS: 11000001 11000010

> Look up the characters A and B in the chart in appendix 3 and verify that these are truly the 8-bit 360 and 370 codes for A and B.

2. ANSWER   DC   C'YES'

> There are three characters between the apostrophes, so the length associated with the symbol ANSWER is three bytes. Each byte contains the 8-bit code for a letter.

> > ANSWER: 11101000 11000101 11100010

3. REFUSE   DC   C'NO'

> The length of the constant is two bytes, and the contents of those two bytes are:

> > REFUSE: 11010101 11010110

For legibility, instead of using the 8-bit binary code to represent the contents of storage, we will use two hexadecimal digits. The first four binary bits in a byte will be represented as one hexadecimal digit and the last four bits by a second hexadecimal digit. So REFUSE, instead of being represented as 11010101 11010110 would appear as D5 D6. Storage still contains the same 16 bit settings.

4. NUT   DC   C'CASHEW'

          NUT:C3 C1 E2 C8 C5 E6

5. FRUIT   DC   C'APPLE'

          FRUIT: C1 D7 D7 D3 C5

Check the 8-bit codes in appendix 3, use the IBM System/360 Reference Data Card (GX20-1703), or use the IBM System/370 Reference Summary Card (GX20-1850).

Further examples:

NUMS   DC   C'3048'

          NUMS: F3 F0 F4 F8

The 8-bit code for a number consists of all 1s in the first 4 bit positions and the binary equivalent of the digit in the fifth through eighth bits. This makes the 8-bit code for a zero character 11110000 rather than 00000000. Keep this fact in mind when it comes time to do arithmetic, and you will be able to see why arithmetic cannot be performed on character constants. Arithmetic is performed on numbers in binary, decimal, or floating-point format (discussed in chapters 7, 9, and 10, respectively).

SPECIALS   DC   C'#$@*'

          SPECIALS: 7B 5B 7C 5C

Special characters are treated just like any other characters and are translated into their 8-bit codes.

BLNK   DC   C'TRY IT'

          BLNK: E3 D9 E8 40 C9 E3

A blank character is like any other special character. Its 8-bit code is 01000000 or, in hexadecimal shorthand, 40.

Combining alphabetic, numeric and special characters into one example illustrates the wide use this type of constant will have in your programs:

MSG   DC   C'PRICE IS $1.00'

MSG: D7 D9 C9 C3 C5 40 C9 E2 40 5B F1 4B F0 F0

The apostrophe (') and the ampersand (&) are two special characters that require special handling, but they may be used. Whenever the programmer wishes to represent an apostrophe or an ampersand in a character string, he should place *two* apostrophes or *two* ampersands in that location of the value subfield. Only *one* is placed in storage.

The reason for the double characters in the value to represent one 8-bit code in storage is that these two characters have special meanings to the assembler. The ampersand means something special to the macro language portion of the assembler. Using two ampersands tells the assembler that rather than using its macro language facilities, the programmer wishes one ampersand in storage as part of this character string. Example:

COLORS   DC   C'BLACK && WHITE'

COLORS: C2 D3 C1 C3 D2 40 50 40 E6 C8 C9 E3 C5

You must be able to understand the assembler's need for two apostrophes to represent one 8-bit code for an apostrophe in storage. What character is used at the beginning and end of the value subfield in a DC instruction? Precisely, an apostrophe. If two apostrophes are not used to indicate an apostrophe embedded in a character string, the assembler has no other alternative but to consider the single apostrophe as the end of the value subfield of the DC instruction. Example:

DBL   DC   C'DON''T'

DBL: C4 D6 D5 7D E3

If a length modifier is used with a character constant, then it specifies the number of bytes the constant is to occupy in storage, and this length is associated with the symbolic name of the constant. A maximum length of 256 may be specified. A length modifier may be larger or smaller than the number of bytes required to hold the number of characters in the value subfield. If the specified length of the field is larger, the assembler left-justifies the characters from the value subfield in the allocated space and pads the rest of the allocated space with blanks. That is, it places the 8-bit code for a character blank (hexadecimal 40) in each of the unfilled bytes. Example:

PAD   DC   CL5'NONE'

PAD: D5 D6 D5 C5 40

Notice above that the first character from the value subfield of the DC (the letter N) is placed in the first byte of the allocated space—it is left-justified in the allocated space. If the specified length is smaller, the value subfield will have to be truncated. The assembler program simply ignores the rightmost characters as if they were not part of the value subfield. The important thing to remember is that the assembler can fill only the number of bytes the programmer describes as the size of the constant. In all cases the assembler left-justifies. Example:

TRUNC   DC   CL5'1234567'

TRUNC: F1 F2 F3 F4 F5

To anticipate what the assembler will do, remember these rules:

> left-justify,
> truncate on the right,
> pad with blanks on the right.

The length that is associated with both of the symbols PAD and TRUNC is 5 bytes. Why 5 rather than 4 for PAD or 7 for TRUNC? Because a length modifier takes precedence over the length based on the number of characters in the value subfield (the implied length).

Use of the duplication factor is illustrated in the following examples. The same general rules apply to these examples. One rule is added: The constant is assembled, then it is duplicated.

DUPL   DC 2C'AB'

DUPL: C1 C2 C1 C2

The constant in this example is C1 C2; this constant is then duplicated so that there are two identical copies of it: C1 C2 C1 C2. The length associated with the symbolic name DUPL is the length of the constant—in this case two bytes. Four bytes of storage are allocated.

TPL   DC 3C'123'

TPL: F1 F2 F3 F1 F2 F3 F1 F2 F3

The same repetition happens with this example; three copies of the constant are made, and the length associated with the symbol TPL is three bytes. Nine bytes of storage are allocated.

BTH   DC 3CL4'XYZ'

BTH: E7 E8 E9 40 E7 E8 E9 40 E7 E8 E9 40

This example may seem a little tricky at first. But follow the same four rules:

1. left justify
2. truncate on the right
3. pad with blanks on the right
4. assemble the constant, then duplicate it

Left-justify—therefore the 8-bit code for the X goes in the first byte, Y in the second, and Z in the third. Normally, three bytes would have been used for XYZ, but a length modifier of 4 was specified for BTH; thus, four bytes are used for the constant and a length of 4 is associated with the symbol BTH. Three bytes of this four byte area are filled with XYZ and a hexadecimal 40 is inserted in the fourth byte. The constant is then completely assembled. It is now duplicated twice, so the result is:

BTH: E7 E8 E9 40 E7 E8 E9 40 E7 E8 E9 40

Before continuing to the next type of constant, consider the following instructions to reinforce your understanding of character-type constants. In addition to figuring out what storage will contain for each, calculate the length associated with each symbolic name (the implied length). Try not to refer back to previous examples, but apply the four rules we have learned.

1. CENTS   DC   C'36¢'
2. TRY   DC   CL5'YES'
3. NO   DC   C'CAN"T'
4. THIS   DC   CL4'NEWSPAPER'
5. PASS   DC   2CL4'NOW'
6. CHECK   DC   3CL3'12345678'

Answers:

	Symbolic Name	Storage Contents	Length
1.	CENTS	F3 F6 4A	3
2.	TRY	E8 C5 E2 40 40	5
3.	NO	C3 C1 D5 7D E3	5
4.	THIS	D5 C5 E6 E2	4
5.	PASS	D5 D6 E6 40 D5 D6 E6 40	4
6.	CHECK	F1 F2 F3 F1 F2 F3 F1 F2 F3	3

Fixed-Point Constants (F and H)

In programming, certain instructions require the data manipulated by them to be in fixed-length fields. These fixed-length fields must be located on integral boundaries. In review, a boundary is considered to be integral when its storage address is a multiple of the length of the field in bytes. For example, fullwords (4 bytes in length) must have addresses which are an even multiple of 4; halfwords (2 bytes in length) must have addresses that are multiples of 2.

A checking mechanism is built into the mechanics of each of these fixed-length field instructions. Before one of these instructions performs its operation, this mechanism checks to ensure that the data it is referencing in storage is on the proper storage boundary. If the checking mechanism encounters an incorrect boundary alignment, execution of the program is halted.

The instructions that perform fixed-point binary arithmetic expect data to be in fixed-length fields. Some of these instructions require data to be on fullword boundaries and some require halfword boundaries. So in this section, two types of constants will be discussed: one that defines fixed-point binary constants on fullword boundaries and a second that defines fixed-point binary constants on halfword boundaries. The type code for a fullword fixed-point constant is F, and the type code for a halfword fixed-point constant is H.

A fixed-point constant is written as a signed or unsigned integer decimal number enclosed in apostrophes. If no sign is specified, the number is assumed to be positive. The assembler program converts the decimal number to a binary number and assembles it into the proper field of main storage.

An implied length of 4 bytes for fullwords (F) or 2 bytes for halfwords (H) is assumed, and alignment is always provided on the proper fullword or halfword boundary if no length modifier is specified (we will not use length modifiers in this text with the definition of F or H types of constants). Example:

$$\text{FULL} \quad \text{DC} \quad \text{F}'12'$$

In binary a twelve is represented as 1100, with the leftmost 1 having a place value of 8 and the right 1 a place value of 4 (8 + 4 = 12). This constant is defined as a fullword. Therefore, it occupies 4 bytes or 32 bits in storage.

```
        ┌─sign bit
FULL:   0000 0000 0000 0000 0000 0000 0000 1100 (memory contents)
        fwb (fullword boundary)
```

Notice that the *high-order* (leftmost) bit is the sign bit (0 for positive, 1 for negative). This is referred to as a 32-bit signed integer; it is really a 31-bit integer with a sign bit. If the hexadecimal shorthand is used to represent this binary number, the contents of FULL is:

```
        FULL: 00 00 00 0C
              fwb
```

Try another example:

$$\text{FULL2} \quad \text{DC} \quad \text{F}'35'$$

Converting the decimal 35 to a binary 35:

```
FULL2: 0000 0000 0000 0000 0000 0000 0010 0011
```

and using the hexadecimal shorthand to represent this binary value yields:

```
        FULL2: 00 00 00 23
               fwb
```

Now let's look at this from a different viewpoint. If you wish to place the following constant in storage in a fullword named REVS, how should you set up the value subfield for the DC statement?

REVS: 00 00 01 B6
fwb

Remember that the 00 00 01 B6 above is the hexadecimal shorthand for the 32 binary bits that make up this fullword constant. Two alternatives are available for computing the value subfield for the DC. First, each of the hexadecimal digits can be converted into its 4-bit binary equivalent, and then the place values for each of the 1s can be added to find the decimal equivalent.

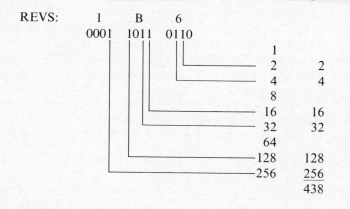

REVS: DC   F'438'

Second, the place values for each of the hexadecimal digits can be multiplied by the digit in that position and the products summed to yield the decimal equivalent.

$$REVS: \quad 1 \quad B \quad 6$$
$$6 \times 1 \; = \quad 6$$
$$B \times 16 \; = \; 176$$
$$1 \times 256 = \underline{256}$$
$$438$$

This second method can also be illustrated using the expanded form:

$$1B6 = 1 \times 16^2 + B \times 16^1 + 6 \times 16^0$$
$$= 1 \times 256 + B \times 16 \; + 6 \times 1$$
$$= 256 \quad\;\; + 176 \quad\;\; + 6$$
$$= 438$$

REVS: DC   F'438'

Use whichever method is easiest for you. You may have difficulty appreciating the necessity of learning to perform the above operations. The necessity is minimal in the process of coding, but you will not always code error-free programs. Someday you will be faced with the problem of debugging. The ability to convert data could be necessary when debugging.

If a negative number has been indicated by the use of a minus sign preceding the decimal number, the constant is assembled in storage in its two's complement form. Try a few negative values:

1. NEG   DC   F'-10'

      The decimal value 10 when converted to binary is: 0000 0000 0000 0000 0000 0000 0000 1010. To review the process for complementing the value of binary 10 requires two steps.

          1) All the bits are flipped—all 0s are made 1s and conversely, all 1s are made 0s.
          2) A binary value of 1 is added to the result from step 1.

      Using the example of NEG:

```
0000 0000 0000 0000 0000 0000 0000 1010
1111 1111 1111 1111 1111 1111 1111 0101
                                    + 1
1111 1111 1111 1111 1111 1111 1111 0110
```

      Represented in the hexadecimal shorthand this number becomes:

      NEG: FFFFFFF6
           fwb

2. NEG1   DC   F'-1'

      Calculation of the two's complement:

```
0000 0000 0000 0000 0000 0000 0000 0001
1111 1111 1111 1111 1111 1111 1111 1110
                                    + 1
1111 1111 1111 1111 1111 1111 1111 1111
```

      In hexadecimal shorthand:

      NEG1: FFFFFFFF
           fwb

Let's look at negative fixed-point constants from the other viewpoint also. How would the DCs look that would describe the following fields:

NEGA: FFFFFF4A
fwb

NEGB: FFFC
hwb

The notation hwb below NEGB's contents indicates that this area is on a halfword boundary.

What you see above is the hexadecimal shorthand for the two's complement of the numbers desired. To calculate the actual binary number when given the two's complement, perform the same two steps that are performed when calculating the original two's complement: (in other words, recomplement the number): (1) flip the bits, and (2) add one to the result.

```
NEGA:   F    F    F    F    F    F    4    A
NEGA: 1111 1111 1111 1111 1111 1111 0100 1010
      0000 0000 0000 0000 0000 0000 1011 0101
                                           + 1
      ─────────────────────────────────────────
      0000 0000 0000 0000 0000 0000 1011 0110
```

Hexadecimal shorthand:

NEGA: 00 00 00 B6

Use the expanded form of this hexadecimal number to calculate its decimal equivalent.

NEGA   DC   F'-182'

```
NEGB:   F    F    F    C
NEGB: 1111 1111 1111 1100
      0000 0000 0000 0011
                       + 1
      ────────────────────
      0000 0000 0000 0100
```

Hexadecimal shorthand:

NEGB: 00 04

NEGB   DC   H'-4'

An important point to remember is that the high-order (leftmost) bit of the fixed-point field being examined is the sign bit. If that bit is 0, the number is positive and can be converted in a straightforward manner from binary to decimal, or from the hexadecimal shorthand for binary to decimal. If that sign bit is 1, the field contains a negative number in two's complement form and it must be recomplemented prior to conversion to decimal. If you are having difficulties handling the various conversions or two's complement notation in this section, a review of the number systems section in chapter 4 might be helpful.)

If a duplication factor is present, the duplication is performed after the constant is assembled.

```
TWICE    DC   2F'32'
     TWICE: 00 00 00 20 00 00 00 20

AGAIN    DC   3F'0'
     AGAIN: 00 00 00 00 00 00 00 00 00 00 00 00
```

Remember that the length associated with each of the symbols is four bytes, the implied length of a fullword fixed-point binary constant. The maximum and minimum values for fixed-point constants are:

Length	Maximum	Minimum
2	$2^{15} - 1$	-2^{15}
4	$2^{31} - 1$	-2^{31}

Regardless of how many bits it takes to represent a particular number, those bits are right-justified in the field and the unused, leftmost, bits in the field are set equal to the sign of the number. If the value of the number requires more bits to represent it than the implied length, the leftmost binary bits are truncated. This causes the loss of the most significant digits as well as the sign bit. The value is assembled into the field once the binary value is truncated to the proper length. For example:

```
TRBL    DC   H'139264'
```

The maximum value a halfword can hold is $2^{15} - 1$, or 32,767. What happens is that the above subfield is converted to binary 100010000000000000, the binary number is right-justified in the halfword space, and the leftmost two bits are truncated, placing in the storage area the value of 0010000000000000. The value in the halfword located at TRBL is now equivalent to a decimal 8192 rather than the 139,264 indicated in the DC value subfield.

Try the following without referring back to previous examples:

What are the contents of storage (in hexadecimal) generated by the following DCs:

```
1. EX1      DC   F'24'
2. FORTY    DC   H'40'
3. NEGS     DC   H'-21'
4. NOW      DC   F'16'
5. T2       DC   H'75011'
6. THIS     DC   2F'100'
```

Write the DC statements that would cause the following to be created in storage:

7.	FIRST:	00000086
		fwb
8.	SECOND:	FFFFFF76
		fwb
9.	THIRD:	016B
		hwb
10.	FOURTH:	FFFF
		hwb

Answers to previous questions:

1.	EX1:	00000018
		fwb
2.	FORTY:	0028
		hwb
3.	NEGS:	FFEB
		hwb
4.	NOW:	00000010
		fwb
5.	T2:	2503
		hwb
6.	THIS:	0000006400000064
		fwb
7.	FIRST	DC F'134'
8.	SECOND	DC F'-138'
9.	THIRD	DC H'363'
10.	FOURTH	DC H'-1'

SUBMITTING YOUR FIRST JOB TO THE SYSTEM

To check that your answers to the previous questions are correct, punch the ten DC statements into cards. Punch the special cards indicated in figure 5-1 and add your DC cards where indicated. Then submit your deck to be run on the system. This will give you a way to familiarize yourself with the procedure for submitting machine runs in your installation and will give you your first example of what kind of printed output you can expect to receive from the computer.

You must keep in mind one factor about your installation before we can proceed: what operating system is to be used with your computer system. An *operating system* is a collection of programs that makes it possible for your programs to execute. You, as a programmer, know what you want to do. For example, you want to write a program in assembler language, have it trans-

```
        under DOS                          under OS

//  JOB                      //jobname     JOB
//  EXEC  ASSEMBLY           //            EXEC  ASMFC†
    ·insert your             //ASM.SYSIN   DD      *
    ·DC statements                         ·insert your
    ·here                                  ·DC statements
    END                                    ·here
                                           END
 /*                               /*
```

†ASMFC is shorthand used by the system to designate the F-level
assembler. This level may vary with your installation.

Fig. 5-1 Job control cards for assembler translation only

lated into machine language, and then have that machine language executed.
However, you must communicate to the operating system what you want to
do and also the order in which you want things done.

NECESSARY JOB CONTROL LANGUAGE

A special language is used to communicate with the operating system. This
language is called Job Control Language (JCL) and it varies with the operating
system being used. The two categories of operating systems that will be used
and explained in this book are referred to as OS and DOS. The same basic
functions are provided by either. (*OS* implies OS-based systems: MFT, MVT,
VS1 and VS2. *DOS* implies both DOS and DOS/VS.)

The Job   The basic unit of work for either system is the Job. A Job is the deck
of cards you submit to be run on the computer. Your job will be placed in a
stack of jobs that forms the job stream for the operating system. At the beginning of each job is a special JCL card. This is called the *JOB* card. It must
always be placed as the first card in your deck. Every card that follows your job
card in the input stream until the next job card or the end of the input stream is
encountered belongs to your job.

The Step   Each job may be divided into a series of steps. Each step specifies
some action to be taken. At the beginning of each step is a special JCL card
called an (*EXEC*) Execute card. The steps are always executed in the sequence
in which the EXEC cards appear in the job. The order of the EXEC cards in
your job communicates to the operating system the order in which you want
things done.

The usual assembler job consists of three steps (as explained at the end of chapter 3), but in this particular case, we want only one step: assembler program translation of each of the operands of our DC statements into the form in which the data would be placed in storage. Since this is only one step, we need only one EXEC card. Figure 5-1 shows the job control cards for this job.

You can observe that the two operating systems, while providing the same general functions, differ in the manner in which you communicate with them; that is, the job control language differs. You will note in the above that all job control statements begin with a slash (/) in column one, and most have a slash in column two. These slashes are followed by at least one blank column (except in the case of the OS job card where you must specify a jobname and the card containing "ASM.SYSIN" immediately after the slashes), then the keyword, which identifies the type of control card. The keyword must be separated from the operand (ASSEMBLY, ASMFC, and *) by at least one blank.

INFORMATION AVAILABLE IN A LISTING

Figure 5-2 shows an example of the printed output you will receive from a DOS system. This particular printed output, also called a *listing*, consists of five pages. (The five pages have been cut down and placed one after the other to facilitate ease of examination on your part.)

Page 1 contains copies of the contents of the JOB and EXEC cards. Page 2 contains information that has no useful purpose to you right now; its contents will be explained later. Page 3 contains the display of your *source* statements and the *object* code that corresponds to the source statements. This code has been generated by the assembler. Each source statement is given a statement number, which is displayed along with the source code and the object code. For example, statement 4 is the define constant statement for a fixed-point binary fullword of 32. The contents of that fullword are displayed in the column labeled *object code*: the hexadecimal shorthand for a binary of 32 is 00000020.

To the left of the object code section in the listing you will notice a column labeled LOC. This column contains the location within the block of object code of the first byte that the assembler allocates on that line. For example, the halfword labeled NEG begins at byte 6 in the object module (6 is evenly divisible by 2 and is therefore a halfword boundary).

In addition to the types of information displayed on page 3 of the listing, you'll notice one other interesting item. Take a look at the object code portion of the listing for statements 5 and 6. Notice that there is a line skipped between the printing of source statements 5 and 6, and that two bytes of zeros are shown in the object code portion of the line that is skipped.

The location of the area labeled TEST is at C within the object module. This statement defines a halfword, so this halfword occupies the bytes at locations C and D. The next statement the assembler encounters is statement 6, a definition of two fullwords, each containing the fixed-point binary equivalence

PAGE 1

```
//      JOB       TUGGLE  STRAIGHT  BINARY
//      EXEC      ASSEMBLY
```

```
                                                      PAGE 2
                                   EXTERNAL  SYMBOL  DICTIONARY

SYMBOL  TYPE ID  ADDR  LENGTH LD ID


        PC   01  000000  000018
```

```
                                                      PAGE 3


LOC   OBJECT CODE    ADDR1 ADDR2  STMT   SOURCE STATEMENT

000000 00000010                    1 AB        DC     F'16'
C00004 003C                        2 SIXTY     DC     H'60'
000006 FFE6                        3 NEG       DC     H'-26'
000008 00000020                    4 IT        DC     F'32'
00000C 02EE                        5 TEST      DC     H'750'
00000E 0000
000010 0000005700000057            6 TIS       DC     2F'87'
                                   7           END
```

```
                                                      PAGE 4
                                   CROSS-REFERENCE

SYMBOL    LEN  VALUE  DEFN

AB        00004 000000 00001
IT        00004 000008 00004
NEG       00002 000006 00003
SIXTY     00002 000004 00002
TEST      00002 00000C 00005
TIS       00004 000010 00006


NO STATEMENTS FLAGGED IN THIS ASSEMBLY
```

```
                                                      PAGE 5
ECJ TUGGLE
```

Fig. 5-2 Example of printed output for DOS

of a decimal 87. When the assembler scans this statement, the next byte it has available to allocate is at location E. But E is not the location of a fullword boundary (E_{16} or 14_{10} is not evenly divisible by 4). Because of this the assembler must skip two bytes to arrive at the next available fullword boundary (10). When the assembler skips bytes to align for the allocation of a constant, it sets the contents of those skipped bytes to zero. If the assembler skips bytes to align for a storage area that it doesn't initialize to any value (using the DS statement explained later in this chapter), it leaves the contents of the skipped bytes at their original contents—it does not set them to zero.

Page 4 contains an alphabetic listing of every symbol used in the source program. The length attribute that is associated with each symbol is displayed along with the number of the statement in which that symbol was defined— defined, in that the symbol appeared in the name field of that statement. The value column on this page corresponds to the location counter value displayed (page 3 of the listing) on the same line that the symbol is defined. The cross-reference table states that the symbol SIXTY is defined in statement number 2; that the symbol SIXTY has a length of 2 associated with it (it's a halfword constant); and the value associated with this symbol is 000004, the location of the first byte of this halfword within the object module. One other piece of information that appears on page 4 is a notation that 'no statements were flagged in this assembly.' This means that the source statements in this program followed the assembler's syntax rules.

Page 5 of the printed output simply contains a notation that this is the end of the job. The TUGGLE following the EOJ is taken from the operand field of the job card. This end of job message can be used in the separation of the paper produced by this job and the following job.

Syntax-Error Example

The example we have been examining contains no errors in the source statements. That is, none of the source statements violated any of the syntax rules of the assembler. The next example (DOS once more) will illustrate the differences in the printed output when syntax errors are present. Pages 1 and 2 remain unchanged.

An addition to page 3 is a notation of an error encountered in the previous statement. The presence of an error is indicated by the word ERROR printed on the next line in the object code column (***ERROR***). Page 4 contains the same type of information as the first example.

Preceding page 5 with its EOJ TUGGLE message, is an additional page of diagnostics which explain the error notations made on the assembler listings on page 3. Such diagnostic messages will not pinpoint the exact cause of the error in all cases, but they give a good indication of the field of the instruction in which the error can be found.

Using figures 5-3 and 5-4, try your hand at figuring out the errors in the source statements by using the diagnostics.

The diagnostic messages indicate that statements 2, 3 and 4 have not followed the assembler's rules for standardization of symbolic names. In statement 2 the symbol is more than 8 characters in length. In statement 3 the symbol does not begin with an alphabetic character, and a special character is used in the name field of statement 4.

Statement 5's problem is that the combination of characters appearing in

```
  LOC  OBJECT CODE     ADDR1 ADDR2  STMT   SOURCE STATEMENT

000000 D9C9C7C8E3                     1  GOOD      DC    C'RIGHT'
000005 000000
000008 00000006                       2  TOOOOLONG DC    F'6'
       *** ERROR ***
00000C 000000A5                       3  6NUM      DC    F'165'
       *** ERROR ***
000010 0002                           4  AB+C      DC    H'2'
       *** ERROR ***
                                      5  TRY       DCS   F'36'
       *** ERROR ***
000012 273B                           6  TOOBIG    DC    H'9652348731'
       *** ERROR ***
000014                                7  MISSING   DC    C
       *** ERROR ***
000014                                8  TYPE      DC    G'42'
       *** ERROR ***
000014                                9  APOS      DC    F(65)
       *** ERROR ***
000014                               10  CONS      DC    F'6A7'
       *** ERROR ***
000014                               11  PRETTY    DC    F ' 6 '
       *** ERROR ***
                                     12  NOTHERE   DC    C'VALUE OF B IS
       *** ERROR ***
                                     13            END
```

```
                                                             DIAGNOSTICS

STMT   ERROR CODE     MESSAGE

   2   IJQ016         INVALID NAME
   3   IJQ016         INVALID NAME
   4   IJQ016         INVALID NAME
   5   IJQ088         UNDEFINED OPERATION CODE
   6   IJQ017         DATA ITEM TOO LARGE
   7   IJQ039         INVALID DELIMITER
   8   IJQ031         UNKNOWN TYPE
   9   IJQ039         INVALID DELIMITER
  10   IJQ039         INVALID DELIMITER
  11   IJQ039         INVALID DELIMITER
  12   IJQ087         NO ENDING APOSTROPHE

 11 STATEMENTS FLAGGED IN THIS ASSEMBLY
```

Fig. 5-3 DOS diagnostic error messages

the opcode field do not comprise one of the combinations that the assembler considers a valid mnemonic opcode. The G used in the type subfield of statement 8 creates the same sort of problem for the assembler; it does not recognize G as one of its acceptable type codes.

The error in statement 6 is that the value presented to the assembler in the value subfield of the operand is a number that takes more than 15 bits and a sign bit to hold it in its binary format. Since a halfword can hold only 16 bits, an overflow condition has occurred.

Statements 7, 9, 10, and 11 have the same diagnostic error message, IN-VALID DELIMITER. This message can be the result of a wide variety of similar causes. This diagnostic is produced when the assembler does not encounter the operand field structure it expects. Once the assembler recognizes

```
LOC    OBJECT CODE  ADDR1 ADDR2  STMT  SOURCE STATEMENT

000000 D9C9C7C9E3                  1 GOOD      DC    C'RIGHT'        NOTHING WRONG
00C005 000000                      2 TOOOOLONG DC    F'6'            MORE THAN 8 CHARACTERS IN LABEL
000008 00000006               *** ERROR ***
00000C 000000A5                    3 6NUM      DC    F'165'          LABEL BEGINS WITH NON-ALPHABETIC
                              *** ERROR ***
000010 0002                        4 AB+C      DC    H'2'            LABEL CONTAINS A SPECIAL CHARACTER
                              *** ERROR ***
                                   5 TRY       DCS   F'36'           DCS IS NOT THE CORRECT PSEUDO-OP
000012 273B                   *** ERROR ***
                                   6 TOOBIG    DC    H'9652348731'   VALUE WON'T FIT IN 16 BITS
                              *** ERROR ***
                                   7 MISSING   DC    C               NO VALUE SUBFIELD PRESENT
                              *** ERROR ***
                                   8 TYPE      DC    G'42'           INCORRECT TYPE SUBFIELD
                              *** ERROR ***
                                   9 APOS      DC    F(65)           PARENS USED TO SURROUND VALUE
                              *** ERROR ***
                                  10 CONS      DC    F'6A7'          NON-DECIMAL DIGIT IN VALUE SUBFIELD
                              *** ERROR ***
                                  11 PRETTY    DC    F ' 6 '         BLANKS EMBEDDED IN OPERAND
                              *** ERROR ***
                                  12 NOTHERE   DC    C'VALUE OF 8 IS  ENDING APOSTROPHE MISSING
                              *** ERROR ***
                                  13        END
```

DIAGNOSTICS

```
STMT  ERROR CODE  MESSAGE
 2    IEU016      INVALID NAME
 3    IEU016      INVALID NAME
 4    IEU016      INVALID NAME
 5    IEU088      UNDEFINED OPERATION CODE
 6    IEU017      NEAR OPERAND COLUMN    3--DATA ITEM TOO LARGE
 7    IEU107      NEAR OPERAND COLUMN    3--INVALID OPERAND
 8    IEU031      NEAR OPERAND COLUMN    1--UNKNOWN TYPE
 9    IEU107      NEAR OPERAND COLUMN    2--INVALID OPERAND
10    IEU107      NEAR OPERAND COLUMN    4--INVALID OPERAND
11    IEU107      NEAR OPERAND COLUMN    2--INVALID OPERAND
12    IEU087      NO ENDING APOSTROPHE
```

11 STATEMENTS FLAGGED IN THIS ASSEMBLY
12 WAS HIGHEST SEVERITY CODE
STATISTICS SOURCE RECORDS (SYSIN) = 13
OPTIONS IN EFFECT LIST, DECK, NOLOAD, NORENT, XREF, NOTEST, ALGN, OS, NOTERM, LINECNT = 55
58 PRINTED LINES

Fig. 5-4 OS diagnostic error messages

the mnemonic opcode, it knows whether the opcode represents a machine instruction or an instruction to the assembler (a *pseudo-op*), and this indicates how the assembler is to interpret the operand field of the instruction. In this case the mnemonic opcode indicates that the operand field describes the definition of a constant.

As the assembler scans the operand field of a DC statement, it expects to encounter either a duplication factor or one of its acceptable type codes. If the assembler encounters a decimal number first in the operand field, it takes this decimal number as the duplication factor. If the assembler encounters an alphabetic character, it checks to ensure that this represents one of its valid types of constants. Statement 8 shows you the action the assembler takes when it doesn't recognize the character as one of its valid type codes.

After encountering a valid type code, the assembler looks for either a length modifier or the apostrophe that begins the value subfield. If neither of these is encountered, as in the assembler's scan of statements 7 and 9, the invalid delimiter message is printed. In statement 7 no apostrophe was found, and in statement 9 the type code was followed by a left parenthesis rather than an apostrophe.

Once the apostrophe is found, the assembler can scan and interpret the value subfield based on what the type code indicates should be found in that subfield. In statements 10 and 11 the assembler found invalid characters in the value subfields. In both cases the assembler is expecting decimal digits only. It encounters an A in statement 10 and a blank in statement 11. Remember, the blank is a special character. In statement 12 the assembler does not know where the value subfield portion of the operand should end, because there is no ending apostrophe.[†]

INTRODUCTION TO DEFINING STORAGE AREAS

The Define Storage (opcode DS) instruction is used to reserve storage areas and to assign symbolic names to those areas. There are times when space is needed for a work area, an intermediate result of an operation, an input record, or an output message. The general format of the DS instruction is similar to the general format of the DC instruction:

symbol or blank   DS   one or more operands

The operand field is identical to that of the DC instruction. The same subfields may be used and they are specified in the same order:

[†]For further explanations of the information produced by the assembler in the listing see chapter 12 or chapter 16.

1	2	3	4
duplication factor	type	modifier	value or constant

In the DS statement, however, only one subfield is mandatory, the type subfield:

```
LOC     DS   C
        DS   H
        DS   F
```

The first DS above sets aside one byte of storage, the second sets aside two bytes, and the third four bytes. These lengths are implied by the type of the constant that is specified. The first DS assigns the name LOC to the first byte of the storage area that is reserved.

The implied length of a particular type of constant can be overridden through the use of a length modifier, just as in a DC instruction:

```
LOC1    DS   CL6
LOC2    DS   6C
```

The first example defines an area 6 bytes in length and gives it the name LOC1. The second example, while it sets aside 6 bytes of storage and gives it the name LOC2, is not an area 6 bytes in length, but 6 separate 1-byte areas. The 6 is a duplication factor. The length attribute associated with the symbol LOC2 is one.

```
INAREA     DS   CL80
```

This DS instruction sets aside space in storage to be used as an input area. Eighty columns of data can be read from a punched card, converted into the 8-bit codes for those 80 characters, and placed in the 80 bytes set aside by the DS. It would be wasteful to initialize this 80-byte area to anything by using a DC instruction; the read operation would merely destroy the initialization.

A value or constant may be specified in subfield 4 of the operand. If present, and no length modifier is used, the assembler uses the value subfield to determine the amount of storage to be reserved. The constant is not assembled and the reserved storage is not initialized. The value subfield enables the assembler to calculate the length of the area to be reserved, but is otherwise ignored.

```
MSG     DS   C'OUTPUT MESSAGE'
```

A length attribute of 14 bytes is associated with the symbolic name MSG, because there are 14 characters (including one blank character) between the apostrophes.

> ERR   DS   CL6'ERROR ENCOUNTERED'

The symbolic name ERR, on the other hand, does not have associated with it a length attribute equal to the number of characters within the apostrophes (17). Since a length modifier is given, the assembler ignores the value subfield. The length attribute associated with the symbol ERR is 6.

A valuable use of the DS instruction is to force boundary alignment prior to the allocation of storage space for a type of area that does not imply any alignment. For example, a character type of constant is not automatically aligned on any special boundary. If a record is read into an input area and you know that the first four bytes of that area are going to be referenced by instructions that manipulate data in fixed-length fields (fullwords for instance), you must ensure that the first four bytes of the 80-byte area are on a fullword boundary. An instruction of INAREA   DS   CL80 would cause the assembler program to allocate the next available 80 bytes and to associate the symbolic name INAREA with the first of those 80 bytes. The first byte of the 80 has only one chance out of four of being on a fullword boundary. Using an instruction of DS 0F just prior to DS for INAREA ensures that the next available byte the assembler program has to allocate when it sees INAREA is on a fullword boundary.

> DS 0F
> INAREA   DS   CL80

The DS   0F uses the alignment capability of the assembler, but because the duplication factor is zero, no fullwords are allocated. In other words, the DS   0F causes the assembler to skip bytes until the next byte that is available for allocation is a byte with an address evenly divisible by 4 (a fullword boundary). The assembler then proceeds to handle the next instruction, which is the allocation of a character type constant. It allocates the next available 80 bytes to this constant; the first byte, which has the name INAREA, is on a fullword boundary.

In way of review, what length attribute is associated with each of the following symbols?

1. AREA   DS   3C
2. LOC   DS   H
3. PLACE   DS   C'MESSAGE'
4. OUTPUT   DS   CL40
5. LOCS   DS   3CL7
6. IN   DS   3F

Answers to previous DS questions:

Symbol	Length Attribute
1. AREA	1
2. LOC	2
3. PLACE	7
4. OUTPUT	40
5. LOCS	7
6. IN	4

QUESTIONS

1. What are the four subfields that can be used in the operand field of a DC instruction?

   1) DUPLICATION FACTOR 2) TYPE 3) MODIFIER 4) VALUE OR CONSTANT

2. Which of the DC subfields are mandatory and which are optional?

   TYPE AND VALUE

3. What boundary alignment is provided by the assembler for each of the following types of constants: (a) F-type, (b) C-type, and (c) H-type?

   a) FIXED-POINT, SIGNED BINARY NUMBER, A FULLWORD b) CHARACTER, ONE 8-BIT BINARY CODE PER CHARACTER c) FIXED-POINT, SIGNED BINARY NUMBER, HALFWORD

4. What is meant by implied length? Use examples in your discussion.

   THE LENGTH ASSOCIATED WITH THE SYMBOL

5. What character is used for padding purposes if the space allocated to a character constant is larger than the number of characters in the value subfield of the DC instruction?

   A BLANK

6. Is a character constant right or left-justified in the allocated space?

   LEFT-JUSTIFIED

7. What two characters require special handling when used in the value subfield of a DC for a character constant? What special handling is required?

   ' AND & PLACE 2' OR 2& IN THAT LOCATION OF THE VALUE SUBFIELD

8. Why are there two different types of constants for defining fixed-point binary fields?

9. Why do we not use length modifiers with the definition of F or H-type constants?

   BECAUSE AUTOMATIC ALIGNMENT WILL BE OVER RIDDEN

10. The sign bit for a positive fixed-point constant is __*0*__ and for a negative fixed-point constant it's __*1*__.

11. In what form is a negative fixed-point number kept in storage?

   COMPLEMENTERARY FORM

12. Is a fixed-point binary number left- or right-justified in the field? What are unused bits set to? ~ZERO~

13. What action is taken if the value subfield of an H-type constant contains a value greater than 32,767?

14. What are the differences between the DC instruction and the DS instruction? ~ONLY ONE SUBFIELD MANDATORY, THE TYPE~

15. What purpose could the value subfield possibly have if specified on a DS instruction?

EXERCISES

1. What storage contents are generated by the following?

    a. FULL   DC   F'78'
    b. CHARS   DC   C'OUT MSG'
    c. HALF   DC   H'-18'
    d. HERE   DS   F

2. If you wanted to generate the following in storage, what DC and DS instructions would be required?

    a. ONE: 00000B74
                 fwb
    b. TWO: C3D6E6
    c. THRE: FFC6
                 hwb

3. What length (in bytes) is associated with each of the following symbols?

    a. NOW   DC   C'65283' ~5~
    b. DUPL   DC   3F'82' ~3~
    c. LTS   DC   CL5'ABC' ~5~
    d. ANIMAL   DS   C'DOGHOUSE' ~8~

4. In addition to figuring out what storage will contain for each of the following, calculate the length associated with each symbolic name.

    a. TRY   DC   2CL3'1F'
    b. IT   DS   C'MAYBE'
    c. NEWS   DC   CL5'WHITEHOUSE'
    d. CK   DC   3H'-5'
    e. RES   DC   2F'7892'

CHAPTER 6

Information
Move Instructions

THE THREE BASIC GROUPS
OF INSTRUCTIONS TO MOVE DATA

Every computer has instructions that move information from one location to another. In addition to being your first executable instructions, the different move instructions can be used to illustrate the different types, or classes, of instructions in assembler language.

Data may reside in an area of computer storage reserved for it, namely, in a general purpose register, or as part of an instruction that is in storage. In Systems/360 and 370, there are three basic groups of instructions that move data (see figure 6-1):

1. from one register to another
2. from one location in storage to another location in storage
3. between a register and a location in storage

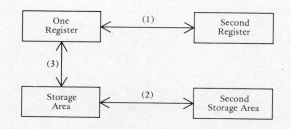

Fig. 6-1 Directions of data movement

There are times when it is necessary to place data in particular registers. For example, some of the arithmetic instructions demand that data be in even-numbered or odd-numbered registers. For this reason, Systems/360 and 370 have instructions that move data from one register to another and between storage locations and registers.

REGISTER-TO-REGISTER MOVE INSTRUCTION

This instruction belongs to a class of instructions called RR-type instructions. An easy way to recognize RR-type instructions is that the mnemonic opcodes of most RR-type instructions end with the letter R. Another thing to remember is that any instruction that moves information into a register is called a *load* instruction, and that all the opcodes for load instructions begin with the letter L. One RR-type instruction that can be used to load a register is:

LR   Load from Register

The general format of an RR-type instruction is:

[NAME]   OPCODE   R1,R2

The brackets around NAME indicate that when you use the instruction the inclusion of a symbolic name is optional. The first operand, R1, is the receiving register (R = register, 1 = first operand—this symbolism is important, as you will see later). The contents of the second operand register, R2, is the data that is moved. *The original contents of R1 are destroyed by the execution of the instruction.* Example:

	R1	R2
Original contents	Reg6: 0000000A	Reg10: 00000008
	LR 6,10	
Contents after execution	Reg6: 00000008	Reg10: 00000008

A register contains 4 bytes (32 bits) of data. Rather than show 32 binary digits when illustrating the contents of a register, we can represent each group of 4 bits by its hexadecimal equivalent. Therefore, the contents of each register are illustrated by 8 hexadecimal digits.

In the instruction, LR   6,10, R1 (register 6) is the receiving register; R2 (register 10) contains the information that is moved. The contents of R2 (register 10) remain unchanged after the execution of the instruction. It is more accurate to say that the contents of R2 are copied into R1, rather than to say that the contents of R2 are moved to R1.

The format used in the previous example will be used in all following examples of the use of move instructions. The first item that appears in the example is the original contents of any registers or storage areas that participate in the operation. The instruction or instructions follow. The last portion of the example shows the contents of the same registers and storage areas after the execution of the instructions. Example:

Reg4: 0000000A   Reg9: FFFFFFF9

LR   4,9

Reg4: FFFFFFF9   Reg9: FFFFFFF9

This LR instruction moves a copy of the contents of R2 (register 9) into R1 (register 4). Remember that rather than show all 32 bits in binary when illustrating the contents of a register, we represent each group of 4 bits by its hexadecimal equivalent. The contents of register 9 are:

in hexadecimal: F   F   F   F   F   F   F   9
in binary: 1111 1111 1111 1111 1111 1111 1111 1001

Since the first bit (bit 0) in register 9 is a 1, the number represented by the contents of register 9 is a negative number (the two's complement of the number). We recomplement the contents of register 9, to the actual value represented:

1111 1111 1111 1111 1111 1111 1111 1001
0000 0000 0000 0000 0000 0000 0000 0110
+ _____ 1

0000 0000 0000 0000 0000 0000 0000 0111

Register 9 contains a negative 7. After the execution of the LR 4,9, register 4 also contains a negative 7.

INSTRUCTIONS TO MOVE DATA BETWEEN REGISTERS AND STORAGE

This group of instructions loads registers from locations in storage or stores the contents of registers into designated storage locations. These instructions are useful, because all data must reside in the computer's storage prior to being operated on, but arithmetic operations and other manipulations are performed on data in registers. These move instructions perform the important task of placing data into registers before manipulations and placing data into storage after manipulations are complete.

The opcodes of instructions that store register contents into storage start with the letters ST. Two instruction types, or classes, are used: The RX- and the

RS-types. There are four RX-type instructions concerned with register-storage transfers:

L Load (from storage)
ST STore (into storage)
LH Load Halfword (from storage)
STH STore Halfword (into storage)

The general format of an RX-type instruction is:

[NAME]   OPCODE   R1,D2(X2,B2)

R1 is either the receiving register or the register whose contents are being stored. The D2, X2, and B2 in the second operand refer to the three items of data which make up an address in the Systems/360 and 370. We will not consider these address items now; instead we will use a symbolic name and let the assembler compute the address. Therefore, our second operand is S2 (S = symbolic name, 2 = second operand), and the general format used throughout the next few chapters is:

[NAME]   OPCODE   R1,S2

The Load and Store instructions require that the address represented by the second operand be a fullword boundary. If the second operand is not at a fullword boundary, the computer determines that an error has been made. Execution of the program is stopped. (Precisely what takes place when execution is stopped is explained in the chapter on debugging.)

When halfword instructions are used, additional facts must be remembered. Halfwords are two bytes long, but registers hold four bytes. On the Store Halfword instruction, only the contents of the low-order (rightmost) two bytes of the register are stored. If the field named in a Store Halfword instruction is a fullword, the contents of two bytes are placed in the high-order (leftmost) bytes of that word. For example, register 6 contains 00541295. If a STH instruction referenced register 6 in its first operand, 1295 would be stored:

Reg6: 00541295   SPOT: 0008
                                   hwb

              STH   6,SPOT

Reg6: 00541295   SPOT: 1295
                                   hwb

or: Reg6: 00541295   LOC: 00018475
                                   fwb

              STH   6,LOC

Reg6: 00541295   LOC: 12958475
                                   fwb

On the Load Halfword instruction, the sign of the halfword is propagated throughout the high-order two bytes of the register, into which data is loaded. That is, the sign of the halfword is extended to form a fullword and then that fullword is loaded into the register:

Reg9: 8D6598A6   LOC: 0001
                                   hwb

LH   9,LOC

Reg9: 00000001   LOC: 0001
                                   hwb

If the first hexadecimal digit of the halfword located at LOC is broken down into bits (0 =0000), the sign of the halfword, the first bit, is 0 (the number is positive) and sixteen zero bits are added to the left hand side of the halfword. This does not change the value of the halfword in storage. It still contains a binary 1, and the contents of the register after execution of the load instruction are also a binary 1. Example:

Reg9: 8D6598A6   SPACE: FFF4
                                     hwb

LH   9,SPACE

Reg9: FFFFFFF4   SPACE: FFF4
                                     hwb

In this case, the address represented by the second operand is the address of SPACE. The sign of this halfword is extended to make a fullword, and this fullword is loaded into register 9, just as it was in the previous example. To go through the process once more, break the first hexadecimal digit of this half-word down into its binary bits (F = 1111). The sign or first bit in this case is 1 (the number is negative). Sixteen one bits are added to the left side of the half-word, and this fullword (FFFFFFF4) is loaded into register 9. The halfword contains a − 12, and so does register 9 after the propagation of the sign and the loading of the resultant fullword. Examples of the STH instruction (The following are the original contents):

Reg2: 00658113   LOCAT: 0028   FIN: 00000012
                                  hwb   fwb
                         STH   2,LOCAT
                         STH   2,FIN
Reg2: 00658113   LOCAT: 8113   FIN: 81130012
                                  hwb   fwb

Because these are both store instructions, the contents of register 2 are not affected.

In the above examples, the symbolic locations LOC, LOCAT, and FIN must be on halfword boundaries. If they are not on halfword boundaries, execution is halted. In the case of STH   2,FIN, FIN is defined as a fullword, its address is evenly divisible by 4. If this address is evenly divisible by 4, it is also evenly divisible by 2; the STH instruction stores into two bytes beginning with the byte at FIN. Since the instruction is a STH instruction, only those two bytes are affected.

Two RS-type instructions are concerned with storage-register transfers:

LM   <u>L</u>oad <u>M</u>ultiple (from storage)
STM   <u>ST</u>ore <u>M</u>ultiple (into storage)

The general format of an RS-type instruction is:

[NAME]   OPCODE   R1,R3,D2(B2)
or
R1,R3,S2

The RS-type of information move instructions cause the movement of several words at a time between consecutive registers and consecutive fullwords in storage. R1 specifies the first register of the block of registers. R3 specifies the last register of the consecutive block. The D2 and B2 in the second operand refer to address portions. We will not consider these now. Instead we will use a symbolic name and let the assembler compute the address. Therefore, our second operand is S2.

In general terms, the execution of the instruction LM   5,6,LOC is as follows. This instruction loads consecutive registers from 5 through 6 with fullwords beginning with the word at location LOC in storage. That is, register 5 is loaded with the fullword at LOC and register 6 with the fullword four bytes past LOC in storage (the next fullword in storage). An example, using actual contents:

Reg6: 00000000   Reg7: 00000140   Reg8: 00556000
PLACE: 00000008 00000850 00000054 00000340
       fwb

LM   6,8,PLACE

Reg6: 00000008   Reg7: 00000850   Reg8: 00000054
PLACE: 00000008 00000850 00000054 00000340
       fwb

In the case of an instruction such as LM   6,6,PLACE, when the beginning and the end of the block of registers is the same register, only one register is loaded. The result is the same as using L   6,PLACE.

The instruction LM   14,1,PLACE illustrates the wrap-around capability of this instruction. When R1 is a higher register number than R3, register 0 is considered to follow register 15. To put it another way, every register has a successor. The above instruction will load four consecutive registers: 14, 15, 0 and 1. Example:

```
Reg15: 00000005   Reg0: 00000056   Reg1: 00000987
LOC: 00000008 000A0006 C1C2C3C4 0000000C
      fwb
```

```
            LM    15,1,LOC
            STM   0,1,LOC
            STH   0,AREA
```

The following DC statements could be used to define the four word area beginning at LOC:

```
        LOC      DC      F'8'
        SCD      DC      H'10'
                 DC      H'6'
        AREA     DC      C'ABCD'
                 DC      F'12'
```

```
Reg15: 00000008   Reg0: 000A0006   Reg1: C1C2C3C4
LOC: 000A0006 C1C2C3C4 0006C3C4 0000000C
      fwb
```

The area beginning with the byte referenced by the symbolic name LOC is exhibited as it is above to point out that the assembler program allocates storage areas in contiguous, or adjacent, groups of bytes. The symbolic name SCD refers to the fourth byte after the byte with the symbolic name LOC, and the symbolic name AREA refers to the eighth byte after the byte with the symbolic name LOC.

If the STH instruction was changed to, STH   0,SCD the resultant change in the area beginning at LOC would be:

```
LOC: 000A0006 0006C3C4 C1C2C3C4 0000000C
```

The fact that the contents of the two bytes beginning with the byte at SCD had just been placed there by the STM instruction is of no concern to the computer. It will execute the STH instruction, regardless of the effect on the two bytes beginning at SCD. It is the programmer's responsibility to ensure that his instruction overlays only the storage locations in which he wants new data to be stored.

STORAGE-TO-STORAGE MOVE INSTRUCTIONS

There are two types of storage-to-storage move instructions, SS- and SI-type. One SS-type of information move instruction handles most requirements. This is the Move Character instruction, for which the opcode is MVC. The general format is:

$$[NAME] \quad MVC \quad D1(L,B1),D2(B2)$$

or, using symbolic operands instead of address elements,

$$[NAME] \quad MVC \quad S1(L),S2$$

The first operand is the receiving location; the second operand is the source. The name of the instruction is a misnomer, because the data is copied rather than moved. Unless the fields overlap, the second operand remains unchanged.

The RR, RS, and RX instructions discussed so far use either fullword or half-word data, implying 4 or 2 bytes of length, respectively. In fact, these instructions assume either 2 or 4 bytes of data plus a particular boundary alignment of that data. SS instructions accept data on any boundary, and—depending on the instruction—can handle as small a string as one byte or as long a string as 256 bytes. The MVC instruction can move a *maximum* of 256 bytes. Because SS-type instructions handle a variable length of data, a length (in bytes) should be specified as part of the operand. This length indicates the number of bytes whose contents are to be copied from the second operand location to the first.

The length is specified as a decimal number, enclosed in parentheses, following the symbolic name of the first operand location. The instruction (MVC TO (6), FROM) will copy six bytes beginning with the byte at location FROM into six contiguous bytes, beginning with the byte at location TO. Movement is from left to right through each field, one byte at a time.

This instruction can be used to move items from an input to an output area. It can be used to construct error messages when things go wrong with a program. It can even be used to move data that is not on a proper boundary to a location that is before an instruction which requires a particular boundary alignment (i.e., a load or a store instruction) is used. Assume that the following DC instructions set up storage for all examples below:

```
FROMAREA      DC   C'AB'
LOC1          DC   C'C123JKL678'
TOAREA        DC   CL11' '
```

Example:
```
                    ┌─LOC1
                    ↓
FROMAREA:  C1 C2 C3 F1 F2 F3 D1 D2 D3 F6 F7 F8
TOAREA:    40 40 40 40 40 40 40 40 40 40 40

           MVC   TOAREA(4),FROMAREA

                    ┌─LOC1
                    ↓
FROMAREA:  C1 C2 C3 F1 F2 F3 D1 D2 D3 F6 F7 F8
TOAREA:    C1 C2 C3 F1 40 40 40 40 40 40 40
```

Using the same original contents of the storage areas, what is the result of the following instruction?

MVC   TOAREA(6),LOC1
TOAREA: C3 F1 F2 F3 D1 D2 40 40 40 40 40

There is a second way to represent the second operand location of the above example. The storage location represented by the symbolic name LOC1 can also be referred to by its relationship to the byte with the symbolic name FROMAREA (see the DCs above). FROMAREA + 2 is the same byte location as LOC1. This *relative addressing* is specified in bytes and is represented by a decimal number separated from the symbol by a plus (+) or minus (−) sign with no blanks inserted before or after the sign. Some examples of relative addressing are:

FROMAREA + 1 is the letter B
TOAREA − 3 is the number 6
FROMAREA + 6 is the letter J

What you are doing is stating a beginning byte (FROMAREA or TOAREA) and then giving a new byte location relative to the beginning byte. Thus the instruction MVC   TOAREA(6),LOC1 could be expressed:

MVC   TOAREA(6),FROMAREA + 2

Using relative addressing on both operands, try the following:

MVC   TOAREA + 3(6),FROMAREA + 2
TOAREA: 40 40 40 C3 F1 F2 F3 D1 D2 40 40

In the following, the second operand location, the source, is changed, because the receiving field overlaps the source field by two bytes.

MVC   FROMAREA(7),FROMAREA + 5
FROMAREA: F3 D1 D2 D3 F6 F7 F8 D2 D3 F6 F7 F8

Remember, movement is from left to right through each field (source and receiving), one byte at a time. In this example, seven bytes are moved. Figure 6-2 shows the contents of FROMAREA as *each* of the seven bytes contents is moved.

Notice that the first and second bytes of the source area are changed by the instruction execution (from F3 D1 to F7 F8). This occurs because the source field and the receiving fields overlap. Carrying the concept of overlapping fields on a little farther (using the original contents of FROMAREA):

MVC   FROMAREA + 1(11),FROMAREA
FROMAREA: C1 C1 C1 C1 C1 C1 C1 C1 C1 C1 C1 C1

receiving field   source field

FROMAREA Original: C1 C2 C3 F1 F2 F3 D1 D2 D3 F6 F7 F8

F3 C2 C3 F1 F2 F3 D1 D2 D3 F6 F7 F8   FROMAREA+5 to FROMAREA

F3 D1 C3 F1 F2 F3 D1 D2 D3 F6 F7 F8   FROMAREA+6 to FROMAREA+1

F3 D1 D2 F1 F2 F3 D1 D2 D3 F6 F7 F8   FROMAREA+7 to FROMAREA+2

F3 D1 D2 D3 F2 F3 D1 D2 D3 F6 F7 F8   FROMAREA+8 to FROMAREA+3

F3 D1 D2 D3 F6 F3 D1 D2 D3 F6 F7 F8   FROMAREA+9 to FROMAREA+4

F3 D1 D2 D3 F6 F7 D1 D2 D3 F6 F7 F8   FROMAREA+10 to FROMAREA+5

F3 D1 D2 D3 F6 F7 F8 D2 D3 F6 F7 F8   FROMAREA+11 to FROMAREA+6

source field

FROMAREA Result: F3 D1 D2 D3 F6 F7 F8 D2 D3 F6 F7 F8

receiving field

Fig. 6-2 The contents of FROMAREA

This example illustrates that the operation of this instruction is from left to right, one byte at a time. The fact that the instruction moves one byte at a time allows the first character to be moved into the second byte, then the contents of the second byte (the original first byte) to be moved to the third byte location, and so on until the contents of 11 bytes have been moved. This is an easy way to propagate a character through an area (for example, all zero or all blank). Clearing an output area so that no unwanted characters are printed is a common use of this capability.

If no length is specified as part of the first operand of an MVC instruction, the length attribute associated with the first operand symbol is used. As explained in the discussion of the DC and DS assembler instructions (chapter 4) a length attribute is associated with each symbolic name defined in an assembler language program. For a fullword, this length attribute is usually 4, and for a halfword it is usually 2. For a symbol representing the location of a character constant, the length attribute is either the number of characters in the constant or the number specified in the length modifier. Example:

```
LOC: C1 C2 C3 C4 C5 C6      AREA: D9 D9 D9 D9 D9 D9 D9 D9
        MVC   LOC,AREA
          .
          .
          .
LOC      DC      C'ABCDEF'
AREA     DC      8C'R'
```

In the above example the vertical ellipsis is used to indicate the separation between the executing instruction (MVC) and the DC statements that define the data for the MVC instruction. The DC and DS statements in a program cannot be intermixed with the executing instructions or the constants defined by them will be interpreted as executing machine-code instructions when the program is executed. The ellipsis is used to indicate that a portion of the program is not included here.

The result of the execution of the previous instruction is the movement of 6 bytes from AREA to LOC (because there are 6 characters between the single quotes in the LOC operand field and no length modifier is used).

LOC: D9 D9 D9 D9 D9 D9   AREA: D9 D9 D9 D9 D9 D9 D9 D9

If the instruction had been MVC AREA,LOC, only one byte would have been moved, because there is only one character between the quotes in the definition of AREA. Remember, the 8 in the operand field of AREA is a duplication factor, not a length modifier.

There is one SI-type information move instruction, the MVI instruction. The general format is:

$$[NAME] \qquad MVI \quad D1(B1),I2$$
$$or$$
$$S1,I2$$

The first operand is the receiving location; the second operand is one byte of immediate data. An immediate operand is immediately available to the computer from the instruction itself; the data rather than the address of the data is actually part of the instruction. The immediate data, the I2, may be specified in one of the following ways:

decimal   . . . ,20
character   . . . ,C'A'

Example:

MVI   CODE,C'F'
.
:
.
CODE   DS   C

This instruction moves an F to the byte with the symbolic name of CODE. Another MVI instruction in the program could be used to move an M into CODE. Thus CODE could be for the purpose of remembering the sex of a respondent to a questionnaire (M or F).

The MVI instruction can create problems if it's not used with care. It can move one byte of data to any byte location within your program. This instruction, therefore, can destroy constants, intermediate results, and even instructions. The following is an example of just how harmful this instruction can be:

$$MVI \quad CONS+2,10$$

$$\vdots$$

CONS   DC   F'6'
CONS (before): 00000006   CONS (after): 00000A06
                     fwb   fwb

This instruction will move a decimal 10 (translated into a binary 1010, or Hex A) into the third byte of the fullword beginning at CONS. This changes the value of that fullword from a decimal 6 to a value of 2566. If any other instruction refers to CONS expecting it to contain a decimal 6, an error will occur—an error with rather unpredictable results. Correctly used, the MVI instruction can be very useful. For example:

$$MVI \quad LOC,C'-' \quad \text{move minus to value}$$

$$\vdots$$

LOC   DS   C
AMT   DC   C'7.98'

           ┌─AMT   ┌─AMT
LOC(before): GGF74BF9F8   LOC(after): 60F74BF9F8

The GG in the first byte of LOC before execution indicates that this byte was set aside or allocated by a DS statement—it was not initialized. The GG stands for *garbage*, data to which no meaning has been assigned for this particular usage. The above is the same as:

$$MVC \quad LOC(1),MINUS$$

$$\vdots$$

LOC   DS   C
AMT   DC   C'7.98'
MINUS   DC   C'-'

The MVI used in conjunction with the character-propagation capabilities of the MVC instruction does an efficient job of clearing an area. One output area can be used for several purposes in the same program. For example, any of several different messages can be built in the same output area, depending on conditions that arise during the execution of the program. Before each use, the area must be set to blanks. The following instructions do just that:

```
          MVI    OUTAREA,C' '              SET FIRST TO BLANK
          MVC    OUTAREA + 1(79),OUTAREA   PROPAGATE BLANK
          .
          .
          .
OUTAREA   DS     CL80
```

Use the following as the contents before execution in each of the following instructions or sets of instructions which does not contain its own DC instructions. Show the contents of any registers or storage areas which change as a result of the execution of the instructions.

PLACE: F1 F2 F3 F4 F2 F2 F2 F2   TEMP: 00 00 00 00 00 00 00 00
       fwb   fwb

SPOT: 00007000 LOC: 00000012 AREA: 00056000 LOCAT: 00000000
  fwb   fwb   fwb   fwb

DEXT: C1 C2 C3 C4 00 00 08 00 F8 F6 F5 F5
      fwb

```
1.           L      1,LOC
             LR     5,1
2.           LM     6,8,DEXT
             STH    8,SPOT
3.           MVI    DEXT + 1,C'S'
             MVC    AREA(4),DEXT
4.           LM     9,10,PLACE
             ST     9,LOCAT
             STH    10,LOCAT
5.           LH     2,AREA
             LH     3,PLACE
             STM    2,3,DEXT + 4
6.           MVC    PLACE + 3(5),PLACE + 2
7.           MVC    AREA2,AREA1
             .
             .
             .
   AREA1     DC     CL7'GOODBYE'
   AREA2     DC     C'PLAC'
8.           MVC    LOC2,LOC1
             .
             .
             .
   LOC1      DC     C'4567890'
   LOC2      DC     6C'AB'
```

Answers:
1. Reg1: 00000012   Reg5: 00000012
2. Reg6: C1C2C3C4   Reg7: 00000800
   Reg8: F8F6F5F5   SPOT: F5F57000

3. DEXT: C1 E2 C3 C4 00 00 08 00 F8 F6 F5 F5
   AREA: C1 E2 C3 C4
4. Reg9: F1 F2 F3 F4 Reg10: F2 F2 F2 F2
   LOCAT: F2 F2 F3 F4
5. Reg2: 00000005   Reg3: FFFFF1F2
   DEXT: C1 E2 C3 C4 00 00 00 05 FF FF F1 F2
6. PLACE: F1 F2 F3 F3 F3 F3 F3 F3
7. AREA2: C7 D6 D6 C4
8. LOC2: F4F5

Figure 6-3 gives the fourth review question solved in an executed program. The pages of the listing that contain valuable information are shown.

System/370 offers one information move instruction in addition to those available on System/360. This is the Move Long instruction. It is an RR-type of instruction with the opcode MVCL. It is one of the few exceptions to the rule that all RR-type opcodes end with R. The MVCL instruction can be used to move more data than the MVC instruction, which is limited to a maximum of 256 bytes. The MVCL instruction has the ability to fill the first operand area with a padding character when the second operand is shorter than the first one. (This move instruction can have operands of *different* lengths.) The MVCL instruction is explained more fully in chapter 18.

SUBMITTING YOUR JOB FOR ASSEMBLY AND EXECUTION

To double check what you have predicted to be the contents of the affected storage areas and registers after the execution of the previous review instructions, submit them as a job to your computing system. This time, put your job through all steps (assembly, linkage editing, and execution). This means you will need three EXEC JCL cards: one to execute the assembler program, one to execute the linkage editor program, and one to execute your own program.[†] The control cards necessary to run your job are as follows:

```
        DOS                                OS

// JOB                    //jobname  JOB
// OPTION   LINK          //         EXEC    ASMFCLG
// EXEC     ASSEMBLY      //ASM.SYSIN DD      *
   ·insert your              ·insert your
   ·source program          ·source program
   ·here                    ·here
   END                      END
/*                        /*
// EXEC     LNKEDT
// EXEC
```

[†]If using OS, ASMFCLG appearing on the EXEC control card will generate the other required EXEC card images. As noted in the previous chapter be sure of the level of your assembler (ASMFCLG indicated F level).

```
     LOC    OBJECT CODE       ADDR1 ADDR2   STMT     SOURCE STATEMENT

     C00000                                 1                CSECT
                                            2                PRINT NOGEN
                                            3                FIRST BEGIN=PLACE,END=LOCAT+4
     C0000C  989A C022              00024   10               LM    9,10,PLACE
     000010  5090 C02A              0002C   11               ST    9,LOCAT
     000014  40A0 C02A              0002C   12               STH   10,LOCAT
                                            13               LAST  BEGIN=PLACE,END=LOCAT+4
     000024                                 20               DS    0F
     000024  F1F2F3F4F2F2F2F2               21       PLACE   DC    C'12342222'
     00002C  00000000                       22       LOCAT   DC    F'0'
                                            23               END
     000030  5B5BC2D7C4E4D4D7               24                     =CL8'$$BPDUMP'
     000038  0000002400000030               25                     =A(PLACE,LOCAT+4)
```

CROSS-REFERENCE

```
     SYMBOL     LEN   VALUE  DEFN

     LOCAT      00004 00002C 00022   0008   0011   0012   0016   0025
     PLACE      00008 000024 00021   0008   0010   0016   0025
```

NO STATEMENTS FLAGGED IN THIS ASSEMBLY

```
         TUGGLE                04/25/74

     GR 0-7   00001E38 00001E30 00007FFF 00001E00   00007F84 FFFFFF7C 00000000 00001DB8
     GR 8-F   00003946 0A0107F1 00001E10 00001E10   40001E02 00003DF8 000001C0 0000007B
     FP REG   41300000 00000000 41300000 00000000   42640000 00000000 43316000 00000000

     001E20            F1F2F3F4 F2F2F2F2 00000000
```

```
         TUGGLE                04/25/74

     GR 0-7   00001E38 00001E30 00007FFF 00001E00   00007F84 FFFFFF7C 00000000 00001DB8
     GR 8-F   00003946 F1F2F3F4 F2F2F2F2 00001E10   40001E02 00003DF8 000001C0 0000007B
     FP REG   41300000 00000000 41300000 00000000   42640000 00000000 43316000 00000000

     001E20            F1F2F3F4 F2F2F2F2 F2F2F3F4
```

EOJ TUGGLE

Fig. 6-3 Executed solution to fourth question

For your use during this stage of the course, some easy-to-use sets of assembler instructions that can be called into use by a few higher-level *macro* instructions in your program are provided. These will relieve you of the necessity of providing your own dumps of storage and your own input and output operations. Check appendix 1 for detailed instructions on these special instructions and how to make them available. The opcodes for these instructions are FIRST and LAST. They are placed in your program as the first and last executable instructions, respectively.

In the name field of the instruction with the opcode FIRST, place the symbolic name of your routine, if any. Several operands can be specified for this instruction, but you need specify only two now. The first operand, BEGIN, is a keyword operand in which you should specify the symbolic label that you used on your first DC or DS statement. The second operand, END, is a keyword operand in which you should specify the symbolic label on your last DC or DS statement. Follow this symbolic name immediately by a plus sign and the length, in bytes, of this last storage area:

[name]   FIRST   BEGIN=symbol,END=symbol+length

These two operands are used as the beginning and ending points of a display (dump) of storage. In addition to a display of what is in the storage between these two points, the contents of the registers will also be displayed. The LAST instruction can also have several operands, but you need specify only the same two operands as those in the FIRST instruction at this time.

A dump will be taken before any of your instructions execute and after your last instruction has executed. These dumps will give you a "before-and-after-picture" of the areas affected by the execution of your instructions. Add two instructions at the beginning of your source program and you are ready to execute. These two instructions are:

```
                CSECT
                PRINT    NOGEN
```

Your entire source program should look like the following:

```
                CSECT
                PRINT    NOGEN
    MYPROG      FIRST    BEGIN=TWO,END=RESULT+4
                  .
                  .      executable instructions
                  .
                LAST     BEGIN=TWO,END=RESULT+4
    TWO         DC       F'2'
                  .
                  .      other constants and
                  .      storage areas
    RESULT      DS       F
                END
```

CHAPTER 6 QUICK REFERENCE TO INSTRUCTIONS DISCUSSED IN THIS CHAPTER

Name	Type	Mnemonic and Form		Object Code Form†	See Page
special	macro	FIRST	BEGIN= END=	not discussed	101
Load	RX	L	← Reg,Stor	58 | R1 | X2 | B2 | D2	90
special	macro	LAST	BEGIN= END=	not discussed	101
Load Halfword	RX	LH	← Reg,Stor	48 | R1 | X2 | B2 | D2	91
Load Multiple	RS	LM	← Reg,Reg,Stor	98 | R1 | R3 | B2 | D2	92
Load Register	RR	LR	← Reg,Reg	18 | R1 | R2	88
Move Character	SS	MVC	← Stor(Length),Stor	D2 | L | B1 | D1 | B2 | D3	94
Move Immediate	SI	MVI	← Stor,Immediate	92 | I2 | B1 | D1	97
Store	RX	ST	→ Reg,Stor	50 | R1 | X2 | B2 | D2	90
Store Halfword	RX	STH	→ Reg,Stor	40 | R1 | X2 | B2 | D2	90
Store Multiple	RS	STM	→ Reg,Reg,Stor	90 | R1 | R3 | B2 | D2	92

Arrows in this column
indicate direction of
data flow

†This is the form of the instruction you will see in the object-code column of the assembler listing.

QUESTIONS

1. Explain an easy way to recognize RR-type mnemonic opcodes.

2. What sort of restrictions do the L and LH mnemonic opcodes place on the data they reference in storage?

3. What occurs when a halfword is loaded into a register that holds four bytes of data?

4. Which bytes of a register's contents are stored as a result of a STH instruction?

5. What is meant by the term wrap-around in terms of the LM and STM instructions?

6. Which operand of the MVC instruction serves as the receiving location?

7. Is the length of the move for the MVC instruction specified with the first or second operand?

8. What are the maximum and minimum number of bytes that can be moved by an MVC instruction?

9. Explain what happens as a result of the execution of the following instruction:

    MVC   LOC+1(26),LOC

10. If no length is specified as part of the first operand of an MVC instruction, what determines how many bytes will be moved when the instruction executes?

11. The contents of how many bytes are moved as the result of an MVI instruction?

12. What is meant by an immediate operand?

13. If the contents of two bytes in storage were described as:

    LOC: GGGG
         hwb

    What would this indicate to you?

EXERCISES

1. Given an input area (INAREA) that contains:

Bytes	Contents
1–15	student name
16–17	class (i.e., 77)
18–19	code for major
20–24	⎤
25–29	
30–34	course codes
35–39	
40–44	⎦

   Write instructions which will create an output area (OUTAREA) with the following, more legible, format:

Bytes	Contents
10–25	student name
35–39	⎤
40–44	
45–49	course codes
50–54	
55–59	⎦
70–71	code for major
78–79	class

   Remember that unused bytes in OUTAREA should be set to blanks.

2. Give two different instructions or sequences of instructions that will change:

   LOC: C1 C2 F1 F2 00 00 02 35 40 40 40 40
         fwb

   to:

   LOC: C1 C2 F1 F2 00 00 02 35 C1 C2 F1 F2
         fwb

3. Given: Reg5: 48215896

   Write instructions to change AREA from:

   AREA: 00 00 06 53 F1 F2 F3 F4 00 00 00
         hwb

to:

> AREA: C1 00 06 53 F1 F2 58 96 00 53 F1

Register 5 can be used, but its contents should remain unchanged.

4. Given: Reg5: 00001050   Reg6: 00529865
Reg10: 00000018
AREA: 00 00 00 65 00 00 06 75 00 C1 C2 C3
          fwb

What are the contents of these registers and storage areas after the following instructions have been executed?

    STM   5,6,AREA
    STH   10,AREA
    LH   10,AREA+6
    MVC   AREA+3(2),AREA+10
    MVI   AREA+9,C'4'

Treat the instructions as a group of instructions, not individually. (Each successive instruction uses the contents of AREA the way that the previous instruction's execution left the contents of AREA.)

5. Write instructions (not DC instructions) that will set all the 123 bytes, beginning with the byte located at PLACE, to blanks (hexadecimal 40s).

6. Using the following as the contents before execution in each of the instructions or (series of instructions), show the contents—after execution—of any altered registers or storage areas.

    LOC: 00074861   R6: 00000526
         fwb

    AREA: C1C2C3F5   PL: 40404040D4D6D6D5
          fwb   fwb

       a.   L   6,LOC
             STH   6,AREA
       b.   LH   7,AREA
             STM   6,7,PL
       c.   MVI   AREA+2,C'T'
       d.   MVC   PL+3(2),AREA+1

Fixed-Point Binary Arithmetic Instructions

You have now reached the point in your introduction to programming and computers where entirely new experiences may be opened to you. In chapter 5 you learned how to define constants in storage with which you can work and to set aside areas of storage to hold the results of your work. You learned the procedure for submitting a job to be run on your system. You also learned how to interpret portions of the assembler listing returned to you from your computer run.

In chapter 6 you learned how to code your first executable assembler language instructions (the information move instructions) and how to use the constants you defined in conjunction with these instructions. You learned that a normal job submitted to the computer goes through three steps: assembly, link edit/load, and execution. Through the execution of your own program on your system you learned that each of these steps can contribute portions of the printed output you receive. You were able to see that the instructions actually work because you saw, displayed in a dump, the contents of storage areas and registers affected by your instructions both before and after they moved data from one location to another within the computer.

In this chapter you will have an opportunity to familiarize yourself with one of the three classes of arithmetic operations available to you on Systems/ 360 and 370. Once you are able to successfully code the exercises included with this chapter, you should be able to tackle any simple arithmetic algorithm.

GENERAL REQUIREMENTS FOR
BINARY ARITHMETIC OPERATIONS

Of the three modes of arithmetic operations (binary,[†] decimal, and floating-point), binary is the fastest. To achieve this speed, certain requirements are placed on the data. For instance, the data must be standardized in several ways, and the operation itself is always performed in general purpose registers, which can be accessed more rapidly than main storage areas.

The data is standardized in that it always occupies a fixed-length area of storage—either a fullword or a halfword of storage. There is one group of fixed-point binary arithmetic instructions that handles fullwords, and one group that handles halfwords. You can add, subtract, multiply, or divide. You merely choose the opcode for the instruction, and in doing so describe the type of data the operation is to expect. For example, for an add there is a full-word add (A) or a halfword add (AH).

The data used with this class of arithmetic instructions is in fixed-point binary format. The data is always treated as signed integers. To review what this means, fixed-point data consists of a sign-bit (bit 0) and 31 integer bits (in the case of a fullword), or a sign-bit and 15 integer bits (in the case of a halfword).

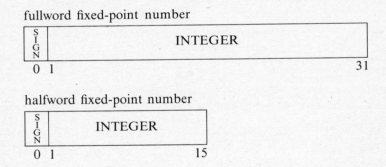

fullword fixed-point number

halfword fixed-point number

The fixed-point binary arithmetic instructions are executed with the most speed because, as mentioned earlier, they use the general purpose registers. At least one of the binary numbers must be loaded into a register before the execution of the binary arithmetic instruction. The data may already reside in a general purpose register as a result of a previous operation. If the data occupies a fullword or halfword in storage, a load instruction (L or LH) can be used to move the fullword or halfword into the register, respectively.

The register holding one of the binary numbers is always specified as the first operand in the arithmetic operation. This register, the first operand, always receives the result after the completion of the operation. The second operand

---

[†]The terms *binary* and *fixed-point binary* are used interchangeably in this text when referring to the instruction set.

represents the location of the second piece of data that participates in the arithmetic operation. If the second piece of data also resides in a register, the opcode you use indicates an RR-type of arithmetic operation:

AR	R1,R2	for addition
SR	R1,R2	for subtraction
MR	R1,R2	for multiplication
DR	R1,R2	for division

If the second piece of data resides in a storage location, you use an RX-type opcode that indicates not only that the second operand represents data in a storage location, but also whether that storage location is a fullword or a halfword.

A	R1,S2	for fullword addition
S	R1,S2	for fullword subtraction
M	R1,S2	for fullword multiplication
D	R1,S2	for fullword division
AH	R1,S2	for halfword addition
SH	R1,S2	for halfword subtraction
MH	R1,S2	for halfword multiplication

(The computer does not perform halfword division operations.)

BINARY ADDITION AND SUBTRACTION

Binary addition instructions add the second operand contents (these are the register contents if AR is the opcode, fullword-storage contents if A is the opcode, and halfword-storage contents if AH is the opcode) to the contents of the first operand register. The sum is placed in the first operand register. The second operand remains unchanged by the execution of the instruction. The following series of instructions performs the addition of two plus two and places the result in a fullword, symbolically named ANS:

I		*II*		*III*	
L	6,TWOF	LH	6,TWOH	L	6,TWOF
A	6,TWOF	AH	6,TWOH	AR	6,6
ST	6,ANS	ST	6,ANS	ST	6,ANS
.		.		.	
.		.		.	
.		.		.	
TWOF	DC F'2'	TWOH	DC H'2'	TWOF	DC F'2'
ANS	DS F	ANS	DS F	ANS	DS F

In halfword addition and halfword subtraction instructions, the second operand is expanded (internally—not in the source storage location) from a halfword to a fullword by placing copies of the sign bit in each of the leftmost or high-order 16 bit positions before the operation execution. The sign is propagated just as it is in the execution of the already familiar LH instruction.

Different combinations of the above instructions can also be used. For instance:

	IV		*Register 6:*	
	LH	6,TWOH	00000002_{16}	
	A	6,TWOF	00000004_{16}	
	ST	6,ANS	00000004_{16}	
	:		*BEFORE:*	*AFTER:*
TWOH	DC	H'2'	0002	0002
TWOF	DC	F'2'	00000002	00000002
ANS	DS	F	GARBAGE	00000004

All of the foregoing combinations of instructions will get the job done. You need only keep in mind the alignment of your data. The important things to remember are:

1. Move one of the pieces of data into the register in which you wish to perform the arithmetic and obtain the result.
2. Use the addition opcode that fits the location of your second piece of data.
3. When the operation is completed, the result can be found in the first operand register. You may then leave the result in the register or move it to any location you wish.

If the location to which you wish to move the result is a halfword rather than a fullword, change the opcode of the store instruction from ST to STH. Keep in mind that the maximum value containable in a halfword is $2^{15} - 1$, or 32,767.

If both of your pieces of data reside in registers, use of the RR-type of opcode results in an even faster operation than the RS-type L and LH, because there is no need to make a relatively time-consuming access of data in storage. RR-type operations always execute fastest.

You will notice that in the case of Example III, the use of the RR-type opcode (AR), there is the one exception to the rule that the second operand remains unchanged by the execution of the arithmetic instructions. In the case where the second operand register is the same register as the register specified in the first operand, it serves as the receiving register; and thus its original contents are destroyed by the execution of the instruction. Only when R1 and R2 are identical are the second operand register's contents altered by the execution of the instruction.

Code a series of instructions to solve each of the following arithmetic problems:

$$
\begin{array}{ccccc}
32 & 18 & 12 & 215 & 18 \\
+\ 16 & +\ 22 & 8 & +\ (-24) & +\ (-6) \\
 & & 37 & & \\
 & & +\ 68 & &
\end{array}
$$

In each case place the result in a different halfword. The last two arithmetic problems are really no different from the three other problems. For example, in the case of the last problem, two DC statements are coded—one for a positive 18, and the other for a negative 6. The positive 18 is loaded into a register; the negative 6 is added to that register's contents, and the result (a positive 12) replaces the positive 18 in that register. An instruction sequence that would perform these operations is:

			Register 5	
	L	5,FIRST	00000012_{16}	
	A	5,SECOND	$0000000C_{16}$	
	STH	5,ANS5	$0000000C_{16}$	
		.		
		.	*BEFORE:*	*AFTER:*
FIRST	DC	F'18'	00000012_{16}	00000012_{16}
SECOND	DC	F'-6'	$FFFFFFFA_{16}$	$FFFFFFFA_{16}$
ANS5	DS	H	GARBAGE	$000C_{16}$

The requirements for subtraction instructions are identical to the ones for addition. One piece of data must already be in a register. This register is specified in the first operand, and it is this register that receives the result of the operation. One other item must be remembered by the programmer in the case of subtraction operations—the algebraic sign rule: When you subtract a negative number, the operation will increase, rather than decrease, the first operand value. For example:

			Register 8	
	L	8,NUM1	00000014_{16}	
	S	8,NUM2	$0000001D_{16}$	
	ST	8,ANS	$0000001D_{16}$	
		.		
		.	*BEFORE:*	*AFTER:*
NUM1	DC	F'20'	00000014_{16}	00000014_{16}
NUM2	DC	F'-9'	$FFFFFFF7_{16}$	$FFFFFFF7_{16}$
ANS	DS	H	GARBAGE	$001D_{16}$

When you subtract a negative 9 from a positive 20, the result is 29, not 11.

This can be more easily understood by becoming aware of how the subtraction operation is performed by the computer. The execution of the instruction begins with the computer (internally) taking the two's complement of the second operand. Once this is accomplished, the second operand is added to the first. Therefore, if you subtract a positive 8 from a positive 13, the positive 8 becomes a negative 8; a negative 8 added to a positive 13 results in a positive 5. Whereas if you subtract a negative 8 from a positive 13, the negative 8 becomes a positive 8 when complemented; a positive 8 added to a positive 13 results in a positive 21. Try coding the series of instructions needed to solve the following set of equations:

1. ANS1 = A + B − C
2. ANS2 = D − B + 3
3. ANS3 = ANS1 − C
4. ANS4 = ANS1 − ANS3

Use the following as values for the variables if you desire:

$$A = 46 \quad B = -4 \quad C = 12 \quad D = -26$$

Remember, submit your solutions to the computer in the form of a job to check your answers.

BINARY MULTIPLICATION AND DIVISION

Binary multiplication and division are similar in many ways to addition and subtraction. There is, however, one striking difference. Consider a fullword multiplication instruction. Whether it is an RR-type or an RX-type instruction, one piece of data is 4 bytes long and resides in a register, and the other piece is four bytes long and resides in a register or a fullword of storage. This means that a 31-bit integer plus a sign bit will be multiplied by a 31-bit integer plus a sign bit. If the numbers are the largest possible to be represented in 31 bits, the product of the multiplication operation will not fit in one register. To solve this problem, Systems/360 and 370 use two consecutive registers to hold the product.

These two consecutive registers are called an even-odd coupled register pair. That is, the first register of the pair is an even-numbered register, and the second register is the odd register whose register number is one higher than the number of the even one. For instance, registers 6 and 7 and registers 10 and 11 and registers 0 and 1 can be used as even-odd coupled register pairs; but registers 7 and 8, or 5 and 6, cannot be used, even though they are consecutive. In preparing for multiplication, the data that is to be moved into a register is placed in the odd register of the even-odd coupled register pair. For instance, if you choose to use registers 8 and 9 as your register pair, you must load the data into register 9. When specifying the first operand of the multiplication instruction, however, you specify the even register of the pair.

The best way to explain these instructions is through examples. One sequence of instructions that will multiply 68 by 14 is:

			Register 6	Register 7
	L	7,SIXTY8	UNKNOWN	00000044_{16}
	M	6,FOURTEEN	00000000_{16}	$000003B8_{16}$
	ST	7,ANS	00000000_{16}	$000003B8_{16}$
	.			
	.		BEFORE	AFTER
SIXTY8	DC	F'68'	00000044_{16}	00000044_{16}
FOURTEEN	DC	F'14'	$0000000E_{16}$	$0000000E_{16}$
ANS	DS	2F	GARBAGE	$000003B8_{16}$

The load instruction sets up for the multiplication instruction by moving the 68 into register 7.

As the multiply instruction executes, the contents of the fullword located at FOURTEEN are multiplied by the contents of the odd register of the even-odd coupled register pair indicated in the first operand (register 7). The product of this operation is placed in the even-odd register pair specified in the first operand, registers 6 and 7. The original contents of register 6 are unimportant, since they do not participate in the operation, but the original contents are destroyed by the operation. Register 6 serves to hold the leftmost 31 bits of the product along with the sign of the product.

The sign of the product is determined by the rules of algebra, from the signs of the multiplier and multiplicand:

Multiplier		Multiplicand		Product
positive	$\times$	positive	=	positive
positive	$\times$	negative	=	negative
negative	$\times$	positive	=	negative
negative	$\times$	negative	=	positive

A product of zero is always positive.

Since we, as programmers, defined the data used in this problem, we were aware of the magnitude of the product, 68 times 14 is 952.[†] This product, 952, is well below the maximum positive number that can be represented in 31 integer bits. Therefore, we can ignore the contents of the even register of the

---

[†]An axiom not to be taken lightly that is applicable here is: "Know your data."

pair, register 6, because it merely contains 32 bits equivalent to the sign bit. So the contents of register 7 are stored in ANS as the result of the problem. If the product had been too large to be contained in the odd register of the pair, the even register would have held some significant bits of the product. An STM instruction could have been used to store the contents of both registers in two consecutive fullwords beginning with the fullword labeled ANS.

The halfword multiplication instruction does NOT use an even-odd coupled register pair. It uses only one register, and any even or odd register can be used. The multiplicand must be in this register before the execution of the MH instruction. This register is specified in the first operand of the instruction, and the multiplier (specified in the second operand) occupies a halfword in storage. The product replaces the multiplicand.

To be more explicit, the multiplicand of the MH instruction and the product, which replaces the multiplicand, are both 32-bit signed integers—and they may occupy any of the general-purpose registers. The multiplier is a 16-bit signed integer that occupies a halfword in storage. The multiplier is expanded to 32 bits—internally (not in storage), before the multiplication operation takes place—by propagating its sign-bit value throughout the 16 high-order bit positions. The resultant 32-bit multiplier and the multiplicand are multiplied, and the 32-bit product replaces the multiplicand.

The previous example (68 multiplied by 14) could have been coded using the halfword multiply, since the multiplier can be represented in a halfword, and the product easily fits into 4 bytes.

```
        L    7,SIXTY8   or LH 7,SIXTY8H
        MH   7,FORTENH
        ST   7,ANS
        .
        .
        .

SIXTY8    DC    F'68'     or SIXTY8H    DC    H'68'
FORTENH   DC    H'14'
ANS       DS    F
```

Care must be taken to ensure that the product can always be represented in 31 integer bits. If the product is too large, the most significant digits will be lost.

Given: A = 6, B = 4, C = 3, D = 2, and X = 5. Try putting together instructions you have learned so far to code programming solutions of the following equations:

1. $A + B - C + D$

Multiplication can be indicated in one of four different ways:

a. by using the symbol $\times$

    2. $A \times B + C$

b. by using a dot or period (to avoid confusion when an $\times$ is used as a symbol in the expression)

    3. $A \cdot X - D$

c. by using parentheses

    4. $A(B)$

d. by simply placing the letters next to each other without using any symbol.

    5. $AB + D$
    6. $3AC - 2BD$

Parentheses can be used to group various operations. When parentheses are used, the operations within the parens are performed, and the resultant number participates for the entire group:

    7. $A(B + C - X)$
    8. $B + C(D - A) - C$

Parentheses can be *nested*; that is, each pair can be enclosed within another pair. In this case, the contents of the innermost pair are evaluated, then the contents of the next most inclusive pair of parentheses, and so on, until the evaluation is complete.

$$A + C(B + A(C - D) - A)$$

1. D is subtracted from C.
2. The result from step 1 is multiplied by A.
3. B is added to the result from step 2.
4. Then A is subtracted from the result of step 3.
5. The result of step 4 is multiplied by C.
6. A is added to the product of the multiplication.

Placing the result in a fullword called ANSER, the code to evaluate this expression would be:

			Register 6	Register 7
L	7,C		UNKNOWN	00000003_{16}
S	7,D	$(C-D)$	UNKNOWN	00000001_{16}
M	6,A	$A(C-D)$	00000000_{16}	00000006_{16}
A	7,B	$B+A(C-D)$	00000000_{16}	$0000000A_{16}$

				Register 6	*Register 7*
S	7,A	$(B+A(C-D)-A)$		00000000_{16}	00000004_{16}
M	6,C	$C(B+A(C-D)-A)$		00000000_{16}	$0000000C_{16}$
A	7,A	$A+C(B+A(C-D)-A)$		00000000_{16}	00000012_{16}
ST	7,ANSER			00000000_{16}	00000012_{16}

.
.
.

A	DC	F'6'
B	DC	F'4'
C	DC	F'3'
D	DC	F'2'
ANSER	DS	F

The divide instructions require an even-odd coupled registered pair, just as the fullword multiply instructions. (There is no halfword divide instruction.) The dividend occupies the entire 64 bits of the register pair. The sign-bit is the leftmost, high order, bit of the even register; and there are 63 integer bits. The even register of the pair is specified in the first operand of the Divide instruction. The divisor occupies one of the other general purpose registers or a fullword in storage. The location of the divisor is specified in the second operand of the Divide instruction. When the execution of the instruction is completed, the quotient is placed in the odd register of the pair, and the remainder in the even register.

The sign of the quotient is determined by the rules of algebra. The remainder has the same sign as the dividend.

Dividend		*Divisor*		*Quotient*	*Remainder*
positive	÷	positive	=	positive	positive
positive	÷	negative	=	negative	positive
negative	÷	positive	=	negative	negative
negative	÷	negative	=	positive	negative

A quotient of zero or a remainder of zero is always positive.

The execution of your program will be stopped for a "fixed-point divide" exception if either of the following should occur: (1) you request a division operation to be performed with a divisor value of zero, or (2) the dividend and divisor values you use generate a quotient that is too large to be represented in 32 bits. Remember, an exception means that you have caused an error condition to arise as your instructions are executing. When this occurs, the operating system stops the execution of your program and gives you a dump. For example, the value of P where $P = A \times B/C$ is calculated by the following series of instructions:

```
        L    7,A
        M    6,B
        D    6,C
        STM  6,7,P
         .
         .
         .
P       DS   2F
A       DC   F'2'
B       DC   F'9'
C       DC   F'3'
```

Notice that in this example the multiplication of A times B places the product in the even-odd coupled register pair 6 and 7. The leftmost or high-order bit of register 6 is the sign of the product, and the remaining 31 bits of register 6, along with all 32 bits of register 7, are the product. Therefore, before the Divide instruction executes, the dividend is occupying the even-odd coupled register pair. After execution, the remainder is stored in the fullword at P and the quotient in the fullword at P + 4.

What happens when the logic of the program does not have a Multiplication instruction preceding the Divide to set up the dividend in the register pair? Simply loading the dividend into the odd register of the pair won't work, even if the dividend can be represented in less than 31 bits. The Divide instruction treats the entire 64 bits in the coupled register pair as the dividend and its sign. For example, given that registers 2 and 3 contain:

$$\text{Register 2: } 00000002 \qquad \text{Register 3: } 00001674$$

we load the dividend, a positive 265, into register 3.

```
        L    3,DIVND
        D    2,DIVSR
         .
         .
         .

DIVND   DC   F'265'†
DIVSR   DC   F'21'
```

When the Divide instruction executes, it will be using the contents of the coupled register pair, 2 and 3, as the dividend. The dividend is then a great deal larger than we want.

$$\text{Register 2: } 00000002 \qquad \text{Register 3: } 00000089$$

The dividend is 0000000200000089_{16}.

In this case we could have avoided this problem by zeroing out register 2's

---

†Remember, the 265 in the DC statement is a decimal 265, whereas the 89 in register 3 is the hexadecimal shorthand for the binary equivalent to 265.

contents. This could be accomplished by loading a fixed-point binary constant of zero into register 2:

```
            L    2,ZERO
            .
            .
            .
ZERO        DC   F'0'
```

or by subtracting register 2's contents from itself, thus zeroing it prior to the division instruction.

```
            SR   2,2
```

This solution, however, makes one possible faulty assumption—that the dividend is always a positive number. What happens if this solution is taken and the dividend is negative?

```
            L    3,DIVND
            SR   2,2
            D    2,DIVSR
            .
            .
            .
DIVND       DC   F'-26'
DIVSR       DC   F'2'
```

The load instruction places FFFFFFE6 in register 3, which is the hexadecimal shorthand for the two's complement of 26. The Subtract instruction places a value of zero in register 2. The Divide instruction treats the entire contents of the register pair as the dividend, with the leftmost, high-order, bit of register 2 automatically being taken as the sign of the dividend. What is this leftmost bit? A zero, making the dividend a positive number (as far as the divide instruction is concerned). A small negative number, a −26 has become a very large positive dividend, a number in the billions.

If your dividend may be negative, we have one way, using the instructions you already know, of ensuring that the dividend is correctly represented in the entire 64 bits of the register pair. The number of unknown sign is moved into the odd register of the pair. A Multiply instruction is used to multiply the now 32-bit number by a positive value of 1, placing the product in the even-odd register pair.

```
            L    5,DIVND
            M    4,ONE
            D    4,DIVSR
            .
            .
            .
DIVND       DC
ONE         DC   F'1'
DIVSR       DC
```

The result of the Multiply instruction is that the sign bit from the odd register is propagated throughout the even register. Remember, this same sort of process takes place automatically when you use an LH instruction and the sign of that halfword is propagated or duplicated to expand that halfword to a fullword before it is loaded into the register.

If DIVND happens to be a positive 12, register 5 contains 0000000C after the Load instruction executes. After the Multiply instruction executes, the product $(1 \times 12 = 12)$ fills the register pair:

Register 4:   00000000   Register 5: 0000000C

If DIVND happens to be a negative 12, register 5 contains FFFFFFF4 after the Load instruction executes. After the Multiply, the register pair contains:

Register 4: FFFFFFFF   Register 5: FFFFFFF4

This is, for now, your best approach for setting up the dividend. If you use it, you will never get caught by the one exception to your expected sign of the dividend: your code will correctly handle both positive and negative values. Given the following:

A: 00000012   B: 0003   C: 00000009
   fwb   hwb   fwb

D: 0004   E: FFFFFFF9
  hwb   fwb

Evaluate the following equations (in each case where division is involved, the quotient is considered the result):

$$\text{ANS1} = A \times B \div C$$
$$\text{ANS2} = B + C$$
$$\text{ANS3} = \text{ANS2} \times B + D$$
$$\text{ANS4} = \text{ANS2} + D$$
$$\text{ANS5} = A \times B + (C - B) \div B$$
$$\text{ANS6} = \frac{D \times C + (A - B \times D)}{C - E}$$

CHAPTER 7 QUICK REFERENCE

Name	Type	Mnemonic and Form	Object Code Form†	See Page
Add	RX	A Reg,Stor (←)	5A | R1 | X2 | B2 | D2	109
Add Halfword	RX	AH Reg,Stor (←)	4A | R1 | XB | B2 | D2	109
Add Register	RR	AR Reg,Reg (←)	1A | R1 | R2	109
Divide	RX	D Reg,Stor (←)	5D | R1 | X2 | B2 | D2	116
Divide Register	RR	DR Reg,Reg (←)	1D | R1 | R2	116
Multiply	RX	M Reg,Stor (←)	5C | R1 | X2 | B2 | D2	112
Multiply Halfword	RX	MH Reg,Stor (←)	4C | R1 | X2 | B2 | D2	114
Multiply Register	RR	MR Reg,Reg (←)	1C | R1 | R2	112
Subtract	RX	S Reg,Stor (←)	5B | R1 | X2 | B2 | D2	111
Subtract Halfword	RX	SH Reg,Stor (←)	4B | R1 | X2 | B2 | D2	111
Subtract Register	RR	SR Reg,Reg (←)	1B | R1 | R2	111

†This is the form of the instruction you will see in the object-code column of the assembler listing.

Arithmetic Conversions

The arithmetic instructions you learned in chapter 7 perform their operations on data in fixed-point binary format. We have been using DC statements of the F and H type to cause the assembler to set up the required binary numbers in storage. This assumes that we always know exactly what numbers we need prior to assembly time. This assumption easily becomes an impractical requirement to meet, as you can see from the following discussion.

The logical sequence of steps necessary in solving a problem can be the same, regardless of what values the symbolic names represent. For example, equation $A = B \times C - D + 5$ requires the following five instructions:

1. an information move instruction to load the value of B into a general purpose register
2. a multiply instruction to perform the $B \times C$ operation
3. a subtract instruction to subtract the value of D from the product generated in step 2
4. an add instruction to add 5 to the result from step 3
5. an information move instruction to store the value of the entire expression in a location in storage labeled A

At this point in your programming experience, you could use DC statements to assign values to the symbolic names B, C, and D, to give a symbolic name to a constant of value 5, as well as to set aside space for the answer and give this space the symbolic name A. Your program could then be executed with the values you have chosen for B, C, and D.

What would happen if you wanted to execute your program a second time using new values for B, C, and D? You would have to change the operands of the three DC statements defining B, C, and D. Then you would have to assemble your program again before you could execute it and calculate the new value for A based on the new values for B, C, and D. Just think of the time you would have to spend repunching—and the computer time involved in re-assembling your program if you wanted to use twenty different values for each of the constants (treating the constants like variables) in solving for twenty possible values of A!

INTRODUCTION TO THE INPUT AND OUTPUT
OF A DATA PROCESSING SYSTEM

Two of the five basic functions provided by all data processing systems can be used here to alleviate the problem of handling multiple values for variables. These are the functions of Input and Output (I/O). Your program can be coded using the same sequence of steps, but this time, DS statements can be used to set aside space for the values of B, C, and D. The code will, as before, treat these locations in storage as if they actually contained values for B, C, and D. Preceding this code, however, will be input instructions to read in the values to be placed in B, C, and D. So, by the time your load, multiply, and subtract instructions are executed there will be one value at B, one at C, and one at D.

The values are punched into a card. As the program is executed, the values are read from the card and placed in the reserved storage areas. At this point, it seems that it might be an easy task to take these values and use them in the arithmetic operations. But, there is one catch; the numbers as read in are not in the proper format—they are *not* fixed-point binary numbers.

Each number read from the card is a character symbol that can be translated into a unique 8-bit EBCDIC code. The 8-bit codes for the numbers 0–9 are as follows:

Number on Card	8-bit EBCDIC Code Placed in Byte of Storage	Hexadecimal Shorthand
0	11110000	F0
1	11110001	F1
2	11110010	F2
3	11110011	F3
4	11110100	F4
5	11110101	F5
6	11110110	F6
7	11110111	F7
8	11111000	F8
9	11111001	F9

The number 26 read in from a card would look like this in storage:

1111001011110110

Two steps are required to change the 26 as represented in EBCDIC to the binary representation of 26. Each of the steps involves a change in the format of the number:

1. The first step involves changing a number in zoned-decimal format to a number in packed-decimal format.
2. The second step involves changing the packed-decimal number to a number in binary format.

ZONED-DECIMAL FORMAT

Numeric characters read from a card and translated into EBCDIC can be said to be stored in *zoned-decimal format*. Each character occupies one byte of storage. The leftmost 4 bits (the first hex digit) are called the zone portion of the byte. The rightmost 4 bits (second hex digit) are called the digit portion. The number 26 appears as:

characters punched into card:	2		6	
EBCDIC representation:	1111	0010	1111	0110
hexadecimal shorthand:	F	2	F	6
portions of bytes:	ZONE	DIGIT	SIGN	DIGIT

The sign of a zoned-decimal number is not shown by prefixing a plus or minus character in front of the number. Instead the sign is carried over the low-order digit in the number. Stated in different terms, the sign of a zoned-decimal number is the zone portion of the rightmost digit of that number. The F(1111) in the zone portion of the least significant byte (the byte containing a digit portion of 6) is the sign of the zoned-decimal representation of 26. The zone portions of the other bytes are unimportant. A zoned-decimal number has the following format:

ZONE	DIGIT		ZONE	DIGIT	SIGN	DIGIT

The zone portions of the least significant byte indicates the following:

Positive Sign	Negative Sign
1010 or A	1011 or B
1100 or C	1101 or D
1110 or E	
1111 or F	

No other bit combinations are recognized as valid signs.

PACKED-DECIMAL FORMAT

In packed-decimal format, the sign of the number is stored in the rightmost 4 bits of the least significant byte, and the digits are stored in successive groups of 4 bits to the left of the sign. There are no zone portions to the bytes. Each byte, except the low-order, contains two digits; the low-order byte contains the last digit and the sign. A packed-decimal number has the following format:

DIGIT	DIGIT		DIGIT	DIGIT	DIGIT	SIGN

The various combinations of bits that make up the sign in a packed-decimal number are interpreted in the same way as a zoned-decimal number. Hexadecimal A, C, E, and F are positive signs; B and D are negative signs.

THE INPUT CONVERSION PROCESS

A number is read in from a card. That number is converted from the Hollerith punch code that represented the number on the card into the EBCDIC that is the internal representation of characters in Systems/360 and 370. This conversion is performed automatically. The number is in zoned-decimal format in storage when your code first begins to handle it. You use two instructions: the PACK instruction and the CVB instruction, to convert the zoned-decimal number to a binary number. Figure 8-1 shows this process in diagram form.

Check in appendix 3 and assure yourself that the automatic conversion was done correctly for each of the characters. Notice the F in the leftmost hex digit of the low-order byte of the first number. A sign of F means this is a positive 1265. Notice also that the sign of the second number in zoned-decimal format is a D, indicating that the second number is a negative 639.

Remember that a minus sign cannot be prefixed to the number punched into the card to indicate the number is negative. Instead, the sign is carried over the low-order digit in the number. Well, when you want to punch a negative number, do just that! Add the punch hole that represents a minus sign on top of the punch hole that represents a 9 and what do you get? A minus sign is represented in the Hollerith code as one punch in the 11-row. A 9 is represented as one punch in the 9-row. Combine an 11-punch with a 9-punch, and what does this combination of punch holes represent? The letter R. Therefore, the letter R punched in column 27 indicates not only that the last digit in the number is a 9, but also that the entire number is negative. The R becomes D9 in storage; the D in the zone portion of the low-order byte of the number indicates that it is a negative zoned-decimal number.

The first number we are examining (the 1265 punched in columns 1–4) becomes 1265F in its packed-decimal format. The F indicates that the number

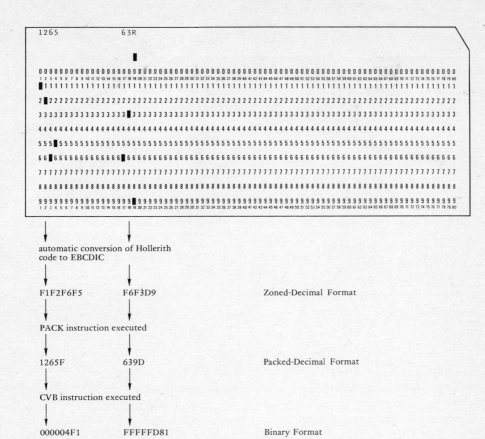

Fig. 8-1 The input conversion process

has a positive decimal value of 1265. The last step in the conversion process takes this number in the base of 10 and converts it to a number in the base of 2 (a binary number). Figure 8-2 reviews this conversion process, converting the decimal 1265 to binary. This binary number is represented in its hexadecimal shorthand as follows:

$$100 \quad 1111 \quad 0001_2$$
$$4 \qquad F \qquad 1_{16}$$

As shown in figure 8-3, converting the second number to binary follows the same steps. Once the binary value is reached, the two's complement of this binary number is computed because the number is negative.

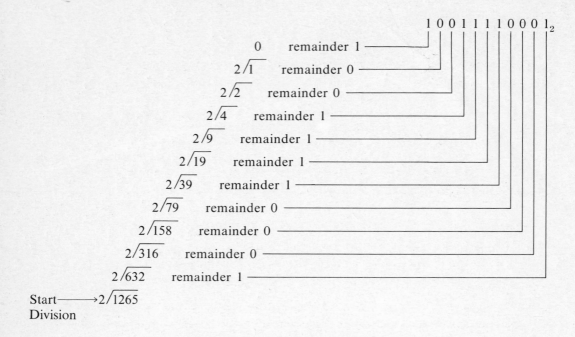

Fig. 8-2 Converting the decimal 1265 to binary

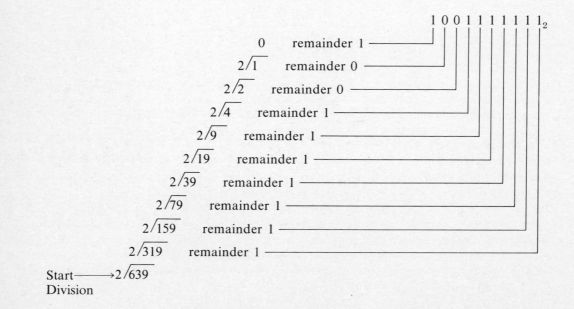

Fig. 8-3 Converting the decimal −639 to binary

Calculation of the two's complement:

$$01001111111_2$$
$$10110000000$$
$$\underline{\qquad\qquad +\ 1}$$
$$110110000001_2$$
$$\text{D} \qquad 8 \qquad 1$$

THE PACK INSTRUCTION

The pack instruction converts a zoned-decimal number into a packed-decimal number. The general format for a PACK instruction is:

$$\text{PACK} \quad \text{S1(L1),S2(L2)}$$

where: S1 is symbolic name of the packed-decimal number
L1 is length of the packed-decimal number, in bytes
S2 is symbolic name of the zoned-decimal number
L2 is length of the zoned-decimal number, in bytes

The format of the data indicated by the second operand is changed from zoned decimal to packed decimal. The result, the packed-decimal number, is placed in the location indicated by the first operand.

Each operand may be from 1 to 16 bytes in length. The operands do not have to be the same length. This is why both L1 and L2 are specified. There are two reasons for having operands of different lengths. First, it takes less storage to represent a number in packed-decimal format than it does to represent the same number in zoned-decimal format (for example, 239582765F and F2F3F9F5F8F2F7F6F5, 5 bytes and 9 bytes, respectively). Second, while the PACK instruction requires no specific length for its data and no special boundary alignment of that data, the CVB instruction requires that its data be a doubleword and aligned accordingly. As a programmer, you should anticipate the requirements of instructions later in a coding sequence when setting up current coding.

You've already had examples of ways to anticipate requirements with the multiply and divide instructions that require even-odd coupled register pairs. If you know your next operation is multiplication, set up your addition or subtraction instruction so that it places the result of its operation in the odd register of the coupled pair. By doing so, you set the result up for use as required in the multiply operation.

In the case of the PACK instruction, you should anticipate the CVB instruction requirement for a doubleword. It may be possible to represent the packed-decimal number in less than 8 bytes, but you should choose a length of 8. Zero digits will be generated to "pad out" the excess bytes to the left of the packed-decimal number. With the ability to specify a length for each operand, it doesn't matter whether your zoned-decimal number is one or 16 bytes long. **Remember, however, that the maximum length field that the PACK instruction can handle is 16 bytes!**

As you use the PACK instruction, you will discover that it is a "trusting" instruction. It makes no checks to see if the bit combinations in the digit portions of the bytes represent valid digits. Further, it makes no check to see whether the sign in the low-order byte is valid. The action of the PACK instruction continues regardless of what bit combinations it encounters; no checks are made, and no error conditions are noted. The action of the PACK instruction is as follows:

1. The sign of the EBCDIC number is placed in the rightmost four bits of the low-order byte of the field designated by the first operand:

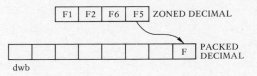

2. The digit portions of each byte, from right to left, are placed in successive positions of the receiving field (also right to left):

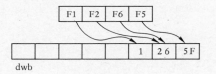

3. If the digits in the second operand are insufficient to fill the first operand, zero digits are used to complete ("pad out") the packed-decimal number:

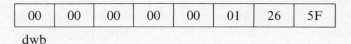

4. If the first operand field is too short to contain all significant digits of the second operand, the high-order digits which do not fit are ignored. There is no way for the computer to inform your program that this has occurred. Once again, it's the programmer's axiom—you must *know your data*.

Try your hand at packing the following zoned-decimal fields:

1. F6F2F8F3F1
2. F2F2D6
3. F1F8F3F6F6F7F2F9F6F4F5

If no length is specified on an operand of a PACK instruction, the length associated with the symbol specified in the operand is used as the length of that operand. What are the contents of AREA2 after the execution of the following instructions?

```
              PACK   AREA2,AREA1
                :
                :
    AREA1     DC    CL5'16523'
    AREA2     DS    D
```

THE CONVERT TO BINARY INSTRUCTION (CVB)

The CVB instruction changes the base of the second operand from decimal to binary. The resultant binary number is placed in the register indicated in the first operand. The number is treated as a right-aligned, signed integer both before and after conversion. The general format for the Convert to Binary Instruction is:

$$[\text{NAME}] \quad \text{CVB} \quad \text{R1,S2}$$

During the execution of the CVB instruction, many tests or checks are made automatically to verify that the requirements of the instruction have been met:

1. The second operand, the packed-decimal number, must be contained in a doubleword. Therefore, the address represented by the second operand is checked to ensure that it is evenly divisible by 8.
2. The low-order 4 bits of the second operand are checked to ensure that they contain one of the six combinations of bits which are considered valid signs. To review, the valid positive signs are 1010, 1100, 1110, and 1111 (hexadecimal A, C, E, and F). The valid negative signs are 1011 and 1101 (hexadecimal B and D). Any of the remaining ten possible bit combinations are considered invalid.
3. Each of the remaining 15 groups of 4 bits in the doubleword of the second operand is checked to ensure that it represents a valid digit 0000_2-1001_2 (0-9).

If any of these checks fail to verify that any requirement has not been met, the execution of the program is stopped. If the requirements have been met, the result of the conversion (the binary number) is placed in the register indicated by the first operand. The second operand is unaffected by the execution of the instruction.

Examples of the conversions of both a positive and a negative packed-decimal number follows:

before: AREA1: 00000000 0000012F
                         dwb
                 AREA2: 00000000 0000105D
                         dwb
                 REG6:   00000000   REG7: 00000000
                         CVB   6,AREA1
                         CVB   7,AREA2

after: AREA1: 00000000 0000012F
                         dwb
                 AREA2: 00000000 0000105D
                         dwb
                 REG6:   0000000C   REG7: FFFFFF97

Since the PACK instruction can handle up to a maximum of 16 bytes and the second operand of the CVB instruction must be a doubleword, the packed-decimal number for the CVB instruction could be a value as large as 999,999,-999,999,999 (16 bytes will hold 15 digits and a sign in packed-decimal format). Yet, the maximum value that can be converted to binary and still be contained in a register is 2,147,483,647, and the minimum number is −2,147,483,648. The number you wish to convert can be outside this range and still pass all verification checks of the CVB instruction. In this case, the CVB instruction will execute; the 32 low-order binary bits of the resultant number will be placed in the first operand register, but the execution of your program will then be stopped.

Once the conversion process is complete, the number is in the proper format (fixed-point binary) for use with the fixed-point binary arithmetic instructions. In fact, the setup for the arithmetic operation is complete because one of the participating numbers is already in a register. If you wish to try your hand at coding these instructions and submitting them to the system for execution to check out whether you really understand them, use C-type constants to create your zoned-decimal data. The following is a solution to this equation:

$$ANS = A \times B$$

where A and B are defined by C-type constants.

A and B could also be defined by hexadecimal (X-type) constants. The general format for hexadecimal constants is:

[symbol]   DC   X'value'

X is the type code for a hexadecimal constant. The value subfield is enclosed in apostrophes, and it may contain any of the 16 hexadecimal digits (0 through 9 and A through F), up to a maximum of 512 digits, or 256 bytes.

```
HEX1    DC  X'C6D2F8E3'
HEX2    DC  X'F6F7'
```

In the case of an odd number of digits, a hexadecimal zero is added on the left to fill out the last byte:

```
HEX3    DC  X'7B2'        HEX3: 07B2
```

A duplication factor may be used with this type of constant. A length modifier may also be specified. If no length modifier is present, the implied length associated with the symbol is equal to half the number of hexadecimal digits in the value subfield. If a length modifier is used and padding or truncation is found necessary, it will occur on the leftmost portion of the constant.

In figure 8-4, the constants of A and B could be defined in either of the following manners:

```
A    DC  C'12'
B    DC  C'3'
     or
A    DC  X'F1F2'
B    DC  X'F3'
```

STATEMENTS NECESSARY FOR PROVIDING THE INPUT FUNCTION

At this point you know the two-step process involved in converting EBCDIC numbers into numbers in binary format. Now we shall consider how to use instructions generated by the exit macro (LAST) so that we can read successive values for variables from fields in punched cards. The reading of data from cards into the computer's storage and the writing of values from storage onto the listing are rather complicated and advanced functions. At present, we can do two things.

The first is to request the assembler to allocate an 80-byte area in your program. This area will hold the EBCDIC representation of any characters punched in the 80 columns of the input card. Any unpunched columns contain blanks and are represented by hexadecimal 40s in your 80-byte area. These bytes can be ignored in your program, but the space for them must still be allocated as part of this area.

The second thing to do is to branch to an instruction generated by your exit macro (LAST), which requests the actual read operation. This branch is generated by coding MREAD in the opcode field and the keyword INTO, followed by an equal sign and the name of your 80-byte area, in the operand. When the read operation has been completed, the next instruction to be

```
       LOC   OBJECT CODE     ADDR1 ADDR2  STMT    SOURCE STATEMENT

       000000                                1            CSECT
                                             2            PRINT  NOGEN
                                             3     FIRST  BEGIN=A,END=ANS+4
       00000C  F271 C036 C030 00038 00032   10            PACK   PACKA,A
       000012  F270 C03E C032 00040 00034   11            PACK   PACKB,B
       000018  4F70 C036       00038        12            CVB    7,PACKA
       00001C  4F90 C03E       00040        13            CVB    9,PACKB
       000020  1C69                         14            MR     6,9
       000022  5070 C046       00048        15            ST     7,ANS
                                            16     LAST   BEGIN=A,END=ANS+4
       000032  F1F2                         23  A         DC     C'12'
       000034  F3                           24  B         DC     C'3'
       000038                               25  PACKA     DS     D
       000040                               26  PACKB     DS     D
       000048                               27  ANS       DS     F
                                            28            END
       000050  5B5BC2D7C4E4D4D7             29                   =CL8'$$BPDUMP'
       000058  000000320000004C             30                   =A(A,ANS+4)
```

```
                                               CROSS-REFERENCE

       SYMBOL   LEN   VALUE   DEFN

       A        00002 000032  00023   0008  0010  0019  0030
       ANS      00004 000048  00027   0008  0015  0019  0030
       B        00001 000034  00024   0011
       PACKA    00008 000038  00025   0010  0012
       PACKB    00008 000040  00026   0011  0013
```

```
       NO STATEMENTS FLAGGED IN THIS ASSEMBLY
```

```
                TUGGLE         04/25/74                    BEFORE EXECUTION

       GR 0-7   00001E58 00001E50 00007FFF 00001E00   00007F84 FFFFFF7C 00000000 00001DB8
       GR 8-F   00003946 0A0107F1 00001E10 00001E10   40001E02 00003DF8 000001C0 0000007B
       FP REG   41300000 00000000 41300000 00000000   4264000C 00000000 43316000 00000000

       001E30   0A0EF1F2 F3E4D4D7 00001E24 00001E30   C0000014 80001F08 00000041
```

```
                TUGGLE         04/25/74                    AFTER EXECUTION

       GR 0-7   00001E58 00001E50 00007FFF 00001E00   00007F84 FFFFFF7C 00000000 00000024
       GR 8-F   00003946 00000003 00001E10 00001E10   40001E02 00003DF8 000001C0 00000000
       FP REG   41300000 00000000 41300000 00000000   42640000 00000000 43316000 00000000

       001E30   0A0EF1F2 F3E4D4D7 00000000 0000012F   C0000000 0000003F 00000024
```

Fig. 8-4 Coding solution of ANS $= A \times B$ using defined constants

executed will be the one immediately following the MREAD statement in your program.

The best way to show you how this works is through the use of a coding illustration. The equation $A = B \times C$ will be solved. (See figures 8-5 and 8-6.)

This is a simple example, but there are many new things to examine. First, let's examine how we requested the assembler to allocate our 80-byte area. In chapter 5 there was a discussion of how a duplication factor of zero could be

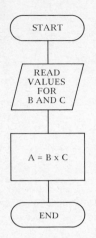

Fig. 8-5 Flowchart for A = B × C using values from input record

```
LOC     OBJECT CODE      ADDR1 ADDR2   STMT    SOURCE STATEMENT                                              DO

000000                                   1               CSECT
                                         2               PRINT   NOGEN†
                                         3               FIRST   BEGIN=PACKB,END=C+5,IO=YES
                                        18               MREAD   INTO=INAREA
000026  F275 C236 C24A  00238 0024C      21     CALC     PACK    PACKB(8),B(6)
00002C  4F70 C236             00238       22             CVB     7,PACKB
000030  F274 C23E C253  0C240 00255       23             PACK    PACKC,C
000036  4F20 C23E             00240       24             CVB     2,PACKC
00003A  1C62                              25             MR      6,2
00003C  5070 C246             00248       26             ST      7,A
                                          27     EOF      LAST    BEGIN=PACKB,END=C+5,ASMDATA=NO,EOFRTN=EOF,   X
                                                                  I=YES,O=YES
000238                                   102     PACKB    DS      D
000240                                   103     PACKC    DS      D
000248                                   104     A        DS      F
00024C                                   105     INAREA   DS      0CL80
00024C                                   106     B        DS      CL6
000252                                   107     SKIP     DS      3C
000255                                   108     C        DS      CL5
00025A                                   109     PAD      DS      66C
                                         110              END
0002A0  5B5BC2D7C4E4D4D7                 111                      =CL8'$$BPDUMP'
0002A8  000002380000025A                 112                      =A(PACKB,C+5)
0002B0  5B5BC2D6D7C5D540                 113                      =C'$$BOPEN '
0002B8  5B5BC2C3D3D6E2C5                 114                      =C'$$BCLOSE'
```

Several operands must be added to the FIRST and LAST macros. In addition to BEGIN= and END=, the operand IO=YES should be added to the FIRST macro. This specification makes the input data set ready for reading and the output data set ready for printing. Four new operands should be added to the LAST macro.

ASMDATA=NO indicates that all the data used by this program is not produced by DCs.
I=YES,O=YES cause code to be generated to handle the actual reading and writing operations.
EOFRTN=EOF specifies the name that appears on the instruction (EOF) which is to be given control when the end of file condition is encountered on the input file.

†The instruction PRINT NOGEN is an instruction that tells the assembler not to print the instructions generated by the FIRST and LAST macros. You will notice that due to this some statement numbers are missing on the source listing page of your printed output. This is nothing to worry about. The printing of these instructions at this point would only add needless confusion.

Fig. 8-6 Coding solution of A = B × C using values from input record (Part 1 of 2)

CROSS-REFERENCE

SYMBOL	LEN	VALUE	DEFN			
$CARD	00006	000070	00050	0015	0037	0068
$INPUT	00004	0000A4	00067	0061	0063	
$LINE	00006	000108	00076	0016	0044	0096
$OUTPUT1	00121	000138	00094	0087		
$OUTPUT2	00121	0001B1	00095	0092		
$READ	00004	0000F4	00068	0020		
$WRITE	00004	00022A	00096			
A	00004	000248	00104	0026		
B	00006	00024C	00106	0021		
C	00005	000255	00108	0008	0023	0030	0112
CALC	00006	000026	00021			
EOF	00004	000040	00029	0062		
IJCX0010	00008	000090	00063	0053		
IJJC0007	00004	000050	00036			
IJJC0008	00004	000060	00043			
IJJO0003	00004	000010	00014			
IJJZ0010	00001	0000A2	00066			
IJJZ0012	00001	000138	00093			
INAREA	00080	00024C	00105	0019		
PACKB	00008	000238	00102	0008	0021	0022	0030	0112
PACKC	00008	000240	00103	0023	0024	
PAD	00001	00025A	00109			
SKIP	00001	000252	00107			

NO STATEMENTS FLAGGED IN THIS ASSEMBLY

```
          TUGGLE            04/25/74

GR 0-7  000020A8 000020A0 00007FFF 00001E00    00007F84 FFFFFF7C 00000000 00001DB8
GR 8-F  00003946 0A0107F1 00001E10 00001E10    40001E02 00003DF8 000001C0 0000007B
FP REG  41300000 00000000 41300000 00000000    42640000 C0000000 43316000 00000000

002030                    C23A4700 0002D200    D189C23B 47000002 D200D18A C23C4700
002050  0002D200 D18BC23D 47000002
```

```
          TUGGLE            04/25/74

GR 0-7  000020A8 000020A0 0000000F 00001E00    00007F84 FFFFFF7C 00000000 00000159
GR 8-F  00003946 0A0107F1 00001E10 80001E26    40001E02 00003DF8 80001F00 000020C0
FP REG  41300000 00000000 41300000 00000000    42640000 00000000 43316000 00000000

002030                    00000000 C000023F    00000000 0000015F 00000159 F0F0F0F0
002050  F2F34040 40F0F0F0 F1F54040
```

Fig. 8-6 (Part 2 of 2)

used in the operand of a DS statement to cause alignment on a particular integral boundary. For example, the two statements:

```
              DS   0F
INAREA        DS   CL80
```

assure that the first byte of INAREA is a fullword boundary, permitting load instructions to move successive groups of 4 bytes into registers.

In this coding example, a duplication factor of zero is used on the DS statement with the label INAREA itself. This allows the name INAREA to be used in referring to an area 80 bytes in length. The 80 bytes are not actually allocated by this particular DS statement. The 4 DS statements that follow actually allocate the 80 bytes and indicate the breakdown of the 80-byte area into fields.

The first field, which contains the value for B, is 6 bytes in length, indicating that the value for B can be up to 6 characters long; and these characters will be right aligned in columns 1–6 of the card. The symbols INAREA and B are synonyms in that they refer to the same exact byte in storage. They are different in that INAREA has a length attribute of 80 and B a length attribute of 6. The next field of interest to the problem is columns 10–14 of the card. This field contains the value for C. A dummy field labeled SKIP is set up between the DS for B and the DS for C. This dummy field merely contains the three bytes between the two fields of importance. The space must be allocated to ensure the symbol C will refer to the tenth byte in the 80-byte area. The DS with the label, PAD, allocates the 66 bytes necessary to complete the 80-byte area. They will be ignored, but they still must be allocated. The read operation will read 80 columns of information from the card and will place any EBCDIC characters in those columns into 80 consecutive bytes of storage beginning with the byte labeled INAREA.

When the instruction labeled CALC is executed, the read operation has been completed by the code generated by the MREAD and LAST macros. If the card contained the following:

```
columns 1 2 3 4 5 6 7 8 9 10 11 12 13 14 15 16 17  .  .  . 79 80
contents 0 0 0 0 2 3 ƀ ƀ ƀ  0  0  0  1  5 ƀ  ƀ  ƀ  .  .  .  ƀ  ƀ
```

The 80 bytes beginning with the byte labeled INAREA would contain:

INAREA

F0F0F0F0F2F3404040F0F0F0F1F5404040 . . . 4040

⎵⎵⎵⎵⎵⎵⎵⎵⎵   ⎵⎵⎵⎵⎵⎵⎵⎵⎵
      B   C

The PACK instructions convert B and C to 00000000 0000023F and 0000-0000 0000015F, respectively. Notice that lengths are specified for the operands of the first PACK instruction, but not for the operands of the second PACK instruction. In these cases the PACK operations could have been done either way. Each of the symbols had the correct length of the field associated with it. In the case of B and C, length modifiers were used in the operand field rather than duplication factors (6C would have allocated 6 bytes the same as CL6, except that in the first case the length associated with the symbol would have been one). Both types of operand specifications are given in the example so you can see that they work.

The CVB instructions convert the 23 and 15 in packed decimal to their binary equivalents (00000017_{16} and $0000000F_{16}$, respectively). The multiply instruction places 00000000 00000159 in registers 6 and 7, and the store instruction moves 00000159 into the fullword at A. Thus completing the problem, you exit the code at LAST.

PREPARING TO WRITE OUTPUT

The result of the example in the previous section was stored in a fullword labeled A. To write that value out on the printer instead of storing it in A, you have to go through the same sort of conversion process you performed on the original data when you read it in. The result of the arithmetic operation is in binary format. This binary number must be converted to a decimal number in packed-decimal format, and then the packed-decimal number must be unpacked to generate a number in zoned-decimal format suitable for writing.

There are two instructions that perform these two conversion operations: Convert to Decimal (CVD) and Unpack (UNPK).

CONVERT TO DECIMAL INSTRUCTION (CVD)

The CVD instruction changes the base of the first operand from binary to decimal. The resultant decimal number is stored in the second operand location. This is one of the few instructions in the repertoires of Systems/360 and 370 where the second operand, rather than the first, receives the result. This is an important fact to remember.

There are many similarities between this instruction and the CVB instruction. Both require that the second operand be a doubleword. Both treat the low-order 4 bits of this doubleword as the sign of the packed-decimal number. On converting the binary number to a decimal number, the CVD instruction prefers 1100 (C) as the sign for a positive number and 1101 (D) for a negative number. The other combinations which are considered valid signs by the CVB instruction are not used by the CVD. Example:

before: REG7: 00000159   AREA1: F0F0F0F0F0F0F0F0
                                  dwb

CVD   7,AREA1

after: REG7: 00000159   AREA1: 000000000000345C[†]
                                  dwb

[†]Notice the preferred sign of C in the low-order 4 bits of AREA1.

There is no possibility of an overflow condition occurring with the execution of the CVD instruction. The largest binary number that can fit in a register is 2,147,483,647. Since only $5\frac{1}{2}$ bytes are required to represent this number in packed-decimal format and the second operand of the CVD instruction must be a doubleword (or 8 bytes), there is no possibility of not having sufficient room in the second operand location.

THE UNPACK INSTRUCTION (UNPK)

The Unpack instruction changes the format of the second operand from packed decimal to zoned decimal and places the zoned-decimal number in the first operand location. This direction of the flow of the data must be remembered by you. Because the Pack instruction works from second operand to first, it is easy to think that the Unpack instruction, which performs the reverse conversion, works with its operands in the reverse order. Not so. **Both the Pack and the Unpack instructions take their original data from the second operand location and place their result in the first operand location.**

The action involved in the format change is just the reverse of that taken in the execution of the Pack instruction. The low-order two groups of four bits reverse their positions. This places the sign of the number back in a position over the least significant digit in the number. A zone of F is added to the left of each of the other groups of 4 bits. The fields are processed from right to left. For example:

before: AREA1: 000000000000345C   AREA2: 00000000

UNPK   AREA2(4),AREA1(8)

after: AREA1: 000000000000345C   AREA2: F0F3F4C5

If the number in the second-operand location takes less space when unpacked than is available in the first operand, the second operand is extended with high-order zeros before the unpacking. If the first operand field is too short to contain all significant digits of the second operand when it is unpacked, the remaining high-order digits are ignored. Try your hand at unpacking the following packed-decimal fields:

1. 82356C
2. 712D
3. 5108237C

Our zoned-decimal result of the above UNPK instruction is: F0F3F4C5. If we tried to write this number out on the printer, the result would be 034E. We would like to print 0345. Why the difference in the last digit? Remember the explanation of the CVD instruction. What was the positive sign that the computer preferred in this case? C, not F. It is F5 that we would like to have as the contents of the low-order byte of the output field. This would print as a 5. The CVD instruction, however, will never produce an F for a positive sign. It produces a C (or D if the number is negative). We have to include another instruction to change the sign of our zoned-decimal number from a C to an F.

THE MOVE ZONES INSTRUCTION (MVZ)

The Move Zones instruction can solve our problem of having a zoned-decimal number with the machine's preferred positive sign (C) when we want the sign of F for printing.[†]

The Move Zones instruction (MVZ) is an SS-type instruction. Its general format is:

MVZ   S1(L),S2

This instruction can have operands that are up to a maximum of 256 bytes in length. We will be using a length of one, however, since we are only worried about the zone portion of one byte (the low-order byte).

The execution of the MVZ instruction moves the zone portion of each byte in the second operand field to the zone portion of the corresponding byte in the first operand field. Since these operands can both be part of one field, it allows us to move the zone portion of one byte in our field into the zone portion of another byte (in this case, the low-order byte). In other words, we can move one of the zones containing an F to replace the machine's preferred sign (C) in the zone portion of the low-order byte.

In this example, assume again that the fullword labeled AREA2 contains F0F3F4C5. We know if we print this field we get 034E. Using the MVZ instruction that follows:

MVZ   AREA2+3(1),AREA2+2

we can change the contents of AREA2

from: F0F3F4C5

to: F0F3F4F5

When the field AREA2 is printed now, it will print as 0345. Two problems generally come to mind at this point:

[†]The Or Immediate instruction (OI) can also be used to solve this problem. This instruction is discussed in Chapter 17.

1. If the number in AREA2 had been only one significant digit, where would we get the F zone from as a source?
2. What if the number in AREA2 had been negative?

The first problem can be solved easily. While the resultant number may only have one significant digit, the field receiving the result contains more than one byte, and the remaining high-order bytes would be set to F0s. One of the zones from these bytes would serve the purpose.

The second problem is also easy to solve. There is an instruction (LTR) that can check the contents of the register containing the result of the multiplication operation. This instruction can indicate whether the contents of the register are positive, negative, or equal to zero. A branch instruction can then be used to decide between a group of instructions that handle positive numbers or a group of instructions that handle negative numbers. (Both the LTR instruction and the branch instruction are explained in chapter 11. Should you ever be placed in a situation of handling negative numbers, look ahead to chapter 11 for explanations of how to code these instructions.)

STATEMENTS NECESSARY TO PERFORM THE WRITE OPERATION

Two things must be done to use the simplified method of writing. You had to do the same two things for reading: 1) allocate an output area and divide the area into fields, and 2) branch to the instruction generated by the exit macro (LAST).

The line you have at your disposal on the printer is longer in number of columns than the punched card. In this text you will have the possibility of printing 121 characters on one line. Therefore, allocate a 121-character area for your output area.[†] In this case, however, use DC instead of DS instructions to define areas you are skipping or areas needed to pad out to the 121-character length. You use DC instructions because each character in these areas should be set to a blank character. This makes your output more legible.

For reasons to be explained later, you must have a blank in column one of your output area. You may use any of the other 120 bytes in your output area for whatever data you wish. Just make sure you have a blank in the first byte.

To cause the branch to take place, the action on your part is similar to the action you take to read. You place "MRITE" in the opcode field and "FROM =", followed by the name of your 121-byte output area, in the operand field. When the write operation is completed, your next sequential instruction will be given control.

[†]Some systems have the capability of printing greater than 121 characters on one line, however, using the special instruction MRITE, you will be restricted to 121-character lines.

```
LOC    OBJECT CODE    ADDR1 ADDR2  STMT    SOURCE STATEMENT
000000                                1            CSECT
                                      2            PRINT NOGEN
                                      3    FIRST   BEGIN=PACKB,END=AREA2+4,IO=YES
                                     18            MREAD INTO=INAREA
000026 F275 C246 C266 00248 00268    21    CALC    PACK  PACKB(8),B(6)
00002C 4F70 C246            00248    22            CVB   7,PACKB
000030 F274 C24E C26F 00250 00271    23            PACK  PACKC,C
000036 4F20 C24E            00250    24            CVB   2,PACKC
00003A 1C62                          25            MR    6,2
00003C 4F70 C25E            00260    26            CVD   7,AREA1
000040 F337 C2C7 C25E 002C9 00260    27            UNPK  AREA2(4),AREA1(8)
000046 D300 C2CA C2C9 002CC 002CB    28            MVZ   AREA2+3(1),AREA2+2
                                     29            MRITE FROM=OUTAREA
                                     32    EOF     LAST  BEGIN=PACKB,END=AREA2+4,ASMDATA=NO,EOFRTN=EOF,  X
                                                         I=YES,O=YES
000248                              107    PACKB   DS    D
000250                              108    PACKC   DS    D
000258                              109    A       DS    F
000260                              110    AREA1   DS    D
000268                              111    INAREA  DS    0CL80
000268                              112    B       DS    CL6
00026E                              113    SKIP    DS    3C
000271                              114    C       DS    CL5
000276                              115    PAD     DS    66C
000288                              116    OUTAREA DS    0CL121
000288 40                          117    FIRSTBYT DC   C' '
000289 E3C8C540C1D5E2E6            118    MSG     DC    CL16'THE ANSWER IS'
0002C9                             119    AREA2   DS    CL4
0002CD 4040404040404040           120    PAD2    DC    CL100' '
                                   121            END
000338 5B5BC2D7C4E4D4D7           122            =CL8'$$BPDUMP'
000340 00000248000002CD           123            =A(PACKB,AREA2+4)
000348 5B5BC2D6C7C5D540           124            =C'$$BOPEN '
000350 5B5BC2C3D3D6E2C5           125            =C'$$BCLOSE'
```

Explanatory notes:

a. Statement 18 requests that the card be read.
b. Statements 21–24 perform the conversions necessary to convert the values for B and C to binary numbers.
c. Statement 25 performs the multiplication.
d. Statements 26–28 convert the binary number and get it ready for printing.
e. And statement 29 branches to request that OUTAREA be written on the printer.

Fig. 8-7 Full example of coding involved in reading records and printing results (Part 1 of 2)

Putting this example all together in one location complete with all the conversions necessary for printing results in the program given in figure 8-7.

Let's review all these new instructions and put them into perspective by using them in another program. The Little Thumper Manufacturing Company wants an inventory taken of the number of spools of raw material it has in stock. The stockboys have carefully counted the number of boxes of spools in the stockroom and recorded these numbers on slips of paper, along with the size of the box. Depending on the supplier, some of the boxes contain 4 spools

CROSS-REFERENCE

```
SYMBOL    LEN  VALUE   DEFN

$CARD     00006 000080 00055   0015  0042  0073
$INPUT    00004 000084 00072   0066  0068
$LINE     00006 000118 00081   0016  0049  0101
$OUTPUT1  00121 000148 00099   0092
$OUTPUT2  00121 0001C1 00100   0097
$READ     00004 000104 00073   0020
$WRITE    00004 00023A 00101   0031
A         00004 000258 00109
AREA1     00008 000260 00110   0026  0027
AREA2     00004 0002C9 00119   0008  0027  0028  0028  0035  0123
B         00006 000268 00112   0021
C         00005 000271 00114   0023
CALC      00006 000026 00021
EOF       00004 000054 00034   0067
FIRSTBYT  00001 0002B8 00117
IJCX0011  00008 0000A0 00068   0058
IJJC0008  00008 0C0064 00041
IJJC0009  00004 000074 00048
IJJ00003  00004 000010 00014
IJJZ0011  00001 0000B2 00071
IJJZ0013  00001 000148 00098
INAREA    00080 000268 00111   0019
MSG       00016 0002B9 00118
OUTAREA   00121 0002B8 00116   0030
PACKB     00008 000248 00107   0008  0021  0022  0035  0123
PACKC     00008 000250 00108   0023  0024
PAD       00001 000276 00115
PAD2      00100 0002CD 00120
SKIP      00001 00026E 0C113
```

NO STATEMENTS FLAGGED IN THIS ASSEMBLY

```
          TUGGLE            04/25/74

GR 0-7   00002140 00002138 00007FFF 00001E00   00007F84 FFFFFF7C 00000000 00001DB8
GR 8-F   00003946 0A0107F1 00001F10 00001E10   40001E02 00003DF8 000001C0 0000007B
FP REG   41300000 00000000 41300000 00000000   42640000 00000000 43316000 00000000

002040                     D200D18A C23C4700   0002D200 D18BC23D 47000002 D200D18C
002060   C23E4700 0002D200 D18DC23F 47000002   D200D18E C2404700 0002D200 D18FC241
002080   47000002 D200D190 C2424700 0002D200   D191C243 47000002 D200D198 C22A4700
0020A0   5B5BC2D7 C4E4D4D7 00002038 0000205A   5B5BC2D6 D7C5D540 40E3C8C5 40C1D5E2
0020C0   E6C5D940 C9E24040 40F0F01A 0A404040
```

THE ANSWER IS   0345

```
          TUGGLE            04/25/74

GR 0-7   00002140 00002138 0000000F 00001E00   00007F84 FFFFFF7C 00000000 00000159
GR 8-F   00003946 0A0107F1 00001E10 90001E54   40001E02 00003DF8 90002046 000021D0
FP REG   41300000 00000000 41300000 00000000   42640000 00000000 43316000 00000000

002040                     00000000 0000023F   00000000 0000015F 47000002 D200D18C
002060   00000000 0000345C F0F0F0F0 F2F34040   40F0F0F0 F1F54040 40404040 40404040
002080   40404040 --SAME--
0020A0   40404040 40404040 40404040 40404040   40404040 40404040 40E3C8C5 40C1D5E2
0020C0   E6C5D940 C9E24040 40F0F3F4 F5404040
```

Fig. 8-7   (Part 2 of 2)

each, some 6, some 10, and some 12. The information from the slips has been punched into cards with the following format:

Columns	Contents
1–3	Number of boxes
10–11	Number of spools per box

The flowchart in figure 8-8 displays the logic involved in producing the inventory. This flowchart is implemented in the following code:

```
        CSECT
        PRINT   NOGEN
        FIRST   BEGIN=INPUT,END=MSG+63,IO=YES
        SR      3,3
RDIT    MREAD   INTO=INPUT
        PACK    BOXP,BOXES
        CVB     7,BOXP                          NO. OF BOXES
        PACK    SPLP,SPOOLS
        CVB     9,SPLP                          NO. OF SPOOLS PER BOX
        MR      6,9                             SUBTOTAL OF SPOOLS
        AR      3,7                             TOTAL NO. OF SPOOLS
        B       RDIT
EOF     CVD     3,RESULT                        PREPARE
        UNPK    TOTINV,RESULT                   FOR
        MVZ     TOTINV+7(1),TOTINV              OUTPUT
        MRITE   FROM=OUTPUT                     PRINT INVENTORY
        LAST    BEGIN=INPUT,END=MSG+63,I=YES,                        X
                O=YES,ASMDATA=NO,EOFRTN=EOF
INPUT   DS      0CL80
BOXES   DS      CL3
PAD     DS      CL6
SPOOLS  DS      CL2
PAD2    DS      CL69
BOXP    DS      D
SPLP    DS      D
RESULT  DS      D
OUTPUT  DS      0CL121
PAD3    DC      CL50' '
TOTINV  DS      CL8
MSG     DC      CL63' TOTAL INVENTORY'
        END
```

You will notice in the code for this problem that some of the process blocks are implemented by an entire series of instructions, one block in the flowchart may, but does not necessarily, involve just one assembler language instruction. An example of multiple instructions being generated for one flowchart block would be the implementation of the block in which the number of boxes is multiplied by the number of spools per box.

Before these two numbers can be multiplied, the fields read from the input card must be packed and converted to the binary format. These types of con-

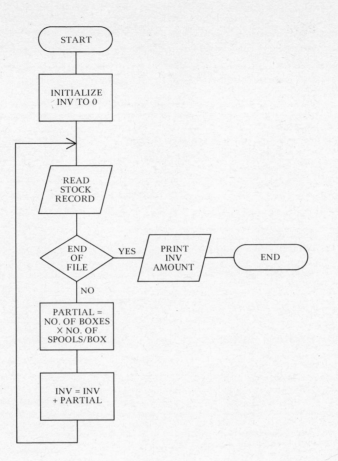

Fig. 8-8 Flowchart for Little Thumper Manufacturing problem

version operations never appear in a flowchart. A program flowchart is a dia-gramatic solution of a problem; it is independent of the programming language used to solve the problem. The PACK and Convert to Binary instructions are peculiar to the assembler language (there's no equivalent instructions in Fortran or PL/1 for example).

You will also note in the coding solution that some flowchart blocks require no instructions to implement them (i.e., the decision block that checks for the end of file condition). When all records in a file have been read, it is the system that recognizes this fact, not the programmer. In our case the instruction labeled EOF (the CVD instruction) will be branched to when the end of the file is reached. As the programmer, you informed the system which instruction to branch to when you specified the operand EOFRTN=EOF on the LAST instruction.

A third item you will notice in the implementation of the flowchart into code is the handling of the flowline that takes the logic of the flowchart back up to the read input and output block. This transfer of control operation is accomplished by the unconditional branch instruction:

B   RDIT

Every time this instruction is executed, it will cause the instruction labeled RDIT to be the next instruction executed rather than the next sequential instruction (the CVD).

Chapter 8 Quick Reference

Name	Type	Mnemonic and Form		Object Code Form†	See Page
Convert to Binary	RX	CVB	←Reg,Stor	4F R1 X1 B2 D2	131
Convert to Decimal	RX	CVD	→Reg,Stor	4E R1 X1 B2 D2	138
special	macro	FIRST	BEGIN= END= IO=YES	not discussed	135
special	macro	LAST	BEGIN= END= ASMDATA=NO EOFRTN=EOF I=YES O=YES	not discussed	135
special	macro	MREAD	INTO=	not discussed	133
special	macro	MRITE	FROM=	not discussed	141
Move Zones	SS	MVZ	←Stor(Length),Stor	D3 L B1 D1 B2 D2	140
Pack	SS	PACK	←Stor(Length),Stor(Length)	F2 L1 L2 B1 D1 B2 D2	129
Unpack	SS	UNPK	←Stor(Length),Stor(Length)	F3 L1 L2 B1 D1 B2 D2	139

†This is the form of the instruction you will see in the object-code column of the assembler listing.

QUESTIONS

1. Explain how the use of input and output statements, in addition to conversion instructions, adds a great amount of flexibility to your programs' handling of data.

2. What format are numbers read from an input card translated into before being placed in storage? Why is it not possible to perform arithmetic operations on data in this format?

3. Explain the zoned-decimal and packed-decimal formats. Use example data in your discussion.

4. How do you input a negative number from a field on an input card?

5. Explain the execution of the PACK instruction in changing the following fields from zoned decimal to packed decimal.

    a. LOC1: F6F8F2F7
    b. LOC2: F8F0F6F1F3D2

6. Since the PACK instruction is an SS-type instruction, under what condition or conditions may a length, or lengths, not be specified as part of the operand specifications?

7. What special requirements must be met by the source data for the CVB instruction?

8. What happens if the requirements of the CVB instruction for source data are not met?

9. What two types of data constants can be used to define your zoned-decimal data within your program? What are the differences in these two types of constants?

10. Which operand of the unpack instruction contains the packed-decimal number that serves as the source data for the execution of the instruction?

11. What is wrong with using the following as a zoned-decimal field in an output area, and how can the problem be corrected?

    F6F7F0C8

EXERCISES

1. Using the following as the initial contents in each case, give the contents of any registers or storage areas which are altered by the execution of the instruction.

    FLD: F6F2F3F8F0F1F6D2
        dwb
    REG2: 00000A63   REG3: FFFFFF82
    LOC: 000000000005719C
        dwb

       a. MVZ   FLD+7(1),FLD+6
       b. PACK   LOC(8),FLD+2(4)
       c. CVD   2,LOC
       d. UNPK   FLD(6),LOC+4(4)
       e. CVD   3,LOC
          UNPK   FLD(8),LOC(8)
       f. PACK   LOC(8),FLD+5(3)
          CVB   2,LOC

2. Write a program to read in three values from successive 4 column fields beginning with the first value in columns 1–4. Calculate and print the sum and the product of these three values and the difference between the product and the sum.

3. Write a program to read in values for A (from columns 3–7) and B (from columns 20–22). Using these values, calculate the value of the following expression and print the result.

    $4A+6AB-B^2$

4. Use as input a file containing records in the following format:

Columns	Contents
1–20	Employee Name
30–31	Employee Age

    Write a program to print each employee's name and age and the average age of all employees appearing in the file.

CHAPTER 9

Packed-Decimal Arithmetic

The two preceding chapters discussed fixed-point binary instructions. These instructions are available on all Systems/360 and 370 computers, and they perform operations on data in the binary format. Since data read from cards is in the zoned-decimal format, it must be packed and converted to binary before fixed-point arithmetic instructions can be used.

A second set of arithmetic instructions available for Systems/360 and 370 performs arithmetic operations on data in packed-decimal format. This group of instructions is known as the decimal feature and is an option that may or may not be selected by an individual installation. These instructions perform operations in storage on variable-length fields of data rather than on fixed-length data in registers, as occurs with fixed-point binary instructions. All numbers are treated as integers; for example, 1624, 1.624, 16.24, and 162.4 are all handled as 1624.

ADVANTAGES

Decimal arithmetic is most useful in those applications in which there are many input and output operations but few computations to be performed on each piece of data. Many commercial applications fit this description. An example is the preparing of monthly statements for a company's accounts-receivable department. Much of the input is in the form of debits applied to a particular account number for that month. These debits are added to the balance at the end of the previous month. Any payments are deducted, and an itemized statement is prepared. Most of the processing time is involved with reading in data in zoned-decimal format from cards and printing the statement, again using zoned decimal.

Although arithmetic operations performed by the decimal instructions are generally slower than those performed by the fixed-point binary ones, the small amount of processing time that could be saved by doing calculations in binary does not always warrant the time it takes to convert the decimal input to binary and later convert the binary back to decimal for printing. However, because the packed-decimal arithmetic instructions perform their operations on data in variable-length fields, the data is processed one byte at a time. It becomes clear that if the number of uses that a particular value serves in the program is high, it probably pays to convert the number to binary and use the faster, fixed-point instructions. If, however, few operations are performed on a particular item of data, then it is better to avoid the conversion process and instead use the decimal instruction.

Another advantage of packed-decimal arithmetic, and one of the most important ones, is the ability for extra precision. The largest positive value possible in the fixed-point binary format is $2^{31} - 1$, or 2,147,483,647. A number in packed-decimal format can occupy a maximum of 16 bytes, since each byte except the low-order byte contains two digits, the 16 byte can contain a maximum of 31 digits and a sign.

THE PACKED-DECIMAL FORMAT

The packed-decimal format was introduced in chapter 8. A review of this format is included here to refresh your memory. Each field consists of a four-bit sign in the rightmost four bits of the low-order byte. The leftmost four bits in the low-order byte, along with all other bytes in the variable-length field, contain decimal digits. These digits are binary coded, and each occupies four bits. Therefore, every byte except the low-order one in the field contains two digits; the low-order byte contains one digit and the sign.

digit	digit		digit	digit	digit	sign

low-order byte

The valid digits are 0–9. A, C, E, and F are valid positive signs; B and D are valid negative signs. The numbers are always right-aligned in the field and are always integers.

GENERAL STRUCTURE OF THE DECIMAL INSTRUCTIONS

All decimal arithmetic instructions belong to the SS class of instructions. A length may be specified with both operands, and both do not have to be the same length. They process the numbers in their operand fields from right to left, assume that the fields of data on which they operate contain packed-decimal numbers, and produce results in the packed-decimal format. The decimal arithmetic instructions are:

Name	*Mnemonic*
Zero and Add (packed)	ZAP
Add Decimal	AP
Subtract Decimal	SP
Multiply Decimal	MP
Divide Decimal	DP

DECIMAL CONSTANTS (P-type)

The decimal constant provides a way of introducing data into your job in a form suitable for use with the decimal instruction set. P (for *packed*) is the type-code to be used, and a duplication factor is allowed. The value subfield is a decimal number enclosed within apostrophes. Each digit within the apostrophes is converted into its four-bit binary equivalent. If there is a + sign inside the value subfield or if there is no sign (in which case the value is assumed to be positive), a sign code of C is assembled into the rightmost four-bits of the low-order byte of the field being defined.

DEC1　　DC　P'624'
　　　DEC1:　624<u>C</u> (Representation in hexadecimal)

If a negative value is indicated in the subfield, a sign code of D is assembled.

DEC2　　DC　P'-821'
　　　DEC2:　821D

If a decimal point appears in the value subfield, it is ignored. The value subfield is assumed to define an integer.

DEC3　　DC　P'64.823'
　　　DEC3:　64823C

The implied length associated with this type of constant is the number of bytes necessary to hold the digits and sign, two bytes in the cases of DEC1 and DEC2; three for DEC3. No special alignment of the field is made. If a length modifier is used and the digits to be stored do not fill all of the bytes, the unfilled bytes on the left are padded with binary zeros. If the length modifier does not provide a sufficient number of bytes to hold the value subfield digits, excess digits are truncated at the left.

```
DEC4    DC   PL4'174'
        DEC4:  0000174C
DEC5    DC   PL2'-2354'
        DEC5  354D
```

THE DECIMAL INSTRUCTIONS

ZERO AND ADD INSTRUCTION (ZAP)

This instruction is used to initialize a storage area that is to be used to accumulate the results of a series of decimal instructions. If the decimal instructions used registers, you could prepare an accumulator by setting the contents of a register to zero, but the results of the execution of decimal instructions are placed in storage. Therefore, the ZAP instruction allows you to initialize an area of storage large enough to hold the maximum result, besides giving you a way to place the first participating number in this area.

The action of the ZAP instruction is to set the entire first operand area to packed-decimal 0s, then add the second operand to the zeroed area. In effect, the second operand is moved to a new location, and any excess space preceding it in the first operand is set to zeros. If the first operand field is of insufficient size to hold the second operand number, truncation occurs on the left. An overflow condition is signalled, and execution may be halted. An example of the use of the Zero and Add instruction follows:

```
        ZAP   RESULT,LOC
        .
        .
RESULT  DS    PL9
LOC     DC    P'64289'

before:  RESULT:  "GARBAGE"          LOC:64289C
after:   RESULT:  00000000000064289C  LOC:64289C
```

The second operand is checked to ensure that it contains valid packed-decimal data. If it does not, a data exception occurs, execution is terminated, and a dump is taken.

ADD AND SUBTRACT DECIMAL (AP AND SP)

The second operand is added to (AP) or subtracted from (SP) the first operand, and the result is placed in the first operand location. Both operands are checked for valid signs and digits. A data exception, a halt of execution, and a dump occur if invalid combinations of bits are encountered. The operation is algebraic in nature, and the sign of the result is determined by the laws of algebra. For example:

$$-691 + 426 = -265$$
$$-2476 - (-648) = -1828$$

```
              ZAP   RESULT1,DEC6
              AP    RESULT1,DEC7
              ZAP   RESULT2,DEC8
              SP    RESULT2,DEC9
              .
              .
              .
RESULT1       DS    PL4
RESULT2       DS    PL4
DEC6          DC    P'-691'
DEC7          DC    P'426'
DEC8          DC    P'-2476'
DEC9          DC    P'-648'
```

MULTIPLY DECIMAL (MP)

In the decimal multiply instruction, the first operand (multiplicand) is multiplied by the second operand (multiplier), and the product replaces the multiplicand in the first operand location. Besides making sure that the multiplicand and the multiplier are both in packed-decimal format, you must be careful of the size of the first operand field when using this instruction. This area has to be large enough to hold the multiplicand, because that is its first function. But remember that it must *also* be large enough to hold the result of the multiplication operation—the product. The product is almost always larger, in number of digits, than the multiplicand. The multiplier is limited to a maximum size of 15 digits with a sign. There is also the requirement that the multiplier contains fewer bytes than the multiplicand. Therefore, if the length of the second operand is larger than, or equal to, the length of the first operand, or greater than 7, the operation is suppressed—and the execution of the program is interrupted.

There is a rule of thumb to help you calculate the necessary size for the first operand area. Always have as many high-order bytes filled with zeros in the first operand as there are total bytes in the multiplier. For example, if the multiplicand is 6 bytes long and the multiplier 4 bytes, the first operand should be 10 bytes long. The high-order 4 bytes should be set to zeros, and the low-order 6 bytes should contain the multiplicand. If you follow this rule, your product will never overflow (be too big to be contained within) the first operand field.

Should the situation arise where your multiplicand does not have a sufficient number of leading zeros, you have a practical need for the Zero and Add instruction. The ZAP instruction may be used to move the multiplicand to a larger field and zero its high-order bytes. This larger field containing the correct number of leading zeros can then be used as the first operand of the multiply instruction.

```
                    ZAP    LRGR,MULTCAND
                    MP     LRGR,MULTPLR
                    :
                    :
        LRGR        DS     PL7
        MULTCAND    DC     P'4788651'
        MULTPLR     DC     P'16572'
```

Divide Decimal (DP)

In the Divide Decimal instruction, the first operand (the dividend) is divided by the second operand (the divisor), then the first operand is replaced by the quotient and remainder. Within the first operand, the remainder is right-justified in the field and occupies the same number of bytes as the divisor. The remaining bytes in the field are occupied by the quotient. For example, if 13 (6 bytes) is divided by 5 (2 bytes) the resultant first operand would look like:

$$0000002C003C$$

Both the remainder and the quotient are signed. The sign of the remainder is the same as the sign of the dividend. The sign of the quotient is determined by the rules of algebra and depends on the signs of both the dividend and the divisor. An example of the use of the Divide Decimal instruction might be to calculate the average monthly sales for a retail store given the total amount of sales for the year:

```
                    ZAP    AREA,SALES
                    DP     AREA,TWELVE
                    :
                    :
        AREA        DS     PL6
        SALES       DC     P'6576128'
        TWELVE      DC     P'12'
```

After the divide instruction has executed, the remainder occupies the two bytes at AREA+4 and AREA+5. The quotient occupies the bytes in AREA through AREA+3. Now a question arises: Was the original amount of sales $6,576,128. or $65,761.28? Remember that the decimal arithmetic instructions handle all operands as integers. It is the programmer's responsibility to keep track of the location of any implied decimal point.

For example, suppose you want to divide 2769 by 48, and you would like the quotient to be accurate to two decimal places. Simply dividing 2769 by 48 will yield no decimal places in the result. However, by multiplying the dividend by 100 before performing the division operation, the accuracy of this division problem can be extended to yield the two decimal places.

```
                    ZAP    AREA,DIVIDEND
                    MP     AREA,HUNDRED
                    DP     AREA,FORTY8
                    :
        AREA        DS     PL7
        DIVIDEND    DC     P'2769'
        HUNDRED     DC     P'100'
        FORTY8      DC     P'48'
```

The result of the execution of the divide instruction is a quotient of 5768 and a remainder of 36. So even though we have our answer to two decimal places, it could really be more exact: 57.69 rather than 57.68. This answer can be forced by adding one more digit of precision (multiplying the original dividend by 1000 instead of 100). This will yield a quotient with three decimal places. A 5 can be added to that third decimal place, thus forcing the rounding up of the second digit if the third decimal place is 5 or greater. In code this would look like:

```
                    ZAP    AREA,DIVDEND
                    MP     AREA,THOUSND
                    DP     AREA,FORTY8
                    AP     AREA(5),FIVE
                    :
        AREA        DS     PL7
        DIVDEND     DC     P'2769'
        THOUSND     DC     P'1000'
        FORTY8      DC     P'48'
        FIVE        DC     P'5'
```

An explicit length is specified for the AP instruction, because the length implied by the first operand symbol (AREA) is seven bytes. The implied length (one byte) is used for the second operand. The remainder from the division operation is in the low-order bytes of these 7 bytes. We do not want the remainder to participate in the addition operation, so we specify a length of 5 on the first operand to indicate that the add operation is to use only that portion of AREA that contains the quotient (AREA through AREA+4).

PRINTING THE RESULTS
OF DECIMAL ARITHMETIC OPERATIONS

To be printed, a field must be in the EBCDIC format. The packed-decimal results from your program must be unpacked. The zone portion of the low-order byte must be changed from the sign code (a C or a D)† to zone of F, which is necessary to properly print the least significant digit. Once this is done, a decimal point can be inserted in the field, and a dollar or minus sign may be affixed to the front of the field if desired.

In this chapter, UNPK, MVZ, MVC, and MVI instructions will be used to convert the field to a printable form. (When you read chapter 18 you will learn the EDIT instruction, which is a rather complicated and powerful special-purpose instruction used to do these same things.)

Using OUTAREA as the location that is to be printed, the following series of instructions calculate the result of dividing 2769 by 48 and produce that result to two decimal places, rounded. A dollar sign is affixed to the front of the result:

			Receiving Field
ZAP	AREA,DIVDEND		0000000002769C
MP	AREA,THOUSND		0000002769000C
DP	AREA,FORTY8		000057687C024C
AP	AREA(5),FIVE		000057692C
UNPK	ZONED,AREA+2(3)		F5F7F6F9C2
MVC	OUTAREA+1(2),ZONED		—F5F7——
MVC	OUTAREA+4(2),ZONED+2		—F5F7—F6F9
MVI	OUTAREA,C'$'		5BF5F7—F6F9
MVI	OUTAREA+3,C'.'		5BF5F74BF6F9
	:		
	:		
AREA	DS	PL7	
DIVDEND	DC	P'2769'	
THOUSND	DC	P'1000'	
FORTY8	DC	P'48'	
FIVE	DC	P'5'	
ZONED	DS	CL5	
OUTAREA	DS	CL6	

The MVZ instruction (as explained in chapter 8) does not have to be used in this particular case, because the low-order byte of the area called ZONED, which is the byte carrying the sign code of C, is the byte that is truncated.

---

†Although the programmer usually knows his data, there are times when you must check to determine whether a result is negative or not. To be able to do this requires that you use either of two special instructions: the Test Under Mask (TM) discussed in chapter 17, or the Edit and Mark (EDMK) discussed in chapter 18.

CHAPTER 9 QUICK REFERENCE

Name	Type	Mnemonic and Form	Object Code Form†	See Page
Add Decimal	SS	AP Stor(Length),Stor(Length)	FA L_1 L_2 B_1 D1 B_2 D2	152
Divide Decimal	SS	DP Stor(Length),Stor(Length)	FD L_1 L_2 B_1 B1 B_2 D2	154
Move	SS	MVC Stor(Length),Stor	D2 L B_1 B1 B_2 D2	156
Move Immediate	SI	MVI Stor,Immediate	92 I2 B_1 B1	156
Multiply Decimal	SS	MP Stor(Length),Stor(Length)	FC L_1 L_2 B_1 D1 B_2 B2	153
Subtract Decimal	SS	SP Stor(Length),Stor(Length)	FB L_1 L_2 B_1 B1 B_2 B2	152
Zero and Add Decimal	SS	ZAP Stor(Length),Stor(Length)	FB L_1 L_3 B_1 D1 B_2 B2	152

QUESTIONS

1. When would you use the packed-decimal arithmetic instructions? What advantage do these instructions have over the binary ones?

2. The decimal arithmetic instructions belong to which of the classes of instructions?

3. Is data processed by decimal arithmetic instructions from left to right or from right to left?

4. What type of constant may be used to define data used by the decimal arithmetic instructions?

5. What is the function of the Zero and Add instruction (ZAP), and when would you use it?

6. What requirements are placed on the operands of AP and SP instructions? What action is taken by the system if these requirements are not met?

---

†This is the form of the instruction you will see in the object-code column of the assembler listing.

7. Other than the same requirements specified for AP and SP operands, what special requirement is made of the first operand field for the MP instruction? What is the rule of thumb that can help you to ensure that this requirement is met?

8. Which operand of the DP instruction is replaced by the quotient and remainder, and what portion of that operand is occupied by each?

9. Since the numbers used by the decimal instructions are treated as integers, what can be done to ensure a greater precision if that is desired?

EXERCISES

1. What contents are set up in storage for each of the following DC statements?

    a. D1   DC P'65283'
    b. D2   DC P'4281'
    c. D3   DC P'-865'
    d. D4   DC P'97.844'

2. Using the following as the initial contents in each of the sets of instructions, show the contents of any areas altered by the execution of the instructions.

    NUM: 02679C   VAL: 013C   LOC: 026D
    AREA: 00000840000C

    a. ZAP   AREA(4),NUM(3)
    b. DP   AREA(6),LOC(2)
    c. ZAP   AREA(6),NUM(3)
       MP   AREA(6),VAL(2)
    d. SP   LOC(2),VAL(2)

3. What is wrong with the following instruction, and what can be done to eliminate the problem?

    MP AREA,LOC
     .
     .
     .
    AREA   DC P'817C'
    LOC   DC P'65C'

4. Write a program to calculate the total payroll of the Zip Manufacturing Company. As input to your program, use a file containing records in the following format.

Columns	Contents
1–6	Employee's ID Number
15–16	Number of hours worked (fractional hours are not recorded)
20–23	Hourly pay rate ($$¢¢)

5. Write a program to read a sequence of cards, each containing an amount of sales for one month. When you have read all the monthly sales amounts, calculate and print the average monthly sales (to two decimal places) and the number of months' sales used in the calculations.

6. Write a program to calculate the volume of a sphere. Use the equation

$$\text{volume} = \pi H^2 \, \frac{C^2 + 4H^2}{8H} - \frac{H}{3}$$

where H = Height of the segment
     C = Length of the chord of the segment
Read values for H and C from a card having the following format:

Columns	Contents
10–13	Height (to two decimal places)
20–23	Length of cord (to two decimal places)

7. A boy wants to know how many revolutions his bicycle tire makes when he travels the two miles between his house and his friend's house. Use the following, if they might be of assistance to you in your solution:

1 mile = 5280 ft.
diameter of bike tire = 27 inches
circumference of circle = $2\pi R$
π = 3.14

8. Two cars are traveling the same road. One travels at a rate of 50 mph and the other at 65 mph. If the slower car gets a two-hour head start, how long does it take the faster car to catch up?

CHAPTER 10

Floating-Point Arithmetic

The use of floating-point numbers is advisable when the values involved in arithmetic calculations cover a wide range, or the results of such operations need to be scaled to preserve precision. Another great advantage in using the floating-point instruction set is that the computer automatically keeps track of the decimal point and performs any alignment necessary as operations progress.

All floating-point numbers occupy fixed-length fields; they are either 4 or 8 bytes long. A value of 7×10^{75} can be represented in 4 bytes in floating-point format; to represent the same value in packed-decimal format would take 30. No estimates need to be made by the programmer as to the number of bytes needed to hold a floating-point value.

THE FLOATING-POINT FORMAT

Floating-point numbers occupy fixed-length fields, either fullwords, which are referred to as *short form*, or doublewords, which are referred to as *long form*.

To understand these formats, we will pause to review scientific notation, because floating-point numbers are represented in a format that is similar to scientific notation. Both very small and very large numbers can be represented

160

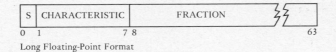

Short Floating-Point Format

Long Floating-Point Format

Fig. 10-1 Floating-point formats

in scientific notation because the numbers are reduced to significant digits multiplied by 10 raised to a particular power. For example:

$$1,000,000 \text{ becomes } 1.0 \times 10^6$$
$$6,400 \text{ becomes } 6.4 \times 10^3$$
$$.0000127 \text{ becomes } 1.27 \times 10^{-5}$$

The above format is generally used in scientific notation; one significant digit is to the left of the decimal point. In Systems/360 and 370, the first significant digit is placed just to the right of the decimal point; hence, the above numbers are represented as $.1 \times 10^7$, $.64 \times 10^4$, and $.127 \times 10^{-4}$, respectively. Represented in this particular manner, the numbers are said to be in their *normalized* form. When normalized, a number has a nonzero, high-order digit. This permits it to be represented with greatest precision.

To return to our examination of the two floating-point formats, the first bit indicates whether the fraction portion of the number being represented is positive (contains a zero) or negative (contains a one). Bits 1–7 contain the exponent or characteristic.

The exponent is handled by a special technique in Systems/360 and 370: the number is represented by its binary equivalent plus 64. (An exponent of $+3$ is represented by a 67; an exponent of -4 is represented by a 60.) This special method of storing exponents is called *excess sixty-four binary notation*. It eliminates the need for a second sign in the format (the sign in the first bit of the format is the sign of the fraction) and still permits a range of -64 through $+63$ for the exponent. In Systems/360 and 370 representation of the characteristics is in their hexadecimal equivalents, rather than decimal, to be consistent with the fraction portion of the format. See figure 10-2 for an example.

The fraction portion occupies the remainder of the format, 6 hexadecimal digits for short floating-point, and 14 hexadecimal digits for long floating-point. The number of digits that comprises the fraction has no effect on the range of

	Normalized Scientific Notation	Excess Sixty-four Binary Notation of Exponent	
Actual Number		Decimal	Hexadecimal
56,780.0000	$.5678 \times 10^5$	45	69
546,000,000.	$.546 \times 10^9$	49	73
27.842	$.27842 \times 10^2$	42	66
.0068	$.68 \times 10^{-2}$	3E	62
.00000917	$.917 \times 10^{-5}$	3B	59

Fig. 10-2 Characteristics of floating-point numbers

the floating-point number—this is controlled by the characteristic, which permits ranges of −64 through +63. The greater number of digits in the long floating-point format merely means there is a possibility of more precision—but still within the same range.

FLOATING-POINT CONSTANTS

While it is nice to understand the internal format for floating-point numbers, Systems/360 and 370 assemblers provide us with ways to specify floating-point constants without knowledge of their representation. DC instructions permit the introduction of data in a format suitable for use by the floating-point instruction set. There are two types—the E-type, which establishes short floating-point constants, and the D-type, which establishes long floating-point constants.

The floating-point number is specified as a signed or unsigned decimal number in the value subfield of the operand. It may be specified as an integer, a fraction, or a mixed number. It may or may not be followed by a decimal exponent (Refer to figure 10-3 to see the object code generated for the following):

DC E'-.65'   Signed value with decimal point before
                    number (fraction).

DC E'84.652'   Unsigned value (positive assumed) with
                    decimal point within (mixed).

DC E'67812'   Signed value with no decimal point (integer).

If an exponent is specified, it immediately follows the decimal number number and is specified in the format "En", where n may be signed or unsigned.

```
LOC    OBJECT CODE    ADDR1 ADDR2  STMT   SOURCE STATEMENT

000000                              1         CSECT
000000 C0A66666                     2         DC    E'-.65'
000004 4254A6E9                     3         DC    E'84.652'
000008 45108E40                     4         DC    E'67812'
00000C 441EB400                     5         DC    E'7.86E3'
000010 3D58C399                     6         DC    E'84.652E-6'
000014 00000000
000018 464BEE4800000000             7         DC    D'4976.2E3'
000020 C4200000                     8         DC    E'-8192'
000024 00000000
000028 46180000200E5604             9         DC    D'1572864.176'
                                   10         END
```

NO STATEMENTS FLAGGED IN THIS ASSEMBLY

Fig. 10-3 Examples of DC statements for floating-point constants

DC E'7.86E3'   Unsigned mixed number with unsigned
                             exponent (plus sign assumed for both
                             number and exponent).

DC E'84.652E-6'   Unsigned mixed number with signed
                             exponent.

DC D'-4976.2E3'   Signed mixed number with unsigned
                             exponent.

The E-type constants occupy 4 bytes each and are aligned on fullword boundaries; the D-type constants occupy 8 bytes each and are aligned on doubleword boundaries. Do not use length modifiers with the definition of these types of constants because you will override boundary alignments; the fields will not be aligned on the proper boundaries.

The constant defined in statement number 2 ($-.65$) has a one in the sign bit to indicate that the value is negative, and a characteristic of 40 (hexadecimal), which is equivalent to 0 plus 64 in decimal (excess sixty-four binary notation). The sign and the characteristic combine to make the first byte of the floating-point format.

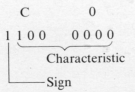

The fraction portion of this constant (A66666) is the hexadecimal equivalent of a decimal .65 taken from the Hexadecimal and Decimal Fraction Conversion table in appendix 6. Following this fraction example through, looking down the decimal column for bits 0,1,2, and 3 in byte one, we locate the decimal value closest to the .65 but not greater than it (.6250 decimal, equivalent to .A hexadecimal). Subtracting this value (.6250) from the value of the constant .65 leaves a remainder of .0250. Moving over to the column for bits 4,5,6, and 7 of byte one in the conversion table, we perform the same operation looking for the decimal value closest to our remaining value of .025 (.0234 decimal, equivalent to .06 hexadecimal). This yields the second hexadecimal digit for the fraction portion of the floating-point format. We now have a fraction portion of A6. Continuing this process yields a 6-digit hexadecimal fraction portion of A66666.

Let's examine one more of these constants, the one defined in statement number 3. In this case the value is specified as a mixed number. This time the sign bit is zero, because the value is positive and the characteristic is a hexadecimal 42 (2 digits left of the decimal point—2 + 64 = 66 in excess sixty-four binary notation, and 66 in decimal is equivalent to 42 in hexadecimal). Converting the integer portion of the value from decimal to hexadecimal, using the Hexadecimal and Decimal Conversion table in appendix 3 yields 54 in hexadecimal. Converting the fraction portion of the value (.652 yields .A6E9).

$$8 \quad 4 \quad . \quad 6 \quad 5 \quad 2$$
$$4 \quad 2 \quad 5 \quad 4 \quad A \quad 6 \quad E \quad 9$$

FLOATING-POINT INSTRUCTIONS

The floating-point feature is an optional hardware feature. When it is installed, four special floating-point registers are available to the programmer. These registers are numbered 0,2,4, and 6. They are not the same as the general purpose registers with the same numbers. Each floating-point register holds 64 bits. The opcode used for an operation indicates to the computer whether it should use all 64 bits (long floating-point arithmetic) or only the high-order 32 of them (short floating-point arithmetic).

NORMALIZATION PROCESS

All of the floating-point instructions do not use normalization in the same exact manner. Some do not involve any normalization. Some normalize before performing their operation—*prenormalization*, some normalize only the result of their operation—*postnormalization*, and some instructions involve both.

Since the fraction is expressed in base 16, this means that the first hexadecimal digit in the fraction portion of a normalized number is not a zero. The process of normalization may involve the shifting of the fraction portion with a corresponding change in the characteristic. But don't forget—the characteristic is also in hexadecimal, so a change of one value in the characteristic reflects a movement of the radix, or decimal point, one hexadecimal, or four binary positions.

For example, the value $-8,192$ in decimal is equivalent to -2000 in hexadecimal. In normalized floating-point format this value is represented by:

C 4 2 0 0 0 0 0

11000100

exponent of 68_{10} (excess sixty-four binary notation)
actual exponent (68–64) is 4

sign of fraction portion is negative

Notice that the first hexadecimal digit of the fraction position, the 2, is nonzero:

C 4 2 0 0 0 0 0

fraction portion

It is not the first binary digit that is zero. There are actually 2 high-order binary zeros.

The following is a list of the floating-point instructions discussed in this chapter:

Name	RR Mnemonic	RX Mnemonic
Add Normalized (Long)	ADR	AD
Add Normalized (Short)	AER	AE
Add Unnormalized (Long)	AWR	AW
Add Unnormalized (Short)	AUR	AU
Subtract Normalized (Long)	SDR	SD
Subtract Normalized (Short)	SER	SE
Subtract Unnormalized (Long)	SWR	SW
Subtract Unnormalized (Short)	SUR	SU
Multiply (Long)	MDR	MD
Multiply (Short)	MER	ME
Divide (Long)	DDR	DD
Divide (Short)	DER	DE
Load (Long)	LDR	LD
Load (Short)	LER	LE
Store (Long)		STD
Store (Short)		STE
Halve (Long)	HDR	
Halve (Short)	HER	

Referring to figure 10-4, let us examine the execution of these instructions through code that implements the following formula:

$$\text{ANS} = \left(\frac{A + B}{6} - 3 \right)^2$$

                                    Contents of Register 2

            LE   2,A   4241E45A
            AE   2,B   441E23E4
            DE   2,KSIX   43505FB5
            SE   2,KTHREE 43502FB5
            MER   2,2   46191DDA
            STE   2,ANS
             .
             .
                                    Contents of Storage
            .
    A   DC   E'65.892' 4241E45A
    B   DC   E'.765E4' 441DE200
    KSIX   DC   E'6'   41600000
    KTHREE DC   E'3'   41300000
    ANS   DS   F
            END

Fig. 10-4 Coding example of short floating-point instructions

Short floating-point values are used in this series; they provide faster processing and require only half as much space as long floating-point numbers. Floating-point register 2 is used throughout this series of instructions, and its contents after execution are shown in figure 10-4 to the right of each instruction affecting it. It is capable of holding 64 bits of information, but only the leftmost 32 bits are used. The rightmost 32 bits are either ignored or left unchanged, depending on the operation performed.

The first instruction loads the floating-point constant that occupies the fullword at location A (4241E45A) into floating-point register 2 (leftmost 32 bits). The second instruction adds the fullword second operand to floating-point register 2. The add operation requires that the decimal points of the two operands be aligned prior to their addition. To check to see if the decimal points are aligned, the characteristics of the two operands are compared. If they are equal, the operands are "lined up," and the add operation is performed. If the characteristics are unequal, as they are in this case, the fractional portion of the operand with the smaller characteristic is shifted to the right.

As each hex digit is shifted one place, the characteristic is increased by one. This shifting continues until the characteristics match; then the addition operation is performed:

Original 1st operand	4241E45A
Fraction portion shifted two places and characteristic increased by two	440041E4
Addition operation	
aligned 1st operand	440041E4
2nd operand	441DE200
	441E23E4

After the addition operation, the sum may be shifted to the left to normalize the result. This involved reducing the characteristic by the number of hex digits shifted and inserting hex zeros in the vacated low-order digit positions. The sign of the sum is determined by the rules of algebra.

In the divide operation, the dividend is in the first operand (register 2 in this case), and the divisor is in the second operand (location KSIX). The dividend is replaced by the quotient. Both the divisor and the dividend are normalized prior to the operation. The fractions are divided, and the characteristics are subtracted. A decimal 64 is added to the resultant characteristic to maintain excess sixty-four binary notation. The sign of the quotient is determined by the rules of algebra and the quotient replaces the dividend. There is no remainder as a result of this divide operation. Divide fractions:

$$
\begin{array}{r}
. 5\,05FB5 \\
600000\,\overline{\smash{\big)}\,1E23\,E40\,00\,00} \\
\underline{1E00\,0\,00} \\
23\,E40\,00 \\
\underline{1E0\,00\,00} \\
5\,E40\,000 \\
\underline{5\,A00\,000} \\
4\,40\,000\,0 \\
\underline{4\,20\,000\,0} \\
20\,000\,00 \\
\underline{1E000\,0\,0} \\
2\,000\,0\,0
\end{array}
$$

subtract characteristics ($44-41=3$) and add decimal 64 to maintain excess sixty-four binary notation ($3+64=67$). Sixty-seven in decimal is 43 in hexadecimal. The result of the division operation is 43505FB5.

The subtraction instruction is similar to the addition instruction except that the sign of the second operand is reversed (positive to negative and vice versa) and the fraction is complemented prior to the alignment and addition of the two operands.

The only remaining operation to be performed at this point is the squaring of the resultant value of the subtraction. Squaring a number means you are multiplying that number by itself. The multiply operation consists of adding the exponents and subtracting 64 from the result and then multiplying the fractions. Both operands are normalized prior to the operation. The product is normalized and replaces the multiplicand in the first operand register.

Add the exponents $(43+43 = 86)$ and subtract 64 in decimal which is 40 in hexadecimal $(86-40 = 46)$, then multiply the fractions:

$$
\begin{array}{r}
5\,02\,FB5 \\
5\,02\,FB5 \\
\hline
1\,9\,14\,8\,89 \\
3\,7\,20\,8\,38 \\
4\,B2\,CBCB \\
A\,0\,5\,F6A \\
190\,EE8\,9 \\
\hline
191DDA0\,43\,709
\end{array}
$$

The contents of floating-point register 2 are 46191DDA043709 after the multiplication operation. This product is in the D rather than the E format. The mutliplier and the multiplicand each contained 6 hexadecimal digits—therefore, the product contains 12 hexadecimal digits. Since the floating-point registers can hold a 14-digit product, the rightmost two digits are always set to zero.

The Store instruction takes the contents of the first half of the first operand register (46191DDA) and places it at the location specified in the second operand. We see that, given values of 65.892 and 7650 for A and 3, respectively, the result of the sequence of operations is: 1,646,042 available at ANS.

The long floating-point operations differ from the short ones in that they use fraction portions of 14 hexadecimal digits rather than 6. The differences in the two types of operations can be seen in the contents of floating-point register 2; refer to the short form in figure 10-4 and the long form in figure 10-5. In this case (figure 10-5) the answer has greater accuracy: 1,646,042.812317.

The Guard Digit   The execution of the short form Add, Subtract, and Divide floating-point operations involves the use of a spare hexadecimal digit, which improves precision. This extra digit serves as the seventh digit in the fraction portion of the floating-point numbers without altering the contents of the low-order 4 bytes of the floating-point register, which are not used in short form operations. This extra hexadecimal character is called a *guard digit*.

```
                                      Contents of Register 2
              LD    2,A               4241E45A 1CAC0831
              AD    2,B               441E23E4 5A1CAC08
              DD    2,KSIX            43505FB6 45A1CAC0
              SD    2,KTHREE          43502FB6 45A1CAC0
              MDR   2,2               46191DDA CFF47735
              STD   2,ANS
               .
               .
               .                     Contents of Storage
  A           DC    D'65.892'         4241E45A 1CAC0831
  B           DC    D'.765E4'         441DE200 00000000
  KSIX        DC    D'6'              41600000 00000000
  KTHREE      DC    D'3'              41300000 00000000
  ANS         DS    D
              END
```

Fig. 10-5 Coding example of long floating-point instructions

The guard digit is set to zero at the beginning of an operation. During prenormalization, the fraction portion of the operand with the smaller characteristic is shifted to the right and the characteristic adjusted to reflect this shift. As this shift takes place, the last digit moved out of the fraction is saved as the guard digit. This guard digit is then allowed to participate in the actual execution of the operation and should a left shift be required after execution (postnormalization) the guard digit can be moved back into the six hexadecimal digits that make up the fraction portion of the number. So, the guard digit may be created as a result of the shifting involved in prenormalization, it participates in the execution of the operation of the instruction, and possibly becomes an actual part of the fraction as a result of the shifting involved in postnormalization.

For example, examine the following addition operation:

$$AE \quad 4,A$$

where register 4 contains:	46104418	
and the fullword at A contains:	C36B3724	
alignment of A yields	460006B3	(7)
addition operation		

		Guard Digit
1st operand	46 10 0 4 1 8	(0)
2nd operand	46 00 0 6 B3	(7)
result	460 EE D6 4	(9)
postnormalization	45EED6 49	

UNNORMALIZED ADDITION AND SUBTRACTION

If the programmer wishes to control the normalization of his operands he may use the Add Unnormalized (AW, AWR, AU, AUR) or the Subtract Unnormalized (SW, SWR, SU, SUR) Instructions. Prenormalization takes place with these instructions just as it does in the case of the normalized add and subtract operations, but the resultants value of the operation is not post-normalized to eliminate any leading zeros. For example, given:

F.P.Reg4:   46103A82 66804317
CNS: C48725C3

                    AU   4,CNS

Prenormalization of the second operand results in the following addition operation:

		Guard
		Digit
10 3 A82		(0)
00 8 7 25		(C)
0FB3 5C		(4)

Replacing the sign and characteristic (46) results in:

F.P.Reg4:   460FB35C 66804317

To aid you in remembering the mnemonic opcodes for these instructions just remember that a U for unnormalized replaces the E for short-form or single-precision operations; and a W (sound alike for double-U) for long-form or double-precision operations.

HALVE OPERATIONS (HDR AND HER)

These two instructions perform a shift operation on the fractional portion of a number in a floating-point register. The fractional portion of the floating-point number in the second operand register are shifted to the right one bit position. No normalization is performed and the result is placed in the first operand register (characteristic and sign unchanged). For example:

```
            LD    2,AREA
            HDR   0,2
            STD   0,AREA2
             .
             .
AREA        DC    D'22'
AREA2       DS    D
  AREA:   42160000 00000000
  AREA2:  420B0000 00000000
```

The result is the same as regular division by a value of 2, except that no post-normalization is performed.

CHAPTER 10 QUICK REFERENCE

Name	Type	Mnemonic and Form	Object Code Form[†]	See Page
Add Norm (Long)	RX	AD ←Reg,Stor	6A | R1 | X2 | B2 | D2	169
Add Norm (Long)	RR	ADR ←Reg,Reg	2A | R1 | R2	169
Add Norm (Short)	RX	AE ←Reg,Stor	7A | R1 | X2 | B2 | D2	166
Add Norm (Short)	RR	AER ←Reg,Reg	3A | R1 | R2	166
Add Unnorm. (Short)	RX	AU ←Reg,Stor	7E | R1 | X2 | B2 | D2	170
Add Unnorm. (Short)	RR	AUR ←Reg,Reg	3E | R1 | R2	170
Add Unnorm. (Long)	RX	AW ←Reg,Stor	6E | R1 | X2 | B2 | D2	170
Add Unnorm. (Long)	RR	AWR ←Reg,Reg	2E | R1 | R2	170
Divide (Long)	RX	DD ←Reg,Stor	6D | R1 | X2 | B2 | D2	169
Divide (Long)	RR	DDR ←Reg,Reg	2D | R1 | R2	169
Divide (Short)	RX	DE ←Reg,Stor	7D | R1 | X2 | B2 | D2	166
Divide (Short)	RR	DER ←Reg,Reg	3D | R1 | R2	166
Halve (Long)	RR	HDR ←Reg,Reg	24 | R1 | R2	170
Halve (Short)	RR	HER ←Reg,Reg	34 | R1 | R2	170
Load (Long)	RX	LD ←Reg,Stor	68 | R1 | X2 | B2 | D2	169
Load (Long)	RR	LDR ←Reg,Reg	28 | R1 | X2 | B2 | D2	169
Load (Short)	RX	LE ←Reg,Stor	78 | R1 | X2 | B2 | D2	166

[†]This is the form of the instruction you will see in the object-code column of the assembler listing.

Name	Type†	Mnemonic and Form	Object Code Form	See Page
Load (Short)	RR	LER	Reg,Reg ←	38 | R_1 | R_2	166
Multiply (Long)	RX	MD	Reg,Stor ←	6C | R_1 | X_2 | B_2 | D2	169
Multiply (Long)	RR	MDR	Reg,Reg ←	2C | R_1 | R_2	169
Multiply (Short)	RX	ME	Reg,Stor ←	7C | R_1 | X_2 | B_2 | D2	166
Multiply (Short)	RR	MER	Reg,Reg ←	3C | R_1 | R_2	166
Subtract Norm. (Long)	RX	SD	Reg,Stor ←	6B | R_1 | X_2 | B_2 | D2	169
Subtract Norm. (Long)	RR	SDR	Reg,Reg ←	2B | R_1 | R_2	169
Subtract Norm. (Short)	RX	SE	Reg,Stor ←	7B | R_1 | X_2 | B_2 | D2	166
Subtract Norm. (Short)	RR	SER	Reg,Reg ←	3B | R_1 | R_2	166
Subtract Unnorm. (Short)	RX	SU	Reg,Stor ←	7F | R_1 | X_2 | B_2 | D2	170
Subtract Unnorm. (Short)	RR	SUR	Reg,Reg ←	3F | R_1 | R_2	170
Store (Long)	RX	STD	Reg,Stor →	60 | R_1 | X_2 | B_2 | D2	169
Store (Short)	RX	STE	Reg,Stor →	70 | R_1 | X_2 | B_2 | D2	166
Subtract Unnorm. (Long)	RX	SW	Reg,Stor ←	6F | R_1 | X_2 | B_2 | D2	170
Subtract Unnorm. (Long)	RR	SWR	Reg,Reg ←	2F | R_1 | R_2	170

QUESTIONS

1. When is it advantageous to use floating-point arithmetic instructions?

2. Explain the following terms:

    a. Characteristic
    b. Fraction
    c. Short form

    d. Long form
    e. Guard digit
    f. Normalization

3. What is the difference between prenormalization and postnormalization?

4. Explain what is meant by excess sixty-four binary notation, and why it is used in Systems/360 and 370.

5. If it's necessary, how are the operands of an add instruction "lined up" prior to the performance of the operation?

EXERCISES

1. Show the object code generated by the following DC statements:

    a. DC   E'678962'
    b. DC   E'.795'
    c. DC   E'86.2271'
    d. DC   E'-49056.79'
    e. DC   E'823.6E2'
    f. DC   D'42626.43E-3'
    g. DC   D'-1736E4'

2. Using the following as the initial contents before each execution

    F.P.Reg2: C4315786 201298B8
    F.P.Reg4: 46829000 00000000
          A: 41620000
          B: C37A2C43
          C: 446B4010 7238BA74

    what is the result of the operation of each of these instructions?

    a. AE   4,C
    b. DER   2,4
    c. SD   2,C
    d. ME   4,A
    e. SE   2,B

CHAPTER 11

Transfer of Control: Branches and Jumps

INTRODUCTION TO CONDITION CODES

Up to this point, our programs have been coded with what could be called straight-line logic. Except for the FIRST and LAST macro, we have done nothing to alter the computer's normal sequence of instruction execution, accessing and executing one instruction right after the other, in the sequential order that they are placed in storage. Your program is loaded into the computer's storage; the first instruction is accessed (fetched) and executed; then the second instruction is fetched and executed; and so on until finally the last instruction has been fetched and executed.

A difficulty arises when problems do not lend themselves to this simple straightforward logical sequence. Most problems involve either repetition of some of the instructions, or decision making regarding which groups of instructions should be executed and in what order. As a programmer, you must analyze the problem. You must express the problem as groups of instructions, each of which will perform one or more of the functions necessary in solving the problem. You must decide which groups of instructions need to be executed repeatedly—and under what conditions this repetition should continue. You must determine when a decision must be made among alternate groups of instructions and what considerations are involved in making this decision.

There are a variety of conditions that arise as a result of the execution of certain instructions in the Systems/360 and 370 repertoires. For example, the result of an addition or subtraction operation may be a positive or negative value, or a value of zero. Which of these three conditions actually results from this operation is indicated in a field of control information in the CPU. This field, two bits in length, is called the *condition code*.[†] (Since it consists of two bits, the condition code can represent up to four different conditions: 00, 01, 10, 11).

Once the condition code is set to one of its four possible values by the execution of an instruction, it remains at that value until another instruction that sets the condition code is executed. Not every instruction affects the condition code. The value of the condition code cannot be directly altered by the programmer, but only by the execution of particular instructions.

If a programmer wishes a decision to be based on the value in the condition-code field, he can use an instruction that will test for particular values of the condition code and branch, or not branch, as a result of that test. With the branch (or jump), control is not given to the next sequential instruction; instead, control is transferred to an instruction elsewhere in the computer's storage. This is why instructions which cause control to jump around (branch) in storage are referred to as transfer of control operations. These transfer of control operations test for one or more of the four possible condition codes (0, 1, 2, or 3). Because of this, they are often referred to as "Branch on Condition" instructions.

DECIDING AMONG ALTERNATE GROUPS OF INSTRUCTIONS

Some arithmetic instructions cause the condition code to be set. Branches can be made accordingly. In the following example, payment received on account is subtracted from the customer's balance. If the result is negative, the resultant value is indicated as a credit, and this result is placed in a full-word named ANS. If the result of the original subtraction is positive, the result is indicated as the customer's new balance (which is assumed to be capable of being represented in 31 bits) and is placed in ANS. If the result of the subtraction is zero, the fullword referred to as ANS should also be set to a value of zero and the indication set that the account is paid in full.

Figure 11-1 illustrates this problem in flowchart form with the explanatory sentences from the preceding paragraph placed to the right of each block in the chart. Code to implement this flowchart is given in figure 11-2.

EXTENDED MNEMONICS

The BM, BP, and Bs in figure 11-2 are examples of extended mnemonic codes. These codes are provided as an aid for the programmer. They allow you to specify two things: (1) the fact that you wish to place a branch instruc-

[†]For further explanation on the storage of the condition code, see chapter 16, "Dumps and Debugging."

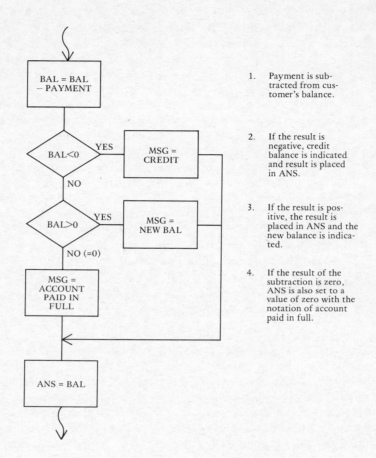

Fig. 11-1 Flowchart for customer's-balance problem

1. Payment is subtracted from customer's balance.

2. If the result is negative, credit balance is indicated and result is placed in ANS.

3. If the result is positive, the result is placed in ANS and the new balance is indicated.

4. If the result of the subtraction is zero, ANS is also set to a value of zero with the notation of account paid in full.

tion in your code at this point, and (2) the condition or conditions on which the branch is to be taken.

The use of the BM (Branch on Minus) extended mnemonic indicates that you want to branch to the instruction labeled MINUS if the result of the subtract instruction is less than zero. In other words, you want the instruction symbolically named MINUS to be the next instruction executed. The BM handles the question expressed in the first decision block.

When the BM instruction tests the condition code, if it finds that the result of the subtract operation was not a negative value, no branch is taken, and the BP extended mnemonic is the next instruction to be executed. To put it another way, if the condition (or conditions) being tested for by the extended mnemonic has not been met, the execution "drops through" this branch

```
              .
              .
              .
              L     7,BAL
              S     7,PAYMENT           BAL-PAYMENT
              BM    MINUS               RESULT WAS NGATIVE
              BP    POS                 RESULT WAS POSITIVE
ZERO          MVC   MSG,PAID            RESULT WAS ZERO
              B     CONTINUE
MINUS         MVC   MSG,CREDIT          RTN WHICH HANDLES
              B     CONTINUE            NEGATIVE RESULTS
POS           MVC   MSG,NEWBAL          RTN WHICH HANDLES
*                                       POSITIVE RESULTS
CONTINUE      ST    7,ANS
              .
              .
              .

ALIGN         DS    0F
MSG           DS    CL24
ANS           DS    F
PAID          DC    CL24'ACCOUNT PAID IN FULL'
CREDIT        DC    CL24'CREDIT DUE'
NEWBAL        DC    CL24'NEW CURRENT BALANCE'
              .
              .
              .
```

Fig. 11-2 Code for customer's-balance problem

instruction to the next sequential instruction in the program. The branch is taken *only* when the conditions tested for are met.

The extended mnemonic BP (Branch on Plus) handles the question expressed in the second decision block. The BP causes a branch to the instruction labeled POS if the subtract operation resulted in a value greater than zero. If the condition of a resulting value greater than zero is not met, the next sequential instruction, the one labeled ZERO, is the next instruction executed. This means that the code handling the condition of a result of zero is executed. The logic of this program is such that if the result is not less than zero (branch to NEG not taken), and the result is not greater than zero (branch to POS not taken), then the result must be equal to zero. Therefore, the instruction labeled ZERO will be executed only when the subtract operation results in a zero value.

In this example there are five groups of instructions. Each performs its own particular function or functions necessary in solving the problem. In any one execution of the program, not all of the groups of instructions will be executed. The first group (the Load and Subtract instructions) will always be executed, as will the fifth group, the Store instruction labeled CONTINUE. But only one of the other three groups of instructions will be executed for a particular set of values for BAL and PAYMENT. You build into your code the ability to decide which of the three groups gets executed by your inclusion of instructions with extended mnemonics in the opcode field. You determine when these decisions need to be made by where you place the branch instructions in your code.

At the end of the group of instructions that handle the result of zero and also at the end of the group that handles a negative result, you will notice the extended mnemonic for an unconditional branch (B). This indicates that a branch to the instruction whose label appears in the operand field (CONTINUE in this case) is to be taken regardless of whatever condition is indicated in the condition code.

Why does this program need unconditional branches? The group of instructions that handles negative results immediately follows, in storage, the group of instructions that handle results of zero. If there was no unconditional branch instruction at the end of the zero group, the negative group of instructions would be executed. Therefore, the wrong message would be moved, destroying the correct message previously stored there. You not only have to set up the branch instructions that decide between alternate groups of instructions; you also must ensure that you provide code at the end of the execution of the instructions in any group that correctly determines the next group of instructions to be executed (unless the desired group happens to be the next sequential set of instructions, as is the case with the group that stores the contents of register 7 at ANS, following the group that handles positive values).

A list of the extended mnemonics you can use to check the result of arithmetic operations follows:

BO†	Branch on Overflow
BP	Branch on Positive
BM	Branch on Minus
BZ	Branch on Zero
BNP	Branch on Not Positive
BNM	Branch on Not Minus
BNZ	Branch on Not Zero

If the statement of our problem is changed so that the result of the subtraction operation is the new balance message whenever that result is negative or positive, then the BNZ extended mnemonic can be used to check for both of these conditions. The code would be changed to that given in figure 11-3.

In this coding example, the instruction labeled POSORNEG is executed if the value resulting from the subtract operation is greater than or less than

---

†The first extended mnemonic in this list (BO) will be discussed in the next section in the chapter. The last three extended mnemonics permit the checking of two different conditions with one instruction.

```
                    .
                    .
                    .
              L     7,BAL
              S     7,PAYMENT              BAL-PAYMENT
              BNZ   POSORNEG               NONZERO RESULT
ZERO          MVC   MSG,PAID               RTN WHICH HANDLES
              B     CONTINUE               ZERO BALANCE
POSORNEG      MVC   MSG,NEWBAL             NEW BALANCE RTN
CONTINUE      ST    7,ANS

                    .
                    .
                    .

ALIGN         DS    0F
MSG           DS    CL24
ANS           DS    F
PAID          DC    CL24'ACCOUNT PAID IN FULL'
NEWBAL        DC    CL24'NEW CURRENT BALANCE'
                    .
                    .
                    .
```

Fig. 11-3   Code for altered customer's-balance problem

zero. If neither of these conditions is met, the next sequential instruction (labeled ZERO) is executed. If the branch was not taken to POSORNEG, the only condition which can be met is that the result is equal to zero.

THE OVERFLOW CONDITION

Overflow occurs when the resulting value of an addition or subtraction operation requires more bits than are available in the field set aside to accept the result. Since the results of binary addition and subtraction operations are placed in registers, and registers hold 31 data bits and a sign bit, the result of an addition or subtraction operation must be capable of representation in 31 bits. If 32 or more bits are necessary, the resultant value cannot be confined within a single register, and an overflow condition occurs.

When an overflow condition arises, it has priority over any other condition code that would have been set in the absence of overflow. For example, if a subtraction operation results in a positive value, but that positive value cannot be correctly represented in 31 bits, then the condition code is set to reflect an overflow, rather than the condition of a positive result.

It is a good coding practice to avoid any possibility of your code causing an overflow condition. If you make no check for this condition, your program could continue execution using erroneous data resulting from an overflow operation. If you make no check for this condition (using the BO extended mnemonic), you usually prevent any further execution with the erroneous value. The operating system will be notified of the condition by the computer and will in turn terminate the execution of your program. Your best practice is to *know your data* and logic well enough to prevent this condition from occurring.

REPETITION OF GROUPS OF INSTRUCTIONS

At design time, when the programmer breaks up his solution to a problem into groups of instructions, he can recognize when it might be advantageous to execute a particular group of instructions more than once. This reuse of a group of instructions is called a *program loop*.

LOOP STRUCTURE

To review, there are four parts to every loop: (1) initialization, (2) body, (3) adjustment and test, and (4) exit. Some loops may have more than one of these performed by a single instruction, and other loops may require the execution of several instructions to perform a single part of the structure. The order in which the four parts of the loop are performed may vary with the needs of each loop structure, but all four parts will be there.

The *initialization* part of the loop prepares any areas or quantities that must be set before the first iteration of the loop. The portion of the program which is reused or repeated as the result of the loop is called the *body* of the loop. The body consists of all instructions that perform the function or functions provided by the loop.

Each loop contains, in addition to instructions that provide the functions of the loop, some way of determining when the computer should stop executing instructions within it and execute another segment of the program. The instructions that help make this determination are called the *loop control*.

The loop-control portion consists of two parts: the adjustment and the exit. The loop-control test consists of a check to see if a particular condition or event has occurred. This condition might be that the end-of-file (end-of-data) condition has occurred on an input data file, the desired degree of accuracy has been reached, or that the loop has been executed the desired number of times. The test is made for the presence or absence of the desired condition by a conditional branch instruction. When the condition arises, the branch is taken, thus exiting the loop and allowing execution to continue with another segment of the program. As long as the necessary condition does not arise, execution of the loop is allowed to continue.

The *adjustment* part of the loop control contains instructions that update quantities for the next repetition of the loop. It may involve the increment or decrement of a counter that keeps track of the number of times the instructions in the body of the loop have been repeated or the change of some field used in the execution of the body of the loop (or both). The *exit* from the loop consists of the conditional branch instruction, which actually makes the test that determines whether or not to leave the loop. A more complex loop structure may have several conditions that can cause an exit to be taken from the loop. Each condition must then have a corresponding conditional branch instruction, which would check for the occurrence of the condition.

FLOWCHART EXAMPLES OF LOOPS

Example 1: Powers of Numbers   To illustrate the four parts of a loop, we will use the example of raising a positive number "N" to any positive power "P" greater than zero. See figure 11-4.

In this example four variables are used: N, P, COUNTER, and SUM. The variable N contains the value to be raised to the power contained in P. The variable SUM contains the products of the successive multiplication operations. SUM is initialized to *one*, because any number left at its zero power

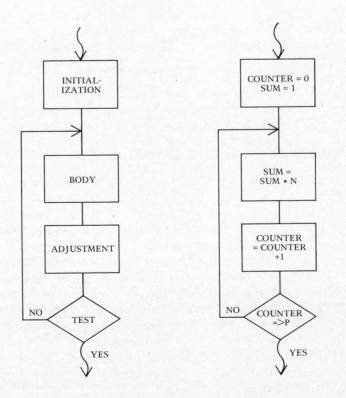

Fig. 11-4   Flowchart for powers-of-numbers problem (trailing decision)

results in a value of 1. The variable COUNTER is used to ensure that the value of N is raised to the correct power.

For example, take the values of N $= 3$ and P $= 4$. The following is a listing of values contained in each variable as each iteration of the loop occurs.

	N	P	COUNTER	SUM
initial value	3	4	0	1
results of 1st iteration	3	4	1	3
results of 2nd iteration	3	4	2	9
results of 3rd iteration	3	4	3	27
results of 4th iteration	3	4	4	81

When the test is made at the end of the fourth iteration, the value (4) contained in COUNTER is equal to the value (4) contained in P. The exit is taken from the loop, and the value contained in the variable SUM is equal to $3^4 = 81_{10}$. Take any other set of values for the variables N and P and follow the flowchart through the iterations to test the logic flow.

The variable P must be a power greater than zero, because this is a *trailing-decision loop*. This means that the decision that makes the exit part of the loop follows the body of the loop. If P has a value of zero, by the time a test could be made to determine whether the loop has been executed the correct number of times, it would have already been executed one iteration too many. In such a case, when the exit is taken from the loop, the variable SUM would contain a value equal to the value N, and it should contain a value of one.

As shown in figure 11-5, this problem solution can be modified by changing the loop into a *leading-decision loop*. Place the test for exit before the body of the loop. If P is zero, you will exit from the loop while SUM still has a value of one and before the body of the loop changes that value.

A leading-decision loop structure has this one advantage: in the special case where the body of the loop should not be executed even a single time, this is handled correctly by the test for exit. No extra test is necessary to catch this special case. (To make the trailing-decision loop work correctly, we would have had to add a special test at the beginning to determine whether P is equal to zero.)

Example 2: Determining Whether a Given Number Is Even or Odd (without Division)   Using figure 11-6, determine whether a given number N is even or odd (without destroying N's value). In this example, the set-up, or initializa-

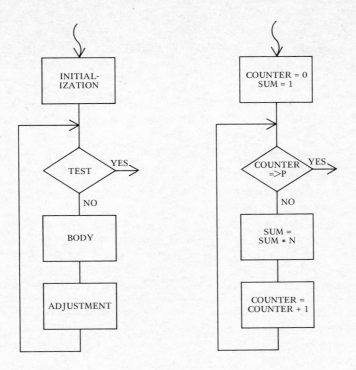

Fig. 11-5 Flowchart for powers-of-numbers problem (leading decision)

tion, for the loop involves assigning the value represented by the variable N to another variable. This preserves the original value of N, even though the adjustment part of the loop uses the value to control the loop. Here we have our first example of two parts of the general loop structure being combined in one block of the flowchart. The body of the loop actually includes the adjustment part of the loop.

The function of this loop is to continually subtract a value of two from the given number until the point at which that number has been reduced to zero or a negative one (-1). At this point, the test part of the loop allows an exit to be taken. After the loop has performed its function, a check of the current value of R reveals whether the original number is even or odd. If R has a value of zero, the original number is even. If R has a value of negative one, the original value is odd.

A good practice for you to follow is to carefully check a flowchart to make sure it expresses the logic that actually solves a problem. To do this, you should assume actual values for any given variables in the flowchart and follow the logic through with those values to ensure that the desired result is reached.

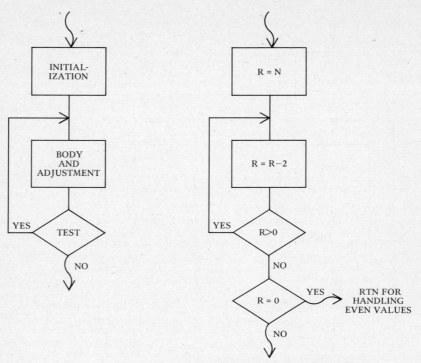

Fig. 11-6 Flowchart for even- or odd-number problem

In the case of the previous flowchart, we need to use two different values for N—One odd, and one even:

	N(odd)	*N(even)*
initial value	5	6
results of 1st iteration	3	4
results of 2nd iteration	1	2
results of 3rd iteration	−1	0

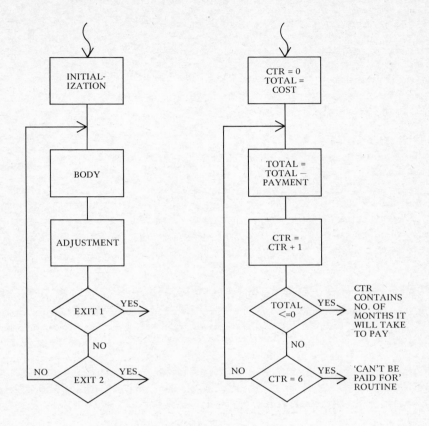

Fig. 11-7   Flowchart for two-exit loops

Example 3: Loop with Two Exits   Given the cost of an item purchased and the amount of the payment per month, determine how many months the payment will have to be made before the item is paid for. (If the item cannot be paid for in six months, then terminate your calculations at that point).

In this example, which is illustrated in figure 11-7, the execution of the loop can be terminated either by the cost of the item being paid for in six or less payments, or the counter reaching a maximum value of 6. Remember, always substitute values for variables and follow the flow of the logic through the chart. This is sometimes referred to as "playing computer." Do just as the computer would do—follow the simple steps one by one:

| | PAYMENT$_1$ + $25 | | PAYMENT$_2$ = $15 | |
	CTR$_1$	TOTAL$_1$	CTR$_2$	TOTAL$_2$
initial value	0	100	0	125
1st iteration	1	75	1	110
2nd iteration	2	50	2	95
3rd iteration	3	25	3	80
4th iteration	4	0	4	65
5th iteration			5	50
6th iteration			6	35

Using the first set of values and the logic of the flowchart, it can be determined that four payments will be sufficient to cover the cost of the item. In the case of the second set of values, the item cannot be paid for in six months. The "can't-be-paid-for" routine will have to take action to indicate this condition.

Programming the Decision for Exit from the Loop

In the first sections of this chapter you learned that the fixed-point add and subtract instructions set the condition code, indicating the results of the arithmetic operations.

Example 4: Determining Whether a Given Number Is Even or Odd   To review, refer to figure 11-8 and let us examine one set of instructions that implement the logic in the flowchart for example 2.

```
EVNODD      CSECT
            FIRST
            L       7,N              NUMBER TO BE CHECKED
            L       8,FULLWD2        CONSTANT TO BE SUBTRACTED
LOOP        SR      7,8              DECREMENT NUMBER BY 2
            BP      LOOP             BRANCH TO DECREMENT AGAIN
            BZ      EVEN             BRANCH, NO. IS EVEN
ODD         .                        NUMBER IS ODD
            .
            .
            B       ENDIT
EVEN        .
            .
            .
ENDIT       LAST
FULLWD2     DC      F'2'
N           DC      F'76'
```

Fig. 11-8   Code for even- or odd-number problem

The subtract instruction sets the condition code to reflect the result of the subtraction operation. The next sequential instruction tests that condition code to see whether its result was a positive value—a number greater than zero. If so, the branch to the instruction labeled LOOP is taken, so another subtraction can be performed.

If the condition code does not indicate that a positive result was present, execution "drops through" to the next sequential instruction (rather than taking the branch). This instruction test for a zero condition. If the condition is met, a branch is taken to the instruction labeled EVEN. This instruction is the first one in the routine that handles even numbers. This routine gets control when it has been determined that N is evenly divisible by 2, an even number.

If the branch to the instruction labeled EVEN is not taken, the next sequential instruction is executed (the one labeled ODD). At this point in the logic of the program, the original value of N placed in register 7 has been reduced by a value of two repetitively, until the value in register 7 is now either a zero or a negative one.

If the BZ instruction test for the zero condition was not met, then the value in register 7 must be negative one. This indicates that the original value of N was not evenly divisible by 2; it was an odd number. The next sequential instruction after the BZ instruction is the first instruction in the routine that handles odd values of N.

Example 5: Powers of Numbers This example can be programmed from either the leading-decision or trailing-decision loop flowchart in a manner similar to the even or odd example. The set of instructions given in figure 11-9 implements the trailing-decision flowchart.

```
                 CSECT
1.               FIRST
2.               SR      6,6          INITIALIZE COUNTER TO VALUE OF ZERO
3.               L       9,FWDSUM     SET UP SUM FOR FIRST MULTIPLICATION
4. LOOP          M       8,N          RAISE TO NEXT POWER
5.               A       6,ONE        INCREMENT COUNTER
6.               L       2,P          LOAD DESIRED POWER
7.               SR      2,6          HAS COUNTER REACHED DESIRED VALUE OF P?
8.               BP      LOOP         BRANCH IF DESIRED POWER NOT REACHED
9. CONTINUE      ·
                 ·
                 ·
                 LAST
   FWDSUM        DC      F'1'
   ONE           DC      F'1'
   P             DC      F'the power to which N is to be raised'
   N             DC      F'the value for N'
                 END
```

Fig. 11-9 Code for even- or odd-number problem (trailing decision)

You may ask why we test in such a round-about way for the condition necessary to exit the loop. Examine what would happen if we eliminated the need for instruction 6 by changing instruction 7 to: S 6,P:

```
1.                FIRST
2.                SR     6,6          INITIALIZE COUNTER TO ZERO
3.                L      9,FWDSUM     SUM FOR FIRST MULTIPLICATION
4. LOOP           M      8,N          RAISE TO NEXT POWER
5.                A      6,ONE        INCREMENT COUNTER
6.                S      6,P          HAS COUNTER REACHED DESIRED VALUE OF P?
7.                BZ     LOOP         BRANCH IF DESIRED POWER NOT REACHED
8. CONTINUE       ·
                  ·
                  ·
                  LAST
FWDSUM            DC     F'1'
ONE               DC     F'1'
P                 DC     F'4'
N                 DC     F'3'
                  END
```

This would properly subtract the value of P (which is the power which N is to be raised) from the counter. It would set the condition code to reflect whether the result of that operation was a positive, negative, or zero value. The mnemonic opcode for the branch is changed to a BZ because we are subtracting P from the current value of the counter rather than the current value of the counter from P, but it looks as if the loop would work.

But would the loop really work? Whenever you change instructions in a program, play computer to ensure that the *new* series of instructions reflects the logic of the flowchart. Try using the original values we used for N and P in checking out the logic of the flowchart (3 and 4, respectively):

			(register 6) COUNTER	(register 9) SUM	(flowchart checkout) COUNTER
initial value	3	4	0	1	0
results of 1st iteration	3	4	−3	3	1
results of 2nd iteration	3	4	−6	9	2
results of 3rd iteration	3	4	−9	27	3
results of 4th iteration	3	4	−12	81	4
results of 5th iteration	3	4	−15	243	

At the end of the fourth iteration, we know from the original value of P that we should exit the loop, but this has not happened.

Compare the resulting values of these iterations with those received on the checkout of the flowchart. You see that something is definitely wrong. The resulting values for the COUNTER (register 6 in this case) just don't agree. In fact, you don't even have to refer to the old resultant values for the counter. The fact that you have a negative value in the counter after you have completed the first iteration of the loop indicates an error condition. The counter is being used to count the number of trips through the loop. It should start out with a value of zero and increase by a value of one each iteration of the loop until it reaches a value equal to the value of P.

What has caused the counter to contain negative values? The negative values result from the fact that the first operand register receives the result of a subtract operation. In our newly coded instruction: S 6,P, the first operand, register 6, is being erroneously altered as the test for exit from the loop is being extablished.

This is why the original set of instructions was used in programming this flowchart. The value for P is loaded into register 2, and the current value of the counter (register 6's contents) is subtracted from the contents of register 2, which places the resultant value in register 2. This destroys the value of P that we loaded into register 2 and sets the condition code. However, we still have the value of P in the fullword of storage labeled P. We can load P from this fullword in storage into register 2 every time we execute the instructions of the loop. The value of P in storage is unaffected by the load operation.

What is even more important, the value of the counter remains unchanged by the execution of the SR instruction. It contains the value that resulted from the execution of instruction 5 on this iteration (the A instruction) until the add instruction executes on the next iteration of the loop.

SETTING THE CONDITION CODE
USING THE COMPARE INSTRUCTIONS

Fortunately, there is a more straightforward way to solve the problem of testing for the condition necessary to exit a loop than that which was presented in the preceding section. This straightforward approach to our problem is accomplished by using compare instructions.

The compare instructions will set the condition code, but *will not change* the contents of either of the operands participating in the comparison. The sole use for the compare instructions is to compare two operands and set the condition code based on the result of this compare.

The result indicated in the condition code after such a comparison reflects whether:

1. the two operands are equal.
2. the first operand is less than the second operand.
3. the first operand is greater than the second operand.

No overflow condition can result from a compare operation as it can from an addition or subtraction operation because there is no arithmetic result in comparison operations. The extended mnemonics you may use to check the result of a comparison operation are listed below.

Extended Mnemonic	Meaning
BH	Branch on (first operand) High
BL	Branch on (first operand) Low
BE	Branch on (operands) Equal
BNH	Branch on (first operand) Not High
BNL	Branch on (first operand) Not Low
BNE	Branch on (operands) Not Equal

There are fourteen different opcodes for performing compare operations; these are as follows:

Mnemonic opcode	Data treated as	Instr. type	Chapter discussed[†]	Available on S/360	S/370
CR	signed binary	RR	11	X	X
C	signed binary	RX	11	X	X
CH	signed binary	RX	11	X	X
CP	packed decimal	SS	11	X	X
CDR	floating-point	RR	11	X	X
CD	floating-point	RX	11	X	X
CER	floating-point	RR	11	X	X
CE	floating-point	RX	11	X	X
CLC	logical	SS	11 & 17	X	X
CLI	logical	SI	17	X	X
CL	logical	RX	17	X	X
CLR	logical	RR	17	X	X
CLM	logical	RS	18		X
CLCL	logical	RR	18		X

ALGEBRAIC COMPARES (CR, C AND CH)

These three instructions perform algebraic comparisons:

CR	R1,R2	Compare Register
C	R1,S2	Compare Fullword
CH	R1,S2	Compare Halfword

[†]The first nine of these instructions will be discussed in this chapter; the remaining five are discussed in the chapters indicated under the column heading, *Chapter discussed*.

They treat both *comparands* (operands being compared) as 32-bit signed integers. In the case of the CH instruction, the sign of the halfword is propagated internally to extend the halfword to a fullword before comparison. The contents of both operand fields are unchanged by the execution of the instruction. Using the following:

$$\text{Reg2: 0000007A} \quad \text{A: 00721AF3} \quad \text{C: FFF4}$$
$$\text{fwb} \qquad\qquad \text{hwb}$$

```
C    2,A
CH   2,C
```

The results would be first operand low in the case of the C and first operand high for the CH (remember, any positive number is greater than any negative number in an algebraic comparison).

Example: Powers of Numbers   Figure 11-10 illustrates the use of the compare instructions in the powers of numbers program.

```
POWERS    CSECT
          FIRST
          SR    6,6            INITIALIZE COUNTER TO ZERO
          L     9,FWDSUM       SET UP SUM FOR FIRST MULTIPLICATION
LOOP      M     8,N            RAISE TO NEXT POWER
          A     6,ONE          INCREMENT COUNTER
          C     6,P            Q: COUNTER = P
          BL    LOOP           A: BRANCH IF COUNTER < P
CONTINUE  .
          .
          .
          LAST
FWDSUM    DC    F'1'
ONE       DC    F'1'
P         DC    F'4'
N         DC    F'3'
          END
```

Fig. 11-10   Code for powers-of-numbers problem using compare instructions

DECIMAL COMPARISON (CP)

There is one instruction for comparing fields containing data in the packed-decimal format:

```
CP   S1(L1),S2(L2)      Compare Decimal
```

Comparison is algebraic, with the signs and all digits of both operands participating. The same checking mechanism built into the other decimal instructions also operates with the decimal compare—each sign and digit is checked for validity.

Since this instruction can have a length specified with each operand, there is the possibility of comparison of two fields of unequal length. Should this occur, the shorter field is extended (internally) with high-order zeros. Fields containing all zero digits but opposite signs are considered equal—a negative packed-decimal zero (D0) is not considered to be less than a positive zero (C0, F0).

```
ABC: 0045219C    XYZ: 0007184C
        CP   ABC(4),XYZ(4)
        BL   FIRST
        BH   SECOND
```

The result of the execution of the preceding CP instruction is that the branch to the instruction labeled SECOND is taken.

FLOATING-POINT COMPARISONS

There are four instructions that perform comparisons on data in the floating-point format. These are:

```
CD     R1,S2     Compare (Long)
CDR    R1,R2     Compare Register (Long)
CE     R1,S2     Compare (Short)
CER    R1,R2     Compare Register (Short)
```

The comparison made is algebraic; that is, the sign, fraction, and exponent are all considered part of the comparand. The comparison is performed similar to normalized floating-point subtraction:

```
        LD   4,FLD1
        CD   4,FLD2
        BL   LOW
        BH   HIGH
        .
        .
        .
FLD1    DC   D'78.452'
FLD2    DC   D'-19.73'
```

The preceding instructions will cause a branch to be taken to the instruction labeled HIGH, because the comparison is algebraic, and FLD1 is positive, FLD2 negative.

LOGICAL COMPARISONS (CLC)†

The basic difference between this comparison operation and all the preceding ones is that a logical comparison does not recognize an algebraic sign. Every bit in a logical comparison participates like any other bit. Both operands are treated as unsigned binary fields. The comparison operation proceeds from left to right in each field, and the first inequality of bits that is encountered causes the condition code to be set.

The CLC instruction is the all-purpose instruction for the comparison of nonnumeric data in storage. The CLC: CLC   S1(L), S2   Compare Logical can compare fields in storage up to a length of 256 bytes. A frequent use of this instruction might be the comparison of alphabetic names to ensure that an update record was matched with the corresponding record in the master file. For example, a hardware store keeps an alphabetical file of the statements of account for all credit customers. Every time a customer makes a purchase, an update record is made to reflect it. The master alphabetic file is searched to find the master record for that customer, and this record is altered to reflect the new purchase. Figure 11-11 shows how the section of the hardware store's program for handling these transactions would look in flowchart form.

---

†Only one of the logical compare instructions will be discussed here. The others (CLR, CL, CLI) will be discussed in chapter 17 and (CLCL, CLM) in chapter 18.

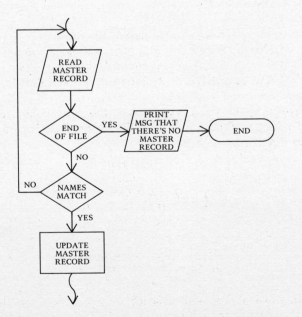

Fig. 11-11   Flowchart for hardware-store problem

The decision block that checks whether the names match could be implemented by the following CLC instruction:

```
      CLC   MSTRNM(15),UPDTNM          CORRECT ACCOUNT?
      BE    MATCH                      YES
      B     READNEXT                   NO, BRANCH TO
*                                      READ NEXT MASTER
```

Where MSTRNM is the symbolic name of the 15-byte field in the input area containing the master file record, and UPDTNM is the symbolic name of the 15-byte field containing the customer's name whose account we wish to update.

This example can be extended to include one more built-in efficiency. As the solution stands right now, the name from every record in the master file will be compared to the update name. If for any reason the update name is incorrect and does not match any of those in the master file, this important fact will not be known until end of file is reached on the master file. If the master file contains 5000 records and the name on the update is Adams, this approach will result in a lot of wasted reading and comparisons just to find out that an error condition exists. This inefficiency can be eliminated by considering the fact that the master file is in *collating sequence*.

By collating sequence, we mean that the EBCDIC codes that make up the name fields are in ascending order (the file is alphabetically arranged). The letter A (11000001) is logically less in comparison to the letter B (11000010), and B is less than the letter C (11000011), and so on through the entire alphabet.

This sequence makes it possible to determine if an update record has no matching master record as soon as the comparison performed by the CLC indicates that the first operand is greater than the second. Remember, the CLC instruction compares left to right with all bits participating in the comparison (no sign). As soon as an inequality is encountered, the condition code is set. If the two fields that are being compared contain the following:

MSTRNM: C1D2D6D9D5404040 . . . 40
UPDTNM: C1C4C1D4E2404040 . . . 40

the comparison of the second bytes (D2 and C4) will stop the comparison and cause the condition code to be set to reflect the fact that the first operand is high. The letter K (D2) is higher in the collating sequence than the letter D (C4). We are past the point in the master file where the record for ADAMS should have been located. Changing the code to:

```
      CLC   MSTRNM(15),UPDTNM
      BE    MATCH
      BH    NOTAVAIL
      B     READNEXT
```

allows the branch to be taken to NOTAVAIL as soon as possible, rather than waiting for end-of-file.

OTHER INSTRUCTIONS THAT SET THE CONDITION CODE

In the previous sections of this chapter you learned that the add, subtract, and compare instructions set the condition code based on the results of their execution. Those of you who are using the decimal or floating-point instruction set will be happy to learn that the decimal and floating-point add, subtract, and compare instructions set identical condition codes.

THE LOAD AND TEST (LTR)

Another fixed-point arithmetic instruction that sets the condition code is helpful in certain programming applications. This is the Load and Test instruction. It belongs to the RR class of instructions, and its general format is:

LTR   R1,R2

The action of this instruction is to load the contents of the second operand register into the first. The contents of the second operand register are not changed in any manner. The LTR instruction is different from the L, LH, and LR instructions in that as it moves the contents of R2 to R1, it examines, or tests, these contents to see if they are equal to zero, less than zero, or greater than zero (no overflow condition can arise). The same extended mnemonics used to test the condition code set by the fixed-point add and subtract (except BO, Branch on Overflow) can be used for testing the condition code setting of the LTR instruction.

Now the question arises, when would such an instruction be of use to a programmer? Well, one good example is the setup for a division operation. Division by zero is not permitted on Systems/360 and 370. Let us assume that your program has been performing a series of arithmetic operations in register 5, and you now want to use the contents of this register as the divisor in a fixed-point divide operation. You want to assure yourself that register 5 does not contain zero. You could define a fixed-point binary constant of zero and compare this zero to the contents of register 5. But why waste the 2 or 4 bytes necessary to hold that constant? Why not just use:

```
LTR  5,5
BZ   NODIVIDE
```

It is clear in the above instructions exactly what you are doing. You are testing the contents of register 5 without wasting another register, and you are branching to an instruction labeled NODIVIDE if the test indicates a value of zero in register 5. Otherwise execution will drop through to the next sequential instruction which will be your divide instruction.

FLOATING-POINT LOAD AND TESTS (LTDR AND LTER)

The floating-point instruction set has two instructions which perform a similar function with data residing in floating-point registers:

LTDR	R1,R2	Load and Test (Long)
LTER	R1,R2	Load and Test (Short)

These instructions set the identical condition codes to the fixed-point LTR instruction:

1. equal to zero (zero fraction)
2. less than zero (sign of fraction is negative)
3. greater than zero (sign of fraction is positive and not zero)

Other instructions also set the condition code as a result of their execution. These condition code settings will be discussed as the new instructions are introduced. (A complete list of all instructions that set the condition code and all the resultant condition-code settings can be seen in appendix 3.)

TESTING THE CONDITION CODE USING THE BC INSTRUCTION

The Branch on Condition instructions (BC and BCR) are an alternative to using extended mnemonics for branching instructions. The Branch on Condition instructions allow you to specify explicitly the condition or conditions on which you wish to branch. You specify the conditions you wish tested by creating what is called a *mask*. The mask consists of 4 bits, and each bit in the mask corresponds to a particular condition-code setting. The first bit in the mask corresponds to a setting of 0, the second bit in the mask corresponds to a condition-code setting of 1, and so on.

Each bit that is on (contains a value of 1) in the 4-bit mask field will cause the corresponding condition-code setting to be tested. The easiest way to think of the mask is as if it were a 4-bit binary number. To test whether the first of the four bits is on, the binary number represented by the mask would have to be equivalent to a decimal 8, or 1000_2. The condition code tested by this mask is one of 0. To test for a condition code of 3, the mask would have to be 0001, or equivalent to a decimal 1. To test for both a condition code of 0 or a condition code of 3, the mask would have to be 1001 or the equivalent of a decimal 9. The relations between masks and condition-code values are shown below.

mask	1 0 0 0	0 0 0 1	1 0 0 1
tests	↓	↓	↓ ↓
cond. code	0-1-2-3	0-1-2-3	0-1-2-3

When you used one of the extended mnemonics, the assembler created a 4-bit mask that tested for the conditions your mnemonic requested. For instance, if you specified: BM NEG after a subtract instruction, the assembler took the extended mnemonic BM and translated it into the opcode BC and the mask of 0100, or the equivalent of a decimal 4. Why a decimal 4? The relationship of the actual conditions resulting from a subtract operation and the condition code settings are as follows:

Condition Resulting from Operation	Condition-Code Setting
result was zero	0
result was negative	1
result was positive	2
overflow occurred	3

To put this in a tighter perspective, let us examine the format of the BC instruction: BC M1,S2 The BC instruction belongs to the RX class of instructions, which normally means that the first operand is a register number and the second operand a symbolic reference to a location in storage. In the case of the BC instruction, however, the first operand is used to specify the mask to be used in testing the condition code:

The instruction BC 8,LOOP
has the same effect as BZ LOOP   or,
BE LOOP

The following two instructions are also equivalent:

BC   7,NOTEQ
BNE   NOTEQ

Either of the above instructions causes a branch to be taken to the instruction labeled NOTEQ if any condition is met other than an equal condition. The condition-code setting for compare instructions are:

Condition Resulting from Operation	Condition-Code Setting
two operands are equal	0
first operand < second operand	1
first operand > second operand	2
unused	3

Even though the condition code of 3 is unused by the compare instructions, the mask you create specifies all conditions *except* the one that you do not wish to cause a branch. (This makes it more obvious that you are excluding this condition as a valid cause for a branch.)

TESTING THE CONDITION CODE USING THE BCR INSTRUCTION

The BCR instruction is similar to the BC. The mask is specified in the first operand, and the address of the instruction to which the branch is to be taken if the condition is met is specified in the second. The difference lies in the fact that the BCR is an RR class of instruction. This means that the address of the instruction to branch to must be *in the register* specified in the second operand. In other words, instead of specifying the symbolic name of the instruction in the second operand, the actual address of that instruction must have previously been placed in a register, and it is this register that is specified in the second operand of the branch instruction.

If the address of the instruction labeled LOOP is contained within register 6, the instruction, BCR   8,6 if placed after a subtract instruction, would branch to the one labeled LOOP, providing the result of the subtraction was a value of zero. The only problem with the BCR instruction is that we have not yet discussed any method of obtaining an actual address of anything in storage, much less how to put that address into a register.

INTRODUCTION TO THE LOAD ADDRESS INSTRUCTION (LA)

A useful instruction in the repertoires of Systems/360 and 370 that can be used at this point is the Load Address instruction, opcode LA. Belonging to the RX class of instructions, its function is to take the address specified by the second operand, place it in the low-order three bytes of the register specified by the first, and zero the high-order byte in that register: LA   R1,S2 Load Address Notice the difference between the L and LA instructions. Both belong to the RX class of instructions, yet their functions differ. Using the following instructions as examples, we can see exactly what that difference is:

$$L \quad 6,TXP$$
$$LA \quad 6,TXP$$

The Load instruction (L) calculates the address represented by the symbol TXP. It then checks to see if that address is on a fullword boundary. If the address designates a fullword boundary, the contents of the fullword at that address are loaded into register 6.

The Load Address instruction (LA) calculates the address represented by the symbol TXP and places this address into register 6. In contrast to the Load instruction, no check is made for any particular boundary alignment, and no access of the storage contents at that address is made. The address is merely calculated, and that address is placed in the first operand register.

For the sake of this example, the second operands specified in the instructions were identical (TXP). In actual programming situations, they would probably not be. The symbol in the second operand of a Load instruction would tend to be the symbol on a constant, and the symbol in the second operand of a Load Address would usually be the label of an executable instruction. With our instruction: BCR 8.6 all we have to do to make it work is to precede the BCR instruction with a load address instruction as follows: LA 6,LOOP where LOOP is the label on the instruction that is to be given control if and when the execution of the Subtract instruction results in a value of zero, and the condition code is set to zero.

THE BRANCH ON COUNT INSTRUCTIONS (BCT AND BCTR)

There are several instructions in the Systems/360 and 370 instruction repertoires that provide for rather powerful loop control—single instructions that provide the adjustment and test functions of the loop control, as well as the decision on whether or not to exit from the loop. Two of these specialized branching instructions are explained in this section.

In the Branch on Count instructions, the first operand register holds the counter that is used as the control for the count-controlled loop. The second operand contains the address of the next instruction to be executed if the counter controlling the loop specifies that the loop should be executed again. In the case of the BCT instruction, the address is specified in the second operand in the form of the symbolic name of an instruction. In the BCTR instruction, a register is specified in the second operand, which contains the address.

> BCT R1,S2 Branch on Count
> BCTR R1,R2 Branch on Count Register

The action taken when either of the Branch on Count instructions executes is relatively straightforward. The action involves the following steps:

1. The contents of the first operand register is algebraically reduced by a value of 1.
2. The new contents of the first operand register is compared to a value of zero.

   a. If the new contents are not equal to zero (contents of R1 $\neq$ 0), the branch is taken to the instruction specified in the second operand.

   b. If the new contents are equal to zero (contents of R1 = 0), the next sequential instruction after the Branch on Count instruction is the next instruction to be executed. In other words, no branching takes place when the count in the first operand register has been reduced to a value of zero.

The Branch on Count instructions do not alter or check the value of the condition code in any way. Whether or not they cause a branch to be taken is solely dependent on the contents of the first operand register.

Let's examine the use of the Branch on Count instruction to control a read loop in which the number of records to be read is known before the start of the execution of the loop. The number of records is read from a parameter card that precedes the regular records in the data set.

Notice that in figure 11-12, the number of records read in from the parameter card is checked for a value of zero before allowing the loop to be entered for the first time. Why is this necessary? Well, it's a safety measure that should be taken by any programmer before he uses the contents of a register as the first operand of either Branch on Count instruction. Remember, the action of these instructions is to check the contents of R1 for a value of zero after the algebraic reduction has occurred. Notice that the check is for a value *equal* to zero, not equal to or less than zero.

Starting with a value of zero in the R1 register would cause the contents of this register to be algebraically reduced by one to a value of -1 before the first check for zero is made. The branch would be taken. The next time the BCT instruction was executed, the result in R1 would be a -2, and so on until the maximum negative number (hex) was reached. The following reduction would turn the value into the largest positive value (hex), and this would be algebraically reduced by one each time through the loop until a value of zero was finally reached in that R1 register. (This would take a long time!)

In this particular coding example, the read instruction would have encountered the end-of-file condition long before all this could occur. This would result in the printing of ERRMSG2, but why let the program perform all the needless calculations if the LTR instruction can catch a parameter value of zero before the first time?

Keeping this one difficulty of the Branch on Count instructions in mind, these are good instructions for the efficient handling of loop control. If a value of 12 is read from the parameter card, the five instructions (READ through BCT) that make up the loop will be executed twelve times before the BCT instruction encounters a value of 0 in register 6 after reduction; and the branch is not taken, allowing the CVD instruction to be executed.

```
          CSECT
          PRINT   NOGEN
          FIRST   BEGIN=PKFLD,END=ERRMSG+121,IO=YES
          MREAD   INTO=PARMRCD                          READ NUMBER OF DATA RECORDS
          PACK    PKFLD,NORCDS                          PACK AND
          CVB     6,PKFLD                               CONVERT NUMBER TO BINARY
          LTR     6,6                                   CHECK FOR NUMBER OF ZERO
          BZ      NOLOOP                                BRANCH TO PRINT ERROR MESSAGE
          SR      8,8                                   ZERO FOR SUM
LOOP      READ    INTO=INAREA                           READ A RECORD
          PACK    PKFLD,AMT                             PACK AND
          CVB     4,PKFLD                               CONVERT AMOUNT TO BINARY
          AR      8,4                                   ADD AMOUNT TO SUM
          BCT     6,LOOP                                BRANCH IF RECORDS LEFT TO READ
          CVD     4,PKFLD                               CONVERT AND
          UNPK    TOTAL,PKFLD                           UNPACK SUM FOR OUTPUT
          .
          .
          .
          MRITE   FROM=OUTAREA                          PRINT TOTAL
          B       FINISH
INSUFRCD  MRITE   FROM=ERRMSG2                          PRINT INSUFF. RECORDS MESSAGE.
          B       FINISH
NOLOOP    MRITE   FROM=ERRMSG                           PRINT ZERO PARAMETER MESSAGE
FINISH    LAST    BEGIN=PKFLD,END=ERRMSG+121,ASMDATA=NO,I=YES,           X
                  O=YES,EOFRTN=INSUFRCD
PKFLD     DS      D
PARMRCD   DS      0CL80
NORCDS    DS      CL6
          DS      CL74
INAREA    DS      0CL80
AMT       DS      CL5
          DS      CL75
OUTAREA   DS      0CL121
          DC      CL16' THE TOTAL IS'
TOTAL     DS      CL9
          DC      CL76' '
ERRMSG2   DC      CL28' NUMBER READ FROM PARAMETER'
          DC      CL32'RECORD DOES NOT EQUAL NUMBER OF'
          DC      CL61'RECORDS IN DATA SET.'
ERRMSG    DC      CL28' NUMBER READ FROM PARAMETER'
          DC      CL31'RECORD EQUALS ZERO - EXECUTION'
          DC      CL62'STOPPED.'
          END
```

Fig. 11-12 Coding example of the use of a BCT instruction

CHAPTER 11 QUICK REFERENCE

Name	Type[†]	Mnemonic and Form		Object Code Form[††]	See Page
Branch Unconditionally	E.M.	B	Stor	47 M_1 X_2 B_2 D2	178
Branch on Condition	RX	BC	Mask,Stor	47 M_1 X_2 B_2 D2	196
Branch on Condition Register	RR	BCR	Mask,Reg	07 M_1 R_2	198
Branch on Count	RX	BCT	Reg,Stor	46 R_1 X_2 B_2 D2	199
Branch on Count Register	RR	BCTR	Reg,Reg	06 R_1 R_2	199
Branch on A Equal B	E.M.	BE	Stor	47 M_1 X_2 B_2 D2	190
Branch on A High	E.M.	BH	Stor	47 M_1 X_2 B_2 D2	190
Branch on A Low	E.M.	BL	Stor	47 M_1 X_2 B_2 D2	190
Branch on Minus	E.M.	BM	Stor	47 M_1 X_2 B_2 D2	176
Branch on A Not Equal B	E.M.	BNE	Stor	47 M_1 X_2 B_2 D2	190
Branch on A Not High	E.M.	BNH	Stor	47 M_1 X_2 B_2 D2	190
Branch on A Not Low	E.M.	BNL	Stor	47 M_1 X_2 B_2 D2	190
Branch on Not Minus	E.M.	BNM	Stor	47 M_1 X_2 B_2 D2	178
Branch on Not Plus	E.M.	BNP	Stor	47 M_1 X_2 B_2 D2	178
Branch on Not Zero	E.M.	BNZ	Stor	47 M_1 X_2 B_2 D2	178
Branch on Overflow	E.M.	BO	Stor	47 M_1 X_2 B_2 D2	179
Branch on Plus	E.M.	BP	Stor	47 M_1 X_2 B_2 D2	178
Branch on Zero	E.M.	BZ	Stor	47 M_1 X_2 B_2 D2	178
Compare	RX	C	Reg,Stor	59 R_1 X_2 B_2 D2	190

[†]E.M. stands for Extended Mnemonic.
[††]This is the form of the instruction you will see in the object code column of the assembler listing.

Name	Type	Mnemonic and Form	Object Code Form	See Page
Compare (long)	RX	CD Reg,Stor	69 R_1 X_2 B_2 D2	192
Compare Register (long)	RR	CDR Reg,Reg	29 R_1 R_2	192
Compare (short)	RX	CE Reg,Stor	79 R_1 X_2 B_2 D2	192
Compare Register (short)	RR	CER Reg,Reg	39 R_1 R_2	192
Compare Halfword	RX	CH Reg,Stor	49 R_1 X_2 B_2 D2	190
Compare Logical Character	SS	CLC Stor(Length),Stor	D5 L B_1 D1 B_2 D2	193
Compare Decimal	SS	CP Stor(L),Stor(L)	F9 L_1 L_2 B_1 D1 B_2 D2	191
Compare Register	RR	CR Reg,Reg	19 R_1 R_2	190
Load Address	RX	LA Reg,Stor ←	41 R_1 X_2 B_2 D2	198
Load and Test (long)	RR	LTDR Reg,Reg ←	22 R_1 R_2	196
Load and Test (short)	RR	LTER Reg,Reg ←	32 R_1 R_2	196
Load and Test	RR	LTR Reg,Reg ←	12 R_1 R_2	195

QUESTIONS

1. Is the condition code set as a result of the execution of each and every instruction?

2. Why are branch instructions referred to as transfer of control operations?

3. What two things does an extended mnemonic allow you to specify?

4. If the extended mnemonic BM is used following a subtract instruction, under what conditions will the execution "drop through" to the next sequential instruction, rather than the branch being taken?

5. Why might a program need unconditional branch instructions?

6. Explain what is involved in the overflow condition.

7. What are the four parts of loop structure?

8. What are meant by the terms leading-decision and trailing-decision loop?

9. What is meant by "playing computer", and when would you use the technique?

10. What advantage do you gain by using a compare instruction?

11. How do the LTR, L, and LA instructions differ from one another?

12. Explain what a mask is on the BC and BCR instructions, and what function it plays in the execution of the instruction.

13. What condition codes are checked for by the following masks?

   a. 1000   b. 0110   c. 1111

14. How can you get the address of the instruction labeled AGAIN into register 4 before the execution of the following instruction?

   BCR   8,4

15. Discuss the execution of the BCT instruction.

EXERCISES

1. Given the following as the original contents for each group of instructions, how many times will each of the loops be executed?

   AREA: C1C2C3C4   Reg 5: 00000006   Reg 9: 00000018
         fwb
   TWO: 0002
        hwb

   a. LOOP1   MR   8,5
                AR   9,9
                BCT   5,LOOP1
   b. LOOP2   SH   9,TWO
                BP   LOOP2
                L   8,AREA
   c. LOOP3   SR   4,4
                AR   4,5
                CR   4,9
                BL   LOOP3

```
d. LOOP4    LH    5,AREA
            ST    5,AREA
            CLC   AREA(2),AREA+2
            BNE   LOOP4
```

2. Find the amount of money involved when $500 is compounded quarterly at the annual rate of 8% for a period of 3 years.

   The interest must be calculated every period (four times for each of the three years in this case). The interest for period one is added to the original principal amount, this new principal is multiplied by the rate, calculating the interest for the second period. This amount is added to the principal amount. The process is continued until the compound interest has been calculated for the total number of periods.

3. Code a program to read a value N and calculate N! (N! is "N factorial," which is $1 \times 2 \times 3 \times \ldots \times (N - 1) \times N$.) For a value of N of 4, N! would be $1 \times 2 \times 3 \times 4$ or a value of 24.

4. A man has a charge card at a local department store. At Christmas time he charged a total of $400 worth of presents. If the department store charges interest at a rate of $1\frac{1}{2}\%$ per month and the man makes monthly payments of $50, what will be the balance due on the account after the man has made 6 payments?

   Changing this problem slightly, determine the total number of monthly payments the man will have to make to clear his account and exactly what amount he would have to pay the last month to leave his account with a zero balance.

5. The sum-of-the-years' digits method is a popular technique used by businesses in computing depreciation on capital equipment for tax purposes. The method involves taking the number of years of useful life remaining divided by the factorial of the total number of years in the life of the equipment. This fraction multiplied times the original depreciable cost yields the depreciation for that particular year.

   An example would be a $600 typewriter with a useful life of 5 years. The denominator of the fraction is $5 + 4 + 3 + 2 + 1 = 15$. The numerator for the first year would be 5, and the depreciation allowable for the first year would be $\frac{5}{15} \times \$600$ or $200.

   Write a generalized program that will read the cost of a new piece of capital equipment and its useful life, and print the allowable depreciation for each year of the useful life of the equipment.

6. Since purchasing a house is one of the largest purchases an individual ever makes in his lifetime, it is not paid for in cash but through a mortgage.

The monthly payment that will be paid throughout the life of the mortgage can be calculated by the following:

$$M = \frac{P \times R}{1 - \left(\dfrac{1}{1 + R}\right)^N}$$

Where: M = the monthly payment
  P = the initial amount of the mortgage
  R = the annual interest rate divided by 12
  N = total number of monthly payments

Write a program to calculate the monthly payment for a mortgage of $30,000 for a period of 20 years at an annual interest rate of 8½%. Also calculate the total amount of interest that would be paid over the life of the loan. (You'll be surprised to find out how much it costs in interest to borrow this large a sum of money.)

PART III

Program Management and the Assembly Process

The Assembler and the Assembly Process

This chapter is a discussion of the process the assembler program goes through in translating your source program into one in the machine's language. You will be introduced to the way in which the assembler scans each of your instructions in order to determine what you want to do.

Do not read this chapter for *total* understanding the first time. Rather, you should acquire a feeling for the assembler's need to establish certain syntax rules. For greatest benefit, use chapter 12 as a reference when you encounter diagnostic error messages from the assembler. Gain an appreciation for the job the assembler is doing, and you will be ready for independent work that much sooner. The programmer who is able to figure out the *why* behind his errors can better discipline himself to eliminate them.

THE ASSEMBLER PROGRAM

The assembler program processes the source statements that you code in assembler language. This processing relieves you, the programmer, of the responsibility of handling the great amount of clerical tasks and detail otherwise necessary in programming a computer. The assembler permits you to use a meaningful symbol (rather than a string of numbers) to represent the location of an instruction or of data. It permits you to specify operations through the use of meaningful mnemonic opcodes and translates these into numeric machine opcodes. The assembler allocates storage space for instructions and data, and it keeps track of the location of each piece of the program.

In addition to the object program, the assembler produces a printed listing that provides you with the following useful information about your program:

1. A copy of the source statements that make up your assembler language program, sequentially numbering your statements as it prints them
2. The corresponding machine language program (object code) generated by the assembler
3. Diagnostic error messages in order to aid you in the elimination of any mistakes encountered in your source statements
4. A table of information, cross-referencing each symbol defined in your program with the statement numbers of all source statements that refer to the symbol in their operand field

Figure 12-1 shows a sample of printed listing information produced by the assembler.

THE ASSEMBLER'S SCANNING PROCESS

Your source program is the input file (or data set) to the assembler program. The assembler reads the program one statement at a time. It examines each statement by scanning it from left to right. If the assembler finds an asterisk (*)

```
   LOC  OBJECT CODE      ADDR1 ADDR2   STMT   SOURCE STATEMENT
 000000                                   1           CSECT
                                          2           PRINT NOGEN
                                          3           FIRST BEGIN=TWO,END=RESULT+4
                                         10  *   PRINTED LISTING EXAMPLE
 00000C  5870 C022          00024        11           L     7,TWO
 000010  5A70 C022          00024        12           A     7,TWO
 000014  5070 C026          00028        13           ST    7,RESULT
                                         14           LAST  BEGIN=TWO,END=RESULT+4
 000024  00000002                        21  TWO      DC    F'2'
 000028                                  22  RESULT    DS    F
                                         23           END
 000030  5B5BC2D7C4E4D4D7                24                 =CL8'$$BPDUMP'
 000038  000000240000002C                25                 =A(TWO,RESULT+4)
```

```
                                      CROSS-REFERENCE

 SYMBOL    LEN   VALUE   DEFN
 RESULT   00004 000028 00022   0008  0013  0017  0025
 TWO      00004 000024 00021   0008  0011  0012  0017  0025


 NO STATEMENTS FLAGGED IN THIS ASSEMBLY
```

Fig. 12-1 Sample assembler listing

in the first column of the statement, it recognizes it as a comment statement and examines no further. It merely assigns a number to the comment statement and prints both on the listing. An example is statement 10 in figure 12-1. If there is no asterisk in the first column of the source statement, the assembler checks to see if it contains a blank—or a character other than a blank. If the column is blank, the source statement has no symbolic name associated with it and the assembler scans until it encounters the first nonblank character.

If the first column is not blank, the assembler collects each successive character in its scan until it encounters a blank. The characters it has collected make up the symbolic name associated with the machine instruction (or assigned to the first byte of an area if the statement defines a storage area or a constant). Statement 21 in figure 12-1 is a DC statement that assigns the symbolic name TWO to the first byte of the fullword area. The assembler checks to ensure that the characters it has collected comply with its syntax rules for valid symbols. It checks the symbol for eight characters or less, determines if the first character is alphabetic (A–Z) or national (@, #, or $), and that each of the remaining characters is either alphabetic or numeric. If the assembler discovers that it has collected more than eight characters, or that any of these violate syntax rules, it generates a diagnostic error message.

If the symbol collected is valid, the assembler skips all succeeding blanks until it encounters the first nonblank character—the same action it took when no label was used in the source statement. In the case of the statement with the label TWO, the assembler skips spaces 4 through 9 before it encounters the D in column 10.

It then collects characters for the mnemonic opcode in the same manner it collects name field characters. Then it compares the opcode with its list of valid mnemonics. An invalid mnemonic causes the assembler to generate a diagnostic error message. The blanks between the opcode and the operand field are skipped, and the operand is scanned. The valid syntax for the operand field is determined by the opcode.

The comment field is *not* examined. Once the entire statement has been scanned, the entire source statement, complete with comments, if present, is printed on the assembler listing, along with any diagnostic error messages generated for that statement by the assembler. Figure 12-2 is an example of an assembler listing which includes diagnostic error messages.

INTRODUCTION TO THE ASSEMBLER'S TWO PASSES

In the previous section you read how the assembler scans each source statement from left to right. In this section you will learn that the assembler does not necessarily make a complete scan of each source statement the first time it sees it. In fact, the assembler sees each source statement twice. It makes *two* passes over the source program, one instruction at a time. On the first pass, the

```
LOC   OBJECT CODE      ADDR1 ADDR2  STMT    SOURCE STATEMENT
000000                                1             CSECT
                                      2             PRINT NOGEN
                                      3             FIRST BEGIN=TWO,END=RESULT+4
                                     10 *   PRINTED LISTING EXAMPLE WITH DIAGNOSTICS
00000C 5870 C022             00024   11             L     7,TWO
                                     12             ADD   7,TWO
        *** ERROR ***
000010 5070 C026             00028   13             ST    7,RESULT
                                     14             LAST  BEGIN=TWO,END=RESULT+4
000020 00000002                      21 2          DC    F'2'
        *** ERROR ***
000024 00000002                      22 TWO         DC    F'2'
000028                               23 RESULT      DS    F
                                     24             END
000030 5B5BC2D7C4E4D4D7              25                   =CL8'$$BPDUMP'
000038 000000024000000002C           26                   =A(TWO,RESULT+4)
```

```
                                                   DIAGNOSTICS

STMT   ERROR CODE    MESSAGE

  12  IJQ088         UNDEFINED OPERATION CODE
  21  IJQ016         INVALID NAME


  2 STATEMENTS FLAGGED IN THIS ASSEMBLY
```

Fig. 12-2   Sample assembler listing including diagnostic error messages

assembler performs the following basic functions:

1. It *allocates space* for the machine code, constants, and storage areas you wish to establish.
2. It builds a table called a *cross-reference* (symbol) *table* and makes an entry in this table for every symbol it encounters in the name field.

On the second pass, the assembler performs the following basic functions:

1. It *resolves any symbolic references* to storage locations appearing in the operands of instructions by referring to the information stored in the cross-reference table on the first pass.
2. It *translates the source statements* into machine code and constants and thus fills the space it has allocated.
3. It *produces the assembler listing*, complete with diagnostic error messages and other programmer aids.

The Location Counter

The assembler uses a location counter to keep track of the address of the next byte it has available for allocation in the object module. (To review, the object module is the block of machine code created by the assembler as it translates your source code.) As it begins each pass over the source program, the value of the location counter is set to zero. As a source statement is scanned, the assembler determines how many bytes must be allocated in the object module to hold the machine code or data generated by its translation of that source statement. The value in the location counter is incremented by the number of bytes allocated.

How does the assembler know how many bytes to allocate? Remember that if the source statement is a machine instruction, the opcode places the instruction in one of five classes of instructions. Each instruction belonging to a particular class occupies a predefined number of bytes:

Class	Bytes Occupied
RR	2
RX	4
RS	4
SI	4
SS	6

For example, the opcode L belongs to the RX class of instructions; every time the assembler sees an L in the opcode field of an instruction, it increments the location counter by a value of four. The opcode MVC, on the other hand, belongs to the SS class of instructions; every appearance of an MVC in an opcode field causes the addition of a value of 6 to the location counter value.

If the source statement contains an opcode of DC or DS, the assembler must examine the operand field to determine the number of bytes it must allocate. The following is a copy of statements 22 and 23 from the assembler listing printed in figure 12-2:

```
LOC   OBJECT CODE    ADDR1 ADDR2 STMT   SOURCE STATEMENT


000024  00000002                   22 TWO     DC   F'2'
000028                             23 RESULT  DS   F
```

Notice that the value (hexadecimal) contained in the location counter is displayed on the extreme lefthand side of the assembler listing shown at the beginning of this chapter. This value is the location within the object module of the first byte of the area allocated for the translation of a particular source statement.

When the assembler started its scan of the DC statement, the next byte it had to allocate was the one at location 24. The operand field of this DC statement informs the assembler that it needs to allocate 4 bytes; so it allocates bytes 24, 25, 26, and 27, and then increments the location counter by a value of 4. The location counter value preceding the next statement indicates that the next available byte is at location 28. What is the next location counter value available after RESULT? Simply: $28_{16} + 4_{16} = 2C_{16}$.

The Symbol (Cross-Reference) Table

The symbol table that the assembler builds contains every valid symbol appearing in the name field of a statement within the source program. In addition to the symbol, several other pieces of information about that symbol are included in the table. These include: (1) DEFN—the statement number of the source statement in which this symbol appeared in the name field (i.e., was defined); (2) VALUE—the value associated with that symbol, which (in the majority of cases) is the location counter value associated with the first byte of that instruction or area; and (3) LEN—the length attribute associated with that symbol (specified in base ten). Examine the symbol table entries in the assembler listing given in figure 12-3. Notice that the symbol TWO, defined in statement 25, is referenced by (appears in the operand of) statements 12, 13, and 15, and has a length of 4 bytes associated with it, because it is the name on a DC requiring a fullword.

```
   LOC   OBJECT CODE        ADDR1 ADDR2   STMT    SOURCE STATEMENT

 000000                                     1              CSECT
                                            2              PRINT NOGEN
                                            3              FIRST  BEGIN=MLTPLR,END=RESULT+4
                                           10  *    SYMBOL TABLE EXAMPLE LISTING
 00000C 5870 C032               00034      11              L     7,MLTPLR
 000010 5C60 C036               00038      12              M     6,TWO
 000014 5A70 C036               00038      13              A     7,TWO
 000018 D204 C03A C03F 0003C    00041      14              MVC   LOC(5),AREA
 00001E 5C60 C036               00038      15              M     6,TWO
 000022 5070 C046               00048      16              ST    7,RESULT
                                           17              LAST   BEGIN=MLTPLR,END=RESULT+4
 000032 0000
 000034 00000006                           24  MLTPLR  DC    F'6'
 000038 00000002                           25  TWO     DC    F'2'
 00003C                                     26  LOC     DS    5C
 000041 C1C2C3C4C5C6C7                      27  AREA    DC    C'ABCDEFG'
 000048                                     28  RESULT  DS    F
                                            29              END
 000050 5B5BC2D7C4E4D4D7                    30              =CL8'$$BPDUMP'
 000058 000000340000004C                    31              =A(MLTPLR,RESULT+4)
```

```
                                                          CROSS-REFERENCE

   SYMBOL    LEN    VALUE   DEFN

   AREA     00007  000041  00027    0014
   LOC      00001  00003C  00026    0014
   MLTPLR   00004  000034  00024    0008   0011   0020   0031
   RESULT   00004  000048  00028    0008   0016   0020   0031
   TWO      00004  000038  00025    0012   0013   0015
```

```
NO STATEMENTS FLAGGED IN THIS ASSEMBLY
```

Fig. 12-3 Sample symbol (or cross-reference) table

THE FIRST PASS IN DETAIL

At this point let us put together everything we have learned about the first pass of the assembler. The assembler scans source statements one at a time. If there is an asterisk in the first column, there is no symbol for the assembler to enter into the symbol table, and there is no opcode to be examined. If the scan reveals a valid symbol in the name field, a check is made to ensure that this symbol has not yet been placed in the symbol table, because duplicate symbols are not permitted in assembler language. If no duplicate exists, the symbol is placed in the table. If it is already there, this appearance of the symbol is flagged with a diagnostic error message. The remainder of that source statement is scanned and handled by the assembler. Notice that any references to the duplicate symbol are cross-referenced, with the first definition of the symbol LOOP in the cross reference table. The second definition is placed in the symbol table, but it is never used to resolve any operand references.

The scan continues, and the mnemonic opcode is examined. If it represents a valid machine instruction and there is a symbol in the name field, the current value of the location counter is placed in the symbol table with the symbol. The class of instruction that the opcode belongs to determines the number of bytes necessary to hold the machine code for that instruction, and the location counter is incremented by this number of bytes. The scan of this source statement is stopped, and the scan of the next instruction is started.

If the next instruction has no symbol in the name field, the blanks are skipped in the scan, and the opcode is collected again. The opcode indicates a machine instruction, so the location counter is incremented by the number of bytes for an instruction belonging to the instruction repertoire.† The assembler cannot allocate space for that instruction, because it has no way of determining the class of the instruction. The location counter is not altered, and a diagnostic error message is generated to indicate this fact on the second pass, because the operand cannot be interpreted and translated into machine language.

When a statement is scanned, a symbol entered in the symbol table, and the opcode is a DC or DS, the assembler will have to continue its scan to the operand field of the instruction. The scan is continued to allow the assembler to determine how many bytes to allocate and whether the first byte of the area needs to be aligned on a particular boundary.

As the assembler scans the operand field, the type subfield tells whether the first byte of the area to be allocated must be on a particular boundary. For instance, if the type is F, then a fullword boundary is needed. The assembler will examine the location counter value to determine if it is evenly divisible by 4. If it is and no duplication factor is used in the operand, then the location

---

†The opcode may be the name of a macro, which is a special case. This possibility will be ignored in the present discussion.

counter is incremented by 4. If a duplication factor is present, then the location counter is incremented by a value equal to 4 times the duplication factor.

If the type subfield is F and the location counter is not evenly divisible by 4, the assembler will increment the location counter value until its value is evenly divisible by 4. This value is placed in the symbol table with the corresponding symbol from this source statement, and the location counter is incremented in one of the ways used above, depending on whether a duplication factor is present or not. When this happens, some bytes are skipped.[†]

When there is a C in the type subfield, the assembler calculates the number of bytes to allocate by examining the length modifier, if present, or by counting the number of characters between the apostrophes in the operand. No alignment is necessary in the case of character constants, so the current value of the location counter is entered in the symbol table, and the location counter is incremented by the number of bytes allocated.

In the example given in figure 12-4, the length attribute associated with each of the symbols is entered into the symbol table. The length attribute is 2 for RR-type machine instructions, 4 for RX-, RS-, and SI-type machine instructions, and 6 for SS-type machine instructions. For the constants and storage areas, the length attribute is 4 for fullwords, 2 for halfwords, 8 for doublewords, and either the length modifier number or the number of characters in the value subfield for character strings. At the end of the first pass, all necessary space has been allocated, and the symbol table is complete. There is an entry in the table for each symbol defined in the program.

THE SECOND PASS IN DETAIL

As the second pass begins, the assembler has already examined each statement once. Now it resets the location counter back to zero and examines each source statement a second time. **Note:** For those of you who are punching your source statements into punch cards for input, one point should be clarified. The assembler cannot back up the card reader to read the cards containing your source statements a second time. The way this is handled is to read the information from the cards and place the information in successive records on another type of I/O device that can be rewound (like a tape) or repositioned (like a disk) so that each source statement may be read a second time. To repeat, *there is no way to backspace the card reader.* Once a card is read, it is placed in a hopper to await the operator's attention.

As the assembler translates each instruction, it increments the location counter value. If it locates a syntax error in a source statement, it constructs an error message. As it prints the source statement on its listing, it also prints

---

[†]Due to this alignment skipping, experienced programmers usually group their constants to conserve space, starting with doublewords, working down to halfwords, and finally character strings.

```
LOC    OBJECT CODE    ADDR1 ADDR2   STMT    SOURCE STATEMENT

000000                                1             CSECT
                                      2             PRINT NOGEN
                                      3             FIRST BEGIN=FOUR,END=LOC+6
                                     10  *  FIRST PASS EXAMPLE
00000C 5A60 C022          00024      11 LOOP        A      6,FOUR
000010 5A70 C022          00024      12 LOOP        A      7,FOUR
       *** ERROR ***
000014 5060 C036          00038      13             ST     6,ANSWER
                                     14             MXT    8,2
       *** ERROR ***
                                     15 LAST        BEGIN=FOUR,END=LOC+6
000024 00000004                      22 FOUR        DC     F'4'
000028 0000000600000006              23 TWICE       DC     2F'6'
000030 F1F2F3F4F5                    24 AREA        DC     C'12345'
000038                               25 ANSWER      DS     F
00003C E8C5E2404040                  26 LOC         DC     CL6'YES'
                                     27             END
000048 5B5BC2D7C4E4D4D7              28                    =CL8'$$BPDUMP'
000050 0000002400000042              29                    =A(FOUR,LOC+6)
```

CROSS-REFERENCE

```
SYMBOL    LEN    VALUE  DEFN

ANSWER    00004  000038 00025    0013
AREA      00005  000030 00024
FOUR      00004  000024 00022    0008  0011  0012  0018  0029
LOC       00006  00003C 00026    0008  0018  0029
LOOP      00004  00000C 00011
LOOP      00004  00000C 00012
TWICE     00004  000028 00023
```

DIAGNOSTICS

```
STMT    ERROR CODE    MESSAGE

   12 IJQ023          PREVIOUSLY DEFINED NAME
   14 IJQ088          UNDEFINED OPERATION CODE


   2 STATEMENTS FLAGGED IN THIS ASSEMBLY
```

Fig. 12-4 Sample symbol or cross-reference table for listing, including diagnostic error messages

an indication of the error message to come. After the assembler has printed the entire listing of the source statements with all error indications, it prints the information it has stored in its symbol table (the cross-reference) in alphabetical order and then the error messages that were indicated as it printed the source statements.

The page of the listing containing the error messages is labeled *Diagnostics*. At the end of the list of error messages is a notation of how many statements were flagged (error indications added) in this assembly. If an assembly listing contains no errors in syntax, a message to this effect immediately follows the cross-reference table in the listing. This message is: 'No statements flagged in this Assembly'. This is the message you should watch for in your listings.

By following the program in figure 12-5 through the assembler's first pass as it would, you can construct the symbol table. Can you recognize the error the assembler would catch on its first pass? As the assembler scans statement 13, it will be unable to allocate space in the block of machine code based on the mnemonic opcode it encounters in this instruction. (DIV is not one of the

```
LOC   OBJECT CODE     ADDR1 ADDR2   STMT   SOURCE STATEMENT

000000                                 1            CSECT
                                       2            PRINT NOGEN
                                       3            FIRST BEGIN=BASE,END=AREA+2
                                      10 *   AREA OF A TRIANGLE
00000C 5850 C026       00028          11            L     5,BASE
000010 0000 0000       00000          12            M     4,ONE
       *** ERROR ***

       *** ERROR ***
                                      13            DIV   4,TWO
000014 0000 0000       00000          14            M     5,HEIGHT
       *** ERROR ***
000018 5050 C040       00042          15            ST    5,AREA
       *** ERROR ***
                                      16            LAST  BEGIN=BASE,END=AREA+2
000028 00000008                       23 BASE       DC    F'8'
00002C 00000002                       24 TWO        DC    F'2'
000030 0000000C                       25 HEIGHT     DC    F'12'
000034 E3C8C540C1D9C5C1               26 MSG        DC    C'THE AREA IS  '
000042                                27 AREA       DS    H
                                      28            END
000048 5B5BC2D7C4E4D4D7               29                  =CL8'$$BPDUMP'
000050 0000002800000044               30                  =A(BASE,AREA+2)
```

```
                                                 CROSS-REFERENCE

SYMBOL    LEN   VALUE   DEFN

AREA      00002 000042 00027    0008  0015  0019  0030
BASE      00004 000028 00023    0008  0011  0019  0030
HEIGHT    00004 000030 00025    0014
MSG       00013 000034 00026
ONE                             0012
TWO       00004 00002C 00024
```

```
                                                 DIAGNOSTICS

STMT   ERROR CODE    MESSAGE

   12  IJQ024        UNDEFINED SYMBOL
   13  IJQ088        UNDEFINED OPERATION CODE
   14  IJQ010        INVALID SPECIFICATION OF REGISTER OR MASK FIELD
   15  IJQ033        ALIGNMENT ERROR


4 STATEMENTS FLAGGED IN THIS ASSEMBLY
```

Fig. 12-5 Assembler listing for working through the assembler's two passes

assembler's valid mnemonic opcodes.) The assembler will record this error so it will not try to examine the operand of this instruction on its second pass and so it can also indicate and print an undefined operation code error message on its listing.

There will be five symbols entered in the symbol table at the end of the first pass. These five symbols appear in the name fields of statements 23 through 27 and are: BASE, TWO, HEIGHT, MSG, and AREA.

On the assembler's second pass, it locates the remaining three syntax errors in this program. As it scans the operand field of statement 11, it encounters the symbol BASE. It looks for this symbol in its symbol table. When it locates the entry for BASE, it changes the symbolic storage reference to an address of a storage location. It then converts both the number 5 and the address to binary and fills the allocated space with these binary values. Exactly *how* the symbol is converted to an actual address is unimportant now.

As the assembler scans the operand field of statement 12, it encounters the symbol ONE. It looks for this symbol in its symbol table but does not find it. If an entry for a particular symbol does not appear in the symbol table, this means that the assembler did not encounter it in the name field of any of the source statements scanned on its first pass. In other words, the symbol was never defined; it was never assigned a location counter value.

This undefined symbol is placed in the symbol table, but the only piece of information the assembler can place in the table along with the symbol is the fact that it is referenced in the operand field of statement 12. The assembler cannot associate any specified length with the symbol nor any value or statement number of the definition, because the symbol ONE never appeared in the name field of any instruction it examined on the first pass. Statement 13 is not examined on the second pass because of the syntax error encountered on the first pass (the invalid mnemonic opcode—DIV).

The next syntax error encountered by the assembler is in statement 14. The error message printed by the assembler in its listing is 'Invalid specification of register or mask field'. (This message might be phrased a little differently, depending on which operating system you use, but the existence of an invalid specification of a portion of the operand field is indicated in any case.) The opcode of the instruction in error here is M, for a fullword multiply instruction. HEIGHT is the symbol assigned to a fullword in storage; therefore, the second operand is correctly specified.

What are the syntax requirements for specifying the first operand of a multiply instruction? Except for the MH opcode, all the multiplication instructions require an even-odd coupled register pair. The even register of this pair must be specified in the first operand. Although the quotient from the divide instruction is in register 5 and this is the number that is to participate in the multiplication operation, register 4 must be specified in the first operand of the multiply instruction.

The last error the assembler encounters on its second pass occurs in statement 15. The opcode of this instruction (ST) indicates an RX instruction. It also indicates that the second operand should be a fullword. To be a fullword, the address represented by the symbol AREA must be evenly divisible by 4. Take a look at the symbol table entry for AREA. The location counter value assigned to this symbol is 42. This value is not evenly divisible by 4; therefore the assembler indicates and prints an alignment error message. The programmer has specified an operand address that is not compatible with the expected operand address; it does not meet the boundary alignment requirements of the ST instruction.

Examine the following source program as if you are the assembler program going through its two passes over the data. Construct the symbol table as the assembler does on its first pass and check for any syntax errors on both passes:

```
              CSECT
              PRINT   NOGEN
              FIRST   BEGIN=WIDTH,END=PERIMETER+4
*AREA OF RECTANGLE
              LH      7,LENGTH            LOAD LENGTH OF RECTANGLE
              M       6,WIDTH             MULTIPLY LENGTH TIMES WIDTH
              STH     7,AREA              STORE AREA OF RECTANGLE
*PERIMETER OF RECTANGLE
              L       5,LENGTH            RELOAD LENGTH OF RECTANGLE
              A       5,WIDTH             ADD WIDTH TO LENGTH
              M       4,TWO               CALCULATE PERIMETER
              ST      5,PERIMETER         STORE PERIMETER OF RECTANGLE
              LAST    BEGIN=WIDTH,END=PERIMETER+4
WIDTH         DC      F'6'
AREA          DS      H
LENGTH        DC      H'9'
PERIMETER     DS      F
              END
```

HANDLING AND ADDRESSING OF OPERANDS

In understanding the assembler and the assembly process, it is of great help to consider the variety of expressions possible within the operand field. Operands can be specified as single expressions or as combinations of expressions forming a more complex one.

An expression is a term, or an arithmetic combination of terms, representing a value. The expression may be a complete operand or a portion of an operand such as: 1) the address; 2) the mask; 3) the length specification of a storage-to-storage instruction; or 4) the duplication factor for a DC or DS assembler instruction.

The value of an expression within an operand can be one of two types—either the value is absolute or relocatable. An absolute value has a value inherent in the term itself. This value is always the same. A relocatable value is assigned to the term by the assembler; it is not inherent in the term itself. The relocatable value always has a relationship to the beginning of the block of code the assembler generates on its second pass. The assembler calculates this relation. Later, the relocatable value is adjusted to reflect where the beginning of the block of code generated by the assembler is placed when that block of code is loaded into the computer's storage for execution. The relocatable value reflects the location in storage of the block of code. If the block of code is moved to a different location in storage, the relocatable value is changed to reflect this relocation, thus the name *relocatable*.

ABSOLUTE VALUES—SELF-DEFINING TERMS

An *absolute value* is fixed; no change needs to be made to an absolute value if a block of code is relocated. As our definition states, a self-defining term has its value inherent in the term itself. The assembler does not assign its value to it.

While it is natural for you to use decimal self-defining values, binary, hexadecimal, and character self-defining values may also be used. Regardless of which kind of self-defining terms you use, the assembler converts each one into its binary equivalent and places it in the proper field of the machine instruction it is building.

Self-defining terms can be used to represent length modifiers, duplication factors, masks, register numbers, immediate operands of SI-type instructions, and portions of addresses (when you learn to specify operands explicitly, as well as symbolically). The following examples show use of self-defining terms:

```
        L     3,AREA              register number (3)
        MVI   LOC,C'$'            immediate operand (C'$')
        .
        .
        .
FLWDS   DC    4C'ABC'             duplication factor (4)
MSG     DC    CL11'**ERROR**'     length modifier (11)
```

SYMBOLS: RELOCATABLE AND ABSOLUTE

To review, a symbol is a character or combination of characters that can be used to represent storage location or arbitrary values. A symbol can be from one to eight characters in length. The first character must be alphabetic or national (A–Z, @, #, or $), and the remaining characters must be alphameric (alphabetic or numeric). A symbol may be defined only once in an assembly. Each symbol appearing in the name field of an instruction in an assembler language program must be unique; a symbol may be defined only *once* in a program.

A symbol is defined, or assigned a value, at assembly time when it appears in the name field of a source statement. If the values are assigned to symbols that identify storage areas, instructions, constants, or control sections (the name given to the entire block of code generated by the assembler), the addresses represent the leftmost byte of the field containing those items. Since *these addresses may change* upon loading the block of machine code into storage for execution, these symbols are considered to be *relocatable* terms. Examples of relocatable terms are present in every program you have written.

```
MINE       CSECT
           PRINT   NOGEN
           FIRST   BEGIN=INITVALU,END=ANS+4
           L       6,INITVALU              ZERO LOOP COUNTER
           L       9,ONE                   REG. 9 = 1
LOOP       M       8,N                     MULTIPLY REG. 9 BY 3
           A       6,ONE                   ADD 1 TO LOOP COUNTER
           C       6,EIGHT                 Q: 8 TIMES THRU LOOP?
           BNE     LOOP                    A: NO, GO TO LOOP
           ST      9,ANS                   A: YES, STORE RESULT
           LAST    BEGIN=INITVALU,END=ANS+4
INITVALU   DC      F'0'
ONE        DC      F'1'
N          DC      F'3'
EIGHT      DC      F'8'
ANS        DS      F
           END
```

In the above example, ANS is the name of a storage area; LOOP is the name of an instruction; INITVALU, ONE, N, and EIGHT are names of constants; and MINE is the name of the entire block of code. The assembler has assigned each of these symbols a value based on the location of the first byte of the area the symbol represents in relation to the first byte in the entire block of code.

Using the Equate (EQU) to Assign a Value to a Symbol   A symbol may also appear in the name field of an equate statement. The equate statement (opcode EQU) is an assembler instruction (pseudo-op) which allows you to assign a value to a symbol. The symbol in the name field of an EQU statement is assigned the value that appears in the operand portion of that instruction. The operand field can contain either absolute or relocatable values or symbols: therefore the symbol EQUated can be either absolute or relocatable.

The EQU statement has several advantages. It allows you to give a symbolic name to absolute values, and all symbolic references made to those values will appear in the assembler's cross-reference Table. This is most advantageous, because you can refer to a particular register by symbolic name. For example, if you are using register 6 to hold a counter that controls your loop, you can equate the symbolic name LOOPCTR with a decimal self-defining value of 6. Then you can use the symbol LOOPCTR wherever you would have used the 6 in your program. The code is the previous example would now look like:

```
LOOPCTR    EQU   6
           L     LOOPCTR,INITVALU
           L     9,ONE
LOOP       M     8,N
           A     LOOPCTR,ONE
           C     LOOPCTR,EIGHT
           BNE   LOOP
```

The assignment of the single absolute value of 6 to the symbol LOOPCTR made this small program easier to understand, even without comments, on quick examination. Imagine how the equate statement can ease the programmer's job in a long program, by making it unnecessary to remember (on page 5 of a listing) which register is used for a particular purpose (on page 1).

One important thing to remember about equates is that you are assigning a value to a symbol. Wherever that symbol is used in the operand of an instruction, the assigned value will be substituted in place of the symbol. When the symbol LOOPCTR is used in an operand where a register number is expected, the 6 that is substituted means register 6. Use the symbol LOOPCTR where a length is specified in a storage-to-storage instruction, and when the 6 is substituted it indicates a length of 6 bytes:

MVC   LOC2(LOOPCTR),LOC1

When the equate statement assigns the value of 6 to a symbol, it does not mean that that symbol is equated with register 6. Therefore, the same symbol can be used for several purposes. Care must be taken, however, so that the multiple use of a symbol does not lead to errors or confusion.

Another advantage of the EQU is that it makes changes easier. Assume you have used the following equate statements:

```
LOOPCTR    EQU   8
BLOCK      EQU   5
DIVDEND    EQU   6
CHANGE     EQU   2
SUM        EQU   8
```

Further assume that you discover at the end of coding that you have used register 8 for two purposes. You can correct the error by simply changing the operand on one of the equate statements to a different register number. Because you have used a symbolic name in the assembly, every symbolic reference to that register number is changed to another register automatically, as the assembler makes its passes over the source.

Figure 12-6 illustrates one type of error that can be caused by the multiple use of one register.

This program will execute successfully but will not calculate the correct

```
DUPUSE      CSECT
            PRINT   NOGEN
            FIRST   BEGIN=KTWO,END=ANS+4
*  SUMS OF SUCCEEDING POWERS OF 2
TWO         EQU     7
SUM         EQU     8
RESULT      EQU     7
            SR      SUM,SUM                   ZERO SUM REG.
            L       TWO,KTWO                  SET UP VALUE FOR MULTIPLY
LOOP        MR      6,TWO                     DOUBLE CONTENTS OF REG. 7
            AR      SUM,RESULT                ADD RESULT TO SUM
            C       RESULT,ENDVALU            Q: RESULT = 512
            BNE     LOOP                      A: NO, LOOP AGAIN
            ST      SUM,ANS                   A: YES, STORE RESULT
            .
            .
            .
            LAST    BEGIN=KTWO,END=ANS+4
KTWO        DC      F'2'
ENDVALU     DC      F'512'
ANS         DS      F
            END
```

Fig. 12-6 Error caused by multiple use of a register

answer. Why? Because register 7 is used for two purposes: 1) to hold a value of 2 for each successive multiplication, and 2) to hold each new power of 2 as the multiplication operation is completed. This means that what actually happens is each successive resultant value is squared—multiplied by itself, rather than by a value of two. This problem can be solved merely by changing the operand on the equate statement for the symbol TWO from 7 to 9 (or any other unused register). Doing this causes the assembler to substitute a value of 9 in any instruction where the symbol TWO appears. This in turn causes register 9 to receive a value of 2, and through the entire program, register 9 contains that value.

Without the use of equates, a discovery of this type of error necessitates a search of the entire program for instructions referring to the doubly used register. Then a decision must be made as to which use of the register should be changed, and each affected instruction must be recoded (and repunched if the error is not discovered until after keypunching).

Assigning Synonyms with the Equate Statement The EQU statement can also be used to assign a synonym or synonyms for previously defined symbols. By previously defined, we mean that the symbol appearing in the operand field of an EQU statement must have appeared in the name field of an instruction that the assembler has previously handled on this pass. In other words, to use a symbol in the operand of an EQU statement, that symbol must already be entered in the assembler's symbol table.

```
COUNTER    EQU   3
TIMES      EQU   COUNTER
```

Register 3 can be referred to by the symbolic name COUNTER, when it is used in the function of loop control, and by the symbolic name TIMES, when the exit is taken from the loop. (In addition, it can be referred to in the case where the number of times the loop was executed is used by instructions in a later section of the program.)

The operand of an equate statement can also be a relocatable symbol:

```
DOLLAR     EQU   C'$'
           MVC   AREA2+1(6),AREA1
           MVI   LOC,DOLLAR
             .
             .
             .
AREA1      DC    C'627.45'
AREA2      DS    CL7
LOC        EQU   AREA2
```

The two move instructions fill the 7 bytes of AREA2. The 6 characters of the constant AREA1 are placed in bytes 2–7, and the hexadecimal representation of the dollar sign is placed in byte 1. The rule about previously defined symbols in the operand holds for relocatable symbols as well as absolute symbols.

RELOCATABLE VALUES: LOCATION COUNTER REFERENCES

Earlier in this chapter we learned that the assembler keeps a location counter that it uses to assign addresses to statements in a program. The programmer can refer to the current value of this location counter in any DC, DS, EQU, or machine instruction in his source module. This reference is made by specifying an asterisk (*) as a term in an operand.

To review how the assembler keeps the location counter value, let's examine what happens as each machine instruction or data area is assembled. The location counter is set to a value of zero at the start of each pass of the assembler. As each statement is assembled, the location counter is first adjusted to the proper boundary, if necessary. Then it is incremented by the length of the assembled item. Thus the location counter always points to the next byte available for allocation. It is the address of this byte that is substituted wherever an asterisk is used as a term in an operand.

In other words, using an asterisk in an operand is the same as placing a symbol in the name field of the instruction and then using that symbol in the operand of that statement:

```
HERE      LA  R6,HERE
```
is the same as:
```
HERE      LA  R6,*
```

RELOCATABLE VALUES: LITERALS

The use of literals is an alternative to using constants as a means to introduce data into a program. A literal is coded exactly as the operand of a DC statement, and its specification is preceded by an equal sign ($=$). The following code illustrates the use of a literal and of an identical constant:

```
L    6,=F'26'
L    7,FULL26
         .
         .
         .
FULL26   DC  F'26'
```

As can be observed in this example, the literal represents data, rather than a reference to data. This is one of the advantages of literals. The data used by an instruction is visible in it. The use of constants does not permit this immediate verification (on our part) of the data being used by the instruction. The use of a literal in an MVC instruction illustrates this convenience. (The advantage may not be as apparent here as in your programs, where the number of instructions coded makes it necessary to place the constants on a page different from the instructions referring to those constants.)

```
MVC  OUTAREA(11),=C'***ERROR***'
```

would accomplish the same as:

```
MVC  OUTAREA(11), MSG
         .
         .
MSG      DC    C'***ERROR***'
```

The assembler handles a literal by assembling the data specified in it into a special area of storage called a *literal pool*. This special area is created immediately following your block of code. It is aligned on a doubleword boundary, and the literals are arranged in the pool in the most efficient manner: doublewords, words, halfwords, and then odd-length literals. This ensures proper boundary alignment for data that demands it and minimizes the space needed for the literal pool.

There are two other things to keep in mind when using literals: (1) Only one literal is allowed in a given machine language instruction, and (2) a literal cannot be combined with any other term.

In general a literal may be used wherever a storage address is permitted as an operand. The exception is that a literal cannot be used as the *receiving* field in an instruction that modifies storage in any way, or any I/O, or in shift instructions (discussed in chapter 17). If you examine what the assembler does with a literal, the reason for this restriction becomes apparent.

The assembler performs the function of storing the data for you. It constructs the literal pool, and control of the data in that pool is its responsibility. If you use two identical literals in your program, the assembler assembles *only one* into the literal pool and puts the address of this one literal into both instructions containing the literal specification. Therefore, it cannot allow you to alter anything within the literal pool at execution time.

Note: There is one big drawback to the use of literals. This is the fact that most assembler programs do not cross reference literals. The programmer must keep track of all uses of literals. If changes need to be made, he must ensure that *all* statements affected are changed.

THE EVALUATION OF EXPRESSIONS

An *expression* has been defined as being a term or an arithmetic combination of terms representing a value. It was also explained that the expression may have either the attribute absolute or relocatable. If the expression consists of a single term, it takes the attribute of the term. If the expression consists of several terms, its attribute and validity is determined by the following rules:

1. Relocatable + or − absolute = relocatable
2. Relocatable − relocatable = absolute
3. Absolute + or − absolute = absolute
4. Absolute × absolute = absolute
5. Absolute ÷ absolute = absolute
6. A multiterm expression may not contain a literal (a literal represents data rather than a reference to data).
7. Multiplication or division cannot involve relocatable terms.
8. If more than one relocatable term appears in an expression, all but one must be paired (to be paired they must have opposite signs).
9. All relocatable expressions must be positive.

```
EQUAL   EQU   8
LOW     EQU   4
SIX     EQU   6
TWO     EQU   2
GRN     EQU   X'26'
BLU     EQU   X'14'
        MVC   AREA+4(SIX),LOC+SIX
```

In the group above: AREA+4   is relocatable+absolute,
                     (SIX)   is absolute, and
                     LOC+SIX   is relocatable+absolute;

In: CLI   AREA,GRN+BLU

           AREA   is relocatable, and
           GRN+BLU   is absolute+absolute;

In: MVC   LOC(SIX−TWO),AREA+TWO

           LOC   is relocatable,
           SIX−TWO   is absolute−absolute, and
           AREA+TWO   is relocatable+absolute;

And finally in: BC   EQUAL+LOW,LOOP

           EQUAL+LOW is absolute+absolute

Using these symbols:

           relocatable symbols   A, B and C
           absolute symbols   G and H

The following are absolute expressions:

           G   *−B+2
           B−A+X'C1'   37
           H+24   B−C

The following are relocatable expressions:

           A   =F'2765'
           +4   G(H+A−B)+C

The following expressions are invalid for the reasons given:

=F'678'+4   literal in multiterm expression
2*A−B   multiplication involving a relocatable term
A+B−G   pairing rule violated

Examine the assembler statements in figure 12-7 for their use of absolute and relocatable expressions.

QUESTIONS

1. Give some examples of the useful information provided for you by the assembler in the listing it provides.

2. In general explain the assembler's scanning process.

```
LOC     OBJECT CODE      ADDR1 ADDR2   STMT   SOURCE STATEMENT

C00000                                   1            CSECT
                                         2            PRINT NOGEN
                                         3     FIRST  BEGIN=FIVE,END=SPOT+100


000006                                  11 SIX    EQU   6
000004                                  12 FOUR   EQU   4
00000C  5870 C02E              00030    13        L     7,AREA+FOUR
000010  5C60 C026              00028    14        M     SIX,FIVE
000014  D20E C05E C02A   00060 0002C    15        MVC   SPOT(L),AREA


                                        17 LAST   BEGIN=FIVE,END=SPOT+100

000026  0000                            24 FIVE   DC    F'5'
000028  00000005                        25 AREA   DC    C'ERR 6728 CAUGHT'
00002C  C5D9D940F6F7F2F8                26 LUC    DS    CL20
00003B                                  27 L      EQU   LOC-AREA
00000F
00004F  00
000050  00000008                        28 TAB    DC    F'8'
000054  00000010                        29        DC    F'16'
000058  00000018                        30        DC    F'24'
00005C  0000000C                        31        DC    F'12'
000060  4040404040404040                32 SPOT   DC    CL100' '
                                        33        END
0000C8  5B5BC2D7C4E4D4D7                34               =CL8'$$BPDUMP'
0000D0  00000028000000C4                35               =A(FIVE,SPOT+100)
```

Fig. 12-7 Examples of uses for absolute and relocatable expressions

3. What action is taken if the assembler finds an asterisk (*) in column 1 of a coding line?

4. What is meant by the statement, "The assembler makes two passes over the source program."?

5. List the basic functions provided by the assembler on each of its two passes.

6. Why is the location counter so important to the assember in its translation process?

7. How does the assembler know how many bytes to allocate for a particular instruction?

8. Describe the difference between an absolute and a relocatable value.

9. Give some examples of the use of self-defining terms.

10. What advantages are there to the use of equate statements?

11. What restriction is placed on the use of a symbolic name in the operand field of an equate statement?

12. Does a location counter reference result in an absolute or a relocatable value?

13. Give one advantage and the major disadvantage of the use of literals for defining data within a program.

EXERCISES

1. How many bytes will the assembler allocate for each of the following source program instructions?
   a. an MVC instruction
   b. AREA   DC   C'ERROR MESSAGE'
   c. an MH instruction
   d. SEVEN   DC   F'7'
   e. an STM instruction
   f. INAREA   DS   DCL80
   g. an MVI instruction
   h. LOC   DC   CL7'ABCDEFGHIJ'

2. Using the following cross-reference table,

SYMBOL	LEN	VALUE	DEFN			
AMOUNT	00004	000138	00118	0024	0105	0136
BILLS	00004	0006A3	00212	0017	0145	
COMP	00006	000300	00170			
HOLD	00047	000309	00173			
PKT	00002	000304	00314	0016		

   answer these questions:

   a. In what statement number is the symbol BILLS defined?
   b. The symbol AMOUNT appears in the operand field of how many instructions?
   c. If the symbol HOLD appeared in the name field of a DC statement for a character-type constant, what length was specified in the length modifier subfield of the operand?
   d. If PKT is the name of a machine instruction, to which of the five general classes of machine instructions does this instruction belong?
   e. Could the symbol BILLS have appeared in the name field for the definition of a fullword constant?

3. Explain the syntax errors the assembler has located in its translation of the source program on the following page.

```
LOC   OBJECT CODE      ADDR1 ADDR2  STMT    SOURCE STATEMENT

                                      1            PRINT NOGEN
                                      2            FIRST  BEGIN=SIX,END=SAVE+8
000002                                9 LOC        EQU    2
00000C                               10 SAME       EQU    IN
           *** ERROR ***
00000C 5870 0002          00002      11            L      7,LOC
           *** ERROR ***
000010 4890 C03A          0003C      12            LH     9,SIX
000014 0000 0000          00000      13            M      9,FO
           *** ERROR ***
000018 0000 0000 0000 00000 00000    14            MVC    OUT(SIX),IN
           *** ERROR ***
00001E 4F40 C057          00059      15            CVB    4,NUM
           *** ERROR ***
                                     16            DH     4,SIX
           *** ERROR ***
000022 0000 0000 0000 00000 00000    17            MP     NUM,TRY
           *** ERROR ***
000028 0000 0000          00000      18            B      LOOP
           *** ERROR ***
00002C 0000 0000          00000      19            STM    6,SAVE
           *** ERROR ***
                                     20            LAST   BEGIN=SIX,END=SAVE+8
00003C 0006                          27 SIX        DC     H'6'
00003E                               28 OUT        DS     CL15
00004D 000000
000050 00000004                      29 FO         DC     F'4'
000054                               30 IN         DS     CL5
000059 658C                          31 NUM        DC     P'658'
                                     32 TRY        DC     P'875136
           *** ERROR ***
00005C                               33 SAVE       DS     2F
                                     34            END
000068 5B5BC2C7C4E4D4D7              35                   =CL8'$$BPDUMP'
000070 0000003C00000064              36                   =A(SIX,SAVE+8)
```

CROSS-REFERENCE

```
SYMBOL    LEN    VALUE  DEFN

FO        00004 000050 00029   0013
IN        00005 000054 00030   0010  0014
LOC       00001 000002 00009   0011
LOOP                           0018
NUM       00002 000059 00031   0015  0017
OUT       00015 00003E 00028   0014
SAME      00001 00000C 00010
SAVE      00004 00005C 00033   0007  0019  0023  0036
SIX       00002 00003C 00027   0007  0012  0014  0023  0036
TRY                            0017
```

DIAGNOSTICS

```
STMT   ERROR CODE    MESSAGE

   10  IJQ021        SYMBOL NOT PREVIOUSLY DEFINED
   11  IJQ033        ALIGNMENT ERROR
   13  IJQ010        INVALID SPECIFICATION OF REGISTER OR MASK FIELD
   14  IJQ003        LENGTH ERROR
   15  IJQ033        ALIGNMENT ERROR
   16  IJQ088        UNDEFINED OPERATION CODE
   17  IJQ024        UNDEFINED SYMBOL
   18  IJQ024        UNDEFINED SYMBOL
   19  IJQ010        INVALID SPECIFICATION OF REGISTER OR MASK FIELD
   19  IJQ039        INVALID DELIMITER
   32  IJQ087        NO ENDING APOSTROPHE
```

10 STATEMENTS FLAGGED IN THIS ASSEMBLY

CHAPTER 13

Fundamentals of Systems/360 and 370 Addressing

THE CONCEPT OF ADDRESSING

Thus far we have been using meaningful symbols to refer to constants, storage areas, and instructions in a program. The assembler has been converting these symbolic references into the actual addresses of specific bytes in the computer's storage area. Up to this point, the entrance macro (FIRST) has been causing the assembler to set this up for you. Now it is time to learn exactly how locations in storage are addressed and exactly what must be done to accomplish this.

In chapter 12, two types of symbols were discussed in the section on "Handling and Addressing of Operands." These are symbols to which an absolute value has been assigned, and those to which a relocatable value has been assigned. It is the relocatable symbols we are discussing in this chapter. The assembler created a block of code (machine code) from your source statements. This block of code is loaded into the computer's storage for execution. Another name for this block of code is a *Control SECTion*, or CSECT, for short.

When the assembler built the CSECT, it used a location counter to keep track of how much space it had used in the block. As it allocated space in the CSECT for each instruction, it incremented the value in the location counter to point to the next available byte in the CSECT.

As the assembler encountered a symbol in the name field, it used the current value in the location counter to note where in the block of code it encountered that symbol. It placed this value, along with the symbol, into its symbol table. When it encounters this same symbol in the operand field of an instruction, the assembler knows exactly what byte the symbol refers to in the block of code by referring to the location counter value for it in the symbol table. For example, if the assembler encounters the following instruction: LOOP   A 6,FOUR and the current value of the location counter is 8, the assembler knows that the machine instruction it generates for this add instruction will be located nine bytes from the beginning of the block of code.

The assembler's counter begins with a value of zero; in other words, it uses zero-origin rather than one-origin referencing, just as the computer's storage is based on a zero-origin. Bytes in the computer's storage are addressed in hexadecimal (base 16) just as the assembler's location counter values are. Figure 13-1 shows what this would look like in picture form.

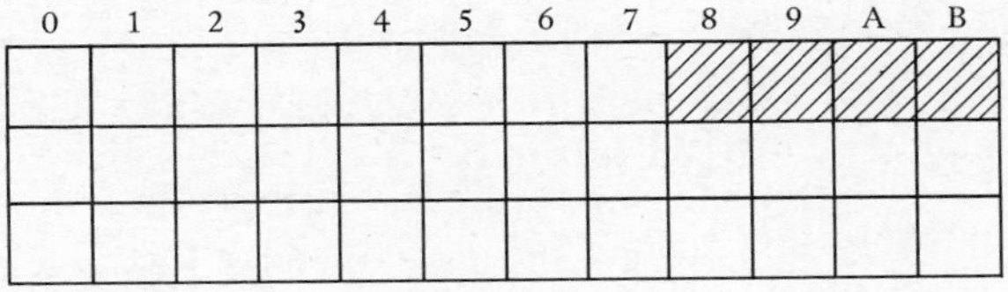

Fig. 13-1 Example of computer storage

By the time the assembler scanned the add instruction, it had allocated the first eight bytes in the CSECT it was creating. This add instruction is an RX type and occupies 4 bytes; therefore, it occupies the bytes with the location counter values of 8, 9, A, and B. When the assembler scans the following instruction on its second pass: BE LOOP and it encounters the symbol LOOP in the operand, it searches its symbol table and finds the symbol LOOP with a value of 8 associated with it. This value is substituted for the symbol LOOP in the machine instruction. The result is a branch instruction that will cause a branch to the byte with the address 8, the location of the add instruction.

The add instruction will always be in the same location in relation to the beginning of the CSECT. Every time the assembler encounters the symbol LOOP in an S1 or S2 operand of an instruction, it will substitute an 8 for that operand in the machine instruction.

THE NEED FOR RELOCATION

While the locations referred to by symbols remain constant in relation to the beginning of the block of code (CSECT) generated by the assembler, the entire block of code is not always loaded at the beginning of storage (address zero). That is, the assembler allocates space in the CSECT relative to zero (the original setting of the location counter), but the block of code may be loaded beginning at storage location 1000, 2000, 8A00, or any other double-word boundary.

Your reaction may be to ask why the block of code isn't always loaded at the beginning of storage—at address zero. To begin with, there must be a program already in storage that can load your block of code. There also has to be a program or programs that can handle any error conditions arising as your program executes. And these are but a few examples of the programs that must also occupy storage.

Note: Those of you using Disk Operating System/Virtual Storage, Operating System/Virtual Storage 1 or Operating System/Virtual Storage 2 (DOS/VS OS/VS1 and OS/VS2 for short) will find that your program, or parts of your program, will be relocated several times at different storage locations by the Dynamic Address Translation facility. How this happens and why this happens will be explained more fully in chapter 23. The only fact you must realize now is that your program will be relocated, that it won't be in storage beginning at address zero, and that you must account for this in some manner.

THE MEANS FOR RELOCATION

You should always expect your program to be relocated to an area of storage other than the location at address zero. Exactly where need never be known by you if you reference locations symbolically. The computer adds the address of where the beginning of the block is loaded into storage to the location counter value the assembler substituted for the symbol in the operand when it translated the instruction.

For example, if the block of code containing the Add and Branch instructions were loaded beginning at location 3000, the Branch instruction would have to branch to address 3008—the address of the first byte containing the machine code for the Add instruction. Since the program must always be assembled before it can be loaded into storage for execution, there is no way to know at assembly time at what address the block of code will be loaded.

Without knowing the beginning address, the assembler must still build machine code instructions, containing addresses, to reference the locations within your program that you referenced symbolically. To accomplish this the assembler uses one of the general purpose registers. This register will be used to hold the base (beginning) address for the block of code, and it is therefore referred to as the *base register*. The assembler will use the number of this register as it builds the machine code, under the assumption that one of the first executable instructions the programmer has in the program will fill that base register with the correct storage address.

THE PROCESS OF ESTABLISHING ADDRESSABILITY

At this point, how addressability with relocation can be accomplished may seem confusing. Keep the following things in mind:

1. The programmer has responsibilities in setting up the base register.
2. The assembler has the job of building machine code to reflect the programmer's responsibilities.
3. At execution time, the work of the assembler and the programmer is fulfilled.

THE PROGRAMMER'S RESPONSIBILITIES

The programmer must choose a general purpose register for the assembler to use for relocation purposes and inform the assembler which register he has chosen. This register is known as the base register because it will contain the base address from which all relationships are calculated for all relocatable symbols that the assembler must resolve.

The programmer must also inform the assembler what address will be in this base register. This address may point to the first byte in the CSECT when it is loaded, or it may point to another byte. The important thing to remember here is that the address in the base register must be closer to the beginning of the program than any byte referenced by a symbol. This ensures that the relation between the address in the base register and the address of any location referenced by a symbol is a positive one. The assembler must be able to calculate a positive number which, when added to the value in the base register, defines the actual address of the byte in storage referenced by the symbol. This positive number added to the contents of the base register is called the *displacement*.

Once you indicate which general-purpose register the assembler may use as a base register and what address will be in that register, it is imperative that you abide by these indications.

FULFILLING THE PROGRAMMER'S RESPONSIBILITIES

There is a special instruction to the assembler called the USING instruction. This instruction informs the assembler which register it may use as the base and what value will be in that register at execution time. The assembler pseudo-op† USING is placed in the opcode field. In the first operand, you specify the address the assembler can assume will be in the base register at

---

†An assembler pseudo-op is an instruction to the assembler. It does not cause the assembler to generate a machine code instruction. It merely gives the assembler some information.

execution time, and in the second operand you specify the base register number. For example:

```
            USING   *,12
BEGIN       L       6,AREA
```

This USING instruction gives the assembler two pieces of information:

1. It may use register 12 as the base register.
2. It should build machine code addresses as if the base register (register 12 in this case) contains the current value of the location counter (the asterisk denotes this). This is the address of the first byte allocated to the Load instruction (the same address that is associated with the symbol BEGIN).

The Assembler's Job   Adding a few other instructions to our example in the previous section:

```
0   PROG        CSECT
0               SR      8,8
2               USING   *,12
2   BEGIN       L       6,AREA
                 .
                 .
                 .
24  AREA        DC      F'7'
```

As the assembler makes its first pass, it builds the following symbol table:

Symbol	Value	Length
PROG	0	
BEGIN	2	4
AREA	24	4

As it begins its second pass, the assembler sets its location counter back to zero and examines each instruction in sequence. It allocates the bytes with location counter values of 0 and 1 to the SR instruction, builds the machine code, and increments its location counter to a value of 2. The USING instruction informs the assembler that it may use register 12 as the base (also called relocation) register. It informs the assembler that the actual storage address equivalent to the current value in the location counter will be in register 12 at execution time. This is the address of the byte that is 2 bytes from where the CSECT is loaded into storage.

Since USING is an assembler pseudo-op, no machine code is generated; therefore, no space is allocated in the block of machine code. The assembler merely records the two important pieces of information it has been given; the location counter remains unchanged.

The assembler examines the next instruction (L), notes that it belongs to the RX-type of instructions, and allocates four bytes in the block of machine code (location counter values 2, 3, 4, and 5). As it builds the machine code for this instruction, it resolves the address for the symbol AREA in the operand.

To resolve the address for a symbol, the assembler finds that symbol in its symbol table and locates the value associated with it. In the case of the symbol AREA, that value is 24. Now the assembler takes the information it was given in the USING statement and calculates the displacement for the symbol AREA. Remember, the displacement is the positive number that when added to the contents of the base register results in the address associated with the symbol being resolved. What positive number can be added to the contents of Register 12 to calculate a value of 24?

desired value of:	24
− assumed contents of register 12:	2
displacement	22

Once the assembler has calculated the displacement, it builds it, along with the base register number, into the machine code for the load instruction and proceeds to handle the next instruction. An RX-type instruction occupies 4 bytes of storage. The format of the machine code for an RX-format instruction is:

Where: Bits 0–7 contain the machine code for the operation to be performed.

Bits 8–11 contain the hexadecimal equivalent of the first operand register number.

Bits 12–15 contain the hexadecimal equivalent of the index register number for the second operand (explained in chapter 14).

Bits 16–19 contain the hexadecimal equivalent of the base register for the second operand.

Bits 20–31 contain the displacement value for the second operand (in hexadecimal).

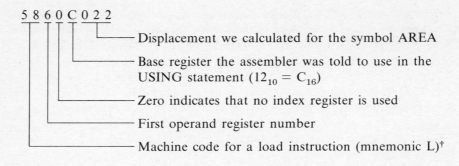

5 8 6 0 C 0 2 2

— Displacement we calculated for the symbol AREA

— Base register the assembler was told to use in the USING statement ($12_{10} = C_{16}$)

— Zero indicates that no index register is used

— First operand register number

— Machine code for a load instruction (mnemonic L)[†]

[†]For a complete list of machine code opcodes see appendix 3, the IBM System/360 Reference Data Card (GX20-1703), or the IBM System/370 Reference Summary Card (GX20-1850).

Fig. 13-2 First machine-code example

Figure 13-2 shows how our Load instruction would look in machine code. The machine code formats for the other types of instructions can be seen in figure 13-3.

EXECUTION TIME, CALCULATION OF EFFECTIVE ADDRESSES

When it comes time to execute an instruction that contains a reference to storage, the process is straightforward. The number of the base register and the displacement are fetched from the instruction where the assembler placed them. The displacement and the contents of the base register are added to calculate an *effective address*. This is the actual storage address of where this operand is located. For instance, let's use the machine code for our Load instruction as an example: 5 8 6 0 C 0 2 2.

The number of the base register (C) and the displacement (022) are fetched from the instruction where the assembler placed them—bits 16–19 and bits 20–31, respectively. This displacement, and whatever the contents of the base register happen to be, are added to calculate the effective address. One thing to remember with effective addresses is that in Systems/360 and 370 they are 24 bits long. Only the low-order three bytes of the base register participate in the calculation of the effective address; the high-order byte is ignored.

The above discussion of the computer's straightforward calculation of effective addresses brings to mind the promises the programmer made in the USING statement: not only that the assembler could use register 12 as the base register, but also that in that register at execution time would be the base storage address. That base register must be filled before any instruction that requires the computer to calculate an effective address executes.

RR Format

OPCODE	R1	R2

0　　　　　7 8　11 12 15

RX Format

OPCODE	R1	X2	B2	D2

0　　　　　7 8　11 12 15 16 19 20　　　31

RS Format

OPCODE	R1	R3	B2	D2

0　　　　　7 8　11 12 15 16 19 20　　　31

SI Format

OPCODE	I2	B1	D1

0　　　　　7 8　　　15 16 19 20　　　31

SS Format　　　　　　L

OPCODE	L1	L2	B1	D1	B2	D2

0　　　　　7 8　11 12 15 16 19 20　　　31 32 35 36　　　47

Where　R　= register
　　　　B　= base register
　　　　D　= displacement
　　　　X　= index register
　　　　I　= immediate area
　　　　L　= length
　　　　1　= first operand
　　　　2　= second operand
　　　　3　= third operand

Fig. 13-3　Machine-code formats

So far we have not filled our base register with the base address. If we fail to fill register 12 with the address of where that load instruction is actually placed in storage, the computer uses whatever register 12 happens to contain as part of the effective address calculations.

To understand the method used to fill the base register with the correct address, you must realize that the central processing unit (CPU) of the computer has acces to an *instruction address counter*. This address counter provides a function for the CPU that is similar to the function provided for the assembler by the location counter.

The location counter keeps track of the next byte the assembler has available for allocation in the CSECT it is building. The instruction address counter keeps track of the storage address of the beginning of the next instruction that is to be executed. It contains the actual address of the first byte of the next instruction to be fetched, interpreted, and executed. (In System/370 it can contain what is called a logical instruction address, explained in chapter 23.)

An instruction called the Branch and Link Register, opcode BALR, can be used to pick up the contents of the instruction address counter and place this contents in a general purpose register. The BALR instruction belongs to the RR-class of instructions. Its general format is: BALR   R1,R2.

R1 is the register into which the contents of the instruction address counter is placed. R2 is used as the branching register. It usually contains the address of the next instruction to be executed. (This instruction is generally used for a special type of branching operation that will be explained more fully in chapters 14 and 15.) We do not wish to use the branching capability of the BALR instruction, so we will specify register zero in the second operand.

Register zero can never be used for the purpose of addressing. Whenever a zero appears in any portion of an instruction where part of a storage address is to appear, what is indicated is that that portion of the storage address is not to participate in the calculation of the effective address. Remember the example of the machine code for the Load instruction in figure 13-2, where bits 12–15 contained a value of zero to indicate that no index register was used, since we have not yet discussed index registers.

When a zero appears in the second operand of the BALR instruction, it means that R1 is to receive the current contents of the instruction address counter (the address of the next sequential instruction), and then the next sequential instruction in the program is to be fetched and executed. The second operand is register 0. Register 0 cannot be used for addressing purposes, so no branch takes place. Figure 13-4 shows how the previous example looks with the base register properly initialized.

On its first pass, the assembler placed the symbols EXAMPL, FIRST, and AREA in its symbol table along with the location counter values associated with these symbols; 0, 2, and 24, respectively. As the assembler begins its second pass, it resets its location counter to zero. It allocates the first two bytes for the BALR instruction and builds the machine code (05C0). It then scans the USING instruction and receives two important pieces of information: (1) It may use register 12 as the base register in resolving any symbolic references the programmer might make to storage locations; and (2) The address in register 12 will be the address of the actual byte of storage where the load instruction begins.

```
0   EXAMPL    CSECT
0             BALR    12,0
2             USING   *,12
2   FIRST     L       6,AREA
              AR      6,6
                .
                .
                .
24  AREA      DC      F'8'
              END
```

Fig. 13-4 Initialization of the base register

In handling the next instruction (the Load) on its second pass, the assembler allocates four bytes in the CSECT for the instruction (it belongs to the RX-class). The assembler resolves the operand portion of this instruction by looking up the symbol AREA in its symbol table. It then calculates the displacement necessary for computation of an effective address at execution time equivalent to a location counter value of 24 at assembly time.

$$
\begin{array}{lr}
\text{desired location counter value} & 24 \\
- \text{ assumed contents of base register} & 2 \\
\hline
\text{displacement} & 22
\end{array}
$$

A displacement of 22 is built into the second operand portion of the machine instruction, along with the fact that register 12 is the base register: 5860C022. The assembler builds the machine code for the remainder of the program, and the object module is loaded and executed.

Let us assume that the instruction address counter contains 3000, the beginning address of the block of code (the CSECT). The instruction at the address indicated by the address counter (the BALR) is fetched, interpreted, and executed. As the BALR instruction is fetched, the address counter is incremented by the length of the fetched instruction (two bytes in this case). Therefore, as the BALR instruction executes, it causes the current value in the address counter (3002) to be placed in the first operand register, register 12. This is the actual equivalent to the address (0002) pledged by the programmer in the USING statement.

The instruction at the address indicated by the address counter is now fetched, the address counter is updated (to 3006), and the Load instruction is interpreted and executed. The displacement portion of the second operand (16 in this case) is added to the contents of the base register (register 12), and the effective address is generated.

$$
\begin{array}{lr}
\text{actual base register contents} & 3002 \\
+ \text{ displacement} & \underline{022} \\
\text{effective address} & 3024
\end{array}
$$

The fullword located at effective address 3024 (the 00000008) is loaded into register 6. The instruction at the address indicated by the address counter (the AR) is now fetched, interpreted, and executed. And so it goes through the the end of the program.

You should begin to see now just how important it is that you fulfill the promises made to the assembler in the USING statement. Without a USING statement, you cannot symbolically reference storage; and once you have placed a USING statement in your program, you have caused an automatic process to take place at execution time.

Effective addresses are generated for each operand of every instruction that references storage locations. If you don't fill the base register with the promised value, fill it with the wrong value, or mistakenly use the base register for another purpose in your program, you will cause addressing errors at execution time.

Once your program starts to execute, the base register number has been built into every instruction that references storage. As each of those instructions executes, the displacement is added to the contents of the low-order three bytes of the base register, and the resultant value will be used as an effective address.

Depending on the opcode of the instruction involved and the particular erroneous effective address calculated, the results can be catastrophic when you destroy a base register. You can attempt to store the contents of a register in an area of storage that does not belong to you. You can cause a specification error because an effective address with an invalid boundary alignment was generated. You may even cause the invalid execution of an instruction to destroy other instructions or data. Base registers are an important and integral part of the structure of the S/360 and S/370 computers, and they should be treated as such.

USE OF THE FIRST AND LAST MACROS

Now that you can establish addressability for the relocatable symbols in your programs, you no longer have to depend on the macros to perform this service for you. You can indicate this fact by placing the keyword operand SETUP=NO in the operand portion of the FIRST macro. This will prevent the macro from generating the BALR and USING instructions. You will continue to specify the beginning (BEGIN=) and ending (END=) addresses for the purpose of dumping the contents of storage before execution. Your source program will now look similar to this:

```
EXAMPL   CSECT
         PRINT   NOGEN
         BALR    12,0
         USING   *,12
         FIRST   SETUP=NO,BEGIN=AREA,END=LOC+2
STRT     L       6,AREA
         AR      6,6
         LAST    BEGIN=AREA,END=LOC+2
AREA     DC      F'8'
LOC      DS      H
         END
```

QUESTIONS

1. What is the difference between absolute and relocatable symbols?

2. Is the computer's storage addressing one- or zero-origin?

3. On which of its two passes does the assembler resolve symbolic references to storage?

4. Why is relocation necessary, and how is it accomplished?

5. What two pieces of information does the USING instruction give to the assembler?

6. How may the base register be loaded with the base address at execution time?

EXERCISES

1. What are the effective addresses that will be generated when the following instructions are executed? Register 12 contains a value of 00007500.

   a. 5AA0C0BC
   b. 5020C7C4
   c. D274C49BCA60
   d. 5D90C540
   e. 92C3C0F1

2. Why does the relation between the address in the base register and that of a location referenced by a symbol always have to be a positive one?

3. What is the effect of not placing the BALR and USING instructions in the following section of code?

```
PROB2    CSECT
         USING    *,12
         BALR     12,0
         L        8,LOC
         AR       8,8
         ST       8,LOC2
          .
          .
          .
LOC      DC       F'278'
LOC2     DS       F
         END
```

4. How do you think the execution of the following program will be stopped?

```
PROB4    CSECT
         BALR     *,12
         USING    12,0
         L        8,AREA
         SR       12,12
         ST       8,LOC
          .
          .
          .
AREA     DC       F'681'
LOC      DS       F
         END
```

Data Structures, Looping, and Address Modification

In chapter 13 you learned the basics of the Systems/360 and 370 addressing structures. In this chapter you will learn what an index register is and how to use one in references to collections of data. You will learn how to specify addresses explicitly, rather than implying addresses symbolically; you will learn address modification and special branching instructions.

REFERENCING COLLECTIONS OF DATA

There are times in programming when we are working with large amounts of similar data. This demands that we organize it. Either we collect this similar data into contiguous storage locations (a table), or we connect similar groups of information by linking each group to the next (a list, or queue). Having done so, we can use a general algorithm to retrieve any piece of information from the data structure. What algorithm we use depends on how we organize the data.

INTRODUCTION TO TABLES

A *table* consists of collections of related data items. Each collection of information within the table is called an *element*. The table is given a symbolic name which refers to the beginning of the table. A reference can be made to a particular element within a table by giving its relation to the symbolic name. For example, consider figure 14-1. This table contains four elements of

TAB

Fig. 14-1   A conceptual view of a table

data. Each element is four bytes long and contains one word of data. This means that the entire table occupies 16 bytes of storage. You are already aware that the 16 bytes of contiguous storage looks conceptually like figure 14-2.

The structure in figure 14-1 is generally used to represent a table, because it is easier for the programmer to visualize the relations between the elements. Always keep in mind, however, that the space a table occupies in computer storage is more closely reflected by illustrations such as figure 14-2.

Regardless of which way you visualize this table, each element in it is referred to by referencing its relative position within the table. The first element (the beginning of the table) can be referenced simply by using the symbol TAB. The second element is referenced by TAB+4, indicating that the first byte in the second element of the table TAB is 4 bytes from the one represented by the symbol TAB. If a program were coded to sum the contents of the four elements of TAB, it might contain one Load and three Add instructions. For example:

```
L   7,TAB
A   7,TAB+4
A   7,TAB+8
A   7,TAB+12
```

When the third Add instruction has been executed, register 7 contains the sum of the values in the 4 elements of the table called TAB.

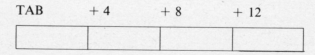

Fig. 14-2   An actual view of a table in storage

USING INDEX REGISTERS IN ADDRESS MODIFICATION

Extend the above example to sum the values contained in a table that has 50 elements. Using the above approach to coding, we must write one Load and 49 Add instructions! "Bad coding," you say. "There must be another method." Well, you are right. There is a method whereby we can use one Add instruction instead of forty-nine. This approach uses a concept known as *indexing*. A general purpose register will be used to hold a value that can be added to the address represented by the symbol TAB. If register 6 is the index register, the Add instruction appears as follows: A   7,TAB(6). Whatever value register 6 contains when this Add instruction executes will be used as an increment to the address represented by the symbol TAB. If register 6 contains 00000004, the instruction will add the value in the second element of the table (TAB) to the contents of register 7. It has the same effect as: A   7,TAB+4.

The advantage of using an index register is that its value can be changed at execution time. For example, if the Add instruction: A   7,TAB(6) is part of a loop of instructions, another instruction within this same loop can add a value of 4 to the contents of register 6: Each time the Add instruction is executed to calculate the sum, it contains a value 4 more than the last time it was executed (as is shown in figure 14-3).

Each time statement 3 is executed, the value from one element in the table is added to the contents of register 7. Statement 3 is the body, or functional portion, of this loop. Statements 1 and 2 initialize the index register and the sum to zero. Statements 4, 5, and 6 comprise the control portion of the loop. Statement 4 is sometimes referred to as the modification, or adjustment portion, of the loop. It modifies the contents of register 6 that is used not only as an index register but also as the register containing the control value for the loop.

```
1              SR    6,6             INITIALIZE INDEX REGISTER
2              SR    7,7             INITIALIZE SUM REGISTER
3 LOOP         A     7,TAB(6)        ADD ONE ELEMENT VALUE TO SUM
4              A     6,FOUR          INCREMENT INDEX REGISTER
5              C     6,TWOHUND       CHECK FOR TERMINAL INDEX VALUE
6              BNE   LOOP            BRANCH TO ADD ANOTHER ELEMENT
7              ST    7,ANS           ALL ELEMENTS SUMMED, STORE RESULT
               .
               .
               .
   FOUR        DC    F'4'            INDEX REGISTER INCREMENT VALUE
   TWOHUND     DC    F'200'          TERMINAL INDEX VALUE
   ANS         DS    F               LOCATION FOR STORING RESULT
```

Fig. 14-3 Summing the elements of a fifty-element table

This loop has finished its execution when the contents of the fiftieth element of TAB has been added to the sum in register 7, which occurs when statement 3 has executed with a value of 200 in the index register. Statement 5 tests for this particular condition in register 6. If the condition is not found, a branch is taken to instruction 3, and another iteration of the loop takes place. If 200 has been reached when statement 6 checks, then an exit is taken from the loop, and statement 7 will store the sum in ANS. This problem appears in flowchart form in figure 14-4.

As in every loop, the things to be careful about are the initialization of values for the first execution of the loop and the test for exit from it. This test must ensure that the last element in the table is handled correctly, that the loop is

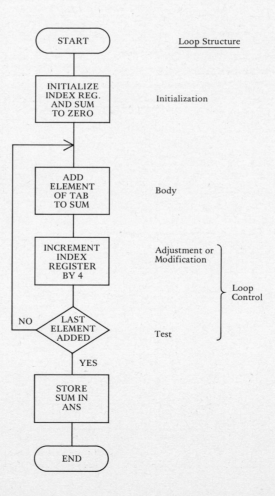

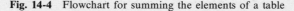

Fig. 14-4 Flowchart for summing the elements of a table

not exited after the forty-ninth element has been added, or that the loop makes no attempt to add the nonexistent fifty-first element to the sum.

SEARCH-REFERENCE AND DIRECT-REFERENCE TABLES

Conceptually, we will be using two different types of tables—the search-reference table and the direct-reference table.

The tables in figures 14-5 and 14-6 each have three elements. The only difference is that in the search-reference table, each element is divided into an argument portion and a function portion, while each element in the direct-reference table contains only a function portion.

SEARCH-REFERENCE TABLES

It is easiest to think of each element in the search-reference table as having a key in its argument portion. If you are looking for the information in a particular element, you use that element's key to locate it. For example, the payroll department has a table of salary information. To locate the salary of a particular employee, you must know that employee's identification number (ID), the key (argument portion). Figure 14-7 shows how this table would look.

Argument	Function

Fig. 14-5 The search-reference table

Function

Fig. 14-6 The direct-reference table

ID No.	Salary
7916	0017550C
1094	0012500C
2237	0008525C
6410	0025775C

Fig. 14-7 Table of salary information

The programming in this problem is much the same as the steps you would take if you were seeking salary information from the table. You must know the ID number of the individual whose salary you want to know. You take this number and compare it, one by one, to ID numbers in the table. When you find a matching number in the first column, you look at the corresponding value in the second column (the salary). If you cannot find the ID number you are looking for in the first column, then you know that there is a mistake somewhere; either you do not have the person's correct ID number, the individual is not an employee of this firm, or his number has inadvertently been omitted from the table.

In programming, everything is given special names, but you do the same exact tasks in everyday life. You compare a search argument (the ID number for the employee whose salary you are seeking) to the argument portion of successive elements in the table. This is done by starting with an index value of zero and incrementing it by the number of bytes in an element each time you look at a new argument. Should you find a match, an equal condition (sometimes referred to as a *hit*), you increment your index register by the number of bytes in the argument portion, and you access the function portion of that element. You are serially searching this table for an argument that matches your search argument. If the index register is incremented to a value that when added to the address represented by the symbolic name of the table generates an address beyond the end of the table, then you know your search argument is not in the table. This serial search of a search reference table is given in flowchart form in figure 14-8.

The only things to watch for in coding this problem—in addition to the things you normally watch on coding any loop—are the increments of the index register.

WAGES

ID Number	Salary
7916	0017550C
1094	0012500C
2237	0008525C
6410	0025775C

The argument portion of each element in the above table contains 4 bytes of data. The function portion of each contains a 4-byte packed-decimal number with two implied decimal places. The table is to be named WAGES. The DC statements needed to set up this table are:

```
WAGES    DC    F'7916'
         DC    PL4'17550'
         DC    F'1094'
         DC    PL4'12500'
         etc.
```

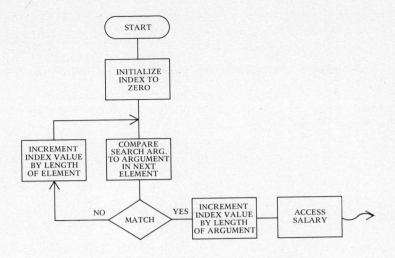

Fig. 14-8 Flowchart for serial search

Because the ID number is 4 bytes long, is in fixed-point binary format and aligned on fullword boundaries, the opcode C can be used to compare the ID number we are searching for to the one in the argument portion of each successive element. Figure 14-9 shows one series of statements that will perform a serial search of the table called WAGES.

Register 8 is used as the index register. The symbol TRYAGAIN is the label on the group of instructions that searches the table; MATCH is the label on the first instruction of the group that handles the salary when the correct ID number is found in the table; and NOTIN is the label on the instruction that gets control when the entire table has been searched and a match for the required ID number is not found.

DIRECT-REFERENCE TABLES

The elements in a direct-reference table contain only function portions (no arguments) as illustrated below. In this type of table the key is used directly to reference a particular element in the table. For example, the following table contains interest rates charged to various categories of customers.

0600
0700
0750
0850
0925

```
SEARCH      CSECT
            BALR    12,0            ESTABLISH
            USING   *,12             ADDRESSABILITY
            SR      8,8             INITIALIZE INDEX REGISTER
            L       9,SRCHARG       FETCH I.D. FOR SEARCH ARGUMENT
TRYAGAIN    C       9,WAGES(8)      COMPARE I.D.'S
            BE      MATCH           BRANCH IF I.D.'S MATCH
            A       8,EIGHT         INCREMENT INDEX REGISTER
            C       8,END           ALL I.D.'S CHECKED
            BE      NOTIN           YES, SEARCH ARG. NOT IN TABLE
            B       TRYAGAIN        CHECK NEXT I.D.
MATCH       A       8,FOUR          INCREMENT INDEX REGISTER TO
*                                   ACCESS SALARY
                    .
                    .
                    .

NOTIN
                    .
                    .
                    .
SRCHARG     DC      F'2237'         I.D. SEARCHED FOR
EIGHT       DC      F'8'            SIZE OF ELEMENT
FOUR        DC      F'4'            SIZE OF ARGUMENT
END         DC      F'32'           TERMINAL INDEX VALUE
            END
```

Fig. 14-9 Code for serial search of table

Each customer has a credit rating between 1 and 5. Whenever a request for a loan by a customer is read into the computer, his credit rating is also read. A credit rating of 2 entitles the customer to a loan at 6% interest, a rating of 3 a loan at $7\frac{1}{2}\%$ interest, a rating of 4 a loan at $8\frac{1}{2}\%$, and so on. If the symbolic name of the table is INTTAB, and each element in the table occupies a halfword, multiplying the credit rating, minus 1, by a value of 2 and using the result as an index value, the proper element within INTTAB can be referenced directly.

After the execution of the second Load instruction in figure 14-10, register 9 contains the interest rate of $8\frac{1}{2}\%$, the interest for a customer who has a credit rating of 4.

Another frequent use for direct-reference tables is in the tabulation of responses to questionnaires. The questionnaires are designed to permit the expression of each answer as a numeric digit (multiple-choice responses). The answers to each question are stored in a table, with the first element containing the total of the answers of 1 for that question, the second element the total count of the two answers to that question, and so on. The input card giving responses for a particular questionnaire might have the format given in figure 14-11.

```
        L     7,RATING        FETCH CREDIT RATING
        S     7,ONE           MANIPULATE CREDIT RATING TO
        M     6,TWO            OBTAIN INDEX VALUE
        LH    9,INTTAB(7)     ACCESS TABLE
        .
        .
        .

RATING  DC    F'4'            CREDIT RATING
ONE     DC    F'1'
TWO     DC    F'2'
* THE DIRECT REFERENCE INTEREST RATE TABLE
INTTAB  DC    H'600'
        DC    H'700'
        DC    H'750'
        DC    H'850'
        DC    H'925'
        END
```

Fig. 14-10   Code for using direct-reference table

Column	Contents	Indication of Digit
1	Sex:	1–male 2–female
2	Marital Status:	1–single 2–married 3–other
5	Income Bracket:	1–$5,000-$8,000 2– 8,001-10,000 3–10,001-15,000 4–15,001-20,000 5–20,001-25,000 6–over $25,000
10	Education Level:	1–through 8th grade 2–through 12th grade 3–Associate Degree 4–Bachelor's Degree 5–Graduate Degree

Fig. 14-11   Questionnaire input-card format

The table to keep track of the income brackets would contain six elements, because there are six possible choices in answer to that question. To tabulate this part of the questionnaire, the cards in the input file are read into INAREA, and the steps given in figure 14-12 are taken.

```
* CODE TO HANDLE INCOME BRACKETS
          PACK    INCOM,MONEY       PREPARE THE INCOME VALUE TO BE
          CVB     7,INCOM              CALCULATED AS A RESPONSE
          C       7,MAXINDEX        IS THIS A VALID RESPONSE
          BNL     ERROR             NO, BRANCH TO PRINT ERROR MSG.
          S       7,ONE             CONTINUE PREPARING THE INCOME
          M       6,TWO                VALUE
          LH      2,INCBRAC(6)      FETCH RESPONSE RECORD
          A       2,ONE             INCREMENT RESPONSE RECORD
          STH     2,INCBRAC(6)      REPLACE INCREMENTED RESPONSE RCD.
          .
          .
          .
INAREA    DS      0CL80             INPUT AREA FOR RESPONSES
SEX       DS      C
MARITAL   DS      C
SKIP      DS      CL2
MONEY     DS      CL2
MONEY     DS      C
          .
          .
          .
ONE       DC      F'1'
TWO       DC      F'2'
MAXINDEX  DC      F'6'              HIGHEST VALID BRACKET
INCOM     DS      D
INCBRAC   DC      6H'0'             DIRECT REFERENCE TABLE FOR STORING
*                                   INCOME BRACKET RESPONSES
```

Fig. 14-12   Questionnaire code (direct-reference table)

The code to handle each of the questions would be similar to that displayed in figure 14-12 (for handling income brackets). The response must be converted to binary, checked to make sure the response is a valid digit (a value between 1 and 6 in this case), a 1 subtracted from the digit to allow for the zero origin of the table, multiplied by the size of the element in the table, and the resulting value used to access and increment the contents of the element in the table that holds the count of that particular response to the question.

When the end-of-file is reached on the input file, each of the tables contains the breakdown of responses to its question. Averages and percentages can be calculated and printed reports made.

EXPLICIT ADDRESSING

Our two coding examples on the use of tables were made easy because the payroll example used a table with elements of two words each, and the questionnaire example used tables with halfword elements. This made it possible to access the elements, or the portions of the elements, by using fullword and halfword instructions.

There are, however, many cases when the information to be stored in tables does not conform to this sort of regimen. For instance, the payroll example could have had an argument portion that contained social security rather than ID numbers. Social security numbers are of the format: XXX-XX-XXXX; and since they contain special characters, this portion of the element would have to be in character, rather than binary or packed-decimal format.

The argument portion of the table would occupy 11 bytes. Once this change has been made to the table, the C and CH instructions can no longer be used to search the arguments for a match to the search argument. The CLC instruction is needed. The CLC (Compare Logical Character) instruction belongs to the SS-class of instructions. It therefore can compare arguments of greater length and not depend on those arguments being aligned on any special integral boundary.

Because the CLC is an SS-type of instruction, an index register cannot be used. The instructions belonging to the RX-class of instructions are the only ones in the repertoire of Systems/360 and 370 that have the capability of using registers for the purpose of indexing. This does not mean, however, that the CLC instruction does not have the ability to use addresses that can be altered dynamically at execution time. This can be accomplished by explicitly specifying the address.

Explicit addressing permits the programmer to accept the responsibility for referencing storage that he has previously relegated to the assembler. *Implicit addressing* has permitted the programmer to symbolically reference storage locations and to depend on the assembler to resolve the references to storage implied by the symbols. Such an address is established at assembly time (a displacement and the contents of a base register), and its resolution at execution time is fixed. The programmer cannot, at execution time, request the assembler to alter the address in any manner.

Through explicit addressing the programmer picks the base register he wishes to use for the execution of an individual instruction. He can fill this register with any value he wants at execution time, and he can alter its contents at execution time whenever he desires. The following is an example of DC statements that could establish the payroll table containing social security numbers in the argument portion of the table.

```
WAGES    DC    CL11'672-34-7916'
         DC    PL4'17550'
         DC    CL11'452-68-1094'
         DC    PL4'12500'
         etc.
```

If the social security number we are searching for has been read into an 11-byte area labeled SARG, the code given in figure 14-13 could be used to search the argument portion of the table.

```
SEARCH      CSECT
            BALR    12,0                ESTABLISH
            USING   *,12                  ADDRESSABILITY
            .
            .

            .
            LA      6,WAGES             ADDRESS OF SALARY INFO. TABLE
TRYAGAIN    CLC     SARG(11),0(6)       CHECK FOR DESIRED ARGUMENT
            BE      MATCH               BRANCH IF A MATCH IS FOUND
            A       6,FIFTEEN           INCREMENT INDEX REGISTER
            C       6,END               END OF TABLE?
            BE      NOTIN               YES, ARG. NOT IN THE TABLE
            B       TRYAGAIN            CHECK NEXT ARGUMENT
MATCH       A       6,ELEVN             INCREMENT INDEX REGISTER TO REACH
*                                         FUNCTION
            .
            .

            .
FIFTEEN     DC      F'15'               SIZE OF ELEMENT
ELEVN       DC      F'11'               SIZE OF ARGUMENT
            END
```

Fig. 14-13   Explicit-addressing coding example

As the assembler examines the CLC instruction, it resolves the symbolic reference to storage in the first operand by using the base register it was given in the USING statement (register 12) and calculating the displacement for the symbol SARG, using the address promised in the USING statement (by the programmer) to be in the base register at execution time. These two numbers, along with the length of the field, are placed in the machine code generated by the assembler for this CLC instruction. Because the second operand was not specified symbolically, the assembler does not examine it; it simply places the displacement (000_{16}) and the base register (register 6) in the machine code.

Because the programmer has chosen to specify the second operand address explicitly, it is his responsibility to ensure that the correct address is generated at execution time. This is accomplished by the Load Address (LA) instruction, which at execution time places in register 6 the actual address of the beginning of the payroll table. After the LA instruction executes, register 6 contains the actual effective address for the table.

Nothing needs to be added to the address in register 6 to access the first social security number in the table. However, you will notice that a displacement is specified in the second operand portion of the CLC instruction. Even though a displacement of zero is needed, the zero *must* still be present to enable the second operand to be syntactically correct. (The assembler cannot interpret a left parenthesis immediately following the comma.)

Let us extend our discussion of explicit addressing with additional examples, since this technique can be used in any operand that references storage. Take, for example, the case where you already have the address of a table in register 5. You know that the table is aligned on a fullword boundary and that each element in the table is a fullword. What you wish to accomplish is to compute the average of the fifteen elements in the table. This can be accomplished by the following segment of code.

```
              LR    9,5           GET SECOND COPY OF TABLE ADDRESS
              A     9,SIXTY       COMPUTE END OF TABLE ADDRESS
              SR    7,7           INITIALIZE SUM TO ZERO
SUMAGIN       A     7,0(5)        ADD ELEMENT TO SUM
              A     5,FOUR        INCREMENT INDEX REGISTER
              CR    5,9           END OF TABLE?
              BL    SUMAGIN       NO, BRANCH TO ADD NEXT ELEMENT
              M     6,ONE         SET UP FOR DIVISION
              D     6,FIFTN       COMPUTE AVERAGE
              .
              .
              .
SIXTY         DC    F'60'         TERMINAL VALUE FOR INDEX
FOUR          DC    F'4'          SIZE OF ELEMENT
ONE           DC    F'1'
FIFTN         DC    F'15'         NUMBER OF ELEMENTS IN TABLE
              END
```

The instruction labeled SUMAGIN is an Add instruction belonging to the RX-class of instructions. Notice that the general format for the operand portion of an RX instruction is: R1,D2(X2,B2). This format indicates that if we are going to explicitly specify a base register for the second operand, it should syntactically follow the comma within the set of parentheses. In other words, our Add instruction should have looked like: A   7,0(0,5).

Remember that register zero cannot be used for addressing purposes. Whenever a zero appears in an operand in a location where an address is expected, it indicates that that portion of the address is not to participate in the calculation of the effective address. If register 5 contains 00006500, the calculation of the effective addresses for both Add instructions follows:

	A 7,0(5)	A 7,0(0,5)
base register	———	006500
index register	006500	———
displacement	000	000
	006500	006500

Notice that the effective address calculated in each case is identical (006500). An effective address in the case of an RX instruction is calculated by adding the contents of the low-order 24 bits of the base register, if used; the contents of the low-order 24 bits of the index register, if used; and the 12-bit displacement. (If it helps you to keep things straight in your mind, use 0(0,5), but 0(5) will generate the same effective address.)

The following are the general formats of all types of instructions except the RR-type, which does not reference storage:

Type	*Operand Format*
RX	R1,D2(X2,B2)
RS	R1,R3,D2(B2)
SI	D1(B1),I2
SS	D1(L,B1),D2(B2)
	or
	D1(L1,B1),D2(L2,B2)

Using the following register contents:

Reg. 0: 00007800   Reg. 4: 00000014   Reg. 7: 00010578
Reg. 9: 00000270   Reg. 10: 00006800

what effective addresses are generated when the following instructions execute?

(A)	ST	6,6(10)
(B)	S	8,0(4,7)
(C)	MVC	2(4,10),7(7)
(D)	M	2,8(0,10)
(E)	L	1,8(4)
(F)	LM	1,3,12(10)
(G)	CLI	5(7),C'B'
(H)	PACK	0(5,7),2(4,10)

Some of the above instructions have operands specifically designed to test your knowledge. Certain ones will be discussed more, but here are the effective addresses you should have calculated:

(A)   006806
(B)   01058C
(C)   006802 and 01057F
(D)   006808
(E)   00001C
(F)   006A7C
(G)   01057D
(H)   010578 and 006802

Question A is very straightforward. B should bring to mind the fact that addresses are in hexadecimal, because $8 + 4 = C$. C reminds you that SS instructions contain two effective addresses and that in the case of the MVC instruction, the number of bytes to be moved is specified in the first operand immediately following the left parenthesis (4 in this case). A length will usually appear in operands of SS instructions, which are specified explicitly. No length can possibly be implied from the definition of a symbol if no symbol is used in the operand. (If no length was specified in question C, a length of one would be assumed.)

The trick to D is to make sure you do not add the contents of register zero in the calculation of the effective address. Don't forget that register zero cannot be used for addressing purposes.

Although you may think that the effective address that is generated when the Load instruction in E executes is not a valid address, it really is—00001C is a fullword boundary (required by the opcode L), so the fullword located at 1C will be loaded into register 1. If this had been a Store instead of a Load instruction, the program would have abended because of a protection exception. Locations 1C–1F do not belong to this program (they belong to the operating system), so this instruction will not be permitted to alter their contents. In fact, in a few computers (those equipped with fetch protection) the Load instruction would not have been allowed to execute either, but in most cases it would.

Questions F and G are straightforward. The only thing to remember about the PACK instruction in H is that it is one of the SS instructions that has a separate length specification for each operand.

SPECIAL USES FOR INSTRUCTIONS

THE LA INSTRUCTION

Two things we have learned can be combined to provide new and convenient uses for the Load Address instruction (LA). Up to this point we have used the LA instruction to place the address represented by a symbol into a register: LA   7,AREA loads the address represented by the symbol AREA into register 7.

In the previous section we learned that a base register, an index register, and a displacement can be specified explicitly instead of letting the assembler figure them out. The action of the LA instruction can be combined with the ability to specify addresses explicitly, and the result gives us an efficient means of either loading a positive constant into a register or adding a positive value to the contents of a register without having to define a constant. Examine the execution of the following instruction: LA   6,4(6).

It takes the contents of register 6, adds to its contents a value of 4, placing the result in the first operand register (register 6), zeroing the high-order byte. If register 6 contains 00007C00 before the execution of the instruction, it will contain 00007C04 afterwards. The effective address generated by the second operand replaces the original contents of the first operand register. Because the same register number is specified in both operands, the result is that the contents of the register is incremented by the value in the displacement sub-field of the second operand. Since the maximum displacement allowed is 4095, the contents of any register (besides register zero) can be incremented by a value from 1 to 4095. Now examine the execution of this instruction: LA   8,4.

The effective address generated by the second operand is 000004:

base register	———
+ index register	———
+ displacement	004
effective address	000004

Any valid displacement (maximum of 4095) can be used to place the corresponding constant value in a register. The alternative would be to define a constant and then load that constant into a register, thus wasting the storage space occupied by the constant.

THE BCTR INSTRUCTION

In chapter 11, the Branch on Count Register Instruction (BCTR) was introduced with its regular function of controlling the execution of instructions within a loop. In addition, the BCTR instruction can be used to give an efficient means of subtracting a value of one from the contents of a general purpose register.

Reviewing the execution of the BCTR instruction reveals the two actions normally taken: (1) the contents of the register specified in the first operand is algebraically reduced by a value of one; and (2) if the resultant value in the first operand register is not equal to zero, a branch is taken to the location whose address is contained in the register specified in the second operand. Examine the following:

```
            L      8,TEN
            LA     6,LOOP
LOOP        A      4,LOC(3)
            .
            .
            .
            BCTR   8,6
            .
            .
TEN         DC     F'10'
```

The preceding BCTR instruction subtracts one from register 8. Since the result is not equal to zero (it is 9), the branch is taken to the instruction labeled

LOOP. This branch will be taken every time the BCTR instruction executes, until the contents of register 8 has been reduced to zero. When this happens, the branch is not taken. Instead, execution continues with the next sequential instruction in the program. This is an example of the normal use of a BCTR instruction.

The special use of the BCTR involves the algebraic decrement of the first operand register's contents but not the branching capability. The following accomplishes just that: BCTR 9,0. In this case, the content of register 9 is reduced by one, but no branching takes place, because register 0 is specified in the second operand (register 0 can never be used for the purpose of addressing). Thus, the BCTR instruction is an extremely efficient means to subtract a value of one from the contents of a register. No storage space is needed to hold the constant (H'1' or F'1'); no access of storage needs to be made to fetch the constant; and, furthermore, the BCTR instruction being an RR-type instruction occupies only two bytes of storage itself.

SPECIAL BRANCHING INSTRUCTIONS

THE BRANCH AND LINK INSTRUCTIONS (BAL,BALR)

Several different instructions may be used to branch to a common group of instructions that provides a useful function in a program—then branches back automatically when it has finished that function. An example of this might be a program that prints a variety of error messages. Rather than have a separate set of instructions at each point in the program where an error message needs printing, one set of instructions is established to print the error message whose address is contained in register 6.

At every place in the program where an error message needs printing, an instruction will load register 6 with the error message address and *branch and link* to the beginning of the group of instructions that print the message. After the printing is accomplished, another branch instruction will return control to the next sequential instruction following the Branch And Link instruction in the mainline routine.

Figure 14-14 shows a flowchart for the branch and link problem.

The general formats for the branch and link instructions are:

| Branch And Link | BAL | R1,D2(X2,B2) |
| Branch And Link Register | BALR | R1,R2 |

As each of these instructions executes the following occurs:

1. The address of the next sequential instruction is placed in R1.
2. A branch is taken to the address specified in the second operand.

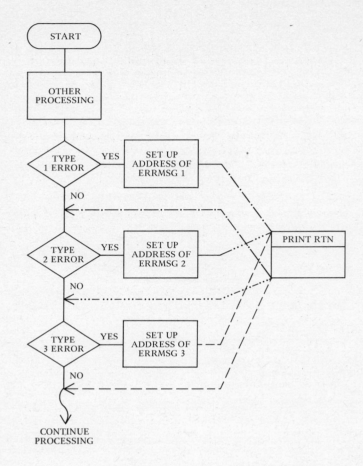

Fig. 14-14 Flowchart for branch and link problem

The code for the error-message problem (specified earlier in this section) is given in figure 14-15.

If this coding finds that an error of "type 1" has been discovered, the instruction LA 6,ERRMSG1 will be executed, and then the Branch And Link will be executed, transferring control to the instruction labeled PRINTRTN. ERRMSG1 will be printed, and a branch will then be taken to the address contained in register 8. The next instruction to be executed will be the Store instruction labeled NPL. Whenever the instruction labeled PRINTRTN is given control, the data whose address is contained in register 6 will be printed; and then a branch will be taken to the address contained in register 8.

The printing routine never knows which of the four error routines passed control—nor does it need to. When the print routine has completed its function, it simply returns control via register 8. The next instruction to execute may be

```
                      .
                      .
                      .
                LA    6,ERRMSG1         SET UP ADDRESS OF ERRMSG 1
                BAL   8,PRINTRTN        BRANCH TO PRINT ROUTINE
       NPL      ST
                      .
                      .
                      .
                LA    6,ERRMSG2         SET UP ADDRESS OF ERRMSG 2
                BAL   8,PRINTRTN        BRANCH TO PRINT ROUTINE
                A
                      .
                      .
                      .
                LA    6,ERRMSG3         SET UP ADDRESS OF ERRMSG 3
                BAL   8,PRINTRTN        BRANCH TO PRINT ROUTINE
                S
                      .
                      .
                      .
                LA    6,ERRMSG4         SET UP ADDRESS OF ERRMSG 4
                BAL   8,PRINTRTN        BRANCH TO PRINT ROUTINE
                M
                      .
                      .
                      .
   PRINTRTN     MWRIT FROM=0(6)         PRINT THE ERROR MESSAGE
                BR    8                 BRANCH BACK
                      .
                      .
                      .
   ERRMSG1      DC
   ERRMSG2      DC
   ERRMSG3      DC
   ERRMSG4      DC
                      .
                      .
                      .
```

Fig. 14-15   Coding example of the branch and link instruction

a Store, an Add, a Subtract, or a Multiply; the print routine does not know which one it will be. This routine blindly branches back using register 8, thus it is imperative that the integrity of the address in the return register be maintained. The reason behind the names for these instructions is obvious. Not only do they cause a branch to be taken, but before they do they set up the link for the return branch. The RR-format branch and link instruction (BALR) plays a big role in the transfer of control between separately assembled CSECTS. (This will be explained fully in chapter 15.)

There are branching instructions in the repertoires of Systems/360 and 370 that will increment and test an index value and branch or not based on the resultant index value. For example, take the case when we want to sum the elements in a table labeled CAP. Each element occupies one halfword of storage, and the table contains twenty elements.

BRANCH ON INDEX LOW OR EQUAL (BXLE)

This instruction belongs to the RS-class of instructions and has the general format of: BXLE   R1,R3,D2(B2). There are four items used in the execution of this instruction:

1. an index value
2. an increment
3. a comparand
4. a branch address

Figure 14-16 shows how the execution of this instruction looks in flow-chart form.

The BXLE instruction is usually placed at the end of a trailing-decision loop.

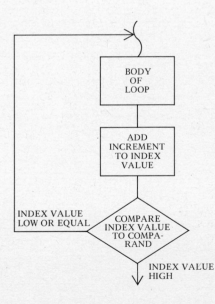

Fig. 14-16   Flowchart for execution of the BXLE instruction

The index value is kept in R1; the increment in R3. The comparand is always contained in an odd-numbered register. This can be the same register that is used to hold the increment if the increment register (R3) is an odd-numbered register, or it can be the register whose number is one greater than the number of the increment register if the register specified as R3 is an even number:

$$
\begin{array}{ll}
\text{index value} & \text{(R1)} \\
\text{increment} & \text{(R3)} \\
\text{comparand} & \text{(R3 if R3 is odd)} \\
& \text{(R3 + 1 if R3 is even)}
\end{array}
$$

For example, figure 14-17 gives the instructions to implement the addition of the elements in CAP discussed earlier. As the BXLE executes, the contents of the increment register (register 8) is added to the index (register 6). The new contents of the index register is then compared to the comparand (in register 9). If the comparison results in the contents of the index register being lower or equal to the contents of the comparand register, the branch is taken to the instruction labeled LOOP to add the next element to the sum. If the comparison results in the contents of the index register being higher than the comparand register's contents, the next sequential instruction (the ST) is then executed, and the execution of the loop is thus terminated.

```
          .
          .
          .
          L      9,ENDVALU      LOAD COMPARAND (40)
          LA     8,2            LOAD INCREMENT VALUE (2)
          SR     6,6            INITIALIZE INDEX REGISTER
          SR     2,2            INITIALIZE SUM
LOOP      AH     2,CAP(6)       ADD ELEMENT TO THE SUM
          BXLE   6,8,LOOP       INCREMENT AND CHECK INDEX REGISTER
          ST     2,SUM          STORE SUM WHEN LOOP COMPLETE
          .
          .
          .
ENDVALU   DC     F'40'          COMPARAND
SUM       DS     F
CAP       DC     H'6'
          DC     H'83'
          DC     H'26'
          .
          .
          .
```

Fig. 14-17 Adding elements in a table using the BXLE

BRANCH ON INDEX HIGH (BXH)

This instruction executes in a manner similar to the BXLE, uses the same register setup, and is part of the same general class of instructions (RS-type). It differs in that it branches when the index register contains a value that is higher than the comparand (rather than low and equal). Figure 14-18 shows how this execution looks in flowchart form.

The elements in the table labeled CAP can be summed using a BXH to control the execution of the loop. In this case the elements will be summed from the "bottom up." The increment can be of any magnitude, and the comparand and increment can be contained in the same register, therefore making this efficient solution possible. (The index value will initially be set to forty to add the last element to the sum first.)

```
              .
              .
              .
         L    6,LASTEL      INITIALIZE INDEX REGISTER
         L    9,NEG4        INCREMENT AND COMPARAND VALUE
         SR   2,2           INITIALIZE SUM
LOOP     AH   2,CAP(6)      ADD ELEMENT TO SUM
         BXH  6,9,LOOP      DECREMENT AND CHECK INDEX REGISTER
         ST   2,SUM         STORE SUM WHEN LOOP COMPLETE
              .
              .
              .
LASTEL   DC   F'40'         INITIAL INDEX VALUE
NEG4     DC   F'-4'         INCREMENT VALUE
SUM      DS   F
CAP      DC   H'6'
         DC   H'83'
         DC   H'26'
              .
              .
              .
```

Notice that this solution requires the use of one less register. This may be an important efficiency in a large program in which the availability of registers is low.

INTRODUCTION TO CHAINED LISTS OR QUEUES

There are times when you will want to use a collection of data items when they do not occupy contiguous storage space. Therefore, they cannot be referenced as you would reference elements in a table, by indexing into the table. These noncontiguous elements can, however, be connected to one another by their addresses and can be referenced using explicit addresses.

The concept involved here can be illustrated with a simple example. Customers of the barber shop are served on a first-come, first-served basis. As

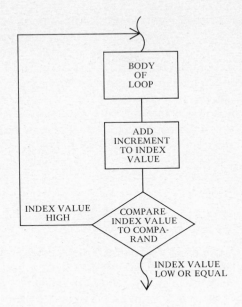

Fig. 14-18 Flowchart for execution of the BXH instruction

each customer enters the shop, he remembers the person ahead of him who is in line for service. It does not matter where the customers sit while waiting their turn—in fact, customers may move around, holding different conversations or looking for magazines. Each customer merely keeps track of the customer who precedes him, and when that customer has been served he knows he is next for the chair.

So it is with *chained lists*. While the data items that comprise a chained list may be spread throughout storage, each one in the list contains some sort of identifier for locating the next. The field within the data item that contains the identifier is generally referred to as the *link field*, and the process of chaining, or queuing up, data items into a list involves a system for establishing this link field.

These systems involve conventions regarding where in the chain a new data item should be added (at the beginning or end), which data item should be removed from the chain (the first or the last), and whether the data items in the group should have a single link field each, or two link fields each. In the case where there are two link fields, one keeps track of the next data item in the list (*forward pointer*), the other link field keeps track of the following data item (*back pointer*).

Two general systems for handling of chained lists will be discussed in this chapter. They are referred to as FIFO and LIFO. FIFO handles a list on a "First In-First Out" basis. New data items are added to the end of the chain and items are removed from the beginning of it. Thus regardless of how many items there are in a chain, the first item added to it will be the first one removed and handled.

The easiest way to describe the "Last In-First Out" (LIFO) system of handling a list is to have you imagine a waiting line for a show, only where breaking into the line is an accepted practice. In this case, the person who pushes in at the head of the line gets into the show first. Not very fair you say. Well, it has its place in programming. Think of the situation where you want your data items to be chained, but you want the ability to give priorities to the most important items. By priorities, we mean that you desire those particular data items to be handled first. In this case, items are added at the beginning of the list rather than at the end.

CONSTRUCTION OF A CHAINED LIST

Figure 14-19 is an example of a chained list. The first 4 bytes in each block (or data item) contains the link field. Notice that the last block has a zero pointer—a general convention for the end of a chain.

Each chained list has a *header*, which keeps track of the beginning of it. The header contains the address of (points to) the first data item in the list. The first four bytes in the first block (the link field) *points to* (contains the address of) the second block; the link field in the second block points to the third block; and the link field in the third block contains a zero, indicating that it is the end or last block in the chain.

Another way of handling the chained list, shown in figure 14-19, is that the

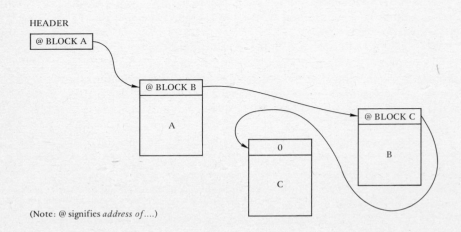

(Note: @ signifies *address of....*)

Fig. 14-19 Illustration of a chained list

header may contain two addresses—the addresses of the first and last blocks in the chain. In this case, the new type of header would look like:

@BLOCK A
@BLOCK C

Using this type of header can make it easier to reference the chained list. For instance, if both addresses in the header are the same, it indicates that there is only one block of data in the chain. If the two addresses are not identical, it is an indication that there are at least two. Zeros in the first pointer (or both) of the header indicate that the chain is empty—contains no data items. (Whether both pointers or only one must be zero to indicate an empty chained list depends on the programmer's preference.)

ADDING AND REMOVING DATA ITEMS IN CHAINED LISTS

Data items are always removed from the beginning of a chained list. After removing a block from the chained list displayed in figure 14-19, the remaining chain looks like figure 14-20.

Data items may be added to a chained list in one of two ways—either the new item (block D) may be added to the end of the chain (figure 14-21), or as illustrated in figure 14-22, the new item (block E) can be pushed in at the beginning of the chain. Block D and block E are each added to the chained list first illustrated in figure 14-19.

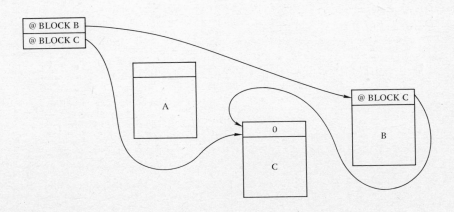

Fig. 14-20 Chained list with block A removed

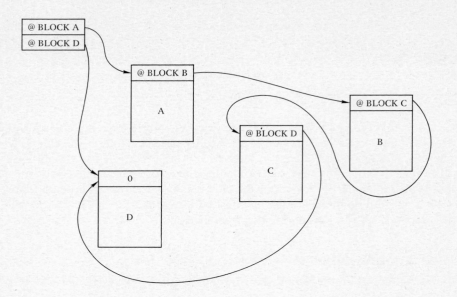

Fig. 14-21 Chained list with block D added

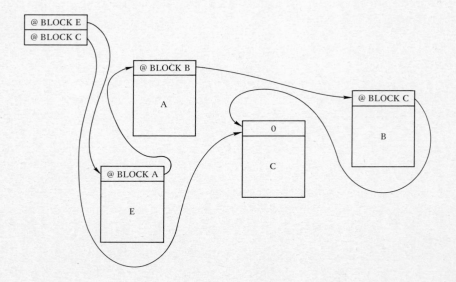

Fig. 14-22 Chained list with block E pushed

DOUBLE-THREADED CHAINED LISTS

There is one problem with a single-threaded chained list such as the ones shown in figures 14-19 through 14-22. This is the problem of a disconnection in the chain. In all these examples there is one continuous thread that connects all the blocks of data in the list, the chain of addresses. Should this chain be broken for any reason, all the blocks following the break are lost! They still exist, but there is no way to really get to them—their addresses are lost.

The loss of data may be minimized by using a *double-threaded chain*. One chain of addresses starts at the beginning of the list and proceeds to the end. The other chain starts at the end of the list and proceeds backward to the beginning of the list. Thus if the chain gets broken for any reason, it can be reconstructed by following each chain of pointers to the point at which the chain is broken. Figure 14-23 shows a double-threaded chained list containing three blocks of data.

The unbroken line of arrows that begins in the first header is the chain of forward pointers. The broken line of arrows that begins in the second header is the chain of backward pointers (often simply referred to as *back pointer* or *back chain*).

One last term to be familiar with occurs when this type of collection of data items is referred to as a *queue*. The term is *queue-control words* (which is another term for *headers*). The collection is referred to as a queue; the header is the control of the queue, and each address in the header occupies a word of storage.

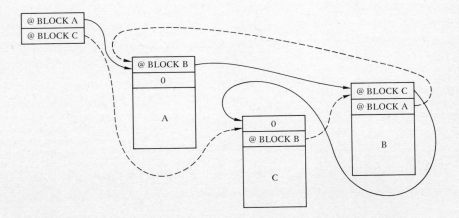

Fig. 14-23   Double-threaded chained list

Chapter 14 Quick Reference

Name	Type	Mnemonic and Form	Object Code Form	See Page
Branch and Link	RX	BAL R1,D2(X2,B2)	45 | R1 | X2 | B2 | D2	261
Branch and Link Register	RR	BALR R1,R2	05 | R1 | R2	261
Branch on Count Register	RR	BCTR R1,R2	06 | R1 | R2	260
Branch on Index High	RS	BXH R1,R3,D2(B2)	86 | R1 | R3 | B2 | D2	266
Branch on Index Low or Equal	RS	BXLE R1,R3,D2(B2)	87 | R1 | R3 | B2 | D2	264
Load Address	RX	LA R1,D2(X2,Bc)	41 | R1 | X2 | B2 | D2	259

QUESTIONS

1. What advantage do we gain grouping information into tables and queues?

2. Define the following:
   - a. Table
   - b. Element
   - c. Argument
   - d. Search argument
   - e. Function
   - f. Forward pointer
   - g. Back pointer

3. Explain what an index register is and how it is used to reference elements within a table.

4. What is the difference between a search-reference and a direct-reference table?

5. Using examples, explain conceptually how you would serially search a table.

6. What is meant by explicit addressing, and why do we use it?

7. Why can't you use register 0 as an index register?

8. What is the error in each explicitly specified operand in the following instructions?

    a. L   7,(8)
    b. MVC   4(2),8(6)
    c. A   4,1(5)

9. What does register 3 contain after the execution of each of the following?

    a. BAL   3,LOC
    b. LA   3,6
    c. LA   3,4(3)
    d. BCTR 3,0

10. What is the maximum displacement that you can explicitly specify in an operand?

11. What is the difference between the execution of the BXH and BXLE instructions?

12. What is the link field used for in data items that are part of a chained list?

13. Explain the differences between handling a chained list on a FIFO and LIFO basis.

14. What purpose does the header of a chained list serve, and what is another name by which it is sometimes referred?

15. What does it mean when a header contains zeros?

16. Discuss the difference between a single-threaded and a double-threaded chained list.

EXERCISES

1. Using the contents of the following registers:

    Reg. 0: 00000012   Reg. 2: 00008750   Reg. 7: 0000002C
    Reg. 8: 00005A66   Reg. 10: 000002B3

what are the effective addresses generated when the following instructions execute?

    a. ST   3,12(7,2)
    b. AH   1,6(0,2)
    c. MVC 10(8,2),20(8)
    d. LA   9,6

2. Code a routine to sort the halfword elements in a 20-element table labeled XYZ into ascending order.

3. Code a routine to find the smallest value in a 12-element table named TAB. (Each element in the table occupies a fullword.)

4. Write a program that will calculate the amount of change needed for a sale. Use a table named AVAIL in which the first element contains the total number of quarters you have, the second element the total number of dimes, the third element nickels, and the fourth pennies. Each sale is limited to a maximum of $1.00, and the amount tendered will always be $1.00.

5. Use a BXH or BXLE instruction to control a loop which sums the values in a 65-element table.

6. Program routines to handle a single-threaded chained list. You should be able to handle both FIFO and LIFO lists. You will, therefore, need routines to add a data item to the end of the chain, push a data item in at the head of the chain, and remove one from the beginning of the chain.

7. If register 5 contains 07000104, before execution, what will it contain after the execution of the instruction LA   5,6(5)?

8. Write a program to process orders for auto parts and produce bills for the customers. The orders consist of the customer's name, the number of the part he wishes to order, and the quantity of that part he desires. The program should work with a search-argument table, consisting of arguments containing the part numbers available in the inventory and functions containing the price per unit for those parts. The bills produced should contain all pertinent information, including any error messages if errors are encountered as the orders are processed.

CHAPTER 15

Program Sectioning and Linking

INTRODUCTION

There are many instances in programming when the solution to a job can be divided into a series of separate functions, each defined by a different programmer. These functions can even be programmed in several programming languages, with the programmer choosing the most appropriate language for each. There are only two things that are necessary to make this division of labor possible. First, a means for dividing the functions to be performed must be established; and second, a means of communicating between the sections or divisions of programming must be devised. Division of the function into what we call control sections can, with planning, be accomplished easily. The communications capability is provided by developing a standard means of passing control and information between the control sections.

TERMINOLOGY USED

A *control section* (*CSECT* for short) is a block of coding that can be relocated, independent of other coding, without altering or impairing the logic of the program. It is loaded into storage starting at any doubleword boundary. The beginning of a control section is identified by the assembler pseudo operation code CSECT in the opcode field of an instruction. Its name is specified in the name field of this instruction, and the operand is left blank. The end of a control section is identified by the appearance of an END instruction—or by an instruction that defines another control section. For now we will use the END

275

instruction. (The alternative is used in complicated situations which will be discussed later.)

Each of the CSECTS may be considered a *subroutine* (the terms *subroutine* and *routine* are used interchangeably here); each is a block of code that performs a particular function and is essentially complete and separate from the rest of the program. It is possible for any subroutine to pass control to (or call) another routine. In illustration form, this could look like:

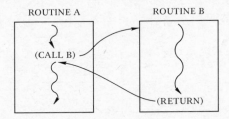

Routine A receives control from the supervisor after it is loaded. The instructions in Routine A execute until one is encountered that requests control to be transferred to Routine B (Call B). The form of this statement may not be the same under all operating systems, but some instruction or sequence of instructions will be available that causes control to leave a routine. Routine A is considered a *calling routine*—a subroutine that calls or passes control to another routine. Routine B, on the other hand, is referred to as the *called routine*. It is a subroutine that is called or receives control.

Once passed control, Routine B performs the function for which it was designed. Then it returns control to the routine that called it—Routine A. Here again, the statement used to indicate Routine B's return of control (RETURN) may not be the same under all operating systems. Once control is returned to Routine A, at the next sequential instruction after the "call", it continues to perform its function. When it is complete, control is returned to the supervisor. Thus Routine A is a subroutine of the operating system. It receives control from the supervisor, and it returns control to the supervisor when its function is completed. To illustrate:

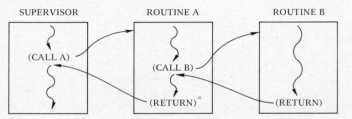

The supervisor "calls" or passes control to Routine A. The supervisor is the calling routine, and the act of calling involves a transfer of control to Routine

A, which performs a portion of its function and at a particular point calls Routine B. Routine A becomes the calling routine, and it passes control to Routine B—now the called routine. Routine B performs the function or functions for which it was designed, and it then returns control to the routine that called it—Routine A, which completes its function and returns control to the routine that in turn called it—the supervisor.

The transfer of control between separately assembled CSECTS is an orderly affair. For now, we may consider that the only main routine in the computer is the supervisor. Every problem program is a subroutine of the supervisor. Each routine must wait to receive control before it can execute, and each called routine must return control to its calling routine. There is one exception to this established chain of transfer and return of control. Should any subroutine, regardless of its position in the chain, cause an error condition as it executes, it can cause the ABEND procedure to be taken immediately. This makes it possible for the last subroutine in a chain to abnormally terminate the execution of all routines that precede it in the chain. This is the case because an error must be responded to by the operating system as soon as it is encountered, so that all the possible causes of the error are still available and can be located in a dump.

There is a difference between OS- and DOS-based systems when it comes to transferring control. The difference occurs at the time of the first transfer of control, the transfer between the supervisor and your first subroutine. Since transfers between all other subroutines are similar, we will examine these first.

NEED FOR STANDARD LINKAGE CONVENTIONS

USE OF SAVE AREAS

There are 16 general purpose registers in Systems/360 and 370 for use by all routines, supervisor, or problem program. They are shared by all. With this restriction in mind, Routine A should not destroy the contents of the supervisor's registers; and Routine B should not destroy the contents of Routine A's. Therefore, the first thing a routine should do when it receives control is to save the contents of the 16 registers for its caller.

It establishes a convention as to where the contents of the registers should be stored. Under one approach, each routine establishes a save area. These save areas are 18 fullwords in length and serve as the areas where the contents of that routine's own registers are stored. The first thing a subroutine does when it gets control is to store the original contents of the 16 registers, and the last thing a routine does before it returns control is to restore the original contents of the 16. Assuming our earlier example, the makeup of the three save areas is as shown in figure 15-1.

The symbol @ stands for the word "address." The second word of each save

	Supervisor Save Area	Routine A Save Area	Routine B Save Area
	unused	unused	unused
Backward Pointer →		← @ Sup's save area ←	@ A's save area
Forward Pointer →	@ A's save area →	@ B's save area →	
	contents R14	contents R14	
	contents R15	contents R15	
	contents RØ	contents RØ	
	contents R1	contents R1	
	contents R2	contents R2	
	contents R3	contents R3	
	contents R4	contents R4	
	contents R5	contents R5	
	contents R6	contents R6	
	contents R7	contents R7	
	contents R8	contents R8	
	contents R9	contents R9	
	contents R10	contents R10	
	contents R11	contents R11	
	contents R12	contents R12	

Fig. 15-1 Makeup of the three save areas

area is referred to as the *backward pointer*, and the third word is referred to as the *forward pointer*.

REGISTER USAGE

In addition, it is helpful to establish conventions for registers used in the passing of control and parameters. Such conventions, established by programmers for the use of programmers, are referred to as Standard Linkage Conventions.

These conventions set aside particular registers for specific purposes involved in the use of subroutines. The four registers used under OS and DOS Standard Linkage Conventions—and the use established for each—are as follows:

Register	Use
1	address of parameter list
13	address of the save area
14	address in calling routine to which control is to be returned
15	entry point address of the called routine

The best way to study the use of Standard Linkage Conventions is to examine the code that performs linking:

```
RTNA      CSECT
          EXTRN   RTNB
          STM     14,12,12(13)      SAVE SUPERVISOR'S REGISTERS
          BALR    12,0              ESTABLISH ADDRESSABILITY
          USING   *,12              "                "
          ST      13,SAVE+4         SAVE @ SUP'S SAVE AREA IN OWN SAVE AREA
          LA      15,SAVE           GET @ OF OWN SAVE AREA
          ST      15,8(13)          SAVE @ OWN SAVE AREA IN SUP'S SAVE AREA
          LR      13,15             PUT @ OWN SAVE AREA IN R13
          .
          .
          .
          LA      1,PARM            @ PARAMETER LIST IN R1
          L       15,ADRRTNB        @ ROUTINE B IN R15
          BALR    14,15             BRANCH TO ROUTINE B
          .                         CONTROL IS RETURNED HERE
          .
          .
          L       13,SAVE+4         GET @ SUP'S SAVE AREA
          LM      14,12,12(13)      RESTORE SUP'S REGISTERS
          BR      14                RETURN TO SUPERVISOR
SAVE      DC      18F'0'
ADRRTNB   DC      A(RTNB)
PARM      DC
          .
          .
          .
          END
```

The CSECT statement defines this code as a division of function, a subroutine. We will ignore the EXTRN statement for now. The STM instruction stores the contents of 15 registers, registers 14 through 12 (remember that the STM instruction has a wrap-around feature, and register 0 is stored immediately after register 15). Where are the contents stored? Twelve bytes past the address in register 13. When Routine A receives control by Standard Linkage

Conventions, what is contained in register 13? The address of the save area. Whose save area? The supervisor's. So the contents of these 15 registers are stored in words 4–18 of the supervisor's save area. The contents in the registers are for the supervisor's use, so the most logical place to store the contents of these, as used by the supervisor, is in the calling routine's (the supervisor's) save area.

Now the contents of all but one register have been stored—register 13. It is Routine A's only key to the location where it stored the original contents of the registers when it received control. This address must, therefore, be stored in a very safe place. Routine A has to be able to use this address to restore the original contents of the registers before returning control.

Routine A saves this important address in the second word of its own save area. To do this it must use a symbolic reference to the location of its save area in storage. In order for A to be able to make this symbolic reference to storage, addressability must first be established for the CSECT. This is why the BALR and USING instructions that establish addressability must immediately follow the STM and precede the ST of register 13's contents.

How come we could store the contents of the other 15 registers before we had established addressability? We did not use a symbolic reference to storage in the operand portion of that STM instruction. Since we are using Standard Linkage Conventions, we can depend on the address of the calling routine's save area being in register 13 when we receive control. We can use this register's contents in explicit addressing, with a displacement of 12, to generate the address of the fourth word in the supervisor's save area. The general format for the STM instruction, an RS-type of instruction, is: STM R1,R3,D2(B2). Register 13 is the base register for this instruction. The effective address is calculated as the contents of the low-order three bytes of the base register plus the value of the displacement:

base register contents = @ sup's save area
displacement   = C (addresses are in hexadecimal)
effective address   @ sup's save area + C

Let's look again at the instructions in Routine A. Now that addressability has been established, the address of the supervisor's save area can be stored in the second word of Routine A's save area:

```
RTNA    CSECT
        EXTRN   RTNB
        STM     14,12,12(13)    SAVE SUPERVISOR'S REGISTERS
        BALR    12,0            ESTABLISH ADDRESSABILITY
        USING   *,12            "                      "
        ST      13,SAVE+4       SAVE @ SUP'S SAVE AREA IN OWN SAVE AREA
        LA      15,SAVE         GET @ OF OWN SAVE AREA
        ST      15,8(13)        SAVE @ OWN SAVE AREA IN SUP'S SAVE AREA
        LR      13,15           PUT @ OWN SAVE AREA IN R13
```

The next instruction loads the address of Routine A's save area into register 15. Why not register 13 where it belongs by Standard Linkage Conventions? We still have to fill the third word of the supervisor's save area (the forward pointer). This word should contain the address of the called routine's save area (Routine A). So once more we use the original contents of register 13 (the address of the supervisor's save area), this time with a displacement of 8, to save the address of Routine A's save area in the third word of the supervisor's.

We no longer need the original contents of register 13, so we can now move the address of A's save area from its temporary location in register 15 to its proper Standard Linkage position in 13. This done, the entry code requirements of Standard Linkage Conventions are fulfilled. The program may now proceed with its processing. Part of this processing may involve the calling of another subroutine.

(For now, we will skip the code for calling another subroutine.) When processing is complete, control must be returned to the supervisor. The code involved in the return of control is referred to as the *exit code*. The contents of the calling routine's registers must be restored. In order to accomplish this, the second word of Routine A's save area is returned to register 13. Remember, this is the address of the supervisor's save area, and that it is the only pointer Routine A has to the original contents of the registers.

An LM instruction is then used with the same operands as used on the original STM, to restore the remaining 15 registers. Then Routine A returns control to the supervisor by branching via the contents of register 14. In fact, once the supervisor's registers have been restored, Routine A can do nothing that involves their use. The LM has destroyed Routine A's base register, so any symbolic reference to its storage is invalid. All the registers contain the supervisor's data that Routine A must not destroy.

DIFFERENCES UNDER DOS-BASED SYSTEMS

The difference between OS- and DOS-based systems lies in the fact that the initial transfer of control under DOS, between the supervisor and the first subroutine, does not follow the Standard Linkage Conventions. The supervisor saves its own registers before it calls a subroutine, and it does not establish the contents of the linkage registers as done otherwise. The routine that receives control from the DOS supervisor begins by establishing its own addressability. It does not save the original contents of the registers in the supervisor's save area, and it does not establish the forward and backward save area chains in the second and third words of them. It merely performs its defined functions.

When the time comes for the first subroutine to return control to the DOS supervisor, it does not restore the registers, since they were never stored. It does not return control by branching via the contents of register 14, because the supervisor has not placed the return address in it. Instead, to return control to the supervisor, the called subroutine places the macro name "EOJ" in the opcode field of its last executable instruction. The execution of the code generated by this macro call returns control to the supervisor.

The transfer of control between any two other subroutines under DOS requires the full Standard Linkage Conventions. The difference in linkage between OS and DOS lies in the first transfer of control, the one between the DOS supervisor and the programmer's first routine.

COMMUNICATIONS BETWEEN CONTROL SECTIONS

BRANCHING TROUBLES

Before we examine the code in a calling sequence, we have to examine how communications between control sections are managed. Why is a special means of communication necessary? Well, let's examine the instructions we currently have for branching. We can use an RX- or an RS-branch instruction to branch to a location we can reference symbolically. For instance: B LOOP The problem with this is that the symbol branched to must be defined within this control section. The assembler has to be able to break the symbol down into the contents of a base register and a displacement value. How about the possibility of loading an address into a register and branching via that register? For instance:

```
          LA    6,LOOP
          BR    6
                or
          L     8,ADLOOP
          B     0(8)
          .
          .
          .
ADLOOP    DC    A(LOOP)
```

In the first case, the symbol LOOP that appears in the operand of the LA instruction must be defined (appear in the name field of an instruction within this CSECT). If it does not, the LA instruction will be flagged as containing an undefined symbol. A similar situation exists in the second example. ADLOOP is the name on an address constant (a fullword that at execution time will contain the actual address represented by the symbol in parentheses). Therefore, ADLOOP is defined; but the symbol must also be defined. Therefore, none of the current means of establishing branch targets will work.

Each control section is created by a separate execution of the assembler. The output of each execution consists of an object module and a control dictionary, called the *External Symbol Dictionary* (ESD). In building the object module code, the assembler has resolved all symbolic references to storage locations by reducing the symbols to either a base register and displacement, or to base register, index register, and displacement (dependent on the class of the instruction opcode). By the time the assembler finishes its two passes over the source data, it has created the object module, and none of the symbols, such as those we have discussed, exist. So, these symbols cannot be referred to by this control section or any other. In examining the communication problem even farther, we see that there is no constant relation between CSECTs. Thus knowing the location of one does not mean that we can address locations within another by the techniques of relative addressing.

SYMBOLIC LINKAGE

Control sections can pass control between each other through the use of symbolic linkage. This is accomplished by establishing certain symbols, which will be referenced within this CSECT, but defined externally to it. These are called *external symbols*. Other symbols, defined within this CSECT to be referred to by others, are called *entry symbols*. They can provide the means for other CSECTs to enter this control section, as well as to use data or tables defined in this CSECT.

These special symbols, external and entry, are the only ones that the assembler saves from the source statements. It is these symbols, along with their locations within the source module, which the assembler places in the ESD it builds with the object module for the CSECT. You notify the assembler which symbols are to be placed in the ESD by the use of special assembler pseudo operations. An external symbol is indicated in the operand field of an EXTRN instruction, and an entry symbol is indicated in the operand field of an ENTRY instruction.

The EXTRN and ENTRY statements cause the assembler to place the symbols appearing in their operands in the ESD, but there is one other thing you must do in the case of each type of symbol. In the case of the EXTRN statement, you must provide an address constant for the external symbol. In the case of the ENTRY statement, you must make sure that the symbol you wish to make externally referencable is defined within your CSECT (appears in the name field of a source statement within it). The CSECTs in figure 15-2 illustrate examples of each.

CSECTs ONE and TWO were assembled separately. CSECT ONE refers to the symbol AREA in the operand of a DC instruction, yet AREA is not defined within it. The assembler knew that this symbol would not be defined (because of the EXTRN statement) so it did not flag the DC statement as containing a reference to an undefined symbol. Instead, the assembler places the symbol AREA in the ESD, along with the fact that it is an external symbol, as it encounters the EXTRN instruction and places the location of the address constant, referencing AREA with the symbol in the ESD.

As the assembler creates the object module for CSECT TWO, it encounters the ENTRY statement and places the symbol AREA in the ESD, with the fact that it is an entry symbol. The assembler watches for the symbol AREA to appear in the name field, and when it does encounter the symbol, it places the location of the symbol definition with the notation for the ENTRY AREA

LOC	NAME	OPCODE	OPERANDS
000	ONE	CSECT	
		EXTRN	AREA
		.	
		.	
		.	
		L	6,ADAREA
		L	8,0(6)
		.	
		.	
		.	
108	ADAREA	DC	A(AREA)
		END	
000	TWO	CSECT	
		ENTRY	AREA
		.	
		.	
		.	
06C	AREA	DC	F'26'
		END	

Fig. 15-2 Examples of EXTRN and ENTRY statements

in the ESD. The symbolic names on each of the CSECT instructions are automatically placed in the ESDs as entry symbols. The ESDs contain the following information after the assembler has completed its work:

ESD for CSECT ONE

Symbol	Type	Location
ONE	ENTRY	0
AREA	EXTRN	108

ESD for CSECT TWO

Symbol	Type	Location
TWO	ENTRY	0
AREA	ENTRY	6C

The information in these ESDs is used by the linkage editor as it combines the two object modules and builds its load module. For each symbol of the EXTRN type that the linkage editor encounters in any of the ESDs it is handling, it must locate a corresponding symbol of the ENTRY type in another. As the linkage editor program finds an ENTRY for the EXTRN it is trying to resolve, it places the location of the symbol's definition at the location within the other CSECT where the symbol is referenced.

When the first Load instruction in CSECT ONE is executed, register 6 is loaded with the address of the symbol AREA. This is an address within CSECT TWO placed at location 108 within CSECT ONE by the linkage editor. When the second load instruction in CSECT ONE executes, the fullword (26) defined at location 6C in CSECT TWO is loaded into register 8. The linkage was made symbolically to allow an instruction within CSECT ONE to reference, and access, the contents of a fullword within TWO.

Put in simple terms, the linkage editor resolves the external references between separately assembled CSECTs. As long as the CSECTs that you request the linkage editor to combine contain ENTRY symbols to match all EXTRN symbols, all the symbolic linkages are made for you. (For information on how to tell the linkage editor which CSECTs to combine into a load module, refer to chapter 20.)

PASSING CONTROL AND HANDLING PARAMETERS

A subroutine (that is, a CSECT) must do at least two things and may do a third. It must establish symbolic linkage between the definition of the entry point symbol in the called routine and the address constant for this external symbol in the calling routine. It must also load the address of the called routine's entry point into register 15 (according to Standard Linkage Conventions) and transfer control to the called routine by branching, using register 15's contents. These two steps are required to accomplish the transfer of control.

Optionally, the calling routine may set up and pass parameters. If parameters are passed, register 1, by Standard Linkage Conventions, will hold the address of the parameter list. What the parameter list contains depends on which of two ways is used to pass parameters: *call by value* and *call by name*. In calling by value, the parameter list that is pointed to by register 1 contains the parameters themselves. In calling by name, the parameter list contains the addresses of the parameters. The difference can be illustrated through an example: a man who gives his girlfriend a diamond ring is passing, or calling by value. On the other hand, one who gives his girlfriend the key to a safety deposit box that contains a diamond ring is passing, or calling by name. Using call by name (the preferred manner of passing parameters), the calling sequence looks like:

```
              LA      1,PARMLIST
              L       15,ADRTNB
              BALR    14,15
                .
                .
                .
PARMLIST      DC      A(PARM1)
              DC      A(PARM2)
              DC      A(PARM3)
PARM2         DC      CL12'ERROR'
PARM1         DC      F'6'
PARM3         DC      F'12'
```

The called routine after its entry code could use the following instructions to refer to the parameters:

```
            .
            .
            .
      LM    6,8,0(1)            @ PARM1 IN REGISTER 6
 *                              @ PARM2 IN REGISTER 7
 *                              @ PARM3 IN REGISTER 8
 *   POSSIBLE USES OF PARAMETERS
      L     4,0(6)             PLACES 00000006 IN REG 4
      L     2,0(8)             PLACES 0000000C IN REG 2
      MVC   OUT(12),0(7)       MOVES CHARACTER STRING ERROR
                                 TO AREA CALLED OUT
```

Using explicit addressing, the called routine can refer to and use the parameters in any way it desires.

REVIEW OF SUBROUTINE RESPONSIBILITIES

As a means of review, the following are lists of the responsibilities of routines:

The Calling Routine's Responsibilities

1. Define storage for an 18-word save area and put its address in register 13.
2. Put the address of the called routine in register 15.
3. Set up a parameter list and put its address in register 1 (optional).
4. Put the address of the location in the calling routine where control is to be returned in register 14.
5. Transfer control to the called routine by branching to the address in register 15.

The Called Routine's Responsibilities

1. Store the contents of registers 14 through 12 in words 4 through 18 of the calling routine's save area.
2. Establish addressability.
3. Set up an 18-word save area and store the address of the calling routine's save area in the second word.
4. Store the address of its own save area in the third word of the calling routine's save area.
5. Place address of its own save area in register 13.
6. Return the address of the calling routine's save area to register 13 from the second word of its own save area.
7. Restore the contents of registers 14 through 12 from words 4 through 18 of the calling routine's save area.
8. Return control to the calling routine by branching to the address in register 14.

QUESTIONS

1. What is a control section, and what abbreviation can you use to refer to one?

2. A control section is always loaded into storage at the same integral boundary. Is this a halfword, fullword, or doubleword boundary?

3. How do you identify the beginning and end of a control section and give it a name?

4. Define the term subroutine (or routine).

5. What is the difference between a calling and a called routine?

6. What effect does an ABEND have on the already established chain for return of control.

7. What is the first thing a subroutine should do when it receives control?

8. What rules are referred to as Standard Linkage Conventions?

9. What four general purpose registers are used for Standard Linkage Conventions, and for what purpose is each used?

10. What is the makeup of an 18-word save area?

11. How is it that the STM instruction, which stores the contents of registers 14 through 12, is able to precede the establishment of addressability in a subroutine?

12. What is stored in the forward and backward pointer locations in a save area? Why are these locations so important?

13. Why won't the following work for transferring control (branching) between separately assembled CSECTs?

    a. An RX-type of instruction to branch to a location referenced symbolically

    ```
    B    LOOP
    ```

    b. Loading an address into a register and branching via that register

    ```
    LA  8,LOOP
    BR  8
    ```

    c. Relative addressing

14. Describe what is meant by symbolic linkage. What part does each of the following play in it?

   a. External symbols
   b. Entry symbols
   c. Address constants
   d. ESD

15. What are the purposes of EXTRN and ENTRY statements?

16. How does the linkage editor help in resolving external references between separately assembled CSECTs?

17. What are parameters and how do Standard Linkage Conventions handle them?

18. What is the difference between "call by value" and "call by name"?

EXERCISES

1. Design and write a routine that expects two parameters 1) a table (maximum of 100 halfword elements), and 2) the number of elements in the array. Have your routine calculate and return the average of the values in the array.

2. Code a routine that will sort into ascending order an array of up to 200 fullword elements.

3. Code three subroutines that handle chained lists, one to add a block to the end of the list, one to push a block in at the front of the list, and the third to remove a block from the beginning of it. Then code a calling routine that will invoke the three subroutines to build and access chained lists in both a FIFO and a LIFO manner.

4. Write a subroutine that will generate random numbers that range between any two positive values. Have your routine expect as parameters 1) the lower value for the range of the random number, 2) the upper value for the range, and 3) a location where it is to place the random number to return it to the calling routine.

5. Code a subprogram that receives a frequency distribution containing 10 entries which range from 1 to 25 in magnitude, and produce as output a bar graph reflecting this information.

CHAPTER 16

Dumps and Debugging

IMPORTANCE OF DEBUGGING

The object of debugging is to recognize, locate, and eliminate errors in a program. To recognize the value and importance of developing the ability to debug and troubleshoot problems must be one of the first goals of a new programmer. You have been learning to code in assembler language. But you're not a machine, so you can't expect to write perfect code every time. You have learned by now that there are certain rules you must follow when coding. You've also learned what happens when you don't observe one of these rules: either the assembler gives you a diagnostic error message, or your program abends (terminates execution). In learning to debug, you will learn to recognize the type of error, locate its cause, and prevent it from recurring.

WHEN TO DEBUG

There are three stages at which you should debug, or at least use positive programming habits that help to minimize the number of errors, or "bugs," in your programs. The first phase of debugging occurs when the program is being coded. The process involved at this level is referred to as *desk checking*. The second phase may take place after the coded program has been submitted to the assembler program for translation. Bugs recognized by the assembler program must be corrected at this time. Their locations are pointed out to the programmer through assembler diagnostic error messages. The third phase of debugging takes place after the translated source program has been loaded into the storage of the computer—when machine instructions are fetched and executed. This is the time that most of the troubleshooting involved in debugging takes place.

DESK CHECKING

Few beginning programmers realize the importance of desk checking. The advantages to be gained by careful work at this point in the development of a solution to a problem can eliminate much wasted effort during subsequent phases of debugging. Using a program flowchart to illustrate the logic involved in a solution can help ensure that the basic logic used by a programmer does, in truth, solve the problem. Once a working flowchart has been developed, a programmer needs only to stick close to its logic as he codes the problem solution. After completion of the coding process, the entire body of code can be compared with the working flowchart.

Generous use of comments on the code at this point can reveal some coding errors. It can also be of immeasurable help during later stages of debugging, especially if someone else has to debug your code months (or even years) later. Entire blocks of code, as well as individual instructions that make up the blocks, can be commented. And these block comments can be used as a direct tie to the processing blocks in the flowchart.

Once the entire program is coded, additional checking techniques can be used to catch errors before the source program is translated. Scanning the operand field of the assembler instructions, the programmer can compile a list of all symbols referenced in the operands. He can then make a second scan of the name field of each instruction in the program, checking the symbols in his list as he encounters them. When all instructions have been scanned a second time, the programmer should have checked off every symbol in the *symbols-referenced list*. This type of checking process takes only a short time, but it can reduce the possibility of an undefined, or multiply defined, symbol and a wasted machine run.

Because branching instructions are particularly important in the implementation of logic, an excellent habit is to doublecheck the coding of all branch instructions. It is relatively easy to think "Branch Not Equal" and write "BE". A good approach is to compare the branch instructions you have coded with the decision blocks of the flowchart. One more check should be made before submitting the code for assembly: a "one-for-one" check of the punched cards with the coding sheets. This accomplished, the programmer has done all he can to eliminate bugs at the earliest point—the time of desk checking.

ASSEMBLER DIAGNOSTICS

As the assembler program scans each instruction in the source program, it checks for valid symbols, correct opcodes, and the proper specification of operands based on the opcodes encountered. Regardless of which assembler program and operating system you are using, the assembler will print an indication of error immediately following a statement that contains an error. Some large assemblers actually print the error message at this point; others print the error messages in a list at the end of the listing of the source program. In this type of diagnostic-message listing, the statement number from the source listing is used to connect a particular error message with the statement causing the error.

Figure 16-1 shows an example of assembler diagnostic error messages. The particular type of error message is indicated by a three-letter prefix identifying

```
       LOC   OBJECT CODE     ADDR1 ADDR2   STMT   SOURCE STATEMENT

       000000                                 1          CSECT
                                               2          PRINT NOGEN
                                               3    FIRST BEGIN=LOC,END=FIV+2
       000000 5860 C02E          00030        10          L     6,LOC
       000010 5A60 C034          00036        11          A     6,FIV
              *** ERROR ***
       000014 0000 0000 0000 00000 00000      12          MVC   AREA,SPOT
              *** ERROR ***
       00001A 5060 C02E          00030        13          ST    6,LOC
       00001E 0000 0000          00000        14          ST    20,SLOT
              *** ERROR ***
                                               15          LAST  BEGIN=LOC,END=FIV+2

       00002E 0000                             22 LOC  DC    F'6'
       00003C 00000006                         23 AREA DC    C'AB'
       000034 C1C2                             24 FIV  DC    H'5'
       000036 0005                             25          END
                                               26                =CL8'$$BPDUMP'
       000038 5B5BC2D7C4E4D4D7                 27                =A(LOC,FIV+2)
       000040 0000003000000038
```

```
                               CROSS-REFERENCE

       SYMBOL     LEN   VALUE   DEFN

       AREA     00002 000034 00023   0012
       FIV      00002 000036 00024   0008   0011  0018  0027
       LOC      00004 000030 00022   0008   0010  0013  0018  0027
       SLOT                          0014
       SPOT                          0012
```

```
                                    DIAGNOSTICS

       STMT   ERROR CODE   MESSAGE

        11   IJQ033       ALIGNMENT ERROR
        12   IJQ024       UNDEFINED SYMBOL
        14   IJQ010       INVALID SPECIFICATION OF REGISTER OR MASK FIELD
        14   IJQ024       UNDEFINED SYMBOL


       3 STATEMENTS FLAGGED IN THIS ASSEMBLY
```

Fig. 16-1 Assembler diagnostic-error messages (OS)

it as an assembler diagnostic message (for example, IEU, IFO, IJQ, or so on) followed by a message number. Normally the message provides the programmer with sufficient information to eliminate the bug, but if this message is not sufficient, a publication produced by IBM gives a more thorough explanation.[†]

There is one other way the assembler can communicate that it has encountered an error. This type of error is an undefined label or symbol. The fact that the assembler caught this type of error is indicated in the symbol cross-reference table, which contains five entries for each symbol encountered in the translation process. These five pieces of information are the:

1. symbol itself
2. length attribute associated with the symbol
3. value associated with the symbol
4. number of the statement in which the symbol is defined (appears in the name field)
5. numbers of statements that refer to this symbol in their operands

In the case of an undefined symbol, there will be entries of type 5 above, but no entry of type 4. (Some assemblers print ***UNDEFINED*** below the symbol.)

Errors the Assembler Cannot Catch   There is no way the assembler can catch either an error in the logical sequence of instructions or the misuse of an instruction. For example, the following three instructions pass the assembler's checks of syntax errors, yet an error does exist. Since the error is logical, not syntactical, the assembler cannot recognize it.

```
              CVB   6,LOC
               .   .
               .
               .
    AREA      DC    D'0'
    LOC       DC    C'0006587C'
```

You may have to locate this type of error at the third phase of debugging, after execution (if you do not find it while desk checking). The CVB instruction will cause a data exception as it executes. The second operand not only must be on a doubleword boundary, but must also contain data in the packed-decimal format—not character!

[†]Under OS, this information is given in the *Assembler Programmer's Guide* (there is one for each assembler). Under DOS, it is included in the *Assembler Language Manual*. Each of these manuals contains an appendix with an entry for each diagnostic message. Each entry contains an explanation of the error and suggests any programmer responses that might solve it.

Errors During Execution

As a program executes, it shares the computer's storage with the supervisor of the operating system. The supervisor is the main program in the computer and has responsibility for its operation and gives your program control, allowing it to execute. When your program has finished execution, it returns control to the supervisor; thus it executes as a subroutine of the supervisor.

When your program violates one of the rules of Systems/360 or 370, it causes what is known as an *exception*. When this occurs, execution of your program is interrupted. Control is then seized by the supervisor, which displays the reason for the interrupt (and your program's termination) in an abend dump.

THE INTERRUPT PROCEDURE

The computer works under the control of a special doubleword of information called a Program Status Word (PSW). The CPU uses the contents of the PSW to control the order in which instructions are executed. The PSW also indicates the status of the program at any given point in time. The PSW that contains the status of the program currently executing is referred to as the current PSW. Let's examine the information stored in a PSW by looking at figures 16-2 and 16-3.

SYSTEM MASK	KEY	AMWP	INTERRUPTION CODE
0 7	8 11	12 15	16 31

ILC	CC	PROG MASK	INSTRUCTION ADDRESS
32	34	36 39	40 63

Fig. 16-2   Program status word (System 360)

CHANNEL MASKS	E	KEY	CMWP	INTERRUPTION CODE
0 6	7	8 11	12 15	16 31

ILC	CC	PROG MASK	INSTRUCTION ADDRESS
32	34	36 39	40 63

Fig. 16-3   Program status word (System 370 in BC model)

There is a slight difference between the formats of the PSW in Systems/360 and 370 on page 293, but the portions we will examine are identical in both. The interruption code portion of the PSW (bits 16-31) identifies the action or condition causing the interrupt when an exception occurs. The instruction address part of the PSW (bits 40–63) always contains the address of the next instruction that should be fetched and executed by the CPU. When an exception occurs, a code indicating the cause of it is stored in the interruption code portion of the current PSW, and the entire PSW is stored in a special location in fixed storage locations (becomes the old PSW). A series of *new* PSWs, one for each different type of interrupt that can occur, are also located there.

When an interruption occurs, a *new* PSW is fetched from this series. This actually becomes the current PSW, and execution continues under control of this one. The instruction address part of this PSW contains the address of the first instruction in the supervisor routine for handling this type of interruption. So in the case of a program check, the next instruction fetched and executed starts the routine that examines the problem and causes the dump to be taken. Five different types of interrupts can occur. We are interested in one of these, the *program check interrupt*. It can be caused by exceptions occurring within your program.

The examination made, the action taken, and the form the dump listing takes depends on which operating system you are executing under. Some translate the interruption code into an explanation and print the actual address of the instruction causing the exception at the beginning of the dump (DOS). Other operating systems merely print the contents of the current PSW at the time the exception occurred and the completion code (type of error). They leave it up to the programmer to determine the address of the instruction causing the error—from a printout of the program check old PSW (the one that was stored after the program interruption). Before we examine the differences between the various operating systems, let's examine the similarities in the dumps.

Information Found in a Dump

At the top of each page in the dump three pieces of information can be found (use figures 16-4 and 16-5 as illustrations: Ⓐ the name associated with the job (from the job card), Ⓑ the date the job was run, and Ⓒ the page number of this particular page of the dump.

Just before the actual storage dump, the contents of the registers are displayed (in hexadecimal). The contents of the sixteen general purpose registers are displayed, eight per line, Ⓓ, with the notations "GR 0–7" and "GR 8–F" (DOS-based systems), or "REGS 0–7" and "REGS 8–15" (OS-based systems), just to the left of each line. Together with these two lines are displayed the contents of the floating-point registers, Ⓔ, identified on the left with the notation "FP REG" (DOS-based systems), or "FLTR 0–6" (OS-based).

TUGGLE ⒶA   04/25/74 ⒷB   PAGE   1 ⒸC

Ⓓ { GR 0-7   00001E58 00001E50 00007FFF 00001E00   00007F84 FFFFFF7C 00000000 00001DB8
D   GR 8-F   00000014 0A0107F1 00001E10 00001E10   40001E02 00003DF8 000001C0 0000007B
Ⓔ FP REG   41300000 00000000 41300000 C0000000   4264000C 00000000 43316000 00000000
   COMREG   BG ADDR IS 0001C0   Ⓗ H

Ⓕ F
000000   00000000 00000000 00000000 00000000   00000000 000001C0 FF050000 00000000   ....
000020   FF070007 40001986 FF150007 80001E14   5B5B8C2C5 D6D1F440 FF05000E 80001986   .... $$BEOJ4 ....
000040   00001AA8 08000000 00001A98 00000000   FF000000 00FF0000 00040000 0F001018   ....
000060   00040000 00000288 00040000 00000FE8   00000000 0000076C 00040000 00000254   ....Y
000080   00000000 00000000 000000C0 00000003   00050680 41B80071 45700106 41A0B258   ....
0000A0   41900136 41800F3C 47F000CA 06B00680   06B006B0 06B006B0 06B0418B 00174188   ....O.........
0000C0   00504570 01064180 01369640 A0019120   A00C4710 00E29260 A00195E2 A0024780   .&.............S-....S..
0000E0   09869510 022F0778 94F901FB D7010218   02189680 B2594400 0E660788 947FB259   ....9.P.........
000100   45700EDA 07F842B0 00D748B0 018C9180   A0000717 5890A004 4880018E 90C0901C   .....8..P............
000120   C2089010 01B0D207 90088000 9680A000   07F74570 010ED203 0C420C46 DC030C42   K.....K....... .7....K..
000140   B2481BAA DD030C42 000C43A1 000442A0   01EF41AA B2484400 A0045890 A0044220   ....K.....- .....
000160   A0009140 A0014710 0198D207 01809008   98989010 82000180 956001EF 47800190   ....-....
000180   5890A004 98189030 989B01B0 82000038   9284B2A8 47F00188 9680A000 41100030   ...O..........O...
0001A0   47F00E66 615C4061 504044F0 00FE1E00   00001DA8 00001258 000001C0 10000000   .O../* /& .O.........
0001C0   F0F461F2 F561F7F4 1E001800 C0000000   00000000 00000000 E3E4C7C7 D3C54040   04/25/74.........TUGGLE
0001E0   00007FFF 00001E5F 00001E5F C0000010   00007FFF E0007E90 A8A07ED0 009C1321   ....
000200   13281371 1372138C 1398139C 13A038F0   F4F2F5F7 F4F1F1F5 00001248 00000006   ....O 42574115.
000220   0B980BB6 0C440000 0C4C0000 13140010   5B5BC2D6 00160003 01000C54 12440000   ....)...... $$B0.
000240   00000000 01C01000 0C4C0000 00001A98   000013E2 9238018F 909B01B0 48B001BC   ....S......
000260   4190050C 48B0018C 951001EF 47F0027E   58A0B25C 9018A030 41A0B258 07F941A0   ....* ..9-
000280   B2A89601 A00007F9 909B01B0 922018F   45900264 41900178 95000023 47800316   .....9..........6
0002A0   95230023 47B000AE 48600022 1A664866   B2B507F6 181F1B66 4121000F 45700AAC   -.D.......O.....6
0002C0   48600BC4 1B331823 43201007 47F00364   472000BA 182395OB 100747F0 03604720   ....9......O.-.
0002E0   00889680 1002960C 100407F9 18584143   00024354 00004145 50001A44 4A400BBC   ....9......&..-
000300   95FF4000 477002F2 42840000 07F995FF   03AD0789 1B0095FF 03AD4780 0EEC9560   ....2...9........
000320   01EF4780 02B44160 0010D502 A0050239   47700342 41110000 491001AE 47B00342   ....N...............
000340   1B664121 000F4570 0AAC1B33 43301007   95011006 47700200 4123000B 95161007   ....N....1...
000360   47B000BA 41822000 48700200 43387000   D4031002 B2B44930 01AC47B0 02DE8930   .........O........M...
000380   00034133 B328D5C2 100901F1 47B000B6   440003DE 5870024C 95077000 477003AA   ....N....1...........)...
0003A0   D5027001 01F147B0 00B64180 00024148   80001A44 4A400BBC 41588314 D20003AD   N...&..1.....&.........K..
0003C0   40005010 400092FF 44000220 50004260   50064400 08789560 B2A04770 044CD202   ....-.).-..&.- .&-...-...)K.
0003E0   024D1009 5860024C 95076000 4770044C   D202024D 60015870 024C1B44 43403005   ...-.).-...) K.-.-.).-..1
000400   4C400BB0 5A400250 41440000 D5037C01   4004780 044C9120 100C4710 04469105   ) ... .&...-.N.....1.....
000420   10024770 04469140 60044780 044694BF   60049110 10024780 043E9640 10029614   ....K.......
000440   10029601 100CD203 40007001 95FF3002   477002EC 42803002 91983006 07794820   .....K.......&-..)...
000460   30009500 30004780 04709F00 20000769   91203006 47100092 95503004 47800ACC   ....& .-....
000480   D2020049 1009D300 00485006 9C002000   4770049E 9023B2A0 96803006 07F94730   K....L..&.......9.-
0004A0   07769106 00454770 0A52913F 00454770   048891AF 00440789 4020003A 58600048   ....&.......-.-
0004C0   4A600B74 50600040 47F00550 D2000B08   3005D202 00491009 58700048 18884380   .-.&-. .O.&K....K.....-.
0004E0   30034C80 0B1E4A80 02069500 80004770   048C9504 70004170 0B084780 05025070   .)............K......&.
000500   0048D202 70091009 47F0048C 41900178   91060045 47700A56 94FD0039 41700550   ..K....O......&
000520   D501003A B2A24780 07344560 C73A4820   003A4220 05494560 05484133 0008D500   N.......-..7........-...N.
000540   3000003A 47200680 950E3001 077607F7   457006A2 91020044 47800578 91803006   ...D....D......O.....-
000560   471007C4 95FF3002 477007C4 95623004   47700578 457008F0 91390045 47700788   .-...D....D.....9.......
000580   41600582 91800044 07869604 00044910A   01F90789 95003004 07769580 B2884780   ....9.-.
0005A0   05AA9108 B2904700 05829603 B2884190   01329110 00444710 05CA9500 00440789   ....9...
0005C0   D6020041 00414770 06BA9104 00444770   05E09550 00444770 06809477 300607F9   O.....................&.....9
0005E0   94773006 91043006 47800668 D6011004   00449473 30069180 100C4710 06129550   ....O..............&

```
JOB TUGGLE Ⓐ       STEP GC        TIME 150704    DATE 74241 Ⓑ

COMPLETION CODE    SYSTEM = 0C5

PSW AT ENTRY TO ABEND  FFF5000D 8057C27C

TCB  0236F8  RBP   00023AA0  PIE    00000000  DER  0002343C  TIO 00023C20  CMP 80C5000   TRN 00000000
             MSS   02024CC0  PK-FLG F0850400  FLG  00006F6A  LLS 00023C88  JLB 00000000  JPQ 00023CB0
             FSA   0106EF68  TCB    00000000  TME  00000000  JST 0002360FB NTC 00000000  OTC 0002228
             LTC   00000000  IQE    00000000  ECB  00023A4C  STA 20000000  D-PQE 0002460 SQS 00023C8
             ASTAE 00000000  TCT    80022D28  USER 00000000  DAR 00000000  RESV 00000000 JSCB 87022FD0

ACTIVE RBS

PRB  023E68  RESV  00000000  APSW   8057C27C   WC-SZ-STAB 00040082  FL-CDE 00023EA8  PSW FFF5000D 8057C27C
             Q/TTR 0CC00000  WT-LNK 000236F8

SVRB 023990  TAB-LN 00C8C22C  APSW F9F0F1C3   WC-SZ-STAB 0012D002  TQN 00000000  PSW 00040033 500CA7CA
             C/TTR  0004491C  WT-LNK 00023E68
             RG 0-7  0005FF1C  0005FC86  0023D48   5C023A50  00024228  00023C78  00000000
             RG 8-15 00000000  00022D28  00023A50  8005FC72  0006EF68  4005FD8E  F357C278
             EXTSA   0000298E  8F06EF10  00000000  C4F90C50  00023A0C  00023A14  E2E8E2C9
                     C5C1F0F1  C9C5C1F1  C1C2C5D5

SVRB 02344A0 TAB-LN 001803C8  APSW F1F0F5C1   WC-SZ-STAB 0012D002  TQN 00000000  PSW FF04000C 5006E7A6
             Q/TTR  00004815  WT-LNK 00023990
             RG 0-7  00105BB0  000239F0  8000A6E2  000BB888  00023990  00023990  03026EF8  00023990
             RG 8-15 000236F8  4000A62A  8F06EF10  8F06EF10  00023C50  00023A14  4000B0C4  00000000
             EXTSA   E2E8E2C9  C5C1F0F1  C9C7C3F0  F3F0F3C5  00000000  C0001E0C  00000000  0000C990
                     FFFF7FFF  000234F4  E2C3D9F0  F2F00000

LOAD LIST
NE 00023CC8  RSP-CCE 02023CB0  NE 00023660  NE 00023E60  RSP-CDE C10252F8  NE 00024170  RSP-CCE 010251F8
NF 00000000  RSP-CDF 010251B8

CCE                                                                                                 LN    ADR
NE 00023CC8  ATR1 0F  NCDE 000000    RQC-RB 00023E68  NM GJ       USE 01  EPA 05FC30  ATR2 20  XL/MJ 023F98
023EA8       ATR1 30  NCDE 023EA8    RCC-RB 00000000  NM IGC0A05A USE 02  EPA 06E058  ATR2 28  XL/MJ 023CA0
0252F8       ATR1 80  NCDE 025328    RQC-RB 00000000  NM IGGC19CD USE 01  EPA 07DA38  ATR2 20  XL/MJ 0252F8
0251F8       ATR1 80  NCDE 025228    FCC-RB 00000000  NM IGG019AA USE 01  EPA 07CE40  ATR2 20  XL/MJ 0251E8
0251B8       ATR1 B0  NCDE 0251F8    RQC-RB 00000000  NM IGG019AB USE 01  EPA 07D870  ATR2 20  XL/MJ 0251A8
                      NCDE 0251B8

XL                                          LN        ADR
023F98       SZ 0C00C01C  NO 000CC001  8000030D  0005FC30
023CA0       SZ 00000010  NO 00000001  800007A8  0006E058
0252F8       SZ 0C00C01C  NO 00000001  80000270  0007DA38
0251E8       SZ 00000010  NO 00000001  800001C0  0007CE40
```

Fig. 16-5 Example for dump-reading practice (OS-based systems part 1 of 3)

```
0251AR   SZ 0000010   NO 0000000C1        80000148    00070870

DEB
C23400  00004426 00004426 00000000          00000113 000028E0    00004426 00004426    *....N ....TATE....*
C23420  10000000 8ECCCCCC 8F000000 01000000 68000000 FF06EF10    110C0000 03C236F8    *..............8*
C23440  0000001A 000A001A 0013000A 0C010C01 00000000 00000000    04023418 1A001E0C    *..............BBA*
C23460  C3C40000 CCCCCCCC 00000000 00000000 00000000 00000000    00CC007D C2C2C2C1    *CD............*

TIOT  JOB TUGGLE   STEP GO    PGM=*.CD   PROC ASSEM
 DD  14040140  SYSAREND   002CCC00  8C001E0C
 DD  14040140  SYSIN      0028150C  8C001E0C
 DD  14040100             CC2C1200  8C001E0C

MSS    *********** SPQE ********     *********** DQE *****************   ******** FQE ********
       FLGS NSPQE  SPID  DQE         BLK       FQE      LN       NDQE    NFQE      LN
0246CC  00  0256C8  251  023E88      0005F800 0005FR0C 000008CC CC000000 00000000  00000430
0256C8  00  024?F8  252  023F68      0006F000 0006F000 00000800 00023C90 00000000  000007FA
                                     0006E000 0006E0CC CC00E0CC CC000000 00000000  00000059
0243F8  CO  CCCCCC  000  024C90      0006E800 0006E800 00000800 00023810 00000000  000005D8
024090  60  CCCCCC  000  022ECO      0006D800 0006D800 0C000800 CC000000 00000000  000001A0

C-PQE 00024DD0  FIRST 00023EF0  LAST 0CC23EF0
FQE 023EF0  FFB 00060000  LFB 00060000  NPQ 00000000  PPQ 000CCCC0
            TCB 00024228  RSI 00010000  RAD 0005F800  FLG 0000

FBCE 060000  NFB 00023EF0  PFB 00023EF0  SZ 0000D800

CCB TRACE
MAJ 024DB8  NMAJ 00023CCC  PMAJ C001A9A0  FMIN 00024D98  NM SYSESN
MIN 023D20  FQEL 000237A0  PMIN 00024D98  NMIN 00000000  NM FF SYS1.MACLIB
            NQEL CCCCCCCC  PQEL 80023D20  TCB 00024228  SVRB 00022C00
MAJ 023C00  NMAJ 00000000  PMAJ 00024DB8  FMIN 00023BF8  NM SYSIFA01
MIN 023BF8  FQEL 00023AF8  PMIN 00023C00  NMIN 00000000  NM FO IEA
            NQEL CCCCCCCC  PQEL 00023RE8  TCR 000236F8  SVRR 000234A0

SAVE AREA TRACE

INTERRUPT AT 57C27C
```

Fig. 16-5 (Part 2 of 3)

```
(E) FLTR 0-6      1341CCCC00000053   C8E052D20F74241F          0000000030000000   0000000000000000           PAGE 0069

(D) REGS 0-7      0005FF1C  0005FC86  00023D48  5C023A50   00024488  00024228  00023C78  00000000
    REGS 8-15     CCCC0000  00022D28  0C023A50  8005FC72   4005FC32  0006EF68  4005FD8E  F357C278

LOAD MODULE   GO
                                      (G)                                                              (H)
(F) C5FC20                                               05C00700 4510C01E 000C8420 0005FDFC
 05FC40   00000000 0005FC48 0005FE9C 80060000   92801014 0A330700 4510C032 0005FD24   *....K........ ..................*
 05FC60   8F05FD90 0A131B77 1B884100 C2EA45B0   C1525A80 C26AD278 C296C2EA C503C2EA   *................................*
 05FC80   C2E64780 C0704E80 C3BEF377 C35DC3BE   D300C364 C3634100 C33A45B0 C1BE47F0   *...........B...A...B.K.B.B.N.B.*
 05FCA0   C038F273 C3B6C3C8 4F30C3B6 1A7347F0   C0384E70 C3C6F357 C278C3C6 D300C27D   *BW.......C.3.C.C.L.C.C...C...A..0*
 05FCC0   C27C4100 C26E45B0 C1BE90EC D00C05C0   50D0C188 41F0C184 50FD0008 18DF0700   *..2.C.C...C....0....CF3.B.CFL.B.*
 05FCE0   4510C02C 0000842C 0005FDFC 00000000   0005FCF4 0005FE9C 00060000 92801014   *B...B...A..........A..0A........*
 05FD00   0A330700 4510C03C 8005FD24 0A140700   4510C048 8005FD90 0A1458D0 C18898EC   *..................4.............*
 05FD20   D00C07FE 00000000 00000000 00000000   00000000 00000000 C0000001 00004000   *...........................A...*
 05FD40   00000001 0005FCB2 80000000 D9C5C1C4   C9D54040 02005000 00000001 00000001   *............................... .*
 05FD60   00000050 00000000 00000001 00000001   00000001 00000050 C0000001 00000000   *............READIN  ...........*
 05FD80   00000001 4110C054 58F01030 05FF07FB   00000000 00000000 00000000 00000000   *................................*
 05FDA0   00000000 C0000001 00004000 00000001   00000001 84000000 D7D9C9D5 E3404040   *.........0......................*
 05FDC0   02000050 00000001 00000001 00000079   00000000 00000001 00000001 C0000001   *.......... .............PRINT   *
 05FDE0   00000079 C00000C1 00000000 00000001   4110C0C0 58F01030 05FF07FB 00000000   *................................*
 05FE00   00000000 00000000 00000000 0C000000   00000001 00004000 C0000001 00000001   *.....................0.........*
 05FE20   54000000 E2C5C1D7 C4C44040 02000020   00000001 00000001 00000660 00000000   *.................... ..........*
 05FE40   00000001 00000001 00000001 0000007D   00000001 00000000 00000000 00000000   *....SNAPDD   ....................*
 05FE60   00000000 00000000 00000000 00000000   00000000 00000000 00000000 00000000   *................................*
 05FE80   00000000 C00000CC 00000000 0C000000   00000000 00000000 00000000 00000001   *................................*
 05FEA0   40404040 40404040 40401040 40F01046   40C9E240 E3C8C540 E3D6E3C1 D34B4040   *................................*
 05FEC0   40404040 404C404C 40404040 40404040   40404040 40404040 40404040 40404040   *              .  0.. IS THE TOTAL.  *
      LINE 05FEE0   SAME AS ABOVE                                                           *                                *
 C5FF00   40404040 40404040 40404040 40404040   40404040 40404040 D9C9E3C5 30883088   *                                *
 05FF20   41108516 0A3C912C 40104780 8498417C   000447F0 82944100 00101890 451084A2   *                          RITE....*
 05FF40   0A0AD70F 10001000 41A1000C 50A10000   18A19200 10089220 10C90A28 41108532   *........ ..........0...........*
 05FF60   0A3848EA 000C40EC 30921809 40E3C8C5   D9C540C9 E240C140 C2C1C440 C3D6C4C5   *..P.............................*
 05FF80   40C9D540 C3C1D9C4 40404040 404040CE   00058D28 00150040 40404040 40404040   *...... ..... THERE IS A BAD CODE*
 05FFA0   40404040 40404040 40404040 40404040   40404040 40404040 40404040 40404040   * IN CARD          .......        *
      LINE 05FFC0   SAME AS ABOVE                                                           *                                *
 05FFE0   40404040 40F30000 001A8000 C9C5C6F4   F2F6C940 D8E4C5E4 C540C3D9 C9E3C9C3   *     3......IEF426I QUEUE CRITIC*

LOAD MODULE   IGC0A05A

 06E040                                                           4180D099 18114313
 C6E060   00001A81 41330001 95FF3000 47806068   1BEE1BFF 1B001B11 43E30000 43030001   *.... ..0...........0..........*
 06E080   8CE00004 88F0001C 8C000004 8810001C   1A2044E0 60701A1E 41818001 44F06076   *.........................T.....*
 06E0A0   F384D069 C069CC07 D06962C6 41FFF001   44F0607C 47F066F8 413E3003 47F06010   *.....0.........................0..*
 06E0C0   41330001 47F060E2 D2008000 3002D200   D0692000 D2008000 C0695050 D08C5000   *3.............F..0..0...0.8.....0..*
 06E0E0   D12094FC D1235B00 C1201A10 5800D120   41110003 5010D064 94FCD067 C7C3D06C   *......0.SK.....K......K.........*
 C6E100   D06C1810 5400629C 19014780 60BC1B10   4010D06C 5810D064 4A10D06C 18005D00   *J...J....J.......J...............P...*
 06E120   66804000 D06A1211 4770611C 4810D06A   12114770 60E85850 D08C5860 D12407F5   *................. ...............*
 C6E140   4120D121 45B06236 5820D120 413062C4   48A0D06A 4BA0D06C 88A00002 45B0623E   *.....................Y......J..5*
 06E160   46A06104 9640D112 455062DA 94BFD112   47F060DE 18A15810 C1204B10 D06C5010   *..J.........J....D...............*
 06E180   D0704120 D07145B0 62364810 D06C8810   00011A31 5820D120 45B0623E 5020D120   *..... J........J...0........J.......*
 C6E1A0   9640D112 455062CA 94BFD112 4810D06C   12114770 61984700 615E4110 0001191A   *..........................J......J.*
                                                                                          *. J.......J.......................*
```

Fig. 16-5 (Part 3 of 3)

The main body of the dump is a byte-by-byte display of the contents of storage. Each line of the dump is divided into three separate sections. On the immediate left of each line, Ⓕ is the hexadecimal address in storage of the first byte displayed on that line. The remaining two sections of each line contain a display of storage: one in hexadecimal of the contents in the center, Ⓖ, and a display of any bytes that contain a valid EBCDIC graphic symbol, Ⓗ. If a particular byte contains a bit combination that does not represent an EBCDIC graphic, a period is substituted at that location in the line.

Using figures 16-4 and 16-5, see if you can find the following information:

1. jobname
2. date the job was run
3. contents of general purpose register 8
4. address of the first byte displayed in the second line of the dump
5. contents (hexadecimal) of the byte described in question 4[†]

The next task is to learn to count across a particular line in a dump; that is, how to locate the contents of a byte other than the first one displayed on a line. The hexadecimal-display portion of each line in the dump displays the contents of eight fullwords of storage. The eight hex digits representing each word are grouped and separated from the next eight by a blank. There is a wider separation between the fourth and fifth word.

To locate the beginning of a particular word, count in hexadecimal across a line, starting with the address to the left of that line and incrementing by values of 4. For instance, with the last line displayed on the page we are examining: 0005E0, 5E4, 5E8, 5EC, 5F0, etc., notice that you can calculate the address of the fifth word (the one immediately following the wide gap) by adding a value of 10 (hexadecimal) to the address displayed at the beginning of the line.

What are the contents of the word that begins at address 000250? Proceed down the column at the left until you locate the address closest to, but not greater than, 250. This occurs in the nineteenth line. The address is 000240. What value needs to be added to this address to calculate the address of 250? A value of 10 (hexadecimal). This means the contents of the word that begins at address 000250 is displayed immediately following the large gap in the center of the line. Its contents: 000013E2.

Find the contents of the following locations:

1. fullword located at address 0004C4 (DOS), 05FF84 (OS)
2. doubleword located at address 000258 (DOS), 05FDB8 (OS)
3. byte at address 00047C (DOS), 05FC7C (OS)

[†]The answers to the above questions are (1) TUGGLE, (2) 04/25/74 (DOS), 74241 (OS Julian), (3) 00000014 (DOS), 00000000 (OS), (4) 000020 (DOS), 05FC40(OS), and (5) FF (DOS), 00 (OS).

4. byte at address 00054E (DOS), 05FF6E (OS)
5. halfword at address 00030E (DOS), 05FEAE (OS)
6. 7 bytes beginning with the byte at address 00059D (DOS), 05FC9E (OS)

You should discover the following contents:

1. 50600040 (DOS), C3C1D9C4 (OS)
2. 909B01B0 48B001BC (DOS), D7D9C9D5 E3404040 (OS)
3. 47 (DOS), D5 (OS)
4. 07 (DOS), C8 (OS)
5. 95FF (DOS), 1046 (OS)
6. 88478005AA9108 (DOS), 47F00038F2F3C3 (OS)

LOCATING CAUSE OF ERROR AT EXECUTION TIME

Every operating system has a means of informing the programmer of the first location of his program in storage. This is a point of reference for determining which instruction caused the exception that brought about an abend dump.

The dump shown in figure 16-6 was produced when the supervisor recognized the occurrence of a data exception at location 001E10. To figure out which instruction in the program caused it, the load-point address (1E00 in this case) is subtracted from that of the instruction causing the exception:

$$
\begin{array}{ll}
\text{exception at} & \text{1E10} \\
\text{load point} & \underline{\text{1E00}} \\
& \text{10}
\end{array}
$$

The result of this subtraction is the location within the assembler listing of the source code of the instruction that caused the exception. The instruction at location 10 in the source listing is the CVB instruction. What requirements of the CVB instruction operands might lead to a data exception? The CVB requires that the data specified in the second operand be in packed-decimal format.

The value subfield of the second operand (LOC) looks like a valid sign and valid digits for the packed-decimal format (0005782C). But this is not the correct way to check the actual data in the field. The correct way is to check either the object code as displayed in the source listing or to find the field in the dump and check it there. In this case, the object code displayed in the source listing is sufficient to pinpoint the problem. The object code portion of the source listing shows the contents of the 8-byte field LOC to be: F0F0F0 F5F7F8F2C3. The field actually contains 8 bytes of zoned-decimal data. The problem lies in the type code used in the operand of the DC statement. Instead of a C-type code a P- or X-type code should have been used.

```
LOC    OBJECT CODE    ADDR1 ADDR2  STMT    SOURCE STATEMENT

000000                              1            CSECT
                                    2            PRINT  NOGEN
                                    3       FIRST BEGIN=AREA,END=D+4
00000C 5880 C03E        00040      10            L     8,TWTY
000010 4F60 C036        00038      11            CVB   6,LOC
000014 1C86                        12            MR    8,6
000016 5A90 C046        00048      13            A     9,D
00001A 5090 C042        00044      14            ST    9,ANS
                                   15       LAST  BEGIN=AREA,END=D+4

00002A 000000000000                22  AREA      DC    D'0'
00003C 0000000000000000            23  LOC       DC    C'0005782C'
000038 F0F0F0F5F7F8F2C3            23  LOC       DC    C'0005782C'
000040 00000014                    24  TWTY      DC    F'20'
000044                             25  ANS       DS    F
000048 00000041                    26  D         DC    F'65'
                                   27            END
000050 5B5BC2D7C4E4D4D7            28                  =CL8'$$BPDUMP'
000058 0000000300000004C           29                  =A(AREA,D+4)
```

CROSS-REFERENCE

```
SYMBOL    LEN   VALUE   DEFN

ANS       00004 000044 00025   0014
AREA      00008 000030 00022   0008   0018   0029
D         00004 000048 00026   00C8   0013   0018   0029
LOC       00008 000038 00023   0011
TWTY      00004 000040 00024   0010
```

NO STATEMENTS FLAGGED IN THIS ASSEMBLY

```
04/25/74   PHASE  XFR-AD  LOCORE  HICORE  DSK-AD  ESD TYPE  LABEL       LOADED  REL-FR

           PHASE*** 001E00  001E00  001E5F   4C 06 1  CSECT            001E00  001E00
```

OS031 PROGRAM CHECK INTERRUPTION - HEX LOCATION 001E10 - CONDITION CODE 0 - DATA EXCEPTION
OS00I JOB TUGGLE   CANCELED

```
         TUGGLE            04/25/74

GR 0-7   00001E58 00001E50 00007FFF 00001E00   00007F84 FFFFFF7C 00000000 00001DB8
GR 8-F   00000014 0AC107F1 00001E10 00001E10   40001E02 00003DF8 000001C0 0000007B
FP REG   41300000 00000000 41300C00 00000000   4264000C 00000000 43316000 00000000
COMREG   BG ADDR IS C001C0

000000   00000000 00000000 00000000 00000000   00000000 000001C0 FF050000 00000000
000020   FF070007 40001986 FF150007 80001E14   5B5BC2C5 D6D1F440 FF05000E 80001986
```

Fig. 16-6 Data-exception debugging example

If this program had been executing under a supervisor that does not figure
out the type of exception causing the dump—and the address of the instruction
causing the exception, you could find the same information from the PSW that
was current at the time the exception occurred. Three portions of the PSW
would be of interest to you: (1) the interruption code in bits 16–31, (2) the
instruction length counter in bits 32–33, and (3) the instruction address in

bits 40–63. In the abend dump we are examining, these portions of the PSW would contain the following:

interruption code	7
instruction length counter	2
instruction address	1E14

Remember, the instruction address portion of the PSW contains the address of the next instruction that would have been executed had not the abend occurred. Before the instruction causing the exception was executed, the instruction address in the current PSW was incremented by the length, in bytes, of this instruction. To figure out which instruction caused the exception, the programmer need only subtract this length from the address in the PSW.

The length can be found in the ILC portion of the PSW, bits 32–33. These two bits contain the number of halfwords in the executing instruction (1, 2, or 3). In the case we're examining, the ILC contained 2. So, subtracting 4 (the number of bytes in two halfwords) from the instruction address in the PSW, we calculate that the instruction causing the exception is located at the address 1E10.

The interruption-code field of the PSW indicates the type of exception caused was a data exception. There are fifteen different types of programming exceptions that may be encountered in the interruption-code portion of the PSW. As you can see below, the data exception has an interruption code of 0007.

Code	Type of Exception
0001	operation
0002	privileged operation
0003	execute
0004	protection
0005	addressing
0006	specification
0007	data
0008	fixed-point overflow
0009	fixed-point divide
000A	decimal overflow
000B	decimal divide
000C	exponent overflow
000D	exponent underflow
000E	significance
000F	floating-point divide

OS-based systems aid the programmer by using the interruption code of a program check to build a system completion code. This is displayed on the second line of the dump after the jobname, date, etc. An operation exception would result in a 0C1 System Completion Code; an addressing exception would give 0C5; a data exception would give 0C7, and so on.

DEBUGGING ERRORS IN LOGIC

There are many times when a program seems to execute correctly but provides incorrect results. The following listing illustrates just this situation.

The execution of this program was not interrupted by an exception. In fact, although this program produced six lines of output, they were not the expected ones. When working properly, the program should read in a series of records from a card data set. The format of these cards is as follows:

Columns	*Contents*
1–4	Code indicating that the sum on this card has been checked ("RITE" indicates a checked sum; anything else indicates an incorrect sum.)
5–15	Last name of the customer
16–25	First name of the customer
31–34	Sum of this month's bills for the customer

A count is kept of the number of cards read. A copy of the input card (the input record) is moved to the output area to be printed on the report. As each card is read, columns 1–4 are checked to see if they contain the code RITE. If so, the sum (cols. 31–34) from the card is added to the total sum being calculated for printout at end-of-file. Then a branch is taken back to read another card.

If RITE is not found in cols. 1–4, the number of the card and a message to the effect that there is a bad code in this card is printed, so the error can be eliminated. A branch is then taken to read another card. Did this program execute correctly? We begin our investigation by checking the six lines of output. The first five produced indicate that all five cards read contained bad codes. Looking at the input, we can determine that each of the first five data cards contains the characters RITE in columns 1–4 and also that there are only five cards in the input data set. This means that even though each data card contained the code indicating its sum was checked, every input card was flagged as containing a bad code.

With this fact in mind, let's examine the source code to see what happened. The instruction that checks for valid codes is statement 25. This is a storage-to-storage compare of the four characters at KODE with the four at GOOD.

```
LOC     OBJECT CODE         ADDR1 ADDR2  STMT  SOURCE STATEMENT
C00000                                     1          CSECT
                                           2          PRINT NOGEN
                                           3    FIRST BEGIN=ONE,END=TOT+8,IO=YES
00001E  1677                              18          SR    7,7
000020  1B88                              19          SR    8,8
                                          20    LOOP  MREAD INTO=INAREA
00002A  5A80 C276           00278         23          A     8,ONE
00002E  D278 C2A2 C2F6      002A4 002F8   24          MVC   OUTAREA+40,INAREA
000034  D503 C2F6 C2F2      002F8 002F4   25          CLC   KODE(4),GOOD
00003A  4780 C058           0005A         26          BE    HANDLE
00003E  4E80 C3CE           003D0         27          CVD   8,KTR
000042  F377 C369 C36F      003D0 00371   28          UNPK  PTKTR,KTR
000048  D300 C370 C36F      00372 00371   29          MVZ   PTKTR+7(1),PTKTR+6
                                          30          MRITE FROM=ERRMSG
000056  47F0 C020           00022         33          B     LOOP
00005A  F273 C3C6 C314      003C8 00316   34    HANDLE PACK  PACKSUM,SUM
000060  4F30 C3C6           003C8         35          CVB   3,PACKSUM
000064  1A73                              36          AR    7,3
000066  47F0 C020           00022         37          B     LOOP
00006A  4E70 C3D6           003D8         38    EOF   CVD   7,TOT
00006E  F357 C284 C306      00286 003D8   39          UNPK  PTTOT(6),TOT
000074  D300 C289 C288      00286 0028A   40          MVZ   PTTOT+5(1),PTTOT+4
                                          41          MRITE FROM=OUTAREA
                                          44    LAST  BEGIN=ONE,END=TOT+8,ASMDATA=NO,I=YES,O=YES,  X
                                                      EOFRTN=EOF
000278  00000001                         119    ONE     DC   F'1'
00027C                                   120    OUTAREA DS   0CL121
00027C  40404040404040404040            121    CTLCHR  DC   CL10' '
000286                                   122    PTTOT   DS   CL6
00028C  40C9E240E3C8C540                123            DC   CL104' IS THE TOTAL.'
0002F4  D9C9E3C5                        124    GOOD    DC   CL4'RITE'
0002F8                                   125    INAREA  DS   0CL80
0002F8                                   126    KODE    DS   CL4
0002FC                                   127    MSG     DS   CL26
000316                                   128    SUM     DS   CL4
00031A                                   129    PAD     DS   CL46
000348                                   130    ERRMSG  DS   0CL121
000348  40E3C8C5D9C5540C9               131            DC   CL35' THERE IS A BAD CODE IN CARD'
000373  40404040404040404040            132    PTKTR   DC   CL8' '
0003C8                                   133            DC   CL78' '
0003C8                                   134    PACKSUM DS   D
0003D0                                   135    KTR     DS   D
0003D8                                   136    TOT     DS   D
                                         137            END
0003E0  5B5B6C2D7C4E4D4D7               138            =CL8'$$BPDUMP'
0003E8  0000027B0000003E0               139            =A(ONE,TOT+8)
0003F0  5B5B6C20C7C5D0540               140            =C'$$BOPEN '
0003F8  5B5B6C23D3D6E2C5               141            =C'$$BCLOSE'
```

Fig. 16-7 Debugging logic errors (Part 1 of 3)

SYMBOL	LEN	VALUE	DEFN				
$CARD	00006	0000B0	00067	0015	0054	0085	
$INPUT	00004	0000E4	00084	0078	0080		
$LINE	00006	000148	00093	0016	0061	0113	
$OUTPUT1	00121	000178	00111	0104			
$OUTPUT2	00121	0001F1	00112	0109			
$READ	00004	000134	00085	0022			
$WRITE	00004	00026A	00113	0032	0043		
CTLCHK	00010	00027C	00121				
EOF	00004	00006A	00038	0079			
ERRMSG	00121	000348	00130	0031			
GOOD	00004	0002F4	00124	0025			
HANDLE	00006	00005A	00034	0026			
IJCX0012	00008	0000D0	00080	0070			
IJJC0009	00004	000090	00053				
IJJC0010	00004	0000A0	00060				
IJJD0003	00004	000010	00014				
IJJZ0012	00001	0000E2	00083				
IJJZ0014	00001	000178	0C110				
INAREA	00080	0002F8	00125	0021	0024		
KODE	00004	0002F8	00126	0025	0028		
KTR	00008	0003D0	00135	0027	0037		
LOUP	00004	000022	00021	0033			
MSG	00026	0002FC	00127				
ONE	00121	000278	00119	0008	0023	0047	0139
OUTAREA	00121	00027C	00120	0024	0042		
PACKSUM	00008	0003C8	00134	0034	0035		
PAD	00046	00031A	00129				
PTKTK	00008	00036B	00132	0028	0029		
PTTOT	00006	000286	00122	0039	0040		
SUM	00006	000316	00128	0034			
TOT	00008	0003D8	00136	0008	0038	0047	0139

NO STATEMENTS FLAGGED IN THIS ASSEMBLY

Fig. 16-7 (Part 2 of 3)

```
TUGGLE      04/25/74                                                                                              PAGE   1

GR 0-7   000021E8 000021E0 00007FFF 00001E00   00007F84 FFFFFF7C 00000000 00001DB8
GR 8-F   00003946 UA0107F1 0001E10 00001E10    4001E02 000030F8 00001C0 0000007B
FP REG   41300000 00000000 41300C00 00000000   42640000 00000000 43316000 00000000

002070   E3C8C540 E3D6E3C1 40404040 40404040   40404040 4040D190 C2424700 40C9E240     THE TOTAL....        J.B.... IS
002080   40404040 --SAME-- D34B4040 40404040   40404040 40404040 40404040 40404040
002090   40404040 D9C9E3C5 40404040 40404040   40404040 40404040 40404040 40404040     RITE
0020FC   40404040 --SAME--
002130   40000000 47000002 5B5BC2D7 C4E4D4D7   00002048 40E3C8C5 D9C540C9 E9C9E6F3     ......$$BPDUMP ...... THERE I
002150   F240C140 C2C1C440 C3D6C4C5 40C9D540   C3C1D9C4 40404040 40404040 E9C9E6F3     CARD       FZIW3
002170   030A0A40 40404040 40404040 40404040   40404040 40404040 40404040 40404040
00219C   40404040 --SAME--
0021B0   40404040 40404040 40404040 40404040   40FE615C 00000000 00000000 92011028     ......00.
0021D0   0A320000 0A320000 47F0F01A                                                    ./*..............

THERE IS A BAD CODE IN CARD     00000001
THERE IS A BAD CODE IN CARD     00000002
THERE IS A BAD CODE IN CARD     00000003
THERE IS A BAD CODE IN CARD     00000004
THERE IS A BAD CODE IN CARD     00000005
000000 IS THE TOTAL.            RITETUGGLE      SHARON      0084
```

```
TUGGLE      04/25/74                                                                                              PAGE   1

GR 0-7   000021E8 000021E0 00007FFF 00001E00   00007F84 FFFFFF7C 00000000 00000000
GR 8-F   00000005 CA0107F1 0001E10 B0001E82    4001E02 000030F8 B0002076 00002278
FP REG   41300000 00000000 00000000 00000000   42640000 00000000 43316000 00000000

002070   E3C8C540 E3D6E3C1 40404040 40404040   40404040 F0F0F0F0 F0F0F0F0 40C9E240     THE TOTAL....        000000 IS
002090   40404040 40E3 E2 C8C1D9D6 D5404040    40404040 D9C9E3C5 E3E4C7C7 D3C54040     SHARON               RITETUGGLE
0020D0   40404040 F0F0 --SAME--                 40404040 F8F44040 40404040 40404040                          0084
0020F0   40404040 40E3C8C5 43404040 40404040    C2C1C440 C3D6C4C5 40C9D540 C3C1D9C4     THERE IS A   BAD CODE IN CARD
002110   40404040 F0F0F0F0 40404040 40404040    40404040 40C90540 40404040 40404040              000000        THERE I
002130   40404040 43404040 40404040 40C9D540    40E3C8C5 40E3C8C5 D9C540C9 F0F0F0F0              00000
002150   E240C140 C2C1C440 C3D6C4C5 40C9D540    C3C1D9C4 40404040 D9C540C9 F0F0F0F0     S A BAD CODE IN   CARD       00000
002190   40404040 --SAME--                      40404040 40404040 40404040 40404040     005
0021B0   40404040 40404040 40404040 40404040    40FE615C 00000000 00000000 92011028
0021D0   0000005C 00000000                                                             ./*..........
```

Fig. 16-7 (Part 3 of 3)

KODE is defined as the first four bytes of INAREA, and GOOD is defined in statement 124 as a character constant of length 4 containing the EBCDIC characters RITE.

The CLC instruction is followed by the extended mnemonic BE. This instruction causes a branch to the instruction labeled HANDLE when the four bytes located at KODE equal the four bytes located at GOOD. But in our case, this branch was never taken. Instead, execution dropped through to the next sequential instruction, in every case, causing the error message to be printed five times. The code looks like it should work, but it doesn't.

The next step is to examine the dynamic dump produced just before the job ended. The program did not abend, so we don't have a big dump, but we do have the one produced by the LAST macro. We want to check the areas KODE and GOOD to determine if they contain what we expect. KODE should still contain the first four characters from the last data card, and GOOD should contain the EBCDIC representation of the characters RITE.

How do we locate these two areas in the dump? The program was loaded at address 1E00. The location counter value from the source listing for each of the symbols is added to 1E00 to calculate the location of each symbol within the dump.

Symbol	Loc. Ctr. Value	Load Point Address	Location within Dump	Contents
KODE	2F8	1E00	20F8	D9C540C9
GOOD	2F4	1E00	20F4	40E3C8C5

Instead of both areas containing D9C9E3C5 (RITE) as they should, KODE contains D9C540C9 (RE I), and GOOD contains 40E3C8C5 (THE). If we examine location 20F4 in the dump produced by the FIRST macro, we find that these four bytes contained D9C9E3C5 (RITE) before any of our instructions executed. Our problem now is to determine what happened between the time the FIRST dump was taken and the time when the LAST dump was taken. What destroyed the contents of these two storage areas (KODE and GOOD)?

If we continue our examination of the dump produced by the LAST macro, we find that the eight bytes we are concerned about, together with the next several words of storage, contain the character string, "THERE IS A BAD CODE IN CARD". This string of characters is actually part of what we defined as ERRMSG. It should be located at address 2148 within the dump (1E00 + 348). Examining the dump once more, we find that this string of characters does correctly appear beginning at address 2148. All that can be said at this point is that our program must have moved a copy of this character string from location 2148 to location 20F4.

Our program contains one MVC instruction, statement 24. Its purpose is to move a copy of the input record to the output area for printing. This instruction should therefore move the contents of 80 bytes from INAREA to OUTAREA+40. Is this what the instruction actually does? Examine the object code produced by the assembler for statement 24: D278C2A2C2F6.

The first byte contains the machine opcode for the mnemonic opcode MVC (D2). The second byte contains the length of the move (in bytes). Remember, this length is in hexadecimal. (A hexadecimal 78 is equivalent to a decimal 120.) Also remember that in order to represent the length of the maximum move (256 bytes), the assembler always builds a number one less than the specified length of the move into the machine code, but when that machine code executes, the specified number of bytes will be moved. In this case, 78 is built into the instruction, and 79 (hex) bytes will be moved—79 (hex) = 121 (dec). But we did not expect the MVC instruction to move 121 bytes!

What happened? Well, no length was specified on the first operand of the MVC instruction, so the implied length of the symbol appearing in the first operand was used. Looking up the symbol (OUTAREA) in the cross-reference table, we find that the length the assembler has associated with the symbol OUTAREA is 121. Playing computer with this instruction, we find that 121 bytes did get moved. The 121 bytes, beginning with the byte located at INAREA through the byte located at PTKTR+5, were moved to OUTAREA+40 through PAD+2. This destroyed not only the contents of the area labeled GOOD but also all of the meaningful fields in the input area.

To correct the problem, we simply add a length specification to the first operand of the MVC instruction: MVC OUTAREA+40(80),INAREA. But just because we have solved this problem does not mean that we have accomplished all we can with this run of the problem. We should still closely examine the remainder of the program. Check the execution of the program, instruction by instruction (play computer), to ensure that the instructions that have executed performed as you expected. (Also doublecheck to ensure that any corrections you have made to instructions with bugs do not cause errors in previously error-free instructions.)

Examine the MVC instruction. Notice that whereas we have corrected this particular MVC so that it moves the correct number of bytes, we've used, as the receiving area, the output area that we plan to use for our total message at end-of-file. We should have defined a separate output area for this purpose.

So, we can really catch two errors with this one execution run instead of just one. We realize that we must define another output area, that the symbolic name of this output area should be specified in the first operand of the MVC, and that a length of 80 bytes is not implied—it must be explicitly specified for this operand. Never give up your search for errors until you are relatively sure that your program is executing as you had planned. Do as much debugging as you can on each execution of your programs—and always keep in mind the value of good comments.

DIFFERENT TYPES OF DUMPS

There are two types of dumps: the *abend* and the *dynamic* dump. Abend dumps are produced by the operating system whenever your program causes an exception; they are the end result of your program breaking one of the rules of Systems/360 and 370 at execution time. Once an abend dump is requested, control will *not* be returned to your program. The programmer must provide one thing for an abend dump. Under DOS, he must specify the DUMP option on the OPTION job control language statement. Under OS, the programmer must provide a DD statement with the DDNAME "SYSABEND" or "SYSUDUMP".

Dynamic dumps are produced when your program issues a request for one by invoking the SNAP macro (under OS-based systems) or the PDUMP macro (under DOS-based systems). After a dynamic dump is taken, control is returned to the next executable instruction after the macro call.

Dynamic dumps can be used by the programmer to display the contents of registers and selected areas of storage at any point in the execution of his program. Placed strategically throughout a program, the requests for dynamic dumps can go a long way in helping a programmer check out and debug his program.

The PDUMP Macro

A name may optionally be specified on the PDUMP macro. Only two operands need be supplied, both of which are addresses. They may be specified symbolically or as the contents of registers. These operands are the beginning and ending addresses of the storage area to be dumped. Storage is dumped up to, but not including, the second operand address. Relative addressing can have the dump include the second operand address as well. For example, using the following:

```
INAREA     DS   20F
OUTAREA    DC   CL31' THE RECORD IS'
LOC        DS   CL10
RCD        DS   CL80
PKD        DS   D
```

The following code will display the contents of storage from the beginning of INAREA to the end of RCD:

```
PDUMP   INAREA,PKD
or
LA      6,INAREA
LA      8,PKD
PDUMP   (6),(8)
```

If PKD needs to be displayed also, the PDUMP macro should be used as follows:

```
PDUMP   INAREA,PKD+8
or
LA      6,INAREA
LA      8,PKD+8
PDUMP   (6),(8)
```

THE SNAP MACRO

A name may be optionally specified on the SNAP macro. Four operands are generally specified:

ID=decimal number, PDATA=(REGS), STORAGE= (first,last),   X
DCB=dcbname

The ID operand contains a decimal number used to identify this dump. If your program includes several SNAP macro calls, the use of different ID numbers will help you to identify which macro call invoked a particular dump.

The PDATA operand allows you to specify information in addition to the hexadecimal representation of storage that you would like to have displayed by the SNAP macro. In this case we want to have the contents of registers to be displayed, so we specify PDATA=(REGS). STORAGE=(first,last) indicates the beginning and ending points of the dump. Storage is dumped up to, but not including, the second operand address.

The DCB operand must be used to indicate the name of the Data Control Block (DCB) that describes the SNAP data set. This is a DCB with very special characteristics. Under OS-based systems, the programmer must, in addition to invoking the SNAP macro, define a DCB for the snap data set, provide a DD job control statement for the snap data set, and open the SNAP DCB prior to his first SNAP macro call.[†] In addition to the normal DCB operands, the SNAP DCB must specify the following:

DSORG=PS,RECFM=VBA,MACRF=W,BLKSIZE=882 or 1632,   X
LRECL=125,DDNAME=ddname

[†]For further information on DD, DCB, and other concepts of I/O under OS-based systems, see chapter 21.

The "ddname" specified on the DD job control language statement and in the DDNAME operand of the DCB must be a name other than SYSABEND or SYSUDUMP. A ddname that is easy to remember is SNAPDD.

QUESTIONS

1. What are the three stages at which you can debug your program?

2. How does use of a program flowchart aid in solving a problem?

3. Why are comments important to a program if the assembler doesn't examine them and the computer can't execute them?

4. Describe a method you can use, as you desk check, to ensure that your program does not contain undefined symbols.

5. Which of the following errors can the assembler catch during its scan?

   a. Erroneous use of AH in place of A opcode
   b. Undefined symbols in operand
   c. Operand of 30 in an RR instruction
   d. Symbol beginning with a numeric digit
   e. BE extended mnemonic where BL should have been used
   f. Divide instruction with 5 specified in first operand

6. What type of information can you find in the symbol cross-reference table produced by the assembler?

7. What is the PSW, and why is it so important?

8. Explain what happens when an exception occurs during the execution of a program.

9. If your program has abended, how would you locate the following information?

   a. The type of exception that caused the dump to be taken
   b. Which instruction was executing when the error occurred
   c. Which instruction in the listing corresponds to the instruction at location 3E24 in the dump
   d. Which statements in the program change the contents of the fullword labeled AREA
   e. The contents of register 1 when your program was initially given control
   f. The contents of floating-point register 2 when the abend occurred

EXERCISES

1. Find the cause of the abend dump given on pages 313–318.

2. Locate the contents of the following in the abend dump used above.

    a. the fullword at 0002B0
    b. register 3
    c. the halfword at 001DBA
    d. the byte at 000F85

```
LOC    OBJECT CODE    ADDR1 ADDR2   STMT   SOURCE STATEMENT

000000                                1            CSECT
                                      2            PRINT NOGEN
                                      3     ***********************************************************
                                      4     * *  TITLE - WEATHER                                     *
                                      5     * *                                                      *
                                      6     * *                                                      *
                                      7     * *  FUNCTION - THIS PROGRAM DETERMINES THE HIGH AND LOW FOR 7 DAYS.  A *
                                      8     * *             SUM OF ALL HIGHS AND LOWS IS ALSO CALCULATED.          *
                                      9     * *                                                      *
                                     10     ***********************************************************
                                     11     FIRST   BEGIN=NHNN,END=LOW+4
00000C 1811                          18            SR    1,1            CT = 0
00000E 1B22                          19            SR    2,2            SUM = 0
000010 1B33                          20            SR    3,3            INITIAL WEEKLY HIGH = 0
000012 5840 C052     00054           21            L     4,NHNN         INITIAL WEEKLY LOW = 999
000016 5A21 C05E     00060           22     LOOP   A     2,TABLE(1)     ADDDAY'S HIGH AND
00001A 5A21 C062     00064           23            A     2,TABLE+4(1)   LOW TO SUM
00001E 5931 C05E     00060           24            C     3,TABLE(1)     WKLY HIGH , = TABLE HIGH
000022 47B0 C028     0002A           25            BNL   OK             YES, BRANCH TO OK
000026 5831 C062     00060           26            L     3,TABLE(1)     NO, REPLACE WEEKLY HIGH
00002A 5941 C062     00064           27     OK     C     4,TABLE+4(1)   WKLY LOW )= TABLE LOW
00002E 47D0 C034     00036           28            BNH   FINE           YES, BRANCH TO FINE
000032 5841 C062     00064           29            L     4,TABLE+4(1)   NO, REPLACE WEEKLY LOW
000036 5A10 C056     00058           30     FINE   A     1,ONE          ADD 1 TO INDEX REGISTER
00003A 5910 C05A     0005C           31            C     1,SEVEN        ALL 7 DAYS HANDLED
00003E 4740 C014     00016           32            BL    LOOP           NO, BRANCH TO HANDLE NEXT DAY
000042 9014 C096     00098           33            STM   1,4,ANSWERS    YES, STORE RESULTS
                                     34     LAST   BEGIN=NHNN,END=LOW+4

000052 0000                          41     NHNN    DC    F'999'
000054 000003E7                      42     ONE     DC    F'1'
000058 00000001                      43     SEVEN   DC    F'7'
00005C 00000007                      44     TABLE   DC    F'89'         HIGH DAY 1
000060 00000059                      45             DC    F'55'         LOW
000064 00000037                      46             DC    F'92'         HIGH DAY 2
000068 0000005C                      47             DC    F'50'         LOW
00006C 00000032                      48             DC    F'71'         HIGH DAY 3
000070 00000047                      49             DC    F'45'         LOW
000074 0000002D                      50             DC    F'85'         HIGH DAY 4
000078 00000055                      51             DC    F'37'         LOW
00007C 00000025                      52             DC    F'60'         HIGH DAY 5
000080 0000003C                      53             DC    F'45'         LOW
000084 0000002D                      54             DC    F'55'         HIGH DAY 6
000088 00000037                      55             DC    F'47'         LOW
00008C 0000002F                      56             DC    F'98'         HIGH DAY 7
000090 00000062                      57             DC    F'92'         LOW
000094 0000005C                      58     ANSWERS DS    1F            COUNT OF DAYS
000098                               59     TOTAL   DS    1F            SUM OF ALL HIGHS AND LOWS
00009C                               60     HIGH    DS    1F            WEEKLY HIGH
0000A0                               61     LOW     DS    1F            WEEKLY LOW
0000A4                               62             END
```

LOC   OBJECT CODE   ADDR1 ADDR2 STMT   SOURCE STATEMENT

0000A8 5B58C2D7C4E404D7   63   =CL8'$$BPDUMP'
0000B0 0000005400000A8   64   =A(NHNN,LOW+4)

CROSS-REFERENCE

SYMBOL   LEN VALUE   DEFN

ANSWERS 00004 000098 00058 0033
FINE   00004 000036 00030 0028
HIGH   00004 0000CA0 00060
LOOP   00004 000016 00022 0032
LOW   00004 0000A4 00061 0016 0037 0064
NHNN   00004 000054 00041 0016 0021 0037 0064
OK   00004 00032A 00027 0025
ONE   00004 000058 00042 0030
SEVEN   00004 00005C 00043 0031
TABLE   00004 000060 00044 0022 0023 0024 0026 0027 0029
TOTAL   03004 00009C 00059

NO STATEMENTS FLAGGED IN THIS ASSEMBLY

04/25/74 PHASE XFR-AD LOCORE HICORE DSK-AD ESD TYPE LABEL   LOADED REL-FR

          PHASE*** 001E0C 001E00 001EB7 4C 06 1 CSECT   001E00 001E00

TUGGLE   04/25/74

GR 0-7 00001EB0 00001EA8 0000001E00 00001E00 00007F84 FFFFFF7C 00000000 000010B8
GR 8-F 00003946 0A0107F1 00001E10 00000000 4001EE02 0003DF8 000001C0 0000007B
FP REG 41300000 00000000 00000000 42640000 00000000 43316000 00000000

001E50 000003E7 00000001 00000007 00000059 00000037 0000005C 00000032 ....X.........*.
001E70 00000047 0000002D 00000055 00000025 0000003C 00001F2D 00000037 0000002F ............*..*.
001E9C 00000062 0000005C 0A020700 4110C3F6 4500C0A6 00001F48   ....*....*.....C6

OS03I PROGRAM CHECK INTERRUPTION - HEX LOCATION 001E16 - CONDITION CODE 1 - SPECIFICATION EXCEPTION
OS00I JOB TUGGLE CANCELED

TUGGLE   04/25/74

```
GR 0-7   00001EB0 00000001 00000000 00000059        FFFFF7C  00000000 00001D88
GR 8-F   00003946 0A0107F1 00001E10 00001E10        40001E02 00003DF8 000001C0 0000007B
FP REG   41300000 00000030 41300000                 42640000 00000000 43316000 00000000
COMREG BG ADDR IS 0001C0
```

```
000000  00000000 00000000 00000000 00000000   00000000 000001C0 FF050000 00000000    .............$$BEOJ4 ....
000020  FF070007 40001986 FF150006 9000 1E1A   5B5BC2C5 D6D1F440 FF05000E 0F001018    ...................
000040  00001A A8 08000000 0001A98 00000000   FF000000 00FF0000 00040000 03000254    ...............Y
000060  00040000 00000288 00040000 000000FE8   00000000 0000076C 45700106 41A0B258    ...................
000080  41900136 41800F3C 47F000CA 06900680   06B006B0 06B006B0 06B041BB 001741BB    ...............0...
0000A0  00504570 01064180 01369640 A0019120   A00C4710 00E29260 A00195E2 A0024780    &........9..P..
0000C0  09869510 022F0778 94F901FB D7010218   02189680 B2594400 0E660788 947FB259    .......9..P..
0000E0  45700EUA 07F84B80 00748B80 018C9180   A0000717 5890A004 4880018E 90C0901C    .8..P....0..
000100  D2089010 01B0D207 90088000 9680A000   07F74570 010ED203 0C420C46 DC030C42    K...K...7...K
000120  B24818AA DD030C42 000C43A1 000442A0   01EF41AA B2484400 A0045890 A0044220    .........K....
000140  A0009140 A0014710 0198D207 01B09008   98989010 82000180 956001EF 47800190    ...K......
000160  5890A004 98189030 989B01B0 82000038   92842B2B 47F00188 9680A000 41100030    0........
000180  47F00E66 615C4061 504044F0 00FE1E00   00001DA8 00001258 000001C0 10000000    0.../*/&.0...
0001A0  F0F461F2 1E001800 47F041E0 00001E00   F4F2F5F7 F4F1F1F5 000001C0 D3C54040    04/25/74....42574115.
0001C0  00007FFF 00001EB7 0001 1E87 0000 0010   00007FFF E0007E90 A8A07ED0 009C1321    $$B0...
0001E0  13281371 1372138C 1398139C 13A038F0   F4F2F5F7 00160003 01000C54 12440000    .S....0
000200  09980BB6 0C440000 0C4C0000 001 A098   5B58C2D6 9238018F 909B01B0 4880018C    $$BO...
000220  00000000 01C01000 00001A98 00014148   000013E2 9018A030 41A0B258 07F941A0    ..S...9
000240  41900S0C 48B001BC 95100 1FF 47 7002 7E   5A0B25C 9018A030 41A0B258 07F941A0    .9...*...9
000260  B2A89601 A0000 7F9 909B01B0 9220018F   45900264 41990178 95000023 47800316    ...9...
000280  95230023 47B000AE 48600022 1A664866   B2B607F6 181F1B66 4121000F 45700AAC    .6...9...
0002A0  48600 0C4 1B331823 43201007 47F00364   47200008A 1823950B 10074 7F0 03604720    .D....9.
0002C0  00889680 10029 60C 100407F9 18584143   00024354 00004145 50001A44 A4400BBC    .9....9.
0002E0  95FF4000 47F002F2 42840000 07F995FF   03AD0789 1B0095FF 03AD4780 0EEC9560    ......2..9..
000300  01EF4780 02B44160 00100502 A0050239   47700342 41110000 491001AE 47800342    &...N....
000320  1B664121 000F4570 0AAC1B33 43301007   95011006 47700200 41230008 95161007    M........N..
000340  47B000BA 41822000 4870020C 43387000   04031002 B2844930 01AC47B0 02DE8930    N...L..&..)
000360  00034133 B3280502 100901F1 47B000B6   44003DE 5870024C 95077000 477003AA    N...l...&..)K
000380  D5027001 01F14780 00864180 05037001   80001A44 4A4008BC 4158B314 D20003AD    .6...)..&..)
0003A0  4C400B80 5A400250 41440000 470044C   04044780 100C4710 04469105 0446910S    J...&..N.
0003C0  024D1009 5860024C 95076000 47B0004C   D2022204D 60015870 043E9640 10029614    ...6...K...
0003E0  4C400B80 5A400250 41440000 470044C   044C9120 100C4710 10029614 07794820    &....N...
000400  10029601 100C0203 40007001 95FF3002   47002EC 42803002 91983006 478004CC    K...6....
000420  30009500 30004780 04709F00 20000769   91203006 47100092 95503004 478004CC    .6......9
000440  D2020049 10090300 004B5006 9C002000   4770049E 9023B2A0 96803006 07F94730    ...&.).&.)
000460  07769106 00454770 0A52913F 00454770   04891AF 00440789 4020003A 58600048    K.L.&....
000480  4A000B74 5060040 47F00550 02000B08   3005D202 00491009 58700048 1B884380    .J..&..0.&K.
0004A0  3003C80 0B1E4B0 02069500 80004770   91060045 70004170 00440789 0B084780    K...&...9
0004C0  0048D202 70091009 47F0048C 41990178   003444820 05494560 05484133 100C0550    K..L..&......
0004E0  DS01003A B2A24780 07344560 073A4820   45700A62 9102004 47800578 91803006    N....0...7
000500  3000003A 472006B0 10C0203 07607F7   457006A2 91020044 45700578 477007B8    N......-
000520  471007C4 95FF3002 47007C4 95623004   01F90776 95003004 07769680 2B84780    ...D...D..
000540  41600582 91800044 B2904700 05B29603   132110 00444770 05CA9500 00440789    -....9.
000560  05A9108 B2904700 06BA9104 47800668   05E09550 00444770 06809477 30060789    .&......9
000580  94773006 91043006 47800668   044473 30069180 100C4710 06129550              0...&
```

TUGGLE   04/25/74

```
000600  30044780 07529551 30044780 07529200   30039680 10029101 100C4710 062247F0
000620  065094FE 100C944B 10020701 10041004   44003D0E 5860024C 96406004 91401002
000640  47800648 96101002 94BF1002 47C0069E   92FF5006 43703002 02003002 40000200
000660  430003AD 427003AD 95003000 47C00680   07899198 30064780 069E07F9 40000200
000680  4560073A 45700692 41330008 44000530   072995FF 30020787 91983006 07774170
0006A0  045F1B44 43403002 41548314 1A441A44   4A400BBC 58104000 30024780 30024780
0006C0  0668D201 10000046 D2021000 C041D601   10040044 95015000 47200712 58700040
0006E0  4B700874 D5027001 01F14720 07125877   00000502 70G001A4 4780070A D5027000
000700  01A74770 07129620 30069640 10029601   10049127 00444770 05F29680 30069104
000720  10024780 05F69604 30069500 30044770   068007F9 9823B2A0 07F71B22 4320003A
000740  483001FE 43223000 89200003 41323007   07F61B77 43703003 4C7008BE 4A700206
000760  00470000 47F00612 00E201E2 D2010000   07680729 07680729 U2010044 01AAD202
000780  00410B71 956082A0 47700788 9101100C   47800788 4400003E 5880024C 95078000
0007A0  47700788 944B1002 91401002 47800784   96101002 948F1002 92040843 91090045
0007C0  47800FF2 92040843 58800040 12884770   07E29212 08439104 30064780 080294FD
0007E0  08439120 100C4710 07F29101 10024710   08B895FF 30024780 08029110 100C4710
000800  08884860 0BC2D715 30069800 06064000   01324770 0688495FF 0BC047B0 08984A60
000820  08439204 600A9690 30064186 02076000   00404030 45700A0A 30024770 08429602
000840  00450774 91020843 47800BC0 41800B18   45700A0A 60089F5F 30024770 30049540
000860  B2A04780 09929560 30044780 B0E29562   4780097C 4780087C BBE207F4 47700BA4
000880  457008F0 91020843 91020843 91305006   96201002 4780097C 95623004 47F00580
0008A0  45700844 47800A0A 92206008 41700918   96100B1C 96201002 4780097B 940E0044
0008C0  95060044 47800A0A 9220600B 41700918   96100B1C 41800B18 58000048 48F0003A
0008E0  9C00F000 94EF081C 9D00F000 47200908   07979204 00440FF7 45700AA2 9102600A
000900  47100966 D5024001 0B934780 C9729560   0147940780 09729560 B2A04770 09669101
000920  100C4780 09669101 600C4710 09809130   04544780 096694FE 100C4400 030E5860
000960  024C9640 600441A0 01329601 82984780   0668D205 0056000C 97060987 97010987
000980  D2010002 30009204 30009264 00018200   07689541 30044770 099E94F3 600C9501
0009A0  600C0774 91020843 47100980 96021003   D2070040 60004580 09DE47F0 05804400
0009C0  09804570 0A1247F0 09CA4580 09DE47F0   05549104 600A4780 09B04180 06847F0
0009E0  09F496F0 09DF4930 0BDCD257 07F81828   44000F36 48700BC2 4B70B282 40700BC2
000A00  446F3006 45700AA2 07F81828 4320017E   09225080 00484220 00484220 003A9C00
000A20  20004740 0A329000 20004720 0A264710   08E89106 00454770 0A529139 00457077
000A40  91020044 07179108 00444717 00044770   0A1E4020 003AD201 0000076A 920F0073
000A60  B2000768 D5010BB4 0BC24720 0A84492C4   0BD348F0 0BDC9550 F0044780 0A8292C1
000A80  0BD30A03 92849298 47F00136 41220000   800001AD 9118F006 077E95FF F002477O
000AA0  0A9407FE 4B6001EE 41220000 592001A7   12660787 41110000 591001F0 0A004710
000AC0  47200006 491001AE 474000A6 07F79510   015E92E9 0BD39102 A00047OO A0004710
000AE0  0F4C4110 B7809210 01EF9610 05A79103   0E6694EF 05A79280 05A79280 A00047F0
000B00  01360000 00000000 93000B08 60000001   08000B10 60000001 04000BE0 20000006
000B20  13001268 20000001 1A001268 20000005   16001270 20000004 0700126E 40000006
000B40  39001279 60000006 08000840 40000000   1A001868 50000005 0000B058 30B806C0
000B60  07001270 41000000 3100127B 40000005   08000868 00A01880 86001680 030B06D3
000B80  92000234 20000005 86001B88 60C01168   08000860 00A01880 86001680 600003D8
000BA0  0C2C0BRE 0C000006 00020F28 60C00860   00550000 0BD40902 09B009BE 12FCOF24
000BC0  01000000 00020F28 0F320136 5B5BC1D5   C5D9D940 00000C60 06000000 13381200
000BE0  01000000 00000000 00000000 00000000   00000000 00000000 00000000 00000000
000C00  00000000 --SAME--
000C20  00000000 --SAME--
000C40  0000B484 8C836050 40100000 00000000   00000000 00000000 00000000 FF050002
000C60  0000B608 0C000008 00001258 000001C0   00000000 00000000 00001338 00001600
000C80  00001EB0 00001A88 000001BB 000001C0   00000008 00000C60 000016EA 00000002
000CA0  00000294 48600BC5 92020BC5 92600BEF   42600E25 41201007 45700AAC 4570010E
000CC0  18D44890 0B9602C7 90001000 1B449604   0BA3D503 90000230 4780DCF6 D5010030
```

TUGGLE   04/25/74

```
000CE0  90004780  CCFA955B  9004780   OCF24144  02004144  01004144  01004144  05015040
000D00  B27CD207  CB780B88  45C00DD4  18E94180  9168955C  E0084780  0800D507  9000E008
000D20  47800032  41EOE014  15E84740  0D1247F0  0U085880  E0148880  00085870  L0108870
000D40  0008L200  47800052  18101887  1A994390  0U5618C8  181TD202  B27CE017  0200827C
000D60  B2T09200  B27UD201  0B7E0B5E  1B994390  E0130201  0B5CE01A  4880085E  46900D88
000D80  4880085C  40800B7E  18214570  0AA84880  0B7E0620  1A284570  0AA85010  0B789286
000DA0  0B7B45C0  0DU45810  0B784110  10004A10  0B7E1299  47200D78  95100E25  47700DCE
000DC0  06104910  01C84740  0DCE5010  01E45890  A0040F7D  45E0OA8C  9190F006  47700DE8
000DE0  9180F006  47100A90  45E00E28  800001AD  41F00BA0  0A009180  0BA24780  0DF645E0
000E00  0E289120  0BA34780  0E1C4370  B27C4177  0001A270  02350201  02370826  D204827B
000E20  02344160  00007FC  80000058  48F0B2B0  0704F002  B274D704  B274F002  44000E30
000E40  07FE4570  010E1B00  45400CA4  5860902C  12664780  0E581806  5009900C  D3009009
000E60  0E2547F0  01360502  82500239  47800E78  9500022F  477000AE  948FA001  47800086
000E80  48F0H296  90F10C7C  180F41FF  00085OF0  0C601866  41100000  551001F0  478000B6
000EA0  05021000  00304770  00AE4540  0CA89140  A0014710  01329500  022F4770  013647F0
000EC0  0ECA4400  0E664770  00AE9680  0EDA0717  022F9703  00B04170  01360702  B291825D
000EE0  0702H25D  B29L4400  47200F4C  9284B2A8  068C0680  50800024  47F00132  91010021
000F00  47100AE  95010BD3  45800002  928000F3  07BF92D9  08D24190  01364160  0B04940F
000F20  09DF0IFF  92000DF3  45800002  928000F3  07F99601  02ABU201  00343000  457006A2
000F40  47F005F2  92F10BD3  4570010E  41100DCC  0C485000  9304770  01365880  00244880
000F60  4860016E  44000E66  47700F6E  18664540  10207I9  96020021  07F94570  010E58E0
000F80  0B765080  00249560  01EF4780  C1909180  B25050L8  000C4570  01OE47F0  0ED6D400
000FA0  0C805880  82909001  802C5800  800C4480  0021477O  01E47F0  00055510  01F04780
000FC0  01F91000  07F996C0  01F91000  07F991F0  45900264  95300IEF  47200OAC  90980130
000FE0  0086457O  0AA07F9  909B01B0  4570B03C  47F000AC  95OB01EF  9218018F  12550707
001000  47800OAC  41400C44  41C0OAC   4800178   9601B290  47F00132  47F70008  4570010E
001020  45900264  94F00019  91400018  4770B05C  95B9B288  4770004  4F70008  47F0B09E
001040  41B08258  96018000  4930022E  4770B05C  D21B02C   90105050  90CC1135  47F0B09E
001060  5B93B24C  D2076000  900B8223  6008902C  0223902C  6008D21B  9010602C  10355034
001080  11444570  BOC4457C  010E0203  900C6004  478C09E  12554740  B09E4121  00474570
0010A0  0004TF0   01324140  400007F9  4A400022  48001EE   18538850  0011A45  98564000
0010C0  0AA4900L  400007F9  4A400022  48404213  0B2C9102  B10ED202  B2711OC9
0010E0  07F74370  3003417T  0014270   30039220  B1069IC8  60050717  07179108
001100  5B5CB270  58550002  D2036012  50024170  B1149102  9106600C  4170B1CE  95FF3003
001120  60004710  B16A9101  600C4710  B1949140  07149102  B1081B0  B00477O  4770B19A
001140  91246O0C  07779102  600D0717  9186000C  47F009B0  B2306012  07149050A  30030724
001160  B2469101  60050717  07F49102  C90Z950A  92080B58  4550B230  9101B268  47802224
001180  9686000A  45700AQA  47F008E8  B1A047F0  95138273  47B00B24  5870B270  41770001
0011A0  41800B20  45700004  4B700B74  50700B58  9240002C  41800A28  4570000A  47F008E8
0011C0  0784910F  3003474D  43206000  47F009BE  924000BC  41B000B8  0310C2C7  19000C54
0011E0  95623004  41800B38  43206000  1003b00D  1DA8FFFF  01C00000  0310C2C7  19000301
001200  507C827C  41B00838  43206000  47F009B0  00000000  FF006000  00000000  16000301
001220  07F59620  1003DG00  1003b00D  47F00CE   00010DA8  07001600  84006150  47F00A64
001240  0C00LE0U  24081680  8000C1D9  47F00ACE  0001LDA8  07001600  E420E66  0EFC0F60
001260  5B5BA2C1  L3E3D5C1  8000C1D9  42404022  13500016  IF050000  0B000AE  00AE10A6
001280  0F000000  00001338  84000207  47F00190  0FC60CBE  030E10A6  10800AE  00AE10A6
0012A0  0F440082  0F7A0FA2  0F9A0DAE  0EC20FBE  00AE00AE  00AE00AE  01780178  03001EC8
0012C0  10800178  00AE00AE  00AE0FCE  0AE00AE   FF000000  0D030C00  000EFF00  FFFFFFF
0012E0  02001A88  00001E30  04000000  05000000  22000000  000EFF00  400080FC
001300  0784910F  FFFFFFF0  000000F8  100000FC  0191FF00  000100FC  0192FF00  600200FC
001320  507C827C  41800838  43206000  600000F8  1DA8FFFF  01C00000  00000000  60200FC
001340  07F59620  1003DG00  1003b00D  0190FF01  FF000000  00010000  00000000  0160000
001360  0180FF00  50C300C4  0181FF01  600000FC  FF000000  00100000  00030000
001380  00040000  00050000  00FF0002  0C000000  00000000  00000000
```

TUGGLE   04/25/74

```
0013A0  00FF00FF 01FF02FF 03FF04FF 05FFFFFF   FFFF03FF FFFFFFFF 06FF06FF 06FF04FF   ................
0013C0  00FF01FF 02FF03FF 04FF05FF 05FF05FF   05FF05FF 07FFFFFF 08FF06FF 06FF06FF   ................
0013E0  06FF0000 16000000 00000000 0000C700   0FFF0000 00000000 00000000 00000000   ..............G.
001400  00000000 --SAME--                                                          ........
0016C0  00000000 00000000 00000000 00000000                                        ....
```

LBLTYP   HEX LENGTH IS 0CC0
--BG--

```
001DA0  0000IE10 40001E02 D5D6404D5 C1D4C540   FF150006 90001E1A 0A0107F1 00001E10   .....NO NAME....l...
001DC0  00000059 00000037 00003DF8 000001C0   0000007B 00001EB0 00000001 00000090   ........8.......
001DE0  05C04110 00000037 FFFFFF7C 00000000   00001DB8 00003946 00004040 00000000   ...............
001E00  05C04110 C0A64100 C0AE0A02 1B111B22   1B335840 C0525A21 C05E5A21 C0625931   ...............
001E20  C05E4780 C0285831 C05E5941 C06247D0   C0345841 C0625A10 C0565910 C05A4740   ...............
001E40  C0149014 C0964110 C0A64100 C0AE0A02   0A0E0000 000003E7 00000001 00000007   ...............
001E60  00000059 00000037 0000005C 00000032   00000047 0000002D 00000055 00000025   ...............
001E80  0000003C 0000002D 00001F48 0000002F   00000062 0000005C 0A020700 00000025   ......*......*...
001EA0  4500C0A6 00001F48 5B5BC2D7 C4E4D4D7   00001E54 00001EA8 A020700 4110C3F6   ..*..$$BPDUMP...C6
001EC0  00000000 --SAME--                                                          ........
007FE0  00000000 00000000 00000000 00000000   00000000 00000000 00000000 00000000   ........
```

Coding at the Bit and Byte Level

LOGICAL OPERATIONS ON FULLWORDS

There are times in programming when the programmer needs instructions that can accomplish the more intricate manipulations on individual bits within registers or storage. The instructions discussed in this chapter should give you this ability. There are three different types: (1) logical operations on fullwords—arithmetic and comparison; (2) manipulations involving bytes—move and comparison; and (3) manipulations on individual bits—shifts, logic functions, and testing.

MEANING OF THE WORD *Logical*

Logical, in terms of data type, means unsigned. The first group of instructions deals with fixed-length data (4 bytes, fullwords), but all 32 bits in the field participate in the operation (AL, ALR, SL, SLR, CL, CLR). The leftmost or high-order bit is not considered to be of any special significance. It is not the bit containing the sign of the number. It is merely the leftmost bit of the number itself. There is no way to represent a negative logical value.

ARITHMETIC ON UNSIGNED NUMBERS

The logical add and subtract instructions allow the performance of arithmetic operations on unsigned data. The great advantage in this is that the overflow condition will never arise. This allows the programmer to add fields larger than 31 bits in length, by adding successive pieces of the longer fields. The addition or subtraction of large fields of bits is possible because the logical add and subtract instructions allow all 32 bits to participate in the operation, and these instructions set the condition code based on entirely different conditions from the algebraic adds and subtracts. The four logical arithmetic instructions are:

$$
\begin{array}{ll}
\text{ALR} & \text{R1,R2} \\
\text{AL} & \text{R1,S2} \\
\text{SLR} & \text{R1,R2} \\
\text{SL} & \text{R1,S2}
\end{array}
$$

and they set the condition code based on the presence of the following conditions:

Condition-Code Setting	Operation Result
0	result was zero with no carry
1	result was nonzero with no carry
2	result was zero with a carry
3	result was nonzero with a carry

The method for handling large fields is to add successive low-order words of the two participating fields, checking the condition code setting after each successive operation. If the condition code was set to 2 or 3, a carry of 1 must be added to the next higher-order words to be added. The highest-order words can be added algebraically (using the A or AR instructions) to catch the possibility of overflow in the overall result.

The section of code given in figure 17-1 will add fields (FLD1 and FLD2) up to 95 bits in length and place the result in three consecutive words beginning at ANS.

```
        LM    6,8,FLD1      FLD1 NOW IN REGISTERS 6, 7, 8
        AL    8,FLD2+8      ADD LOW-ORDER 32 BITS
        BC    12,NOADD1     WAS THERE A CARRY OUT?
        AL    7,ONE         YES, ADD ONE TO MIDDLE 32 BITS
NOADD1  AL    7,FLD2+4      NO, ADD MIDDLE 32 BITS
        BC    12,NOADD2     WAS THERE A CARRY OUT?
        AL    6,ONE         YES, ADD ONE TO HIGH-ORDER BITS
NOADD2  A     6,FLD2        NO, ADD HIGH-ORDER BITS
        BO    OVERFLOW      CHECK FOR OVERFLOW IN COMPLETE NO.
        STM   6,8,ANS       NO OVERFLOW, STORE SUM
```

Fig. 17-1 Adding two 95-bit fields

FULLWORD LOGICAL COMPARE INSTRUCTIONS

The CL (RX-type) and the CLR (RR-type) instructions compare two full-words of binary unsigned data. The operation is performed similar to the algebraic compares (C and CR). There is, however, one basic difference between a logical and an algebraic compare instruction—the leftmost bit. The algebraic compare treats this bit as the sign of the field, and the logical compare treats it as merely one of the 32 bits that make up a fullword. Resulting condition-code settings for all of these compare operations are identical:

Condition-Code Setting	Operation Result
0	operands are equal
1	first operand is low
2	first operand is high
3	unused

Let's examine their use through an example:

Reg. 5: 00006152   Reg. 7: FFFFFF64

CR   5,7   would set a condition code of 2
(first operand is high)

CLR   5,7   would set a condition code of 1
(first operand is low)

In the algebraic compare, a positive value will always be greater than a negative one. But in the logical compare the first bits that differ as the instruction compares bit by bit from left to right will set the condition code. A bit that is *on* will immediately make its field greater than the field whose corresponding bit is *off*, regardless of where the differing bits appear in the fields.

CHARACTER OR BYTE MANIPULATION

There are several instructions that handle single bytes or a variable number of bytes.

BYTE TRANSFER OR MOVE INSTRUCTIONS

The MVI and the MVC instructions explained in chapter 6 move one byte, or from one to 256 bytes, respectively. There are two instructions that move one byte between a register and a byte in storage. These are the Insert Character (IC) and the Store Character (STC) instructions. Both belong to the RX-class of instructions:

$$\text{IC} \quad \text{R1,S2}$$
$$\text{STC} \quad \text{R1,S2}$$

The Insert Character instruction takes a byte from the second operand storage location and inserts it in the low-order byte of the general purpose register specified in the first operand. (The remaining three bytes in the register are unaltered.) The action of the Store Character instruction is just the reverse. The low-order byte of the first operand register is moved to the byte whose address is specified in the second operand. In the case of both instructions, no checks are made for boundary alignment of the second operand.

An example of the use of these instructions is the reading of a one-byte code from an input record and the use of it to control the branching within a program. This example, which is given in figure 17-2, involves the maintenance of an inventory file. The code read indicates whether the input record contains information to update a current inventory record (four possible different actions for updating codes 0, 1, 2 & 5); add a new record (code 3); and delete an existing record (code 4).

In this example we have an illustration of the use of a *branch table,* a table in

```
                SR    6,6           INITIALIZE REGISTER FOR CODE
                IC    6,CODE        INSERT THE CODE
                SH    6,D240        IS
                LTR   6,6            THIS
                BM    INVALID         A
                C     6,FIVECODE      VALID
                BH    INVALID           CODE?
                MH    6,FOUR        MULT CODE BY LENGTH OF BRANCH INSTR
                B     RTNS(6)       USE REG 6 AS DISPLACEMENT INTO TABLE
*   BRANCH TABLE
RTNS            B     UPDAT1
                B     UPDAT2
                B     UPDAT3
                B     ADD
                B     DELETE
                B     UPDAT4
                .
                .
                .
D240            DC    H'240'
FIVECODE        DC    F'6'
FOUR            DC    H'4'
```

Fig. 17-2 Use of IC and STC instructions

which each element is a branch instruction. In this example, the branch instruction that is executed depends on the value contained in the code read from the input record. The instructions between the IC and the MH instructions test the code byte from the input record to ensure that it contained a valid code. Subtracting a decimal 240 from the contents will determine whether the code byte contained a character below F0 in the collating sequence. Once the subtraction has been performed, the compare instruction can eliminate all characters above a F5 in the collating sequence.

Once it has been determined that the code is valid, the only thing that needs to be accomplished is to multiply that code by the length of each of the branch instructions in the table. This having been done, the contents of register 6 may be used as a displacement into the branch table labeled RTNS. When the branch to RTNS(6) is taken, control is transferred to one of the six routines that handle the inventory file.

COMPARISON OF CHARACTERS

There are two instructions that compare the binary unsigned contents of individual bytes in storage. The CLI, an SI-type instruction, compares one byte of immediate data to the contents of one byte in storage. The CLC, an SS-type instruction, compares bytes from left to right and sets the condition code when the first two unequal bytes are encountered, or the end of the fields is reached. The condition-code settings are the same as those set by all compare instructions.

BIT MANIPULATIONS

There are instructions in the repertoire of Systems/360 and 370 that can manipulate individual bits of data. Three types of bit-manipulation instructions will be explained in this section: (1) the shifts, (2) the logical operations, and (3) the Test under Mask instruction.

THE SHIFT OPERATIONS

These instructions move bits sideways in registers. There are eight opcodes for shift operations, and they represent the various combinations of the characteristics of shift operations:

1. direction of the shift, right or left
2. number of registers whose contents participate in the shift, single registers or even-odd coupled register pairs
3. manner in which the contents of the register or registers are treated, algebraically or logically

The eight instructions are:

SLL	Shift Left Logical
SRL	Shift Right Logical
SLDL	Shift Left Double Logical
SRDL	Shift Right Double Logical
SLA	Shift Left Algebraic
SRA	Shift Right Algebraic
SLDA	Shift Left Double Algebraic
SRDA	Shift Right Double Algebraic

All of the shift instructions belong to the RS-class. The first operand always specifies the register—or the even register of the even-odd coupled register pair —whose contents are to be shifted. The second operand consists of a displacement and a base register, but the result derived by adding the displacement to the contents of the register is not used as an effective address. Instead, the low-order *six* bits of this resultant value are used as the number of bit positions for the shift operation. The rest of the "effective address" is ignored.

The difference between a logical and an algebraic shift is the manner in which the high-order bit is treated. In the logical shifts, this bit is treated like any other bit in the shift operation. In the algebraic shifts, the high-order bit becomes the sign bit and takes on an important role in the shift operation. This bit is propagated in the case of a shift in the right direction, and it can cause an overflow condition to arise in a shift to the left. In all cases besides the right algebraic shifts, vacated bits are replaced by binary zero. Let's try to clarify all this through a few examples. In each case the following will be used as the original contents of the registers:

Register 2: 4040F1F2   Register 3: F3404040
Register 8: 000005A6   Register 9: FFFFFFF8

1.	SLL	2,16	R2: F1F20000		
2.	SRL	3,24	R3: 000000F3		
3.	SRDL	2,16	R2: 00004040	R3: F1F2F340	
4.	SLDL	2,8	R2: 40F1F2F3	R3: 40404000	
5.	SLA	8,1	R8: 00000B4C		
6.	SRA	8,2	R8: 000002D3		
7.	SRA	9,1	R9: FFFFFFFC		
8.	SLDA	8,4	R8: 00005A6F	R9: FFFFFF80	

The logical shifts are generally used to isolate bytes in the center of fields. The algebraic shifts can be used to multiply or divide an algebraic number by powers of 2. Notice that instruction 5 multiplies the original contents of register 8 by 2, and that instruction 7 divides the original contents of register 9 by 2 (-8 to a -4). Instruction 8 does a similar thing; it multiplies by 8 (2^3) the large positive number that occupies the entire even-odd register pair.

A practical use for the right algebraic shift is involved in the setup of the dividend for the algebraic divide operation. To review, the dividend for an algebraic division operation must occupy the entire 64 bits of the even-odd coupled register pair specified in the first operand. In the following:

Reg.6: 00000000   Reg.7: 00002600   LOC: 00000275
D   6,LOC

the dividend is 0000000000002600. How did this value come to occupy the 64 bits of the two registers? Up to this point it was the result of a multiplication operation. Either a multiply that precedes the division in the solution of the algorithm, or if no multiplication is necessary, the dividend (occupying a single 32-bit register) is multiplied by a value of one. In either case the result of the multiplication is a product occupying the 64 bits of an even-odd coupled register pair:

Previous multiplication			Multiplication by 1		
L	7,AREA		L	7,NUM	
M	6,FOR		M	6,ONE	
D	6,LOC		D	6,LOC	
.			.		
.			.		
.			.		
AREA	DC	F'2432'	NUM	DC	F'9728'
FOR	DC	F'4'	ONE	DC	F'1'
LOC	DC	F'629'	LOC	DC	F'629'

The use of a right algebraic shift instruction will accomplish the identical result. Examine the following:

```
        L      6,NUM
        SRDA   6,32
        D      6,LOC
        .
        .
        .
LOC     DC     F'629'
NUM     DC     F'9728'
```

Contents after the load operation:

Reg.6: 00002600   Reg.7: GGGGGGGG

Contents after the shift operation:

Reg.6: 00000000   Reg.7: 00002600

Why not load NUM into Register 7 and just subtract the contents of Register 6 from itself? Because this would work satisfactorily only in the cases where NUM is a positive number. When NUM happens to be a negative value, the sign bit of 1 must be propogated throughout the even register of the even-odd coupled register pair.

BIT MANIPULATION BASED ON THE FUNCTIONS OF LOGIC

These instructions enable the programmer to initialize or alter the value of any bit or group of bits in a storage location or register. It is best to consider these logical functions at a conceptual level before we examine the actual machine instructions that perform the operations. There are two operands involved in each of these operations. Corresponding bits in each of the operands are compared with one another. Depending on their relation to one another, to zero, and the type of operations used, the corresponding bit in the resultant field is set to either one or zero.

As shown in figure 17-3, there are three types of operations used: (1) the AND, (2) the Exclusive OR, and (3) the inclusive OR. In the AND operations, corresponding bits in both operand fields must be ones in order for the resultant bit to be set to one. In the Exclusive OR operations, only one of the corresponding bits from the operand fields can be a one to set the resultant bit to a one. In the inclusive OR, one of the corresponding bits from the operand fields may be a one, or the corresponding bits from both operands may be ones.

Notice that only one of the four possible bit combinations results in a one bit when an AND operation is used; the bits in the first and second operands *must* be a one. Two of the four bit combinations result in a one bit when an Exclusive OR operation is used. The bit in one operand must be a one—exclusively of the bit in the other operand—or the resultant bit will not be a one.

AND			Exclusive OR			Inclusive OR		
First Operand	Second Operand	Result	First Operand	Second Operand	Result	First Operand	Second Operand	Result
1	1	1	1	1	0	1	1	1
1	0	0	1	0	1	1	0	1
0	1	0	0	1	1	0	1	1
0	0	0	0	0	0	0	0	0

Fig. 17-3 Operations based on the functions of logic

In the case of the inclusive OR, three of the four bit combinations result in a one bit, because in every case where there is at least one one-bit, the resultant bit is a one.

Instructions That Implement the Logic Functions There are four instructions to perform each of the three logic functions—one in each of the following four classes of instructions: RR, RX, SI, and SS. The actions of the instructions are identical, but the location of the data on which the operation is performed is different:

Instruction Type	AND Opcode	EXCLUSIVE OR Opcode	INCLUSIVE OR Opcode
RR	NR	XR	OR
RX	N	X	O
SI	NI	XI	OI
SS	NC	XC	OC

These instructions set condition code as follows.

Condition-Code Setting	Operation Result
0	every bit in the result was zero
1	at least one bit in the result was one
2	unused
3	unused

Using the following as the original contents of registers and main storage areas, let us examine the results of the execution of the following instructions:

REG8: 00005831   REG9: 68149831
LOC: F1F2F3F4   AREA: F6F2F8C6
      fwb

1. NR 8,9   R8: 00001831
2. XR 8,9   R8: 6814C000
3. OR 8,9   R8: 6814D831
4. XR 9,9   R9: 00000000
5. O   8,LOC   R8: F1F2FBF5
6. NI LOC,X'F0'   LOC:F0F2F3F4
7. XC LOC+1(2),AREA LOC:F10401F4
8. OI AREA+3,X'F0'   AREA:F6F2F8F6

Uses for The Logical Functions Notice in example 4 that to Exclusive Or an area to itself sets the entire area to zeros. This is a faster way to zero the contents of a register than to subtract the contents of the register from itself on some System/360 and 370 machines. Also notice that example 8 shows another way to fix the sign over the low-order digit in a zoned-decimal field created by the UNPK instruction.

The logical instructions can be used to alter a series of bit switches. A *switch* is a programming device used to remember a condition. A switch may occupy an entire word, a byte, or a bit within a byte. For instance, one byte in storage can hold eight separate switches; each of the eight bits that makes up the byte can record the condition of one switch by its on or off position. An OI instruction can be used to turn any of the eight switches to an *on* position, leaving the remaining bits unchanged. An NI instruction can be used to turn any of the eight switches off, leaving the remaining bits untouched. An XI instruction can change each of the eight switches to its opposite state.

```
OI    SWS,X'F0'    turns first 4 switches ON
NI    SWS,X'3F'    turns the first + second switch OFF
XI    SWS,X'FF'    flips all switches to opposite state
  .
  .
  .
SWS   DC   X'00'
```

The condition of any or all of these bit switches can be tested through use of the Test Under Mask (TM) instruction.

THE TEST UNDER MASK INSTRUCTION (TM)

Test Under Mask is an SI-type instruction whose byte of immediate data contains the mask under whose control the testing operation is performed. This mask specifies which bits in the byte at the first operand address are to be tested. A mask of X'80' would test the first bit; a mask of X'40' the second bit; and a mask of X'01' the last. The conditions of several bits can also be tested with one TM instruction by specifying several one bits in the immediate operand. A mask of X'F0' would test all of the first four bits.

The results of the Test Under Mask instruction are expressed in the condition code. The condition code will reflect whether all the bits in the first operand chosen for testing by the bits in the mask are all zeros, all ones, or some zeros and some ones. The resulting condition codes are:

Condition-Code Setting	Operation Result
0	selected bits all contain zeros
1	selected bits are a mixture of ones and zeros
2	unused
3	selected bits all contain ones

The contents of the first operand byte are not affected by the execution of the TM instruction; they remain unchanged.

Let's examine an application where a clothing manufacturer keeps a description of a piece of material in one byte of storage (DESC). The first three bits in the byte keep track of the color or colors of the material:

> bit 1   red
> bit 2   yellow
> bit 3   blue

The next two bits record whether the material is solid, striped, or plaid:

> bit 4   striped
> bit 5   plaid

The remaining three bits in the byte record the type of material:

> bit 6   cotton
> bit 7   wool
> bit 8   linen

The instruction that could be used to check to see if there are any pieces of plaid material in stock would be: TM   DESC,X'08'. If we were looking for all the linen in stock we would use the following mask: TM   DESC,X'01'.

If we didn't care what color the material was, but we were looking for all the striped cottons we had in stock, the following would be used:

TM   DESC,X'14'

There is a special set of extended mnemonics for use after a test under mask instruction:

Extended Mnemonic	Condition-Code Setting	Explanation
BO	3	branch if all ones
BM	1	branch if mixed
BZ	0	branch if all zeros
BNO	0, 1 or 2	branch if not all ones (if mixed or all zeros)

Let's examine the case where we are looking for yellow plaid cotton. Using the above three examples you would imagine that the following Test Under Mask instruction would work: TM   DESC,X'4C'. The Branch Instruction: BO   FOUND would transfer control to the instruction labeled FOUND, if the description byte contained the bit settings for yellow plaid cotton. But there is no guarantee that the material is yellow only. The material may be a red and yellow plaid, a blue and yellow plaid, or a red, blue, and yellow one.

The lesson to be learned from this example is that the mask in the Test Under Mask instruction specifies which bits are to be tested. The condition code is set based on the settings of the bits that are tested; it says nothing, however, about the settings of the bits which are not tested. To guarantee that a branch would be taken to the instruction labeled FOUND only when the material is yellow plaid, it would be better to use an instruction that would test the settings of all 8 bits. Such an instruction is the Compare Logical Immediate (CLI). The instructions:

```
CLI   DESC,X'4C'
BE    FOUND
```

would branch to the instruction labeled FOUND only when the material being tested is yellow plaid cotton.

There are some instances where only the CLI instruction will properly test for the desired conditions; there are other instances where only the TM instruction will test correctly. The CLI must be used when a particular combination of bit settings is sought. The TM must be used when one bit or a couple of bits need to be tested while ignoring the settings of the other bits in the byte.

Which instruction, CLI or TM, would you use to locate all the cotton material in the inventory? If the byte immediately following DESC in storage, labeled YDS, contains the amount of yards of each material (maximum of 200 yards), how would you code a routine to yield the total yardage of cotton in the inventory?

As each inventory record is read (see figure 17-4), the contents of the descrip-

```
        SR     8,8              ZERO TOTAL SUM OF YARDS
        SR     6,6              INITIALIZE FOR NUMBER OF YARDS
LOOP    MREAD  INTO=INAREA      READ AN INVENTORY RECORD
        TM     DESC,X'04'       TYPE IS COTTON?
        BZ     LOOP             NO, BRANCH TO READ NEXT RECORD
        IC     6,YDS            YES, GET NUMBER OF YARDS
        AR     8,6              ADD NUMBER OF YARDS TO TOTAL
        B      LOOP             BRANCH TO READ NEXT RECORD
        .
        .
        .
INAREA  DS     0CL80
        .
        .
        .
DESC    DS     C
YDS     DS     C
```

Fig. 17-4   Routine to calculate total yardage of cotton

tion byte is checked for cotton as the type of material. If the one bit tested by the TM instruction (the cotton bit) is a zero, a branch is taken back to LOOP to read another inventory record. If the cotton bit is a one, the number of yards for that cotton material is inserted into register 6, and this amount of yardage is added to the sum of the total yards of cotton being kept in register 8. When the end of the input file is encountered, register 8 will contain the total number of yards of cotton in the inventory.

CHAPTER 17 QUICK REFERENCE

Name	Type	Mnemonic and Form	Object Code Form	See Page
Add Logical	RX	AL R1,D2(X2,B2)	5E | R1 | X2 | B2 | D2	320
Add Logical Register	RR	ALR R1,R2	1E | R1 | R2	320
Compare Logical	RX	CL R1,D2(X2,B2)	55 | R1 | X2 | B2 | D2	321
Compare Logical Immediate	SI	CLI D1(B1),I2	95 | I2 | B1 | D1	330
Compare Logical Characters	SS	CLC D1(L,B1),D2(B2)	D5 | L | B1 | D1 | B2 | D2	323
Compare Logical Register	RR	CLR R1,R2	15 | R1 | R2	321
Insert Character	RX	IC R1,D2(X2,B2)	43 | R1 | X2 | B2 | D2	322
Move Characters	SS	MVC D1(L,B1),D2(B2)	D2 | L | B1 | D1 | B2 | D2	321
Move Immediate	SI	MVI D1(B1),I2	92 | I2 | B1 | D1	321
ANDMMMMMMM	RX	N R1,D2(X2,B2)	54 | R1 | X2 | B2 | D2	327
AND Characters	SS	NC D1(L,B1),D2(B2)	D4 | L | B1 | D1 | B2 | D2	327
AND Immediate	SI	NI D1(B1),I2	94 | I2 | B1 | D1	327
AND Register	RR	NR R1,R2	14 | R1 | R2	327
OR	RX	O R1,D2(X2,B2)	56 | R1 | X2 | B2 | D2	327
OR Characters	SS	OC D1(L,B1),D2(B2)	D6 | L | B1 | D1 | B2 | D2	327

Name	Type	Mnemonic and Form	Object Code Form	See Page
OR Immediate	SI	OI D1(B1),I2 ←	96 | I2 | B1 | D1	327
OR Register	RR	OR R1,R2 ←	16 | R1 | R2	327
Subtract Logical	RX	SL R1,D2(X2,B2) ←	5F | R1 | X2 | B2 | D2	320
Shift Left Algebraic	RS	SLA R1,D2(B2)	8B | R1 | //// | B2 | D2	324
Shift Left Double Algebraic	RS	SLDA R1,D2(B2)	8F | R1 | //// | B2 | D2	324
Shift Left Double Logical	RS	SLDL R1,D2(B2)	8D | R1 | //// | B2 | D2	324
Shift Left Logical	RS	SLL R1,D2(B2)	89 | R1 | //// | B2 | D2	324
Subtract Logical Register	RR	SLR R1,R2 ←	1F | R1 | R2	320
Shift Right Algebraic	RS	SRA R1,D2(B2)	8A | R1 | //// | B2 | D2	324
Shift Right Double Algebraic	RS	SRDA R1,D2(B2)	8E | R1 | //// | B2 | D2	324
Shift Right Double Logical	RS	SRDL R1,D2(B2)	8C | R1 | //// | B2 | D2	324
Shift Right Logical	RS	SRL R1,D2(B2)	88 | R1 | //// | B2 | D2	324
Store Character	RX	STC R1,D2(X2,B2) →	42 | R1 | X2 | B2 | D2	322
Test Under Mask	SI	TM D1(B1),I2	91 | I2 | B1 | D1	328
Exclusive OR	RX	X R1,D2(X2,B2) ←	57 | R1 | X2 | B2 | D2	327
Exclusive OR Characters	SS	XC D1(L,B1),D2(B2) ←	D7 | L | B1 | D1 | B2 | D2	327
Exclusive OR Immediate	SI	XI D1(B1),I2 ←	97 | I2 | B1 | D1	327
Exclusive OR Register	RR	XR R1,R2 ←	17 | R1 | R2	327

QUESTIONS

1. What is the meaning of the word *logical* in Systems/360 and 370?

2. Given   Reg.6: FFFFFF64   Reg.9: 00000A72, discuss the differences in the executions of the following two instructions:

   CLR   6,9   CR   6,9

3. What is a branch table, and how is it used?

4. What are the three ways in which shift instructions differ from one another?

5. How is the second operand of a shift instruction used in the execution of the instruction?

6. What is the difference between a logical and an algebraic shift operation?

7. Why is the SRDA useful in preparation for the divide operation?

8. Explain the difference between an AND, an inclusive OR, and an Exclusive OR operation.

9. Why are twelve different instructions needed to perform the logic functions?

10. What is the difference between the TM and CLI instructions?

EXERCISES

1. Using the following as the initial contents in each case, show the contents of any registers, storage areas, or condition codes affected by the execution of the instructions.

   Reg.0: 00000031   Reg.1: 000063B9
   Reg.4: C1C2C3C4   Reg.5: F6F8F0F2
   LOC: 00006A27   AREA: D6F2C2C5
          fwb   fwb

a. CLR	0,4		f. SLDL	4,8
b. C	1,AREA		g. SRA	5,16
c. ALR	4,5		h. NR	1,5
d. MVI	AREA+1,C'B'		i. XI	LOC+2,X'8E'
e. IC	5,AREA		j. TM	AREA+2,C'B'

Powerful Special-Purpose Instructions

Systems/360 and 370 contain powerful instructions that perform rather complicated functions. One of these instructions does the job of an entire sequence of others. A list of instructions discussed in this chapter and brief explanations of their functions follow:

ED	Edit unpacks a packed-decimal field and makes it ready for printing by inserting desired punctuation.
EDMK	Edit and Mark provides the functions of ED and records the location of the first significant digit.
EX	Execute permits a break in the normal sequential execution of instructions to temporarily alter and then execute one instruction elsewhere in the program.
TR	Translate performs code translation.
TRT	Translate and Test does a character scan, or search.

There is also a series of instructions discussed in this chapter that are available only on System/370. These instructions are:

CLM	Compare Logical Characters Under Mask
CLCL	Compare Logical Long
ICM	Insert Characters Under Mask
MVCL	Move Long
STCM	Store Characters Under Mask

EDITING OF OUTPUT FIELDS

THE EDIT INSTRUCTION (ED)

There are many applications in programming in which the end result is a formal report. Such reports, when they involve financial information, require the insertion of dollar signs, commas, decimal points, minus signs and credit notations in their number fields. The Edit and the Edit and Mark instructions provide the ability to easily create legible reports, with all required punctuation and annotation.

The purpose of the Edit instruction is twofold—it unpacks a packed-decimal field, thus creating a zoned-decimal field; and it makes it more easily readable by inserting punctuation where desired. The Edit instruction is an SS-type of instruction where only one length need be specified as part of the first operand, which is called the *pattern*—a string of characters that controls what is being done with the source data. The length specified with the first operand applies to the length of the pattern.

The second operand specifies the *source field*, containing data in packed-decimal format. The data to be edited by the Edit instruction is not altered, however, by the execution of the instruction. It is fetched one byte at a time and changed to zoned-decimal format. The zoned-decimal format replaces the first operand (the pattern), so the pattern is destroyed, not the source. We will be discussing four different types of pattern characters:

Pattern Character	Bit Configuration
fill character	any combination
digit selector	0010 0000
significance starter	0010 0001
message character	any other combination

As the editing operation is performed, one of three possible things will happen to each of the pattern characters:

1. It might be replaced by a digit from the source field changed to its zoned format.
2. It might be replaced by the fill character.
3. It might be left unchanged.

The easiest way to explain how this instruction works is through examples.

Example 1: The Use of a Message Character We have a field of data defined as: ABC   DC X′26173C′. Remember, the X-type code for the constant indicates a hexadecimal constant. The value subfield contains any of the valid hexadecimal digits (0–9, A–F), and there is no special boundary alignment.

We want to insert a decimal point in the field so that the field will be printed as: 261.73. The pattern that will generate this output is as follows:

PTRN   DC   X'402020204B2020'

and the instruction that will perform the operation is ED   PTRN(7),ABC.

Each byte in the pattern is examined one at a time, beginning with the leftmost byte. The first byte in the pattern has a special purpose and is known as the fill character. This will be discussed later in the explanation of Example 3. The next byte in the pattern is a hexadecimal 20. This is referred to as a digit-selector character. Whenever a digit-selector character is encountered in the pattern, the next digit from the source field is unpacked and replaces the digit-selector character (X'20') in the pattern. The pattern looks like this after the first source digit has been handled.

40F220204B2020

The third byte in the pattern is examined and found to be another digit-selector character. The next digit from the source field is unpacked and replaces the X'20' in the third byte in the pattern. So it goes, with the fourth byte of the pattern also. The pattern at this point looks like:

40F2F6F14B2020

The next byte in the pattern contains a hexadecimal 4B, the hex equivalent of the 8-bit EBCDIC code that represents a decimal point, or period, in Systems/360 and 370. Whenever the contents of a byte in the pattern contains a combination of bits that is not a hex 20 or a hex 21 (explained later), that byte is said to contain a *message character*. Message characters are used to insert the proper punctuation and text where desired in the resultant field. The message character 4B remains unchanged in its original position in the fifth byte of the pattern field.

The next two bytes of the pattern field are examined and found to be digit-selector characters. The next two digits in the source field are unpacked and replace their respective bytes in the pattern. This results in:

40F2F6F14BF7F3 or as printed: 261.73

Notice that the edit instruction does not have the familiar problem with the sign of C or D over the last digit. Each digit selector character causes a hexadecimal F to be affixed to the front of the next digit in the source field. Negative signs are handled in a different manner (as illustrated in Example 5 in this chapter).

Example 2: Several Different Message Characters Included in the Result If we have a source field as follows: SORC   DC   X'398742626C' and we wish to create 3,987,426.26 as the printed output, what pattern would generate the desired output, and what would the Edit instruction look like that performed the operation? Don't forget to put X'40' in the first byte of the pattern. Remember, this fill character must be present. The instruction to perform this edit operation would be: ED   PTRN2(13),SORC where PTRN2 is defined as:

PTRN2   DC   X'40206B2020206B2020204B2020'   (X'6B' is a comma)

Notice that in these first two examples, a length has been specified with the first operand. This is done as a reminder of the length of the pattern used for that Edit instruction. In reality, the implied length associated with the symbol PTRN2 is 13 bytes—sufficient to hold the value subfield in the operand of the DC, symbolically named PTRN2. If the length specification were removed from the first operand of the Edit instruction, the assembler would still recognize the pattern to be 13 bytes in length.

Example 3: Editing Using the Fill Character Suppose there was a need to prepare the contents of register 6 for printer output. We know that register 6 contains the results of a binary arithmetic operation and that its value is greater than zero and less than nine million. We also know that we wish to insert a decimal point and possibly two commas as we did in Example 2. This would mean that the largest value would look like: X,XXX,XXX.XX. Therefore, a pattern identical to the one used in Example 2 can be used here. Since it is not possible to use the same pattern because the operation of the Edit instruction in that example destroyed the original pattern, we will redefine the pattern. The instructions that perform this operation follow:

```
        CVD   6,DBL
        ED    PTRN,DBL+3
         .
         .
         .
DBL     DS    D
PTRN    DC    X'40206B2020206B2020204B2020'
```

The first operation necessary is the conversion of the binary contents of register 6 to the packed-decimal format (the format needed for the source field of the Edit instruction). If the contents of register 6 are: 00056B1A, the result of the CVD instruction will be: DBL: 00000000 0355098C.

Since the maximum value expected is nine million with two decimal places, the value contained in register 6 will be right justified in the last 5 bytes of the doubleword labeled DBL. Therefore, the Edit instruction need only work with bytes DBL+3 through DBL+7. These five bytes will yield sufficient source digits for the 9 digit-selector characters in the pattern. Put another way, there are nine hexadecimal 20s in the thirteen bytes of the pattern, and there must be nine digits in the source field in addition to the sign in the low-order 4 bits of that field.

The ability of the Edit instruction to suppress leading zeros is illustrated in this example. This is accomplished by using a switch, called the *significance indicator*, which is used with the execution of the Edit instruction. Its state of being, on or off, can be used to determine if extraneous zeros and message characters are printed at the beginning of an output field. If the significance indicator is on, all source digits are unpacked and replace their respective digit-selector characters in the pattern field; and all the message characters in the pattern remain unchanged. If the significance indicator is off, all digit selector characters whose selected digits are zero and all message characters in the pattern are replaced by the fill character (from the first byte of the pattern field).

The significance indicator is turned off as the Edit instruction starts to execute. It remains in an off position until a nonzero source digit is encountered. This means that in the case of our example the first four bytes (three digit selectors and one message character) are replaced with the fill character (40) before a nonzero digit (the 3) is examined in the source field. At that point the significance indicator switch is turned on.

Figure 18-1 illustrates the byte-by-byte execution of the Edit instruction. The state of the significance indicator at the beginning and end of handling each pattern byte is shown, as well as the resultant action taken.

And so the execution of the Edit instruction continues until the resultant field (PTRN) looks like: 4040404040F36BF5F5F04BF9F8. This would print

Pattern (byte being handled is underlined)	Significance Indicator		Pattern (resultant byte is underlined)
	Before Execution	After Execution	
40<u>20</u>6B2020206B2020204B2020	OFF	OFF	40<u>40</u>6B2020206B2020204B2020
4040<u>6B</u>2020206B2020204B2020	OFF	OFF	404040<u>20</u>20206b2020204B2020
404040<u>20</u>20206B2020204B2020	OFF	OFF	40404040<u>20</u>206B2020204B2020
40404040<u>20</u>206B2020204B2020	OFF	OFF	4040404<u>040</u>206B2020204B2020
4040404040<u>20</u>6B2020204B2020	OFF	ON	4040404040<u>F3</u>6B2020204B2020
4040404040F3<u>6B</u>2020204B2020	ON	ON	4040404040F3<u>6B</u>2020204B2020
4040404040F36B<u>20</u>20204B2020	ON	ON	4040404040F36B<u>F5</u>20204B2020

Fig. 18-1 Byte-by-byte execution of edit instruction

as: ꞵꞵꞵꞵꞵ3,550.98. You will notice that in this example, as in most uses of the Edit instruction, there is an odd number of digit-selector characters. This occurs because a packed-decimal field always has an odd number of digits, since there is always a sign in the low-order 4 bits of the low-order byte.

Example 4: Need for Significance Starter   When the following instruction executes:

```
          ED   PTN(7),ANS
               .
               .
               .
   ANS    DC   X'00065C'
   PTN    DC   X'402020204B2020'
```

the result when printed will be: ꞵꞵꞵꞵꞵ65.

Since there is a 4B in the pattern, we can assume that a decimal point was desired in the result. The significance indicator was off when the byte containing the 4B was examined in the pattern; therefore, the 4B was replaced with the fill character (40). The significance indicator was not turned on until the 6 was encountered in the source field.

What is needed is a way to force the significance indicator to be turned on regardless of whether or not a nonzero source digit has been encountered. This can be accomplished by placing a X'21', referred to as the *significance starter*, in the pattern at the point at which significance is desired. In this case a pattern of: 402020214B2020 would solve the problem and yield ꞵꞵꞵꞵ.65.

The X'21' in the fourth byte of the pattern serves two purposes: It: (1) selects the next digit from the source; unpacks and replaces the X'21' in the pattern if the source digit is nonzero; replaces the X'21' in the pattern with the fill character if the source digit is a zero; and (2) turns the significance indicator on, regardless of what source digit it encountered.

The significance starter character can be placed anywhere in the pattern. If the .65 in the above example was the answer to a scientific problem, a leading zero might be helpful before the decimal point. What pattern would generate the following printed result? ꞵꞵꞵ0.65.

Example 5: Case Where a Negative Source Field Is a Possibility   In printing results of operations that could be either positive or negative, we should have some way to indicate when a negative amount has been calculated. Such a situation might occur when we are handling account balances. When we generate a negative balance due (in other words, the customer has a credit coming), we would like to be able to indicate this fact by printing the letters CR after the field. The following pattern will cause the letters CR to be printed after a negative value and blanks after a positive value:
PN   DC   X'4020206B2020214B202040C3D9'.

Execute the following:

```
ED    PN(13),FLD
       .
       .
       .
FLD    DC    X'4156028D'
```

and the printed result is 41,560.28♭CR. The same Edit instruction with a positive source field would result in: 41,560.28.

Your question right now is probably what difference does the sign of a field make in the printing or nonprinting of the letters CR. The answer lies in the low-order four bits in the source field. These four bits hold the sign of the packed-decimal field. As each byte is fetched from the source field, the low-order four bits are checked to see if they contain one of the valid sign codes. If a valid sign code is encountered, action is taken after the last source digit is handled. If a positive-sign code is encountered, the significance indicator is turned off. If a negative sign code is encountered, the significance indicator is left on.

Therefore, if the source field is positive, the significance indicator is turned off after the 8 digit is handled in the source field. This means that the fill character replaces all message characters in the pattern following the last digit selector character.

Review The Edit instruction works with two fields of data: (1) the source, and (2) the pattern. The source remains unchanged, but each byte in the pattern is affected in one of the following ways:

1. The byte is replaced by a source digit changed to its zoned-decimal format.
2. The byte is left alone.
3. The byte is replaced by the fill character.

Which action occurs with a particular byte depends on (1) the state of the significance indicator, (2) what the respective pattern character is, and (3) whether or not the source digit being examined is a zero or nonzero digit.

Whether the significance indicator switch is turned on or off or is left as it was at the start of handling a particular pattern byte depends on (1) the source digit being examined, (2) whether the pattern character was a significance starter, and (3) whether the low-order source digit in the byte being examined is a positive sign or not. Figure 18-2 contains a decision table showing the various conditions that can be present and the resultant actions taken when the Edit instruction handles an individual byte in the pattern.

A *decision table* consists of four parts. Above the double horizontal line are the possible conditions the Edit instruction is liable to encounter. On the left is the detailed list containing each condition, and on the right is a checklist of which of those conditions are present for any one particular case. Case 1 has

	1	2	3	4	5	6	7	8	9	10	11	12	13
Conditions													
Digit selector	1		1			1			1		1		
Significance indicator on						1	1	1	1	1			
Significance indicator off	1	1	1	1	1						1	1	1
Message character		1					1						
Significance starter				1	1			1		1		1	1
Source digit of 0	1			1		1			1				1
Source digit of 1–9			1		1			1		1	1	1	
Low-order source digit, positive sign									1	1	1	1	1
Results													
Fill character	1	1		1									1
Zoned source digit			1		1	1		1	1	1	1	1	
Message character							1						
Significance indicator on			1	1	1	1	1	1					
Significance indicator off	1	1							1	1	1	1	1

Fig. 18-2 Decision table for execution of the edit instruction

the following conditions present: (1) the pattern byte being handled is a digit-selector character, (2) the significance indicator is off at the start of handling this pattern byte, and (3) the source digit being examined is a zero. The third and fourth parts of a decision table are found below the double horizontal line. On the left is the list of all possible resultant actions that the Edit instruction can take as it handles a pattern byte. On the right is the checklist of which particular actions are taken in any one individual case. Examine Case 1 again. The conditions were that the significance indicator was off, and we had selected a digit of zero. The action taken is to replace the digit selector character in the pattern with the fill character and to leave the significance indicator in an off position.

Using figure 18-2, see if you can figure out the actions that result when each of the following sets of conditions are present:

1. Significance indicator is on.
   Pattern contains message character.
2. Significance indicator is on.
   Pattern contains a digit-selector character.
   Source digit is a 6.
   Low-order source digit is a positive sign.
3. Significance indicator is off.
   Pattern contains a significance-starter character.
   Source digit is a 0.

What will be the result of the execution of the following instructions?

1.   ED   PTRN1,SORC1
                       .
                       .
                       .

     PTRN1   DC   X'4020206B2020204B2020'
     SORC1   DC   X'6582100C'

2.   ED   PTRN2,SORC2
                       .
                       .
                       .

     PTRN2   DC   X'40202020'
     SORC2   DC   X'000C'

3.   ED   PTRN3,SORC3
                       .
                       .
                       .

     PTRN3   DC   X'40202020202040C4D6D3E240202040C3C5D5E3E2'
     SORC3   DC   X'0083042D'

4.   ED   PTRN4,SORC4
                       .
                       .
                       .

     PTRN4   DC   X'40212020202040D5C5C7'
     SORC4   DC   X'00279D'

Define the patterns that would process the following fields to provide the desired output:

	Field	Desired Output
5.	6824598C	6,824,598
6.	2697123C	26+97=123
7.	000489654C	48.9654

Answers to previous questions:

1. ƀ65,821.00
2. ƀƀƀƀ
3. ƀƀƀ830ƀDOLSƀ42ƀCENTS
4. ƀƀ0279ƀNEG
5. PTRN5   DC   X'40206B2020206B202020'
6. PTRN6   DC   X'4020204E20207E202020'
7. PTRN7   DC   X'4020202020204B20202020'

THE EDIT AND MARK INSTRUCTION (EDMK)

The execution of the Edit and Mark instruction is identical to that of the Edit instruction except that the Edit and Mark provides one additional function. As it changes the format of the source field from packed to zoned decimal under control of the pattern field, it records the address of the first significant character placed in the resultant field. For example, the following Edit and Mark instruction: EDMK PTRN(7),SOURC using these definitions for the two fields:

```
PTRN      DC   X'402020204B2020'
SOURC     DC   X'06582C'
```

generates the following result in the PTRN field;

```
PTRN:     4040F6F54B     F8F2.
```

It also causes the address of the third byte in PTRN to be placed in register 1 (the high-order byte is not affected). PTRN+2 is the address placed in the register, because this byte contains the first significant character. The first significant digit is the first source digit with a hexadecimal F appended to it. It is recognized as such only if the significance indicator is off. Register 1 is untouched if significance was forced by the use of a significance starter in the pattern.

The address in register 1 can be used as a guide to insert a dollar sign into the resultant field if desired. Keep in mind that this address needs slight modification. It is the address of the first significant digit (the F6), but you don't want to move a dollar sign in on top of this digit. So a value of 1 or more must be subtracted from the contents of register 1 before using its contents as the receiving address for a dollar sign. Adding two instructions following the Edit and Mark does the trick:

```
          EDMK   PTRN(7),SOURC
          S      1,ONE
          MVI    0(1),C'$'
              .
              .
              .
ONE       DC     F'1'
PTRN      DC     X'402020204B2020'
SOURC     DC     X'06582C'
```

One important thing to remember when using the EDMK is that no address is placed in register 1 if the significance was forced on before encountering the first significant digit to be converted. Significance is forced when a significance starter appears in the pattern occupying a byte that precedes the digit selector for the source digit containing the actual first significant digit. There are really two conditions that cause the EDMK instruction to place an address in register 1:

1. the resultant byte contains a zoned-decimal character created from a source field character, and
2. the significance indicator is off when the particular character is formed

The same instructions (EDMK, BCTR, and MVI) can be used if register 1 is loaded with the address of the byte following the significance starter in the pattern before the execution of the EDMK instruction. This will ensure that there is a valid address in register 1 for use in the BCTR and MVI instructions, even if significance is forced. If significance is not forced, the address in register 1 will simply be overlaid by the address of the first significant digit. The following group of instructions will work regardless of how significance was started:

```
         LA      1,PTRN+3
         EDMK    PTRN(9),SOURC
         S       1,ONE
         MVI     0(1),C'$'
          .
          .
          .
ONE      DC      F'1'
PTRN     DC      X'4020212020204B2020'
SOURC    DC      X'0006582C'
```

In this example the resultant field contains PTRN: 404040F0F6F54BF8F2 and register 1 contains the address of the fourth byte in PTRN, the byte following the significance starter in the pattern field. The subtract instruction reduces this address by a value of 1, and the dollar sign is moved into the third byte of PTRN.

PTRN: 40405BF0F6F54BF8F2

Change the source field to:

SOURC   DC   X'9246582C'

and the resultant field contains:

PTRN: 40F9F2F4F6F54BF8F2

and register 1 contains the address of the second byte in PTRN. One is subtracted, and the dollar sign is moved into the first byte of PTRN:

5BF9F2F4F6F54BF8F2.

In either case the dollar sign will print immediately before the first digit that prints.

THE EXECUTE INSTRUCTION (EX)

The Execute instruction allows you to break the normal sequential execution of instructions in your program to execute one instruction (the subject instruction) in some other part. Only that one will be executed, and then control will be returned to the instruction immediately following the Execute instruction in sequence. This instruction also performs a second function. In addition to breaking the normal sequential execution of instructions, it has the ability to temporarily alter the one instruction that it causes to execute out of sequence.

The subject instruction is altered for this one execution by "oring" the contents of the low-order byte of the register specified in the first operand with the contents of the subject instruction's second byte. This means that the Execute instruction has the ability to temporarily change the:

1. R1 and R2 fields of an RR instruction
2. R1 and X2 fields of an RX instruction
3. R1 and R3 fields of an RS instruction
4. immediate byte of an SI instruction, or
5. length byte of an SS instruction.

Now, your reaction is, "Fine, but why change the second byte of an instruction?". There is a multitude of reasons for making this temporary change. What if you wish to move an immediate byte of data to location SPOT, but you are not able to determine until execution time what byte you wish to move? By placing the contents of the byte you wish moved into the low-order byte of a register and specifying this register in the first operand of an Execute instruction, your job will be completed. For example, examine the following:

```
                 LTR   8,8
                 BM    NEGSIGN
POSSIGN          IC    6,POS
                 B     EXEC
NEGSIGN          IC    6,MINUS
EXEC             EX    6,MOVESIGN
                 .
                 .
                 .
POS              DC    C'+'
MINUS            DC    C'-'
MOVESIGN         MVI   SPOT,X'00'
```

Notice that the subject instruction, the MVI, is placed with the DC and DS statements in the program. This is because it will be executed by the Execute instruction, and it therefore does not need to be present in the normal body of instructions. Also we would not wish to place it among the normal instructions, because if it did execute in a normal sequence it would move two hexadecimal zeros to location SPOT.

The hexadecimal zeros specified in the second operand of the subject instruction raise another question. Why specify X'00'? Well, something must be specified. The assembler must have a syntactically correct second operand on the MVI or it cannot assemble the instruction into machine code; and it would have to flag it. Therefore, we must specify something in the second operand, but we want it to be something that won't affect the oring operation of the Execute instruction. The two hex zeros would have no effect. The following illustrates what happens when the code beginning at POSSIGN is executed:

```
POS:            4       E
POS:            0100    1110   (in low-order byte of Reg. 6)
ORED WITH:      0000    0000   (in 2nd byte of subject instruction)
RESULT:         0100    1110
```

Let's use a different type of subject instruction—an SS. Assume that we want to move a field of data at execution time, but we don't know the length of this field until execution time. Before using the Execute instruction to perform this variable length move, we must review machine code formats for SS-type instructions. The machine code format for an MVC instruction is:

D2	L	B1	D1	B2	D2
0 7	8 15	16 19	20 31	32 35	36 47

The number of bytes that the MVC instruction can move ranges from a minimum of 1 to a maximum of 256. Notice that there are eight bits in the machine code format to hold the length (bits 8–15); yet it takes nine to represent a decimal 256 in binary (100000000). The assembler can handle this maximum length because it subtracts 1 from the length specified in the first operand of the MVC instruction and assembles this new value into machine code for the MVC instruction. When the MVC instruction executes (normal execution), one more byte than that indicated by the number assembled is moved.

The above fact must be kept in mind when you program the execution of an SS instruction through the use of an Execute (EX). It is not the exact length of the move that is placed in the low-order byte of the first operand register (in the EX instruction), but it is the actual length minus 1.

The following code illustrates the use of the EX with an MVC as the subject instruction. If you know the beginning addresses of two adjacent fields, FLD1 and FLD2, you can calculate the length of FLD1 by subtracting the address of FLD1 from that of FLD2. Register 7 contains the address of FLD1, and register 8 the address of FLD2:

```
          SR     8,7
          BCTR   8,0
          EX     8,MOVE
          L      2,LOC
          .
          .
          .
ONE       DC     F'1'
```

```
MOVE      MVC     OUTAREA+6(0),INAREA
LOC       DC      F'86'
INAREA    DS      0CL80
FLD1      DS      40C
          DS      CL40
```

In this example we see that FLD1 begins with the first byte of INAREA and can have a variable length of up to forty bytes. It is assumed that a scan has been made of this field before the SR instruction to determine its actual length for this application. The MVC instruction will be assembled with a length of zero in bits 8–15. The Execute instruction would cause the length − 1 to be "ored" to this zero length, and one more byte than the "ored" result would be moved. After execution, the MVC instruction remains unchanged (its length field still contains a X'00').

Because the Execute is branching to execute an instruction, the address specified in the second operand is checked to ensure it is even (all instructions must start on halfword boundaries). If an even address is not found, a specification exception occurs. An error condition also occurs if the subject instruction is another Execute instruction. Paradoxical as it might seem, you cannot execute an Execute instruction!

TRANSLATION OF CHARACTER STRINGS (TR)

Systems 360 and 370 have an instruction that can change one 8-bit code into a different one. A string of characters can be translated from one code base to another with the use of one single instruction—the Translate instruction (opcode TR). One way to illustrate the use of this instruction is through an example. Think back to when you were a child, and you used all sorts of special "codes" to pass important notes to your friends. Anyone you didn't consider to be a friend was unable to understand what you were writing.

The Translate instruction is an SS-type instruction. It translates a variable-length field of from 1 to 256 bytes in length, working one byte at a time from left to right in the field. As each byte in the original code field is translated, it is replaced by its equivalent in the new code. The translation process is accomplished using a 256-byte table. The table contains one byte of the new 8-bit code for each of the 256 possible combinations of 8 bits in the original code. Which new 8-bit code from the table replaces a particular one in the original character string depends on the decimal value of the 8 bits that make up the byte in the original character string.

The action of the Translate instruction (see figure 18-3) is to use the decimal equivalent of the first byte in the first operand field (the original code) as a displacement from the beginning of the 256-byte table. The byte at this address is fetched, and a copy of it replaces the first byte in the first operand field. This accomplished, the first byte has been translated, and the decimal equivalent of the second byte of the first operand is used as a displacement to move a copy

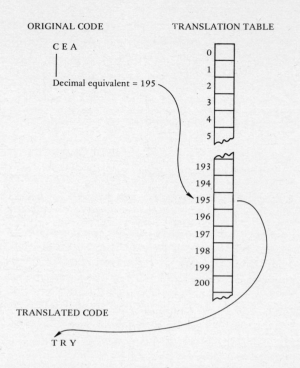

ORIGINAL CODE   TRANSLATION TABLE

C E A

Decimal equivalent = 195

TRANSLATED CODE

T R Y

Fig. 18-3 Illustration of the execution of the translate instruction

from the 256-byte table. So the operation continues until every byte in the first operand field (length specified with the first operand) has been translated.

Let's examine the following section of code. In this example the original code is the reverse alphabet of the translated one. Z translates to an A; a Y translates to a B; an X translates to a C; etc. The numbers are also reversed—a 9 translates to a 0, an 8 to a 1, and so forth. Every other bit combination in the original string should translate to a blank (hexadecimal 40), except the comma, period, dash, and semicolon, which should translate to identical codes. The general format for the translate instruction is: TR   symbol(length),symbol where the first operand is the address of the character string to be translated, and the second operand is the label of the beginning byte of the 256-byte table.

```
         TR   ORIG(59),TABLE
         .
         .
         .
TABLE    DC   75C' '                    TRANSLATION TABLE
         DC   C'.'
         DC   18C' '
         DC   C';'
```

```
              DC   C' '
              DC   C'−'
              DC   10C' '
              DC   C','
              DC   85C' '
              DC   C'ZYXWVUTSR'
              DC   7C' '
              DC   C'QPONMLKJI'
              DC   8C' '
              DC   C'HGFEDCBA'
              DC   6C' '
              DC   C'9876543210'
              DC   6C' '
    ORIG      DC   C'GSRH♭RH♭ZM♭'         FIELD TO BE
              DC   C'VCZNKOV♭LU♭GSV♭'     TRANSLATED
              DC   C'FHV♭LU♭GSV♭GIZMH'
              DC   C'OZGV♭RNHGIFXGRLN.'
```

Let's examine what happens in the translation of the first two characters of ORIG. The first character, a G, has a decimal equivalent of 199.[†]

Use the decimal equivalent of 199 as a displacement from the beginning of TABLE and you find the letter T at this location. The T replaces the G in the original character string, and translation continues with the second character, the S. Its decimal equivalent is 226, and using the 226 as a displacement yields the letter H from the translation table. An H now replaces the S in the original character string. The first part of the original character string now looks like: THRH♭RH♭ZM♭ . . . . Continue translating the 3rd through the 59th characters and see what the translated message has to say.

CHARACTER SCAN OR SEARCH (TRT)

The instruction explained in this section is referred to as the Translate and Test instruction, but its name is a misnomer. The action of this instruction does not involve the translation of any character string from one 8-bit code to another. Instead, it involves a character scan, or search. The Translate and Test instruction scans a character string for a particular combination or combinations of bits in a byte. A 256-byte table is used in conjunction with this instruction. In this case the table holds the clue as to which of the 256 different combinations of 8 bits should stop the scan.

The decimal equivalents of successive bytes from the first operand field are used as displacements to locate in the table particular bytes whose origin is specified in the second operand. So far, this execution of the TRT instruction

---

[†]To assist you in calculating these decimal equivalents use appendix 3, pages 7–10 of the IBM System/360 Reference Data Card (GX20-1703), or pages 9–12 of the IBM System/370 Reference Summary Card (GX20-1850).

is identical to the execution of the TR. But at this point they greatly differ. The Translate instruction fetches a copy of the byte within the table and replaces the byte in the first operand field that was used as a displacement.

The Translate and Test instruction examines the contents of the byte from the table. If this byte contains X'00', no action is taken; and the next byte from the first operand is used as a displacement into the table. This continues from left to right in the first operand until a nonzero byte is encountered in the second operand table, when the scan stops. The address of the first operand byte, which was used as a displacement when the nonzero byte was encountered, is placed in the low-order three bytes of register 1. The nonzero byte from the second operand table that stopped the scan is inserted into the low-order byte of register 2.

For instance, if we were scanning a field to find the end of a sentence, our table could be defined to contain all X'00' in every byte except the 76th one. The 76th byte has a decimal value of 75, which is equivalent to a binary 01001011 (X'4B'), the 8-bit code for a period. If our field contained a maximum of 120 bytes of data, the following instructions would scan the field from left to right until a period was encountered:

```
          LA    4,FLD
          XR    1,1
          XR    2,2
          TRT   FLD(120),TABL
          SR    1,4
          .
          .
          .

FLD       DC    CL120'THIS IS IT.'
TABL      DC    75X'00'
          DC    X'01'
          DC    180X'00'
```

The scan of the TRT instruction will be stopped when the 11th byte of FLD is used as a displacement into TABL. This generates the effective address equivalent to TABL+75. It is the contents of the byte at this address that is placed in register 2(X'01'), and the effective address of FLD+10 is placed in register 1.

For instance, if the first byte of the area labeled FLD is loaded at address 3000, then TABL refers to the byte at location 3078. As the 11th byte of the first operand field was examined (the byte at address 300A), the decimal equivalent of its contents (75) was added to the address of the second operand (3078), generating an effective address of 30ED. The contents of the byte at this effective address was nonzero (X'01'). The scan was stopped. The address 300A was placed in register 1, and the X'01' was inserted into register 2's low-order byte.

In another form, the action of the TRT instruction can be illustrated as follows:

TRT   FLD(120),TABL

FLD: E3C8C9E240C9E240C9E34B	byte from first operand (FLD)
$\rightarrow 4B_{16} = 75_{10}$	decimal equivalent
TABL + 75 ——————	used as displacement
TABL: 00000000...00000100...	into second operand (TABL)
R1: @FLD + 10	address of byte in first operand
R2: XXXXXX01	contents of nonzero byte

Notice that the address of the first byte in FLD was loaded into register 4 before the execution of the TRT instruction. After the execution of the TRT, register 1 contains the address of the byte in FLD that stopped the scan. By subtracting the beginning address of the character string from the address of the byte within the string that stopped the scan, you can calculate the number of characters in the sentence. This number could then be used in conjunction with an Execute instruction whose subject is an MVC, and the entire sentence can be moved to a different location.

In this example, the contents of registers 1 and 2 are set to zero before execution of the TRT instruction, because this instruction affects only the three low-order bytes of register 1 and the low-order byte of register 2. The other bytes are unaffected by the TRT instruction. The condition code is set to reflect the result of a Translate and Test operation. In some cases, these condition-code settings can be very useful. (More will be said about this later.)

Condition Code	Signifies
0	All bytes in first operand were used as displacements, but no nonzero contents were encountered in any of the bytes at those locations within the second operand table.
1	A nonzero byte was encountered in the table prior to the use of the last byte in the first operand as a displacement.
2	A nonzero byte was encountered in the table as the last byte in the first operand was used as a displacement.

The condition code would be set to 1 for the example given earlier. The first operand specified a length of 120 bytes; the nonzero byte was encountered in the table as the eleventh byte of the 120-byte field was used as a displacement. If there had been no period in any of the 120 bytes of the first operand, the condition code would have been set to a value of 0. If the period that was encountered was in the last byte in the first operand (the 120th character), the setting of the condition code would have been 2. This capability of the instruction can be used as a stop measure.

You can always place a character you know will stop the scan in the last byte of the first operand field. The scan will never run out of first operand data before encountering a nonzero value in the table. All you have to do is check the condition-code setting after the TRT executes; a 1 indicates a scan halted by a period; a 2 indicates a scan that your stop character halted.

The above example used only one nonzero byte in its 256-byte table. This can be expanded so that several bytes within the table are filled with different values (say different multiples of 4) and, depending on which nonzero byte stops the scan, different actions can be taken. For example, suppose we were to write the section of code for a compiler that would handle the translation of an expression into machine code. In this case we must recognize the different operators and have a separate code "multiple of 4" in the table at the position for the character which represents the operator.

We must also have a different "multiple of 4" in the table to indicate any valid alphabetic character that might start a symbolic name. The scan thus stopped, and the symbol thus located, could then be passed to a routine that could interpret the symbol. The table could contain 4 in the position for a + sign, 8 in the position for a − sign, C in the position for a * (multiplication) sign, etc. The section of code would look like:

```
        LA    1,EXPR       REGISTER 1 = BEGINNING ADDRESS
  *                        OF EXPRESSION
        XR    2,2          CLEAR HIGH-ORDER BYTES TO ZERO
SCAN    LR    6,1          SET UP ADDRESS FOR SCAN OF
  *                        NEXT CHARACTER
        TRT   0(60,6),TAB  SCAN FOR OPERATOR OR SYMBOLIC
  *                        NAME
        A     1,ONE        SET UP FOR NEXT SCAN
RTN     B     RTN(2)
        B     ADD
        B     SUBT
        B     MULT
        .
        .
        .
        B     STOP
```

The series of branch instructions forms a branch table. Using the multiple of 4, the TRT instruction inserted in register 2 when its scan was stopped, the B instruction labeled RTN, branches to a branch instruction within the branch table. This transfers control to the proper routine for handling the generation of code for the particular operator or symbolic name that stopped the scan. Each of these separate routines would end with a branch to the instruction labeled SCAN, and the scan of the expression would continue from the new point.

Each expression being translated could end with a very special character (like the ";" in PL/1). This special character would stop the scan with a nonzero byte in the table that would cause the last branch in the branch table to be taken (B to the instruction labeled STOP), and the scan of the expression would be terminated at this point.

It is possible to extend this coding example so that any blank source records used merely to make the listing easier to read are skipped. The condition code settings are used. If the TRT instruction were to scan all 60 bytes of the first operand field and not encounter a nonzero corresponding byte in the TRT table, the condition code is set to a value of 0. A branch instruction can be used to check for this condition-code value. If a value of zero is found, a branch is taken back to the beginning of the block of code, which begins the scan of a new statement. This would prevent the branch table from being used erroneously:

```
BEGIN     MREAD
            .
            .
            .
          TRT       0(60,6),TAB
          BC        8,BEGIN
          A         1,ONE
            .
            .
            .
```

INSTRUCTIONS AVAILABLE ONLY ON SYSTEMS/370

Five instructions that are available with System/370 but not System/360 will be discussed in this section. These are not the only new instructions available on System/370, but the others are considered to be beyond the scope of this book. If you wish information on the instructions not discussed here, you should refer to the manual entitled IBM System/370 Principles of Operation (GA22-7000). The five instructions discussed in this chapter are:

MVCL	Move Long
CLCL	Compare Logical Long
CLM	Compare Logical Characters Under Mask
ICM	Insert Characters Under Mask
STCM	Store Characters Under Mask

The Move Long Instruction (MVCL)

This instruction moves a variable number of bytes from the second operand to the first operand location. The two fields may be different in their respective lengths. Any low-order bytes remaining if the first operand is longer will be filled with a padding character. (See figure 18-4.)

The MVCL belongs to the RR-class of instructions. It is one of the few RR instructions with a mnemonic opcode that does not end with the letter R. Each operand specifies the even register of an even-odd coupled register pair. The use of these registers is shown in figure 18-4.

Movement of data is from left to right in the fields, and movement stops when the number of bytes specified in bits 8–31 of R1+1 have been moved. Using the following as the contents before execution, examine the execution of this MVCL instruction:

Reg2: 00004E00 Reg3: 00000350
Reg6: 00006C84 Reg7: 40000276

MVCL 2,6

The receiving field specified in registers 2 and 3 begins at address 004E00 and contains space for 848 (350_{16}) bytes. The source field specified in registers 6 and 7 begins at location 006C84 and contains 630 bytes of data. These 630 bytes are moved to the first 630 bytes of the 848-byte area, which begins at location 004E00, and the remaining 218 low-order bytes of this first operand area are filled with the padding character of 40_{16}, which is specified in the high-order byte of register 7. When the execution of the MVCL instruction is

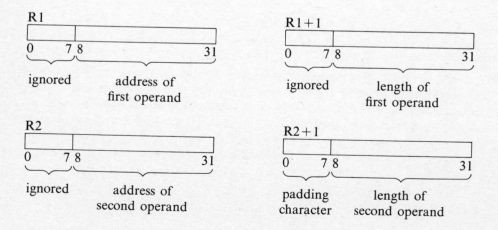

Fig. 18-4 Register usage in the MVCL instruction

complete, the four registers specified in the operands have been altered to reflect the operation:

1. The address in R1 has been incremented by the count value in R1+1 (004E00+350=005150).
2. The count in R1+1 is zero (Reg3: 00000000).
3. The address in R2 has been incremented by the number of bytes that have been moved out of the second operand (006C84+276=006EFA).
4. The count in R2+1 has been reduced by the number of bytes moved out of the second operand (000276−276=000000).

The execution of this instruction is designed to work only if the operands as specified do not destructively overlap as would occur if part of the first-operand location were specified as source data for the move after data has already been moved into that location. Should this condition arise, the condition code is set to 3, and no data movement takes place.

The condition-code settings generated by the execution of this instruction are as follows:

Condition-Code Setting	Operation Result
0	First operand and second operand counts are equal.
1	First operand count is low.
2	First operand count is high.
3	No movement is performed because of destructive overlap.

THE COMPARE LOGICAL INSTRUCTION (CLCL)

This instruction logically compares a variable number of bytes of the first operand to the contents of the second operand location. The two fields may be different in their respective lengths, with the shorter of the two operands being extended with the padding character. The CLCL instruction is similar in many ways to the MVCL. The CLCL belongs to the RR-class. It also is one of the few RR instructions that has a mnemonic opcode that does not end with the letter R. Each operand specifies the even register of an even-odd coupled register pair. (The use of these registers is identical to their use in the MVCL instruction as shown in figure 18-4.)

The comparison is performed from left to right throughout the fields, one byte at a time. Each byte is considered to contain a binary unsigned quantity. The comparison ends as soon as two unequal bytes are compared—or the last byte in the longest operand has been compared. If the comparison is stopped because of an unequal condition, the location of the bytes causing the condition are reflected in the contents of the registers used in the instruction. For example, given:

Reg4: 0000825E   Reg5: 0000000C
Reg6: 000053A2   Reg7: 40000009
00825E: C1E2E8D3C440C7D540E2F3F8
0053A2: C1E2E8D3C440E6F3F9

CLCL   4,6

After execution of the CLCL instruction, registers 4–7 will contain:

Reg4: 00008264   Reg5: 00000006
Reg6: 000053A8   Reg7: 40000003

Registers 4 and 6 now contain the addresses of the two bytes whose inequality stopped the operation, and registers 5 and 7 reflect the location of those bytes with relation to the beginning of the field.

If the operation had terminated because of an inequality caused by comparison with an inserted padding character, the register containing the count for that shorter field would contain a count of zero (rather than a negative number).

The condition codes set by the execution of this instruction are the same as those set by all other compare instructions, with the addition that a condition code of zero also reflects the situation where both fields being compared have lengths of zero specified. The resultant condition codes are:

Condition-Code Setting	Operation Result
0	Operands are equal, or both operands have zero lengths.
1	First operand is low.
2	First operand is high.
3	Unused

CHARACTER OPERATIONS EXECUTED UNDER MASK (CLM, ICM, and STCM)

There are three new instructions available on the IBM S/370 that perform their operations under the control of a mask. All three belong to the RS-class of instructions, and each specifies its mask as the third operand. These instructions are:

CLM	Compare Logical Characters Under Mask
ICM	Insert Characters Under Mask
STCM	Store Characters Under Mask

In each of these instructions the mask occupies 4 bits, and each corresponds to one of the 4 bytes in the register specified in the first operand. The bits correspond, from left to right in the mask, with bytes in the register from left to right; that is, the first bit in the mask refers to the high-order byte in the register, and the last bit in the mask refers to the low-order one. If a particular bit is on in the mask (i.e., contains a 1), the byte that corresponds to that bit will participate in the operation. A mask of 12 has the first and second bits on and the third and fourth bits off ($12_{10} = 1100_2$). This mask would permit the two high-order bytes of the first operand register to participate in the operation.

In the case of the Compare Logical Characters Under Mask (CLM), a mask of 12 would mean that the two high-order bytes of the register would be compared as a two-byte contiguous field with the two bytes beginning with the one whose address is specified in the second operand. For instance:

Reg6: C1C2C3C4   AREA: C1C2D6F3

CLM   6,12,AREA

would compare the C1C2 from the first two bytes of register 6 with the first two bytes at AREA(C1C2). Resultant condition codes are:

Condition-Code Setting	Operation Result
0	Selected bytes are equal, or mask is zero.
1	Selected field of first operand is low.
2	Selected field of first operand is high.
3	Unused

So, with the above CLM instruction, a condition code of zero will be set. Use the same contents for register 6 and AREA but change the instruction to: CLM   6,10,AREA, and this time the condition code will be set to 2. The selected bytes of register 6 (first and third, C1C3) that make up the contiguous field of the first operand contain a higher value than the two bytes located at AREA.

With the Insert Characters Under Mask (ICM) instruction, the contents of bytes from contiguous locations beginning with the byte at the second operand address are inserted into the first operand register in the byte positions indicated by the bits that are on in the mask. For instance:

Register 2: 00000000   LOC: FFFFFFF6

ICM   2,6,LOC

changes register 2's contents to: 00FFFF00.

The condition code settings for the ICM instruction are as follows:

Condition-Code Setting	Operation Result
0	All inserted bits are zeros, or the mask is zero.
1	First bit of inserted field is one.
2	First bit of inserted field is zero, and not all inserted bits are zeros.
3	Unused

The above condition-code settings permit the ICM instruction to be used for the same purpose as a Load and Test (LTR) when the ICM instruction is used with a mask of 15 (all ones, 1111).

The instruction Execution of the Store Characters Under Mask (STCM) is similar to the ICM instruction, except that bytes of the first operand register selected by the mask are stored into successive and contiguous bytes of storage beginning with the byte addressed by the second operand:

Reg3: F2F6F7F3   REC: C1C2C3C4

STCM   3,7,REC

results in: Reg3: F2F6F7F3   REC: F6F7F3C4

The STCM instruction does not set the condition code.

CHAPTER 18 QUICK REFERENCE

Name	Type	Mnemonic and Form	Object Code Form	See Page
Compare Logical Long	RR	CLCL R1,R2	0F | R1 | R2	355
Compare Logical Characters Under Mask	RS	CLM R1,M3,D2(B2)	BD | R1 | M3 | B2 | D2	356
Edit	SS	ED ⟵ D1(L,B1),D2(B2)	DE | L | B1 | D1 | B2 | D2	335
Edit and Mark	SS	EDMK ⟵ D1(L,B1),D2(B2)	DF | L | B1 | D1 | B2 | D2	342
Execute	RX	EX ⟶ R1,D2(X2,B2)	44 | R1 | X2 | B2 | D2	344
Insert Characters Under Mask	RS	ICM ⟵ R1,M3,D2(B2)	BF | R1 | M3 | B2 | D2	356

Name	Type	Mnemonic and Form	Object Code Form	See Page
Move Long	RR	MVCL R1,R2	0E | R1 | R2	354
Store Characters Under Mask	RS	STCM R1,M3,D2(B2) →	BE | R1 | M3 | B2 | D2	356
Translate	SS	TR D1(L,B1),D2(B2) ←	DC | L | B1 | D1 | B2 | D2	347
Translate and Test	SS	TRT D1(L,B1),D2(B2)	DD | L | B1 | D1 | B2 | D2	349

QUESTIONS

1. What two purposes does the Edit instruction serve?

2. What purpose does the pattern serve in the execution of the Edit instruction?

3. In what format must the source field be specified for the Edit instruction?

4. Which field is altered by the execution of the edit instruction, the source or the pattern?

5. Explain the function of the following in the execution of the Edit instruction:

    a. fill character
    b. digit selector
    c. significance indicator
    d. significance starter
    e. message character

6. What makes the EDMK instruction different from the ED?

7. Under what conditions does the Edit and Mark instruction *not* alter the contents of Register 1?

8. If you want to insert a dollar sign in front of an edited field, why can't you use the value placed in register 1 by the EDMK instruction as the address to receive the dollar sign?

9. If there is a possibility that significance may be forced in your pattern field, what can you do to make sure that a dollar sign can still be inserted?

10. Explain, in your own words, the operation of the Execute instruction.

11. Why is the subject instruction of an Execute instruction usually placed among the constants and definitions of storage, and why does the second byte of this instruction usually contain X'00'?

12. Given: Reg3: 7B6C5C5B   AREA: 40F6F1F2F7
    Explain what happens when the following instruction is executed.

            EX   3,MOV
            .
            .

      MOV   MVI   AREA,X'00'

13. What distinguishes the EX instruction from all other branching instructions?

14. Why does the Translate instruction use a 256-byte table?

15. In the execution of the TR instruction, how is a byte of the original code used in the translation process?

16. What makes the Translate and Test instruction differ from the Translate?

17. Explain what a branch table is. Use an example in your explanation.

18. What makes the mnemonic opcodes of the Move Long and Compare Logical Long instructions different from other RR-class instructions?

19. In what way are the ICM and LTR instructions similar?

20. What function does the mask serve in the execution of the CLM, ICM, and STCM instructions?

EXERCISES

1. What is the contents of FLD after each of the following instructions executes?

        a.   ED FLD(7),ONE
                  .
                  .

      FLD   DC X'4020206B202020'
      ONE   DC X'52683C'

b.
```
            ED   FLD(5),TWO
             .
             .
FLD         DC   X'40204B2020'
TWO         DC   X'000C'
```
c.
```
            ED   FLD(7),THRE
             .
             .
FLD         DC   X'402021204B2020'
THRE        DC   X'00075C'
```
d.
```
            ED   FLD(10),FOR
             .
             .
FLD         DC   X'5C20206B21202040C3D9'
FOR         DC   X'00006D'
```

2. Try your hand at setting up the 256-byte table and the necessary instructions to convert form EBCDIC to ASCII code format.

3. How many bytes are moved by each of the following sets of instructions?

a.
```
            SR    8,8
            EX    8,FIRST
             .
             .
FIRST       MVC   LOC2(0),LOC1
```
b.
```
            IC    9,TWO
            EX    9,SCND
             .
             .
TWO         DC    X'02'
AREA2       DS    CL8
AREA1       DC    C'THIS IS A NOTICE'
SCND        MVC   AREA2,AREA1
```

4. Write code to scan a 100-character line for the first nonblank character; then collect all the nonblank characters and move them to an output area and print. The only nonblank characters that should appear are the alphabetic characters A–Z and the numeric digits 0–9. If any other character is present, an error message should be printed.

5. Code a program that will center a heading in a 120-character line, a variable-length heading that can range from four to one hundred characters.

6. Code a program that will justify the margins on a printed page of output. (Justify means that the last letters on each line should line up one above the other the same way the first letters in each line do.) This means your program must insert the correct number of blanks between words in a line. Code your program to handle 65-character lines (expect that each input line will have a maximum of 65 characters). The end of a paragraph is marked by the special character @. You need not justify the last line in a paragraph.

CHAPTER 19

Additional Facilities
of the Assembler

Discussed in this chapter are some of the miscellaneous features and some of the very useful facilities of the assembler. Some instructions that allow the programmer to control the assembler will be discussed. Base registers will also be examined more fully, with a discussion of the use of multiple-base registers, as well as a feature called Dummy Control Sections (DSECTS).[†]

CONTROLLING THE ASSEMBLER PROGRAM

There are assembler instructions that can alter the assembler's predetermined way of performing some of its functions. There are instructions that control the layout and amount of detail the assembler produces in the listing of the source program. There is an instruction to change the standard coding conventions the assembler uses for the format of source statements. There are even instructions to the assembler that can cause it to alter the setting of the location counter.

[†]If after you have read this chapter there remain some features of the assembler that you would still like to explore, examine a copy of *OS/VS and DOS/VS Assembler Language* (GC33-4010), *IBM System/360 Disk and Tape Operating Systems, Assembler Language* (GC24-3414), or *IBM System/360 Operating System Assembler Language* (GC28-6514). In addition you might find the following useful: *System/360 Principles of Operation* (GA22-6821), or *System/370 Principles of Operation* (GA22-7000).

Listing Control

There are four assembler instructions that control the listing of the source program produced: PRINT, TITLE, EJECT and SPACE. The PRINT instruction controls the amount of detail the assembler produces in the listing. Three operands can be specified. The following illustrates the choices available for operands. Those that are underlined are the defaults, the assembler's predetermined choices:

blank   PRINT $\begin{bmatrix} \underline{ON} \\ OFF \end{bmatrix}$ $\begin{bmatrix} ,\underline{GEN} \\ ,NOGEN \end{bmatrix}$ $\begin{bmatrix} ,\underline{NODATA} \\ ,DATA \end{bmatrix}$

If the PRINT instruction is used, at least one of the operands must be specified, and only one operand may appear for each option (i.e., don't specify both GEN and NOGEN). The following contains an explanation of each option:

Option	Explanation
ON	Produce a listing.
OFF	Don't produce a listing.
GEN	Print all statements generated by macro instructions (explained in chapter 22).
NOGEN	Don't print statements generated by macro instructions.
DATA	Print all bytes of constants in object code portion of the listing.
NODATA	Print only first eight bytes of constants in object code portion of listing.

All of the options are not equal in their importance; there is a hierarchial relationship among them. For instance, if OFF is specified, it doesn't matter whether GEN or DATA are. If no listing is produced at all, there is no place to print instructions generated by macros or all the bytes of the constants used.

The TITLE instruction provides a means of printing headings at the top of each page in the listing. Its general format is:

blank   TITLE   character string of up to
100 characters (enclosed
in apostrophes)

The heading starts to be printed at the top of the page following the one that contains the TITLE instruction. Any printable character that appears between the apostrophes will be printed. In order for ampersands and apostrophes to appear as part of the printed heading, double ampersands and apostrophes must appear between the apostrophes in the TITLE instruction. The following show sample TITLE instructions and the headings they generate:

TITLE   'ACCOUNTING ROUTINE'
ACCOUNTING ROUTINE
TITLE   'STITCH && SEW'
STITCH & SEW

The EJECT and SPACE instructions allow the programmer to control the vertical spacing of the listing produced by the assembler. That is, the EJECT causes the source-program instruction following it to be printed at the top of the next page. The appearance of two EJECT instructions immediately following one another causes a blank page to appear in the listing.

The SPACE instruction can be used to separate different sections of code within one listing. In its operand, a programmer specifies a decimal self-defining term, which is the number of lines to be skipped. If the operand field is left blank, one line will be skipped. Should the decimal number be greater than the number of lines remaining to be printed on the page, the effect of the SPACE instruction is identical to that of an EJECT.

Of all the listing-control instructions, only the PRINT instruction appears in the printed listing. The TITLE, EJECT, and SPACE instructions cause the assembler to take the requested actions, but they are not printed as part of the listing.

CHANGING STATEMENT FORMATS

The standard coding conventions for the assembler are:

Column	Use
1	beginning column for instructions
16	continue column for instructions which do not fit on one line
71	end column for instructions

Why would you want to change these standard columns? Well, for one thing, you might want to increase the size of the identification or sequence field (normally columns 73–80). In order to accomplish these objectives, the ICTL instruction is provided. It has the following general format:

blank   ICTL   b[,e][,c]

Operand	Specifies	Range	Rules
b	begin column	1–40	must be equal to or less than $e-5$ must be less than c

e	end column	41–80	must be equal to or greater than b+5
			must be greater than c
c	continue column	2–40	must be greater than b
			must be less than e

For example, ICTL   6,70,21 changes the "begin" column to 6, allowing some identification to occupy columns 1–5. It also changes the "end" column to 70 and the "continue" column to 21. When using the ICTL instruction, the b operand must always be specified, but the e and c may be omitted. If e is omitted, a default of column 71 is used as the end column. If c is omitted, or if e has a value of 80, the assembler assumes that you have no need for lines to be continued.

ALTERATION OF THE LOCATION COUNTER SETTING (ORG)

The ORG instruction can be used to set the value of the location counter used by the assumbler either forward or backward. Both of these will be shown in connection with the definition of the translate table for the TR instruction. In each case, a portion of the control section is redefined.

To review, the TR instruction will translate a source field, one byte at a time, by using the contents of each of the bytes as a displacement into a 256-byte table. For instance take the case where the source is reverse alphabetic—a Z translates to an A; a Y translates to a B; a 9 to a 0; an 8 to a 1; and so on. While this translation needs a table of 256 bytes, only 36 of those bytes contain values other than zero, and those 36 bytes are contained in four blocks. The ORG instruction makes it relatively easy to define this table. The entire 256-byte area can be defined with one DC statement:

```
LOC CTR

2000            TAB    DC   XL256'00'
2100
```

to contain all zeros. Then a series of ORG instructions can be used to set the location counter back to the beginning of each of the four blocks and redefine the bytes in each. The first portion of this code would look like:

```
LOC CTR
    2000        TAB     DC      XL256'00'
                        ORG     TAB+193
    20C0        FRST    DC      C'ZYXWVUTSR'
                        ORG     TAB+209
    20D1                DC      C'QPONMLKJI'
```

The DC statement labeled FRST redefines the nine bytes beginning with the byte at location counter value 20C0, from: 000000000000000000 to: E9E8E7E6E5E4E3E2D9.

Another use of the ORG instruction depends on the programmer thoroughly knowing his data. If he can guarantee that the source field will contain only bytes that generate displacements in a very small range, such as the digits 0–9, he does not have to define an entire 256-byte table to contain a mere 10 non-zero bytes.

The ORG instruction can be used to define only that portion of the table that is really needed. One extra item must be guaranteed in this case—the fact that the ORG statement must be preceded by at least 250 bytes of object module. This is because only the 10 bytes immediately preceding the ORG instruction will be used as part of the table—the 240 bytes preceding those 10 bytes will never be referenced as a translation table but must be present in order to make the source bytes work as the correct displacements. (The first item referenced will be $240_{10} - F0_{16}$ bytes into the table.)

```
            DC    C'¢$#.,+*/?@'      DEFINE TRANSLATE DATA
            ORG   *-250             ORG BACK FOR TABLE ORIGIN
    TAB     DS    0C                NAME THE TABLE
            ORG   *+250             RESET LOCATION COUNTER
```

A source byte of 3 will translate to a period; a source byte of 6 to an asterisk; and so forth.

Pooling Literals (LTORG)

The LTORG instruction causes the assembler to define a literal pool at the point at which the LTORG instruction appears. In the literal pool the assembler collects all the literals it has encountered up to that point in its translation of your source program or since the last LTORG. If no LTORG instruction appears in the source program, the literals will be assembled at the end of the first control section. It is therefore necessary that you make sure the literal pools are included in the control sections to which they belong (the base register must be able to serve for addressing the literals). If you have more than one CSECT in an assembly containing literals, it would be wise to put a LTORG statement at the end of each one.

The space in literal pools is arranged efficiently. All literals with lengths of a multiple of eight are stored first, then those literals with multiples of four bytes in length, then the remaining literals with even lengths, and last all of the literals that are left (those with odd lengths). The beginning of a literal pool is always aligned on a doubleword boundary; therefore, the allocation of space ensures that no bytes are wasted due to skipping for proper alignment.

Under DOS/VS and OS/VS all literals are cross-referenced, thus eliminating the greatest disadvantage of literals. With a cross-reference table it is always easy to find all the references to a particular literal constant if alterations become necessary in the program.

USE OF MULTIPLE BASE REGISTERS

Before we discuss the use of multiple base registers, let's review how addressability is established and what it is. First, the reason for establishing addressability is that it makes it possible for the programmer to refer to locations within storage through the use of symbols in the operands of instructions. In other words, it permits the use of implicit rather than explicit addresses. To establish addressability the programmer must choose a general purpose register that may be used as the base register, and he must also inform the assembler which one he has chosen, besides what address will be in this register. The programmer's last responsibility is to code the instructions that will ensure the base register is actually loaded with the promised value.

The USING assembler instruction is the vehicle for forming the assembler of both the base register number and the contents that register will contain at execution time. The general format of the USING instruction is:

$$\text{USING} \qquad \text{address,reg} \#$$

The assembler uses the two pieces of information you provide it with in the USING instruction to convert each implicit address in your program to a base-displacement form of address. The maximum displacement that the assembler can use is 4,096 bytes—this is known as the USING range.

The *range* of the USING instruction is 4,096 bytes from the address contained in the base register. It has nothing to do with the location counter value at the point in the program where the USING instruction appears. The only mandatory thing about the placement of the USING instruction is that it must precede the first instruction that makes a symbolic reference to storage, which the assembler must resolve. This restriction is in force because of something called the *domain* of the USING instruction. While the range of the USING does not begin where the USING instruction appears in the module, the domain of the USING does. Therefore, it is the domain that makes it necessary for USING to be placed as close as possible to the beginning of the source module. Any implicit address references that are outside the domain of the USING instruction (precede the USING) will not be converted by the assembler.

CONTROL SECTION LONGER THAN 4,096 BYTES

If you are coding a control section that is longer than 4,096 bytes, one base register does not have sufficient range to establish addressability for the entire control section. In this case the USING instruction can be used to establish successive base registers. Examine the following:

```
              BALR   12,0
              USING  HERE,12,3,4
HERE          LM     3,4,ADDRS
                .
                .
                .
ADDRS†        DC     A(HERE + 4096)
              DC     A(HERE + 8192)
```

The USING instruction informs the assembler that register 12 is to be used as the base register for the first 4,096 bytes. When register 12's range is exhausted, the assembler automatically starts using register 3 to address the next 4,096, and so on.

Notice in the above example that the customary BALR instruction loads only the first of the three base registers. The addressability it provides permits the LM instruction to load the two other base registers. Care must be exercised here that the symbol ADDRS and the two address constants are defined within the range of the first base register (register 12).

DUMMY CONTROL SECTIONS (DSECT)

There are times in programming when the programmer needs to refer to whole blocks of data residing outside his own program (i.e., data passed between subroutines). Because of the quantity of data being referenced, it is impractical to use address constants and EXTRN statements to refer to each piece or pass each data item as an individual parameter. Instead, all the data items are collected in contiguous areas that make up a block of data; and one address, the address of the beginning of the block, is passed as a parameter between subroutines. This one address can be loaded into a register and that register used as the base register for a *dummy control section* (a DSECT).

A DSECT is a convenient means that the programmer can use to describe the layout of an area of storage without actually reserving the storage. It is assumed that the storage is reserved elsewhere (most likely in another subroutine). By passing the address of the actual block of data as a parameter, using

---

†The symbol ADDRS must be defined within the range of base register 12, so the assembler can convert it in the LM instruction.

this address as the contents of a register, and specifying that register as the base register for a DSECT, the programmer can symbolically reference areas within the actual block of data that exists elsewhere.

Figure 19-1 illustrates the definition of and establishment of addressability for a dummy control section.

Upon entry to the subroutine shown in figure 19-1, register 1 is expected to contain the address of the data area. Register 12 is used as the base register for the CSECT and register 10 for the DSECT. When the assembler translates the MVC instruction, it uses register 12 and the displacement for the symbol OUT as the explicit first operand. For the second operand, the assembler uses register 10 and a displacement 8 as the explicit second operand. Register 10 will be used as the base register for any symbol resolved that is part of the DSECT.

```
INAREA
        NAME    Man #     GROSS PAY  HRS  RANK


EX              CSECT
                BALR    12,0                ESTABLISH ADDRESSABILITY
                USING   *,12                FOR CSECT
                LR      10,1                REGISTER 1 CONTAINS ADDRESS
    *                                       OF INAREA (PARAMETER)
                USING   INDESC,10           ESTABLISH ADDRESSABILITY
    *                                       FOR DSECT
                  .
                  .
                  .
                MVC     OUT,MANNUM
                  .
                  .
                  .
OUT             DS      CL8
INDESC          DSECT
NAME            DS      CL8
MANNUM          DS      8C
GROSPA          DS      8C
HRS             DS      CL4
RANK            DS      CL4
                END
```

Fig. 19-1 Use of a DSECT, coding example

QUESTIONS

1. What are the standard options (the defaults) of the PRINT instruction?

2. Can the options of OFF, GEN, and DATA be in effect at the same time? Explain.

3. What is the maximum-size heading you can use on a listing?

4. What must be done in order to be able to include ampersands and apostrophes in a heading?

5. When does a SPACE instruction have the same effect as an EJECT instruction?

6. What is the function of the ICTL instruction, and under what circumstances would you use it?

7. What is the result of the execution of each of the following instructions?

    a. ORG   * − 8
    b. LTORG
    c. ORG   HERE + 17

8. In literal pools, why are literals arranged in a prescribed order?

9. What is the maximum displacement that can be assembled into a machine instruction?

10. Why would you need more than one base register in a control section?

11. What is the basic difference between a control section and a dummy control section?

CHAPTER 20

Job Control Language

The Systems/360 and 370 *operating systems* perform major control functions for IBM's most widely used computer systems. Each consists of an organized collection of programs that communicate with one another in standard ways. As a component of the operating system you are using, the assembler uses certain of its services. Among these are the ever-watchful control program, or supervisor, libraries for the storage of macro definitions and other needed modules, input and output facilities, a linkage editor, a loader, and a means of allocating needed storage to programs. To specify which of these services are needed for a particular job, the programmer uses statements of the operating system's job control language.

STRUCTURE OF A JOB

A *job* is a unit of work to the computer. Each job consists of one or more steps, each step involves the execution of a program, and each is identified by an EXEC job control statement. The general makeup of a job is shown in figure 20-1.

The /∗ (delimiter) control statement is used to indicate the end of a data set for a job step, or the end of the job step itself. The /& control statement is used to indicate the end of the job under DOS-based systems; the null statement (// ƀ) is used under OS-based ones. The /∗ (and the /&) are the only job control statements that contain only one slash (/), which is placed in column 1. All other job control statements are identified by slashes (//) in columns 1 and 2.

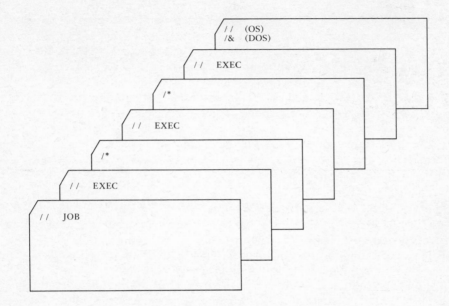

Fig. 20-1 General makeup of a job

The operands used on the JOB and EXEC control statements, as well as the other statements that make up the job control language, differ with the operating system used. The particulars of the job control language will be explained in separate sections for DOS- and OS-based systems.

JOB CONTROL STATEMENTS FOR DOS-BASED SYSTEMS

Ten job control statements will be discussed in this section. A brief explanation of each follows:

Name	Purpose
JOB	indicates the start of control statements for a job
OPTION	specifies options for job control
EXEC	indicates program to be executed
/*	indicates end of a job step or end of a data set
/&	indicates end of a job
ASSGN	assigns a specific I/O device to a symbolic unit name

TLBL	file label information for a tape data set
LBLTYP	defines amount of storage space needed to process labels at link edit time
DLBL	file label information for a data set on a direct-access storage device
EXTENT	defines an area of a data set residing on a direct-access storage device

The JOB statement indicates the beginning of a job. It has the following format:

//   JOB   jobname   [accounting information]

The jobname must consist of from one to eight alphameric characters. It is used as the identification for the job (e.g., if the job abends, the jobname will be displayed at the top of the dump).

The accounting information is an optional part of the JOB statement. The specific requirements of an installation determine whether accounting information must be supplied, and if so, what type of information is required.

The OPTION statement is the programmer's means of specifying the job-control options to be in effect for his job. The general format for this statement is:

//   OPTION   optionl [, option 2, . . .]

The options may be specified in the operand portion of the OPTION statement in any order. Default options are built into each operating system. (Find out what the defaults are for your installation.) Only a few of the many possible options will be explained here. For information on other available options, see the IBM publication, *DOS System Control and Service* (GC24-5036).

DUMP	causes a dump of storage and register contents if an abend occurs
NODUMP	suppresses the production of a dump if an abend occurs
LINK	indicates that the object module which is created is to be link edited
NOLINK	suppresses the LINK option
XREF	requests the assembler to produce a cross-reference list of the symbols used in the source module
NOXREF	suppresses the XREF option

For a normal job, the programmer usually specifies the following options (unless they are the defaults on his system):

//   OPTION   LINK,DUMP,XREF

The EXEC statement specifies that a particular program is to start execution. When this control statement is encountered by the operating system, the specified program is loaded and executed. Therefore all control statements pertaining to the job step must precede the EXEC statement for that step. The general format for the EXEC statement is:

// EXEC [progname]

The *progname* operand specifies the name of the program to be executed. This must be the name of a program in a core-image library. It must be the name of the first (or only) phase of the program in the library. If the program to be executed has just been processed by the Linkage Editor, you can leave the operand portion of the EXEC statement blank.

A job generally consists of three EXEC statements—one to execute the assembler program, one to execute the linkage editor program, and the third to execute the resultant machine language program (the phase created by the linkage editor as it executes).

The /* control statement is used to indicate the end of an input stream data set or data file. The records of the input stream are physically part of your job. They are not data sets on a separate I/O device that are merely connected to your job. When you specify the execution of the program called the assembler, the input data set for the assembler is found in the input stream. The assembly language statements that comprise your source module immediately follow the // EXEC ASSEMBLY control statement and are terminated by a /* control statement. If you include an input data set for your program in the input stream, it immediately follows the // EXEC statement and is terminated by a /* control statement.

The /& is the end of job statement. Physically, it must be the last statement in each job. Try your hand at setting up the control statements for the following job:

1. There are three steps—assembly, link edit, and execution.
2. Jobname is TRYIT.
3. There is no accounting information.
4. XREF is a default option on this system, and you wish the options of LINK, DUMP, and XREF to be in effect for this job.
5. There are two input data sets in the card deck: (1) the source module, and (2) an input data set for the program when it executes.

USING TAPES ON DOS-BASED SYSTEMS

The programmer must do three things to use tape data sets under DOS-based systems:

1. tell the operator to mount the tape volume

2. inform the operating system which data set is mounted on which tape drive
3. provide for processing of labels

The first of these responsibilities is relatively easy. Every installation has a prescribed manner of providing the operator with mount information. Some installations have the programmer inform the operator verbally; some have him use a note either attached to the job or written on the JOB control statement. Before we discuss the second and third requirements for using tapes, the definitions of some new terms must be established.

Each tape volume has a *volume serial number* associated with it. This serial number is unique among all volume serial numbers at an installation. It appears on the outside of the tape reel where the operator can see it; it may also appear on the tape itself so that the operating system can recognize it. Each I/O device in an installation has an address. The address consists of a three-digit hexadecimal number by which the device is known to the system. Addresses vary with the installation, but some examples are:

Address	I/O Device
00C	card reader
00D	card punch
00E	printer
180	tape drive
191	disk drive

Check with the people in charge of your installation to get a list of the addresses associated with the I/O devices available.

Logical unit names allow the programmer to refer to particular classes or groups of I/O devices. It is through the logical unit name that the programmer makes the connection between the actual data set on a particular I/O device and the DTF (the Definition of The File, which describes that data set, within the program). Logical unit names usually begin with the letters "SYS", which are followed by either three letters or three numbers. Each installation has a fixed list of logical unit names, and the logical unit names in this list are permanently assigned to particular I/O devices (using the physical addresses of those devices). Examples of permanent assignments that might be used in your installation follow:

Logical Unit Name	Physical Address of I/O Device
SYSRDR	00C
SYSPCH	00D
SYSLST	00E
SYS004	180
SYS010	191

The ASSGN job control statement is used to temporarily override one of these permanent assignments by assigning a logical unit name to a particular physical device. The term *temporary* means for the duration of the one job. At the end of the job, all assignments revert back to the assignments specified in the installation's permanent assignment list. The general format of the ASSGN statement is:

// ASSGN SYSxxx,address

where SYSxxx is the logical unit name, and address is the physical address of the particular I/O device to be assigned (specified as a hexadecimal constant, X'nnn'). Some examples are:

// ASSGN SYS004,X'180'
// ASSGN SYS011,X'181'

The first assigns the device whose physical address is 180 to the logical unit name of SYS004. The second connects the logical unit name SYS011 to the physical device 181.

The ASSGN control statement fulfills the second responsibility for using tapes on DOS-based systems. It informs the system which data set is on which tape drive.

LABEL PROCESSING

A *label* is a record containing identification information about a data set. Two job control statements are necessary to allow label processing. The first of these is the TLBL statement. It contains information for creating the label for a new data set or checking the label on an existing data set. Its general format is:

// TLBL filename[,'file-id'][,date][,file-serial number]

where *filename* is the unique name associated with the file and is identical to the logical unit name used on the DTF (the definition within the source program) for the file. This operand is the only required operand.

The *file-id* operand is made up of from one to seventeen alphameric characters. Because it is enclosed within apostrophes, it may contain embedded blanks. The file-id is used to identify the file or data set on the volume. If present, it is used in the label-checking procedure for an existing file; otherwise this part of the checking procedure is omitted. If the file-id is omitted, when creating a new (output) file, the fine-name is used for checking.

The date operand is used to indicate a *retention period* on output files. It is specified as a one to four-digit number (0-9999). *If omitted, a retention period of seven days is assumed.* The creation date for the file is always the date currently in use by the system. The retention period specifies that this data set is not to be destroyed for 0-9999 days after the date of creation.

The *file-serial number* operand consists of from one to six alphameric characters. It is used to identify the tape volume. If this operand is omitted when a file is created, the volume serial number is used. On an existing file, omission of this operand causes this portion of the label-checking process to be bypassed.

Although the filename operand is the only operand required on the TLBL statement, it is a good practice to include either the file-id or the file-serial number also. This permits the label-checking portions of the operating system to ensure that the correct tape volume is mounted.

The file-serial number is a positional operand. Some operands are recognizable because they contain keywords, and others (positional operands) are recognizable only because they are the first, second, third, etc. operand specified. If you do not specify the file-id and date operands, you must indicate this by the use of commas. The two alternative statements would look like:

```
//   TLBL      filename,'file-id'
//   TLBL      filename,,,file-serial number
```

The last job control statement necessary for handling tapes under DOS-based systems is the LBLTYP statement. To inform the linkage editor program that your program is going to process tape labels, you place this statement immediately before the EXEC LINKEDT control statement and specify TAPE as an operand. This specification and placement of the LBLTYP statement causes the linkage editor to set aside sufficient space in the phase or module that it is creating, in order to allow for the processing of labels. If this statement is erroneously omitted, the first portion of your load module is *destroyed* as the label processing is accomplished. So be careful!

The following example shows the job control statements to run a three-step job (assembly, link edit, and execution). The program uses a tape input file, as well as a card input file in the input stream. The operator is asked to mount the tape volume with the serial number 000026 on the tape drive with the address 181 (logical unit name SYS005). The DUMP option is specified, because this program is not yet debugged. MASTER is the name used on the DTF for the tape file.

```
//   JOB       EXAMPLE
//   OPTION    LINK,DUMP
//   EXEC      ASSEMBLY
     .
     .                                      source program
     .
/*
//   LBLTYP    TAPE
//   EXEC      LNKEDT
//   ASSGN     SYS005,X'181'
```

```
//   TLBL      MASTER,,,000026
//   EXEC
        .
        .                              input stream data set
        .
/*
```

Using Direct Access Storage Devices on DOS-Based Systems

To use a data set on a direct access storage device (also known as *disk* or *DASD*), the programmer must fulfill responsibilities analogous to those for tape data sets, and one additional responsibility (see 3 below):

1. tell the operator to mount the disk volume on the drive
2. inform the operating system which data set is mounted on which disk drive
3. *inform the operating system where on the disk volume the data set resides*
4. provide for processing of labels

The first and second responsibilities are handled in the same manner as when using tape data sets. The operator is informed by written note or verbally, and the ASSGN control statement is used to assign a logical unit name to a particular physical device, thus informing the system which data set is mounted on that drive. The third and new responsibility is met as part of the label-processing procedure. DASD label processing involves the use of two job control statements—DLBL and EXTENT.

The DLBL control statement provides information for label creation and checking. Its general format is:

$$// \quad DLBL \qquad filename[,'file\text{-}ID'][,date]$$

This statement is similar to the TLBL used for tape data sets. The filename is the only required operand. It is the unique name associated with the file and is identical to the symbolic name used on the DTF for the file. It contains from one to seven alphameric characters, the first of which must be alphabetic.

The file-ID, if present, is the name associated with the file. It can consist of from one to 44 bytes of alphameric data enclosed within apostrophes.

The date operand is used to specify the retention period for a file. If present, it can be specified in one of two ways: (1) from one to four numeric characters that will be used to develop a retention date based on the system's current date, or (2) an absolute expiration date for the file in the format, yy/ddd.

The EXTENT control statement is peculiar to disk files. It defines an *extent*—the area or one of the areas occupied by a file on a direct-access storage device. One or more EXTENT statements must follow each DLBL statement. The general format of this statement follows.

```
//   EXTENT     [logical-unit]
                [,serial-number][,type]
                [,sequence-number]
                [,relative-track]
                [,number-of-tracks]
```

All operands are optional, but keep in mind that they are positional operands; and the absence of any operand preceding an existing operand must be indicated by a *null operand*, a lone comma. The logical unit specified in the first operand position is the logical unit specified in the ASSGN statement for this file. In the second operand, the volume serial number of the disk volume containing this data set is specified.

The third operand is used to specify the type of the extent. We will always specify 1 to indicate a data area. We will specify 0 for the fourth operand, which indicates the sequence of this extent within a multiextent data set. Since our data sets need only one extent, this operand need not be adjusted upward.

The last two operands refer to the location of the data set within the entire disk volume. The relative-track operand points to the beginning of the area, and the number-of-tracks operand tells the size of the area. Both are specified as fields of from one to five characters. The following job control statements are necessary to use a sequential data set on tracks 1 through 30 of the disk with volume serial number 123456 on disk drive address 192. The logical unit name is SYS012.

```
//   JOB       EXDISK
//   OPTION    LINK,DUMP
//   EXEC      ASSEMBLY
     .
     .
     .                                    source program
/*
//   EXEC      LNKEDT
//   ASSGN     SYS012,X'192'
//   DLBL      DSKFILE
//   EXTENT    SYS012,123456,1,0,1,30
//   EXEC
     .
     .                                    input stream data set
     .
/&
```

JOB CONTROL STATEMENTS UNDER OS-BASED SYSTEMS

Five control statements will be discussed in this section. The names of these statements and a brief explanation of each follows:

Name	Purpose
JOB	marks the beginning of a job
EXEC	marks the beginning of a job step, identifies the program to be executed during that step or the procedure to be used
DD	requests the allocation of I/O devices and describes the data sets on the devices
/*	terminates an input stream data set
//	can be used to mark the end of a job

With the exception of the /* (delimiter) statement, all control statements contain slashes in columns 1 and 2. Not all operands for each of the job control statements will be explained in this chapter.[†]

THE JOB STATEMENT

The JOB statement identifies the beginning of a job; a name associated with the job must appear in the name field of this statement. The name must begin in column 3 (following the two slashes), and consists of from one to eight alphameric characters, the first of which is alphabetic. Since this name is the identifier of the job, it should be unique. The general format of the JOB statement is given in figure 20-2.

Whether of not the accounting information and the programmer's name must be specified depends on the requirements of a particular installation.

$$//\text{jobname} \quad \text{JOB} \quad [\,(\,[\text{acct}\#]\,[\text{,accounting information}]\,)\,] \qquad X$$

$$[\text{,programmer's name}]^{\ddagger} \qquad X$$

$$[\text{,MSGLEVEL}=(\left\{\begin{matrix}0\\1\end{matrix}\right\}\left\{\begin{matrix},0\\,1\end{matrix}\right\})\,]$$

Fig. 20-2 General description of the OS JOB control statement

---

[†]If you desire information on any unexplained operands, check the *Job Control Language Reference* (GC28-6704) and *OS/VS JCL Reference* (GC28-0618).
[‡]To continue a JCL statement, place a nonblank character in column 72 of the first card and continue the statement in column 16 of the second card.

(Find out what your installation requires; these operands may be mandatory.) If they are required, keep in mind that they are positional parameters—the accounting information must be specified first, and the programmer's name second. If the programmer's name is required but the accounting information is optional, the absence of the latter must be indicated by a comma preceding the programmer's name.

The *programmer's name*, if present, can consist of up to 20 characters. If he wishes to include special characters (other than periods—blanks for instance), he can do so if the characters are enclosed in apostrophes.

The MSGLEVEL operand entries specify what information is to be printed about a job. The first number inside the parentheses allows you to specify which job control statements are to be printed on your listing. There are three possible choices:

0   Only the JOB statement is displayed (this is the default).

1   All job control statements are displayed, including those generated from a cataloged procedure. (A *cataloged procedure* is a group of control statements that have been given a name and placed in a library of cataloged procedure. They will be explained more fully later.)

2   Only those job control statements appearing in the input stream are displayed (no statements from cataloged procedures).

A 1 is usually the best specification, because just displaying the JOB statement is insufficient in most situations, and suppressing all statements generated by a cataloged procedure is best reserved for routinely run (debugged) programs.

The second number inside the parentheses of the MSGLEVEL operand specifies whether or not I/O device allocation messages are to be printed. A 0 indicates that you want these messages only if your job abends. A 1 (the default) indicates all allocation and termination messages are to be printed, regardless of how the job terminates. Three JOB statements follow:

```
//JOBA    JOB    (16275,'4/10/73'),TUGGLE,           X
                 MSGLEVEL=(1,0)
//JOBB    JOB    ,'S K TUGGLE',MSGLEVEL=(1,1)
//JOBC    JOB    MSGLEVEL=2
```

Note that in the third example above, when the second subparameter of MSGLEVEL is omitted, the parentheses need not be coded.

THE EXECUTE STATEMENT

The EXEC statement begins a job step and is followed by DD (data definition) statements and input-stream data sets for that job step. Its general format is shown in figure 20-3.

If you specify a stepname, it must be unique within the job, and it must begin in column 3 (following the two slashes). The EXEC statement can specify either the program to be executed during this step or the cataloged procedure to be used. Because of the complexity of job control language in OS-based systems, the PGM= option will not be discussed in this chapter. Instead you will be shown how to use a cataloged procedure that will generate the necessary job control statements. You will also be shown how to code DD (data definition) control statements to connect your data sets to your job, as well as the techniques for overriding cataloged procedures to add to or modify the DD statements generated.

$$//\text{stepname} \quad\quad \text{EXEC} \quad\quad \left\{ \begin{array}{l} \text{PGM}=\text{program name} \\ \text{[PROC}=\text{]procedure name} \end{array} \right\}$$

Fig. 20-3 General description of the OS EXEC control statement

USING CATALOGED PROCEDURES

Most of the programming jobs that you execute can be handled by coding one operand on the first (and only) EXEC control statement in the job. This is done by choosing one of the IBM-supplied cataloged procedures and specifying PROC=procedure name (or simply procedure name) in the operand of the EXEC statement. Job control statements for jobs that require the use of many control statements—and/or are run frequently—are generally established as cataloged procedures.

Cataloged procedures are stored in a data set referred to as the system procedure library. This library is named SYS1.PROCLIB and is provided by IBM for users of its systems. Your system procedure library contains several general procedures that can be used to generate the JCL statements for most of your jobs. Two useful procedures follow. Equivalent procedures are provided on your system (if the F level assembler is used), although there may be slight physical differences. These two procedures are as follows:

Name	Purpose
ASMFC	for assembling only (figure 20-4)
ASMFCLG	for assembling, linkage editing, and executing (figure 20-5)

```
//ASM        EXEC   PGM=IEUASM,REGION=50K
//SYSLIB     DD     DSNAME=SYS1.MACLIB,DISP=SHR
//SYSUT1     DD     DSNAME=&SYSUT1,UNIT=SYSSQ,SPACE=(1700,(400,50)),      X
//                  SEP=(SYSLIB)
//SYSUT2     DD     DSNAME=&SYSUT2,UNIT=SYSSQ,SPACE=(1700,(400,50))
//SYSUT3     DD     DSNAME=&SYSUT3,SPACE=(1700,(400,50)),                 X
//                  UNIT=(SYSSQ,SEP=(SYSUT2,SYSUT1,SYSLIB))
//SYSPRINT   DD     SYSOUT=A
//SYSPUNCH   DD     SYSOUT=B
```

Fig. 20-4   The procedure ASMFC

```
//ASM        EXEC   PGM=IEUASM,PARM=LOAD,REGION=50K
//SYSLIB     DD     DSNAME=SYS1.MACLIB,DISP=SHR
//SYSUT1     DD     DSNAME=&SYSUT1,UNIT=SYSSQ,SPACE=(1700,(400,50)),      X
//                  SEP=(SYSLIB)
//SYSUT2     DD     DSNAME=&SYSUT2,UNIT=SYSSQ,SPACE=(1700,(400,50))
//SYSUT3     DD     DSNAME=&SYSUT3,SPACE=(1700,(400,50)),                 X
//                  UNIT=(SYSSQ,SEP=(SYSUT2,SYSUT1,SYSLIB))
//SYSPRINT   DD     SYSOUT=A
//SYSPUNCH   DD     SYSOUT=B
//SYSGO      DD     DSNAME=&LOADSET,UNIT=SYSSQ,SPACE=(80,(200,50)),       X
//                  DISP=(MOD,PASS)
//LKED       EXEC   PGM=IEWL,PARM=(XREF,LIST,NCAL),REGION=96K,            X
//                  COND=(8,LT,ASM)
//SYSLIN     DD     DSNAME=&LOADSET,DISP=(OLD,DELETE)
//           DD     DDNAME=SYSIN
//SYSLMOD    DD     DSNAME=&GOSET(GO),UNIT=SYSDA,SPACE=(1024,(50,20,1)),  X
//                  DISP=(MOD,PASS)
//SYSUT1     DD     DSNAME=&SYSUT1,UNIT=(SYSDA,SEP=(SYSLIN,SYSLMOD)),     X
//                  SPACE=(1024,(50,20))
//SYSPRINT   DD     SYSOUT=A
//GO         EXEC   PGM=*.LKED.SYSLMOD,COND=((8,LT,ASM),(4,LT,LKED))
```

Fig. 20-5   The procedure ASMFCLG

THE DATA DEFINITION (DD) STATEMENT

Any data sets used by your programs must be described in DD statements. These statements must follow the EXEC control statement for the particular step in which the data sets are accessed. DD statements describe the characteristics of, and give the location for, data sets.

A *data control block* (DCB) is established within the source program for each data set. A DCB is a block of information within the source program that describes a data set used by it. Space for the DCB is established in your CSECT by the expansion of the DCB macro, but not all of the information to fill the DCB need come from operands specified in the DCB macro. The data control block can be completed at execution time if the DCB parameter is specified on the DD statement. That is, the DD statement is the latest point in the execution of a job when the programmer can supply information about data sets used in the job. He can omit certain operands from the DCB macro in his source program and instead specify these operands as part of the DD control statement for that data set.

To get an idea of how the connections are made between the instructions that do the reading and writing in the source program and the DCB; the DCB and the DD statement; the DD statement and the actual data set; we can examine figure 20-6.

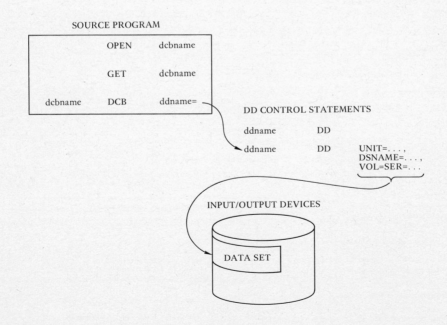

Fig. 20-6 Combining of information about a data set

The initial step in setting up these connections is accomplished when the DCB macro in the source program establishes space for the DCB and gives it a name (dcbname). The OPEN macro causes the data set specified by the dcbname operand to be logically connected to the program and to be initialized.

During the *open process*, the ddname from the DCB (DCBIN, see figure 20-7) is matched with the ddname from one of the DD statements for this job step (READIN, see figure 20-7). One of the operands on this particular DD statement specifies the data set name dsname (MSTR, again see figure 20-7), which permits the actual physical data set to be located. These connections having been made, the GET macro can access a record from the data set whose dcbname appears in the operand of the GET macro. (For more information on these macros, refer to chapter 21.)

The general format for the DD statement is given in figure 20-8.

```
//EX            JOB
//              EXEC       ASMFCLG
//ASM.SYSIN     DD         *
                CSECT
                STM        14,12,12(13)
                BALR       12,0
                USING      *,12
                  .
                  .
                  .
                OPEN       (DCBIN)
LOOP            GET        DCBIN,INAREA
                  .
                  .
                  .
                B          LOOP
                  .
                  .
                  .
DCBIN           DCB        DDNAME=READIN,MACRF=GM,            X
                           RECFM=F,EODAD=EOF,DSORG=PS
                  .
                  .
                  .
                END
/*
//GO.READIN     DD         DSNAME=MSTR,UNIT=2314,             X
                           VOL=SER=666666,                   X
                           DCB=(BLKSIZE=80,LRECL=80),         X
                           DISP=SHR
/*
```

Fig. 20-7 Coding example of sources of information about a data set

$$
// \begin{bmatrix} \text{ddname} \\ \text{procstepname.ddname} \end{bmatrix} \quad \text{DD}
$$

DSNAME=identification,   X
[UNIT=unit information],   X
[VOLUME=SER=serial number],   X
[LABEL=(label information)],   X
[DCB=(attributes)],   X
{ DISP=([status][,disp.][,cond.disp]),   X
  SYSOUT=x,
[SPACE=(units,(quantity,increment))]

Fig. 20-8   General description of OS DD control statement

Within the limited use of JCL used in this text (except in the case of an input stream data set), the DSNAME operand is the only required operand; all the others are considered optional.

The DDNAME Portion of the DD Statement   The ddname is an important part of the DD statement. It is the connection between the information in the DD statement, which results in the data set being allocated to the job step, and the description of the data set specified in the operand of the DCB macro in the source program. The DDNAME connects information in the job control statements with information in the source program. In figure 20-7 the symbol of READIN appears in both the ddname field of the DD control statement and the operand of the DCB in the source program. The ddname must be unique within the job step in which it appears.

If the ddname is specified in the format of "procstepname.ddname", this particular DD statement is taken as an override or addition to the DD statements specified in the cataloged procedure used for this job step.

Input and Output Stream Data Sets   If the data set defined in the DD statement is an input stream data set, you can simply place an asterisk (*) in the operand field of the DD statement. The input stream data set, consisting of 80-byte records, begins immediately following the DD   * statement and is terminated by a delimiter statement (/* in columns 1 and 2).

Just as an asterisk (*) can indicate the presence of a data set in the input stream, the SYSOUT operand of a DD statement can indicate that you wish an output data set routed to the output stream. To specify that you wish to use the normal output-stream data set, code "SYSOUT=A" in the operand of the DD statement.

The DSNAME Operand   The dsname operand is used to identify the data set. In this operand specify the name by which a data set is or will be cataloged. This parameter can be specified DSNAME= or abbreviated DSN=. (See DSNAME=MSTR in figure 20-7.) If the data set is not cataloged, but is described by a previous step in the job, you can specify the dsname operand in the following manner:

DSNAME= ∗.stepname.ddname

replacing stepname and ddname with the name of the job step and DD statement within the job step in which this data set was defined.

In this case, the asterisk (∗) indicates that you are referring to a preceding control statement. Should this statement be part of a procedure, add the procedure name to the DSNAME specification:

DSNAME= ∗.stepname.procstepname.ddname.

The location of a cataloged data set is recorded in the operating system's catalog. The system needs only the name of the data set—and the fact that it is an existing one—to locate it (hence, only the DSNAME operand is required). If the data set is not cataloged, operands such as UNIT and VOLUME may be required.

The UNIT and VOLUME Operands   The UNIT operand specifies information about the I/O device on which the data set resides. The unit can be identified by its address. For example, UNIT=180 could indicate tape unit 180, and UNIT=191 could indicate disk unit 191. The address can also be specified more generally by a type number, which corresponds to disk or tape. This mode of specification increases device independence, because the job is not dependent on the tape having to be mounted on a particular tape drive. Should a particular tape drive be out of order on the day the job is to be run, any of the functioning drives will permit the tape to be mounted. Two examples of type numbers are:

3400	Nine-track magnetic tape drive that can be written in 800, 1600, or 6250 bits per inch
3330	Any 3330 Disk Storage Drive

The VOLUME operand provides the system with information about the particular volume on which the data set resides or will reside. Examples of volumes are tape reels and disk packs. This operand can be abbreviated VOL=. It is specified: VOL=SER=serial number. Serial# is the 1- to 6-character volume serial number associated with the volume.

The UNIT and VOL operands need not be specified for a cataloged data set or a data set described in a previous jobstep (DSNAME=∗.stepname.ddname), because this information is available from other sources (the data set was available to that previous step).

Data Set LABEL Operand Data set labels are used by the operating system in its identification of data sets. Data sets residing on magnetic tape usually have labels, and data sets residing on direct-access volumes (disks) always have labels. Labels precede data sets on tape volumes and are included in the Volume Table of Contents (VTOC) for direct-access data sets. The label operand has the following subparameters:

$$\text{LABEL} = ([\text{sequence number}] \begin{bmatrix} \text{,SL} \\ \text{,SUL} \\ \text{,NSL} \\ \text{,NL} \end{bmatrix} \begin{bmatrix} \text{,EXPDT=yyddd} \\ \text{,RETPD=nnnn} \end{bmatrix})$$

If you are giving label information about a tape data set other than the first data set on the volume, a sequence number must be specified. The sequence number gives the position of this data set in relation to the others on the volume. It allows positioning of the tape volume so this particular data set can be accessed. The second subparameter specifies whether or not labels are used, and, if so, what type of labels they are. The choices are:

NL	no labels
SL	standard labels
NSL	nonstandard labels
SUL	both standard and user labels

Standard labels are processed by the system. If you use nonstandard ones, your installation must provide the routines to process the labels. If this subparameter is omitted, standard labels are assumed.[†]

The third label subparameter is a keyword parameter, indicating either a retention period or an expiration date. The use of either of these specifications permits you to state that the data set is to remain unchanged for some length of time. If RETPD=nnnn is specified, this length of time is nnnn days. If EXPDT=yyddd is specified, you state the actual year (yy) and day (ddd) that you are willing to have the data set deleted or reused. Nonspecification of a retention period or an expiration date results in a retention period of zero days. If either is specified, and the end date so defined has not been reached, the data set may not be modified or deleted without permission of the system console operator.

[†]To find out the items that make up a label or the format of labels, refer to either *Tape Labels* (GC28-6680) manual for tape, or for direct access device labels, *OS/VS Tape Labels* (GC26-3795).

The DCB Operand of the DD Statement   The DCB operand is the mechanism by which the DD control statement can serve as the latest point for supplying information about data sets. The general format is the keyword followed by a list of attributes: DCB=(attributes).

The attributes are specified as keyword subparameters separated by commas. DCB=(BLKSIZE=400,LRECL=80, . . .).

Subparameters that may be specified at this time are BLKSIZE, DSORG, EROPT, LRECL, and RECFM. (For more information see chapter 21.)

Data-Set Status (DISP Operand)   The status of a data set, both before and after a particular job step, can be indicated in the DISP operand. The general format of the operand is:

$$\text{DISP}=\left(\begin{bmatrix}\text{OLD}\\\text{SHR}\\\text{MOD}\\\text{NEW}\end{bmatrix}\begin{bmatrix}\text{,KEEP}\\\text{,PASS}\\\text{,DELETE}\\\text{,CATLG}\\\text{,UNCATLG}\end{bmatrix}\begin{bmatrix}\text{,KEEP}\\\text{,DELETE}\\\text{,CATLG}\\\text{,UNCATLG}\end{bmatrix}\right)$$

One, two, or three terms may follow the keyword. The first term indicates the status of the data set in relation to this job step. There are four choices for this term. The choices and an explanation of each are:

Status	Meaning
OLD	an existing data set used as input only to this step and program
SHR	an existing disk data set that can be shared with other jobs concurrently (for example, the system macro library)
MOD	a partially completed sequential output data set. When opened, this data set is positioned after the last record in the existing data set, to permit extension of the data set with additional records.
NEW	an output data set to be created during this job step

The second term in the DISP parameter specifies the action to be taken with the data set after this job step has reached its normal termination (not an abend). It is like specifying the status of the data set after the job step. There are five possibilities here:

Disposition	Meaning
KEEP	Keep the data set.
PASS	Pass the data set on to a later job

	step that can refer to it by specifying: DSNAME = *.stepname.ddname or explicitly with DISP = OLD and a respecification of serial number and unit information.
DELETE	Delete this existing data set.
CATLG	Catalog and keep the data set.
UNCATLG	Remove this cataloged data set from the catalog, but still keep it.

If this second term is omitted, the data set will have the status it had before this job step. Any data set that existed prior to this job step (OLD,SHR or MOD) will continue to exist; any created during it (NEW) will be deleted.

The third term in the DISP parameter specifies the action to be taken with the data set if this job step should abend. This disposition request is referred to as the *conditional disposition*. Any disposition that can be specified for the second term (except PASS) can be specified here. An example of a use for this third term occurs in the creation of a new data set to be kept and cataloged if the step goes to a normal termination, but deleted if the step abends. This is specified as follows: DISP = (NEW,CATLG,DELETE).

If the conditional disposition is not specified and the step abends, the regular disposition is used. A new data set is cataloged whether it was satisfactorily created or not. Another use for the conditional disposition is to keep a data set that may help in the location of the problem causing an abend but would normally be deleted. This disposition is specified: DISP = (NEW,,KEEP). The second term is not needed, because the normal disposition is to maintain the previous status of the data set. Since the data set did not exist before the job step, it will be deleted if the step goes to normal termination.

Direct Access Storage Device (DASD) Data Sets—the SPACE Operand The SPACE operand is used only when creating a data set on a DASD volume. This operand permits you to request the quantity of space needed for your data set in units of cylinders (CYL), tracks (TRK), or blocks (bytes). The system assigns the specific tracks. Another specification of the SPACE operand is useful if a data set might exceed the amount of space requested. It provides the ability to ensure that extra space will be made available at a later time if necessary. The general format of the SPACE operand is as follows:

$$SPACE = (units,quantity)$$

or

$$SPACE = (units, (quantity,increment))$$

Units is specified as CYL, TRK, or a decimal number; *quantity* is a decimal number specifying the amount of space desired in the units specified; and *increment* is a decimal number indicating the additional amount of space to be allocated each time the existing data space is exhausted. This secondary allocation of space by the operating system is allowed a maximum of fifteen times. After this limit is reached, or where no secondary allocation has been provided, the supervisor will terminate your program with a B37 or end-of-space system abend. Examples of uses of the space parameter are:

$$SPACE=(TRK,30)$$
$$SPACE=(CYL, (100,10))$$
$$SPACE=(360, (200,50))$$

The first example indicates that thirty tracks are to be allocated to this data set. The second example specifies that the primary allocation for the data set should be one hundred cylinders, and that after this space has been utilized, the data set should be extended by ten cylinders. The third example specifies that the initial space for the data set should be sufficient to hold 200, 360-byte blocks, and that the incremental amount whenever the data set needs to be extended is 50, 360-byte blocks.

Before continuing, see if you can figure out what kinds of data sets the following DD statements define:

```
//DD1    DD    DSNAME=MASTER,DISP=(OLD)
//DD2    DD    SYSOUT=A
//DD3    DD    UNIT=3400,DSNAME=ABC,              X
               DISP=(,CATLG,KEEP)
//DD4    DD    UNIT=3330,SPACE=(TRK,20)
//DD5    DD    UNIT=3330,DSNAME=RECORDS,          X
               VOL=SER=000026,DISP=(,KEEP),       X
               SPACE=(CYL,(50,10))
//DD6    DD    DSNAME=OLDMAST,UNIT=3330,          X
               VOL=SER=123456,DISP=(SHR)
//DD7    DD    *
```

DD1 is the ddname of an existing data set that is cataloged. DD2 is an output stream data set. DD3 is a new data set created on a 9-track tape and cataloged under the name ABC. If the job step should abend, the data set ABC is kept but not cataloged. DD4 creates a temporary sequential data set on disk. The system creates a data set name for this data set. It will not exist after this step.

DD5 is a new data set to be kept on disk 000026 with the data set name RECORDS. It is allocated fifty cylinders of space initially and extra space in increments of ten cylinders if necessary.

DD6 is an existing disk data set that is not cataloged; therefore, the unit and volume serial number information is given to help locate it. Because of the disposition, more than one job in the system may retrieve data from this data set concurrently. DD7 is an input stream data set.

OVERRIDING STATEMENTS IN CATALOGED PROCEDURES

To review, cataloged procedures are previously defined sequences of job control statements, but there is no requirement to use those sequences of control statements exactly as defined. The programmer can place statements in the input stream to add to, nullify, or respecify parameters already specified in a cataloged procedure. Overrides are effective only for the duration of the step in which they are specified.

It is the DD statements, within the procedure, that you will desire most often to override. The override process involves coding a control statement in the input stream that specifies the stepname and the ddname of the DD statement to be overridden. The stepname identifies the name on the EXEC statement which serves to mark the beginning of the job step that is to be overridden. The ddname identifies a particular DD statement within that job step. If the specified ddname does not appear within the procedure definition for that step, it is to be considered a DD statement to be added to those in the procedure for that step when the control statements are generated in the input stream.

For example, if the example below is the input stream, a DD statement with the ddname SYSIN would be added to the first step—the step with the stepname of ASM, and a DD statement with the ddname of REPORT would be added to the third step—the step that executes the load module. Notice that stepname.ddname is specified in the name field.

```
//              JOB
//              EXEC      ASMFCLG
//ASM.SYSIN     DD        *
                .
                .         source module
                .
/*
//GO.REPORT     DD        UNIT=3400,DSNAME=ACCTS,          X
                          VOL=SER=006587,DISP=(,KEEP)
```

USING STANDARD CATALOGED PROCEDURES

The cataloged procedure for assembly ASMFC is used to generate the control statements necessary to load and execute the F-level assembler program. This run produces an object deck and an assembler listing. If you place the following job control statements around your source module as shown, the use of the procedure ASMFC will cause the insertion of all the control statements necessary to assemble your source module:

```
//jobname       JOB
//stepname      EXEC      PROC=ASMFC
//ASM.SYSIN     DD        *
                .
                .         source module
                .
/*
```

The EXEC statement above will cause all control statements from the procedure ASMFC to be inserted at this point, as if they had been placed in the input stream. The ASM.SYSIN DD statement is added to the bottom of the control statements generated by the procedure. Why is it added to the bottom? Notice the ddname field. It contains ASM.SYSIN. The ASM. indicates that this statement is to be part of the procedure whose stepname is ASM. Since the ddname of SYSIN does not appear on any of the control statements already in the procedure, this DD statement becomes an additional DD statement in step ASM. Had SYSIN been a duplication of a ddname already in the cataloged procedure, this statement would have been used to override the existing SYSIN DD statement.

The ddname of SYSIN represents the input data set to the assembler. To review, an asterisk (*) in the operand indicates that the data set follows this DD statement in the input stream. The source program must be placed in the input stream immediately following the ASM.SYSIN DD statement.

The cataloged procedure ASMFCLG is used to generate the control statements necessary to run a three-step job that assembles, link-edits, and executes a source program. In using this procedure, you have several options:

1. You can assemble a source module, link edit the object module, and execute the load module.
2. You can assemble a source module, link edit the object module with other object modules, and execute the combined load module.
3. The program can access data from an input stream data set.
4. The program can access data on other devices besides the primary input stream device.

```
//jobname      JOB
//stepname     EXEC     PROC=ASMFCLG
//ASM.SYSIN    DD       *
                .
                .        source program
                .
     /*
```

The following code generates the statements to fulfill option 2:

```
//jobname      JOB
//stepname     EXEC     PROC=ASMFCLG
//ASM.SYSIN    DD       *
                .
                .        SOURCE PROGRAM
                .
     /*
//LKED.SYSIN   DD        *
                .        object module in card form
                .        & optionally linkage editor
                .        control statements
     /*
```

LKED.SYSIN is an additional ddname for the link-edit step, and the data set that follows this DD * in the input stream will be used as additional input to link edit (the linkage editor also receives as input the object module created as output from the assembly step).

The third step generated by the procedure ASMFCLG is the GO step. It involves the execution of the load module created by the linkage editor. As this program executes, it can use an input stream data set or data sets on other devices (options 3 and 4, respectively). The control statements to accomplish this are:

```
//jobname       JOB
//stepname      EXEC      PROC=ASMFCLG
//ASM.SYSIN     DD        *

                          .
                          source program
                          .
/*
//GO.REPORT     DD        UNIT=3400,DSNAME=ACCTS,          X
                          VOL=SER=006587,DISP=(,KEEP)

//GO.BILLS      DD        *

                          .
                          input stream data set
                          .
/*
```

The first DD statement in the GO step (GO.REPORT) specifies a data set created during this step, which resides on tape. The GO.BILLS DD statement permits use of an input stream data set. Either or both types of DD statements can be specified.

THE LINKAGE EDITOR

The linkage editor is an IBM-supplied program that processes object modules, preparing them for execution. It can process the single object module created by the assembly step that precedes it in the job, or it can combine several object modules, some of which were created in other jobs.

OS-Based Systems

The two DD control cards of interest to you in executing the linkage editor are those with the ddnames of SYSLIN and SYSLMOD. SYSLIN is the ddname of the linkage editor's input data set, and SYSLMOD is the ddname of its output data set.

If the linkage editor is processing a single object module created by the assembler in the same job, there is nothing special you have to do. The use of the cataloged procedure ASMFCLG (or your system's equivalent) will ensure that SYSLIN contains the object module and the output (the load module) is placed in SYSLMOD.

There are two possibilities if object modules that were created in a different job are to be used. These involve object modules in deck form and object modules stored in existing data sets. Combining can be accomplished by making SYSLIN a *concatenated data set.* A concatenated data set is actually a group of data sets that are treated as one data set (for the duration of the job step). Any input data sets that have the same block size can be concatenated. (See chapter 21 for more explanation of record format and block size.)

To concatenate the SYSLIN data set, either specify the DSNAME and DISP=OLD as well as UNIT and VOLUME information in the operand of a DD statement with a ddname field of LKED.SYSIN; or place an asterisk in the operand of a DD statement with the same DDNAMES and follow the DD * card with the object module in deck form. Additional object modules may be concatenated to the input data set by following the LKED.SYSIN DD control statement with DD statements containing blank ddname fields. One DD card for each object module with the operands of DSNAME and a DISP of OLD as well as UNIT and VOLUME information.

If no object module is to be used from a previous step in the same job, the cataloged procedure of ASMFCLG (or your system's equivalent) can be used, with the SYSIN statement overriding the SYSLIN DD statement and specifying the data set that contains your object module in the operand.

DOS-BASED SYSTEMS

If the single object module needed by the linkage editor was created by the assembler in this same job, no special statements need be presented. Previously assembled (in other jobs) object modules which have been cataloged in libraries under unique names can be presented to the linkage editor using the INCLUDE statement:

blank INCLUDE cataloged name

If the module you wish to include is to be the first to receive control and execute, the INCLUDE card must immediately follow the //   OPTION card. If the module assembled in this job is to receive control first, the IN-CLUDE card or cards follow the //   EXEC   LNKEDT card.

QUESTIONS

1. Define the following:

    a. Job   c. Job control language
    b. Job step   d. Input stream data set

2. If you use a DOS-based system briefly describe the function of each of the following:

    a. OPTION   c. /*
    b. EXEC   d. /&

3. What extra control statements are needed when your job uses tape data sets on a DOS-based system? When it uses a direct access data set?

4. Why does a DOS job generally consist of three EXEC control statements?

5. Why is it necessary to use a LBLTYP statement in a DOS job that uses a tape data set?

6. What are the four responsibilities a programmer must fulfill to use a disk data set on a DOS job?

7. What is a cataloged procedure, and why is it convenient to use them on an OS-based system?

8. How is the connection made between a GET instruction in a program and the actual data set on the I/O device in an OS-based system?

9. What is the difference between a DDNAME and a DSNAME?

10. What is the value of a retention period or expiration date?

EXERCISES

1. Set up control statements for the following DOS job. Show where you would place the source program and the input stream data set.

    a. Assembly, link edit, and execution steps
    b. Jobname of EXERC1
    c. State that you want the LINK and DUMP options.

2. To the job you set up for exercise 1, add the following tape and disk data sets.

    a. A data set on tape volume 652817, which should be mounted on the physical device 180. Use a logical unit name of SYS006 and the filename of DETAIL.
    b. A data set with the filename of MASTER on disk volume 333333, relative track 27 and it contains 20 tracks of data. Use SYS008 as the logical unit name for this data set.

3. Describe the data sets used by the program in the following DOS-based job.

```
//        JOB        EXERC3
//        OPTION     LINK
//        EXEC       ASSEMBLY
          .
          .                     source program
          .
/*
//        LBLTYP     TAPE
//        EXEC       LNKEDT
//        ASSGN      SYS007,X'181'
//        ASSGN      SYS010,X'190'
//        TLBL       CJ,,,008273
//        DLBL       FILEIN
//        EXTENT     SYS010,666555,1,0,1,50
//        EXEC
683       4965
716       2075
/&
```

4. Set up DD control statements to describe the following data sets:

a. A new disk data set named DA, which is to be created on volume 123456 on a 2314 disk drive. It is to occupy 100 tracks initially with increments of 25 tracks if needed. You want the data set kept only if the job does not abend.

b. an input stream data set

c. An existing cataloged data set named OPAL

d. A tape set to be created and cataloged under the name of AGNES. AGNES is to be kept if the job abends, but not cataloged.

CHAPTER 21

Input and Output through the Operating System

Input and output statements transfer and control the flow of data between the computer's internal-storage and an external-storage media. Some input and output concepts are the same regardless of which external storage media is used. For instance, all input and output data belongs to data sets.[†] A *data set* is a named, organized collection of logically related records that exists on an external-storage media. The transfer of records between the computer's storage and this data on external media is handled by data management routines supplied with the operating system you are using.

GENERALITIES ABOUT DATA SETS

A data set consists of a collection of records that have some relation to one another. What we have been thinking of as a record is more correctly called a *logical record*. It is the basic unit of input and output that will be used in this text.

In some data sets, logical records are grouped together into larger physical units. The reading or writing of data, in these cases, is performed on these larger units, called blocks (or *physical records*). The process of grouping the logical records together is called *blocking*. In a particular data set, all blocks contain the same number of logical records, except the last block which may

---

[†]In higher-level languages (Fortran, PL/I, Cobol) and the Disk Operating System (DOS), the term *data file* is used instead of *data set*.

be short, depending on the total number of logical records in the data set. This fixed number of logical records per block is referred to as the blocking factor of the data set.

Each data set may contain logical records in one of four formats. This chapter discusses only one of these formats: fixed-length (F format). Fixed-length records are illustrated in figure 21-1. In the first example, the logical records are unblocked. In the second, they are blocked, and the blocking factor is 4.

Why block logical records? Simply as a matter of efficiency. Since data is transferred in blocks between internal storage and the I/O device, fewer I/O operations are necessary if the records are blocked. Another efficiency is derived from the fact that each block of data on the external-storage media is separated by an *interrecord gap*. (This is merely a space on the recording media that separates the various blocks in a data set.) Two hundred logical records in an unblocked data set require the use of 199 interrecord gaps to separate them—199 wasted areas on the external-storage media that could have been used to store data. When a blocking factor of 5 is used on this same data set, only 39 interrecord gaps are required to separate the 40 physical records in the data set.

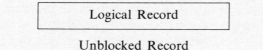

Logical Record

Unblocked Record

or

Logical Record	Logical Record	Logical Record	Logical Record

Blocked Records

Fig. 21-1 Fixed-length records

There is another variation that can be made to the format of records. A control character may precede each logical record in a file. This format is used when the records in the data set will eventually be printed on a printer. This character will then be used to control the carriage on the printer, allowing single spacing, double spacing, and ejects (to the top of the next page) of the output form. Figure 21-2 shows how formats would look.

If the logical records are output to the printer, the carriage-control character is used to control the printer's carriage, but it is not printed. If these same logical records are output to an I/O device other than the printer, the control char-

Logical Record

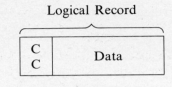

Unblocked Record

Blocked Records

Fig. 21-2 Use of carriage-control characters in logical records

acter is treated as any other data character. The record format, the blocksize, the logical record length, if you choose to block, and whether or not carriage-control characters are part of the logical records are facts that become parts of tables describing the data sets to OS- and DOS-based operating systems.

Some input and output concepts are also identical, regardless of the operating system used. Both OS and DOS relieve the programmer of having to interface directly with the hardware involved in controlling the I/O devices. To use the data management facilities, the programmer need only fulfill a few simple requirements. (Each requirement can be met through the programmer's use of a special I/O macro instruction.) The programmer must:

1. Describe the physical characteristics of the data to be read or written with respect to data set organization, record sizes, and the language level to be used in accessing the data. For each data set to be accessed, a table containing this information must be created as part of the source module. The information is supplied by the programmer; the assembler builds the table. This table is called a *Data Control Block* (DCB), under OS-based systems, and a *Define The File* (DTF) under DOS-based.

2. Logically connect the data set to the program (by using the OPEN macro instruction) and inform the data management routines that the program will be processing this data set. The routines should perform any initializations that may be necessary to the future processing of records in this data set.

3. Access the records in the data set using the correct forms of input (GET) or output (PUT) macros.

4. Inform the data management routines that you have concluded processing of this data set, that you no longer need help, and that this data set may now be logically disconnected from your program. This is accomplished by using the CLOSE macro instruction.

These four requirements must be handled by you in order to handle any data set, regardless of what type of data set it is, on what media the data set resides, and which operating system is used.

DESCRIBING PHYSICAL CHARACTERISTICS OF DATA—DOS

The programmer supplies the information for the description of the data set under DOS-based systems by coding a DTF macro. An example DTF is shown below. This DTF defines an input data set on the card reader.

```
CARDS     DTFCD     DEVADDR=SYSIPT,DEVICE=2540,      X
                    IOAREA1=INAREA,WORKA=YES,         X
                    EOFADDR=EOF
```

There are several DTF macros, one for each type of I/O device. The programmer chooses the DTF macro for the type of device on which his data set resides. He then specifies the keyword parameters required for that particular device. The general format for the DTF macro call is:

filename   DTFxx   keyword parameters

The filename is the symbolic name by which the programmer will refer to this file or data set in his program. This name is referenced by the programmer: (1) when he uses an OPEN macro to logically connect this data set to the program; (2) when he accesses records from the data set (GET and PUT macros); and (3) when he uses the CLOSE macro to inform the supervisor that he is finished processing it. The filename is the programmer's way to connect the action requested of the supervisor with the description of the data to be acted upon.

DTFxx is the macro name. The two small xs are replaced by two characters used to specify a particular type of I/O device. The ones that will be explained in this chapter are:

Macro Name	Defines File On
DTFCD	card device
DTFMT	magnetic tape
DTFPR	printer
DTFSD	sequential direct access storage device

TABLE 21-1 DTF Operands

OPERAND	DTFCD	DTFMT	DTFPR	DTFSD
DEVADDR =	*	*	*	X
IOAREA1 =	*	*	*	*
BLKSIZE =	80	*	121	*
CTLCHR =	X	N/A	X	N/A
DEVICE =	2540	*	1403	2311
EOFADDR =	X	*	N/A	*
RECFORM =	FIXUNB	FIXUNB	FIXUNB	FIXUNB
TYPEFLE =	INPUT	INPUT	N/A	INPUT
WORKA =	X	X	X	X
✳ FILABL =	N/A	NO	N/A	N/A
✳ RECSIZE =	N/A	X	N/A	X
IOAREA2 =	X	X	X	X

NOT NECESSARY

DESCRIBING SEQUENTIAL DATA SETS UNDER DOS

These four DTF's are used for sequential data sets, in which the records are handled in the sequence they are physically stored. For example, in order to read the fifth record in the data set, the first, second, third, and fourth records must be read first.

Table 21-1 lists the possible operands for the various DTFs. An asterisk (*) indicates that the specification of a particular operand is required. An X indicates those operands that may be specified. N/A indicates that that particular operand is *not applicable* for that DTF. Any other number or symbol that appears under the column heading for a particular DTF indicates the default value, which will be assumed if that particular operand is not specified.

The DEVADDR operand must be specified for all types of DTFs. It is in this operand that the symbolic unit name is specified. This same name is used in the job control statements to assign an actual I/O device to the data set. So this is an important operand. It is the connection between the description of the data set and the data set itself. (For more information on the job control language statements (ASSGN and EXTENT) that assign an I/O device to a data set, refer to chapter 20.)

Each system has a fixed list of symbolic unit names. The programmer chooses one that refers to the type of device on which his data set resides. He has a choice between a system logical unit or a programmer logical unit. Examples of system logical units are:

SYSIPT   the primary input device
             for the program

SYSLST   the primary output device
             for printed output

SYSPCH   the primary output device
for punched output

The programmer logical units all begin with the letters SYS, followed by three digits. Programmer logical units are used to refer to all other symbolic units in the system. Each system has a list of standard system units, which associates each symbolic unit name with a particular physical device in the system. The programmer codes his program keeping in mind only a device *type*—not a particular I/O device address. At execution time, the system will assume a particular physical device by using its list of standard system units.

Should the programmer wish to use something other than the system's standard unit assignment, he can use an ASSGN job control statement to temporarily override the system's standard unit assignments. The following are the symbolic unit names most frequently used for particular DTFs.

DTF	*DEVADDR=*
DTFCD	SYSIPT
DTFMT	SYSnnn
DTFPR	SYSLST
DTFSD	SYSnnn

At least one input/output area must be specified for use with each data set. The symbolic name of this area must be specified in the IOAREA1 operand of the DTF statement. If increased efficiency is desired in the I/O process, the symbolic name of a second input/output area can be specified in the IOAREA2 operand.

Another area can be used to hold input and output records. This type of area is called a *work area*, whose use in a program is indicated to the I/O routines by specifying the operand "WORKA=YES". This allows you to process records in several different areas in your program and to specify the name of a particular one when you request a record to be accessed by a GET or PUT macro. For instance, you can have three work areas—one in which you place the results of a normal execution of your loop and two to indicate error conditions you might recognize in it. The I/O routines move a record from the work area you specify in a PUT macro to IOAREA1 (or IOAREA2 if it appeared in the DTF); from there it is transferred to the I/O device. What you are doing when you specify WORKA=YES is to use temporary storage areas. The data management routine moves records from the input area, to or from your work area, to the output area.

The BLKSIZE operand is used to specify the length of IOAREA1 (in bytes). Notice that this operand is required for DTFMT and DTFSD, but it is optional for the other two DTFs. It is optional because a default value is assumed (80 for DTFCD and 121 for DTFPR).

The CTLCHR operand can be specified for only the card punch or the printer, and it is optional. This operand permits you to specify if your logical records contain control characters—and if they do, which of two kinds of control characters you are using. If the CTLCHR operand is missing, the assumption is made by the I/O routines that control characters are not used in this data set. If CTLCHR is specified, indicate CTLCHR=ASA. This indicates that an ASA/ANSI (American National Standards Institute) control character will appear as the first byte of each logical record in the data set, and that the control character will be one of the following:

Control Character	Meaning
(blank)	space one line before printing
1	eject to top of next page before printing
0	space two lines before printing
—	space three lines before printing
+	don't space before printing
V	select stacker 1 ⎱ (for card punch)
W	select stacker 2 ⎰

The DEVICE operand is used to specify the I/O device on which the data set resides (i.e., the fact that DTFPR was used indicates a printer, but DEVICE= specifies which type of printer). The choices are: 1442, 2501, 2520, 2540, 3505, or 3525 for card devices; 1403, 1404, 1443, 1445, or 3211 for printers; and 2311, 2314, 2321 or 3330 for direct access. The underscored choices are the defaults if the DEVICE operand is not specified. To find out what you should specify in this operand, you must ask someone who knows which particular devices are used on your system.

Some of the devices used to hold sequential data sets can hold either input or output data sets. The TYPEFLE operand is used to indicate which. A card punch data set must be indicated by the use of TYPEFLE=OUTPUT with the DTFCD macro. A data set that you are creating rather than reading is indicated by TYPEFLE=OUTPUT on either the DTFMT or DTFSD. If TYPEFLE is not specified, the default is INPUT.

The EOFADDR operand specifies the symbolic name of the first instruction of the routine which is to receive control when the end-of-file condition is encountered on an input data set. This operand must be specified for all sequential input data sets. As an illustration, the DTFs in figures 21-3 and 21-4 define the input and output files used by the macros in this text.

The input data set has the following characteristics:

a. The data set is known by the filename $CARD.
b. It resides on the device known by the logical unit name of SYSIPT.

```
$CARD     DTFCD       DEVADDR=SYSIPT,              X
                      DEVICE=2501,                 X
                      IOAREA1=$INPUT,              X
                      WORKA=YES,                   X
                      EOFADDR=&EOFRTN
```

Fig. 21-3 DTF for input data set used by text macros

```
$LINE     DTFPR       DEVADDR=SYSLST,              X
                      IOAREA1=$OUTPUT1,            X
                      IOAREA2=$OUTPUT2,            X
                      CTLCHR=ASA,                  X
                      WORKA=YES
```

Fig. 21-4 DTF for output data set used by text macros

c. The TYPEFLE operand is not specified; therefore the data set is assumed to reside on a card reader, rather than a card punch; because the default is INPUT.

d. In this case the symbolic unit name SYSIPT is assigned to a 2501 card reader.

e. By default, also, the block size is 80 bytes. This means that $INPUT, which is specified as IOAREA1, is 80 bytes in length.

f. The RECFORM operand is not specified so the records are fixed in length and unblocked. IOAREA1 holds one physical record, and that physical record contains one logical record.

g. Work areas are used, and the symbolic name of the work area to receive the input record is specified in the operand of the GET instruction.

The output data set is described as follows:

a. It is known by the filename $LINE.

b. It resides on the device known by the symbolic unit name of SYSLST: by default, this symbolic name is expected to be assigned to a 1403 printer.

c. I/O areas named $OUTPUT1 and $OUTPUT2 are used to provide extra efficiency on output operations, and each of these areas is 121 bytes in length by default.

d. Work areas are used. The symbolic name of the particular work area which contains the record to be printed on a particular I/O operation is specified in the operand of the PUT instruction.

e. By default, the records are fixed in length and unblocked. Each of these records contains an ASA control character in its first byte which will be used to control the printer. This means that the remaining 120 characters of data will be printed on each line.

DESCRIBING PHYSICAL CHARACTERISTICS OF DATA—OS

The programmer supplies the information for the description of the data set under OS-based systems by coding a DCB macro. This macro is used for all types of I/O devices. The operands used with the macro connect the description with a particular type of I/O device. The general format for the DCB macro is shown in figure 21-5.

Name is the symbolic name by which the programmer will refer to this data set in his program. This name is referenced by the programmer: (1) when he uses an OPEN macro to logically connect the data set to the program; (2) when he accesses records from the data set; and (3) when he uses the CLOSE macro to inform the supervisor that he has finished processing it. This symbolic name is the programmer's way to connect the action requested of the supervisor with the description of the data to be acted upon.

Each of the operands describes one of the characteristics of the data set. The DSORG operand specifies how the records are arranged in it; PS indicates physical sequential. The MACRF operand specifies which macros will be used to access the records in the data set, and, in the case of the GET and PUT

$$\text{name} \quad \text{DCB} \quad \text{DSORG} = \text{PS}, \text{MACRF} = \begin{bmatrix} \text{PM} \\ \text{GM} \end{bmatrix}, \text{RECFM} = \begin{bmatrix} \text{F} \\ \text{FA} \\ \text{FB} \\ \text{FBA} \end{bmatrix} \qquad \text{X}$$

$$\text{DDNAME} = \text{ddname}, \text{BLKSIZE} = \text{decimal} \#, \qquad \text{X}$$

$$\text{LRECL} = \text{decimal} \#, \text{EODAD} = \text{end-of-file addr}, \qquad \text{X}$$

$$\text{EROPT} = \begin{bmatrix} \text{ACC} \\ \text{SKP} \\ \text{ABE} \end{bmatrix}, \text{SYNAD} = \text{I/O errorrtn addr}$$

Note: The brackets indicate that a choice must be made between the parameters that appear within the brackets.

Fig. 21-5 General format for the DCB macro

macros, whether the data is to be moved to or from a special work area indicated by the programmer in the operand of the GET and PUT macros.

The RECFM operand is used to specify whether the records are fixed in length and unblocked (F) or fixed in length and blocked (FB). The letter A may be added to this operand to indicate that ASA control characters are used in each record.

In the DDNAME operand the programmer specifies the symbolic name he used on the DD job control statement that connects the data set on the I/O device to the program. This operand is important—it enables the connection to be made between the description of the data set and the particular data set. (For more information on the job control language statement (DD) which connects an actual I/O device to a job step, refer to chapter 20.)

The BLKSIZE and LRECL operands specify the length (in bytes) of the physical and logical records respectively. If F or FA is specified in the RECFM operand, these two operands must be equal. If FB or FBA is specified in the RECFM operand, BLKSIZE must be an even multiple of the length specified in LRECL.

The EODAD operand is specified only for sequential input data sets. It is the symbolic name of the instruction that is to receive control when the end-of-file condition is encountered on the input data set.

There are times when the I/O device encounters difficulties in trying to perform a requested operation. The programmer has the ability to specify what action should be taken if a serious difficulty that results in an uncorrectable error occurs. He can specify EROPT on his DCB. This operand has three alternatives: ACC, SKP, ABE. It specifies the action to be taken by the system. The three choices are:

> ACC accept the block that caused the error
> SKP skip the block that caused the error
> ABE abend (the default)

Most programmers specify SKP, or ACC and specify a SYNAD routine to print an error message and then continue processing.

In the SYNAD operand, the programmer specifies the address of an error-analysis routine, in which the programmer can print out a message to provide clues to the cause of error and identify the dump. At the end of his error analysis, the programmer must return control to the data management routine to take the action he has specified in the EROPT parameter by branching, via the contents of register 14.[†]

[†]For more information on the use of the SYNAD and EROPT operands in a DCB macro call, see the IBM manuals, *System/360 Operating System Supervisor Services and Macro Instructions* (GC28-6646), *System/360 Operating System Data Management Macro Instructions* (GC26-3796), *System/360 Operating System Data Management Services* (GC26-3746), *OS/VS Data Management Instructions* (GC26-3793), and *OS/VS Data Management Services* (GC26-3783).

As an illustration, the DCBs in figures 21-6 and 21-7 define the input and output data sets described by the LAST macro used under OS.

```
$CARD      DCB       DSORG=PS,MACRF=GM,         X
                     RECFM=F,DDNAME=INDD,       X
                     BLKSIZE=80,LRECL=80,       X
                     EODAD=&EOFRTN
```

Fig. 21-6 DCB for input data set used by text macros

```
$LINE      DCB       DSORG=PS,MACRF=PM,         X
                     RECFM=FA,DDNAME=OUTDD,     X
                     BLKSIZE=121,LRECL=121
```

Fig. 21-7 DCB for output data set used by text macros

OPENING AND CLOSING A DATA SET

There is a great deal of difference in the way data sets are described under OS- and DOS-based systems. But there is great similarity in the manner and form in which the programmer fulfills the other three basic requirements (opening, closing, and accessing). The OPEN macro is used to open all data sets. Both OS- and DOS-based systems permit the opening of several with one OPEN instruction. The only difference between the two types of operating system is that OS systems provide the ability to specify options. The only option we are interested in at this time, is the first option—that is, whether the OS data set is an input or an output one, with the default "INPUT".

To open a data set under DOS-based systems, the programmer need only specify the filename he used on his DTF macro. To open two data sets, two filenames appear in the operand, separated by a comma. To open the two data sets described by the LAST macro's DTF, the statement would be: OPEN $CARD,$LINE.

To open the same two data sets under OS, the statement would be:

OPEN   ($CARD,,$LINE,(OUTPUT)).

Notice that no options are specified for the DCB name $CARD. It is an input file, and the default is input. The omission of options must be indicated by two consecutive commas, indicating a null operand. Options must be specified for $LINE, because it is an output file. The options must be enclosed in parentheses. If each of the data sets were opened separately, the macro calls would appear as:

```
OPEN     ($CARD)
OPEN     ($LINE,(OUTPUT))
```

This should be avoided, however, because it is more efficient to request as much as possible at one time.

Closing data sets is even easier than opening them. You merely use the CLOSE macro with the filename or the dcbname as the operand. There is one difference between the two types of system here. The operands of the OS CLOSE macro are enclosed in parentheses, while the operands of the DOS CLOSE are not. If your program abends, the abend routine will close all your data sets before dumping the contents of storage.

ACCESSING RECORDS IN A DATA SET

The GET and PUT macros for OS- and DOS-based systems are identical. Two operands are specified—the first is the symbol that appears in the name field of the description of the data set, the filename or dcbname. The second operand is the symbolic name of the work area used for this particular I/O operation.

Comprehensive Examples

To illustrate how all of this fits together, the examples given in figures 21-8 and 21-9 show reading from an input file on cards, counting the number of cards read, and printing each record as it is read and the count of cards read when end-of-file is encountered.

```
* INITIALIZATIONS
          OPEN    (DCBIN,,DCBOUT,(OUTPUT))
          SR      6,6                              SET COUNTER TO A VALUE OF ZERO
* READ AND WRITE LOOP
LOOP      GET     DCBIN,INAREA
          LA      6,1(6)                           INCREMENT COUNTER BY VALUE OF ONE
          MVC     OUTAREA+20(80),INAREA            MOVE RECORD TO OUTPUT AREA
          PUT     DCBOUT,OUTAREA                   PRINT A COPY OF THE RECORD READ
          B       LOOP                             BRANCH TO GET ANOTHER RECORD
* END OF FILE PROCESSING
EOF       CVD     6,PKD                            CONVERT THE COUNT
          UNPK    CT,PKD                           AND PREPARE IT
          MVZ     CT+4(1),CT+3                     FOR OUTPUT
          PUT     DCBOUT,CNTMSG
          CLOSE   (DCBIN,DCBOUT)
          .
          .
          .
INAREA    DS      20F
*
OUTAREA   DC      CL20' '
          DS      CL80
          DC      CL21' '
*
PKD       DS      D
*
CNTMSG    DC      CL30' THE NUMBER OF CARDS READ WAS'
CT        DS      CL5
          DC      CL86' '
* DATA CONTROL BLOCKS
DCBIN     DCB     DSORG=PS,DDNAME=READIN,MACRF=GM,BLKSIZE=80,                    X
                  LRECL=80,RECFM=F,EODAD=EOF
*
DCBOUT    DCB     DSORG=PS,DDNAME=PRINT,MACRF=PM,BLKSIZE=121,                    X
                  LRECL=121,RECFM=FA
          .
          .
          .
          END
```

Fig. 21-8 Comprehensive I/O example (OS)

```
* INITIALIZATIONS
          OPEN    CARDIN,PRINTOUT
          SR      6,6                              SET COUNTER TO A VALUE OF ZERO
* READ AND WRITE LOOP
LOOP      GET     CARDIN,INAREA
          LA      6,1(6)                           INCREMENT COUNTER BY VALUE OF ONE
          MVC     OUTAREA+20(80),INAREA            MOVE RECORD TO OUTPUT AREA
          PUT     PRINTOUT,OUTAREA                 PRINT A COPY OF THE RECORD READ
          B       LOOP                             BRANCH TO GET ANOTHER RECORD
* END OF FILE PROCESSING
EOF       CVD     6,PKD                            CONVERT THE COUNT
          UNPK    CT,PKD                           AND PREPARE IT
          MVZ     CT+4(1),CT+3                     FOR OUTPUT
          PUT     PRINTOUT,CNTMSG
          CLOSE   CARDIN,PRINTOUT
          .
          .
          .
INAREA    DS      20F
*
OUTAREA   DC      CL20' '
          DS      CL80
          DC      CL21' '
*
PKD       DS      D
*
$OUT      DS      CL121
*
$INPUT    DS      20F
*
CNTMSG    DC      CL30' THE NUMBER OF CARDS READ WAS'
CT        DS      CL5
          DC      CL86' '
* DATA FILE DESCRIPTIONS
CARDIN    DTFCD   DEVADDR=SYSIPT,DEVICE=2501,IOAREA1=$INPUT,     X
                  WORKA=YES,EOFADDR=EOF
*
PRINTOUT  DTFPR   DEVADDR=SYSLST,IOAREA1=$OUT,CTLCHR=ASA,        X
                  WORKA=YES
          .
          .
          .
          END
```

Fig. 21-9 Comprehensive I/O example (DOS)

QUESTIONS

1. Define the following:

   a. Data set
   b. Logical record
   c. Block
   d. Blocking factor
   e. Fixed-length records
   f. ASA control characters
   g. Sequential data set

2. What are the requirements a programmer needs to fulfill in order to be able to use the operating system's data management facilities?

3. How do you describe the physical characteristics of a data set on your system?

4. Why are the DDNAME and DEVADDR operands so important in a DCB and DTF, respectively?

5. On an OS-based system, why would a programmer want to specify the SYNAD operand on a DCB?

EXERCISES

1. Code a DCB or DTF required by your system to describe a data set with the following characteristics.

   a. An input card data set with the name of RECORDS. Each input record is 80 characters in length and unblocked.
   b. Use INREC as the DDNAME in coding a DCB, and SYSIPT as the logical unit name in coding a DTF.
   c. The name of the end-of-file routine is FINIS.

2. Code the DCB or DTF for the following output data set:

   a. The data set is to reside on tape, each record having a blocking factor of 3 with a logical record length of 100 bytes.
   b. Use SALES as the DDNAME in coding a DCB, and SYS007 as the logical unit name in coding a DTF.

CHAPTER 22

Macros and the Macro Language

INTRODUCTION

Macros are an extremely useful facility of assembler language. A macro is the programmer's means to generate a sequence of instructions and constants at assembly time from a single statement in the source program. This single statement assumes a previously established macro definition. Examples of macros with which you are already familiar are: OPEN, GET and PUT; data management macros provided by the operating system.

The use of macros in assembler language programming offers many advantages. One is convenience. The use of macros requires less training on the part of the programmer. A macro can provide all the code that is necessary for the proper execution of a program, without requiring the programmer to understand the concepts behind this code. The FIRST and LAST macros used in this text are examples of this advantage. The beginning programmer was relieved of the responsibility of understanding the establishment of addressability, the dynamic dumping of storage, and the control of input and output operations.

Another convenience of macros is the adaptation to your needs of generated code for a particular problem; macros allow you the flexibility—through the use of defaults—to generate only the code you need, and to do so with as little specifying of operands as possible. This convenience goes hand in hand with an often overlooked advantage of macros—control. If macros are used, certain important coding conventions and interfaces can be standardized. The format of and parameters used in calling sequences can be more easily controlled.

A final advantage of macros is economy. The number of instructions generated by a macro can be designed to be the most efficient set of instructions to provide the desired functions.

CONCEPT OF MACROS

The use of macros involves the programmer at two separate times. The first is when the macro is defined, and the second is when the macro call causes code to be placed in the source module (at the location of the call). In other words, the macro definition must be in existence for a particular macro name before that particular macro name appears in the opcode field of an instruction in a source program.

A macro definition consists of a stream of assembler language control and machine instructions. The macro definition is made available to a source program either by placing it in a special library of macro definitions or by placing it ahead of the source module in the input stream. The instructions in the macro definition may contain some missing fields or subfields.

When the macro is called (the macro name appears in the opcode field of a source statement), the operands from the macro call instruction will be substituted for the missing fields or subfields in the instructions in the macro definition (similar to parameter substitution in a subroutine call). When the macro is defined, part of the definition process is the specification of how many items are missing in the instructions that make up the macro definition and which items, specified in the operands of the macro call, are to be substituted into what locations for the missing items. Let's examine an illustration:

Macro Definition (*simplified*)		*Macro Call*	
DOT	&A,&B,&C	MVC	X(6),Y
L	6,&A	MVI	X+6,C'*'
MH	6,&B	DOT	FIV,TWO,ANS
A	6,&A	L	7,NIN
ST	6,&C	M	6,ONE
		D	6,ANS

The macro definition specifies that the name of the macro is DOT, and that when it is called, three operands (parameters) are to be specified in the macro call. The macro definition contains a stream of four assembler language instructions, and each of these has an indication of a missing operand; there are four missing fields. The first parameter, that which is specified in the first operand of the macro call instruction, will be substituted wherever &A appears in the instructions in the macro definition (the L and A instructions). As the proper values from the operands are substituted into the instructions in the macro definition, copies of these are inserted in the assembler's input stream in the location defined by the macro call. This process is called the *macro expansion*. The assembler's input stream appears as follows after the expansion of the macro is completed:

```
      MVC   X(6),Y
      MVI   X+6,C'*'
      DOT   FIV,TWO,ANS
+     L     6,FIV
+     MH    6,TWO
+     A     6,FIV
+     ST    6,ANS
      L     7,NIN
      M     6,ONE
      D     6,ANS
```

The four instructions generated by the expansion of the macro DOT are treated just as if they appeared in the original source program. Note, however, that the assembler flags each macro-generated instruction with a plus (+). If this same macro was called at a different point in the source program, and the only difference in the macro call instruction was that SIX was specified in the first operand, the same 4 instructions would be generated. The only differences would be that the symbol SIX would appear wherever &A appeared in the instructions in the macro definition:

```
      DOT   SIX,TWO,ANS
+     L     6,SIX
+     MH    6,TWO
+     A     6,SIX
+     ST    6,ANS
```

In addition to the ability of the assembler to expand instructions at a macro call and insert parameters into predetermined locations within these, it also has the ability to choose which statements within the macro definition it wishes to copy into its input stream—even changing the order in which it copies these from the definition.

ELEMENTS OF MACRO DEFINITIONS

The beginning and end of a macro definition are always indicated by special assembler pseudo-ops. The MACRO pseudo-op (called the *header statement*) indicates the beginning of a macro definition; the MEND pseudo-op (called the *trailer statement*) indicates the end.

Immediately following the MACRO instruction in the definition appears a special statement called the *prototype statement*. This statement gives the name by which the macro definition will be known (specified in the opcode

```
                              ┌→ MACRO
            Prototype ────────→  DOT        &A,&B,&C
                              ┌  L          6,&A
            Body             │   MH         6,&B
Limits                       │   A          6,&A
                             └   ST         6,&C
                              └→ MEND
```

Fig. 22-1 Elements of a macro definition

field) and declares the parameters that will be associated with this macro (specified in the operand field and, optionally, in the name field). In other words, the prototype statement serves as a model of the macro call instruction. In our previous example, DOT   &A,&B,&C would be the prototype statement.

The *body of the macro* follows the prototype statement. This includes all of the assembler instructions which will be generated when the macro is expanded. These are called model statements. Figure 22-1 shows how the MEND instruction ends the body of the macro.

PLACEMENT OF THE DEFINITION

The macro definition must be established before the use of a macro call for that particular macro name, but you have two choices on how to establish it. First, it can be included as part of the source module by placing the definition at the very beginning of the source module (prior to the CSECT instruction). This placement makes it possible to call that macro name from within that source module.

Second, the macro definition can be made available to more than one source module by placing it in a library. This is accomplished by using a special set of job control language statements and the appropriate utility program.

THE PROTOTYPE STATEMENT

The general format of the prototype statement follows:

Name	*Operation*	*Operand*
a name field parameter or blank	a symbol	zero or more symbolic parameters separated by commas

You are already aware of the fact that the symbol in the operation field is the name of the macro. This symbol is restricted, in that you cannot duplicate an existing machine opcode, assembler pseudo-op, or macro name.

The operand entry requires a little more explanation. The general format shows that the operand may consist of zero or more symbolic parameters separated by commas. *Symbolic parameters* are similar to the parameters of a subroutine—they allow you to pass values to the body of a macro definition from the macro call instruction. It is the symbolic parameters that keep track of the locations within the body of the macro where substitutions or insertions are to be made when the macro is called. If no symbolic parameters appear in the operand field, it indicates that the model statements of the macro definition are to be generated as is—no substitution is to occur.

Symbolic parameters are variable symbols and must adhere to the following format: &SYMBOL. The *variable symbol* must begin with an ampersand (&), followed by from one to seven alphameric characters, the first of which is alphabetic. (Note that this meets the normal limit of eight characters.)

POSITIONAL AND KEYWORD PARAMETERS

There are two types of symbolic parameters: positional and keyword. The example at the beginning of this chapter used three positional parameters. If your macro uses only a few parameters and their values will change almost every time you call the macro, it is easier to use positional parameters. To specify a positional parameter in the macro call instruction, you need only specify the value in the proper position in the operand field.

The *positional operands* of a macro call instruction must be specified in the same order as the positional parameters in the prototype statement. Thus they lose their ease of use when a macro has many parameters. For example, if you have a macro name whose prototype statement specifies ten positional parameters, and you wish to specify values for only the fifth and tenth ones, you must indicate that you are not specifying positional parameters 1–4 and 6–9. To accomplish this, a null character string must be specified for each of the missing ones. A *null character string* is a character string, with a length of zero, that can be indicated by leaving no space in the operand field for that value. This can be accomplished by immediately placing the comma that ends that operand and continuing on with the value for the next operand. The fifth and tenth parameters are given values of A and B, respectively, in the following macro call: macroname   ,,,,A,,,,,B.

Blanks appearing between the commas would *not* accomplish the same thing. Blanks cannot be used to indicate an omitted positional operand, because a blank actually occupies a position as a character, and the null character string is one with a length of zero.

Keyword parameters are generally used when all values do not change whenever the macro is called. A normal (or default) value can be specified as part of the prototype statement. This eliminates the need for specifying that particular keyword operand whenever the desired value equals the default value. This indicates one of the great advantages of the use of keyword parameters—the keyword operands may be specified in any order in the macro call instruction. It is the character string making up the keyword that the assembler recognizes and connects with the definition, rather than the position in which that keyword appears in the operand. The general format for the keyword parameters is as follows:

$$\&keyword = default,$$

or

$$\&keyword = ,$$

The keyword follows the rules for variable symbols: it is followed by an equal sign that may be followed by a default value or by a null value. If the keyword does not appear in the operand field of the macro call, the default, if available, is substituted into the model instructions. If no default is available, the null value will be used. If the keyword is specified in the macro call, the value specified overrides the default. The following is an example of a keyword macro definition:

```
            MACRO
&NAME       ESTAB      &REG=12,&ADDR=*
            BALR       &REG,0
            USING      &ADDR,&REG
            MEND
```

The macro ESTAB can now be used to establish addressability for a control section. The macro call: BEGIN   ESTAB would use the defaults for both symbolic parameters, and the following two instructions would be generated:

```
+BEGIN      BALR    12,0
+           USING   *,12
```

whereas the following macro call: ESTAB   REG=10,ADDR=LOC would override both defaults and would result in the generation of these two instructions:

```
+           BALR    10,0
+           USING   LOC,10
```

Notice that the keyword used in the operand of the macro call instruction is identical to the one specified in the prototype statement, except that the &, which indicates a variable symbol, is omitted.

The best of both worlds can be achieved by using both keyword and positional parameters in the same prototype statement (*mixed mode*). This type of macro is referred to as a mixed-mode macro. There is a slight difference between OS- and DOS-based operating systems in the placement of positional parameters and operands. Under DOS-based systems, all positional parameters must precede the first keyword parameter; the same rule applies to the specification of operands in the macro call.

Under OS-based systems, the order in which the positional parameters appear in the prototype statement determines the order in which the positional operands appear in the macro call, but the keyword parameters and operands may be interspersed at will. They do not in any way affect the ordering of the positional parameters and operands. A good rule to follow is to place all positional parameters and operands first; such a macro works under either operating system.

CONDITIONAL ASSEMBLY FEATURES

Our use of macros in this chapter has involved a preset sequence of instructions generated as a result of the macro expansion. Different values were substituted in the instructions because different operands were used in the macro call, but the number of instructions and the order in which they were generated was fixed.

Assembler language contains several conditional features that allow more flexibility in the expansion of macro definitions. They allow for branching inside the macro definition, performance of arithmetic and logic operations within the macro definition as a means for controlling the branching, generation of selected instructions from within the definition, and the changing of the order of generated instructions.

Two elements of the conditional features that make the branching within the macro definition possible are *sequence symbols* and *special branching statements*.

Figure 22-2 shows an example of a macro definition containing a branching instruction which utilizes a sequence symbol.

The function of the macro defined in figure 22-2 is to generate either an ST instruction, if the second parameter is omitted (null), or an STM instruction, if the second parameter is specified. The AIF is the branching instruction and .ST1 is a sequence symbol. Let's examine these more closely.

```
        MACRO
        STORE    &REG1,&REG2,&LOC
        AIF      ('&REG2'  EQ  '').ST1
        STM      &REG1,&REG2,&LOC
        MEXIT
.ST1    ST       &REG1,&LOC
        MEND
```

Fig. 22-2 Branching within macro definition

SEQUENCE SYMBOLS

Sequence symbols provide labels for model statements that serve as the targets for branch instructions within the macro definition. All sequence symbols begin with a period, followed by from one to seven characters. The first character *must* be alphabetic. Any remaining characters *must* be alphameric. Sequence symbols must be defined within the same macro definition that references them. They are useful only within the macro definition for branching; they do not appear in the name field of instructions that are generated by the expansion of the macro.

A sequence symbol cannot appear on any model statement that already contains an entry in the name field. If a name field contains a regular or a variable symbol, there is simply no way to place a sequence symbol in that same field, even though the sequence symbol would not appear on the generated instruction. However, the conditional assembly language *does* supply the programmer with a means of branching to a model statement that cannot hold a sequence symbol. The instruction that permits this is the ANOP instruction. Its general format is:

Name	Operation	Operand
a sequence symbol or blank	ANOP	not required

The ANOP instruction does not perform any operation; it merely provides an instruction that can serve as a target for a branch. An ANOP instruction placed immediately before a model statement that cannot hold a sequence symbol causes this statement to be processed as soon as a branch is taken to the sequence symbol in the name field of the ANOP statement.

For example, if the macro definition shown in figure 22-2 expected to receive a label in the name field when called and to generate this label on the store instruction produced, the definition would have to make use of the ANOP instruction for branching. The changes required in the macro definition can be seen in figure 22-3.

```
          MACRO
&NAME     STORE    &REG1,&REG2,&LOC
          AIF      ('&REG1' EQ '').ST1
&NAME     STM      &REG1,&REG2,&LOC
          MEXIT
.ST1      ANOP
&NAME     ST       &REG1,&LOC
          MEND
```

Fig. 22-3 Use of ANOP within macro definition

THE BRANCHING STATEMENTS

One of the most useful and powerful instructions in the conditional assembly repertoire is the AIF instruction which makes a test for a particular condition. If the condition is met, the AIF instruction permits you to cause a branch to be taken within the macro definition. If the condition is not met, the next sequential instruction in the macro definition is handled. The AIF instruction must be specified in the following format:

Name	*Operation*	*Operand*
a sequence symbol or blank	AIF	(logical expression) sequence symbol

The syntax of the assembler language does not allow for any blanks to be inserted between the right parenthesis and the period that begins the sequence symbol. If the condition tested in the logical expression of the AIF instruction is met, the next one within the macro definition to be processed is the instruction in which the sequence symbol referred to in the AIF instruction appears in its name field.

Let's examine the logical expression portion of the AIF instruction. This is the portion that determines whether or not the branch is taken. The logical expression can consist of: (1) an arithmetic relation that contains two arithmetic expressions separated by a relational operator; (2) the relation between two character strings, as shown by the relational operator that separates them. The following are the relational operators that can be used:

Operator	*Meaning*
EQ	equal
NE	not equal
LE	less than or equal
LT	less than
GE	greater than or equal
GT	greater than

The logical operators can also be used in the logical expression. They are: AND, OR, and NOT. In evaluating a logical expression, the assembler gives each logical term a value of 0 or 1. If the relation is true, a value of 1 is given to it; if the relation is false, a value of 0 is assigned. Everything in the logical expression is finally reduced to one value (a zero or a one). Some rules must be observed in coding logical expressions.

1. The relational or logical operators must be preceded and followed by at least one blank or special character:

   (&A EQ 20)

   > This arithmetic relation checks to see if the value passed for the symbolic parameter &A is equal to a value of 20.

2. A logical expression must not contain two logical terms in succession:

   (&A &B EQ 6)

   > is not a valid logical expression; the logical terms &A and &B must be separated by an operator.

3. A logical expression can contain several operators:

   (&A EQ 5 AND &B NE 5)

   > This logical expression checks for the presence of two conditions, and both must be true before the branch is taken. The value substituted for &A must be 5, and the value substituted for &B must be anything but 5.

Let's examine a macro definition to put some of these rules into a meaningful light. Figure 22-4 shows the definition of a macro named FIRST (for a DOS-based system assembler).

This macro is capable of generating code that performs three important

```
          MACRO
&NAME     FIRST  &SETUP=YES,&DUMP=YES,&BASE=12,&BEGIN=$DBEGIN,        X
                 &END=$DEND,&IO=NO
          AIF    ('&SETUP' EQ 'NO').FIRST01
&NAME     BALR   &BASE,0
          USING  *,&BASE
.FIRST01  AIF    ('&DUMP' EQ 'NO').FIRST02
          AIF    ('&BEGIN' NE '$DBEGIN').FIRST12
          MNOTE    'NO BEGIN SPECIFIED FOR PDUMP-$DBEGIN GENERATED'
$DBEGIN   DS     0H
.FIRST12  AIF    ('&END' NE '$DEND').FIRST13
          MNOTE  1,'NO END SPECIFIED FOR PDUMP-$DEND GENERATED'
$DEND     DS     0H
.FIRST13  PDUMP  &BEGIN,&END
.FIRST02  AIF    ('&IO' EQ 'NO').FIRST03
          AIF    ('&IO' NE 'IONLY').FIRST42
          OPEN   $CARD
          AGO    .FIRST03
.FIRST42  AIF    ('&IO' NE 'OONLY').FIRST43
          OPEN   $LINE
          AGO    .FIRST03
.FIRST43  OPEN   $CARD,$LINE
.FIRST03  ANOP
          MEND
```

Note: The AGO instruction is an unconditional branch to the sequence symbol appearing in the operand.

Fig. 22-4 Definition of the macro FIRST

functions for the programmer: (1) the establishment of addressability, (2) provision of a dump displaying the contents of storage before the execution of the program, and (3) initialization of the data sets if input and output operations are to be used.

The FIRST macro has six keyword parameters. The keywords SETUP, DUMP, and IO control whether or not the three basic functions need to be provided. A default value is assigned to each parameter in the prototype statement so that the beginning programmer need specify only a few operands on the macro call:

```
          FIRST   BEGIN=LOC,END=AREA+2
                  .
                  .
                  .
   BEGIN    DC      CL20'MESSAGES'
   AREA     DC      C'HP'
```

Notice that of the six parameters on the prototype statement, only two are specified in the macro call above. Default values will be used for the others. SETUP controls the establishment of addressability. Its default value, YES, indicates that the macro should generate BALR and USING instructions. The default on the keyword parameter BASE provides the base register number (&BASE=12) to be used.

Statement 3 in the macro definition checks to see if the value associated with the keyword parameter &SETUP is equal to NO. Since our example macro does not specify the keyword SETUP, the default value of YES is used. So the logical expression in the AIF statement is false. The branch to sequence symbol .FIRST01 will not be taken. The next instruction to be examined is the next sequential instruction in the macro definition (the BALR).

The BALR instruction is examined. It permits substitution of two values. The name field was left blank on the macro call, so the name field is left blank on the BALR instruction; the null character string was substituted for the keyword &NAME. The default value of 12 is substituted for &BASE, and BALR instruction is generated into the source program. The USING instruction is handled in a similar manner.

Had the character string value of NO been given to the parameter SETUP in the macro call statement, a branch around the BALR and USING instructions would have been taken (to the sequence symbol .FIRST01). The assumption made in this case is that the programmer will establish addressability.

The AIF specified in statement 6 checks to see if a pre-execution dump is desired. If DUMP=NO had been specified in the macro call, a branch would have been taken to statement 14 (labeled .FIRST02) in the macro definition. This would avoid other related AIF statements and the generation of the PDUMP instruction.

In our case, however, DUMP=NO was not specified, so the branch to .FIRST02 is not taken. &BEGIN and &END contain the addresses used as the start and end points for the dump. Statements 7 and 10 check to ensure that the programmer has specified these two operands. They are specified, so the PDUMP instruction is generated with the operands AREA and LOC.

Had either or both of these parameters been omitted when the value associated with the symbolic parameter DUMP was YES, special labels ($DBEGIN or $DEND) would be generated on DS   0H instructions, so that the PDUMP instruction would not contain syntax errors. You will notice that MNOTE statements are generated if these special labels have to be generated.

The MNOTE instruction can be used whenever there is a need to generate an error message on the assembler listing to indicate an error encountered within the macro expansion process. The general format of the MNOTE statement under DOS-based systems is as follows:

Name	Operation	Operand
sequence symbol or blank	MNOTE	'message'

The message that appears between the apostrophes in the operand is printed on the listing.

The general format of the MNOTE statement under OS-based systems is:

Name	Operation	Operand
sequence symbol or blank	MNOTE	n,'message'

The *n* in the operand gives the programmer the opportunity to specify a severity code. This code can range from a value of 0 to 255. Under OS-based systems this severity code and the error message are printed with the regular diagnostic error messages portion of the listing. They are also printed on the source listing if the assembler option FLAG(nnn) on the EXECute card that invokes the assembler specifies a value for *n* that is less than the severity code in the MNOTE instruction.[†]

The third basic function provided by code generated by the expansion of the FIRST macro (figure 22-4) is the initialization of the I/O routines. Any of four values can be assigned to the symbolic parameter IO. These values are as follows:

Parameter Value	Meaning
NO	Either I/O will not be used in this control section or the programmer will supply initialization instructions.

[†]For a further explanation of the assembler option FLAG, see *IBM System/370 OS/VS Assembler Programmer's Guide* (GC33-4021), or *IBM System/360 Operating System Assembler* (*E*) *or Assembler* (*F*) *Programmer's Guide* (GC28-6595 and GC26-3756, respectively).

YES	Both input and output will be performed; both the data sets must be initialized (opened).
IONLY	Only input routines are needed, initialize the input data set only.
OONLY	Only output routines are needed; initialize the output data set only.

Statement 14 checks for the NO value. If present, it branches around the macro definition instructions that handle this parameter. The statement branched to by statement 14 gives you another illustration of a use for the ANOP statement.

Statements 17 and 20 are unconditional branch instructions that prevent mutually exclusive groups of model statements from being examined. You would not want to generate OPEN statements that request the same data set be opened twice.

EXIT FROM A MACRO DEFINITION

There is one additional macro instruction that could be used in this macro definition. This is the MEXIT (*Macro Exit*) *instruction*. The MEXIT allows you to specify that the assembler can exit from its processing of the macro definition. The MEND provides this function at the end of the definition but cannot provide it within the body of the macro definition. In the definition of the FIRST macro, statements 17 and 20 could both be changed to MEXIT instructions. There is no processing that remains to be done once one of these points in the definition has been reached, so a MEXIT statement at these points would have the same affect as a branch to the MEND statement.

CONCATENATING SYMBOLIC PARAMETERS

Concatenation is the process of combining the characters represented by a symbolic parameter with other characters (or the characters represented by other symbolic parameters). Some examples of concatenation follow:

```
MACRO
EXAM      &X,&B,&LOC    ⎤
L&X       7,&LOC&B      ⎥  definition
M         6,AREA&B      ⎦
MEND

EXAM      H,2,FIELD     ⎤  call

LH        7,FIELD2      ⎤
                        ⎥  generated
                        ⎥  instructions
M         6,AREA2       ⎦
```

There are some conditions under which the assembler must be notified that concatenation is desired. These are situations in which a symbolic parameter is going to precede a left parenthesis, letter, or digit. The means that the programmer has to notify the assembler of one of these forms of concatenation is to immediately follow the symbolic parameter with a period:

```
MACRO
SHOW    &R,&L,&LOC,&AREA  ┐
L       8,&LOC.(&R)       │  definition
MVC     &AREA.(&L),&LOC+7 │
ST      8,&AREA.2         ┘
MEND

SHOW    2,26,INAREA,FIELD ┐  call

L       8,INAREA(2)       ┐
MVC     FIELD(26),INAREA+7 │  generated
                          │  instructions
ST      8,FIELD2          ┘
```

USE OF ASSEMBLER ATTRIBUTES

The assembler associates attributes with each symbol defined in a source program. These attributes are available to, and can be tested by, the conditional assembly instructions (the AIF) within macro definitions. There are six different kinds of attributes, two of which will be discussed in this section: the *type* and *length attributes*.

Each attribute has a particular letter associated with it. To refer to an attribute, this letter is followed by an apostrophe and the symbolic parameter whose attribute is sought. For example, T'&A refers to the type attribute of the symbolic parameter &A, and L'&B refers to the length attribute of the symbolic parameter &B.

An example of the use of the attributes can be seen in figure 22-5. This macro tests the attributes of two symbols passed as parameters on the macro call and generates the correct instructions to multiply the two values represented by those symbols, placing the product at the storage location specified by the third symbolic parameter.

If the values passed are fullwords, the five instructions beginning at the sequence symbol .WORD are generated. If the values passed occupy halfwords, it's the five instructions beginning at .HALF that are generated. Notice that one of the parameters passed is the symbolic name of an area that the macro definition can use to store the contents of any register(s) it uses. This prevents the programmer from having to remember which registers' contents will be destroyed by each macro he uses. The letters associated with the type attributes you may want to use are as follows.

```
        MACRO
        MULT    &MLTCND,&MLTPR,&PROD,&SAVE
        AIF     (T'&MLTCND   EQ   'F').WORD
        AIF     (T'&MLTCND   EQ   'H').HALF
        MNOTE   12,'PARAMETERS NOT OF ACCEPTABLE TYPE'
        MEXIT
.WORD   STM     4,5,&SAVE .      SAVE CONTENTS OF REGISTERS
        L       5,&MLTCND .      SET UP, AND
        M       4,&MLTPR .       MULTIPLY
        STM     4,5,&PROD .      STORE PRODUCT
        LM      4,5,&SAVE .      RESTORE REGISTERS
        MEXIT
.HALF   ST      4,&SAVE .        SAVE REGISTER CONTENTS
        LH      4,&MLTCND .      SET UP, AND
        MH      4,&MLTPR .       MULTIPLY
        ST      4,&PROD .        STORE PRODUCT
        L       4,&SAVE .        RESTORE REGISTER
        MEND
```

NOTE: The periods in the comments field (immediately following the operand in the generated instructions) serve as the first character in the comment. Without this initial character the comment will follow the operand by one blank. All extraneous blanks are removed when the macro definition is placed in the macro library, in order to conserve space.

Fig. 22-5 Macro definition using assembler attributes

Letter	Type of Constant Represented
A	Address
C	Character
D	Long floating-point
E	Short floating-point
F	Fullword fixed-point
H	Halfword fixed-point
P	Packed Decimal
X	Hexadecimal

The length attribute that the assembler has associated with a particular symbol may be referred to by placing the notation L' in front of a symbolic parameter. A length attribute may be referred to in either an AIF statement or a SETA statement (discussed in the next section). For example, the symbol X12 is defined in the name field of a DC statement for a character constant: X12   DC   CL8'MESSAGE'.

The following AIF statement would branch to the sequence symbol .OK, because the length associated with the symbol X12 (passed as first parameter) is less than 15 bytes:

```
        MACRO
        MSG     &A,&B
        .
        .
        .
        AIF     (L'&A LT '15').OK
        .
        .
        .
        MEND
```

SET SYMBOLS

Up to this point, the only variable symbols that have been used in macro definitions have been symbolic parameters. Symbolic parameters, however, do not allow for much flexibility. They are given one specific value when the macro is called, and the only action taken with them is to substitute their values in the predefined locations within the generated instructions. *Set symbols*, on the other hand, are variable symbols whose values can be altered during the expansion of the macro definition.

DEFINING SET SYMBOLS

Set symbols must first be defined and set to an initial value (using a local-LCL-instruction). They then may be reset to any desired value using a SET instruction. There are three types of set symbols—arithmetic, binary, and character. Each type has its own LCL and SET instruction. The general format for the LCL instructions is:

$$
\text{Blank} \quad \begin{bmatrix} \text{LCLA} \\ \text{LCLB} \\ \text{LCLC} \end{bmatrix} \quad \begin{array}{l} \text{One or more variable} \\ \text{symbols, separated} \\ \text{by commas} \end{array}
$$

Examples of the use of each follow:

a. LCLA &NO
   Defines &NO as an arithmetic SET symbol and sets it to an initial value of zero.

b. LCLB &SW
   Defines &SW as a binary SET symbol and sets it to an initial value of zero.

c. LCLC &STRING

   Defines &STRING as a character SET symbol and sets it to a null character value (length zero).

All LCLA, LCLB and LCLC instructions must be placed at the very beginning of a macro definition, immediately following the prototype statement. Never use SYS as the first three letters of a set symbol, as this prefix is reserved for system use.

Assigning Values to Set Symbols

There is a SET instruction for each type of set symbol; SETA for arithmetic, SETB for binary, and SETC for character. The purpose of a SET instruction is to change the value of the set symbol that appears in the set instructions name field. The set symbol contains its new value until another set instruction is processed with that set symbol in its name field. The operand of the SET instruction contains the new value for the set symbol. Figure 22-6 shows the general formats for the SET instructions.

Expressions in the operands of SETA instructions are evaluated in the same way as those in the operands of assembler language statements. SETA operands, however, may contain only self-defining terms, variable symbols, and length attributes:

```
LCLA     &A1,&A2,&A3,&A4
LCLB     &B1,&B2,&B3
LCLC     &C1,&C2,&C3
```

a. &A1   SETA   8

b. &A2   SETA   &A1+2

   If the set symbol &A1 has the value of 8 given it in (a.) above, &A2 is assigned a value of 10.

c. &A3   SETA   L'&AREA

   &AREA is a symbolic parameter. The length associated with the symbol passed in the macro call for &AREA will be assigned to &A3. (If ABC is passed to a macro and defined as a fullword, &A3 will be assigned a value of 4.)

d. &A4   SETA   (L'&AREA+3)*4

   Parentheses may be used in the expression to override the normal hierarchy for the evaluation of the operators.

The logical expressions contained in the operands of SETB instructions may contain arithmetic relations (any expression considered valid in the operand of

An arithmetic SET symbol	SETA	Arithmetic expression (Maximum of $2^{32}-1$, minimum of -2^{31})
A binary SET symbol	SETB	0 or 1 Logical expression enclosed in parentheses
A character SET symbol	SETC	Type attribute Character expression (may contain up to 255 characters, but only 8 may be assigned to set symbol, except in OS/VS where the assignment is only restricted to the 255 character limit.) A SETA symbol Concatenation of character expressions

Fig. 22-6   General formats for SET instructions

a SETA instruction), character relations (two character values connected by a relational operator), or other SETB symbols:

e. &B1   SETB   1

f. &B2   SETB   (T'&LOC EQ T'&AREA)
The set symbol &B2 will be assigned a value of 1 if the logical expression is true (if the type attributes of the two symbolic parameters are identical), and to 0 if the expression is false.

g. &B3   SETB   ('&LOC' NE 'SAVE')

While a character expression appearing in the operand of a SETC instruction may contain up to 255 characters enclosed in apostrophes, only the first eight are assigned to the SETC symbol (except assemblers in OS/VS, which can have a maximum of 255 characters assigned). Several character expressions may be combined (concatenated) into a single character expression by separating each set of expressions with a period:

h. &C1   SETC   'ABCDEFGHIJK'
The set symbol &C1 is assigned a character value of ABCDEFGH.

i. &C2   SETC   'ABCD'.'EFGH'
&C2 receives the same character value as the set symbol &C1.

j. &C3   SETC   '&LOC'.'+4'

If the symbolic parameter &LOC is set to TAB by the macro call, the set symbol &C3 is assigned a setting of TAB+4.

Figure 22-7 shows a macro definition that uses set symbols.

```
            MACRO
            HDG       &CHARS,&RCD,&CTLCHR
            LCLA      &START,&LGR,&LGC
&START      SETA      (L'&RCD − L'&CHARS)/2+1
&LGR        SETA      L'&RCD−2
&LGC        SETA      L'&CHARS
            MVI       &RCD,C'&CTLCHR' .              CONTROL CHAR TO OUTPUT
            MVI       &RCD+1,C' ' .                  CLEAR OUTPUT AREA TO
            MVC       &RCD+2(&LGR),&RCD+1 .          ALL BLANKS
            MVC       &RCD+&START.(&LGC),&CHARS .    MOVE HEADING
            MEND
```

NOTE: For an explanation of the periods following the operands, see note on figure 22-6.

Fig. 22-7   Macro definition using set symbols

The macro defined in figure 22-7 will generate the code necessary to center a heading in an output area and prepare that output area for printing. The name of the macro is HDG, and it expects three parameters when it is called. The first is the symbolic name of the character string that is to be centered as the heading. This symbol must have a length associated with it equal to the number of characters in the heading to be centered. The second parameter is the symbolic name on the output area. This symbol must also have associated with it a length equal to the number of bytes in the area it represents (the output area). The third parameter, the macro HDG expects, is the control character that the programmer wishes in the first byte of the output area.[†] (See chapter 20 for explanation of control characters.)

ADDING MACRO DEFINITIONS TO A LIBRARY

Under OS and OS/VS systems, the following JCL statements cause the IEBUPDTE utility program to place the macro definition for a macro named

_____

[†]If you desire more information on macros or macro definitions see *OS/VS and DOS/VS Assembler Language* (GC33-4010), *IBM System/360 Disk and Tape Operating Systems, Assembler Language* (GC24-3414), or *IBM System/360 Operating System Assembler Language* (GC28-6514).

FIRST in the data set SYS1.MACLIB, the operating system's macro library:

```
//MACAT      JOB          44444,TUGGLE
//STP1       EXEC         PGM=IEUBUPDTE,PARM=MOD
//SYSUT1     DD           DSN=SYS1.MACLIB,DISP=OLD
//SYSUT2     DD           DSN=SYS1.MACLIB,DISP=OLD
//SYSPRINT   DD           SYSOUT=A
//SYSIN      DD           DATA
./          ADD          LIST=ALL,NAME=FIRST,LEVEL=01,SOURCE=0
            MACRO
&NAME       FIRST        &SETUP=YES,&DUMP=YES,...
            .
            .            body of macro definition
            .
            MEND
./          ENDUP
/*
```

Specifying DD DATA, as above, is similar to specifying DD *, except that the data set indicated by the former may contain statements with slashes (//) in columns 1 and 2. The statements that begin with ./ are control statements to the utility program. Notice that a control statement precedes the macro definition. It tells the utility program to add the macro named in the operand to the library. The name specified in the NAME operand must agree with the one appearing in the opcode field of the macro prototype statement. A utility control statement follows the macro definition and serves to define the end of the input to the utility program.

Under DOS and DOS/VS, a macro definition must be placed into the source statement library, where it can be located at assembly time. JCL statements can be used to direct the set of programs used to maintain and service the system libraries in order to accomplish this. An example follows:

```
//          JOB          TUGGLE CATALOG
//          EXEC         MAINT
            CATALS       A.FIRST
            MACRO
&NAME       FIRST        &SETUP=YES,&DUMP=YES,...
            .
            .            body of macro definition
            .
            MEND
/&
```

The CATALS control statement names the macro and the sublibrary of the source statement library into which the definition should be placed. The A in the operand specifies the assembler sublibrary, and the FIRST specifies the name of the macro. The period serves as a separator. The names specified for the macro on the CATALS and prototype statements must agree.

MACRO QUICK REFERENCE

	INSTRUCTION			See
Name	*Opcode*	*Operand*	*Explanation*	*Page*
b̸	MACRO	b̸	Header Statement, indicates the beginning of a macro definition	416
b̸	MEND	b̸	Trailer Statement, indicates the end of a macro definition	417
symbolic parameter or blank	symbol	zero and more symbolic parameters	Prototype Statement, serves as example for macro call statement, gives name of macro and all expected parameters	417
sequence symbol or blank	ANOP	b̸	No Operation Statement, provides a place to put a sequence symbol which can serve as a target for a branch statement	421
sequence symbol or blank	AIF	(log. expr.)seq.symbol	Conditional Branch Statement, tests a logical expression and, if true, branches to sequence symbol	422
sequence symbol or blank	MNOTE	⎡ n,'message' ⎤ ⎣ 'message' ⎦	Macro Note ('n', severity code specified for OS), provides means to print message on listing from inside the macro definition	425
b̸	MEXIT	b̸	Macro Exit, provides exit from middle of definition rather than at MEND statement	426
b̸	LCLA	one or more set symbols	Defines and initializes (to 0) an arithmetic set symbol	429
b̸	LCLB	one or more set symbols	Defines and initializes (to 0) a binary set symbol	429
b̸	LCLC	one or more set symbols	Defines and initializes (to null) a character set symbol	429
arithmetic set symbol	SETA	arithmetic expression	Assigns a value to an arithmetic set symbol	430
binary set symbol	SETB	⎡ 0 or 1 ⎤ ⎣ logical expression ⎦	Assigns a value to a binary set symbol	431
character set symbol	SETC	⎡ type attribute ⎤ character expression a SETA symbol ⎣ concatenated char. expressions ⎦	Assigns a value to a character set symbol	431

QUESTIONS

1. What is the relation between a macro definition and a macro call?

2. Describe the elements of a macro definition. Use examples in your discussion.

3. How is a macro-generated instruction identified in the assembler source listing?

4. Why is the prototype statement so important to the macro definition?

5. What are the rules for defining a variable symbol?

6. Explain the difference between positional and keyword parameters.

7. When is a default value used for a keyword parameter?

8. Using examples, discuss the difference between symbolic parameters, sequence symbols, and set symbols.

9. Why does the macro language have an ANOP instruction?

10. Give a few examples of situations in which it might be advantageous to use an MNOTE instruction; an MEXIT instruction.

11. What is the length attribute and type attribute of a symbol and how do you test either of them?

12. In concatenating symbolic parameters, when is it necessary to use a period, and under what circumstances is it unnecessary?

13. What use are set symbols in a macro definition?

EXERCISES

1. Find the error in each of the following:

   a. symbolic parameters
   1. &INT*   3. &.LOC
   2. &MORTGAGE   4. &6CENTS

   b. sequence symbols
   1. INAREA   3. .953
   2. .CR BAL   4. .SAVEAREA

2. Code the AIF statements to accomplish the following:

    a. See if the symbolic parameter &A represents a fullword.
    b. See if the value passed for the symbolic parameter &NUM is equal to a value of 12.
    c. Check &SYM for a null value.

3. Define a macro called DIVID that expects five parameters for the divisor, dividend, quotient, remainder, and save area for registers used. Your macro should be able to generate code for either binary or packed-decimal division.

4. Define a macro called TSORT that will sort the elements of a table into ascending order. The parameters your macro should expect are the name of the table, number of elements in the table, and element size.

CHAPTER 23

Coding for Virtual Storage

WHY VIRTUAL STORAGE?

To understand the need for virtual storage, one must understand the characteristics and shortcomings of conventional storage management. Under conventional systems, the programmer must design his program within the confines of the available real storage space. The space needed by the program must be allocated to it in one contiguous piece. No other programs may share that portion of storage.

To complicate this problem, the supervisor and other operating system programs that provide needed facilities take storage space also. Storage tends to become fragmented as it is allocated to various programs for their use. (*Fragmentation* is the condition where there are many unused storage locations, but these are spread out all through storage, and there is no one piece of contiguous storage big enough to meet the current need.) As a result, some storage space becomes unsuitable for use by either user or operating system programs.

Even if we could manage to set up storage so that all programs have the space they need and thus eliminate fragmentation, we would still waste storage. For example, a program may need, and be able to secure, 60,000 bytes of real storage. At any one point in the execution of that program, however, only 10,000 bytes of that storage area may be in use. The remaining, unused, 50,000 bytes are, in effect, wasted.

The key to efficient use of real storage is who, or what, has the responsibility for managing its allocation and use. In conventional operating systems, this responsibility is entrusted to the component least capable of handling it—the programmers, or users of the system. Each user is selfish in his approach to system resource use. He does not consider the overall efficiency of the system; he does not try to optimize the use of the available real storage.

To provide the efficiency necessary for handling real storage space, the responsibility for its allocation and use must be taken *from* the user of the system and designed into the system itself. The virtual storage concept is one such step forward. In discussing virtual storage, we will work our way through various forms (or types) of relocation.

THE CONCEPT OF RELOCATION

When you use COBOL, FORTRAN, or Assembler language, you code in a symbolic language. Your input and output areas are referred to by symbolic names. Your data constants—and even the instructions that you branch to—are referred to by using symbols. The block of space occupied, or defined, by your source program is referred to as a *symbolic name space*. You refer to specific locations of items within this name space by the symbolic names you have given to the items.

As your source program goes through the translation process, real addresses are substituted for symbolic names, changing the block that solves the problem from a symbolic name space to an *address space*. Generally, addresses are assigned contiguously, beginning at location zero (relative to the beginning of the CSECT). The address space is the output of the compiler or assembler; it is referred to as the object module. In the object module, all symbolic references have been translated to addresses.

Object modules, or address spaces, are further resolved or combined with other address spaces by the linkage editor. Once object modules have been handled by the linkage editor, they are ready to be loaded into the computer's storage (real storage) for execution. The loading process involves the allocation of a portion of the computer's storage to the program and placement of the program's address space in this allocated storage space.

There are several ways in which a program's address space can be placed in the computer's storage space for execution. The process, known as *relocation*, involves the translation of addresses in the program's address space to specific locations within the computer's storage. The several ways in which this is accomplished depend on the time (link-edit, load, or execution) at which the translation occurs.

TYPES OF RELOCATION

We will discuss two types of relocation and give examples of each. The two types refer to the point in time at which the relocation process takes place, the time at which the address space of the program is firmly *bound* to actual storage locations. Our further analysis will include:

1. Static relocation, which involves binding by the time the program is loaded.

   Example 1: the stand-alone programs of the 1401
   Example 2: DOS on System/360
   Example 3: OS on System/360

2. Dynamic relocation, which involves binding as the program is executing.

   Example 1: conceptual view of a segmentation system
   Example 2: conceptual view of a segmentation and paging system

STATIC RELOCATION

In explaining static relocation, we begin with an example that involves no relocation. In the case of the 1401, all programs translated for use were loaded into storage, beginning at location one. No changes were made to the addresses in the program's address space as it was loaded into storage. The symbolic name space was translated into an address space with one origin, and this address space was loaded, as is, at storage location one.

Under the Disk Operating System (DOS) on System/360, one intermediate step was added to the 1401 process. The symbolic name space was translated by a compiler or assembler to an address space reflecting an origin of zero; but this address space was processed by another program before being loaded into storage. This program, the linkage editor, bound the address space to actual storage addresses. Under DOS, an address space is not always loaded at location zero. After a program has been link-edited, it is loaded beginning at the address established by the linkage editor. To change this real storage address, the program must be re-link edited, but at least there is a way of doing so.

Under the Operating System (OS) on System/360, the binding time has been moved to an even later point in the time line for execution of a program. The program still goes through a link edit step, but the address space is not bound to actual storage locations at this point. The linkage editor can be used to combine several address spaces (object modules) into one larger block or address space. But even this larger address space is still relocatable. All the addresses are specified in relation to zero; but this zero is relative to the beginning of the load module, rather than to any one of the object modules. All addresses are still unbound. It is not until the program is actually loaded into the computer's storage that the addresses in the address space are bound to actual storage addresses.

Under this relocation system, the program, once loaded, is bound to its particular real storage location until it finishes execution. This system is much more efficient than either the 1401 or DOS system at allocating storage space, but, being static or fixed, it still has no way of compensating for gross inefficiencies that may arise once execution has begun. There is no way to move a program around in storage during the execution of that program. Thus the need for dynamic relocation, which is the very foundation for the virtual storage concept.

DYNAMIC RELOCATION

Dynamic relocation switches the time of binding to its latest possible point. The addresses when the program is loaded are relative ones. It is not until a portion of the program is actually needed, at execution time, that these relative addresses are translated into absolute real storage locations.

This late time of relocation requires the presence of a special hardware facility called *Dynamic Address Translation* (DAT). Since this DAT facility translates addresses automatically at the moment of execution, the program's address space is never bound to real storage addresses. Thus the program can be moved to different storage locations as it is executing. This permits compensating actions by the operating system at execution time; such actions are simply not available in a static relocation system.

Two other techniques for managing storage become important when the system uses dynamic relocation: (1) segmentation, which involves dividing a program's address space into one or more variable-size segments; and (2) paging, where the segments are divided into one or more smaller fixed size units called pages.

Conceptual View of a Segmentation System   Under static relocation systems, a program cannot be executed until contiguous storage sufficient to accept the entire address space of the program is available. For example, a program may require 40K (K = 1024 bytes) of storage, and there may be more than that available and ready for use; but if, because of fragmentation, there is no contiguous 40K block of storage available, the program cannot be loaded. Subdividing the 40K address space into smaller parts, or segments, could make it possible to use the fragments of real storage space that are available.

Assume that the 40K address space is divided into three segments of 16K, 12K, and 12K by the operating system. The largest contiguous real storage space that is needed now is 16K—a good deal smaller than the original 40K. The three segments are loaded into storage with all the addresses in each segment remaining relative addresses (relative to the beginning of that particular segment). These relative addresses are resolved by the DAT feature.

To understand how the DAT facility resolves addresses at execution time, let us examine the two things it has to work with: (1) the *segment table* for the program (a table which has the function of mapping segment origins in real storage), and (2) the relative addresses within the program.

As each of the segments of a program's address space is loaded into real storage, an entry is made in the segment table. This entry contains an identifier as to which segment this is, within the total address space (segment number), and the beginning real storage address of this segment. For our example program, let us take a conceptual look at the segment table containing entries for the three segments after the program has been loaded:

Segment Table

Segment Number	Real Storage Location
1	20,000
2	65,000
3	92,500

Each relative address within the program, instead of taking the form of a real storage address, is represented as a segment number and the displacement within that segment of the item to be addressed. For the following examples, let us assume that the relative address takes the form:

segment no.	displacement

Remember that the addresses that appear in each segment are related only to that segment; they are relative to the origin of the segment. They do not reflect the real storage addresses of the locations in which they are loaded. Relative addresses for data outside of a given segment contain the segment number where the data may be located. The translation process accomplished by the DAT facility involves the following steps:

1. A relative address is encountered as the program is executing.
2. The segment number portion of the relative address is used by the DAT to locate within the segment table the real storage location of the beginning of that segment.
3. The displacement from the relative address is added to the real storage location from the segment table to calculate the absolute address.

Using the segment table established for the three segments of our original 40K address space, the relative address

translates to an absolute address of 68,500 (as shown on the following page).

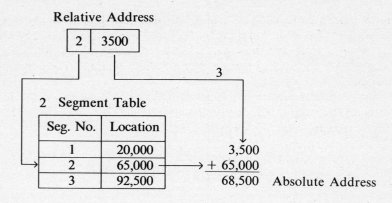

Relative Address

2 Segment Table

Seg. No.	Location
1	20,000
2	65,000
3	92,500

Try your hand at translating the following relative addresses:

a. | 3 | 1,350 |

b. | 1 | 12,764 |

c. | 1 | 8,626 |

Your results should be a. 93,850; b. 32,764; and c. 28,626.

This type of addressing structure permits the operating system to move segments as a program is executing and then update the segment table to reflect the new origins of the segments. All addresses within a segment are relative to the beginning of that segment; therefore, no changes need be made internal to the segment.

One other item within the hardware that makes dynamic address translation possible is called the *Segment Table Origin Register* (STOR). We have discussed the dynamic relocation of just one 40K program, but more than one program is in real storage at any given point in time. The STOR always points to the origin of the segment table for the program that is currently being executed. To change the program that is currently being executed (should some pause be required, for example, to allow an I/O request to be serviced) requires only that the contents of the STOR be changed, thus allowing the dynamic translation of addresses within a different program.

Conceptual View of a Segmentation and Paging System Segmentation and dynamic address translation help to alleviate some of the waste caused by fragmentation, but a much better solution is yet to be discussed. This better solution involves the division of each segment into smaller units called *pages*, which are uniform in size.

The programmer's only responsibility is to design his symbolic name space. The operating system software divides it into segments, subdivides the segments into pages, and builds the segment table, page tables, and all of the relative addresses. All of actual storage is divided into page-size pieces called *page frames*. At load time, pages are loaded into the first available page frames, and the tables are set to reflect their addresses. During execution, the system hardware (DAT facility) automatically translates the relative addresses to absolute ones.

To implement a segmentation scheme complete with paging, an additional portion is added to the structure of the relative address, and a page table is used as a supplement to the segment table.

segment number	page number	displacement

The segment table in this type of implementation contains the origins of the page tables for the various segments, rather than the real storage locations of the origins of the segments. Figure 23-1 shows how this structure looks in illustration form. Our original three-segment program is divided into 4K pages.

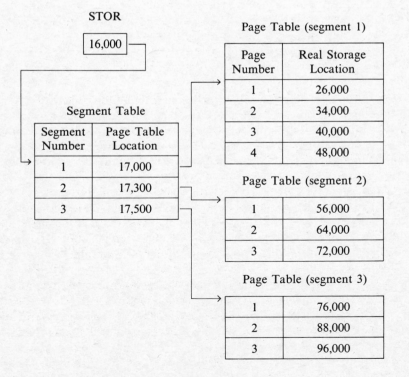

Fig. 23-1 Segment and page-addressing structure

The relative address

3	2	1,736

translates to the real storage location 89,736 (88,000 + 1,736). The STOR locates the beginning of the segment table. The first portion of the relative address, the 3, is used to locate the beginning of the correct page table (17,500). The second portion of the relative address, the 2, is used to locate the real storage location of the origin of the page (88,000) that contains the location that the relative address is referencing. The displacement from the relative address (1,736) is added to the origin of the page from the page table to calculate the absolute address.

Try your hand at calculating the absolute addresses from the following relative addresses (use the preceding segment and page tables):

a.	3	3	3,333
b.	1	4	768
c.	1	3	2,500

Your resulting addresses should be: a. 99,333; b. 48,768; and c. 42,500.

VIRTUAL STORAGE

Virtual storage enables a program to acquire an address space that is larger than the amount of real storage space available on the computer. A computer with a 24-bit address structure has the capability of addressing approximately 16 million bytes. This is the theoretical limit on the size of the System/370 storage. Yet, real storage on the majority of systems doesn't even approach this size.

Since virtual can be much larger than real storage, there is no way to place the entire virtual address space in storage at one time. Therefore the large address space that represents virtual storage is divided into page-size pieces, and these page-size pieces are stored in auxiliary storage called *external-page storage*. The divisions of this type of auxiliary storage are called *slots*, and each slot will hold one page.

In order to be executed, instructions and all data they refer to must be in real storage. Since all pages of virtual storage will not fit in the real storage space, the concept of *demand paging* is used. The theory behind this concept is that when an instruction in real storage makes a reference to either an instruction or data not in real storage, the page containing it is brought into storage. The DAT facility recognizes when this condition exists by its encounter of a relative address that translates to a location within a page not currently residing in real storage.

How does the DAT feature know that a particular page does not currently reside in real storage? An indicator is added to each entry in a page table. Its function is to indicate whether a given page resides in real storage or not. If it does not reside in real storage when a demand is encountered for it by DAT, it must be paged into an available page frame of real storage.

How does the system know whether or not a page frame in real storage is available? It has a table of information called the *page-frame table*. All of real storage is divided into pages of equal size. There is one entry in the page-frame table for each page frame that exists. It contains information such as the number of the page frame; a status indicating whether the page frame is available or not; if it is occupied, the program ID, the segment and page number of the page in the frame, and some extra indications noting not only the activity involving this page frame, but also the type of that activity.

Once a page frame into which the desired page may be loaded has been located, how does the system know which slot in external-page storage that page occupies? You guessed it—another set of tables, *external-page tables*. In fact, there is an external-page table that corresponds to each internal-page one.

Let us see just how all of this new structure works. First, let's examine the process the DAT feature goes through in determining that it is translating an address for a page that does not reside in real storage. We will take two relative addresses—one that translates to a location within a page currently in real storage, and one that translates to a location within a page currently in external-page storage. The following are examples of virtual addresses (similar to segment and page relative addresses):

a. | 1 | 1 | 2,600 |
b. | 1 | 2 | 1,324 |

The virtual addressing structure is illustrated in figure 23-2.

The two states of the indicator bit added to each page entry are:

0 indicates page is in real storage
1 indicates page is in external-page storage

The first virtual address (a) translates to a real storage address of 66,600. The second virtual address, however, cannot be translated; the indicator bit is a one. Even if there had been an address in the page frame location portion of that entry, it could not have been used. This condition is referred to as a *page fault*. What must happen now is that the needed page must be loaded into a real storage page frame from its slot in external page storage. This requires several steps:

1. A page frame of real storage must be selected to hold the needed page.
2. The needed page must be located in the external-page storage.

Segment Table   Page Table

Segment Number	Page Table Location		Page Number	Real Storage Location	Indicator Bit
1	56,000	→	1	64,000	0
2	57,000		2		1
			3	76,000	0
		→	1	84,000	0
			2	92,000	1

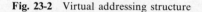

Fig. 23-2 Virtual addressing structure

3. A copy of the needed page must be moved from its slot in external-page storage to the selected page frame location in real storage.
4. The page table and the page frame table entries for this page must be changed to reflect the move made in step 3.
5. The virtual address is translated.
6. Regular execution is resumed.

The following is an explanation of the six steps involved in resolving the second virtual address. (See figure 23-3.)

Step 1: A search is made of the page-frame table. A zero status indicates available, and a status of one indicates filled. Page frame 4 is found to be available to hold the needed page, since its status bit contains a zero.

Step 2: The entry in the external-page table that corresponds to the entry in the page table indicated by the virtual address (2) is used to find the location of the page slot in which page 2 of segment 1 of our program is stored in external-page storage.

Step 3: A copy of the page is moved from its slot in external-page storage to frame 4 of real storage.

Step 4: The fourth entry in the page frame table is changed to reflect this move:

4	A	1	2	1

The page table for segment 1 of our program is changed to reflect

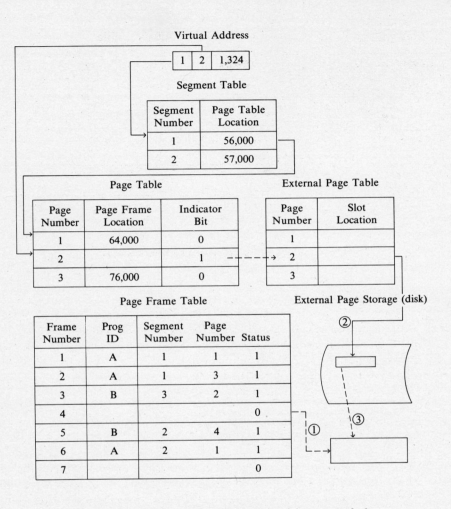

Fig. 23-3   Translation of virtual address involving a page fault

the fact that this page is now residing in real storage—and *where* it is residing, page frame 4.

1	64,000	0
2	72,000	0
3	76,000	0

Step 5: The virtual address is now translated to 73,324.
Step 6: Execution continues.

Suppose Step 1 encountered a situation in which all of the page frames in the system were in use when our page needed to be loaded. This would require some additional logic in Step 1. A determination would have to be made as to which of the pages now occupying the page frames had been referenced the least recently—it would be the best choice to be replaced.

An additional check would have to be made to see whether or not the contents of this page had been changed while it was residing in real storage. If no changes had been made to the page, the copy of this page, still stored in a slot of external-page storage, is still good. If changes have been made to it, the page stored in the slot of external-page storage is no longer valid; a copy of the changed page from the page frame must be moved (paged-out) to update its corresponding slot in external-page storage, before moving (paging-in) the newly demanded page into the page frame currently occupied. This is done to ensure that the slots of external-page storage always contain the most recent contents of pages not currently residing in real storage.[†]

CODING PRACTICES FOR VIRTUAL STORAGE

A programmer using a conventional static storage system usually tries his best to conserve the amount of real storage space he uses, as well as to improve the speed of the execution of his program. A programmer using a virtual storage system, on the other hand, does not have to worry about the amount of storage he uses, but he should still be concerned with the execution speed. How he designs the various parts of his program can have a great effect on how efficiently real storage space can be managed and thus the amount of waiting the program will experience during execution.

The programmer who uses virtual storage can gain efficiency by thoroughly considering the flow of logic through and between the various routines or portions of his program. This involves the placement of sections of code within his program, rather than control of the overall size of it. The most important goal for today's programmer is the minimization of page faults, and thus paging.

One of the best ways to minimize page faults is to change your habits for defining the data that your program uses. Instead of separating all the data definition statements in your program from your executing instructions, define data as close to the instructions that reference it as practical, considering that more than one section of your code may be making references.

If possible, avoid unnecessary accesses to storage areas for data. For example, use a BCTR instruction to reduce the contents of a register by a value of 1, rather than subtracting a value of 1 that you have defined somewhere else

---

[†]For further information on virtual storage concepts and information on the implementation of virtual storage by the various operating systems, see the IBM publication, *Introduction to Virtual Storage in System/370* (GR20-4260).

in storage. Use the LA instruction and the machine's ability to perform address arithmetic to increment the contents of a register by a value ranging up to 4095 (i.e., LA 6,1(6)). This prevents the need to access data in storage as part of an addition operation.

Do not be afraid to use virtual storage space. It is better to define a large direct-access table and be able to make a reference to a particular data item with one instruction than it is to pack data into a small amount of space and then have to make a serial search for a particular data item. The amount of space that a table occupies is not as important as the number of accesses to storage that are necessary to use the information stored in it.

If there is no way to avoid a serial search, arrange your search so that you are accessing items in the sequence in which they are stored. For example, if you are referencing a table which you defined row by row, reference it in that order, rather than column-wise. The point here is to avoid searching for data in storage, if possible; but if you must search, do it sequentially.

This sequential processing concept should be applied to executable instructions, as well as to data. Subprograms, for instance, if short and used only once or twice during the normal execution of your program, should be coded inline. Again, the emphasis is on less page faults at the expense of more use of virtual storage space. This emphasis applies to all routines that are executed in the normal sequence of instruction execution.

Error handling and exceptional condition handling routines do not belong in normal logic sequence. These routines are executed infrequently—generally when the normal execution of instructions has been broken. Since they occupy real storage needlessly (much of the time) if coded inline, they should be coded as subprograms. Then, generally, they occupy real storage only when the unusual conditions they handle occur.

Minimizing the amount of real storage needed by each program in the system allows more programs to be executing at one time. Break your routine into small modules (about 2048 bytes is best, as a maximum size, for DOS/VS and OS/VS1, and 4096 bytes for OS/VS2); have everything necessary for the execution of the instructions within that module inside that module. Just remember, the whole point in coding for virtual storage is not to minimize the amount of real storage that your program uses, but to pack as much related code and data as practical into this minimum (page-sized) space as possible.

QUESTIONS

1. What does it mean when storage is fragmented?

2. Discuss the difference between symbolic name space and address space.

3. What is the difference between a segment and a page?

4. What is the DAT facility, and how is the STOR used?

5. Discuss virtual storage and its advantages.

6. What is a page fault, and how is it handled?

7. Is a programmer using virtual storage concerned with the speed with which his program executes?

8. Why shouldn't all DC and DS statements be collected in one location at the end of the machine instructions when using virtual storage?

EXERCISES

1. Using the information provided in the tables on the opposite page, translate the following virtual addresses:

   a. | 2 | 3 | 2,000 |

   b. | 1 | 2 | 1,84A |

   c. | 1 | 1 | 650 |

   d. | 2 | 2 | 12 |

   e. | 2 | 4 | 1,4B3 |

Segment Table
(address 30,000)

Segment Number	Page Table Location
1	36,000
2	40,000

Page Table
(address 36,000)

Page Number	Page Frame Location	Indicator Bit
1	54,000	0
2	60,000	0

Page Table
(address 40,000)

Page Number	Page Frame Location	Indicator Bit
1		1
2	50,000	0
3	64,000	0
4	46,000	0

The FIRST, LAST, MREAD, and MRITE Macros

The following macros provide support of the input and output functions, establishment of addressability, and provision for dumps—both before and after execution. The various functions of the macros are written in such a way that they relieve the beginning assembler language programmer of the burden of mastering these areas of programming before he can use them.

All operands of the four macros that provide these functions are keyword parameters. This means that each parameter is specified by coding a string of characters that the assembler will recognize as a legitimate operand identifier for a particular macro instruction. Each keyword is followed by an equals sign ($=$) and the parameter you wish to specify. Because the assembler recognizes the specific combination of characters that make up the keyword, it does not matter in what order the keywords appear in the operand.

When using these macros, keep in mind that most of the keyword parameters have *defaults*. If the programmer chooses not to specify a particular operand, the default will be used. The functions are listed below, with the parameters of the various macros that invoke these functions. The defaults, if available, are underlined.

DYNAMIC DUMPS BEFORE AND AFTER EXECUTION

FIRST macro
    DUMP = YES or NO
    BEGIN = $DBEGIN or symbol
    END = $DEND or symbol+constant

LAST macro
    DUMP = YES or NO
    BEGIN = $DBEGIN or symbol
    END = $DEND or symbol+constant

If the programmer does not wish dumps to be provided, he merely specifies DUMP=NO in the operand of either the FIRST macro (to prevent the before execution dump), or the LAST macro (to prevent the after execution dump), or both, if neither is required.

The programmer who wants a dump supplies two operands, BEGIN=symbol and END=symbol+constant. The symbol specified in the BEGIN operand is usually the one associated with the first DC or DS instruction in the program. In the END operand the programmer specifies the symbol associated with the last DC or DS instruction. This symbol is followed by a plus sign (+) which is followed by the constant that represents the length in bytes, of the area defined by the last DC or DS. These two locations are used as the beginning and ending points for the dump. (Make sure the address represented by the symbol in the END operand is larger than the address represented by the symbol in the BEGIN operand.)

Since the FIRST macro generates the code that produces the dump before execution and the LAST macro the code that produces the dump after execution, these operands are generally specified in the same way in both cases. The DUMP operand need not be specified when dumps are desired, because the default in the case of both macros is YES.

The defaults of $DBEGIN and $DEND for the BEGIN and END parameters, respectively, are used to prevent an error condition. If the programmer makes the mistake of not specifying any of these three parameters, the default of YES for the DUMP keyword will cause the code for a dump to be generated. If this should occur, the symbols $DBEGIN and $DEND will be generated as labels within the macro generated code. These will be used as the beginning and ending points for the dump. The result will be that no storage contents will be dumped, but at least the dump program will not come to an abnormal end (ABEND).

ESTABLISHING ADDRESSABILITY

FIRST macro
SETUP = YES or NO
BASE = 12 or register number

At first, the student programmer need not even be aware that there is anything such as addressability to worry about. He simply does not specify either of these operands. Register 12 will be established as the base register, and the BALR instruction to properly load register 12 at execution time will be generated using the defaults.

If the programmer wishes to establish his own addressability once he has learned to handle this responsibility, he makes this desire known to the assembler by specifying SETUP=NO. If, for some reason the programmer does not wish to establish his own addressability, but does not want the generated code to use register 12 as the base register, the base register can be changed by specifying the desired register number in the BASE operand of the FIRST macro.

THE INPUT AND OUTPUT FUNCTION

```
FIRST macro
   IO = NO, YES, IONLY, or OONLY
LAST macro
   ASMDATA = YES or NO
   I = NO or YES
   O = NO or YES
   EOFRTN = NONE or symbol
MREAD macro
   INTO = symbol
MRITE macro
   FROM = symbol
```

For the sake of simplicity, both the input and output files are physical sequential in nature. The MREAD macro provides the input function and the MRITE macro the output function. Should the programmer not want the input and output functions, he need specify nothing. The MREAD and MRITE macros are not used, and the defaults of the IO and ASMDATA operands ensure that no code is generated to provide the functions of input and output.

If the I/O functions are desired, several operands have to be specified. Specifying IO=YES in the operand portion of the FIRST macro causes the code to be generated that initializes both the input and output routines. If only one I/O function is desired, code either IONLY or OONLY.

ASMDATA=NO must be specified in the operand of the LAST macro to indicate that all the data this program uses is not generated by the assembler in the form of DC and DS statements—some data will either be read from an input device (I=YES) or written on an output device (O=YES). Specifying either I=YES or O=YES, or both, will cause all the code to be generated to describe the data set(s) and the code to perform the actual I/O operation.

The output data set resides on the printer. Because the output data will be printed, the area from which a record will be written must be 121 characters in length. The first character of the area will be used as a carriage-control character. The characters that will be expected for control of the vertical spacing of the printer are as follows:

1	Eject to top of next page before printing line
ƀ	(blank) advance to next line before printing
0	Double space before printing
+	Don't advance the paper before printing

These control characters are those approved by the American National Standards Institute.

The input data comes from the card reader. The area into which the input record is read must be large enough to hold all 80 characters from the card, regardless of whether all 80 are used in the program.

One other thing must be specified for the input file. This is the symbolic label on the instruction that is to be given control when the end of the file is encountered. This symbol must be specified in the EOFRTN parameter. If there is no operation that must be performed when end of file is encountered, place a label in the name field of the LAST macro and specify this symbol as the EOFRTN parameter.

Whenever you desire to have a record read from the card file, place the MREAD macro at that location within your program and specify the parameter INTO=symbol. The symbol is the label assigned to your 80-byte input area. To specify that you wish a record written on the printer, place the MRITE macro with the parameter FROM=symbol in the desired location. The symbol you specify must be the label on a 121-byte output area.

Both of these macros cause instructions to be generated that will branch to a routine within the code generated by the LAST macro, which handles the specified input or output function. The programmer can expect that the record has already been read or written when his next sequential instruction after the MREAD or MRITE macro executes.

> **Note: When using any of these four macros, don't use registers 0, 1, or 11–15 for any purpose within your code! The generated code produced by the macros may destroy the contents of these registers.**

Figures A1-1 through A1-4 are printouts of the FIRST, LAST, MREAD, and MRITE macros for a DOS-based system; figures A1-5 and A1-6 are printouts of the FIRST and LAST macros for an OS-based system. Be sure that you use the macro definitions for your particular operating system.

```
              MACRO
&NAME         FIRST  &SETUP=YES,&DUMP=YES,&BASE=12,&BEGIN=$DBEGIN,        X
                     &END=$DEND,&IO=NO
              AIF    ('&SETUP' EQ 'NO').FIRST01
&NAME         BALR   &BASE,0
              USING  *,&BASE
.FIRST01      AIF    ('&DUMP' EQ 'NO').FIRST02
              AIF    ('&BEGIN' NE '$DBEGIN').FIRST12
              MNOTE  'NO BEGIN SPECIFIED FOR PDUMP-$DBEGIN GENERATED'
$DBEGIN       DS     0H
.FIRST12      AIF    ('&END' NE '$DEND').FIRST13
              MNOTE  'NO END SPECIFIED FOR PDUMP-$DEND GENERATED'
$DEND         DS     0H
.FIRST13      PDUMP  &BEGIN,&END
.FIRST02      AIF    ('&IO' EQ 'NO').FIRST03
              AIF    ('&IO' NE 'IONLY').FIRST42
              OPEN   $CARD
              AGO    .FIRST03
.FIRST42      AIF    ('&IO' NE 'OONLY').FIRST43
              OPEN   $LINE
              AGO    .FIRST03
.FIRST43      OPEN   $CARD,$LINE
.FIRST03      ANOP
              MEND
```

Fig. A1-1 The FIRST macro for a DOS-based system

```
              MACRO
&NAME         LAST   &DUMP=YES,&BEGIN=$DBEGIN,&END=$DEND,&ASMDATA=YES,    X
                     &EOFRTN=NONE,&I=NO,&O=NO
              AIF    ('&DUMP' EQ 'NO').LAST01
&NAME         PDUMP  &BEGIN,&END
              AGO    .LAST31
.LAST01       ANOP
&NAME         DS     0H
.LAST31       AIF    ('&I' EQ 'NO').LAST11
              CLOSE  $CARD
.LAST11       AIF    ('&O' EQ 'NO').LAST21
              CLOSE  $LINE
.LAST21       ANOP
.LAST02       EOJ
              AIF    ('&ASMDATA' EQ 'YES').LAST05
              AIF    ('&I' EQ 'NO').LAST03
              AIF    ('&EOFRTN' EQ 'NONE').LAST04
$CARD         DTFCD  DEVADDR=SYSIPT,                                      X
                     DEVICE=2501,                                        X
                     IOAREA1=$INPUT,                                     X
                     WORKA=YES,                                          X.
                     EOFADDR=&EOFRTN
$INPUT        DS     20F
$READ         LA     1,$CARD
              GET    (1),(0)
              BR     11
.LAST03       AIF    ('&O' EQ 'NO').LAST05
$LINE         DTFPR  DEVADDR=SYSLST,                                     X
                     IOAREA1=$OUTPUT1,                                   X
                     IOAREA2=$OUTPUT2,                                   X
                     CTLCHR=ASA,                                         X
                     WORKA=YES
$OUTPUT1      DS     CL121
$OUTPUT2      DS     CL121
$WRITE        LA     1,$LINE
              PUT    (1),(0)
              BR     11
              MEXIT
.LAST04       MNOTE  '*** EOFRTN= MUST BE SPECIFIED FOR INPUT FILE.'
.LAST05       ANOP
              MEND
```

Fig. A1-2 The LAST macro for a DOS-based system

```
          MACRO
&NAME     MREAD  &INTO=
          AIF    ('&INTO' NE '').MREADOK
          MNOTE   '*** KEYWORD INTO= NOT SPECIFIED - CRITICAL ERROR **'
          MEXIT
.MREADOK  ANOP
&NAME     LA     0,&INTO
          BAL    11,$READ
          MEND
```

Fig. A1-3 The MREAD macro for a DOS-based system

```
          MACRO
&NAME     MRITE  &FROM=
          AIF    ('&FROM' NE '').MRITEOK
          MNOTE   '*** KEYWORD FROM= NOT SPECIFIED - CRITICAL ERROR **'
          MEXIT
.MRITEOK  ANOP
&NAME     LA     0,&FROM
          BAL    11,$WRITE
          MEND
```

Fig. A1-4 The MRITE macro for a DOS-based system

```
          MACRC
&NAME     FIRST  &SETUP=YES,&DUMP=YES,&BASE=12,&BEGIN=$DBEGIN,        X
                 &END=$DEND,&IO=NO
          AIF    ('&SETUP' EQ 'NO').FIRST01
&NAME     BALR   &BASE,0
          USING  *,&BASE
.FIRST01  AIF    ('&DUMP' EQ 'NO').FIRST02
          AIF    ('&BEGIN' NE '$DBEGIN').FIRST12
          MNOTE  1,'NO BEGIN SPECIFIED FOR PDUMP-$DBEGIN GENERATED'
$DBEGIN   DS     OH
.FIRST12  AIF    ('&END' NE '$DEND').FIRST13
          MNOTE  1,'NO END SPECIFIED FOR PDUMP-$DEND GENERATED'
$DEND     DS     OH
.FIRST13  SNAP   PDATA=(REGS),STORAGE=(&BEGIN,&END),DCB=SNAPDCB
.FIRST02  AIF    ('&IO' EQ 'NO').FIRST03
          AIF    ('&IO' NE 'IONLY').FIRST42
          OPEN   (DCBIN)
          AGO    .FIRST03
.FIRST42  AIF    ('&IO' NE 'OONLY').FIRST43
          OPEN   (DCBOUT,(OUTPUT))
          AGO    .FIRST03
.FIRST43  OPEN   (DCBIN,,DCBOUT,(OUTPUT))
.FIRST03  ANOP
          MEND
```

Fig. A1-5 The FIRST macro for an OS-based system

```
          MACRO
&NAME     LAST    &DUMP=YES,&BEGIN=$DBEGIN,&END=$DEND,&ASMDATA=YES,        X
                  &EOFRTN=NONE,&I=NO,&O=NO
          STM    14,12,12(13)
          BALR   12,0                          LOAD ADDR OF NSI INTO REG 12
          USING  *,12                          SET UP BASE REG.
          ST     13,$SAVE+4
          LA     15,$SAVE
          ST     15,8(13)
          LR     13,15
*
          AIF    ('&DUMP' EQ 'NO').LAST01
&NAME     SNAP   PDATA=(REGS),STORAGE=(&BEGIN,&END),DCB=SNAPDCB
          AGO    .LAST31
.LAST01   ANOP
&NAME     DS     0H
.LAST31   AIF    ('&I' EQ 'NO').LAST11
          CLOSE  (DCBIN)
.LAST11   AIF   ('&O' EQ 'NO').LAST21
          CLOSE  (DCBOUT)
.LAST21   ANOP
.LAST02   L      13,$SAVE+4
          LM     14,12,12(13)
          BR     14
          AIF    ('&ASMDATA' EQ 'YES').LAST05
          AIF    ('&I' EQ 'NO').LAST03
          AIF    ('&EOFRTN' EQ 'NONE').LAST04
DCBIN     DCB    DSORG=PS,DDNAME=READIN,MACRF=GM,BLKSIZE=80,               X
                 LRECL=80,RECFM=F,EODAD=&EOFRTN

$READ     LA     1,DCBIN
          GET    (1),(0)
          BR     11
.LAST03   AIF    ('&O' EQ 'NO').LAST05
DCBOUT    DCB    DSORG=PS,DDNAME=PRINT,MACRF=PM,BLKSIZE=121,               X
                 LRECL=121,RECFM=FA
$WRITE    LA     1,DCBOUT
          PUT    (1),(0)
          BR     11
SNAPDCB   DCB    DSORG=PS,RECFM=VBA,MACRF=W,BLKSIZE=1632,                  X
                 LRECL=125,DDNAME=SNAPDD
$SAVE     DC     18F'0'
          MEXIT
.LAST04   MNOTE  16,'*** EOFRTN= MUST BE SPECIFIED FOR INPUT FILE.'
.LAST05   ANOP
          MEND
```

Fig. A1-6   The LAST macro for an OS-based system

Answers to Selected Chapter Exercises

Chapter 1

1. 6, C, +, blank

Chapter 2

1. See figure A2-1.
3. See figure A2-2.
5. See figure A2-3.

Chapter 3

1. Valid   a, d, i
   Invalid   b, c, f, and g; all contain special characters (%, +, ', and blank, respectively)
   Invalid   e; contains too many characters
   Invalid   g; does not begin with alphabetic character

Chapter 4

1. a. 10000_2 c. 101100_2 e. 11101011111100_2
   g. 1001111_2
2. a. 75_{16} c. $1565B_{16}$
3. c. 428_{10} e. 2175_{10}
4. b. 10011010_2
5. a. 11011111_2 d. $9D565_{16}$
   b. $ACF9_{16}$ e. 10001100_2
   c. 10011000_2 f. $6C7A_{16}$

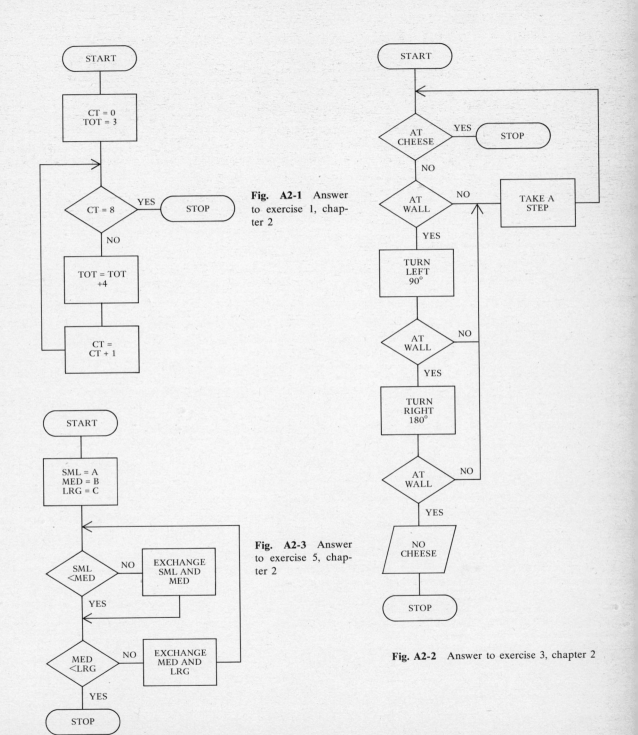

Fig. A2-1 Answer to exercise 1, chapter 2

Fig. A2-3 Answer to exercise 5, chapter 2

Fig. A2-2 Answer to exercise 3, chapter 2

Chapter 5

1. a. FULL: 0000004E
               fwb

   d. HERE: GGGGGGGG (Garbage, not initialized)
               fwb

2. c. THRE   DC H'−58'

3. a. 5   b. 4   c. 5

   d. 8 (while the characters are not placed in storage, the number of characters are used to establish the length)

Chapter 6

2. MVC   LOC+8(4),LOC
               or
   L   6,LOC
   ST   6,LOC+8

4. REG10:   FFFF9865
   AREA: 00 00 00 C2 C3 52 98 65 00 F4 C2 C3
              fwb

5. MVI   PLACE,C' '
   MVC   PLACE+1(122),PLACE

Chapter 7

1. After D   REG2: 00000004   REG3: 00000005
   After MR   REG2: 00000000   REG3: 00000019

3.
```
        LH   7,DIVDND    6784
        M    6,ONE
        D    6,EIGHT     6784/8
        LH   3,TWO3      23
        M    2,EIGHT     23 * 8
        SR   7,3         6784/8 − 23*8
        ST   7,ANSW
         .
         .
         .
DIVDND  DC   H'6784'
ONE     DC   F'1'
EIGHT   DC   F'8'
TWO3    DC   H'23'
ANSW    DS   F
```

7.
```
        LH   7,LNGTH
        MH   7,WIDTH
        M    6,HIGHT     AREA IN TANK
        D    6,GALON     NUMBER OF GALLONS
        ST   7,ANS
```

```
                    .
                    .
    LNGTH    DC   H'22'
    WIDTH    DC   H'12'
    HIGHT    DC   F'7'
    GALON    DC   F'231'
    ANS      DS   F
```

Chapter 8

1. b. LOC: 000000000003801F
   e. LOC: 000000000000126D
      FLD: F0F0F0F0F0F1F2D6

3.
```
            CSECT
            PRINT   NOGEN
            FIRST   BEGIN=FOUR,END=SIX+4,IO=YES
            MREAD   INTO=INAREA            READ A AND B
            PACK    PA,A                   PACK A
            PACK    PB,B                   PACK B
            CVB     5,PA                   REG5 = A
            CVB     7,PB                   REG7 = B
            LR      3,5                    REG3 = A
            MH      3,FOUR                 REG3 = 4A
            MR      4,7                    REG5 = AB
            M       4,SIX                  REG5 = 6AB
            MR      6,7                    REG7 = B * B
            AR      3,5                    4A + 6AB
            SR      3,7                    4A + 6AB − B*B
            CVD     3,PANS
            UNPK    ANS,PANS
            MVZ     ANS+7(1),ANS+6
            MRITE   FROM=OAREA
    END     LAST    BEGIN=FOUR,END=SIX+4,I=YES,             X
                    O=YES,EOFRTN=END,ASMDATA=NO
    FOUR    DC      H'4'
    INAREA  DS      0CL80
            DS      2C
    A       DS      CL5
            DS      12C
    B       DS      CL3
            DS      58C
    OAREA   DS      0CL121
    CTLCHR  DC      C'1'
            DC      C'THE RESULT IS     '
    ANS     DS      CL8
            DC      CL96' '
    PA      DS      D
    PB      DS      D
    PANS    DS      D
    SIX     DC      F'6'
            END
```

Chapter 9

1. a. D1: 65283C   c. D3: 865D
3. Receiving field does not contain sufficient bytes to hold the product. A large enough receiving area can be defined and the contents of AREA moved into the receiving area by a ZAP instruction.

Chapter 10

1. a. 45A5C320
   d. C4BFA0CA
   f. 422AA05DB76B3BB8

Chapter 11

1. a. six times   c. two times

```
3.              CSECT
                PRINT   NOGEN
                FIRST   BEGIN=IN,END=ONE+4,IO=YES
                MREAD   INTO=IN              READ N
                MVC     NUM2(3),NUM          MOVE N FOR OUTPUT
                PACK    PN,NUM               PACK N
                CVB     7,PN                 N IN BINARY
                LR      5,7                  SET UP LOOP CONTROL
                S       5,ONE                PREPARE FOR MULT.
        AGAIN   MR      7,5
                BCT     5,AGAIN              FACTORIAL CALC.
                CVD     7,PFACT              YES, PREPARE
                UNPK    FACT,PFACT             FOR OUTPUT
                MVZ     FACT+7(1),FACT+8     FIX LOW-ORDER SIGN
                MRITE   FROM=ANS
        HR      LAST    BEGIN=IN,END=ONE+4,I=YES,O=YES,        X
                        EOFRTN=HR,ASMDATA=NO
        IN      DS      0CL80                INPUT FORMAT
        NUM     DS      CL3                  NUMBER FOR CALC.
                DS      CL77
        ANS     DS      0CL121               OUTPUT FORMAT
                DC      C'1'                 CONTROL CHAR.
        NUM2    DS      CL3                  N FOR OUTPUT
                DC      C' FACTORIAL IS '
        FACT    DS      CL8
                DC      CL95' '
        PN      DS      D
        PFACT   DS      D
        ONE     DC      F'1'
                END
```

Chapter 12

1. a. 6; it's an SS-type instruction.
   f. none; the duplication factor is zero
2. a. 212   b. 3

Chapter 13

1. a. 0075BC   d. 007A40
3. The base register will be loaded with a value two greater than the assembler was promised. This will cause all the effective addresses calculated at execution time to be incorrect. The first instruction containing a symbolic reference to storage, the Load, will abend because the location referenced is not a fullword boundary.

Chapter 14

1. b. 008756 (register zero does not participate)
   c. 00875A and 005A7A (displacements are specified in decimal in the operands and must be converted to hexadecimal)

```
3.              SR     6,6          ZERO INDEX REGISTER
                L      8,TAB(6)     ASSUME FIRST EL. SMLST
       NEXT     LA     6,4(6)       INCREM. FOR NEXT EL.
                C      8,TAB(6)     NEW SMALLEST?
                BNL    AROUND       NO
                L      8,TAB(6)     YES, PICK UP NEW SMLST
       AROUND   C      6,LAST       ALL ELS. CHECKED?
                BE     FINISH       YES
                B      NEXT         NO, CHECK NEXT EL.
       FINISH   ST     8,SMLST
                  .
                  .
                  .
       LAST     DC     F'96'        INDEX FOR LAST EL.
       TAB      DC     F'8'
                DC     F'12'
                DC     F'786'
                  .
                  .
                  .
                DC     F'86'
                DC     F'3'
       SMLST    DS     F
                END
```

7. 0000010A; remember that the Load Address instruction zeros the high-order byte of the first operand register.

Chapter 15

```
1.              CSECT
                STM    14,12,12(13)
                BALR   12,0          ESTABLISH
                USING  *,12          ADDRESSABILITY
                ST     13,SAVE+4
                LA     15,SAVE
                ST     15,8(13)
                LR     13,15
```

```
         LM      2,4,0(1)          PICK UP PARAMETERS
         LR      4,3               SAVE NO. OF ELS. FOR AVE
         SR      9,9               INITIALIZE SUM
         L       6,INIT            INITIALIZE INDEX REG.
NEXT     LA      6,4(6)            INCREM. INDEX REG.
         A       9,0(6,2)          ADD EL. TO SUM
         BCT     3,NEXT            MORE ELEMENTS?
         M       8,ONE             NO, SET UP FOR DIV.
         DR      8,4               CALCULATE AVERAGE
         ST      9,0(4)            STORE AVERAGE
         L       13,SAVE+4
         LM      14,12,12(13)      RESTORES REGS
         BR      14                RETURN CONTROL
SAVE     DC      18F'0'            SAVE AREA
INIT     DC      F'-4'             INDEX REG INIT VALUE
ONE      DC      F'1'
         END
```

Chapter 17

1. b. condition code set to 2
   e. REG5:   F6F8F0D6
   i. LOC: 0000E427

Chapter 18

1. a. FLD: 40F5F26BF6F8F3
   c. FLD: 404040F04BF7F5
3. a. one   b. three

Chapter 20

```
1.  //   JOB       EXERC1
    //   OPTION    LINK,DUMP
    //   EXEC      ASSEMBLY
                     source program
    //   EXEC      LNKEDT
    //   EXEC
                   input data set
    /&
```

```
4. a. //DDA     DD      DSNAME=DA,VOL=SER=123456,      X
                        UNIT=3330,DISP=(,KEEP),        X
                        SPACE=(TRK,(100,25))
   c. //DDC     DD      DSNAME=OPAL,DISP=(OLD)
```

Chapter 22

1. a.
```
      RECORDS   DTFCD     DEVADDR=SYSIPT,WORKA=YES,        X
                          IOAREA1=IN,EOFADDR=FINIS
      RECORDS   DCB       DSORG=PS,DDNAME=INREC,           X
                          MACRF=GM,BLKSIZE=80,             X
                          LRECL=80,RECFM=F,                X
                          EODAD=FINIS
```

Chapter 23

1. a. 66,000   c. 54,650

APPENDIX 3

System/370 Reference Summary

Third Edition (March 1974)　　　　　**GX20-1850-2**

This edition supersedes GX20-1850-1. It includes new machine instructions and control register functions associated with multiprocessing, and the new instructions CS, CDS, CLRIO, IPK, and SPKA. To the extent that space allows, additional non-TP devices most often attached to System/370s have been added to the I/O command code tables.

The card is intended primarily for use by S/370 assembler language programmers. It contains basic machine information on Models 115 through 168 summarized from the *System/370 Principles of Operation* (GA22-7000), frequently used information from *OS/VS and DOS/VS Assembler Language* (GC33-4010), command codes for various I/O devices, and a multi-code translation table. The card will be updated from time to time. However, the above manuals and others cited on the card are the authoritative reference sources and will be first to reflect changes.

The names of instructions essentially new with S/370 are shown in italics. Some machine instructions are optional or not available for some models. For those that are available on a particular model, the user is referred to the appropriate functional characteristics manual. For a particular installation, one must ascertain which optional hardware features and programming system(s) have been installed. The floating-point and extended floating-point instructions, as well as the instructions listed below, are not standard on every model. Monitoring (the MC instruction) is not available on the Model 165.

Conditional swapping	CDS, CS
CPU timer and clock comparator	SCKC, SPT, STCKC, STPT
Direct control	RDD, WRD
Dynamic address translation	LRA, PTLB, RRB, STNSM, STOSM
Input/output	CLRIO, SIOF
Multiprocessing	SIGP, SPX, STAP, STPX
PSW key handling	IPK, SPKA

Comments about this publication may be sent to the address below. All comments and suggestions become the property of IBM.

MACHINE INSTRUCTIONS

NAME	MNEMONIC	OP CODE	FORMAT	OPERANDS
Add (c)	AR	1A	RR	R1,R2
Add (c)	A	5A	RX	R1,D2(X2,B2)
Add Decimal (c)	AP	FA	SS	D1(L1,B1),D2(L2,B2)
Add Halfword (c)	AH	4A	RX	R1,D2(X2,B2)
Add Logical (c)	ALR	1E	RR	R1,R2
Add Logical (c)	AL	5E	RX	R1,D2(X2,B2)
AND (c)	NR	14	RR	R1,R2
AND (c)	N	54	RX	R1,D2(X2,B2)
AND (c)	NI	94	SI	D1(B1),I2
AND (c)	NC	D4	SS	D1(L,B1),D2(B2)
Branch and Link	BALR	05	RR	R1,R2
Branch and Link	BAL	45	RX	R1,D2(X2,B2)
Branch on Condition	BCR	07	RR	M1,R2
Branch on Condition	BC	47	RX	M1,D2(X2,B2)

MACHINE INSTRUCTIONS (Contd)

NAME	MNEMONIC	OP CODE	FORMAT	OPERANDS
Branch on Count	BCTR	06	RR	R1,R2
Branch on Count	BCT	46	RX	R1,D2(X2,B2)
Branch on Index High	BXH	86	RS	R1,R3,D2(B2)
Branch on Index Low or Equal	BXLE	87	RS	R1,R3,D2(B2)
Clear I/O (c,p)	CLRIO	9D01	S	D2(B2)
Compare (c)	CR	19	RR	R1,R2
Compare (c)	C	59	RX	R1,D2(X2,B2)
Compare and Swap (c)	CS	BA	RS	R1,R3,D2(B2)
Compare Decimal (c)	CP	F9	SS	D1(L1,B1),D2(L2,B2)
Compare Double and Swap (c)	CDS	BB	RS	R1,R3,D2(B2)
Compare Halfword (c)	CH	49	RX	R1,D2(X2,B2)
Compare Logical (c)	CLR	15	RR	R1,R2
Compare Logical (c)	CL	55	RX	R1,D2(X2,B2)
Compare Logical (c)	CLC	D5	SS	D1(L,B1),D2(B2)
Compare Logical (c)	CLI	95	SI	D1(B1),I2
Compare Logical Characters under Mask (c)	CLM	BD	RS	R1,M3,D2(B2)
Compare Logical Long (c)	CLCL	0F	RR	R1,R2
Convert to Binary	CVB	4F	RX	R1,D2(X2,B2)
Convert to Decimal	CVD	4E	RX	R1,D2(X2,B2)
Diagnose (p)		83		Model-dependent
Divide	DR	1D	RR	R1,R2
Divide	D	5D	RX	R1,D2(X2,B2)
Divide Decimal	DP	FD	SS	D1(L1,B1),D2(L2,B2)
Edit (c)	ED	DE	SS	D1(L,B1),D2(B2)
Edit and Mark (c)	EDMK	DF	SS	D1(L,B1),D2(B2)
Exclusive OR (c)	XR	17	RR	R1,R2
Exclusive OR (c)	X	57	RX	R1,D2(X2,B2)
Exclusive OR (c)	XI	97	SI	D1(B1),I2
Exclusive OR (c)	XC	D7	SS	D1(L,B1),D2(B2)
Execute	EX	44	RX	R1,D2(X2,B2)
Halt I/O (c,p)	HIO	9E00	S	D2(B2)
Halt Device (c,p)	HDV	9E01	S	D2(B2)
Insert Character	IC	43	RX	R1,D2(X2,B2)
Insert Characters under Mask (c)	ICM	BF	RS	R1,M3,D2(B2)
Insert PSW Key (p)	IPK	B20B	S	
Insert Storage Key (p)	ISK	09	RR	R1,R2
Load	LR	18	RR	R1,R2
Load	L	58	RX	R1,D2(X2,B2)
Load Address	LA	41	RX	R1,D2(X2,B2)
Load and Test (c)	LTR	12	RR	R1,R2
Load Complement (c)	LCR	13	RR	R1,R2
Load Control (p)	LCTL	B7	RS	R1,R3,D2(B2)
Load Halfword	LH	48	RX	R1,D2(X2,B2)
Load Multiple	LM	98	RS	R1,R3,D2(B2)
Load Negative (c)	LNR	11	RR	R1,R2
Load Positive (c)	LPR	10	RR	R1,R2
Load PSW (n,p)	LPSW	82	S	D2(B2)
Load Real Address (c,p)	LRA	B1	RX	R1,D2(X2,B2)
Monitor Call	MC	AF	SI	D1(B1),I2
Move	MVI	92	SI	D1(B1),I2
Move	MVC	D2	SS	D1(L,B1),D2(B2)
Move Long (c)	MVCL	0E	RR	R1,R2
Move Numerics	MVN	D1	SS	D1(L,B1),D2(B2)
Move with Offset	MVO	F1	SS	D1(L1,B1),D2(L2,B2)
Move Zones	MVZ	D3	SS	D1(L,B1),D2(B2)
Multiply	MR	1C	RR	R1,R2
Multiply	M	5C	RX	R1,D2(X2,B2)
Multiply Decimal	MP	FC	SS	D1(L1,B1),D2(L2,B2)
Multiply Halfword	MH	4C	RX	R1,D2(X2,B2)
OR (c)	OR	16	RR	R1,R2

MACHINE INSTRUCTIONS (Contd)

NAME	MNEMONIC	OP CODE	FORMAT	OPERANDS
OR (c)	O	56	RX	R1,D2(X2,B2)
OR (c)	OI	96	SI	D1(B1),I2
OR (c)	OC	D6	SS	D1(L,B1),D2(B2)
Pack	PACK	F2	SS	D1(L1,B1),D2(L2,B2)
Purge TLB (p)	PTLB	B20D	S	
Read Direct (p)	RDD	85	SI	D1(B1),I2
Reset Reference Bit (c,p)	RRB	B213	S	D2(B2)
Set Clock (c,p)	SCK	B204	S	D2(B2)
Set Clock Comparator (p)	SCKC	B206	S	D2(B2)
Set CPU Timer (p)	SPT	B208	S	D2(B2)
Set Prefix (p)	SPX	B210	S	D2(B2)
Set Program Mask (n)	SPM	04	RR	R1
Set PSW Key from Address (p)	SPKA	B20A	S	D2(B2)
Set Storage Key (p)	SSK	08	RR	R1,R2
Set System Mask (p)	SSM	80	S	D2(B2)
Shift and Round Decimal (c)	SRP	F0	SS	D1(L1,B1),D2(B2),I3
Shift Left Double (c)	SLDA	8F	RS	R1,D2(B2)
Shift Left Double Logical	SLDL	8D	RS	R1,D2(B2)
Shift Left Single (c)	SLA	8B	RS	R1,D2(B2)
Shift Left Single Logical	SLL	89	RS	R1,D2(B2)
Shift Right Double (c)	SRDA	8E	RS	R1,D2(B2)
Shift Right Double Logical	SRDL	8C	RS	R1,D2(B2)
Shift Right Single (c)	SRA	8A	RS	R1,D2(B2)
Shift Right Single Logical	SRL	88	RS	R1,D2(B2)
Signal Processor (c,p)	SIGP	AE	RS	R1,R3,D2(B2)
Start I/O (c,p)	SIO	9C00	S	D2(B2)
Start I/O Fast Release (c,p)	SIOF	9C01	S	D2(B2)
Store	ST	50	RX	R1,D2(X2,B2)
Store Channel ID (c,p)	STIDC	B203	S	D2(B2)
Store Character	STC	42	RX	R1,D2(X2,B2)
Store Characters under Mask	STCM	BE	RS	R1,M3,D2(B2)
Store Clock (c)	STCK	B205	S	D2(B2)
Store Clock Comparator (p)	STCKC	B207	S	D2(B2)
Store Control (p)	STCTL	B6	RS	R1,R3,D2(B2)
Store CPU Address (p)	STAP	B212	S	D2(B2)
Store CPU ID (p)	STIDP	B202	S	D2(B2)
Store CPU Timer (p)	STPT	B209	S	D2(B2)
Store Halfword	STH	40	RX	R1,D2(X2,B2)
Store Multiple	STM	90	RS	R1,R3,D2(B2)
Store Prefix (p)	STPX	B211	S	D2(B2)
Store Then AND System Mask (p)	STNSM	AC	SI	D1(B1),I2
Store Then OR System Mask (p)	STOSM	AD	SI	D1(B1),I2
Subtract (c)	SR	1B	RR	R1,R2
Subtract (c)	S	5B	RX	R1,D2(X2,B2)
Subtract Decimal (c)	SP	FB	SS	D1(L1,B1),D2(L2,B2)
Subtract Halfword (c)	SH	4B	RX	R1,D2(X2,B2)
Subtract Logical (c)	SLR	1F	RR	R1,R2
Subtract Logical (c)	SL	5F	RX	R1,D2(X2,B2)
Supervisor Call	SVC	0A	RR	I
Test and Set (c)	TS	93	S	D2(B2)
Test Channel (c,p)	TCH	9F00	S	D2(B2)
Test I/O (c,p)	TIO	9D00	S	D2(B2)
Test under Mask (c)	TM	91	SI	D1(B1),I2
Translate	TR	DC	SS	D1(L,B1),D2(B2)
Translate and Test (c)	TRT	DD	SS	D1(L,B1),D2(B2)
Unpack	UNPK	F3	SS	D1(L1,B1),D2(L2,B2)
Write Direct (p)	WRD	84	SI	D1(B1),I2
Zero and Add Decimal (c)	ZAP	F8	SS	D1(L1,B1),D2(L2,B2)

Floating-Point Instructions

NAME	MNEMONIC	OP CODE	FORMAT	OPERANDS
Add Normalized, Extended (c,x)	AXR	36	RR	R1,R2
Add Normalized, Long (c)	ADR	2A	RR	R1,R2
Add Normalized, Long (c)	AD	6A	RX	R1,D2(X2,B2)
Add Normalized, Short (c)	AER	3A	RR	R1,R2
Add Normalized, Short (c)	AE	7A	RX	R1,D2(X2,B2)
Add Unnormalized, Long (c)	AWR	2E	RR	R1,R2
Add Unnormalized, Long (c)	AW	6E	RX	R1,D2(X2,B2)
Add Unnormalized, Short (c)	AUR	3E	RR	R1,R2
Add Unnormalized, Short (c)	AU	7E	RX	R1,D2(X2,B2)

c. Condition code is set.
n. New condition code is loaded.
p. Privileged instruction.
x. Extended precision floating-point.

Floating-Point Instructions (Contd)

NAME	MNEMONIC	OP CODE	FORMAT	OPERANDS
Compare, Long (c)	CDR	29	RR	R1,R2
Compare, Long (c)	CD	69	RX	R1,D2(X2,B2)
Compare, Short (c)	CER	39	RR	R1,R2
Compare, Short (c)	CE	79	RX	R1,D2(X2,B2)
Divide, Long	DDR	2D	RR	R1,R2
Divide, Long	DD	6D	RX	R1,D2(X2,B2)
Divide, Short	DER	3D	RR	R1,R2
Divide, Short	DE	7D	RX	R1,D2(X2,B2)
Halve, Long	HDR	24	RR	R1,R2
Halve, Short	HER	34	RR	R1,R2
Load and Test, Long (c)	LTDR	22	RR	R1,R2
Load and Test, Short (c)	LTER	32	RR	R1,R2
Load Complement, Long (c)	LCDR	23	RR	R1,R2
Load Complement, Short (c)	LCER	33	RR	R1,R2
Load, Long	LDR	28	RR	R1,R2
Load, Long	LD	68	RX	R1,D2(X2,B2)
Load Negative, Long (c)	LNDR	21	RR	R1,R2
Load Negative, Short (c)	LNER	31	RR	R1,R2
Load Positive, Long (c)	LPDR	20	RR	R1,R2
Load Positive, Short (c)	LPER	30	RR	R1,R2
Load Rounded, Extended to Long (x)	LRDR	25	RR	R1,R2
Load Rounded, Long to Short (x)	LRER	35	RR	R1,R2
Load, Short	LER	38	RR	R1,R2
Load, Short	LE	78	RX	R1,D2(X2,B2)
Multiply, Extended (x)	MXR	26	RR	R1,R2
Multiply, Long	MDR	2C	RR	R1,R2
Multiply, Long	MD	6C	RX	R1,D2(X2,B2)
Multiply, Long/Extended (x)	MXDR	27	RR	R1,R2
Multiply, Long/Extended (x)	MXD	67	RX	R1,D2(X2,B2)
Multiply, Short	MER	3C	RR	R1,R2
Multiply, Short	ME	7C	RX	R1,D2(X2,B2)
Store, Long	STD	60	RX	R1,D2(X2,B2)
Store, Short	STE	70	RX	R1,D2(X2,B2)
Subtract Normalized, Extended (c,x)	SXR	37	RR	R1,R2
Subtract Normalized, Long (c)	SDR	2B	RR	R1,R2
Subtract Normalized, Long (c)	SD	6B	RX	R1,D2(X2,B2)
Subtract Normalized, Short (c)	SER	3B	RR	R1,R2
Subtract Normalized, Short (c)	SE	7B	RX	R1,D2(X2,B2)
Subtract Unnormalized, Long (c)	SWR	2F	RR	R1,R2
Subtract Unnormalized, Long (c)	SW	6F	RX	R1,D2(X2,B2)
Subtract Unnormalized, Short (c)	SUR	3F	RR	R1,R2
Subtract Unnormalized, Short (c)	SU	7F	RX	R1,D2(X2,B2)

EXTENDED MNEMONIC INSTRUCTIONS[†]

Use	Extended Code* (RX or RR)	Meaning	Machine Instr.* (RX or RR)
General	B or BR	Unconditional Branch	BC or BCR 15,
	NOP or NOPR	No Operation	BC or BCR 0,
After Compare Instructions (A:B)	BH or BHR	Branch on A High	BC or BCR 2,
	BL or BLR	Branch on A Low	BC or BCR 4,
	BE or BER	Branch on A Equal B	BC or BCR 8,
	BNH or BNHR	Branch on A Not High	BC or BCR 13,
	BNL or BNLR	Branch on A Not Low	BC or BCR 11,
	BNE or BNER	Branch on A Not Equal B	BC or BCR 7,
After Arithmetic Instructions	BO or BOR	Branch on Overflow	BC or BCR 1,
	BP or BPR	Branch on Plus	BC or BCR 2,
	BM or BMR	Branch on Minus	BC or BCR 4,
	BNP or BNPR	Branch on Not Plus	BC or BCR 13,
	BNM or BNMR	Branch on Not Minus	BC or BCR 11,
	BNZ or BNZR	Branch on Not Zero	BC or BCR 7,
	BZ or BZR	Branch on Zero	BC or BCR 8,
After Test under Mask Instruction	BO or BOR	Branch if Ones	BC or BCR 1,
	BM or BMR	Branch if Mixed	BC or BCR 4,
	BZ or BZR	Branch if Zeros	BC or BCR 8,
	BNO or BNOR	Branch if Not Ones	BC or BCR 14,

*Second operand not shown; in all cases it is D2(X2,B2) for RX format or R2 for RR format.

[†]For OS/VS and DOS/VS; source: GC33-4010.

EDIT AND EDMK PATTERN CHARACTERS (in hex)

20—digit selector	40—blank	5C—asterisk
21—start of significance	4B—period	6B—comma
22—field separator	5B—dollar sign	C3D9—CR

CONDITION CODES

Condition Code Setting	0	1	2	3
Mask Bit Value	8	4	2	1

General Instructions

Add, Add Halfword	zero	<zero	>zero	overflow
Add Logical	zero, no carry	not zero, no carry	zero, carry	not zero, carry
AND	zero	not zero	—	—
Compare, Compare Halfword	equal	1st op low	1st op high	—
Compare and Swap/Double	equal	not equal	—	—
Compare Logical	equal	1st op low	1st op high	—
Exclusive OR	zero	not zero	—	—
Insert Characters under Mask	all zero	1st bit one	1st bit zero	—
Load and Test	zero	<zero	>zero	—
Load Complement	zero	<zero	>zero	overflow
Load Negative	zero	<zero	—	—
Load Positive	zero	—	>zero	overflow
Move Long	count equal	count low	count high	overlap
OR	zero	not zero	—	—
Shift Left Double/Single	zero	<zero	>zero	overflow
Shift Right Double/Single	zero	<zero	>zero	—
Store Clock	set	not set	error	not oper
Subtract, Subtract Halfword	zero	<zero	>zero	overflow
Subtract Logical	—	not zero, no carry	zero, carry	not zero, carry
Test and Set	zero	one	—	—
Test under Mask	zero	mixed	—	ones
Translate and Test	zero	incomplete	complete	—

Decimal Instructions

Add Decimal	zero	<zero	>zero	overflow
Compare Decimal	equal	1st op low	1st op high	—
Edit, Edit and Mark	zero	<zero	>zero	—
Shift and Round Decimal	zero	<zero	>zero	overflow
Subtract Decimal	zero	<zero	>zero	overflow
Zero and Add	zero	<zero	>zero	overflow

Floating-Point Instructions

Add Normalized	zero	<zero	>zero	—
Add Unnormalized	zero	<zero	>zero	—
Compare	equal	1st op low	1st op high	—
Load and Test	zero	<zero	>zero	—
Load Complement	zero	<zero	>zero	—
Load Negative	zero	<zero	—	—
Load Positive	zero	—	>zero	—
Subtract Normalized	zero	<zero	>zero	—
Subtract Unnormalized	zero	<zero	>zero	—

Input/Output Instructions

Clear I/O	no oper in progress	CSW stored	chan busy	not oper
Halt Device	interruption pending	CSW stored	channel working	not oper
Halt I/O	interruption pending	CSW stored	burst op stopped	not oper
Start I/O, SIOF	successful	CSW stored	busy	not oper
Store Channel ID	ID stored	CSW stored	busy	not oper
Test Channel	available	interruption pending	burst mode	not oper
Test I/O	available	CSW stored	busy	not oper

System Control Instructions

Load Real Address	translation available	ST entry invalid	PT entry invalid	length violation
Reset Reference Bit	R=0, C=0	R=0, C=1	R=1, C=0	R=1, C=1
Set Clock	set	secure	—	not oper
Signal Processor	accepted	stat stored	busy	not oper

CNOP ALIGNMENT

DOUBLEWORD							
WORD				WORD			
HALFWORD		HALFWORD		HALFWORD		HALFWORD	
BYTE	BYTE	BYTE	BYTE	BYTE	BYTE	BYTE	BYTE
0,4		2,4		0,4		2,4	
0,8		2,8		4,8		6,8	

ASSEMBLER INSTRUCTIONS†

Function	Mnemonic	Meaning
Data definition	DC	Define constant
	DS	Define storage
	CCW	Define channel command word
Program sectioning and linking	START	Start assembly
	CSECT	Identify control section
	DSECT	Identify dummy section
	DXD*	Define external dummy section
	CXD*	Cumulative length of external dummy section
	COM	Identify blank common control section
	ENTRY	Identify entry-point symbol
	EXTRN	Identify external symbol
	WXTRN	Identify weak external symbol
Base register assignment	USING	Use base address register
	DROP	Drop base address register
Control of listings	TITLE	Identify assembly output
	EJECT	Start new page
	SPACE	Space listing
	PRINT	Print optional data
Program Control	ICTL	Input format control
	ISEQ	Input sequence checking
	PUNCH	Punch a card
	REPRO	Reproduce following card
	ORG	Set location counter
	EQU	Equate symbol
	OPSYN*	Equate operation code
	PUSH*	Save current PRINT or USING status
	POP*	Restore PRINT or USING status
	LTORG	Begin literal pool
	CNOP	Conditional no operation
	COPY	Copy predefined source coding
	END	End assembly
Macro definition	MACRO	Macro definition header
	MNOTE	Request for error message
	MEXIT	Macro definition exit
	MEND	Macro definition trailer
Conditional assembly	ACTR	Conditional assembly loop counter
	AGO	Unconditional branch
	AIF	Conditional branch
	ANOP	Assembly no operation
	GBLA	Define global SETA symbol
	GBLB	Define global SETB symbol
	GBLC	Define global SETC symbol
	LCLA	Define local SETA symbol
	LCLB	Define local SETB symbol
	LCLC	Define local SETC symbol
	SETA	Set arithmetic variable symbol
	SETB	Set binary variable symbol
	SETC	Set character variable symbol

SUMMARY OF CONSTANTS†

TYPE	IMPLIED LENGTH, BYTES	ALIGNMENT	FORMAT	TRUNCATION/ PADDING
C	—	byte	characters	right
X	—	byte	hexadecimal digits	left
B	—	byte	binary digits	left
F	4	word	fixed-point binary	left
H	2	halfword	fixed-point binary	left
E	4	word	short floating-point	right
D	8	doubleword	long floating-point	right
L	16	doubleword	extended floating-point	right
P	—	byte	packed decimal	left
Z	—	byte	zoned decimal	left
A	4	word	value of address	left
Y	2	halfword	value of address	left
S	2	halfword	address in base-displacement form	—
V	4	word	externally defined address value	left
Q*	4	word	symbol naming a DXD or DSECT	left

†For OS/VS and DOS/VS; source: GC33-4010.
*OS/VS only.

CODE TRANSLATION TABLE

Dec.	Hex	Instruction (RR)	BCDIC	EBCDIC(1)	ASCII	7-Track Tape BCDIC(2)	Card Code	Binary
0	00			NUL	NUL		12-0-1-8-9	0000 0000
1	01			SOH	SOH		12-1-9	0000 0001
2	02			STX	STX		12-2-9	0000 0010
3	03			ETX	ETX		12-3-9	0000 0011
4	04	SPM		PF	EOT		12-4-9	0000 0100
5	05	BALR		HT	ENQ		12-5-9	0000 0101
6	06	BCTR		LC	ACK		12-6-9	0000 0110
7	07	BCR		DEL	BEL		12-7-9	0000 0111
8	08	SSK			BS		12-8-9	0000 1000
9	09	ISK			HT		12-1-8-9	0000 1001
10	0A	SVC		SMM	LF		12-2-8-9	0000 1010
11	0B			VT	VT		12-3-8-9	0000 1011
12	0C			FF	FF		12-4-8-9	0000 1100
13	0D			CR	CR		12-5-8-9	0000 1101
14	0E	MVCL		SO	SO		12-6-8-9	0000 1110
15	0F	CLCL		SI	SI		12-7-8-9	0000 1111
16	10	LPR		DLE	DLE		12-11-1-8-9	0001 0000
17	11	LNR		DC1	DC1		11-1-9	0001 0001
18	12	LTR		DC2	DC2		11-2-9	0001 0010
19	13	LCR		TM	DC3		11-3-9	0001 0011
20	14	NR		RES	DC4		11-4-9	0001 0100
21	15	CLR		NL	NAK		11-5-9	0001 0101
22	16	OR		BS	SYN		11-6-9	0001 0110
23	17	XR		IL	ETB		11-7-9	0001 0111
24	18	LR		CAN	CAN		11-8-9	0001 1000
25	19	CR		EM	EM		11-1-8-9	0001 1001
26	1A	AR		CC	SUB		11-2-8-9	0001 1010
27	1B	SR		CU1	ESC		11-3-8-9	0001 1011
28	1C	MR		IFS	FS		11-4-8-9	0001 1100
29	1D	DR		IGS	GS		11-5-8-9	0001 1101
30	1E	ALR		IRS	RS		11-6-8-9	0001 1110
31	1F	SLR		IUS	US		11-7-8-9	0001 1111
32	20	LPDR		DS	SP		11-0-1-8-9	0010 0000
33	21	LNDR		SOS	!		0-1-9	0010 0001
34	22	LTDR		FS	"		0-2-9	0010 0010
35	23	LCDR			#		0-3-9	0010 0011
36	24	HDR		BYP	$		0-4-9	0010 0100
37	25	LRDR		LF	%		0-5-9	0010 0101
38	26	MXR		ETB	&		0-6-9	0010 0110
39	27	MXDR		ESC	'		0-7-9	0010 0111
40	28	LDR			(		0-8-9	0010 1000
41	29	CDR			)		0-1-8-9	0010 1001
42	2A			SM	*		0-2-8-9	0010 1010
43	2B	SDR		CU2	+		0-3-8-9	0010 1011
44	2C	MDR			,		0-4-8-9	0010 1100
45	2D	DDR		ENQ	-		0-5-8-9	0010 1101
46	2E	AWR		ACK	.		0-6-8-9	0010 1110
47	2F	SWR		BEL	/		0-7-8-9	0010 1111
48	30	LPER			0		12-11-0-1-8-9	0011 0000
49	31	LNER			1		1-9	0011 0001
50	32	LTER		SYN	2		2-9	0011 0010
51	33	LCER			3		3-9	0011 0011
52	34	HER		PN	4		4-9	0011 0100
53	35	LRER		RS	5		5-9	0011 0101
54	36	AXR		UC	6		6-9	0011 0110
55	37	SXR		EOT	7		7-9	0011 0111
56	38	LER			8		8-9	0011 1000
57	39	CER			9		1-8-9	0011 1001
58	3A	AER			:		2-8-9	0011 1010
59	3B	SER		CU3	;		3-8-9	0011 1011
60	3C	MER		DC4	<		4-8-9	0011 1100
61	3D	DER		NAK	=		5-8-9	0011 1101
62	3E	AUR			>		6-8-9	0011 1110
63	3F	SUR		SUB	?		7-8-9	0011 1111

Dec.	Hex	Instruction (RX)	BCDIC	EBCDIC(1)	ASCII	7-Track Tape BCDIC(2)	Card Code	Binary
64	40	STH		Sp Sp	@	(3)	no punches	0100 0000
65	41	LA			A		12-0-1-9	0100 0001
66	42	STC			B		12-0-2-9	0100 0010
67	43	IC			C		12-0-3-9	0100 0011
68	44	EX			D		12-0-4-9	0100 0100
69	45	BAL			E		12-0-5-9	0100 0101
70	46	BCT			F		12-0-6-9	0100 0110
71	47	BC			G		12-0-7-9	0100 0111
72	48	LH			H		12-0-8-9	0100 1000
73	49	CH			I		12-1-8	0100 1001
74	4A	AH		¢ ¢	J	B A 8 2 1	12-2-8	0100 1010
75	4B	SH	.	. .	K		12-3-8	0100 1011
76	4C	MH	⌑)	< <	L	B A 8 4	12-4-8	0100 1100
77	4D		[	((	M	B A 8 4 1	12-5-8	0100 1101
78	4E	CVD	<	+ +	N	B A 8 4 2	12-6-8	0100 1110
79	4F	CVB	‡	| |	O	B A 8 4 2 1	12-7-8	0100 1111
80	50	ST	& +	& &	P	B A	12	0101 0000
81	51				Q		12-11-1-9	0101 0001
82	52				R		12-11-2-9	0101 0010
83	53				S		12-11-3-9	0101 0011
84	54	N			T		12-11-4-9	0101 0100
85	55	CL			U		12-11-5-9	0101 0101
86	56	O			V		12-11-6-9	0101 0110
87	57	X			W		12-11-7-9	0101 0111
88	58	L			X		12-11-8-9	0101 1000
89	59	C			Y		11-1-8	0101 1001
90	5A	A		! !	Z		11-2-8	0101 1010
91	5B	S	$	$ $	[	B 8 2 1	11-3-8	0101 1011
92	5C	M	* •	* *	\	B 8 4	11-4-8	0101 1100
93	5D	D	]	))	]	B 8 4 1	11-5-8	0101 1101
94	5E	AL	;	; ;	^	B 8 4 2	11-6-8	0101 1110
95	5F	SL	Δ	¬ ¬	_	B 8 4 2 1	11-7-8	0101 1111
96	60	STD	-	- -	`	B	11	0110 0000
97	61		/	/ /	a	A 1	0-1	0110 0001
98	62				b		11-0-2-9	0110 0010
99	63				c		11-0-3-9	0110 0011
100	64				d		11-0-4-9	0110 0100
101	65				e		11-0-5-9	0110 0101
102	66				f		11-0-6-9	0110 0110
103	67	MXD			g		11-0-7-9	0110 0111
104	68	LD			h		11-0-8-9	0110 1000
105	69	CD			i		0-1-8	0110 1001
106	6A	AD		| |	j		12-11	0110 1010
107	6B	SD	,	, ,	k	A 8 2 1	0-3-8	0110 1011
108	6C	MD	% (	% %	l	A 8 4	0-4-8	0110 1100
109	6D	DD	γ	_ _	m	A 8 4 1	0-5-8	0110 1101
110	6E	AW		> >	n	A 8 4 2	0-6-8	0110 1110
111	6F	SW	⧧	? ?	o	A 8 4 2 1	0-7-8	0110 1111
112	70	STE			p		12-11-0	0111 0000
113	71				q		12-11-0-1-9	0111 0001
114	72				r		12-11-0-2-9	0111 0010
115	73				s		12-11-0-3-9	0111 0011
116	74				t		12-11-0-4-9	0111 0100
117	75				u		12-11-0-5-9	0111 0101
118	76				v		12-11-0-6-9	0111 0110
119	77				w		12-11-0-7-9	0111 0111
120	78	LE			x		12-11-0-8-9	0111 1000
121	79	CE			y		1-8	0111 1001
122	7A	AE		: :	z	A	2-8	0111 1010
123	7B	SE	# =	# #	{	8 2 1	3-8	0111 1011
124	7C	ME	@ '	@ @	|	8 4	4-8	0111 1100
125	7D	DE	:	' '	}	8 4 1	5-8	0111 1101
126	7E	AU	>	= =	~	8 4 2	6-8	0111 1110
127	7F	SU	√	" "	DEL	8 4 2 1	7-8	0111 1111

1. Two columns of EBCDIC graphics are shown. The first gives standard bit pattern assignments. The second shows the T-11 and TN text printing chains (120 graphics).
2. Add C (check bit) for odd or even parity as needed, except as noted.
3. For even parity use CA.

TWO-CHARACTER BSC DATA LINK CONTROLS

Function	EBCDIC	ASCII
ACK-0	DLE,X'70'	DLE,0
ACK-1	DLE,X'61'	DLE,1
WACK	DLE,X'6B'	DLE, ;
RVI	DLE,X'7C'	DLE,<

CODE TRANSLATION TABLE (Contd)

Dec.	Hex	Instruction and Format	BCDIC	EBCDIC(1)	ASCII	7-Track Tape BCDIC(2)	EBCDIC Card Code	Binary
128	80	SSM -S					12-0-1-8	1000 0000
129	81		a	a			12-0-1	1000 0001
130	82	LPSW -S	b	b			12-0-2	1000 0010
131	83	Diagnose	c	c			12-0-3	1000 0011
132	84	WRD ⎱SI	d	d			12-0-4	1000 0100
133	85	RDD ⎰	e	e			12-0-5	1000 0101
134	86	BXH	f	f			12-0-6	1000 0110
135	87	BXLE	g	g			12-0-7	1000 0111
136	88	SRL	h	h			12-0-8	1000 1000
137	89	SLL	i	i			12-0-9	1000 1001
138	8A	SRA ⎱RS					12-0-2-8	1000 1010
139	8B	SLA ⎰		{			12-0-3-8	1000 1011
140	8C	SRDL		≤			12-0-4-8	1000 1100
141	8D	SLDL		(			12-0-5-8	1000 1101
142	8E	SRDA		+			12-0-6-8	1000 1110
143	8F	SLDA		+			12-0-7-8	1000 1111
144	90	STM					12-11-1-8	1001 0000
145	91	TM ⎱	j	j			12-11-1	1001 0001
146	92	MVI ⎱SI	k	k			12-11-2	1001 0010
147	93	TS -S	l	l			12-11-3	1001 0011
148	94	NI ⎱	m	m			12-11-4	1001 0100
149	95	CLI ⎱SI	n	n			12-11-5	1001 0101
150	96	OI ⎰	o	o			12-11-6	1001 0110
151	97	XI	p	p			12-11-7	1001 0111
152	98	LM -RS	q	q			12-11-8	1001 1000
153	99		r	r			12-11-9	1001 1001
154	9A						12-11-2-8	1001 1010
155	9B			}			12-11-3-8	1001 1011
156	9C	SIO, SIOF ⎱		⊔			12-11-4-8	1001 1100
157	9D	TIO, CLRIO ⎱S		)			12-11-5-8	1001 1101
158	9E	HIO, HDV ⎰		±			12-11-6-8	1001 1110
159	9F	TCH ⎰		■			12-11-7-8	1001 1111
160	A0						11-0-1-8	1010 0000
161	A1		~	o			11-0-1	1010 0001
162	A2		s	s			11-0-2	1010 0010
163	A3		t	t			11-0-3	1010 0011
164	A4		u	u			11-0-4	1010 0100
165	A5		v	v			11-0-5	1010 0101
166	A6		w	w			11-0-6	1010 0110
167	A7		x	x			11-0-7	1010 0111
168	A8		y	y			11-0-8	1010 1000
169	A9		z	z			11-0-9	1010 1001
170	AA						11-0-2-8	1010 1010
171	AB			∟			11-0-3-8	1010 1011
172	AC	STNSM ⎱SI		⌐			11-0-4-8	1010 1100
173	AD	STOSM ⎰		[			11-0-5-8	1010 1101
174	AE	SIGP -RS		≥			11-0-6-8	1010 1110
175	AF	MC -SI		●			11-0-7-8	1010 1111
176	B0			0			12-11-0-1-8	1011 0000
177	B1	LRA -RX		1			12-11-0-1	1011 0001
178	B2	See below		2			12-11-0-2	1011 0010
179	B3			3			12-11-0-3	1011 0011
180	B4			4			12-11-0-4	1011 0100
181	B5			5			12-11-0-5	1011 0101
182	B6	STCTL ⎱RS		6			12-11-0-6	1011 0110
183	B7	LCTL ⎰		7			12-11-0-7	1011 0111
184	B8			8			12-11-0-8	1011 1000
185	B9			9			12-11-0-9	1011 1001
186	BA	CS ⎱RS					12-11-0-2-8	1011 1010
187	BB	CDS ⎰		⌐			12-11-0-3-8	1011 1011
188	BC			⌐			12-11-0-4-8	1011 1100
189	BD	CLM		]			12-11-0-5-8	1011 1101
190	BE	STCM ⎱RS		+			12-11-0-6-8	1011 1110
191	BF	ICM ⎰		—			12-11-0-7-8	1011 1111

Dec.	Hex	Instruction (SS)	BCDIC	EBCDIC(1)	ASCII	7-Track Tape BCDIC(2)	EBCDIC Card Code	Binary
192	C0		?	{		B A 8 2	12-0	1100 0000
193	C1		A	A	A	B A 1	12-1	1100 0001
194	C2		B	B	B	B A 2	12-2	1100 0010
195	C3		C	C	C	B A 2 1	12-3	1100 0011
196	C4		D	D	D	B A 4	12-4	1100 0100
197	C5		E	E	E	B A 4 1	12-5	1100 0101
198	C6		F	F	F	B A 4 2	12-6	1100 0110
199	C7		G	G	G	B A 4 2 1	12-7	1100 0111
200	C8		H	H	H	B A 8	12-8	1100 1000
201	C9		I	I	I	B A 8 1	12-9	1100 1001
202	CA						12-0-2-8-9	1100 1010
203	CB						12-0-3-8-9	1100 1011
204	CC		⌠				12-0-4-8-9	1100 1100
205	CD						12-0-5-8-9	1100 1101
206	CE		¥				12-0-6-8-9	1100 1110
207	CF						12-0-7-8-9	1100 1111
208	D0		!	}		B 8 2	11-0	1101 0000
209	D1	MVN	J	J	J	B 1	11-1	1101 0001
210	D2	MVC	K	K	K	B 2	11-2	1101 0010
211	D3	MVZ	L	L	L	B 2 1	11-3	1101 0011
212	D4	NC	M	M	M	B 4	11-4	1101 0100
213	D5	CLC	N	N	N	B 4 1	11-5	1101 0101
214	D6	OC	O	O	O	B 4 2	11-6	1101 0110
215	D7	XC	P	P	P	B 4 2 1	11-7	1101 0111
216	D8		Q	Q	Q	B 8	11-8	1101 1000
217	D9		R	R	R	B 8 1	11-9	1101 1001
218	DA						12-11-2-8-9	1101 1010
219	DB						12-11-3-8-9	1101 1011
220	DC	TR					12-11-4-8-9	1101 1100
221	DD	TRT					12-11-5-8-9	1101 1101
222	DE	ED					12-11-6-8-9	1101 1110
223	DF	EDMK					12-11-7-8-9	1101 1111
224	E0		‡	\		A 8 2	0-2-8	1110 0000
225	E1						11-0-1-9	1110 0001
226	E2		S	S	S	A 2	0-2	1110 0010
227	E3		T	T	T	A 2 1	0-3	1110 0011
228	E4		U	U	U	A 4	0-4	1110 0100
229	E5		V	V	V	A 4 1	0-5	1110 0101
230	E6		W	W	W	A 4 2	0-6	1110 0110
231	E7		X	X	X	A 4 2 1	0-7	1110 0111
232	E8		Y	Y	Y	A 8	0-8	1110 1000
233	E9		Z	Z	Z	A 8 1	0-9	1110 1001
234	EA						11-0-2-8-9	1110 1010
235	EB						11-0-3-8-9	1110 1011
236	EC		⊣				11-0-4-8-9	1110 1100
237	ED						11-0-5-8-9	1110 1101
238	EE						11-0-6-8-9	1110 1110
239	EF						11-0-7-8-9	1110 1111
240	F0	SRP	0	0	0	8 2	0	1111 0000
241	F1	MVO	1	1	1	1	1	1111 0001
242	F2	PACK	2	2	2	2	2	1111 0010
243	F3	UNPK	3	3	3	2 1	3	1111 0011
244	F4		4	4	4	4	4	1111 0100
245	F5		5	5	5	4 1	5	1111 0101
246	F6		6	6	6	4 2	6	1111 0110
247	F7		7	7	7	4 2 1	7	1111 0111
248	F8	ZAP	8	8	8	8	8	1111 1000
249	F9	CP	9	9	9	8 1	9	1111 1001
250	FA	AP		I			12-11-0-2-8-9	1111 1010
251	FB	SP					12-11-0-3-8-9	1111 1011
252	FC	MP					12-11-0-4-8-9	1111 1100
253	FD	DP					12-11-0-5-8-9	1111 1101
254	FE						12-11-0-6-8-9	1111 1110
255	FF			EO			12-11-0-7-8-9	1111 1111

Op code (S format)

B202 - STIDP	B207 - STCKC	B20D - PTLB
B203 - STIDC	B208 - SPT	B210 - SPX
B204 - SCK	B209 - STPT	B211 - STPX
B205 - STCK	B20A - SPKA	B212 - STAP
B206 - SCKC	B20B - IPK	B213 - RRB

ANSI-DEFINED PRINTER CONTROL CHARACTERS
(A in RECFM field of DCB)

Code	Action before printing record
blank	Space 1 line
0	Space 2 lines
-	Space 3 lines
+	Suppress space
1	Skip to line 1 on new page

MACHINE INSTRUCTION FORMATS

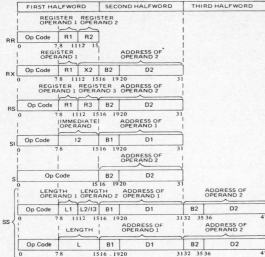

FIRST HALFWORD	SECOND HALFWORD	THIRD HALFWORD

RR

	REGISTER OPERAND 1	REGISTER OPERAND 2
Op Code	R1	R2

0   7,8   1112   15

RX

	REGISTER OPERAND 1			ADDRESS OF OPERAND 2
Op Code	R1	X2	B2	D2

0   78   1112   1516   1920   31

RS

	REGISTER OPERAND 1	REGISTER OPERAND 3		ADDRESS OF OPERAND 2
Op Code	R1	R3	B2	D2

0   78   1112   1516   1920   31

SI

	IMMEDIATE OPERAND		ADDRESS OF OPERAND 1
Op Code	I2	B1	D1

0   78   1516   1920   31

S

		ADDRESS OF OPERAND 2
Op Code	B2	D2

0   1516   1920   31

SS

	LENGTH OPERAND 1	LENGTH OPERAND 2	ADDRESS OF OPERAND 1			ADDRESS OF OPERAND 2
Op Code	L1	L2/13	B1	D1	B2	D2

0   78   1112   1516   1920   3132   3536   47

	LENGTH	ADDRESS OF OPERAND 1			ADDRESS OF OPERAND 2
Op Code	L	B1	D1	B2	D2

0   78   1516 .1920   3132   3536   47

CONTROL REGISTERS

CR	Bits	Name of field	Associated with	Init.
0	0	Block-multiplex'g control	Block-multiplex'g	0
	1	SSM suppression control	SSM instruction	0
	2	TOD clock sync control	Multiprocessing	0
	8-9	Page size control		0
	10	Unassigned (must be zero)	Dynamic addr. transl.	0
	11-12	Segment size control		0
	16	Malfunction alert mask		0
	17	Emergency signal mask		0
	18	External call mask	Multiprocessing	0
	19	TOD clock sync check mask		0
	20	Clock comparator mask	Clock comparator	0
	21	CPU timer mask	CPU timer	0
	24	Interval timer mask	Interval timer	1
	25	Interrupt key mask	Interrupt key	1
	26	External signal mask	External signal	1
1	0-7	Segment table length	Dynamic addr. transl.	0
	8-25	Segment table address		0
2	0-31	Channel masks	Channels	1
8	16-31	Monitor masks	Monitoring	0
9	0	Successful branching event mask		0
	1	Instruction fetching event mask		0
	2	Storage alteration event mask	Program-event record'g	0
	3	GR alteration event mask		0
	16-31	PER general register masks		0
10	8-31	PER starting address	Program-event record'g	0
11	8-31	PER ending address	Program-event record'g	0
14	0	Check-stop control		1
	1	Synch. MCEL control	Machine-check handling	1
	2	I/O extended logout control	I/O extended logout	0
	4	Recovery report mask		0
	5	Degradation report mask		0
	6	Ext. damage report mask	Machine-check handling	1
	7	Warning mask		0
	8	Asynch. MCEL control		0
	9	Asynch. fixed log control		0
15	8-28	MCEL address	Machine-check handling	512

PROGRAM STATUS WORD (BC Mode)

Channel masks	E	Protect'n key	CMWP	Interruption code

0   6 7 8   11 12   15 16   23 24   31

ILC	CC	Program mask	Instruction address

32   34   36   39 40   47 48   55 56   63

0–5 Channel 0 to 5 masks
6 Mask for channel 6 and up
7 (E) External mask
12 (C=0) Basic control mode
13 (M) Machine-check mask
14 (W=1) Wait state
15 (P=1) Problem state

32–33 (ILC) Instruction length code
34–35 (CC) Condition code
36 Fixed-point overflow mask
37 Decimal overflow mask
38 Exponent underflow mask
39 Significance mask

PROGRAM STATUS WORD (EC Mode)

0R00 0TIE	Protect'n key	CMWP	00 CC	Program mask	0000 0000

0   7 8   11 12   15 16   18   20   23 24   31

0000 0000	Instruction address

32   39 40   47 48   55 56   63

1 (R) Program event recording mask
5 (T=1) Translation mode
6 (I) Input/output mask
7 (E) External mask
12 (C=1) Extended control mode
13 (M) Machine-check mask
14 (W=1) Wait state

15 (P=1) Problem state
18–19 (CC) Condition code
20 Fixed-point overflow mask
21 Decimal overflow mask
22 Exponent underflow mask
23 Significance mask

CHANNEL COMMAND WORD

Command code	Data address

0   7 8   15 16   23 24   31

Flags	00	/////	Byte count

32   37 38   47 48   55 56   63

CD—bit 32 (80) causes use of address portion of next CCW.
CC—bit 33 (40) causes use of command code and data address of next CCW.
SLI—bit 34 (20) causes suppression of possible incorrect length indication.
Skip—bit 35 (10) suppresses transfer of information to main storage.
PCI—bit 36 (08) causes a channel program controlled interruption.
IDA—bit 37 (04) causes bits 8–31 of CCW to specify location of first IDAW.

CHANNEL STATUS WORD (hex 40)

Key	0	L	CC	CCW address

0   3 4   5   6 7 8   15 16   23 24   31

Unit status	Channel status	Byte count

32   39 40   47 48   55 56   63

5 Logout pending
6–7 Deferred condition code
32 (80) Attention
33 (40) Status modifier
34 (20) Control unit end
35 (10) Busy
36 (08) Channel end
37 (04) Device end
38 (02) Unit check
39 (01) Unit exception

40 (80) Program-controlled interruption
41 (40) Incorrect length
42 (20) Program check
43 (10) Protection check
44 (08) Channel data check
45 (04) Channel control check
46 (02) Interface control check
47 (01) Chaining check
48–63 Residual byte count for the last CCW used

PROGRAM INTERRUPTION CODES

0001	Operation exception	000C	Exponent overflow excp
0002	Privileged operation excp	000D	Exponent underflow excp
0003	Execute exception	000E	Significance exception
0004	Protection exception	000F	Floating-point divide excp
0005	Addressing exception	0010	Segment translation excp
0006	Specification exception	0011	Page translation exception
0007	Data exception	0012	Translation specification excp
0008	Fixed-point overflow excp	0013	Special operation exception
0009	Fixed-point divide excp	0040	Monitor event
000A	Decimal overflow exception	0080	Program event (code may be
000B	Decimal divide exception		combined with another code)

FIXED STORAGE LOCATIONS

Area, dec.	Hex addr	EC only	Function
0- 7	0		Initial program loading PSW, restart new PSW
8- 15	8		Initial program loading CCW1, restart old PSW
16- 23	10		Initial program loading CCW2
24- 31	18		External old PSW
32- 39	20		Supervisor Call old PSW
40- 47	28		Program old PSW
48- 55	30		Machine-check old PSW
56- 63	38		Input/output old PSW
64- 71	40		Channel status word (see diagram)
72- 75	48		Channel address word [0-3 key, 4-7 zeros, 8-31 CCW address]
80- 83	50		Interval timer
88- 95	58		External new PSW
96-103	60		Supervisor Call new PSW
104-111	68		Program new PSW
112-119	70		Machine-check new PSW
120-127	78		Input/output new PSW
132-133	84		CPU address assoc'd with external interruption, or unchanged
132-133	84	X	CPU address assoc'd with external interruption, or zeros
134-135	86	X	External interruption code
136-139	88	X	SVC interruption [0-12 zeros, 13-14 ILC, 15:0, 16-31 code]
140-143	8C	X	Program interrupt. [0-12 zeros, 13-14 ILC, 15:0, 16-31 code]
144-147	90	X	Translation exception address [0-7 zeros, 8-31 address]
148-149	94		Monitor class [0-7 zeros, 8-15 class number]
150-151	96	X	PER interruption code [0-3 code, 4-15 zeros]
152-155	98	X	PER address [0-7 zeros, 8-31 address]
156-159	9C		Monitor code [0-7 zeros, 8-31 monitor code]
168-171	A8		Channel ID [0-3 type, 4-15 model, 16-31 max. IOEL length]
172-175	AC		I/O extended logout address [0-7 unused, 8-31 address]
176-179	B0		Limited channel logout (see diagram)
185-187	B9	X	I/O address [0-7 zeros, 8-23 address]
216-223	D8		CPU timer save area
224-231	E0		Clock comparator save area
232-239	E8		Machine-check interruption code (see diagram)
248-251	F8		Failing processor storage address [0-7 zeros, 8-31 address]
252-255	FC		Region code*
256-351	100		Fixed logout area*
352-383	160		Floating-point register save area
384-447	180		General register save area
448-511	1C0		Control register save area
512†	200		CPU extended logout area (size varies)

*May vary among models; see system library manuals for specific model.
†Location may be changed by programming (bits 8-28 of CR 15 specify address).

LIMITED CHANNEL LOGOUT (hex B0)

0	SCU id	Detect		Source		000	Field validity flags		TT	00	A	Seq.
0	1 3	4 7	8			12	13 15	16	23	24 26	28	29 31

4 CPU	12 Control unit	24-25 Type of termination
5 Channel	16 Interface address	00 Interface disconnect
6 Main storage control	17-18 Reserved (00)	01 Stop, stack or normal
7 Main storage	19 Sequence code	10 Selective reset
8 CPU	20 Unit status	11 System reset
9 Channel	21 Cmd. addr. and key	28(A) I/O error alert
10 Main storage control	22 Channel address	29-31 Sequence code
11 Main storage	23 Device address	

MACHINE-CHECK INTERRUPTION CODE (hex E8)

MC conditions		000	00	Time	Stg. error	0	Validity indicators
0		8	9	13	14	16 18	19 20 31

0000	0000		0000	00	Val.	MCEL length
32	39	40		45	46 48	55 56 63

0 System damage	14 Backed-up	24 Failing stg. address
1 Instr. proc'g damage	15 Delayed	25 Region code
2 System recovery	16 Uncorrected	27 Floating-pt registers
3 Timer damage	17 Corrected	28 General registers
4 Timing facil. damage	18 Key uncorrected	29 Control registers
5 External damage	20 PSW bits 12-15	30 CPU ext'd logout
6 Not assigned (0)	21 PSW masks and key	31 Storage logical
7 Degradation	22 Prog. mask and CC	46 CPU timer
8 Warning	23 Instruction address	47 Clock comparator

DYNAMIC ADDRESS TRANSLATION
VIRTUAL (LOGICAL) ADDRESS FORMAT

Segment Size	Page Size		Segment Index	Page Index	Byte Index
64K	4K	Bits	8 - 15	16 - 19	20 - 31
64K	2K	0 - 7	8 - 15	16 - 20	21 - 31
1M	4K	are	8 - 11	12 - 19	20 - 31
1M	2K	ignored	8 - 11	12 - 20	21 - 31

SEGMENT TABLE ENTRY

PT length	0000*	Page table address	00*	I
0 3	4 7	8 28	29	31

*Normally zeros; ignored on some models.   31 (I) Segment-invalid bit.

PAGE TABLE ENTRY (4K)

Page address	I	00	
0 11	12	13	15

12 (I) Page-invalid bit.

PAGE TABLE ENTRY (2K)

Page address	I	0	
0 12	13	14	15

13 (I) Page-invalid bit.

HEXADECIMAL AND DECIMAL CONVERSION

From hex: locate each hex digit in its corresponding column position and note the decimal equivalents. Add these to obtain the decimal value.

From decimal: (1) locate the largest decimal value in the table that will fit into the decimal number to be converted, and (2) note its hex equivalent and hex column position. (3) Find the decimal remainder. Repeat the process on this and subsequent remainders.

Note: Decimal, hexadecimal, (and binary) equivalents of all numbers from 0 to 255 are listed on panels 9 – 12.

HEXADECIMAL COLUMNS

6		5		4		3		2		1	
HEX = DEC		HEX = DEC		HEX = DEC		HEX = DEC		HEX = DEC		HEX = DEC	
0	0	0	0	0	0	0	0	0	0	0	0
1	1,048,576	1	65,536	1	4,096	1	256	1	16	1	1
2	2,097,152	2	131,072	2	8,192	2	512	2	32	2	2
3	3,145,728	3	196,608	3	12,288	3	768	3	48	3	3
4	4,194,304	4	262,144	4	16,384	4	1,024	4	64	4	4
5	5,242,880	5	327,680	5	20,480	5	1,280	5	80	5	5
6	6,291,456	6	393,216	6	24,576	6	1,536	6	96	6	6
7	7,340,032	7	458,752	7	28,672	7	1,792	7	112	7	7
8	8,388,608	8	524,288	8	32,768	8	2,048	8	128	8	8
9	9,437,184	9	589,824	9	36,864	9	2,304	9	144	9	9
A	10,485,760	A	655,360	A	40,960	A	2,560	A	160	A	10
B	11,534,336	B	720,896	B	45,056	B	2,816	B	176	B	11
C	12,582,912	C	786,432	C	49,152	C	3,072	C	192	C	12
D	13,631,488	D	851,968	D	53,248	D	3,328	D	208	D	13
E	14,680,064	E	917,504	E	57,344	E	3,584	E	224	E	14
F	15,728,640	F	983,040	F	61,440	F	3,840	F	240	F	15
0 1 2 3		4 5 6 7		0 1 2 3		4 5 6 7		0 1 2 3		4 5 6 7	
BYTE				BYTE				BYTE			

POWERS OF 2

2^n	n
256	8
512	9
1 024	10
2 048	11
4 096	12
8 192	13
16 384	14
32 768	15
65 536	16
131 072	17
262 144	18
524 288	19
1 048 576	20
2 097 152	21
4 194 304	22
8 388 608	23
16 777 216	24

$2^0 = 16^0$	
$2^4 = 16^1$	
$2^8 = 16^2$	
$2^{12} = 16^3$	
$2^{16} = 16^4$	
$2^{20} = 16^5$	
$2^{24} = 16^6$	
$2^{28} = 16^7$	
$2^{32} = 16^8$	
$2^{36} = 16^9$	
$2^{40} = 16^{10}$	
$2^{44} = 16^{11}$	
$2^{48} = 16^{12}$	
$2^{52} = 16^{13}$	
$2^{56} = 16^{14}$	
$2^{60} = 16^{15}$	

POWERS OF 16

16^n	n
1	0
16	1
256	2
4 096	3
65 536	4
1 048 576	5
16 777 216	6
268 435 456	7
4 294 967 296	8
68 719 476 736	9
1 099 511 627 776	10
17 592 186 044 416	11
281 474 976 710 656	12
4 503 599 627 370 496	13
72 057 594 037 927 936	14
1 152 921 504 606 846 976	15

Possible Program Interruptions

The interrupt mechanism permits the CPU to react to conditions within the CPU itself, within the system, or external to the system. The conditions that will be discussed here—program interrupts—are those that can be caused by the program that is executing.

The type of program exception that caused the interrupt is indicated in the interruption-code portion of the PSW (bits 16–31) or spelled out at the beginning of the dump. There are twenty-one different types of exceptions that cause a program interruption. (Some of these will be discussed in detail here; for further information, see GA22-7000, *IBM System/370 Principles of Operation*.)

Operation Exception. Occurs when the first byte in an instruction does not contain a valid operation code.

Privileged-Operation Exception. Occurs when a program is executing in the problem state and the CPU encounters an opcode that represents a privileged operation.

Execute Exception. Occurs when the subject instruction of an Execute (EX) instruction is another Execute instruction.

Protection Exception. Occurs when a main storage location is referenced and that location is protected against references. Two types of protection are recognized: store protection and fetch protection. The first prevents a programmer from altering the contents of a location in main storage; the second maintains the privacy of a storage location from unauthorized access. The protection is accomplished with the comparison of the key associated with the main storage location and the protection key for the program in its PSW.

Addressing Exception. Occurs when the program references a main storage address that does not exist. It's an address beyond the end of the main storage addressed by the CPU. If part of an operand can be addressed and part cannot, the part that can be will participate in the operation, and then execution will be interrupted.

Specification Exception. Can occur in a variety of cases where part of an instruction is incorrectly specified; for instance, if the address of the instruction itself is not on a halfword boundary, or an operand address does not meet the integral boundary requirements of an instruction (for example, L, ST, AH, CVB, or STM). It can also occur if the first-operand field is not longer than the second-operand field in a decimal multiplication or division operation, or if the multiplier or divisor exceeds 15 digits and a sign.

A specification exception can also occur when registers are specified incorrectly; for instance, an odd-register number specified where an even-odd coupled register pair is expected (M, D, CLL, MVCL, and the double shift operations), or a number other than 0, 2, 4, or 6 being specified in a floating-point instruction.

Data Exception. Occurs as the result of errors encountered in the data operated upon by a decimal instruction—the multiplicand doesn't have enough high-order zeros or the product may not fit; an invalid sign or digits in packed-decimal field for the Convert to Binary (CVB) instruction, or any of the decimal instructions. Valid digits are 0–9, valid signs are A–F.

Fixed-Point-Overflow Exception. Occurs in fixed-point arithmetic and left algebraic shift operations when the sign bit (bit 0) is about to be destroyed.

Fixed-Point-Divide Exception. Occurs in fixed-point divide operations when the divisor is zero or the quotient won't fit in one register. Also occurs in the Convert-to-Binary (CVB) operation when the converted number will not fit in the register. Care must be exercised if this is a possibility, because the high-order bits will be ignored, with the remainder of the binary number being placed in the register.

Exponent-Overflow Exception. Occurs when the result of a floating-point operation has a nonzero fraction and an exponent that is greater than 127.

Exponent-Underflow Exception. Occurs when the result of a floating-point operation has a nonzero fraction and an exponent that is less than zero.

APPENDIX 5

Comparison of Assemblers

Language Feature	Assemblers			
	DOS/360 (D)	DOS/VS	OS/360 (F)	OS/VS
1. No. of continuation lines allowed in one statement:	1	2	2	2
2. Location Counter value printed for EQU, USING, ORG (in ADDR2 field):	3 bytes	3 bytes	3 bytes	4 bytes (up to 3 leading zeros suppressed)
3. Self-Defining Terms maximum value:	$2^{24}-1$	$2^{24}-1$	$2^{24}-1$	$2^{31}-1$
number of digits				
binary:	24	24	24	32
decimal:	8	8	8	10
hexadecimal:	6	6	6	8
character:	3	3	3	4
4. Relocatable and Absolute Expressions				
unary operators allowed:	no	yes	no	yes
value carried:	truncated to 24 bits	truncated to 24 bits	truncated to 24 bits	31 bits
number of operators:	15	15	15	19
levels of parentheses:	15	15	15	19
5. Alignment of Constants (with no length modifier) when NOALIGN option specified:	ALIGN/ NOALIGN option not allowed	constants not aligned	constants aligned	constants not aligned
6. Extended Branching Mnemonics for RR format instructions:	no	yes	no	yes

Language Feature	Assemblers			
	DOS/360 (D)	DOS/VS	OS/360 (F)	OS/VS
7. COPY Instruction nesting depth allowed: macro definitions copied:	none no	3 yes	none no	5 yes
8. END Instruction sequence symbol as name entry: generated or copied END instructions:	yes no	yes no	yes no	yes yes
9. All control sections initiated by a CSECT start at location 0 in listing and object deck:	no	yes	no	no
10. External Symbol Dictionary Entries maximum allowed:	255	255	255	399 (including entry symbols identified by ENTRY)
11. DSECT Instruction blank name entry:	no	yes	no	yes
12. DROP Instruction blank operand entry:	not allowed	signifies all current base registers dropped	not allowed	signifies all current base registers dropped
13. EQU Instruction second operand as length attribute: third operand as type attribute:	no no	no no	no no	yes yes
14. DC/DS Instruction number of operands:	one	multiple	multiple	multiple
15. Bit-length specification allowed:	no	yes	yes	yes
16. Literal Constants multiterm expression for duplication factor: length, scale, and exponent modifier: Q- or S-type address constant:	no no no	yes yes no	no no no	yes yes yes
17. Binary and Hexadecimal Constants number of nominal values:	one	one	one	multiple
18. Q-type address constant allowed:	no	no	yes	yes
19. ORG Instruction name entry allowed:	sequence symbol or blank	sequence symbol or blank	sequence symbol or blank	any symbol or blank
20. Literal cross-reference:	no	yes	no	yes
21. CNOP Instruction symbol as name entry:	sequence symbol or blank	sequence symbol or blank	only sequence symbol or blank	any symbol or blank
22. PRINT Instruction inside macro definition:	no	yes	no	yes
23. TITLE Instruction number of characters in name (if not a sequence symbol):	4	4	4	8

Language Feature	Assemblers			
	DOS/360 (D)	DOS/VS	OS/360 (F)	OS/VS
24. OPSYN Instruction:	no	no	yes	yes
25. PUSH and POP Instructions for saving PRINT and USING status:	no	no	no	yes
26. Symbolic Parameters and Macro Instruction Operands maximum number:	100	200	200	no fixed maximum
mixing positional and keyword:	all positional parameters or operands must come first	all positional parameters or operands must come first	all positional parameters or operands must come first	keyword parameters or operands can be interspersed among positional parameters or operands
27. Generated op-codes START, CSECT, DSECT, COM allowed:	no	yes	no	yes
28. Generated Remarks due generated blanks in operand field:	no	no	no	yes
29. MNOTE Instruction in open code:	no	no	no	yes
30. System Variable Symbols &SYSPARM:	yes	yes	no	yes
&SYSDATE:	no	no	no	yes
&SYSTIME:	no	no	no	yes
31. Maximum number of characters in macro instruction operand:	127	255	255	255
32. Type and Count Attribute of SET symbols: &SYSPARM, &SYSNDX, &SYSECT,&SYSDATE,&SYSTIME:	no no	no no	no no	yes yes
33. Set Symbol Declaration global and local mixed:	no, global must precede local	no, global must precede local	no, global must precede local	yes
global and local must immediately follow prototype statement, if in macro definition:	yes	yes	yes	no
must immediately follow any source macro definitions, if in open code:	yes	yes	yes	no
34. Subscripted Set Symbols maximum dimension:	255	255	2500	32,767
35. SETC Instruction duplication factor in operand:	no	no	no	yes
maximum number of characters assigned:	8	8	8	255
36. Arithmetic Expressions in conditional assembly unary operators allowed:	no	yes	no	yes
number of terms:	16	16	16	up to 25
levels of parentheses:	5	5	5	up to 11

Language Feature	Assemblers			
	DOS/360 (D)	DOS/VS	OS/360 (F)	OS/VS
37. ACTR Instruction allowed anywhere in open code and inside macro definitions:	no, only immediately after global and local SET symbol declarations	yes	no, only immediately after global and local SET symbol declarations	yes
38. Options for Assembler Program				
ALIGN:	no	yes	yes	yes
ALOGIC:	no	no	no	yes
MCALL:	no	no	no	yes
EDECK:	no	yes	no	no
MLOGIC:	no	no	no	yes
LIBMAC:	no	no	no	yes

Hexadecimal and Decimal Fraction Conversion Table

				HALFWORD								
BYTE				BYTE								
BITS 0123		4567			0123				4567			
Hex	Decimal	Hex	Decimal		Hex	Decimal			Hex	Decimal Equivalent			
.0	.0000	.00	.0000	0000	.000	.0000	0000	0000	.0000	.0000	0000	0000	0000
.1	.0625	.01	.0039	0625	.001	.0002	4414	0625	.0001	.0000	1525	8789	0625
.2	.1250	.02	.0078	1250	.002	.0004	8828	1250	.0002	.0000	3051	7578	1250
.3	.1875	.03	.0117	1875	.003	.0007	3242	1875	.0003	.0000	4577	6367	1875
.4	.2500	.04	.0156	2500	.004	.0009	7656	2500	.0004	.0000	6103	5156	2500
.5	.3125	.05	.0195	3125	.005	.0012	2070	3125	.0005	.0000	7629	3945	3125
.6	.3750	.06	.0234	3750	.006	.0014	6484	3750	.0006	.0000	9155	2734	3750
.7	.4375	.07	.0273	4375	.007	.0017	0898	4375	.0007	.0001	0681	1523	4375
.8	.5000	.08	.0312	5000	.008	.0019	5312	5000	.0008	.0001	2207	0312	5000
.9	.5625	.09	.0351	5625	.009	.0021	9726	5625	.0009	.0001	3732	9101	5625
.A	.6250	.0A	.0390	6250	.00A	.0024	4140	6250	.000A	.0001	5258	7890	6250
.B	.6875	.0B	.0429	6875	.00B	.0026	8554	6875	.000B	.0001	6784	6679	6875
.C	.7500	.0C	.0468	7500	.00C	.0029	2968	7500	.000C	.0001	8310	5468	7500
.D	.8125	.0D	.0507	8125	.00D	.0031	7382	8125	.000D	.0001	9836	4257	8125
.E	.8750	.0E	.0546	8750	.00E	.0034	1796	8750	.000E	.0002	1362	3046	8750
.F	.9375	.0F	.0585	9375	.00F	.0036	6210	9375	.000F	.0002	2888	1835	9375
1		2			3				4				

GLOSSARY

ABEND.   Abnormal end of job.

ABEND dump.   A display of register contents, storage contents, and any pertinent information that the system can provide at the point where a job cannot be allowed to continue execution because of the occurrence of an exceptional condition.

absolute address.   See *explicit address*.

absolute expression.   An expression whose value is not affected by program relocation. It can represent an absolute address.

absolute term.   A term whose value is not affected by relocation.

absolute value.   A value that is not affected by relocation.

access.   The manner in which files or data sets are referred to by the computer.

access method.   A technique for moving data between main storage and input/output devices.

actual address.   Same as *absolute address*.

address.   The value by which a programmer references a storage location.

address constant.   A constant requested by the programmer and defined by the assembler to contain a complete storage address.

address space.   The complete range of addresses that is available to a programmer.

address translation.   (1) The process of changing the address of an item of data or an instruction to the address in main storage where it is to be loaded or relocated. (2) In virtual storage systems, the process of changing the address of an item of data or an instruction from its virtual storage address to its real storage address.

algebraic shift.   The type of shift in which all bits do not participate equally. The left-most bit is treated as the sign.

algorithm.   A preset procedure designed to create a step by step solution to a problem.

alignment.   See *boundary alignment*.

allocate.   To assign a resource for use in performing a specific task.

alphabetic character.   The characters A through Z and @, #, and $.

alphameric characters. The characters A through Z, digits 0 through 9, and @, #, and $.

ALU. Arithmetic and logic unit. The portion of the hardware that handles arithmetic operations and logical operations such as comparisons.

American National Standards Institute. An organization sponsored by the Business Equipment Manufacturers Association (BEMA) for the purpose of establishing voluntary industry standards. Abbreviated ANSI.

analog. A computer that performs mathematical operations on data received that is converted into electrical impulses. Receives its data in a continuous stream.

ANSI. Abbreviation for American National Standards Institute.

argument. That portion of an element in a search reference table that is checked for a match to the argument being searched for. It is the key to each element.

arithmetic and logic unit. See *ALU*.

ASA. American Standards Association. A former name for the American National Standards Institute.

ASA control characters. Characters placed in the first byte of an output record destined for the printer. It is not printed itself, but is used to control the virtual spacing of the lines; single spacing, double spacing, or eject.

assemble. The translation of a source module in the assembler's symbolic language to an object module in machine language.

assembler. A program that performs the translation of an assembler source module to a machine language object module.

assembler language. A source language that includes symbolic machine language statements in which there is a one-to-one correspondence with the instruction formats and data formats of the computer.

assembler listing. See *listing*.

assembly. The output of an assembler.

assembly time. The time at which an assembler translates the symbolic language statements into their object code form (machine instructions).

asterisk. Refers to the current value of the location counter when used where a relocatable value is expected. A special character (*) that denotes a comment statement (full card comment) when it appears in column one of a source statement.

A-type constant. See *address constant*.

automatic data processing. See *data processing system*.

auxiliary storage. Data storage other than main storage; for example, storage on magnetic tape or direct access device.

background reference. A facility of the job control language that allows the user to copy information or refer to DD statements that appear in an earlier job step.

base address. The beginning address for resolving symbolic references to storage.

base register. A general purpose register that has been designated and contains the base address to be used in resolving symbolic references to storage locations.

basic control (BC) mode. A mode in which the features of a System/360 computing system and additional features, such as new machine instructions, are operational on a System/370 computing system. See also *extended control (EC) mode*.

batch processing. See *stacked job processing*.

batched job. A job that is grouped with other jobs as input to a computing system. Synonymous with *stacked job*.

BAU. The Basic Addressable Unit of Systems/360 and 370, the byte. The smallest piece of storage that can be addressed.

BC mode. See *basic control mode.*

binary-coded decimal character code. A set of 64 characters, each represented by six bits. See also *extended binary-coded decimal interchange code.*

binary number system. A number system containing 2 symbols; 0 and 1. Base 2.

bind. To fix or assign a value to a symbol, parameter, or variable.

binding time. The point in time when a value is fixed or assigned to a symbol, parameter, or variable.

bit. A term generally used to refer to a binary digit.

blank character. On input, a blank will be converted to the EBCDIC representation of a blank, a hexadecimal 40.

block. See *physical record.*

blocking. Combining two or more logical records into one physical record or block.

blocking factor. The number of logical records combined into one physical record or block.

block length. The number of bytes in a physical record or block.

block size. Same as *block length.*

boundary. See *boundary alignment.*

boundary alignment. The position in main storage of a fixed-length field, such as a halfword or doubleword, on an integral boundary for that unit of information. A halfword boundary is a storage address that is evenly divisible by two and a doubleword boundary is a storage address that is evenly divisible by eight.

branch. An instruction that changes the sequence of instruction execution.

branch table. A table in which each element is a branch instruction.

branch target. The subject instruction of the branch instruction. The next instruction that will be executed if the branch is taken.

buffer. An area that data may be read into, while processing continues. Also the I/O area used by the data management routines.

bug. A problem in a program which prevents it from executing successfully. It can be a syntax error, an error at execution time, or an error in the logic of the solution to the problem.

byte. A sequence of eight adjacent binary digits that are operated upon as a unit and that constitute the smallest addressable unit in the computer's storage (BAU).

call. See *subroutine call.*

call by name. Passing the addresses of the parameters to a subroutine.

call by value. Passing the actual values of the parameters to a subroutine.

called routine. A subroutine which is called or receives control.

calling routine. A subroutine which calls or passes control to another routine.

calling sequence. The set up of parameters and actual branch which transfers control.

card field. One or more consecutive card columns assigned to data of a specific nature. For example, card columns 15–20 can be assigned to identification.

carriage-control character. See *ASA control character.*

catalog. (1) The collection of all data set indexes that are used by the control program to locate a volume containing a specific data set. (2) To include the volume identification of a data set in the catalog. Under DOS and TOS, to enter a phase or module into one of the system libraries.

cataloged data set. A data set that is represented in an index, or hierarchy of indexes, that provide the means for locating it.

cataloged procedure. A set of job control statements that has been placed in a procedure library, and can be retrieved by naming it in an execute (EXEC) statement.

central processing unit. That part of the computer system that keeps track of the next instruction to be executed, and interprets and executes all instructions. It can be abbreviated CPU.

chained list. A means of connecting a collection of data items when they are not in contiguous areas of storage. The connection is made through addresses kept in each item or block. See *headers*.

character. An 8-bit code represented in a byte, making 256 different bit combinations possible. EBCDIC.

character expression. A character string enclosed by apostrophes. The enclosing apostrophes are not part of the value represented.

character set. A fixed number of graphic representations, called characters.

closed loop. A group of instructions that are repeated indefinitely. Same as *infinite loop*.

collating sequence. A logical sequence used to order items of data. In the case of the binary contents of bytes representing EBCDIC characters, placing them in ascending order from 00000000 to 11111111 will alphabetize the alphabetic characters, followed by the numeric digits.

comments field. The fourth field of an assembler language statement. It follows the operand field preceded by a blank. It is not checked for syntax errors in the assembler's scan of the statement.

comment statement. A statement used to include information that may be helpful in running a job or reviewing a listing. It is noted to the assembler by the appearance of an asterisk in column one of the statement.

comparison. The examination of the relationship between two items of data. It is usually followed by a decision.

completion code. An indication produced by OS-based systems when a program has abended to show the type of error. For example, a 0C1 is an addressing exception. Also a code set up in OS-based systems where completion status of one step may affect execution of a following step.

computer. An apparatus that receives instructions and data, and produces results using the instructions on the data.

computer program. See *program*.

concatenated data sets. A group of logically connected data sets that are treated as one data set for the duration of a job step.

concatenation character. A period is used to separate character strings that are to be joined together in conditional assembly instructions; for example, (&STRING.ABC).

condition-controlled loop. A loop in which the decision to stop execution is based on the occurrence of a particular condition.

conditional assembly. An assembler facility for altering at pre-assembly time the content and sequence of source statements that are to be assembled.

conditional assembly instruction. An assembler instruction that performs a conditional assembly operation. Conditional assembly instructions are processed at pre-assembly time.

conditional branch. A branch instruction in which a test for a particular condition is made and if the condition is met, the branch is taken.

conditional jump. Same as *conditional branch*.

condition code. A code that reflects the result of a previous arithmetic or logical operation.

constant. A fixed or invariable value or data item.

contiguous. Consecutive bytes in storage. For example, the byte with the address 2 follows the byte with the address 1. Bytes addressed 1 and 2 are contiguous.

control. Part of data processing system that determines the order for performance of basic functions.

control character. See *carriage-control character.*

control section. That part of a program specified by the programmer to be a relocatable unit, all elements of which are to be loaded into adjoining storage locations. It is abbreviated CSECT.

core image library. Under DOS-based systems, a library of phases that have been produced as output from link-editing. The phases in the core image library are in a format that is executable either directly or after processing by the relocating loader in the supervisor.

corner cut. A corner removed from a card for orientation purposes.

count-controlled loop. A loop which is executed a finite number of times.

counter. A location, storage or register, in which a programmer keeps a count of the number of times a particular event has occurred.

CPU. Central processing unit.

cross-reference table. A table produced by the assembler from information encountered in the source module. It contains each symbol, attribute, statement numbers of where the symbol is defined and every statement in which the symbol appears in the operand.

CSECT. Abbreviation for control section.

DASD. See *direct-access storage device.*

DAT. See *dynamic address translation.*

data. Characters that are capable of having meaning assigned to them, by a programmer, for a particular purpose.

data base. A collection of data fundamental to an enterprise.

data control block. A block of constants used by input/output routines in storing and retrieving data. Abbreviated DCB.

data conversion. The process of changing data from one form of representation to another.

data definition name. The name of a data definition (DD) statement, which corresponds to a data control block that contains the same name. Abbreviated ddname.

data definition (DD) statement. A job control statement that describes a data set associated with a particular job step.

data file. A collection of related data records organized in a specific manner. For example, a payroll file (one record for each employee, showing his rate of pay, deductions, etc.). See also *data set.*

data management. A major function of operating systems that involves organizing, cataloging, locating, storing, retrieving, and maintaining data.

data medium. See *medium.*

data organization. The arrangement of information in a data set; for example, sequential organization.

data processing. The handling of data to produce desired results.

data processing system. A network of machine components capable of accepting information, processing this information according to a plan (a program) and producing the desired results.

data protection. A safeguard that prevents the loss or destruction of data.

data set. The major unit of data storage and retrieval in the operating system, consisting of a collection of data in a prescribed arrangement and described by control information to which the system has access.

data set label. A collection of information that describes the attributes of a data set and is normally stored on the same volume as the data set.

data set name. The term or phrase used to identify a data set.

data set organization. See *data organization.*

data set utility programs. Programs that can be used to update, maintain, edit, and transcribe data sets.

DCB. Data control block.

ddname. Data definition name.

DD statement. Data definition statement.

deblock. To remove records from a block.

deblocking. The action of making the first and each subsequent logical record of a block available for processing, one record at a time.

debug. To recognize, locate, and eliminate errors in a program.

decimal number system. A number system containing 10 symbols; 0, 1, 2, 3, 4, 5, 6, 7, 8, and 9. Base 10.

decision. See *branch*.

decision table. A table showing conditions that can be present in a particular situation, and the resultant actions taken.

default value. The choice among exclusive alternatives made by the system when no explicit choice is specified by the user. For example, keyword parameters on a macro call.

define the file. See *DTF*.

delimiter. A character or location that groups or separates words or values in a line or statement. For instance, column 72 is the delimiter for an assembler language statement, and a comma is the delimiter that separates each operand in the statement.

delimiter statement. A job control statement used to mark the end of data (/*), or the end of the job (// in OS-based systems and /& in DOS-based systems).

demand paging. In System/370 virtual storage systems, transfer of a page from external page storage to real storage at the time it is needed for execution.

desk checking. Debugging a program at coding time. Involves use of flowchart, commenting code, undefined symbol check, and a one for one check of keypunching.

device independence. The ability to request I/O operations without regard for the characteristics of specific types of input/output devices. See also *symbolic unit name* or *logical unit name*.

device type. The general name for a kind of device; for example, 1403, 3330, or 3400. See also *group name*.

diagnostic error message. Error messages produced by the assembler following the listing of the source module, explaining problems it has noted as it scanned the instructions.

digital computer. A computer that operates directly on the data it receives. The data is in discrete pieces rather than a continuous stream.

digit punch A punch that occupies a location in rows 0–9 on a punched card.

direct access storage device. A device in which the access time is effectively independent of the location of the data. Abbreviated DASD.

direct reference table. A table in which each element contains only a function portion. The key is used to directly reference a particular element rather than searching a series of arguments in each element.

Disk Operating System. A disk resident programming system that provides operating system capabilities for 16K and larger Systems/360 and 370 computing systems. Abbreviated DOS.

displacement. Positive number which can be added to the contents of the base register to calculate an effective address.

disposition. The status of a data set both before and after a particular job step. Indicated in the DISP operand of the DD statement.

documentation. Supporting information about a program, such as comments, flowcharts, and writeup.

DOS. See *Disk Operating System*.

double threaded. A type of chained list or queue that has a chain of addresses pointing back to the previous blocks as well as forward to the next blocks. See *single threaded.*

doubleword. A contiguous sequence of 64 bits or 8 bytes of storage. It is capable of being addressed as a unit by referencing its first byte which has an address that is evenly divisible by eight.

downtime. The period of time in which the system or a particular device is inoperative.

DSECT. Abbreviation for Dummy Section. Also referred to as Dummy Control Section.

DTF. A macro instruction for defining a file under a DOS-based operating system. It describes the characteristics of the data set, indicates the type of processing to be used with the file, and specifies the main storage areas and routines to be used.

dummy control section. A control section that an assembler can use to format an area of storage without producing any object code. Abbreviated DSECT.

dump. A display of the contents of storage as well as register contents and other pertinent information.

duplication factor. A value that indicates in a DC statement the number of times that the data specified immediately following it is to be generated.

dynamic address translation. In System/370 virtual storage systems, the change of a virtual storage address to a real storage address during the execution of an instruction. Also a hardware facility that performs the translation. Abbreviated DAT.

dynamic dump. A dump of storage and register contents produced whenever a programmer requests one by using the SNAP macro under OS-based systems or PDUMP under DOS-based systems. Control is returned to the next sequential instruction after the dump is produced.

dynamic relocation. A type of relocation which fixes the time of binding to the latest possible point—when it is loaded. Not until a portion of code is needed at execution time is a relative address translated to a real storage address.

EBCDIC. Extended binary coded decimal interchange code.

EC mode. Extended control mode.

edit. The process of inserting characters into an output field to create more legible reports.

effective address. An actual real storage address. A displacement added to the contents of a base register and an index register if one is present.

electronic data processing. Data processing using electronic equipment.

element. A discrete portion of a table that is referenced by its location in relation to the beginning of the table.

eleven-punch. A punch in the second row from the top of a standard punched card. Also the representation of a minus sign.

end-of-file. Condition reached when all the records have been read in a sequential input file. Abbreviated EOF.

end-of-file mark. A code that signals that the last record of a file or data set has been read. Abbreviated EOF.

entry code. The code that handles standard linkage conventions as a routine first receives control, the storing of register contents, establishing addressability, and preparation of a new save area.

entry name. A name within a control section that defines an entry point and can be referred to by any control section.

entry symbol. An ordinary symbol that represents an entry name or control section name.

EOF. Abbreviation for End-of-file.

EQU. Abbreviation for equate.

equate. An assembler pseudo op that allows the assignment of a value to a symbol. The symbol can be either absolute or relocatable depending on the value assigned.

error condition. The state that results from an attempt to execute instructions in a computer program that are invalid or that operate on invalid data.

ESD. External symbol dictionary.

establish addressability. The process of informing the assembler which register it can use as a base register and what value will be in that register. Also the filling of that register with the promised value at execution time.

E-time. See *execution time*.

even-odd coupled register pair. Two consecutive registers, the first having an even number and the second the next higher numbered register. For example, registers 4 and 5, or 8 and 9.

exception. See *error condition*.

excess sixty-four binary notation. A binary notation in which the characteristic component of a floating-point number is represented in storage.

execute. To carry out an instruction or perform a routine.

execute (EXEC) statement. A job control language (JCL) statement that marks the beginning of a job step and identifies the program to be executed or the cataloged procedure to be used.

execution time. The time during which an instruction is decoded and performed. See also *instruction time*. Abbreviated E-time.

exit code. The code that handles linkage conventions as a subroutine is about to return control—restoring registers.

explicit address. An address in which the base register and displacement are coded in the instruction by the programmer rather than coding a symbol and letting the assembler substitute the base register and displacement.

explicit length. A length, in bytes, specified in the operand it refers to rather than letting the implied length of the symbol in that operand apply. Generally used in SS-type instructions.

expression. A term or arithmetic combination of terms representing a value.

extended binary coded decimal interchange code. A set of 256 characters, each represented by eight bits. Abbreviated EBCDIC. See also *binary coded decimal character code*.

extended control (EC) mode. A mode in which all the features of a System/370 computing system, including dynamic address translation, are operational. See also *basic control (BC) mode*.

extended mnemonic. Special mnemonic opcodes that make it easier for the programmer to specify branching instructions. The mnemonic used not only states that this is a branch instruction, but also the mask to be used to determine what conditions.

external page storage. In System/370 virtual storage systems, the portion of auxiliary storage that is used to contain pages.

external page table. In OS/VS2 and VM/370, an extension of a page table that identifies the location on external page storage of each page in that table.

external reference. A reference to a symbol that is defined as an external name in another module. Also, a symbol that is not defined in the module that references it.

external storage. Same as *auxiliary storage*.

external symbol. A control section name, entry point name, or external reference that is defined or referred to in a particular module. An ordinary symbol that represents an external reference.

external symbol dictionary. Control information, associated with an object or load module, that identifies the external symbols in the module. Abbreviated ESD.

externally referencable symbol. See *entry symbol.*

EXTRN. External reference declarative.

fetch. To locate and retrieve something from storage. For example, the next sequential instruction or a word of data for a register.

fetch protection. A storage protection feature that determines the right to access storage by matching a protection key, associated with a fetch reference to storage.

field. A specific group of contiguous bytes in a record which are treated as a unit.

FIFO. A technique for handling a chained list on a first-in-first-out basis.

file. A collection of related records treated as a unit.

fixed-length data. Data of a specific length (two, four, or eight bytes) that reside on integral boundaries (halfword, fullword, and double-word, respectively).

fixed-length record. A data set in which a logical record contains the same number of bytes as every other record in the data set.

fixed-point binary number. Occupy fullwords and halfwords. In each case the first bit in the field is the sign (0 is positive, 1 is negative). A negative number is stored in two's complement form.

floating-point number system. A number system in which very large and very small numbers can be represented because the decimal point can be moved.

flowchart. A pictorial method of displaying the steps involved in the logic of a solution to a problem.

fragmentation. Inability to assign real storage locations because the available spaces, though many, are smaller than needed.

full-line comment. A source statement with an asterisk (*) in column one. It is not scanned by the Assembler and can be used to document the program.

fullword. See *word.*

function. That portion of an element in a search reference table that is referenced for information once the correct element has been found.

fwb. Abbreviation for fullword boundary.

garbage. Data to which no meaning has been assigned for this particular usage.

general purpose register. See *register.*

generate. To produce assembler language statements from the model statements of a macro definition when the definition is called by a macro instruction.

GET. To obtain a logical record from an input file.

group name. A generic name for a collection of I/O devices, for example, DISK or TAPE.

guard digit. Used in execution of short form add, subtract, and divide floating-point operations. One spare hexadecimal digit which serves as extra (seventh) digit to improve precision.

halfword. A contiguous sequence of 16 bits or two bytes, which are capable of being treated as a unit. The first byte of the halfword occupies a storage location whose address is evenly divisible by two.

hard copy. A printed copy of machine output in a visually readable form; for example, printed reports, listings, and documents.

hardware. The mechanical equipment necessary for a computing system.

header statement. The MACRO statement which indicates the beginning of a macro definition to the assembler.

header. Contains the address of the beginning of a chained list. A single-threaded list has one header and a double-threaded list has two headers (second header contains the address of the last element in the chain). Same as *queue control words.*

hexadecimal number system. A number system containing 16 symbols; 0, 1, 2, 3, 4, 5, 6, 7, 8, 9, A, B, C, D, E, and F. Base 16.

hexadecimal shorthand. A means of referring to the contents of a byte as two hexadecimal digits rather than eight binary digits.

high-order. Leftmost. For instance, bit 0 in a register.

hit. See *match.*

Hollerith code. The most widely used punched card code. A subset of EBCDIC.

housekeeping. Operations or routines that do not contribute directly to the solution of the problem, but do contribute directly to the operation of the computer.

hwb. Abbreviation for halfword boundary.

IBM System/360. A large collection of computing system devices that can be connected together in many combinations to produce a wide range of computing systems that share many characteristics including a common machine.

IBM System/370. An upward-compatible extension of the IBM System/360, offering new functions.

IBM System/360 Operating System. A comprehensive collection of control program options, language processors, I/O support, and service routines, designed to meet the needs of users who require the extensive facilities of a large operating system.

immediate data. One byte of data that appears in the instruction itself rather than the symbolic name of the one byte of data. The data is immediately available from the instruction.

implicit address. A symbolic reference to storage that must be converted into its explicit base-displacement form before it can be assembled into the object code of a machine instruction.

implied length. The length associated with a symbol. This length will be used on a variable length operand if a length is not explicitly specified in the operand.

indexing. A technique of address modification implementated by the use of general purpose registers referred to as index registers.

index register. A register whose contents are added to the address derived from a combination of a base address with a displacement or an implicit address converted to a base and displacement.

infinite loop. Same as *closed loop.*

information. Data to which a meaning has been assigned for this particular usage.

initialization. Initial values are assigned outside the loop to all counters, conditions, and variables needed within the body of the loop.

input/output. A general term for the equipment used to communicate with a computer, commonly called I/O. Also the data involved in such a communication.

input stream. The sequence of job control statements and data submitted to an operating system on an input unit especially activated for this purpose by the operator. Synonymous with input job stream, and job input stream.

input stream data set. A data set that physically resides in the input stream.

instruction. A request to the computer to perform one of its basic functions.

instruction classes. The five different (six on System/370) formats of machine instructions used on the computer (RR, RX, RS, SI, and SS with S available only on System 370).

instruction address counter. A location within the CPU where the address of the beginning of the next instruction to be executed is kept.

instruction format. The allocation of bits or characters of a machine instruction to specific classes of instructions.

instruction repertoire. The list of mnemonic opcodes that an assembler recognizes as valid.

instruction time. The time during which an instruction is fetched from storage of a computer into an instruction register. Abbreviated I-time.

integral boundary. A location in main storage at which a fixed-length field, such as a halfword or doubleword, must be positioned. The address of an integral boundary is a multiple of the length of the field in bytes. See also *boundary alignment*.

internal sort. A sorting technique that creates sequences of records or keys, or elements of a table. All the items that participate in the sort in storage as the sort is being accomplished.

interrupt. The supervisor seizing control when an error condition has occurred or assistance is needed to provide I/O.

interruption. A break in the normal sequence of instruction execution. It causes an automatic transfer to a preset location where appropriate action is taken.

I/O. See *Input/Output*.

iterate. To repeatedly execute a loop or series of steps, for example, a loop in a routine.

I-time. Instruction time.

JCL. Abbreviation for job control language.

job. A unit of work to the computer; consists of one or more job steps, and each step involves the execution of a program.

job control language. A programming language used to code job control statements. Abbreviated JCL.

job control statement. Statements which give information to the operating system about what it is supposed to do. Each type of operating system has its own set of job control statements.

jobname. The name assigned to a JOB statement; it identifies the beginning of a job. It identifies the job to the system.

job (JOB) statement. The job control statement that identifies the beginning of a job. It contains such information as the name of the job.

job step. A unit of work associated with one processing program or one cataloged procedure and related data. A job consists of one or more job steps.

jump. See *branch*.

K. 1024 bytes; used in referring to storage capacity.

keyword. One of the significant and informative words in a title or document that describes the content of that document. A symbol that identifies a parameter. A part of a command operand that consists of a specific character string (such as DSNAME=).

keyword parameter. A parameter that consists of a keyword, followed by one or more values. See also *positional parameter*.

label. An identification record for a tape or disk file. A name entry in an assembler language statement.

least significant. The digit with the smallest place value in the number. Rightmost.

left-justify. To align on the left hand side of the field.

length attribute. The length, in bytes, associated with a symbol.

length modifier. A subfield which can be specified in the operand of a DC or DS statement. For example: DS CL6. If used on a fixed length definition (F,H or D) the automatic alignment will be overridden.

LIFO. A technique for handling a chained list on a last-in-first-out basis. Often used for priority queues.

link field. The pointer field in data items in a chained list which connects the data items to each other.

linkage conventions. A set of rules for calling routine responsibilities when using subroutines.

linkage editor. An IBM-supplied program which processes object modules preparing them for execution. It resolves cross references between separately assembled object modules.

listing. A printout, usually prepared by a language translator, that lists the source language statements and contents of a program.

literal. A literal represents data. It can be used in instruction operands to introduce data. It is a means to avoid defined constants and using the symbolic names of these constants in instructions. Literals will be assembled and are relocatable values; but it is the assembler that defines them in literal pools rather than the programmer.

literal pool. An area of storage into which the values of the literals specified in a source module are assembled.

load. To fetch a fullword from storage and place it in a register. Also to place a load module into real storage.

load module. The output of the linkage editor; a program in a format suitable for loading into main storage for execution.

location counter. A value kept by the assembler to tell it which is the next byte available for allocation as it builds the object module. Its value is displayed to the left of each instruction in the source listing.

logical expression. A conditional assembly expression that is a combination of logical terms, logical operators, and paired parentheses.

logical record. A record from the standpoint of its content, function, and use rather than its physical attributes; that is, one that is defined in terms of the information it contains.

logical relation. A logical term in which two expressions are separated by a relational operator. The relational operators are EQ, GE, GT, LE, LT, and NE.

logical shift. The type of shift in which all bits participate equally.

logic error. A case where a program seems to execute correctly but provides incorrect results.

logical unit name. Allows programmer of file description (DTF) to refer to a particular class or group of I/O devices. For example, SYSLST.

loop. A programming technique which permits the reuse of a group of instructions a specified number of times or until a particular condition occurs.

loop body. The instructions which are reused.

loop control. The instructions in the loop which determine when the reuse of the instructions should be stopped.

loop counter. A counter used to prevent excessive looping.

low order. Rightmost. For instance, bit 31 in a register.

machine address. See *absolute address*.

machine language. The language of a particular type of computer. In Systems/360 and 370 machine language, it is a string of binary numbers (1s and 0s).

macro. See *macro definition*, *macro instruction*, and *macro prototype statement*.

macro body. The body is all statements that follow the prototype statement and precede the MEND statement in a macro definition.

macro call. An assembler language statement that causes the assembler to process a predefined set of statements called a macro definition. The statements normally produced from the macro definition replace the macro instruction in the program and they are identified by a plus (+)

sign that precedes each statement. Same as macro instruction.

macro definition. A set of statements that defines the name of, format of, and conditions for generating a sequence of assembler language statements. Contains assembler language control and machine instructions.

macro expansion. The sequence of statements that result from a macro generation operation.

macro-generated instruction. A statement that results at pre-assembly time as the macro definition is being handled.

macro generation. An operation in which an assembler produces a sequence of assembler language statements by processing a macro definition called by a macro instruction. Macro generation takes place at preassembly time. Synonymous with macro expansion.

macro instruction. See *macro call*.

macro instruction operand. An operand that supplies a value to be assigned to the corresponding symbolic parameter of the macro definition called by the macro instruction.

macro library. A library of macro definitions used during macro expansion.

macro prototype statement. A statement used to give a name to a macro definition and to provide a model for the macro instruction, that is, to call the macro definition.

main storage. All program-addressable storage from which instructions may be executed and from which data can be loaded directly into registers. Contrast with auxiliary storage.

mask. A pattern of 4 or more bits used in the testing or alteration of another field. For example, the 4-bit mask in a Branch on Condition instruction or the 8-bit mask in the Test under Mask instruction.

match. An equal condition occurring when two items are compared.

media. The material on which data is recorded, such as magnetic tape, or paper.

microsecond. One-millionth of a second.

millisecond. One-thousandth of a second.

mnemonic operation code. An easy to remember symbol that represents a machine opcode and helps a human understand the nature of the operation to be performed, the type of data used, and the format of the instruction performing the operation.

model statement. A statement in the body of a macro definition from which an assembler language statement can be generated at pre-assembly time. Values can be substituted at one or more points in a model statement; one or more identical or different statements can be generated from the same model statement under the control of a conditional assembly loop.

module. A discrete programming unit. For example, source module, object module, and load module.

most significant. The digit with the largest place value in the number. Leftmost.

multiprocessing system. A computing system employing two or more interconnected processing units to execute programs simultaneously.

multiprogramming system. A system that can process two or more programs concurrently by interleaving their execution.

nanosecond. One-thousand-millionth of a second.

next sequential instruction. Physically the next instruction in storage, the next instruction in the program.

nine-edge. The bottom edge of a punched card.

noise. See *garbage*.

normalized form. A form in which a floating-point number is kept with a non-zero high-order digit. A number can be normalized prior to the execution of the operation (prenormalization), or after the execution (postnormalization), or both before and after.

NSI. Abbreviation for next sequential instruction.

null character string. A character string of length zero. A blank is not a null character string because it has a length of one.

null operand. The absence of an operand. Usually used when passing positional parameters in a macro call. For instance, NAME MAC FIRST,,THIRD where the second parameter is not being passed.

numeric punch. A punch in one of the ten rows numbered 0–9 on a standard punched card.

object module. The block of machine code created by the assembler when it translates the source module.

opcode. The most important part of an instruction. It informs the system what operation is to be performed and the type of data to be used.

open subroutine. A subroutine that lies wholly within the main routine. No special instructions are necessary to pass control to an open subroutine.

operand. The data to be used in an operation or the location of that data.

operating system. The software, programs, that aid in the operation of the mechanical devices, the hardware. They aid in I/O operations, error condition handling, and resource management. For example, DOS, DOS/VS, or OS.

Operation code. See *opcode.*

ordinary symbol. A symbol that represents an assembly-time value when used in the name or operand field of an instruction.

output. The results of the operation of a data processing system.

output stream. Diagnostic messages and other output data issued by an operating system or a processing program on output devices especially activated for this purpose by the system operator. Synonymous with *job output stream, output job stream.*

output stream data set. A data set that resides in the output stream.

overflow. A condition that sets the condition code and at times abends the program. Can occur when the result of an addition or subtraction requires more bits than are available. Also occurs when a left algebraic shift results in shifting into the sign bit position a different value than was there before the operation.

overlapping fields. Fields overlap when at least one byte is common to both fields.

packed-decimal format. Each byte in this format contains two digits, except the right most byte in the field which contains the sign of the number in its rightmost 4 bits.

pad. To fill an area with a prescribed character. For example, unfilled area in a character constant is padded with blanks.

page. In virtual storage systems, a fixed-length block of instructions, data, or both, that can be transferred between real storage and external page storage; also the action of transferring instructions, data, or both, between real storage and external page storage.

page fault. In System/370 virtual storage systems a program interruption that occurs when a page that is marked 'not in real storage' is referred to by an active page. Synonymous with *missing page interruption* and *page translation exception.*

page frame. In System/370 virtual storage systems, a block of real storage that can contain a page. Synonymous with *frame.*

page frame table. In System/370 virtual storage systems, a table that contains an entry for each frame. Each frame table entry describes how the frame is being used.

page-in. In System/370 virtual storage systems, the process of transferring a page from external page storage to real storage.

page-out. In System/370 virtual storage systems, the process of transferring a page from real storage to external page storage.

page table. In System/370 virtual storage systems, a table that indicates whether a page is in real storage and correlates virtual addresses with real storage addresses.

parameter. See *symbolic parameter*.

PDUMP. A dynamic dump on a DOS-based operating system.

phase. Under DOS-based operating systems, the smallest complete unit that can be referred to in the core image library.

physical record. A record from the standpoint of the form in which it is stored, retrieved, and moved; that is, one that is defined in terms of physical quantities. A physical record may contain one or more logical records.

"play computer". To manually execute the instructions of a program in sequence just as the computer would to ensure that the program does what it is expected to do. Substitute values for variables and follow logic through flowchart.

pointer. An address or other indication of location.

positional notation. A means of representing a number by specifying the value of each of its digits by a power of the base of the number raised to the power equal to the position of the digit being evaluated in the number.

positional operand. An operand in a macro instruction that assigns a value to the corresponding positional parameter declared in the prototype statement of the called macro definition.

positional parameter. A parameter that must appear in a specified location, relative to other parameters. See also *keyword parameter*.

postmortem dump. A dump taken when a program has done something in error which causes the supervisor to abend the program.

pre-assembly time. The time at which an assembler processes macro definitions and performs conditional assembly operations.

print control character. See *carriage-control character*.

printer. A device that writes output data from a system on paper or other media.

privileged instruction. An instruction that can be executed only when the central processing unit is in the supervisor state.

problem program. Any program that is executed when the central processing unit is not in the supervisor state. Any program that does not contain privileged instructions.

problem state. A state during which the CPU cannot execute privileged instructions. Contrast with *supervisor state*.

procedure. See *cataloged procedure*.

processing program. A general term for any program that is not a control program.

program. A series of instructions, in a language understood by a computer, which solve a problem. Also the process of creating the series.

program check interruption. An interruption caused by unusual conditions encountered in a program, such as incorrect operands.

program flowchart. See *flowchart*.

programmer. An individual capable of breaking a problem down into discrete steps and expressing those steps in one of the languages understood by the computer.

programming. A skill that requires that problem solutions be broken down into steps and expressed in a language understood by a computer.

programming language. A language understood by the computer and used by the programmer to say which instructions are to be executed and in what order.

program status word. A doubleword in storage used to control the order in which instructions are executed, and to hold and indicate the status of the computing system in relation to a particular program. Abbreviated PSW.

prototype statement. Same as *macro prototype statement*.

pseudo op. An opcode for an instruction that gives information to the assembler. It does not represent a machine instruction.

PSW. Abbreviation for Program Status Word.

QCW. Abbreviation for queue control word.

queue. A waiting line or list formed by items in a system waiting for service; for example, messages to be printed. Also, to arrange in, or form, a queue.

queue control word. See *header*.

radix. A number that is used as the base of a number system.

real storage. In System/370 virtual storage systems, the storage of a System/370 computing system from which the central processing unit can directly obtain instructions and data, and to which it can directly return results.

receiving field. The operand receiving the data that is participating in an operation.

record. A collection of related data items, or fields, which are treated as a unit.

record length. The number of bytes in a logical record.

register. Special areas of storage in the processor.

There are 16 and each holds 32 bits or 4 bytes. They are used in certain operations.

relational operator. An operator that can be used in an arithmetic or character relation to indicate the comparison to be performed between the terms in the relation. The relational operators are EQ (equal to), GE(greater than or equal to), GT (greater than), LE (less than or equal to), LT (less than), and NE (not equal to).

relative address. An address specified as a relationship to a relocatable symbol. The symbol is followed by a plus (+) sign and a decimal number. For example, LOC+6 is an address 6 bytes past the address LOC.

relocatable. The attribute of a set of code whose address constants can be modified to compensate for a change in origin.

relocatable expression. An assembly-time expression whose value is affected by program relocation. A relocatable expression can represent a relocatable address.

relocatable term. A term whose value is affected by program relocation. Its value is assigned by the assembler.

relocation. The modification of address constants to compensate for a change in origin of a module, program, control section, or page.

resource. Any facility of the computing system required by a job or task, including storage, input/output devices, the central processing unit, data sets, and control of processing programs.

right-justify. To align on the right-hand side of the field.

routine. See *subroutine*.

RR-type instruction. An instruction in which both operands are contained in registers.

RS-type instruction. An instruction in which the first (and third, if present) operand is a register and the second a storage address.

RX-type instruction. An instruction in which the first operand is a register and the second a storage address which may be indexed.

save area. An 18-word area used to store the calling routine's register contents when control is received by a subroutine.

scan. The assembler's examination of the syntax of a source statement from left to right across the statement.

search. A systematic check for a particular value or values.

search argument. The value that is used to locate a match, if possible, with an argument in a search reference table.

search reference table. A table in which each element has two parts, an argument and a function.

search key. Same as *search argument*.

secondary storage. Same as *auxiliary storage*.

segment. In System/370 virtual storage systems, a contiguous area of virtual storage that is allocated to a job or system task.

segmentation. The process of dividing a program up into pieces to allow the possibility for part of the program to be in storage and execute without having to have the entire program in storage.

segment table. In System/370 virtual storage systems, a table used in dynamic address translation to control user access to virtual storage segments. Each entry indicates the length, location, and availability of a corresponding page table.

self-defining term. An absolute term whose value is implicit in the specification of the term itself.

semantics. The relationship between symbols and their meanings.

sequence symbol. A symbol used as a branching label for conditional assembly instructions. It consists of a period, followed by one to seven alphameric characters, the first of which must be alphabetic.

sequential access method. Storing and retrieving logical records in a continuous stream. To read the third record, the first and second records must be read first.

sequential data set. A data set whose records are organized on the basis of their successive physical positions, such as a magnetic tape file or a deck of punched cards.

sequential operation. The execution of instructions one after another in the sequence in which they appear in the program. See *NSI*.

SET symbol. A variable symbol used to communicate values during conditional assembly processing.

severity code. A code assigned to an error detected in a source module.

shift. A set of eight instructions which move bits left or right in registers.

SI-type instruction. Instructions with a storage address in the first operand and a byte of immediate data in the second operand.

SS-type instruction. Instructions with storage addresses in both operands. In some, one length is specified with the first operand, and in others, lengths are specified with both operands.

sign bit. Bit 0 in a fixed-point binary field; 0 indicates a positive value and 1 a negative value.

significant digit. A digit whose value is greater than zero.

single threaded. A type of chained list or queue in which each block of data contains a single pointer to the block ahead of it in the chain and the last block contains a zero. See also *double threaded*.

slot. In OS/VS, a continuous area on a paging device in which a page can be stored.

SNAP dump. A dynamic dump on an OS-based system.

software. The programs which aid the problem program in its execution.

sort. A programming routine that orders data.

source field. The operand that provides the data that is to participate in an operation. For example, the data that is moved by an MVC.

source module. The source statements that constitute the input to a language translator for a particular translation.

source statement. A statement written in symbols of a programming language.

special character. A graphic character that is *not* an A–Z, 0–9, @, #, or $.

stacked job. See *batched job.*

stacked job processing. A technique that permits multiple job definitions to be grouped (stacked) for presentation to the system, which automatically recognizes the jobs, one after the other.

standardization. Input media for computers is standardized by set codes on cards, tape, disk, etc. The media themselves are standardized in size, shape, thickness, etc., as they can be handled by machines.

static relocation. Really a case of no relocation at all. All programs are loaded at the same address.

storage. Part of the computer system into which data is entered and stored or from which data is retrieved.

storage fragmentation. See *fragmentation.*

storage protection. A means of preventing a program from writing or storing in areas of storage that don't belong to it. In some cases a program is even prevented from access of such an area.

store. The process of placing data in storage or an auxiliary device.

stored program computer. A computer that is capable of holding not only the data to be operated upon, but the instructions which make up the program that handles the data.

subroutine. A block which implements a section of the logic for solution of a problem. May be part of or separate from the rest of the routine.

subroutine call. The process of passing control to a subroutine.

supervisor. The part of a control program that coordinates the use of resources and maintains the flow of CPU operations.

supervisor call. An instruction that interrupts the program being executed and passes control to the supervisor so that it can perform a specific service indicated by the instruction. Abbreviated SVC.

supervisor state. A state during which the central processing unit can execute input/output and other privileged instructions. Contrast with *problem state.*

SVC. Abbreviation for *supervisor call.*

switch. A programming device used to remember a condition.

symbol. Any group of eight or less alphameric and national characters that begins with an alphabetic or national (#, @, $) character. Same as *symbolic name.*

symbolic address. The specification of an address by using symbols which the assembler resolves into a base register and displacement.

symbolic language. A programming language which permits the programmer to use symbolic names, or mnemonics, to specify opcodes and the data for the operation. This makes the programmer's job much easier.

symbolic linkage. Symbols defined in one csect which can be referred to from another csect. They permit transfer of control in subroutines.

symbolic name. See *symbol.*

symbolic name space. The block of space occupied, or defined, by a source program.

symbolic parameter. A variable symbol declared in the prototype statement of a macro definition. A symbolic parameter is usually assigned a value from the corresponding operand in the macro instruction that calls the macro definition. See also *keyword parameter*, and *positional parameter.*

symbolic unit name. See *logical unit name.*

symbol table. See *cross-reference table.*

syntactically valid. The instruction follows all the rules that govern the structure of the assembler language.

syntax error. A specification in an instruction which does not follow the rules that govern the structure of assembler language. For example, an index register specified in the operand of an MVC instruction.

system completion code. See *completion code.*

system input device. A device specified as a source of an input stream.

system output device. A device assigned to record output data for a series of jobs.

system programmer. A programmer who plans, generates, maintains, extends, and controls the use of an operating system with the aim of improving the overall productivity of an installation. Also, a programmer who designs programming systems.

systems residence volume. The volume or volumes on which the nucleus of the operating system and the highest-level index of the catalog are located.

table. A collection of related data items that are contained in elements which reside in continuous areas of storage.

table argument. See *argument.*

table function. See *function.*

table look up. The process of comparing a search argument to each argument portion in a table to locate a possible match.

target instruction. The instruction that is executed as the result of an execute (EX) instruction.

telecommunications. Data transmission between a computing system and remotely located devices via a unit that performs the necessary format conversion and controls the rate of transmission.

teleprocessing. The processing of data that is received from or sent to remote locations by way of telecommunication lines.

temporary data set. A data set that is created and deleted in the same job.

term. The smallest part of an expression that can be assigned a value.

throughput. The total volume of work performed by a computing system over a given period of time.

time sharing. A method of using a computing system that allows a number of users to execute programs concurrently and to interact with the programs during execution.

time slicing. A feature that can be used to prevent a job from monopolizing the central processing unit and thereby delaying the assignment of CPU time to other jobs. In systems with time sharing, the allocation of time slices to terminal jobs.'

trailer statement. The statement (MEND) that marks the end of a macro definition.

transfer. See *branch.*

troubleshoot. See *debug.*

truncate. Chopped off or ignored. For example, if 87.657 is truncated to 4 digits, the result is 87.65, the 7 is simply ignored.

twelve-edge. The top of a standard punched card.

twelve-punch. A punch in the top row of a standard punched card.

two's complement notation. Representation of negative binary numbers. Created by subtracting each digit of the number from a value of one and then adding one to the least significant digit.

type attribute. The type associated with a symbol. For example, F for fullword, or H for halfword. Can be tested in conditional assembly instructions.

type subfield. A portion of a DC or DS statement that informs the assembler which type of constant is to be defined.

unary operator. An arithmetic operator having only one term. They can be used in absolute, relocatable, and arithmetic expressions. They are positive ($+$) and negative ($-$).

unconditional branch. An instruction which causes a branch to be taken each and every time it is executed.

USASCII. Same as *ASCII.*

utility program. A problem program designed to perform an everyday task, such as transcribing data from one storage device to another.

validity check. A check that a code group is actually a character of the particular code in use. For example, a check to see that the combination of holes punched into a column of a card is a valid combination.

value subfield. The portion of the operand of a DC statement that specifies the constant to be assembled. If specified in the operand of a DS statement it is only used to establish the length of the constant.

variable. A symbolic location that can contain a variety of values.

variable-length data. Data which consists of a string of bytes of no fixed length and located on no specific integral boundary.

variable symbol. A symbol used in macro and conditional assembly processing that can assume any of a given set of values.

virtual address. In virtual storage systems, an address that refers to virtual storage and must, therefore, be translated into a real storage address when it is to be used.

virtual address space. In virtual storage systems, the virtual storage assigned to a job.

virtual machine. A functional simulation of a computer and its associated devices. In VM/370,

a functional equivalent of an IBM System/370 computing system. Each virtual machine is controlled by a suitable operating system. VM/370 controls the concurrent execution of multiple virtual machines.

virtual storage. Addressable space that appears to the user to be real storage, from which instructions and data are mapped into real storage locations. The size of virtual storage is limited by the addressing scheme of the computing system (or virtual machine) and by the amount of auxilliary storage available, rather than by the actual number of real storage locations.

volume. A recording medium that is mounted and demounted as a unit, for example, a reel of tape or a disk pack.

volume serial number. A number in a volume label that is assigned when a volume is prepared for use in the system.

volume table of contents. A table on a direct access volume, that describes each dataset on the volume. Abbreviated VTOC.

VTOC. Abbreviation for volume table of contents.

word. A contiguous series of 32 bits, or four bytes, in storage which can be addressed as a unit. The address of the first byte of the word is evenly divisible by four.

work area. An area used to reference an input record or build an output record. Its name is specified in the GET or PUT instruction.

zone punch. A punch in row 11, 12, or 0 of a standard punched card.

zoned-decimal format. A format in which each character occupies one byte with the first four bits being the zone portion and the second four bits the digit portion. The zone portion of the low-order byte is the sign of the number (A,C,E and F are positive signs, and B and D are negative).

Index